THE YALE EDITION

OF

HORACE WALPOLE'S

CORRESPONDENCE

EDITED BY W. S. LEWIS

VOLUME TWENTY-EIGHT

HORACE WALPOLE'S

CORRESPONDENCE

WITH

WILLIAM MASON

I

EDITED BY W. S. LEWIS

GROVER CRONIN, JR

AND

CHARLES H. BENNETT

NEW HAVEN

YALE UNIVERSITY PRESS

LONDON · GEOFFREY CUMBERLEGE · OXFORD UNIVERSITY PRESS

1955

The two volumes of Walpole's correspondence with Mason have been numbered 28 and 29 in order that the correspondence with Mann may be in continuous series from volumes 17–19. At the present writing, it is expected that there will be seven more Mann volumes, but an allowance has been made to provide for a possible miscalculation.
June 1955

ADVISORY COMMITTEE

LIST OF SUBSCRIBERS

H.M. QUEEN ELIZABETH II

AGNES SCOTT COLLEGE LIBRARY, Decatur, Georgia
ALAMEDA FREE LIBRARY, Alameda, California
ALBERTUS MAGNUS COLLEGE LIBRARY, New Haven, Connecticut
ALLEGHENY COLLEGE, THE REIS LIBRARY, Meadville, Pennsylvania
ALL SOULS COLLEGE LIBRARY, Oxford, England
LLOYD V. ALMIRALL, Esq., New York, New York
JOSEPH W. ALSOP, Jr, Esq., Avon, Connecticut
FRANK ALTSCHUL, Esq., Stamford, Connecticut
AMERICAN INTERNATIONAL COLLEGE LIBRARY, Springfield, Massachusetts.
AMERICAN UNIVERSITY LIBRARY, Washington, D.C.
AMHERST COLLEGE, CONVERSE MEMORIAL LIBRARY, Amherst, Massachusetts
W. ARMYTAGE, Esq., Moyvore, Eire
THE ATHENÆUM CLUB, London, England
ATLANTA UNIVERSITY LIBRARY, Atlanta, Georgia
HUGH D. AUCHINCLOSS, Esq., McLean, Virginia
AUCKLAND UNIVERSITY COLLEGE, Auckland, New Zealand
F. W. BAIN, Esq., London, England
RICHARD B. BAKER, Esq., Providence, Rhode Island
BANGOR PUBLIC LIBRARY, Bangor, Maine
Sir T. D. BARLOW, K.B.E., London, England
BARR-SMITH LIBRARY, University of Adelaide, Adelaide, Australia
W. D. BASTON, Esq., Morpeth, Northumberland
BATH MUNICIPAL LIBRARY, Bath, England
BAVARIAN STATE LIBRARY, Munich, Germany
C. F. BELL, Esq., London, England
BERKELEY COLLEGE LIBRARY, YALE UNIVERSITY, New Haven, Connecticut
BEVERLY HILLS PUBLIC LIBRARY, Beverly Hills, California
THEODORE BESTERMAN, Esq., Paris, France

BIBLIOTECA NACIONAL DE PERÚ, Lima, Peru
Mrs NORMAN H. BILTZ, Reno, Nevada
BIRMINGHAM PUBLIC LIBRARY, Birmingham, England
BOSTON ATHENÆUM, Boston, Massachusetts
BOSTON COLLEGE LIBRARY, Chestnut Hill, Massachusetts
BOSTON PUBLIC LIBRARY, Boston, Massachusetts
BOSTON UNIVERSITY GRADUATE SCHOOL, Boston, Massachusetts
BOWDOIN COLLEGE LIBRARY, Brunswick, Maine
BRANDEIS UNIVERSITY LIBRARY, Waltham, Massachusetts
BRISTOL PUBLIC LIBRARY, Bristol, England
WALLACE BROCKWAY, Esq., New York, New York
BROOKLYN COLLEGE LIBRARY, Brooklyn, New York
BROOKS SCHOOL, North Andover, Massachusetts
RALPH S. BROWN, Jr, Esq., Guilford, Connecticut
BROWN UNIVERSITY, JOHN HAY MEMORIAL LIBRARY, Providence,
    Rhode Island
BRYN MAWR COLLEGE LIBRARY, Bryn Mawr, Pennsylvania
JOHN N. BRYSON, Esq., Oxford, England
BUCKNELL UNIVERSITY LIBRARY, Lewisburg, Pennsylvania
BUFFALO AND ERIE COUNTY PUBLIC LIBRARY, Buffalo, New York
BUTLER UNIVERSITY LIBRARY, Indianapolis, Indiana
CALHOUN COLLEGE LIBRARY, YALE UNIVERSITY, New Haven, Con-
    necticut
CALIFORNIA STATE LIBRARY, Sacramento, California
CAMBRIDGE PUBLIC LIBRARY, Cambridge, England
CAMBRIDGE PUBLIC LIBRARY, Cambridge, New York
CANISIUS COLLEGE BOOKSTORE, Buffalo, New York
CARDIFF PUBLIC LIBRARY, Cardiff, Wales
CARNEGIE LIBRARY OF PITTSBURGH, Pittsburgh, Pennsylvania
RALPH E. CARPENTER, Jr, Esq., Scarsdale, New York
CATHOLIC UNIVERSITY LIBRARY, Washington, D.C.
Mrs RALPH CATTERALL, Richmond, Virginia
CHARLES L. COCKE MEMORIAL LIBRARY, Hollins College, Virginia
CHICAGO PUBLIC LIBRARY, Chicago, Illinois
CINCINNATI PUBLIC LIBRARY, Cincinnati, Ohio
CLAREMONT COLLEGES LIBRARY, Claremont, California
CLEVELAND PUBLIC LIBRARY, Cleveland, Ohio
COE COLLEGE LIBRARY, Cedar Rapids, Iowa
COLBY COLLEGE LIBRARY, Waterville, Maine

COLGATE UNIVERSITY LIBRARY, Hamilton, New York
COLLEGE OF THE CITY OF NEW YORK, New York, New York
COLLEGE OF NEW ROCHELLE LIBRARY, New Rochelle, New York
COLLEGE OF ST THOMAS, St Paul, Minnesota
COLLEGE OF WOOSTER LIBRARY, Wooster, Ohio
COLORADO COLLEGE, COBURN LIBRARY, Colorado Springs, Colorado
COLUMBIA UNIVERSITY LIBRARY, New York, New York
COMMONWEALTH NATIONAL LIBRARY, Canberra, Australia
G. MAURICE CONGDON, Esq., Providence, Rhode Island
CONNECTICUT COLLEGE, PALMER LIBRARY, New London, Connecticut
CONNECTICUT STATE LIBRARY, Hartford, Connecticut
REGINALD G. COOMBE, Esq., Greenwich, Connecticut
Mrs FRANK COOPER, Albany, New York
THOMAS R. COWARD, Esq., New York, New York
HUGH B. COX, Esq., Alexandria, Virginia
CREIGHTON UNIVERSITY, Omaha, Nebraska
E. C. CULL, Esq., Dorking, Surrey
DARTMOUTH COLLEGE, BAKER MEMORIAL LIBRARY, Hanover, New
    Hampshire
DAVENPORT COLLEGE LIBRARY, YALE UNIVERSITY, New Haven, Con-
    necticut
FRANKLIN DAY, Esq., Allendale, New Jersey
DENVER PUBLIC LIBRARY, Denver, Colorado
DES MOINES PUBLIC LIBRARY, Des Moines, Iowa
DETROIT PUBLIC LIBRARY, Detroit, Michigan
Mrs ROBERT CLOUTMAN DEXTER, Belmont, Massachusetts
CHARLES D. DICKEY, Esq., Chestnut Hill, Philadelphia, Pennsylvania
DICKINSON COLLEGE LIBRARY, Carlisle, Pennsylvania
Mrs FRANK F. DODGE, New York, New York
Mrs NELSON DOUBLEDAY, Cleft Road, Oyster Bay, New York
E. H. DOUGLAS-OSBORN, Esq., Barnt Green, Worcestershire
DRAKE UNIVERSITY LIBRARY, Des Moines, Iowa
DREW UNIVERSITY LIBRARY, Madison, New Jersey
DUKE UNIVERSITY LIBRARY, Durham, North Carolina
DULUTH PUBLIC LIBRARY, Duluth, Minnesota
EDINBURGH PUBLIC LIBRARY, Edinburgh, Scotland
EDINBURGH UNIVERSITY LIBRARY, Edinburgh, Scotland
J. M. ELGAR, Esq., Bath, England
ALBERT H. ELY, Esq., Coldspring Harbor, Long Island, New York

EMMANUEL COLLEGE LIBRARY, Cambridge, England
EMORY UNIVERSITY LIBRARY, Emory University, Georgia
ENGLISH LIBRARY EXAMINATION SCHOOLS, Oxford, England
ENOCH PRATT FREE LIBRARY, Baltimore, Maryland
C. G. W. EVE, Esq., London, England
JOHN EVELYN, Esq., Portsmouth, England
FARMINGTON VILLAGE LIBRARY, Farmington, Connecticut
HENRY FIELD, Esq., Cocoanut Grove, Florida
MAURICE FIRUSKI, Esq., Salisbury, Connecticut
Mrs MARGARET MITCHELL FLINT, Westport, Connecticut
FLORIDA STATE UNIVERSITY LIBRARY, Tallahassee, Florida
THE FOLGER SHAKESPEARE LIBRARY, Washington, D.C.
FORBES LIBRARY, Northampton, Massachusetts
FORDHAM UNIVERSITY LIBRARY, New York, New York
FRANKLIN AND MARSHALL COLLEGE LIBRARY, Lancaster, Pennsylvania
FREE LIBRARY OF PHILADELPHIA, Philadelphia, Pennsylvania
DONALD T. GAMMONS, Esq., Boston, Massachusetts
GEORGETOWN UNIVERSITY, RIGGS MEMORIAL LIBRARY, Washington, D.C.
GLASGOW ART GALLERIES, Glasgow, Scotland
GLASGOW UNIVERSITY LIBRARY, Glasgow, Scotland
Mrs WILLIAM GREENOUGH, Newport, Rhode Island
LAUDER GREENWAY, Esq., Greenwich, Connecticut
WILLIAM V. GRIFFIN, Esq., New York, New York
FARNHAM P. GRIFFITHS, Esq., San Francisco, California
GRINNELL COLLEGE LIBRARY, Grinnell, Iowa
GROTON SCHOOL LIBRARY, Groton, Massachusetts
GUILDHALL LIBRARY, London, England
SIDNEY LEWIS GULICK, Esq., San Diego, California
HACKLEY PUBLIC LIBRARY, Muskegon, Michigan
Mrs CHANDLER HALE, Washington, D.C.
ALLEN HAMILTON, M.D., La Jolla, California
HARVARD COLLEGE LIBRARY, Cambridge, Massachusetts
Miss BLANCHE HARVEY, Cleveland, Ohio
HENRY E. HUNTINGTON LIBRARY AND ART GALLERY, San Marino, California
HILDRETH PRESS INCORPORATED, Bristol, Connecticut
HOBART COLLEGE LIBRARY, Geneva, New York
C. B. HOGAN, Esq., Woodbridge, Connecticut

E. C. HOHLER, Esq., Aylesbury, Buckingham, England
Major T. S. HOHLER, Aylesbury, Buckingham, England
HOTCHKISS SCHOOL, Lakeville, Connecticut
HOUSE OF COMMONS LIBRARY, London, England
HOUSE OF LORDS LIBRARY, London, England
ESTATE OF ELTON HOYT, Esq., Cleveland, Ohio
W. H. HUGHES, Esq., London, England
HUNTER COLLEGE LIBRARY, New York, New York
Miss HUNTINGTON, Henley-on-Thames, England
R. M. HYSLOP, Esq., London, England
INCARNATE WORD COLLEGE LIBRARY, San Antonio, Texas
INDIANA STATE LIBRARY, Indianapolis, Indiana
INDIANA UNIVERSITY LIBRARY, Bloomington, Indiana
THE INSTITUTE FOR ADVANCED STUDY, Princeton, New Jersey
STUART W. JACKSON, Esq., Gloucester, Virginia
JACKSONVILLE PUBLIC LIBRARY, Jacksonville, Florida
OLIVER B. JENNINGS, Esq., Coldspring Harbor, Long Island, New York
JOHN CARTER BROWN LIBRARY, Providence, Rhode Island
JOHNS HOPKINS UNIVERSITY LIBRARY, Baltimore, Maryland
Mrs DOUGLAS JOHNSTON, Hazel Green, Alabama
JOINT UNIVERSITY LIBRARIES, Nashville, Tennessee
KANAWHA COUNTY PUBLIC LIBRARY, Charleston, West Virginia
KENYON COLLEGE LIBRARY, Gambier, Ohio
The Right Honourable Lord KENYON, Whitchurch, Shropshire, England
WILLARD L. KING, Esq., Chicago, Illinois
KING COLLEGE LIBRARY, Bristol, Tennessee
KING'S COLLEGE LIBRARY, Cambridge, England
KING'S COLLEGE LIBRARY, Newcastle-on-Tyne, England
KINGSLEY TRUST ASSOCIATION, YALE UNIVERSITY, New Haven, Connecticut
YALE KNEELAND, Jr, M.D., New York, New York
KNOX COLLEGE LIBRARY, Galesburg, Illinois
SEYMOUR H. KNOX, Esq., Buffalo, New York
Miss FRANCES CHRISTIAN KYLE, Belfast, North Ireland
LADY MARGARET HALL LIBRARY, Oxford, England
LAFAYETTE COLLEGE LIBRARY, Easton, Pennsylvania
LEEDS PUBLIC LIBRARIES, Leeds, England
LEEDS UNIVERSITY LIBRARY, Leeds, England

LEHIGH UNIVERSITY LIBRARY, Bethlehem, Pennsylvania
The Reverend J. LEONARD, C.M., Dublin, Eire
A. N. LEWIS, Esq., San Francisco, California
CHARLES L. LEWIS, Esq., San Francisco, California
LIBRARY ASSOCIATION OF PORTLAND, Portland, Oregon
LIBRARY OF THE WOMEN'S COLLEGE OF THE UNIVERSITY OF NORTH
    CAROLINA, Greensboro, North Carolina
HERMAN W. LIEBERT, Esq., New Haven, Connecticut
Mrs A. LINGARD, Bradford, Yorkshire, England
LIVERPOOL PUBLIC LIBRARIES, Liverpool, England
LONDON LIBRARY, St James's Square, London, England
LORAS COLLEGE LIBRARY, Dubuque, Iowa
LOS ANGELES PUBLIC LIBRARY, Los Angeles, California
LOUISIANA STATE UNIVERSITY LIBRARY, Baton Rouge, Louisiana
Miss JULIA McCARTHY, Farmington, Connecticut
SIR COMPTON MACKENZIE, Denchworth Manor, Berkshire, England
McKISSICK MEMORIAL LIBRARY, University of South Carolina, Co-
    lumbia, South Carolina
THE MADISON FUND, San Francisco, California
MANCHESTER PUBLIC LIBRARIES, Manchester, England
ANTHONY F. MARRECO, Esq., London, England
Mrs JOSIAH P. MARVEL, Washington, D.C.
MARY REED LIBRARY, University of Denver, Denver, Colorado
MARYWOOD COLLEGE LIBRARY, Scranton, Pennsylvania
HAROLD R. MEDINA, Esq., MEDINA LIBRARY, Westhampton, New York
MEMPHIS STATE COLLEGE LIBRARY, Memphis, Tennessee
MIAMI UNIVERSITY LIBRARY, Oxford, Ohio
MICHIGAN STATE COLLEGE, East Lansing, Michigan
MILLS COLLEGE LIBRARY, Oakland, California
MINNEAPOLIS ATHENÆUM, Minneapolis, Minnesota
B. I. MISSELBROOK, Esq., Southampton, England
The Reverend HENRY MITCHELL, Wynnewood, Pennsylvania
LAURENCE P. MOOMAU, Esq., Westport, Connecticut
MOUNT HOLYOKE COLLEGE LIBRARY, South Hadley, Massachusetts
MOUNT UNION COLLEGE LIBRARY, Alliance, Ohio
THE MOUNT VERNON LADIES' ASSOCIATION OF THE UNION, Mount
    Vernon, Virginia
MERRILL CALVIN MUNYAN, Esq., Washington, D.C.
EDWARD W. NASH, Esq., Washington, D.C.

NATIONAL GALLERY OF ART, Washington, D.C.
The Right Honourable Lord NATHAN OF CHURT, London, England
THE NATIONAL CENTRAL LIBRARY, London, England
NATIONAL LIBRARY OF IRELAND, Dublin, Eire
NATIONAL LIBRARY SERVICE, Wellington, New Zealand
A. E. NEERGAARD, Esq., M.D., New York, New York
NEWBERRY LIBRARY, Chicago, Illinois
NEW HAMPSHIRE STATE LIBRARY, Concord, New Hampshire
NEW HAVEN PUBLIC LIBRARY, New Haven, Connecticut
NEW JERSEY COLLEGE FOR WOMEN LIBRARY, New Brunswick, New
    Jersey
THE NEW SOUTH WALES LIBRARY OF PARLIAMENT, Parliament House,
    Sydney, Australia
NEW YORK PUBLIC LIBRARY, New York, New York
THE NEW YORK SOCIETY LIBRARY, New York, New York
NEW YORK STATE LIBRARY, Albany, New York
NEW YORK UNIVERSITY LIBRARY, New York, New York
NORFOLK PUBLIC LIBRARY, Norfolk, Connecticut
NORTH TEXAS STATE TEACHERS COLLEGE LIBRARY, Denton, Texas
NORTHERN ILLINOIS STATE TEACHERS COLLEGE, DeKalb, Illinois
NORTHWESTERN UNIVERSITY LIBRARY, Evanston, Illinois
OBERLIN COLLEGE LIBRARY, Oberlin, Ohio
OHIO STATE UNIVERSITY LIBRARY, Columbus, Ohio
OHIO UNIVERSITY LIBRARY, Athens, Ohio
OHIO WESLEYAN UNIVERSITY, CHARLES ELIHU SLOCUM LIBRARY, Dela-
    ware, Ohio
OKLAHOMA AGRICULTURAL AND MECHANICAL COLLEGE LIBRARY, Still-
    water, Oklahoma
ASHLEY W. OLMSTED, Esq., Buffalo, New York
R. HUNT PARKER, Esq., Roanoke Rapids, North Carolina
PASADENA PUBLIC LIBRARY, Pasadena, California
PEABODY INSTITUTE LIBRARY, Baltimore, Maryland
PEMBROKE COLLEGE LIBRARY, Cambridge, England
PENNSYLVANIA STATE COLLEGE LIBRARY, State College, Pennsylvania
PENNSYLVANIA STATE LIBRARY AND MUSEUM, Harrisburg, Pennsyl-
    vania
PHILLIPS ACADEMY LIBRARY, Andover, Massachusetts
PHILLIPS EXETER ACADEMY, DAVIS LIBRARY, Exeter, New Hampshire
THE PIERPONT MORGAN LIBRARY, New York, New York

MISS PORTER'S SCHOOL, Farmington, Connecticut
PORTLAND PUBLIC LIBRARY, Portland, Maine
L. F. POWELL, Esq., Oxford, England
PRINCETON UNIVERSITY LIBRARY, Princeton, New Jersey
PROVIDENCE ATHENÆUM, Providence, Rhode Island
PUBLIC LIBRARY, Sydney, Australia
PUBLIC LIBRARY OF VICTORIA, Melbourne, Australia
PURDUE UNIVERSITY LIBRARY, Lafayette, Indiana
QUEENS BOROUGH PUBLIC LIBRARY, Jamaica, New York
QUEENS COLLEGE LIBRARY, Flushing, New York
QUEENS UNIVERSITY OF BELFAST LIBRARY, Belfast, North Ireland
RANDOLPH-MACON WOMAN'S COLLEGE LIBRARY, Lynchburg, Virginia
READING UNIVERSITY LIBRARY, Reading, England
REDWOOD LIBRARY AND ATHENÆUM, Newport, Rhode Island
REFORM CLUB, London, England
RICE INSTITUTE LIBRARY, Houston, Texas
MRS MARGARET ROCKWELL, Phoenix, Arizona
ROOSEVELT UNIVERSITY LIBRARY, Chicago, Illinois
The Right Honourable LORD ROTHSCHILD, Cambridge, England
THE ROYAL LIBRARY, Stockholm, Sweden
THE ROYAL UNIVERSITY LIBRARY, Upsala, Sweden
RUTGERS UNIVERSITY LIBRARY, New Brunswick, New Jersey
JOHN RYLANDS LIBRARY, Manchester, England
SAGINAW PUBLIC LIBRARIES, Saginaw, Michigan
ST ANDREWS UNIVERSITY LIBRARY, St Andrews, Fife, Scotland
ST BONAVENTURE COLLEGE, FRIEDSAM MEMORIAL LIBRARY, St Bonaventure, New York
ST JOHN'S UNIVERSITY LIBRARY, Brooklyn, New York
ST JOSEPH'S COLLEGE FOR WOMEN LIBRARY, Brooklyn, New York
ST LOUIS PUBLIC LIBRARY, St Louis, Missouri
ST LOUIS UNIVERSITY LIBRARY, St Louis, Missouri
ST MARY'S COLLEGE LIBRARY, Notre Dame, Indiana
ST MARY'S COLLEGE, Strawberry Hill, Middlesex, England
ST OLAF COLLEGE LIBRARY, Northfield, Minnesota
ST PAUL PUBLIC LIBRARY, St Paul, Minnesota
ST PETER'S COLLEGE LIBRARY, Jersey City, New Jersey
MRS JAMES SALLADE, Ann Arbor, Michigan
SAN BERNARDINO VALLEY JUNIOR COLLEGE LIBRARY, San Bernardino, California

SAN FRANCISCO PUBLIC LIBRARY, San Francisco, California
SEATTLE PUBLIC LIBRARY, Seattle, Washington
ERIC H. L. SEXTON, Esq., Rockport, Maine
GEORGE SHERBURN, Esq., Middlebury, Vermont
THE SIGNET LIBRARY, Edinburgh, Scotland
SKIDMORE COLLEGE LIBRARY, Saratoga Springs, New York
RICHARD SMART, Esq., London, England
SMITH COLLEGE LIBRARY, Northampton, Massachusetts
Mrs THEODORE J. SMITH, Geneva, New York
WILLARD SMITH, Esq., Oakland, California
P. H. B. OTWAY SMITHERS, Esq., Alresford, Hampshire, England
SOMERVILLE COLLEGE LIBRARY, Oxford, England
SOUTH AFRICAN PUBLIC LIBRARY, Capetown, Union of South Africa
SOUTHERN METHODIST UNIVERSITY LIBRARY, Dallas, Texas
SOUTHWESTERN COLLEGE LIBRARY, Memphis, Tennessee
STANFORD UNIVERSITY LIBRARIES, Stanford, California
STATE UNIVERSITY OF IOWA LIBRARIES, Iowa City, Iowa
STEPHENS MEMORIAL LIBRARY, SOUTHWESTERN LOUISIANA INSTITUTE,
    Lafayette, Louisiana
JAMES STRACHEY, Esq., London, England
STRATFORD LIBRARY ASSOCIATION, Stratford, Connecticut
Miss L. STUART SUTHERLAND, Lady Margaret Hall, Oxford, England
SWARTHMORE COLLEGE LIBRARY, Swarthmore, Pennsylvania
SYRACUSE UNIVERSITY LIBRARY, Syracuse, New York
HENRY C. TAYLOR, Esq., Coldspring Harbor, Long Island, New York
J. T. TEMPLE, Esq., Harrogate, Yorkshire
TEMPLE UNIVERSITY LIBRARY, Philadelphia, Pennsylvania
TEXAS STATE COLLEGE FOR WOMEN LIBRARY, Denton, Texas
THACHER SCHOOL LIBRARY, Ojai, California
DAY THORPE, Esq., Alexandria, Virginia
TOLEDO PUBLIC LIBRARY, Toledo, Ohio
TRANSYLVANIA COLLEGE LIBRARY, Lexington, Kentucky
BENJAMIN HARTSHORNE TRASK, Esq., New York, New York
TRINITY COLLEGE LIBRARY, Washington, D.C.
TULANE UNIVERSITY LIBRARY, New Orleans, Louisiana
ROBERT TUNSTILL, Esq., Bradford-on-Avon, Wiltshire
UNION COLLEGE LIBRARY, Schenectady, New York
UNIVERSITY COLLEGE, Leicester, England
UNIVERSITY COLLEGE, Ibadan, Nigeria

UNIVERSITY COLLEGE, Southampton, England
UNIVERSITY COLLEGE LIBRARY, Hull, England
UNIVERSITY COLLEGE LIBRARY, London, England
UNIVERSITY COLLEGE OF THE GOLD COAST, Achimota, Gold Coast
UNIVERSITY OF ALABAMA LIBRARY, University, Alabama
UNIVERSITY OF ARIZONA LIBRARY, Tucson, Arizona
UNIVERSITY OF ARKANSAS, GENERAL LIBRARY, Fayetteville, Arkansas
UNIVERSITY OF BASEL PUBLIC LIBRARY, Basel, Switzerland
UNIVERSITY OF BIRMINGHAM LIBRARY, Birmingham, England
UNIVERSITY OF BRITISH COLUMBIA LIBRARY, Vancouver, British Columbia
UNIVERSITY OF BUFFALO, LOCKWOOD MEMORIAL LIBRARY, Buffalo, New York
UNIVERSITY OF CALIFORNIA AT LOS ANGELES LIBRARY, West Los Angeles, California
UNIVERSITY OF CALIFORNIA LIBRARY, Berkeley, California
UNIVERSITY OF CAPE TOWN, Rondebosch, Union of South Africa
UNIVERSITY OF CHICAGO LIBRARIES, Chicago, Illinois
UNIVERSITY OF CINCINNATI LIBRARY, Cincinnati, Ohio
UNIVERSITY OF COLORADO LIBRARY, Boulder, Colorado
UNIVERSITY OF CONNECTICUT LIBRARY, Storrs, Connecticut
UNIVERSITY OF DELAWARE LIBRARY, Newark, Delaware
UNIVERSITY OF DURHAM LIBRARY, Durham, England
UNIVERSITY OF FLORIDA LIBRARY, Gainesville, Florida
UNIVERSITY OF GEORGIA LIBRARIES, Athens, Georgia
UNIVERSITY OF ILLINOIS LIBRARY, Urbana, Illinois
UNIVERSITY OF KANSAS CITY, Kansas City, Missouri
UNIVERSITY OF KANSAS LIBRARY, Lawrence, Kansas
UNIVERSITY OF KENTUCKY LIBRARY, Lexington, Kentucky
UNIVERSITY OF LIVERPOOL LIBRARY, Liverpool, England
UNIVERSITY OF LONDON LIBRARY, London, England
UNIVERSITY OF MANCHESTER LIBRARY, Manchester, England
UNIVERSITY OF MARYLAND LIBRARY, College Park, Maryland
UNIVERSITY OF MELBOURNE, Melbourne, Australia
UNIVERSITY OF MICHIGAN LIBRARY, Ann Arbor, Michigan
UNIVERSITY OF MINNESOTA LIBRARY, Minneapolis, Minnesota
UNIVERSITY OF MISSISSIPPI LIBRARY, University, Mississippi
UNIVERSITY OF MISSOURI LIBRARY, Columbia, Missouri
UNIVERSITY OF NEBRASKA LIBRARY, Lincoln, Nebraska

UNIVERSITY OF NEVADA LIBRARY, Reno, Nevada

UNIVERSITY OF NEW HAMPSHIRE, HAMILTON SMITH LIBRARY, Durham, New Hampshire

UNIVERSITY OF NEW MEXICO LIBRARY, Albuquerque, New Mexico

UNIVERSITY OF NORTH CAROLINA LIBRARY, Chapel Hill, North Carolina

UNIVERSITY OF NORTH DAKOTA LIBRARY, Grand Forks, North Dakota

UNIVERSITY OF NOTRE DAME LIBRARY, Notre Dame, Indiana

UNIVERSITY OF OKLAHOMA LIBRARY, Norman, Oklahoma

UNIVERSITY OF OMAHA LIBRARY, Omaha, Nebraska

UNIVERSITY OF OREGON LIBRARY, Eugene, Oregon

UNIVERSITY OF OSLO LIBRARY, Oslo, Norway

UNIVERSITY OF OTAGO, Dunedin, New Zealand

UNIVERSITY OF PENNSYLVANIA LIBRARY, Philadelphia, Pennsylvania

UNIVERSITY OF PITTSBURGH LIBRARY, Pittsburgh, Pennsylvania

UNIVERSITY OF RHODE ISLAND LIBRARY, Kingston, Rhode Island

UNIVERSITY OF RICHMOND LIBRARY, Richmond, Virginia

UNIVERSITY OF ROCHESTER LIBRARY, Rochester, New York

UNIVERSITY OF SHEFFIELD LIBRARY, Sheffield, England

UNIVERSITY OF SOUTHERN CALIFORNIA LIBRARY, Los Angeles, California

UNIVERSITY OF SYDNEY, Sydney, Australia

UNIVERSITY OF TENNESSEE LIBRARY, Knoxville, Tennessee

UNIVERSITY OF TEXAS LIBRARY, Austin, Texas

UNIVERSITY OF TOLEDO LIBRARY, Toledo, Ohio

UNIVERSITY OF TORONTO LIBRARY, Toronto, Canada

UNIVERSITY OF TÜBINGEN LIBRARY, Tübingen, Germany

UNIVERSITY OF UTAH LIBRARY, Salt Lake City, Utah

UNIVERSITY OF VERMONT, UNIVERSITY LIBRARIES, Burlington, Vermont

UNIVERSITY OF VIRGINIA LIBRARY, Charlottesville, Virginia

UNIVERSITY OF WASHINGTON LIBRARY, Seattle, Washington

UNIVERSITY OF WICHITA LIBRARY, Wichita, Kansas

UNIVERSITY OF WISCONSIN LIBRARY, Madison, Wisconsin

UNIVERSITY OF WYOMING LIBRARY, Laramie, Wyoming

VASSAR COLLEGE LIBRARY, Poughkeepsie, New York

VERMONT STATE LIBRARY, Montpelier, Vermont

VIRGINIA STATE LIBRARY, Richmond, Virginia

A. P. VLASTO, Esq., King's College, Cambridge, England

GEORGE WAHR, Esq., Ann Arbor, Michigan
Mrs CHRISTOPHER WARD, Greenville, Delaware
WASHINGTON UNIVERSITY LIBRARY, St Louis, Missouri
WATKINSON LIBRARY, TRINITY COLLEGE, Hartford, Connecticut
WAYNE UNIVERSITY LIBRARY, Detroit, Michigan
M. E. WEATHERALL, Esq., South Clifton, Guernsey
VANDERBILT WEBB, Esq., New York, New York
WELLESLEY COLLEGE LIBRARY, Wellesley, Massachusetts
WELLS COLLEGE LIBRARY, Aurora, New York
WESLEYAN UNIVERSITY LIBRARY, Middletown, Connecticut
WEST VIRGINIA UNIVERSITY LIBRARY, Morgantown, West Virginia
WALDEMAR WESTERGAARD, Esq., Los Angeles, California
WESTERN COLLEGE LIBRARY, Oxford, Ohio
WESTERN KENTUCKY STATE TEACHERS COLLEGE LIBRARY, Bowling
    Green, Kentucky
WESTERN RESERVE UNIVERSITY, FLORA STONE MATHER LIBRARY,
    Cleveland, Ohio
WESTERN RESERVE UNIVERSITY LIBRARY, Cleveland, Ohio
WESTERN STATE TEACHERS COLLEGE LIBRARY, Kalamazoo, Michigan
WESTMINSTER PUBLIC LIBRARY, Westminster, England
WHEATON COLLEGE LIBRARY, Wheaton, Illinois
WHEATON COLLEGE LIBRARY, Norton, Massachusetts
HENRY WADE WHITE, Esq., Boston, Massachusetts
PETER A. WICK, Esq., Boston, Massachusetts
WILLIAM AND MARY COLLEGE LIBRARY, Williamsburg, Virginia
WILLIAMS COLLEGE LIBRARY, Williamstown, Massachusetts
WITTENBERG COLLEGE LIBRARY, Springfield, Ohio
YALE CLUB LIBRARY, New York, New York
YALE UNIVERSITY LIBRARY, New Haven, Connecticut
MAURICE F. YORKE, Esq., Green Craig, Aberlady, East Lothian, Scot-
    land
WILLIAM ZIMMERMAN, Esq., Washington, D.C.

TABLE OF CONTENTS

VOLUME I

LIST OF ILLUSTRATIONS

VOLUMES I AND II

Grateful acknowledgment is made to the British Museum, Harvard University, the Master and Fellows of Pembroke College, Cambridge, Mrs D. V. Garstin, and Mr Philip Gaskell for permission to reproduce illustrations listed here that are owned by them.

INTRODUCTION

EACH of Walpole's major correspondences has characteristics and qualities peculiar to itself. When writing to his close friends he felt that he was in their presence: he was aware of their position in life, their interests, their turn of mind; above all, of their turn of wit or humour. This is why when reading only his side of a correspondence we are able to form such a clear picture of the person to whom he is writing. Were we to read 'new' letters to Cole or Montagu or Mason that had no obvious clue to the identity of the recipients, we should have little difficulty in assigning the letters correctly. In the present correspondence there is a tone that makes it readily distinguishable, a cynical, a querulous, at times a savage tone, the tone that Mason contributed. The cause of this tone is not far to seek: Mason was a gifted and pushing man whose promising clerical start gradually petered out.

He was born in a vicarage at Hull in 1725, was admitted pensioner at St John's, Cambridge, in 1742 and became a Fellow of Pembroke in 1749. There he was taken up by Gray who found that he had 'much fancy, little judgment, and a good deal of modesty. I take him for a good and well-meaning creature; but then he is really *in simplicity a child,* and loves everybody he meets with: he reads little or nothing, writes abundance, and that with a design to make his fortune by it.'[1] The present editors find Mason's vanity, ambition, and indolence plainly visible, but suggest that his modesty, simplicity, and loving kindness require study and charity to discover. Professor Garrod's summary of him, 'Nobody likes him, and nobody trusts him,'[2] may be

1. Gray to Wharton, 5 June 1748, *Gray's Correspondence,* ed. Toynbee and Whibley, Oxford, 1935, i.307.
2. H. W. Garrod, 'Note on the Composition of Gray's *Elegy,*' *Essays on the Eighteenth Century Presented to David Nichol Smith,* Oxford, 1945, p. 116.

a little sweeping, but in the gallery of Walpole's chief correspondents it is agreed, I think, that Mason is the least attractive.

He took Orders in 1754. Lord Holdernesse was his patron and gave him the living of Aston in Yorkshire. Mason also secured a King's Chaplaincy, two prebends, and a supplementary rectorship, and in due course became a Canon Residentiary at York and Precentor of that cathedral. When Holdernesse failed (through declining influence) to secure for him the Deanship of Canterbury, Mason was unable to forgive him. Confined by his parish and prebendal duties to the solitudes of Yorkshire, except for occasional visits to London, to Wentworth, and, best of all, to the Harcourts at Nuneham, he settled down on his annual £1500[3] and increased the pain of his situation by composing mordant and anonymous verses. He was married in the mid-1760's for less than two years, his wife, Mary Sherman of Hull, dying of consumption at the age of twenty-eight.

The world at large was unaware of Mason's authorship of the *Heroic Epistle* and his other satires, but it held his acknowledged works, particularly *Elfrida* and the *Memoirs of Gray,* in the highest regard. No one shared this appraisal with more conviction than Horace Walpole, although he did not admire Mason at first. Gray brought them together as early as 1751 when he asked Walpole to read *Elfrida*.[4] Since Gray destroyed Walpole's letter, we do not know what was in it, but his opinion of Mason may be guessed by what he said when *Caractacus* appeared eight years later, that 'Mason in imitation of Gray, *will cry and roar all night* without the least provocation.'[5]

In 1756 Mason and Gray hoped that Walpole would speak to Henry Fox or the Duke of Bedford, 'or any other great man' on behalf of James Brown's aspiration to succeed Roger Long as Master of Pembroke.[6] Walpole's solicitation, if he made any, came to nothing, and it is not wonderful that friendship did not immedi-

3. Richard Gough in Nichols, *Literary Anecdotes,* ii.241.
4. GRAY ii.47.
5. MONTAGU i.239.
6. GRAY ii.89.

ately succeed acquaintance; yet in May 1761 we find Mason and Gray at Strawberry listening to the nightingales till one o'clock in the morning, and Walpole's first letter to Mason, of December 1763, makes it clear that in the previous year he had sent Mason the first two volumes of the *Anecdotes of Painting*. That letter shows a considerable advance towards friendship, but the correspondence does not really begin until Gray's death nearly eight years later. When Mason and Walpole met it was determined that Mason, Gray's executor, should write the life of their friend. Walpole promised to contribute a selection of his letters from Gray and to add such notes as would make them intelligible. At this point the correspondence may be said to have begun. Gray in his death brought about what had not been accomplished when he was alive. Mason as the biographer of Gray became one of Walpole's major correspondents.

Once the two men began corresponding regularly their rôles were soon reversed: the dominant correspondent became Mason. We can even see when the change-over occurred. It is in Walpole's letter of 17 April 1774, where he takes Mason to task for signing himself 'with the most perfect respect.'[7] Mason did not assume humility again, either in writing or in any other way; from then on Walpole is the giver, Mason the receiver.

Why, we may ask, did Walpole go under so completely to this man? I suggest that it was because at the outset he made Mason the surrogate for Gray in his epistolary scheme. What more natural than for Walpole to write to the friend and biographer of Gray? During the first years of their correspondence Walpole's news was predominantly literary, but with the writing of the *Heroic Epistle* Mason appeared to Walpole to be the most powerful satirist since Pope, and a Whig in the great Lord Russell–Algernon Sidney tradition. From then on Walpole became Mason's chief supplier of political news with special attention to persons to be satirized. In doing this he believed that he was serving his country as well as his vanity. 'You have a vein of irony

7. *Post* i.155.

and satire,' he wrote, 'that the best of causes bleeds for having wanted.'[8]

Walpole was not alone in his estimate of Mason's genius. Boswell and Temple as young men sat up all night to read *Elfrida* and talk of 'that elegant knot of worthies, Gray, Mason, and Walpole.'[9] William Hayley wrote:

> Say! Mason, judge and master of the lyre!
> Harmonious chief of Britain's living choir! [10]

In an unpublished preface to Mason's Dufresnoy,[11] Sir Joshua Reynolds wrote: 'I consider it as one of the greatest honours of my life to have my name united as it here is with the greatest poet of his age and whose skill in the sister arts both of painting and the theory and practice of music appears to be little inferior to that by which he has been so much distinguished in the literary world.' Even George Steevens praised Mason, and Dr Johnson found *Elfrida* 'exquisitely pretty.'[12] Barry placed Mason in his 'Elysium' next to Gray in the neighbourhood of Erasmus, Cervantes, Sterne, Pope, and Dryden. Today Mason is chiefly remembered as the correspondent of Gray and Walpole and the biographer of Gray.[13]

Between 1773 and 1784 Walpole wrote Mason more than 200 letters containing whatever he thought would interest him, especially derogatory news of the enemies of 'the cause,' the old romantic Whig cause of liberty. It is illuminating to compare these letters with Walpole's letter to the Duke of Richmond of 27 October 1775: 'You have not been a very active opposition, but may plead in excuse that you could do no good. *Now* you can— or never. Give the ministers no respite,' etc., etc. In the same spirit Walpole urged Mason to 'brand the guilty and reward the

8. 27 March 1773, *post* i.77.

9. *Letters of James Boswell*, ed. C. B. Tinker, Oxford, 1924, i.217, to Temple, 4 April 1775.

10. William Hayley, *An Essay on Epic Poetry in Five Epistles to the Rev. Mr Mason, with Notes*, 1782, Epistle I, ll. 13–14.

11. Kindly lent us by its owner, Professor Hilles.

12. Hester Lynch Thrale Piozzi, *Anecdotes of Dr Johnson*, 1786, p. 37.

13. Professor Draper shows how Mason's reputation continued to the end of the next century, when with the criticism of Saintsbury and Lounsbury it sank to its present low rating (*Mason*, pp. 11–14).

good; and since the fountain of honour is now the channel of corruption, wrench the chalice from his hand and dispense the waters to the deserving.'¹⁴ Walpole knew he was not the generalissimo of the opposition forces; he saw himself, rather, as the head of the planning and information services, with Conway, the Duke of Richmond, and Mason the leaders in the field. 'Mr Mason . . . provoked at the enemies of his country, exerted the light but sharp weapon of gay satire to reclaim a prostitute and sinking nation.'¹⁵ Mason was not only 'my ghostly father,' and 'my confessor in literature,' he was also the saviour of his country.

Walpole must have been a good deal of a trial to his friends politically. He was demanding and immoderate but he could not be ignored, because he did bring together, somehow, a great deal of useful information. And he was Horace Walpole, a person of consequence in many fields and for many reasons. Mason did not lose sight of that when he became openly bored with him.

Mason's boredom is evident almost at once. In return for Walpole's two or three long, eager, letters he would send a delayed perfunctory reply, even when Walpole had opened his heart to him as he opened it to few others. This went on for several years before Walpole's patience gradually gave out. 'I must be encouraged, or I cannot write even newspapers. . . . However, as I expect to be indemnified for your silence, I will consent to send you three letters for one, provided you give me a satisfactory account hereafter of your having been better employed than in answering mine. I certainly shall do nothing better than writing to you, and therefore whenever I have anything worth telling you, you shall hear it, and I shall not consider whether it is worth posterity's knowing or not.'¹⁶

It is not surprising that posterity was constantly in Walpole's mind in this correspondence. Was he not writing to the man who

14. 28 Aug. 1778, *post* i.441.
15. Walpole's note in Mason's *Satirical*

Poems, ed. Paget Toynbee, Oxford, 1926, p. 32.
16. 13 March 1777, *post* i.292.

had 'fixed the method of biography' and the greatest satirist of his day? But awareness of posterity was not enough to keep the correspondence going. Walpole's annoyance first appears 15 May 1778 when he confessed that he 'gulped his anger' at Mason's silence. We have no letter from Walpole to Mason between 11 October 1778 and 9 August 1779. It is possible that, as with Montagu, he got tired of not having replies and that he had let the correspondence drop, but when Mason wrote him once more he continued for another four and a half years in much the same laudatory and conciliatory vein, even though he and Mason reached almost at once the chief cause of their ultimate split, the York Association, in which Mason was a prime mover. In this controversy we find Walpole violently opposed to the Association's demand for annual Parliaments and a reformed mode of representation. What was first needed, he said, was a return to the principles by which his father had been guided and which had given England its happiest hour. The constitution should be restored before it was amended: Mason's associates in this dangerous whimsy were writers of bad English as well as proponents of crude and disputable propositions.

'A certain friend of ours who is at times so spitfire and at times so frighted,' Mason wrote of Walpole to Lord Harcourt.[17] He hoped that he might be able to escape a visit to Strawberry Hill. But Walpole held on. 'I could wish to see more of the few friends I have left, and consequently the one I most admire. . . . Oh, but there is or may be an obstacle that I do fear: Lord Harcourt is to go to Harrowgate, and that journey may detain you in the north! Well! pleasures are not the portion of age! I love you both too well to wish to separate you; and I will be content with your mutual satisfaction if it clashes with mine.'[18] Walpole broke his rule not to approach ministers for favours when Mason asked him to solicit the Duke of Richmond for the storekeepership at Hull for his brother-in-law, and this time his solicitation was successful. Then, on Fox's India Bill, Mason and Harcourt went over to the Court party and Walpole ended the correspondence with dis-

17. 1 June 1780, *post* ii.39 n.1.   18. 25 April 1781, *post* ii.136–7.

patch and bitterness. Mason's political derelictions had come to outweigh his poetical genius.

One cannot read the sarcasms exchanged by Mason and Harcourt at Walpole's expense[19] without, I think, feeling sorry for the ailing and aging man who had given so much of himself to both of them. In one of his letters to Mason, Harcourt describes Walpole in Berkeley Square with 'his usual morning circle of *intimate friends.*' Walpole made a story 'in the old style' upon the figures in a drawing by Lady Diana Beauclerk. Harcourt found the story ridiculous, but he has given us one of the most vivid pictures we have of Walpole in his old age.

Mason finally admitted that he missed Walpole's news, which had been his chief source of satirical inspiration; his letters to Walpole, he confessed, were generally the worst he ever wrote. In 1796 he reinstated himself by sending Walpole a sonnet attacking Payne Knight's *Progress of Civil Society,* which 'presumed' to continue Gray's poem on education and civil government. Walpole who detested Knight's *Landscape,* as Mason knew from Harcourt, was delighted with Mason's attack, and although weak and miserable he dictated an answer at once. Three days later, without waiting for Mason's reply, he 'carved out' a second letter in his own hand. It took him three days to do it, but there was no falling off of spirit. In conclusion he quoted George Canning's brilliant parody of Knight and then wrote his last sentence of the correspondence, 'However, I wish to see much superior wit, and far superior and genuine poetry lanced at the head of this marauder, and in any case I flatter myself our correspondence will not close again while there is a finger left of, dear Sir,

Your sincere humble servant,
Orford.'

In the following year both men were dead.

This is the least amiable of Walpole's major correspondences. It has passages that are quoted for their information and their wit, but Mason brought out Walpole's malice and partisanship.

19. They will be found in Appendix 1,
post ii.352–66.

Still and all, the crack of the lash and the dolorous note of doom that sound throughout Walpole's letters should not distract us from noting that Mason also brought out Walpole's patience, his loyalty to friends, and his passion for what he believed was the welfare of his country.

W. S. L.

MANUSCRIPTS AND BIBLIOGRAPHY

WALPOLE'S correspondence with Mason consists of 217 letters written by Walpole and 116 written by Mason. Five of Mason's letters and one of Walpole's —the unsent letter of 5 May 1783—are here printed for the first time.[1] All the letters but these and seven others (which were printed by Miss Berry, Cunningham, or Toynbee) first appeared in *The Correspondence of Horace Walpole, Earl of Orford, and the Rev. William Mason,* edited by the Rev. John Mitford and published by Richard Bentley in 1851. Since the originals of Walpole's letters to Mason have not been found, our text of them is necessarily derived from Mitford's, emended by Croker, Cunningham, and Toynbee; futher emendation has been provided by Dr Chapman and Mr Ketton-Cremer. Mason's letters are printed from the original manuscripts, which Mr Lewis bought in 1935 from Richard Bentley the younger.

Walpole died 2 March 1797 and Mason the following 7 April, before Walpole's executors, Mrs Damer and Lord Frederick Campbell, had sent back Mason's letters, in accordance with Walpole's testamentary request that letters to him from living correspondents be returned to them at his death. Two years later one of the trustees of Mason's estate, the Rev. John Dixon, was still trying to recover the letters,[2] but he failed to do so. They remained among Walpole's papers that passed to the Waldegrave family, and 'formed part of the collection of manuscripts purchased of the [5th] Duke of Grafton, as executor of the late Earl of Waldegrave.'[3] The purchaser, Richard Bentley, acquired the collection some time between October 1846 and March 1848. Mason's letters to Walpole were passed on to John Mitford, a clergyman and writer who had edited Gray and other poets for

1. See List of Letters, *post* pp. xlvii–lvi.
2. Letter from Dixon to Malone de-
scribed in Sir James Prior, *Life of Edmond Malone,* 1860, p. 307.
3. Mitford's Preface, i. p. vii.

Pickering's Aldine edition, and who was the editor of the *Gentleman's Magazine* from 1834 to 1850. Mitford wrote to Bentley 9 March 1848, 'I have just finished the transcript of Mason's letters, and will bring the originals to town when I come. But what I want to know is, where are Walpole's answers? *Transcripts* of Walpole's answers are at Aston, but Mr Alderson won't let me have them.'[4]

The owner of Walpole's letters was the Rev. William Alderson, son of Christopher Alderson, Mason's executor and successor at Aston, and the manuscripts that he was reluctant to give Mitford were not transcripts but the originals, as Mitford was to learn when he finally saw them. In October 1848 William Alderson seems to have abandoned his decision to keep the letters to himself, and, through Archdeacon Charles Parr Burney's mediation, invited Mitford to Aston to see them. But for some unexplained reason it was not until early February 1850 that Mitford at last arrived at Aston and was able to examine Walpole's letters.[5] He spent a 'most agreeable week' there, as he wrote to Burney, and was gratified when 'after some deliberation Mr Alderson was kind enough to entrust me with the letters I wanted to complete my publication.' He returned on February 9th to London, where on the 15th he signed an agreement with Bentley by the terms of which he sold the copyright for £300; he was to have another £100 if a second edition was demanded.[6]

What became of Walpole's letters to Mason after their publication in 1851 is not known. Willam Alderson at his death in

---

4. From photostat of manuscript in the University of Illinois Library, kindly sent to us by Professor Gordon Ray. As early as 1828 Alderson seems to have briefly considered permitting publication of the letters, for at that time he apparently sent at least the first volume of the four in which the manuscripts were bound to John Murray the publisher, who passed it on to J. W. Croker for his advice. Croker wrote to Murray 7 May 1828 that he found them 'the least amusing' of Walpole's letters, but 'well worthy of the press' (Samuel Smiles, *A Publisher and His Friends*, 1891, ii.294–5). For some reason the project was dropped. In 1836 Mitford himself had by some means procured at least partial though very inaccurate texts of the letters of 2 March 1773 *bis* and 27 March 1773; see *post* i.68 n.12 and i.76, head-note.

5. Letters from Burney to Mitford 5 and 12 Oct. 1848 in the possession of W. S. Lewis; photostats of letters from Mitford to Burney ca 1 Oct. 1848 and 11 Feb. 1850 (*penes* Leonard Whibley in 1935).

6. Photostat of manuscript in the University of Illinois Library.

1852 bequeathed to the Rev. Alleyne FitzHerbert 'all the books, manuscripts and other papers known or reputed formerly to have belonged to the Rev. W. Mason.'[7] Presumably Walpole's letters, if still in existence, would have formed a part of this bequest. Descendants of Alleyne FitzHerbert, notably Mr Nicholas H. Fitz Herbert and Mr Cuthbert FitzHerbert, have made every effort to find them for us, but have failed to do so. It seems not unlikely that the letters were destroyed some time between 1851 and 1900, either through carelessness or through ignorance of their identity and value.

Mitford never got his additional hundred pounds. When the *Correspondence* appeared, early in 1851, it was received coldly by reviewers and public alike. Accustomed to the graces and geniality of the letters to Montagu, Mann, and Lady Ossory, readers of this correspondence were repelled by its tone. And Mitford, who was approaching retirement when he undertook the edition,[8] had been notably remiss in watching over the press and in preparing his 'Illustrative Notes.' Croker, in a withering review in the *Quarterly* for June–Sept. 1851, justly condemned the notes as being generally useless. He pointed out that they added confusions of their own, and he poked fun at Mitford's suggested remedy, which was that, since the notes were 'less perfect' than he could have wished, no doubt 'readers will be able to supply themselves with original information' or 'derive assistance from the learned editors of works by Walpole previously published.'[9]

Fortunately, Mitford's preparation of the text on which subsequent editors have been forced to rely seems to have been a performance of greater distinction. On the surface it does not inspire confidence, since it is sprinkled with misprints, and here and there a letter is obviously misdated or out of its proper order. But the misprints can in most cases be readily corrected and the strayed letters returned to their places; these shortcomings were presumably the fault of the inadequately supervised printer.

7. Passage from Alderson's will, supplied to Mr Whibley in 1935 by Mr Frederick Page of the Oxford Press.
8. He was born in 1781, retired from the editorship of the *Gentleman's Magazine* at the end of 1850, and died in 1859.
9. Mitford's Preface, i. p. viii.

There is good reason to believe that Mitford's transcript from which the letters were printed was basically sound. As an editor and transcriber he was experienced and respected. D. C. Tovey, who took much of his material for *Gray and His Friends* from Mitford's transcripts that are preserved in the British Museum, commented, 'Fortunately his handwriting, though minute, is generally clear. . . . It may be inferred that he is generally faithful even to the punctuation, for this was his principle in copying; and I believe that access to the originals, had that been possible for me, would not have improved the present volume to any appreciable extent, wherever I have had Mitford to depend on.'[10] We have been able to test Mitford's accuracy by comparing his printed texts of Mason's letters with the original manuscripts, and we have found, in general, exemplary faithfulness.

The passages in Walpole's letters, with a few from Mason's, that Mitford felt obliged to alter or omit for propriety's sake—about twenty in all—he conscientiously jotted down in a notebook that is among his papers in the British Museum (Add. MSS 32563). Mrs Toynbee printed most of the passages; the few remaining ones that we print for the first time are indicated in the head-notes to the letters.

Although two-thirds of the Walpole-Mason correspondence, unlike any that we have yet published, no longer has manuscript authority, we have in general, for the reasons given above, considered Mitford's text worthy of being treated with the same respect that we accord Walpole's manuscripts. Therefore, as in our previous volumes, the punctuation of Walpole's letters has not been revised, except where it is ambiguous or obviously un-Walpolian. Mason's irregular punctuation has been freely altered, however. In all the letters, the hyphenization and capitalization have been modernized. The spelling has also been modernized (for lists of Walpole's obsolete spellings see COLE i. p. xliii and MONTAGU i. p. xxxiii), except that of proper names, which are spelled as in our source, whether manuscript or printed.

Sources quoted in the biographical footnotes may be assumed

10. Duncan C. Tovey, *Gray and His Friends,* Cambridge, 1890, p. viii.

to be supplemented by the *Dictionary of National Biography*, the *Complete Peerage* and *Complete Baronetage*, and the *Nouvelle biographie générale*. All English books mentioned in the references, unless otherwise specified, are assumed to have been published in London; French books are assumed to have been published at Paris.

Square brackets indicate editorial emendations; angular brackets, the restoration of the manuscript where it has been damaged.

C. H. B.

ACKNOWLEDGMENTS

WE are under particular obligation to Viscount Harcourt for permission to print large extracts from the Harcourt Papers, several of them for the first time. The readiness of owners to undertake the trouble and bother of having their manuscripts photostated and used makes our work possible. None has complied with our frequent importunings more generously than Lord Harcourt.

As indicated in 'Manuscripts and Bibliography' we are also greatly indebted to Mr Nicholas Fitz Herbert of the Hall, Somersal Herbert, Derby, for his very extended efforts, alas unavailing, to run down the originals of Walpole's side of this correspondence.

The Rev. Canon R. A. Wilson very kindly gave us permission to photostat and use Mason's unpublished letters to his curate, Christopher Alderson.

Once again we have to express our indebtedness to Messrs Chapman, Ketton-Cremer, Knollenberg, Hazen, and the late Leonard Bacon, who read our proofs and, as always, made many improvements. Our colleagues Messrs Warren H. Smith and George L. Lam have given much help in time of need.

Our student assistants on bursary appointments from Yale College, who rendered excellent service, were Messrs Michael J. Clifford, William N. Free, Laurence R. Veysey, and Thomas C. Witherspoon, Jr. The untiring help of the Yale Library staff is once more duly acknowledged. In addition we wish to thank the following:

Mr Frederick B. Adams, Jr, Pierpont Morgan Library; Mr A. W. Aspital, British Museum; Mr Frederick J. Boardman, Rotherham Public Library; Dr Curtis B. Bradford, Grinnell College; Sir Russell Brain, Royal College of Physicians; Professor Ralph S. Brown, Yale Law School; Dr Richard T. Burgi, Yale

University; Professor James L. Clifford, Columbia University; Dr Thomas W. Copeland, University of Chicago; Dr Lewis P. Curtis, Yale University; Dr Philip B. Daghlian, Indiana University; Mr Godfrey Davies, Henry E. Huntington Library; Mr Bertrand Davis, Dickinson College; Dr Archibald S. Foord, Yale University; Professor John F. Fulton, Yale Medical School; Mr Philip Gaskell, King's College, Cambridge; Mr F. R. Goff, Library of Congress; Mr Joseph V. Guerinot, Yale University; Professor Frederick W. Hilles, Yale University; Professor Ross Hoffman, Fordham University; Mr Charles Beecher Hogan, Yale University; Mr David Holland, West Horsley, Surrey; the Earl of Home; Mr Arthur A. Houghton, Jr, New York City; Mr William A. Jackson, Houghton Library, Harvard University; Dr Gerrit P. Judd IV, Hofstra College; Dr N. J. M. Kerling, London; Dr Mary E. Knapp, Western College, Oxford, Ohio; Dr Daniel F. Levy, New Haven; Mr Herman W. Liebert, Yale University; Dr Andrew Lossky, University of California; Messrs T. Lyth and Ewart Simard, Josiah Wedgwood & Sons, Ltd, Barlaston, Stoke-on-Trent; Professor Maynard Mack, Yale University; Miss Mabel Martin, Farmington; Mrs Louis L. Martz, New Haven; the McGraw-Hill Book Company; Miss Julia T. McCarthy, Farmington; Dr Robert F. Metzdorf, Yale Library; the late Sir Ellis H. Minns; Dr Leon Nemoy, Yale Library; Mr Leslie M. Oliver, Houghton Library, Harvard University; Mr James M. Osborn, Yale University; Dr William D. Paden, University of Kansas; Miss Rose Phelps, University of Illinois Library School; Professor Frederick A. Pottle, Yale University; Dott. Ferdinando Sartini, Florence; Professor George Sherburn, Middlebury, Vermont; Mr Robert A. Smith, Yale University; Professor William D. Templeman, University of Southern California; Professor Stith Thompson, Indiana University; Mr William Van Lennep, Harvard Library; the Earl and Countess Waldegrave; Professor A. Dayle Wallace, Wayne University.

W. S. L.

CUE-TITLES AND ABBREVIATIONS

Add. MSS . . . Additional Manuscripts, British Museum.

Alderson . . . Mason's unpublished letters (1763–95) to Christopher Alderson, in the possession of Canon Rowland A. Wilson, Hartlebury, Kidderminster, Worcs; photostats in the possession of W .S. Lewis.

Anecdotes, Works iii . Horace Walpole, *Anecdotes of Painting in England,* in *The Works of Horatio Walpole, Earl of Orford,* 1798, vol. iii.

Army Lists . . . [Great Britain, War Office,] *A List of the Officers of the Army and of the Corps of Royal Marines.*

BERRY . . . . *The Yale Edition of Horace Walpole's Correspondence: The Correspondence with Mary and Agnes Berry,* New Haven, 1944, 2 vols.

Bibl. Nat. Cat. . . Catalogue de la Bibliothèque nationale, Paris, 1897—.

BM Cat. . . . British Museum Catalogue of Printed Books.

BM Cat. of Engraved British Portraits . F. O'Donaghue and H. M. Hake, *Catalogue of Engraved British Portraits . . . in the British Museum,* 1908–25, 6 vols.

BM, *Satiric Prints* . . British Museum, Department of Prints and Drawings, *Catalogue of Prints and Drawings . . . Political and Personal Satires,* prepared by F. G. Stephens, E. Hawkins, and M. Dorothy George, 1870–1955, 11 vols.

'Book of Materials' . Three manuscript volumes, the first two entitled by Walpole 'Book of Materials,' the third entitled 'Miscellany,' begun in 1759, 1771, and 1786 respectively; now in the possession of W. S. Lewis.

Boswell, *Johnson* . . *Boswell's Life of Johnson,* ed. George Birkbeck Hill, revised by L. F. Powell, Oxford, 1934–51, 6 vols.

Boswell Papers	. .	*Private Papers of James Boswell,* ed. Geoffrey Scott and Frederick A. Pottle, privately printed, 1928–34, 18 vols.
Burke, *Landed Gentry* .		Sir John Bernard Burke, *A Genealogical and Heraldic History of the Landed Gentry of Great Britain.*
Burke, *Peerage*	. .	Sir John Bernard Burke and Ashworth P. Burke, *A Genealogical and Heraldic History of the Peerage and Baronetage.*
CHATTERTON	. .	*The Yale Edition of Horace Walpole's Correspondence: The Correspondence with Thomas Chatterton, Michael Lort, John Pinkerton, John Fenn and Mrs Fenn, William Bewley, Nathaniel Hillier, and Henry Zouch,* New Haven, 1951.
Cobbett, *Parl. Hist.*	.	*The Parliamentary History of England,* ed. William Cobbett and John Wright, 1806–20, 36 vols.
Coke, Lady Mary, MS Journal . .	.	Photostats of unpublished journals (1775–91) of Lady Mary Coke, now in the possession of Lord Home. Indexed by Dr Curtis B. Bradford.
COLE . .	. .	*The Yale Edition of Horace Walpole's Correspondence: The Correspondence with the Rev. William Cole,* New Haven, 1937, 2 vols.
Collins, *Peerage*	. .	Arthur Collins, *The Peerage of England,* 1768, 1779, 1812 (ed. Sir Samuel Egerton Brydges).
Corr. Geo. III	. .	*The Correspondence of King George the Third from 1760 to December 1783,* ed. Sir John Fortescue, 1927–8, 6 vols.
Country Seats	. .	*Horace Walpole's Journals of Visits to Country Seats, &c.,* ed. Paget Toynbee, published by the Walpole Society, Oxford, vol. xvi, 1928.
Cunningham	. .	*The Letters of Horace Walpole, Earl of Orford,* ed. Peter Cunningham, 1857–9, 9 vols.
Daily Adv. .	. .	*Daily Advertiser.* Film, 1731–95, in the Yale University Library, from the file in the Library of Congress.
DALRYMPLE .	. .	*The Yale Edition of Horace Walpole's Correspondence: The Correspondence with Sir Da-*

		vid Dalrymple, Conyers Middleton, the Earl of Buchan, Daniel Lysons, Samuel Lysons, William Robertson, Robert Henry, William Roscoe, James Edwards, William Beloe, and Robert Nares, New Haven, 1951.
Davies, *York Press*	.	Robert Davies, *A Memoir of the York Press, with Notices of Authors, Printers, and Stationers,* Westminster, 1868.
Delany Correspondence i–vi . . .	.	*The Autobiography and Correspondence of Mary Granville, Mrs Delany,* ed. Lady Llanover, 1861, 3 vols. Second series, 1862, 3 vols.
'Des. of SH,' *Works* ii .		Horace Walpole, 'A Description of the Villa of Mr Horace Walpole at Strawberry Hill near Twickenham,' in *The Works of Horatio Walpole, Earl of Orford,* 1798, vol. ii.
DNB . . .	.	*Dictionary of National Biography,* ed. Leslie Stephen and Sidney Lee.
Draper, *Mason* .	.	John W. Draper, *William Mason: A Study in Eighteenth-Century Culture,* New York, 1924.
DU DEFFAND .	.	*The Yale Edition of Horace Walpole's Correspondence: The Correspondence with Mme du Deffand,* New Haven, 1939, 6 vols.
Foster, *Alumni Oxon.*	.	Joseph Foster, *Alumni Oxonienses: The Members of the University of Oxford, 1500–1714,* Oxford, 1891–2, 4 vols; *1715–1886,* London, 1887–8, 4 vols.
Gaskell . .	.	Philip Gaskell, *The First Editions of William Mason,* Cambridge, 1951 (Cambridge Bibliographical Society, Monograph No. 1).
GEC . . .	.	George Edward Cokayne, *The Complete Peerage,* revised by Vicary Gibbs *et al.,* 1910—; *The Complete Baronetage,* Exeter, 1900–9, 6 vols.
'Genesis of SH' .	.	W. S. Lewis, 'The Genesis of Strawberry Hill,' *Metropolitan Museum Studies,* vol. v, pt i, June, 1934.
Genest . .	.	John Genest, *Some Account of the English Stage,* Bath, 1832, 10 vols.
GM . . .	.	*The Gentleman's Magazine.*

GRAY	*The Yale Edition of Horace Walpole's Correspondence: The Correspondence with Thomas Gray, Richard West, and Thomas Ashton,* New Haven, 1948, 2 vols.
Gray's Corr. . . .	*Correspondence of Thomas Gray,* ed. Paget Toynbee and Leonard Whibley, Oxford, 1935, 3 vols.
Grimm, *Correspondance*	Friedrich Melchior, Freiherr von Grimm, *Correspondance littéraire, philosophique et critique par Grimm, Diderot, Raynal, Meister, etc.,* ed. Maurice Tourneux, 1877–82, 16 vols.
Grove's *Dictionary* of *Music* . . .	Sir George Grove, *Dictionary of Music and Musicians,* ed. H. C. Colles, 1927–8, 5 vols.
Harcourt Papers . .	*The Harcourt Papers,* ed. Edward William Harcourt, privately printed, Oxford, n.d. [ca 1876–1903], 13 vols.
Hazen, *Bibliography of HW*	A. T. Hazen, *A Bibliography of Horace Walpole,* New Haven, 1948.
Hazen, *SH Bibliography*	A. T. Hazen, *A Bibliography of the Strawberry Hill Press,* New Haven, 1942.
Hist. MSS Comm. . .	Historical Manuscripts Commission.
HW	Horace Walpole.
Journal of the Printing-Office . .	Horace Walpole, *Journal of the Printing-Office at Strawberry Hill,* ed. Paget Toynbee, 1923.
Ketton-Cremer, *Walpole*	R. W. Ketton-Cremer, *Horace Walpole. A Biography,* 2d edn, 1946.
Last Journals . .	*The Last Journals of Horace Walpole during the Reign of George III from 1771–1783,* ed. John Doran and A. Francis Steuart, 1910, 2 vols. (Quotations have been collated with photostats of the original MS, now in the possession of Lord Waldegrave.)
London Past and Present	*London Past and Present: Its History, Associations, and Traditions,* ed. Henry B. Wheatley and Peter Cunningham, 1891, 3 vols.
Mason's *Satirical Poems*	*Satirical Poems Published Anonymously by William Mason, with Notes by Horace Wal-*

pole, Now First Printed from His Manuscript, ed. Paget Toynbee, Oxford, 1926. The MS of Walpole's commentary and notes is now in the Harvard Library. An incomplete draft in Walpole's hand, headed 'Notes to Mr W. Mason's later poems, by Mr Horace Walpole, 1779,' is now in the possession of W. S. Lewis.

Mason's *Works* . . *The Works of William Mason, M. A.,* 1811, 4 vols.

Mem. Geo. II . . Horace Walpole, *Memoirs of the Reign of King George the Second,* ed. Henry R. V. Fox, Lord Holland, 1847, 3 vols.

Mem. Geo. III . . Horace Walpole, *Memoirs of the Reign of King George the Third,* ed. G. F. Russell Barker, 1894, 4 vols.

Mem. Gray . . . *The Poems of Mr Gray, to which are Prefixed Memoirs of His Life and Writings by W. Mason, M.A.,* York, 1775.

Mitford . . . *The Correspondence of Horace Walpole, Earl of Orford, and the Rev. William Mason, Now First Published from the Original MSS,* ed. John Mitford, 1851, 2 vols. Mitford's own copy, including his MS corrections, marginalia, and related correspondence, is now in the possession of W. S. Lewis.

MONTAGU . . . *The Yale Edition of Horace Walpole's Correspondence: The Correspondence with George Montagu,* New Haven, 1941, 2 vols.

MS Cat. . . . Horace Walpole, 'Catalogue of the Library of Mr Horace Walpole at Strawberry Hill, 1763,' unpublished MS in the possession of Lord Walpole, Wolterton Park, Norfolk; photostatic copy in the possession of W. S. Lewis.

N&Q . . . . *Notes and Queries.*

NBG . . . . *Nouvelle biographie générale,* ed. Jean-Chrétien-Ferdinand Hoefer, 1852–66, 46 vols.

Nichols, *Lit. Anec.* . John Nichols, *Literary Anecdotes of the Eighteenth Century,* 1812–15, 9 vols.

Nichols, *Lit. Illus.* . . John Nichols, *Illustrations of the Literary History of the Eighteenth Century,* 1817–58, 8 vols.

OED	*A New English Dictionary on Historical Principles,* ed. Sir James A. H. Murray *et al.,* Oxford, 1888–1933.
Royal and Noble Authors, Works i . .	*A Catalogue of the Royal and Noble Authors of England,* in *The Works of Horatio Walpole Earl of Orford,* 1798, vol. i.
Sandwich Papers . .	*The Private Papers of John, Earl of Sandwich, First Lord of the Admiralty 1771–1782,* ed. G. R. Barnes and J. H. Owen, 1932–8, 4 vols. (Publications of the Navy Records Society, vols. 69, 71, 75, and 78.)
Scots Peerage . .	*The Scots Peerage,* ed. Sir James Balfour Paul, Edinburgh, 1904–14, 9 vols.
SH	Strawberry Hill.
SH Accounts . .	*Strawberry Hill Accounts . . . Kept by Mr Horace Walpole from 1747 to 1795,* ed. Paget Toynbee, Oxford, 1927.
'Short Notes' . .	Horace Walpole, 'Short Notes' of his life, printed in *The Yale Edition of Walpole's Correspondence with Thomas Gray,* i. 3–51.
Sold London . .	*A Catalogue of the Collection of Scarce Prints* [also MSS and books] *Removed from Strawberry Hill,* 13–23 June 1842. The number following each entry is the lot number in the sale.
Sold SH . . .	*A Catalogue of the Classic Contents of Strawberry Hill Collected by Horace Walpole,* 25 April–21 May 1842. The roman and arabic numerals that follow each entry indicate the day and lot number in the sale.
TLS	*The Times* (London) *Literary Supplement.*
Toynbee . . .	*The Letters of Horace Walpole,* ed. Mrs Paget Toynbee, Oxford, 1903–5, 16 vols.
Toynbee *Supp.* . .	*Supplement to the Letters of Horace Walpole,* ed. Paget Toynbee, Oxford, 1918–25, 3 vols.
Venn, *Alumni Cantab.* .	*Alumni Cantabrigienses,* Part I, to 1751, ed. John Venn and J. A. Venn, Cambridge, 1922–7, 4 vols; Part II, 1752–1900, ed. J. A. Venn, Cambridge, 1940–54, 6 vols.

Vict. Co. Hist. . . *The Victoria History of the Counties of England.*

Walpoliana . . . John Pinkerton, *Walpoliana* [1799], 2 vols.

Works . . . . *The Works of Horatio Walpole, Earl of Orford,* 1798, 5 vols.

WSL (now WSL) . . In the possession of W. S. Lewis.

Wyvill, *Political Papers* . *Political Papers, Chiefly Respecting the Attempt of the County of York . . . to Effect a Reformation of the Parliament of Great Britain,* ed. Christopher Wyvill, York, [1794–1802], 4 vols.

LIST OF LETTERS

THE dates of the letters to Walpole are printed in italics. Letters printed here for the first time are marked by a dagger (†) after the date; missing letters are marked by an asterisk.

		YALE	MITFORD	TOYNBEE	CUNNINGHAM
1756	*1 Aug.*	i. 1		*Supp.* iii. 140	
1763	29 Dec.	i. 2	i. 1	v. 423	iv. 156
1764	*6 Jan.*	i. 4	i. 2		iv. 157
1765	*14 April*	i. 5	i. 4		iv. 343
	17 April	i. 6	i. 5	vi. 213	iv. 343
1769	5 April	i. 7	i. 7	vii. 265	v. 153
	8 May †	i. 9			
	11 May	i. 16	i. 9	vii. 278	v. 165
1771	*28 Aug.*	i. 18	i. 11		v. 335
	9 Sept.	i. 19	i. 12	viii. 85	v. 335
	21 Sept.	i. 21	i. 14		v. 336
	25 Sept.	i. 23	i. 17	viii. 88	v. 339
1772	*?14 April*	i. 26	i. 21		v. 384
	9 May	i. 27	i. 21	viii. 160	v. 384
	17 May	i. 32	i. 25		v. 389
	25 May	i. 34	i. 27	viii. 169	v. 388
	6 July	i. 36	i. 29	viii. 180	v. 397
	ca 18 July *				
	21 July	i. 38	i. 30	viii. 182	v. 399
	24 Aug.	i. 42	i. 33	viii. 195	v. 405
	9 Sept.	i. 44	i. 34		v. 411
	19 Sept.	i. 45	i. 36	viii. 201	v. 409
	*ca 1 Oct.**				
	6 Oct.	i. 49	i. 40		v. 414
	13 Oct.	i. 51	i. 41	viii. 208	v. 414
	5 Nov.	i. 52	i. 42		v. 418
	10 Nov.	i. 52	i. 43	viii. 213	v. 418
	26 Nov.	i. 53	i. 44	viii. 216	v. 419
	1 Dec.	i. 54	i. 39, 44 misdated		v. 419
1773	9 Jan.	i. 57	i. 47	viii. 226	v. 426
	14 Jan.	i. 59	i. 49		v. 427

		YALE	MITFORD	TOYNBEE	CUNNINGHAM
1773	1 Feb.	i. 61	i. 51	viii. 232	v. 431
	23 Feb.	i. 62	i. 52		v. 432
	2 March	i. 65	i. 55	viii. 243	v. 440
	2 March	i. 66	i. 62	viii. 249	v. 445
	20 March	i. 72	i. 63		v. 445
	27 March	i. 76	i. 74	viii. 257	v. 465
			misdated		misdated
	7 May	i. 81	i. 66		
	15 May	i. 84	i. 69	viii. 275	v. 462
	28 June	i. 89	i. 81		v. 479
	28 June	i. 92	i. 79	viii. 299	v. 478
	5 July	i. 94	i. 84	viii. 301	v. 480
	16 July	i. 96	i. 87		v. 482
	29 July	i. 99	i. 89	viii. 310	v. 487
	3 Sept.	i. 103	i. 94	viii. 331	v. 499
	12 Sept.	i. 105	i. 96		v. 501
	17 Sept.	i. 107	i. 98	viii. 335	v. 502
	19 Nov.	i. 109	i. 100	viii. 360	vi. 13
	23 Nov.	i. 111	i. 102		vi. 14
	27 Nov.	i. 114	i. 104	viii. 361	vi. 14
	1 Dec.	i. 117	i. 109	viii. 371	vi. 22
	3 Dec.	i. 118	i. 110		vi. 23
	8 Dec.	i. 119	i. 111	viii. 376	vi. 25
	ca 11 Dec.*				
	14 Dec.	i. 122	i. 113	viii. 382	vi. 30
1774	4 Jan.	i. 123	i. 116		vi. 31
	14 Jan.	i. 125	i. 118	viii. 400	vi. 45
	15 Jan.	i. 128	i. 122		vi. 47
	21 Jan.	i. 129	i. 123	viii. 407	vi. 49
	3 Feb.	i. 132	i. 126		vi. 51
	14 Feb.	i. 134	i. 128	viii. 422	vi. 59
	3 March	i. 136	i. 131		vi. 61
	19 March	i. 138	i. 133	viii. 430	vi. 66
	23 March	i. 139	i. 134	viii. 431	vi. 66
	7 April	i. 143	i. 137	viii. 439	vi. 72
	ca 13 April	i. 147	i. 286		vi. 431
			misdated		misdated
	17 April	i. 151	i. 141	viii. 443	vi. 75
	23 April	i. 157	i. 148		vi. 78
	ca May	i. 159		xii. 171	viii. 159
				misdated	misdated
				Supp. ii. 163	

		YALE	MITFORD	TOYNBEE	CUNNINGHAM
1774	19 July	i. 161	i. 153	ix. 16	vi. 97
	9 Aug.	i. 163	i. 157		vi. 98
	23 Aug.	i. 165	i. 154	ix. 35	vi. 109
	16 Sept.	i. 167	i. 159	ix. 45	vi. 117
	2 Oct.	i. 170	i. 163		vi. 118
	Oct.	i. 173	i. 160	ix. 65	vi. 119
1775	29 Jan.	i. 175	i. 20		v. 384
			misdated		misdated
	18 Feb.	i. 176	i. 165	ix. 166	vi. 190
	28 Feb.	i. 179	i. 167	ix. 168	vi. 191
	3 March	i. 181	i. 169		vi. 192
	7 March	i. 183	i. 172	ix. 170	vi. 193
	3 April	i. 184	i. 173	ix. 173	vi. 196
	ca 10 April *				
	14 April	i. 190	i. 177	ix. 179	vi. 201
	7 May	i. 194	i. 181	ix. 194	vi. 210
	18 May	i. 198	i. 184		vi. 212
	27 May	i. 201	i. 187	ix. 200	vi. 216
	12 June	i. 205	i. 151	ix. 208	vi. 90
			misdated		misdated
	17 June	i. 207	i. 194		vi. 229
	10 July	i. 210	i. 190	ix. 216	vi. 227
	31 July	i. 214	i. 196		vi. 230
	7 Aug.	i. 216	i. 199	ix. 227	vi. 237
	6 Sept.	i. 219	i. 202	ix. 240	vi. 247
	22 Oct.	i. 223	i. 206		vi. 249
	25 Oct.	i. 225	i. 208	ix. 270	vi. 270
	27 Oct.	i. 228	i. 211	ix. 272	vi. 271
	20 Nov.	i. 230	i. 213		vi. 273
	27 Nov.	i. 232	i. 216	ix. 286	vi. 284
	16 Dec.	i. 234	i. 218		vi. 285
	21 Dec.	i. 236	i. 221	ix. 305	vi. 298
1776	ca 1 Feb.*				
	6 Feb.	i. 240	i. 226	ix. 323	vi. 307
	15 Feb.	i. 241	i. 227		vi. 307
	18 Feb.	i. 241	i. 228	ix. 328	vi. 310
	29 Feb.	i. 248	i. 232	ix. 332	vi. 313
	ca 7 March *				
	11 March	i. 251	i. 235	ix. 335	vi. 315
	25 March	i. 254	i. 237		vi. 316
	ca 1 April *				
	ca 4 April *				

		YALE	MITFORD	TOYNBEE	CUNNINGHAM
1776	8 April	i. 257	i. 241	ix. 343	vi. 322
	10 April	i. 259	i. 243		vi. 323
	14 April	i. 260	i. 244	ix. 345	vi. 324
	20 April	i. 262	i. 247	ix. 351	vi. 328
	21 April	i. 264	i. 248	ix. 352	vi. 329
	23 April	i. 266	i. 250	ix. 353	vi. 330
	1 May	i. 266	i. 250		vi. 330
	4 May	i. 268	i. 252	ix. 357	vi. 334
	ca 9 May *				
	14 May	i. 270	i. 254	ix. 359	vi. 336
	20 May	i. 271	i. 255	ix. 363	vi. 338
	28 May	i. 272	i. 256		vi. 339
	7 June	i. 273	i. 257		vi. 339
	n.d. [?1776] †	i. 273			
	17 Sept.	i. 274	i. 257	ix. 412	vi. 373
	ca 5 Oct. *				
	8 Oct.	i. 276	i. 263	ix. 418	vi. 379
	?Nov.	i. 278	i. 259	ix. 436	vi. 374
			misdated		misdated
1777	17 Feb.	i. 281	i. 265	x. 14	vi. 412
	27 Feb.	i. 284	i. 267	x. 20	vi. 416
	ca 9 March *				
	13 March	i. 288	i. 270	x. 26	vi. 420
	28 March	i. 293	i. 274	x. 29	vi. 422
	5 April	i. 295	i. 276	x. 34	vi. 425
	14 April	i. 298	i. 279		vi. 427
	18 April	i. 301	i. 282	x. 38	vi. 428
	2 May	i. 305	i. 291	x. 46	vi. 436
	12 May	i. 306	i. 291		vi. 436
	16 May	i. 307	i. 371	x. 50	vii. 66
			misdated		misdated
	26 May	i. 310	i. 293		vi. 437
	10 June	i. 312	i. 380	x. 58	vii. 80
			misdated		misdated
	21 June	i. 316	i. 296		vi. 438
	6 July	i. 318	i. 298	x. 73	vi. 451
	27 July	i. 320	i. 301		vi. 453
	4 Aug.	i. 323	i. 303	x. 88	vi. 462
	18 Sept.	i. 327	i. 306	x. 112	vi. 481
	21 Sept.	i. 328	i. 308	x. 115	vi. 483
	23 Sept.	i. 331	i. 310		vi. 485

		YALE	MITFORD	TOYNBEE	CUNNINGHAM
1777	24 Sept.	i. 333	i. 313		vi. 486
	5 Oct.	i. 335	i. 314	x. 127	vi. 493
	22 Oct.	i. 337	i. 317		vi. 494
	24 Oct.	i. 338	i. 318	x. 142	vi. 505
	26 Oct.	i. 340	i. 320		vi. 506
1778	17 Jan.	i. 341	i. 321	x. 176	vii. 20
	20 Jan.	i. 343	i. 324		vii. 21
	24 Jan.	i. 345	i. 325	x. 178	vii. 22
	4 Feb.	i. 348	i. 329	x. 181	vii. 24
	6 Feb.	i. 351	i. 332		vii. 26
	8 Feb.	i. 352	i. 333		vii. 26
	12 Feb.	i. 353	i. 334	x. 186	vii. 28
	18 Feb.	i. 356	i. 337	x. 189	vii. 30
	23 Feb.	i. 361	i. 342		vii. 33
	4 March	i. 363	i. 344	x. 195	vii. 36
	ca 9 March *				
	13 March	i. 367	i. 352		vii. 43
	16 March	i. 370	i. 348	x. 203	vii. 40
	21 March	i. 375	i. 355		vii. 44
	26 March	i. 375	i. 356	x. 209	vii. 46
	8 April	i. 378	i. 358	x. 214	vii. 49
	18 April	i. 382	i. 361	x. 220	vii. 53
	April	i. 386		x. 224	vii. 55
				Supp. ii. 156	
	12 May	i. 390	i. 364	x. 236	vii. 62
	15 May	i. 394	i. 368	x. 239	vii. 65
	24 May	i. 397	i. 373		vii. 68
	31 May	i. 399	i. 376	x. 252	vii. 71
	26 June	i. 404	i. 383	x. 268	vii. 84
	1 July	i. 406	i. 385		vii. 85
	4 July	i. 408	i. 387	x. 270	vii. 86
	16 July	i. 412	i. 391	x. 281	vii. 94
	18 July	i. 414	i. 393	x. 283	vii. 95
	19 July	i. 417	i. 396		vii. 97
	24 July	i. 419	ii. 1	x. 288	vii. 100
	10 Aug.	i. 425	ii. 6	x. 294	vii. 105
	14 Aug.	i. 427	ii. 9		vii. 107
	ca 22 Aug.	i. 430	ii. 376		vii. 116
	25 Aug.	i. 432	ii. 11	x. 305	vii. 114
	ca 25 Aug.	i. 435	ii. 377		vii. 117
	28 Aug.	i. 439	ii. 14	x. 308	vii. 119

		YALE	MITFORD	TOYNBEE	CUNNINGHAM
1778	17 Sept.	i. 442	ii. 20	x. 318	vii. 125
	7 Oct.	i. 444			vii. 139
	11 Oct.	i. 444	ii. 22	x. 332	vii. 139
1779	Feb.	i. 449	ii. 381		vii. 119
	May *				
	May †	i. 450			
	July *				
	1 Aug.	i. 452	ii. 26		vii. 237
	9 Aug.	i. 453	ii. 26	xi. 9	vii. 237
	18 Aug.	i. 457	ii. 29	xi. 12	vii. 241
	21 Aug.	i. 459	ii. 31		vii. 242
	23 Aug.	i. 460	ii. 32	xi. 15	vii. 244
	5 Sept.	i. 462	ii. 34	xi. 20	vii. 247
	14 Sept.	i. 463	ii. 35	xi. 23	vii. 250
	18 Sept.	i. 464	ii. 37		vii. 251
	28 Sept.	i. 466	ii. 39	xi. 28	vii. 254
	21 Oct.	i. 468	ii. 40	xi. 38	vii. 261
	12 Nov.	i. 471	ii. 42		vii. 262
	16 Nov.	i. 473	ii. 44	xi. 55	vii. 276
	ca 19 Nov.	i. 475	ii. 46	xi. 57	vii. 277
	29 Nov.	i. 479	ii. 49	xi. 70	vii. 286
	7 Dec.	i. 483	ii. 53		vii. 288
	11 Dec.	i. 485	ii. 56	xi. 76	vii. 291
	25 Dec.	i. 488	ii. 58	xi. 84	vii. 297
	28 Dec.	i. 489	ii. 59		vii. 297
	31 Dec.	i. 491	ii. 60		vii. 298
1780	4 Jan.	ii. 1	ii. 61	xi. 91	vii. 302
	17 Jan.	ii. 3	ii. 63	xi. 106	vii. 313
	22 Jan.	ii. 7	ii. 66	xi. 108	vii. 315
	29 Jan.	ii. 8	ii. 67	xi. 116	vii. 321
	30 Jan.	ii. 9	ii. 68	xi. 117	vii. 322
	22 March	ii. 12	ii. 71	xi. 145	vii. 343
	7 April	ii. 17	ii. 74	xi. 149	vii. 345
	9 April	ii. 19	ii. 77		vii. 347
	13 April	ii. 21		xi. 154	vii. 350
	17 April	ii. 26	ii. 79	xi. 159	vii. 353
	25 April	ii. 29	ii. 82	xi. 165	vii. 357
	19 May	ii. 32	ii. 84	xi. 167	vii. 359
	20 May	ii. 39	ii. 89		vii. 362
	24 May	ii. 41	ii. 92	xi. 177	vii. 367
	28 May	ii. 43	ii. 94	xi. 178	vii. 368

		YALE	MITFORD	TOYNBEE	CUNNINGHAM
1780	31 May	ii. 50	ii. 99		vii. 371
	4 June	ii. 51	ii. 100	xi. 190	vii. 378
	9 June	ii. 55	ii. 104	xi. 208	xii. 390
	29 June	ii. 61	ii. 109	xi. 231	vii. 407
	12 July	ii. 66	ii. 114		vii. 410
	15 July	ii. 68	ii. 116	xi. 242	vii. 415
	8 Aug.	ii. 72	ii. 119	xi. 254	vii. 424
	20 Aug.†	ii. 73			
	24 Aug.	ii. 75	ii. 121	xi. 261	vii. 429
	31 Aug.	ii. 78	ii. 122	xi. 265	vii. 431
	20 Sept.	ii. 79	ii. 123		vii. 432
	24 Sept.	ii. 81	ii. 125	xi. 280	vii. 441
	13 Oct.	ii. 83	ii. 128	xi. 300	vii. 452
	ca 29 Oct.*				
	1 Nov.	ii. 85	ii. 130	xi. 308	vii. 455
1781	4 Jan.	ii. 89	ii. 133	xi. 362	vii. 491
	21 Jan.	ii. 92	ii. 135		vii. 492
	27 Jan.	ii. 95	ii. 139	xi. 374	vii. 503
	ca 30 Jan.*				
	3 Feb.	ii. 100	ii. 144	xi. 379	vii. 508
	5 Feb.	ii. 103	ii. 147	xi. 382	vii. 510
	9 Feb.	ii. 106	ii. 150	xi. 389	viii. 3
	19 Feb.	ii. 108	ii. 152	xi. 400	viii. 9
	28 Feb.	ii. 112	ii. 156		viii. 11
	3 March	ii. 114	ii. 158	xi. 408	viii. 14
	9 March	ii. 117	ii. 161	xi. 411	viii. 17
	29 March	ii. 119	ii. 163		viii. 18
	30 March	ii. 122	ii. 165	xi. 422	viii. 22
	1 April	ii. 126	ii. 168	xi. 424	viii. 24
	14 April	ii. 128	ii. 170	xi. 426	viii. 26
	21 April	ii. 131	ii. 173		viii. 27
	25 April	ii. 134	ii. 175	xi. 430	viii. 29
	6 May	ii. 137	ii. 178	xi. 438	viii. 35
	15 May	ii. 140	ii. 181		viii. 37
	22 May	ii. 143	ii. 184	xi. 454	viii. 43
	14 June	ii. 145	ii. 186	xii. 13	viii. 53
	ca 30 June *				
	3 July	ii. 148	ii. 188	xii. 18	viii. 59
	16 Aug.	ii. 149	ii. 190	xii. 38	viii. 70
	9 Sept.	ii. 151	ii. 191	xii. 48	viii. 77
	19 Sept.	ii. 153	ii. 194		viii. 78

		YALE	MITFORD	TOYNBEE	CUNNINGHAM
1781	25 Sept.	ii. 155	ii. 195	xii. 57	viii. 84
	1 Oct.	ii. 157	ii. 197		viii. 85
	9 Oct.	ii. 160	ii. 201	xii. 64	viii. 90
	7 Nov.	ii. 161	ii. 202	xii. 83	viii. 102
	9 Nov.	ii. 163	ii. 203		viii. 103
	13 Nov.	ii. 165	ii. 205	xii. 91	viii. 108
	26 Nov.	ii. 166	ii. 207	xii. 104	viii. 115
	28 Nov.	ii. 168	ii. 208	xii. 107	viii. 118
	16 Dec.	ii. 168	ii. 209		viii. 118
	20 Dec.	ii. 170	ii. 210	xii. 122	viii. 127
1782	3 Jan.	ii. 173	ii. 213	xii. 140	viii. 138
	*ca 7 Jan.**				
	10 Jan.	ii. 174	ii. 215	xii. 143	viii. 141
	7 Feb.	ii. 176	ii. 216	xii. 157	viii. 149
	9 Feb.	ii. 181	ii. 220		viii. 151
	14 Feb.	ii. 183	ii. 221	xii. 165	viii. 155
	23 Feb.	ii. 186	ii. 225	xii. 174	viii. 161
	24 Feb.	ii. 189	ii. 227		viii. 162
	28 Feb.	ii. 191	ii. 229	xii. 183	viii. 168
	10 March	ii. 194	ii. 231		viii. 170
	14 March	ii. 196	ii. 234	xii. 194	viii. 177
	15 March	ii. 199	ii. 238	xii. 199	viii. 180
	21 March	ii. 201	ii. 239	xii. 203	viii. 183
	23 March	ii. 203	ii. 244		viii. 186
	23 March	ii. 205	ii. 242	xii. 206	viii. 185
	26 March	ii. 208	ii. 247	xii. 210	viii. 190
	30 March	ii. 211	ii. 251		viii. 192
	1 April	ii. 214	ii. 253	xii. 213	viii. 193
	2 April	ii. 217	ii. 256	xii. 216	viii. 195
	6 April	ii. 220	ii. 260		viii. 197
	6 April	ii. 222	ii. 262	xii. 220	viii. 198
	10 April	ii. 226	ii. 267		viii. 201
	11 April	ii. 229	ii. 270		viii. 202
	13 April	ii. 230	ii. 271	xii. 231	viii. 207
	14 April	ii. 233	ii. 275	xii. 234	viii. 209
	22 April	ii. 236	ii. 279	xii. 238	viii. 211
	24 April	ii. 240	ii. 282		viii. 213
	25 April	ii. 240	ii. 283		viii. 214
	27 April	ii. 242	ii. 284	xii. 241	viii. 214
	7 May	ii. 243	ii. 285	xii. 246	viii. 218
	8 May	ii. 246	ii. 288		viii. 219

		YALE	MITFORD	TOYNBEE	CUNNINGHAM
1782	18 May	ii. 247	ii. 289		viii. 220
	25 May	ii. 249	ii. 291	xii. 256	viii. 224
	2 June	ii. 251	ii. 293		viii. 225
	4 June	ii. 252	ii. 295	xii. 260	viii. 228
	6 June	ii. 254	ii. 297	xii. 262	viii. 229
	25 June	ii. 255	ii. 298	xii. 272	viii. 235
	1 July	ii. 258	ii. 301	xii. 277	viii. 240
	2 July	ii. 258	ii. 301		viii. 240
	8 July	ii. 260	ii. 303	xii. 289	viii. 250
	10 July	ii. 264	ii. 307	xii. 292	viii. 253
	14 July	ii. 267	ii. 310		viii. 254
	17 July	ii. 268	ii. 312	xii. 297	viii. 257
	4 Aug.	ii. 270	ii. 314	xii. 304	viii. 260
	20 Sept.	ii. 273	ii. 317	xii. 334	viii. 280
	26 Sept.	ii. 274	ii. 318		viii. 281
	23 Nov.	ii. 275	ii. 320		viii. 282
	27 Nov.	ii. 276	ii. 321	xii. 375	viii. 310
	4 Dec.	ii. 277	ii. 322		viii. 311
	7 Dec.	ii. 279	ii. 324	xii. 380	viii. 314
1783	18 Jan.	ii. 280	ii. 327		viii. 317
	?ca 21 Jan.	ii. 281	ii. 325	xii. 381	viii. 315
			misdated	misdated	misdated
	10 Feb.	ii. 284	ii. 329	xii. 403	viii. 332
	5 March	ii. 286	ii. 332		viii. 334
	7 March	ii. 289	ii. 330	xii. 413	viii. 333
			misdated		misdated
	4 May	ii. 290	ii. 335		viii. 335
	5 May †	ii. 292			
	7 May	ii. 297	ii. 337	xii. 439	viii. 360
	11 May	ii. 299	ii. 340	xii. 445	viii. 365
	19 May	ii. 302	ii. 342		viii. 366
	31 May	ii. 304	ii. 344	xiii. 1	viii. 373
	9 June	ii. 308	ii. 349	xiii. 5	viii. 376
	22 Sept.	ii. 311	ii. 351	xiii. 56	viii. 409
	ca 5 Nov.*				
	8 Nov.	ii. 313	ii. 354	xiii. 78	viii. 425
	25 Dec.	ii. 320	ii. 362		viii. 442
	30 Dec.	ii. 322	ii. 359	xiii. 107	viii. 441
			misdated		misdated
1784	28 Jan.†	ii. 324			
	2 Feb.	ii. 326	ii. 363	xiii. 124	viii. 455

From Mason, Sunday 1 August 1756

Printed from Toynbee *Supp.* iii. 140–1. MS bequeathed by Mrs Damer to Sir Wathen Waller, 1st Bt; sold Sotheby's 5 Dec. 1921 (Waller sale), lot 40 (with Mason's letters to HW of 15 and 24 March 1796, and HW's letter to Mason of ca April 1778), to Maggs; offered separately in Maggs Cat. No. 425 (Summer 1922), lot 1474; not further traced. The date is established from Gray's letter to HW 30 July 1756 (Gray ii. 89–91), in which Gray says that Mason will shortly be in London and will call on HW to discuss James Brown's candidacy.

Arlington Street,[1] Sunday.

Sir,

I PROPOSE to dine at Sion Hill[2] tomorrow and will if possible make you an hour's visit in the evening, when we may talk upon the affair mentioned by Mr Gray.[3] At present I can think of nobody on whom the Duke of Bedford[4] or Mr Fox[5] can have any influence except on Mr Delaval,[6] who I fancy is very secure for Mr Brown[7] without it. But I will certainly endeavour to wait upon you tomorrow, and in the mean time think of what steps will be best to take. I am, Sir, with great respect,

Your most obedient servant,

W. Mason

1. On 30 July Mason had come to London, where he was staying with his patron, Lord Holdernesse, in Arlington Street (*Gray's Corr.* ii. 469, 472–3). HW, whose town house was also in Arlington Street, was at Strawberry Hill.

2. Syon Hill, Lord Holdernesse's seat at Isleworth, four miles from SH.

3. The illness of Dr Roger Long, Master of Pembroke College, Cambridge, prompted Mason and Gray to interest themselves in the candidacy of their friend, James Brown (see n. 7 below), for the office. Long did not die until 1770, when Brown succeeded him. See Gray to HW 30 July 1756, Gray ii. 89–90; *Gray's Corr.* ii. 470–3.

4. John Russell (1710–71), 4th D. of Bedford, 1732; statesman and diplomatist.

5. Henry Fox (1705–74), cr. (1763) Bn Holland, was secretary of state from 25 Nov. 1755 to Oct. 1756 in the Newcastle ministry. He was at this time on intimate terms with HW ('Short Notes,' Gray i. 24). The reason for soliciting the interest of Bedford and Fox in Brown's election is made clear in Gray to HW 30 July 1756: 'As among eleven or twelve fellows who elect, there are . . . some that will regard their own interest rather more than his, a word from you to Mr Fox, or the Duke of Bedford, or any other great man, may . . . incline these doubtful people to vote for him' (Gray ii. 89).

6. Edward Hussey Delaval (1729–1814); chemist and author of several scientific works; B.A., Pembroke, 1751; fellow, 1751; F.R.S., 1759.

7. James Brown (ca 1709–84), B.A., Pembroke College, 1730; fellow, 1735; Master 1770–84; Vice-Chancellor 1771–2; D.D., 1771 (*Gray's Corr.* i. 222 n. 1).

To Mason, Thursday 29 December 1763

Printed from Mitford i. 1–2.

In the seven-year interval between the first letter and this one HW and Mason seem to have met infrequently. HW's unflattering reference to Mason's *Caractacus* in his letter to Montagu 2 June 1759 (MONTAGU i. 238–9) does not foreshadow their later intimacy, and in August 1759 HW, writing in his memoirs for Dec. 1757 about Whitehead's laureateship, says, 'His Grace [the Duke of Devonshire] had first designed it for Gray, then for Mason, but was told that both would decline it. . . . Gray, crowned with the noblest wreaths of Parnassus, could not stoop to be dubbed poet by a lord chamberlain; and Mason was too sedulous a copyist of Gray's march, to tread a step beyond the print of his buskin' (from HW's MS in the possession of Lord Waldegrave). HW wrote to Zouch 7 March 1761 (CHATTERTON 44) that Mason's elegies were to be published and that he had seen the one on Lady Coventry. The following letter makes it clear that HW had sent Mason the first two volumes of his *Anecdotes of Painting*, 1762.

Arlington Street, Dec. 29, 1763.

Sir,

YOUR bookseller[1] has brought me the volume of your works,[2] for which I give you a thousand thanks; I have read them again in this form with great satisfaction. I wish in return that I had anything literary to tell you or send you, that would please you half as much. I should be glad to know how to convey to you another volume of my *Anecdotes* and a volume of Engravers,[3] which will be published in a fortnight or three weeks—but they will be far from amusing you. If the other volumes were trifling, these are ten times more so; nothing but my justice to the public, to whom I owed them, could have prevailed over my dissatisfaction with them, and have made me produce them. The painters in the third volume are more obscure, most of

1. Robert Horsfield (ca 1723–98), at the Crown in Ludgate Street (Nichols, *Lit. Anec.* iii. 607; H. R. Plomer *et al.*, *A Dictionary of the Printers and Booksellers . . . 1726 to 1775*, 1932, p. 133; Gaskell 8–13).

2. This first collected edition of Mason's *Poems* was published by Horsfield 4 Jan. 1764 (*Daily Adv.*); it contained nothing that had not been published before except the dedicatory sonnet to Lord Holdernesse (Gaskell 10). 'My book was to have come out before Christmas, but my bookseller has begged to postpone the publication till Mr Wilkes ceases to engross the public attention, to which request I have willingly

condescended, not desiring to divert the public attention from so agreeable an object. However, your Lordship may have a book when you please after the 10th' (Mason to Lord Nuneham 1 Dec. 1763, *Harcourt Papers* vii. 25–6).

3. Mrs Toynbee's emendation; Mitford reads 'Engravings.' The third volume of HW's *Anecdotes of Painting* (printed June–Oct. 1762), and the *Catalogue of Engravers* (printed Oct. 1762–May 1763), were published 6 Feb. 1764 (*Journal of the Printing-Office* 10–12; see also Hazen, *SH Bibliography* 55–68).

them, than those in the former; and the facts relating to them have not even the patina of antiquity[3a] to hide and consecrate their insignificance. The tome of Engravers is a mere list of very bad prints. You will find this account strictly true and no affectation. To make you some amends, it will not be long before I have the pleasure of sending you by far the most curious and entertaining book[4] that my press has produced; if it diverts you as much as it does Mr Gray and me,[5] you will think it the most delightful book you ever read, and yet out of 150 pages[6] you had better skip the fifty first. Are not you impatient to know what this curiosity is and to see it? It is the life of the famous Lord Herbert of Cherbury and written by himself—of the contents I will not anticipate one word. I address this letter to Aston upon the authority of your book.[7] I should be sorry if it miscarried only as it is a mark of my gratitude. I am, Sir,

Your much obliged humble servant,

Hor. Walpole

PS. Have you read Mrs Macauley?[8] I am glad again to have Mr Gray's opinion to corroborate mine that it is the most sensible, unaffected and best history of England that we have had yet.

3a. Previously printed 'ambiguity'; we are indebted to Messrs R. W. Chapman and R. W. Ketton-Cremer for the emendation.

4. *The Life of Edward Lord Herbert of Cherbury, Written by Himself,* was printed between 23 Sept. 1763 and 27 Jan. 1764, but was not distributed until July 1764 (*Journal of the Printing-Office* 12; Hazen, *SH Bibliography* 70).

5. When they read it aloud to Lady Waldegrave at SH in the spring of 1763 they 'could not go on for laughing and screaming' (HW to Montagu 16 July 1764, Montagu ii. 130).

6. The printed book actually comprises 171 pages of text.

7. The dedicatory sonnet contains a reference to Aston, of which Mason had been rector since 1754.

8. Catharine Sawbridge (1731–91), m. (1) (1760) George Macaulay, M.D.; m. (2) (1778) William Graham. Publication of the first volume of her *History of England,* 8 vols, 1763–83, was announced in *Daily Adv.* 1 Nov. 1763. HW's copy was sold SH v. 51. Mrs Macaulay's emphatic Whiggism predisposed HW in her favour, but his esteem for her as a historian later vanished; see *post* 27 March 1773 and 16 March 1778.

From MASON, Friday 6 January 1764

Printed from MS now WSL.

Aston, Jan. 6th, 1764.

Sir,

THE bad weather which has confined me a fortnight longer in this place than I intended has given me an opportunity of receiving your most obliging letter in due time. I cannot help, however, animadverting on your reason for directing it to Aston, which you say was on the authority of my book, that is to say, because I had written a sonnet here the 12th of last May, you concluded I should be here also in the very depth of one of the worst winters[1] in the memory of man. A conclusion this, which would only become a bishop to make, and he, too, ought to be one's diocesan. I know nobody else that should expect a poor rector to keep such strict parochial residence. The fact, however, is on your side, but I must own I am here much against my will and shall therefore move southward whenever I can muster up courage sufficient to wade seven mile to a turnpike.

I am very highly obliged to you for your intention of sending me the concluding volumes of your *Anecdotes on Painting*, but hope to be in town soon enough to receive them there. Should they prove to be merely what you say they are I shall read them with great pleasure, for though I am no antiquarian I have as gross an appetite as any of them, in matters where painting is concerned. Lord Herbert's life will be a feast indeed.

I should as soon have thought of purchasing Aulay MacAulay's *Shorthand*,[2] as Mrs Mackaulay's *History*, on seeing them both advertised. I shall now, however, lead the lady into my library very speedily, where she will find no competitor, for I never met with a history of England yet that I thought worth buying, nor indeed could I ever read one fairly through, except David Hume's.[3] I wish you had told me whether she was a maid, wife or widow. Not that I have any

---

1. 'By the great rains that have fallen for some weeks past, the waters are more swelled in England and Wales than they have been for several years past, and the roads in many parts are thereby rendered almost impassable' (*Daily Adv.* 9 Jan. 1764; see also GM 1763, xxxiii. 613–14; 1764, xxxiv. 44, 93).

2. Aulay Macaulay's *Polygraphy or Shorthand Made Easy* was first published in 1747; 3d edn 1756 (BM Cat.).

3. Hume's *History of England* had been completed (to 1688) and published in six volumes in 1762.

intentions of making my addresses to her; but that I might have known whether she be born of English parents,[4] a fact which I am national enough to be very anxious about. I shall learn this, I hope, when I see Mr Gray at Cambridge, where I mean to stay a week or two, before I come to town.

Believe me to be with very great esteem, Sir,

Your most obliged and faithful humble servant,

W. MASON

From MASON, Sunday 14 April 1765

Printed from MS now WSL.

Aston, April 14th, 1765.

Sir,

THOUGH I neglected returning you my thanks for the present you made me of Lord Herbert's life, and of which, as you favoured me with a view of the proof sheets, I before gave you my sentiments, yet I will not omit thanking you for a more extraordinary thing in its kind,[1] which though it comes not from your press, yet I have episcopal evidence[2] is written by your hand. And indeed less than such evidence would scarce have contented me. For when a friend of mine to whom I had recommended *The Castle of Otranto* returned it me with some doubts of its originality, I laughed him to scorn, and wondered he could be so absurd as to think that anybody nowadays had imagination enough to invent such a story. He replied that his suspicion arose merely from some parts of familiar dialogue in it, which he thought of too modern a cast. Still sure of my point, I affirmed this objection, if there was anything in it, was merely owing to its not being translated a century ago. All this I make it a point of conscience to tell you, for though it proves me your dupe,[3] I should be

---

4. She was.

1. *The Castle of Otranto.*
2. Probably from William Warburton, Bp of Gloucester. A MS note by Mitford in his own copy (now WSL) of the Walpole-Mason correspondence, i. 404, alluding to

The Castle of Otranto, reads 'See Warburton's MS letter *penes me.*'
3. ' "*The Castle of Otranto* duped me, as I told its author. I really took it for an original work." Mason MS letter to W. Whitehead' (Mitford i. 404, MS note by Mitford).

glad to be so duped again every year of my life. I have the honour to be, Sir,

Your much obliged and obedient servant,

W. MASON

To MASON, Wednesday 17 April 1765

Printed from Mitford i. 5–7.

Arlington Street, April 17, 1765.

Sir,

THE unexpected and obliging favour of your letter I own gave me great satisfaction; I published *The Castle of Otranto* with the utmost diffidence and doubt of its success. Yet though it has been received much more favourably than I could flatter myself it would be, I must say your approbation is of another sort than general opinion. The first run for or against a new work is what I am sorry to say ought not much to flatter or discourage an author. Accordingly, self-love hitherto had not blinded me: I will not answer now but it may get a little hold on me; your praise is so likely to make me vain, that I oblige myself to recollect all the circumstances that can abate it, such as the fear I had of producing it at all (for it is not everybody that may in this country play the fool with impunity); the hurry in which it was composed; and its being begun without any plan at all, for though in the short course of its progress I did conceive some views, it was so far from being sketched out with any design at all, that it was actually commenced one evening, from the very imperfect recollection of a dream with which I had waked in the morning.[1] It was begun and finished in less than two months, and then I showed it to Mr Gray, who encouraged me to print it; this is the true history of it; and I cannot but be happy, Sir, that he and you have been pleased with it, yet it is as true, if you will give me leave to say so, that I think your friend judged rightly in pronouncing part of the dialogue too

1. For a more detailed account of the origin and composition of the novel, see HW to Cole 9 March 1765, COLE i. 88. See also Oswald Doughty's edition, 1929, pp. xxviii–xlv.

modern. I had the same idea of it, and I could, but such a trifle does not deserve it, point out other defects, besides some to which most probably I am not [sic] insensible. You must forgive me, if your commendation has already drawn me in to talk too much of a thing of my own; but I am vain of its pleasing *you*, Sir, and what would have fully comforted me if I had miscarried with most readers, is not likely to make me think worse of their judgment when confirmed by your taste. I am, Sir,

Your most obedient and obliged humble servant,

HOR. WALPOLE

PS. It is not my interest to recommend it but in justice to what I owe to your amusement I must advise you to read the *Lettres du Marquis de Roselle*,[3] if you have not yet seen them. They are written by the wife of Monsieur Beaumont[4] who has got so much credit by defending the family of Calas.[5] I do not recommend the boasted *Siege of Calais*[6] to you, though it contains some good lines, but the conduct is woeful.

To Mason, Wednesday 5 April 1769

Printed from Mitford i. 7–8. Whether there were any more letters 1765–9 is uncertain. The change of salutation from 'Sir' to 'Dear Sir' indicates a ripening of

3. A novel by Mme Élie de Beaumont, published in London and Paris in 1764 and reprinted at least four times in the same year (NBG; Bibl. Nat. Cat.). See HW to Mann 20 Dec. 1764. HW's copy of the Paris edition was sold SH ii. 148 and is now in the Bodleian.

4. Jean-Baptiste-Jacques Élie de Beaumont (1732–86), French jurist, m. (1750) Anne-Louise Molin-Dumesnil (1729–83). See NBG and 'Notice sur la vie et les œuvres de Mme Élie de Beaumont,' *Lettres du Marquis de Roselle*, Paris, 1829. He had visited SH in November 1764 and HW had later sent him, for Mme Élie de Beaumont, a copy of *The Castle of Otranto* (HW to Lord Hertford 9 Nov. 1764; HW to Élie de Beaumont 18 March 1765).

5. Jean Calas (1698–1762), a Huguenot merchant of Toulouse, was executed for the supposed murder of his eldest son, who, according to Calas's accusers, had been inclined towards Roman Catholicism. Many contemporary and later observers have regarded the verdict against Calas as unjust, and a flagrant example of religious bigotry. Élie de Beaumont's *Mémoire pour les Calas*, 1762, won the praise of Voltaire, who had greatly interested himself in the case. See F. H. Maugham, *The Case of Jean Calas*, 1928.

6. *Le Siège de Calais* (1765), tragedy by Pierre-Laurent Buirette de Belloy (1727–75). See MONTAGU ii. 150 and n. 3.

friendship, but this may have come about through visits during Mason's spring journeys to London as royal chaplain. Such a visit is mentioned in HW to Cole 16 April 1768 (COLE i. 134). When the present letter was written Mason was again in London on his annual mission.

Arlington Street, April 5, 1769.

Dear Sir,

I HAVE read carefully and with great pleasure your two comedies,[1] and will tell you sincerely my opinion of them. The grave one pleases me the most, and made me shed tears. I think it wants very little improvement: none in the conduct, if any rather more comic, which you have confined too much to Flora and the footman; one point I think wants correction, which is Lucinda's neglect of inquiring after her father till the moment she is ready to depart. The greatest objection I believe could be made, is, that the story, at least the situations, have too much resemblance to *The Conscious Lovers*.[2] When I have spoken so frankly, I trust you will believe me too, when I assure you I think it an excellent comedy, and can see no reason you could have to letting it be acted,[3] concealing the author, which I could not advise, after what I have said on that subject. So far from agreeing with Mr Gray, I like the bastardy, and would have the governor, consistently with the good sense of his character, say more against the cruel prejudice that falls on the innocent instead of the guilty. I will not flatter you more about the other piece. The indelicacy of Lady Fitzharold's character I think too strong; and do not approve Lady Betty's being so easily drawn, contrary to the pride of her ideas, which you make her characteristic, into love for the supposed *valet de chambre*. His part pleases me extremely, is new and would have great effect upon the stage; there are many scenes very well worked up; but the play would want softening in the respects I have mentioned. Still I own the other is my favourite: it requires very little alteration, might easily be improved, and I am sure would please universally. If you concealed your name, I can conceive no objection to your letting it be acted, which I should very much wish to see.—I give you a thousand thanks for trusting them to me, and for the sight of the drawing,[4]

1. Mason had sent HW MS copies of his comedies, 'The Surprise,' written in November 1761, and 'The World of Today,' written in the same year (Mitford i. 404). They were never acted or printed, and the MSS have disappeared.

2. By Sir Richard Steele (1672–1729), first acted at Drury Lane 7 Nov. 1722 (Genest iii. 99) and frequently performed throughout the century.

3. *Sic* in Mitford. Cunningham (followed by Toynbee) changed 'reason' to 'objection.'

4. For an account of Mason as draughtsman and painter, see Draper, *Mason* 303–5.

which lost nothing by my being prepared for it; besides the humour which is admirable, it is excellent as a drawing. I enclose a short advertisement for Mr Hoyland's poems,5 I mean by it to tempt people to a little more charity, and to soften to him, as much as I can, the humiliation of its being asked for him; if you approve it, it shall be prefixed to the edition.

Forgive the freedoms I have taken with you, Sir; I should not, but from esteem, and from believing you above being offended with them. I shall see you, I flatter myself, before you go out of town.

Your most obedient

HOR. WALPOLE

From MASON, Monday 8 May 1769

Printed for the first time from MS now WSL. MS untraced until offered by Tregaskis in *The One Thousandth Caxton Head Catalogue*, 1931, p. 35; bought by WSL, Feb. 1932.

On the back of the letter HW has written in pencil a note on the theme of *The Mysterious Mother:* 'Genuine and rational penitence that did not degenerate into superstitious bigotry.' At the conclusion of the letter HW has written in ink: 'N.B. I did not adopt these alteration[s] because they would totally have destroyed my object, which was to exhibit a character whose sincere penitence was not degraded by superstitious bigotry. The introduction of jealousy was utterly foreign to the subject—and though in my original it is very improbable that a wife on the very night of a beloved husband's death would think of going to bed to her own son, it would be at least as improbable that she should suspect her husband would after an absence of many months think of an intrigue with his maid on the very night of his return. Jealousy would reduce the Countess to a very hacked character, instead of being one quite new on the stage. H. Walpole.'

Mason's alterations were first printed in *The Castle of Otranto and The Mysterious Mother,* ed. Montague Summers, 1924, pp. 268–71, from a copy of the 1768 edition of the play (now WSL) inscribed by HW 'with MS alterations by Mr Mason'

5. *Poems by the Reverend Mr Hoyland* was printed at SH 10–24 April 1769 (Hazen, *SH Bibliography* 85–7). Francis Hoyland (ca 1727–1786), son of James Hoyland of Castle Howard, Yorks, was admitted a pensioner at Magdalene College, Cambridge, in 1744; B.A., 1749; ordained deacon, 1751, and priest, 1753; rector of Little Oakley, Northants, 1769–86; vicar of Weekley 1774–86 (DNB; Venn, *Alumni Cantab.*). In 1763 he had published *Poems and Translations by Francis Hoyland, A.B.;* of the five poems in the SH 1769 edition, two were reprinted from the earlier volume. See also *post* 8 May 1769 and 3 Feb. 1774. HW's advertisement, in which he describes Hoyland's misfortunes, is in Appendix 2.

—presumably the copy returned by Mason to HW in 1781 in which Mason had entered his alterations (see *post* 15 May 1781). There are numerous differences between the alterations as given here and those Mason wrote in his copy of the play, and the latter includes a lengthy 'Postscript to the alterations' (printed by Summers pp. 272–4) that bears little resemblance to the prefatory note here printed.

Aston near Sheffeild, May 8th, 1769.

Dear Sir,

SINCE I came hither I have read your tragedy[1] three or four times over with a good deal of attention, and as the *costume*,[2] the characters and many of the sentiments, etc., please me highly, I cannot help wishing that capital defect in the *dénouement*[3] was amended according to the scheme I proposed to you. To prove the thing feasible, I send you a sketch of such alterations as I think necessary. You will see plainly by the manner in which they are written that it was not so idle a vanity as that of correcting you *as a poet* that prompted me to write them. I trust I had a better motive: it was to show by taking this liberty, that I have an opinion of your candour *as a man;* and that I am with the truest respect, dear Sir,

Your much obliged and obedient servant,

W. MASON

1. *The Mysterious Mother* (*Works* i. 37–129), written Dec. 1766–March 1768, was printed at SH 14 June–6 August 1768 (Hazen, *SH Bibliography* 79–85). Mr Ketton-Cremer's résumé of the plot, which provides a context for Mason's alterations, is as follows: '[The Countess of Narbonne] had secretly taken the place of a maid-servant [Beatrice] with whom her son had arranged an assignation, and had borne him a daughter. . . . The guilty mother . . . [had] exiled her son Edmund to the wars, while bringing up Adeliza, her daughter by him, "fruit of that monstrous night," as her ward. Edmund returns home, unheralded and disguised, and falls in love with Adeliza. Meanwhile Benedict, the Countess's sinister and malignant confessor, professes to have detected heretical leanings in his penitent: and these tendencies, combined with her obstinate refusal to reveal the source of her life-long anguish, determine him to destroy her. She recognizes Edmund as her son, and her horror at his presence causes the friar to suspect the nature of her secret. With devilish malice he urges Edmund and Adeliza to marry immediately, and joins their hands himself. The Countess, distracted by the news of the marriage of her children, reveals the whole hideous secret, and finally stabs herself. Adeliza retires to a nunnery: Edmund returns to the wars' (Ketton-Cremer, *Walpole*, 1946, pp. 251–2).

2. 'The custom and fashion of the time to which a scene or representation belongs' (OED).

3. Mason held that the Countess's plight could not excite pity inasmuch as she had committed incest deliberately. The purpose of his alterations was to make her crime accidental and involuntary, proceeding from jealousy rather than from lust. The only factual change in the story in Mason's version is that the Count's death follows instead of preceding the Countess's crime.

PS. I have just heard from Mr Stonhewer[4] that the edition of poor Mr Hoyland's[5] odes is finished. By the last account I had of him from York, I find his situation is very deplorable, though, when my correspondent wrote, the state of his mind was more sane than it had been; but he is subject to such frequent relapses that I fear he will hardly ever be fit to perform the common duties of his profession. If he be, I fear few of his profession will venture to employ him as their substitute. All this however proves that what you have done for him will not be thrown away.

[Enclosure.]

ALTERATIONS PROPOSED IN *The Mysterious Mother*

By the Reverend William Mason.[6]

The following alterations are founded upon what I would suppose an axiom, viz.: That incest is a crime of so horrid a nature that whoever had committed it even ignorantly and by mistake, would have the same sensations of remorse, feel them in the same degree, and express their contrition in the same manner as if they had done it wilfully. If the person in question was a woman of strong natural sense, cultivated understanding, and unaffected piety, she would forget or overlook the only thing that could alleviate her despair, the thought of its being not intended, especially if ill-grounded jealousy had led her into so dreadful an error; for the consequences of the fact being full as terrible, an ingenuous and virtuous mind would still feel the sting of conscience in the severest degree. If this be allowed, it will follow that the very few alterations proposed to be made, are all that are necessary to make in the following scenes, in order to give the principal character a claim to our pity, without diminishing our terror; and to remove that disgust and indignation which she raises at present, in spite of all the dramatic art which the author has used to prevent it.

N.B. Many of these alterations being verbal or linear only, might

4. Richard Stonhewer (ca 1728–1809), son of a Durham clergyman of the same name; admitted pensioner at Trinity College, Cambridge, 1745; B.A., 1750; fellow of Peterhouse, 1751. He was under-secretary of state for the north 1765–6, and for the south, 1766; appointed private secretary to the Duke of Grafton, his intimate friend, 1766; auditor of excise 1772–89; F.S.A., 1787. He was a close friend of Gray, and Mason bequeathed to him Gray's library and MSS (Venn, *Alumni Cantab.*; *Gray's Corr.* i. 237 n. 38; DNB).

5. Expanded by HW from Mason's 'H.'

6. This line was added by HW.

be inserted by the pen in the present printed copy as errata, and the rest, when properly corrected, would only occasion a few pages to be cancelled, for care has been taken to insert as nearly as possible only the same number of lines.[7]

Act 1st

Page 12th,[8] read the 6, 7, 8, 9 lines thus:

> Ne'er fired her breast save only for her Lord,
> And him she loved with so entire a soul,
> That she had died, e'er wilfully foregone
> The faith she plighted with him at the altar.

Page 17th[9]

Read the last line but one thus:

> There was a time when my full-sated soul—

Page 23d[10]

Dele 16 and 17th lines and insert:

> And that those crimes may be of that dire sort
> As wake remorse eternal, though they spring
> From passion's error, not from horrid guilt
> Premeditated? Shall he teach me spells—

Act 2d

Page 26 and 27[11]

Dele the 18 line and the rest of the page and three lines following in the next, inserting these instead:

7. In the following notes the editors print HW's text; the italicized words are those that Mason proposed to replace with his alterations.

8. 'BENEDICT.

   . . . She owned to me,
That, though of nature warm, the passion love
Did ne'er anticipate her choice. The Count,
Her husband, so adored and so lamented,
Won not her fancy, till the nuptial rites
Had with the sting of pleasure taught her
   passion.'

9. 'COUNTESS.
Alas! must guilt then ground our very virtues?

Grow they on sin alone, and not on grace?
While Narbonne lived, my fully-sated soul
Thought none unhappy—for it did not
   think!'

10. Benedict urges the Countess to confess her sin to another 'holy man'; she protests, and says,

          '. . . Must I learn
That minutes stamped with crimes are past
   recall?
That joys are momentary; and remorse
Eternal? Shall he teach me charms and
   spells,
To make my sense believe against my
   sense?'

11. 'FLORIAN [Edmund's confidant].

Did usher in the morn your father died.

EDMUND.

Well, what of that? sage monitor! 'twas chance
That killed him, not a fit of ling'ring sickness.
And Beatrice and I, some hours, had parted,
Ere tidings came of that his sudden fate.
The maid, as I conjecture, in her fright
(For at the time she 'tended on her mistress)
Did let some word escape which might betray
Our late soft dalliance—Whether thus my mother
Became apprised I know not, etc.

Act 3d

Page 51st[12]

Instead of 8, 9, 10, 11, insert these:

Greater, oh impious!—yet there may be greater.
There may be such as would have dared to do
From very vice, what I—O think it not—
They could not be so blackly criminal.

Act 4th

Page 78[13]

For *adore* read *or love*

Page 79[14]

For *dire* read *blind*

. . . You have often told me,
The night, the very night that to your arms
Gave pretty Beatrice's melting beauties,
Was the same night on which your father died.
'EDMUND.
*'Tis true—and thou, sage monitor, dost thou
Hold love a crime so irremissible?
Wouldst thou have turned thee from a willing girl,
To sing a requiem to thy father's soul?
I thought my mother busied with her tears,
Her faintings, and her masses, while I stole
To Beatrice's chamber.—How my mother
Became apprised, I know not. . . .'*
12. The Countess, soliloquizing, speaks of 'greater sinners' than herself:

'—Greater! oh! impious! *Were the faggots placed
Around me, and the fatal torch applied,
What wretch could view the dreadful apparatus,
And be a blacker criminal than I am?'*
13. The Countess to Adeliza:
'Ha! what a glance was there! it spoke resemblance
To all I hate, *adore—*'
14. The Countess to Adeliza:
'Must thou be left to spoilers? or worse, worse,
To the fierce onset of thy own *dire* passions?'

Page 81st

After the 19th line some such sentiment as this should be added:

> For Adeliza, know in such a state
> Our very happiness is its own bane,
> It conjures up fell doubts that end in crimes—
> —O child, beware, beware of jealousy.

Page 83¹⁵

For line 9, 10, 11 read,

> Hear my last breath. Love not the knight too well
> Ev'n though he be thy husband. It may lead thee
> To crimes which but to think of is perdition.

Page 84¹⁶

Read the 13th line thus:

> That 'tis impossible to check their impulse.

Page 86

For *Passion's* crime read *folly's*

Act 5th

Page 105¹⁷

Latter part of the 2d line and for the third read,

>   Fair deceiver!
> She wakes the monster.¹⁸ See the couch is spread—

Page 111¹⁹

For line 6, 7 read,

15. The Countess to Adeliza:
'Hear my last breath. *Avoid the scorpion pleasure.*
Death lurks beneath the velvet of his lip,
And but to think him over, is perdition!'
16. 'COUNTESS.
Nature! these feelings were thy gift. Thou knowest
How ill I can resist thy forceful impulse.'
17. The Countess, raving:
'He beckons me—I will not—lies my Lord
Not bleeding in the porch? I'll tear my hair
And bathe his wounds—where's Beatrice!—
    monster! monster!
She leads the demon!—see! They spread the couch.'
18. 'Viz. jealousy which she occasioned' (Mason).
19. *'Does my own son then boil with fiercer fires*
Than scorched his impious mother's madding veins?'

Will my own son then with his mother's blindness
Rush on a crime as horrid as her own?

Page 114

Dele line 16th and the rest of the page. *Dele* also the first 8 lines of
the next and insert these:

> Ye know how fondly even to jealousy
> I doted on my Lord. Yes I was jealous,
> Of each fair female, jealous chief of her
> (So would Hell have it) her thy Beatrice,
> O would she had been thine! thou think'st she was—
> —Edmund—she ne'er was thine.

Page 115²⁰

Instead of line 12, 13 and 14 insert,

> More dire than was the deed. My jealous madness
> Falsely surmised that it had traced the time
> The very hour when to the damsel's bed
> My husband meant to steal. That fatal night
> I seized the maid, in yonder tower confined her
> And in her stead—

Same page, *dele* the last line and proceed thus:

> I took the damsel's place, and while my arms
> Twined to my thinking round my husband's waist,
> Thine to thy thinking round young Beatrice—
> Hear Hell and tremble—I did clasp my son
> And thou thy mother—Be that sleep eternal
> Nor let her know the rest, she is thy daughter,
> Fruit of that monstrous night.

>   EDMUND.
> Infernal tale
> My dagger must revenge—but how revenge—

20.   'COUNTESS.
Thou canst not harbour a foreboding
     thought
More dire, *than I conceived, I executed.*
Guilt rushed into my soul—my fancy saw
     thee
Thy father's image—
          'EDMUND.
     Swallow th' accursed sound!

Nor dare to say—
               'COUNTESS.
          Yes, thou polluted son!
Grief, disappointment, opportunity,
Raised such a tumult in my madding blood,
I took the damsel's place,' etc.

Whom shall I strike, myself or her? O father
O injured shade—
      COUNTESS (snatching the sword).
              Thus Edmund I revenge
Both him and thee—

To MASON, Thursday 11 May 1769

Printed from Mitford i. 9–11.

Arlington Street, May 11, 1769.

Dear Sir,

I AM more pleased than surprised at your kindness, and the hurry
with which I answer your letter will I hope in some measure express my gratitude. I thank you for myself, not for my play. I care little
about the latter, in comparison of the satisfaction I receive from your
friendship. I cannot think the play deserved the pains you have bestowed on it, but I am very willing to flatter myself that you felt some
kindness for the author: and I doubt I am one of those selfish parents
that love themselves better than their offspring.

I cannot think of the stage—I believe from pride—and I am weary
of printing and publishing—I suppose from vanity, at least I am sure
I have no better reasons for not making all possible use of your alterations, with which I am so much pleased that I shall correct my own
copy by them.[1] I am astonished to see with how few lines you have
been able totally to change the canvas of a whole play, a play totally
defective in the plan, and I believe not much better in the conduct,
which you would not exert your judgment, or rather your chemistry
to prove; for I must repeat how surprised I am at the *solution* you
have made with so little trouble. I own too my own want of judgment:
I believe I was so pleased with what ought to have prevented my attempting the subject, which was the singularity of it. Unfrequent
crimes are as little the business of tragedy, as singular characters are
of comedy; it is inviting the town to correct a single person. You see
Sir, I am far from being incorrigible, on the contrary, I am willing
to be corrected; but as Mr Gray could tell you, I cannot correct myself.[2] I write I neither know how nor why, and always make worse what

1. HW did not do so; his copy is now in
the Pierpont Morgan Library. His candid
opinion of the alterations is given in the
head-note to the preceding letter.

I try to amend. I have begged him a thousand times to no purpose to correct trifles I have written, and which I really could not improve myself. I am not so unreasonable or so impudent[2a] as to ask the same favour of you, Sir; but I accept with great thankfulness what you have voluntarily been so good as to do for me; and should *The Mysterious Mother* ever be performed when I am dead, it will owe to you its presentation.[3]

When I see Mr Stonhewer, I will know if he would choose another edition of poor Mr Hoyland's poems. I doubt *not,* as when he sent for the last twenty, he said he believed he *could* get off them.[4] I gladly adopt your corrections, but I cannot father your own goodness. It is to you, Sir, Mr Hoyland owes everything.

Dodsley[5] has published a dozen letters of Pope to Mrs Blount;[6] they are evidently real love-letters—and yet they are stiff and unnatural, though he affects negligence in them.

I forgot to reprove you for calling me *a poet.*[7] I wish I had any pretensions to that title. It is true I early wished to be one, but soon found I was not;[8] my prose was like speeches of the members of the House of Commons, who try to talk themselves into titles to which they were not born; you Sir, who found your patent in your cradle, call me *my Lord,* as English peers condescend to give their own appellation to the peers of Ireland, though conscious that the latter are only commoners: for my part I give up all pretensions but to your esteem, with which you have flattered me, and which I beg you to continue by marks of friendship to, dear Sir,

Your much obliged humble servant,

Hor. Walpole

2. See HW to Gray 18 Feb. 1768, Gray ii. 167.

2a. Previously printed 'imprudent'; emended by Dr Chapman.

3. No record of a performance has been found. Joseph Haslewood's statement in Sir Egerton Brydges, *Censura Literaria,* 1805–9, ix. 189, that it was 'publicly represented' in Ireland, has not been confirmed.

4. Three hundred copies had been printed at the SH Press. Another edition was printed in 1769, but not at SH (Hazen, *SH Bibliography* 87).

5. James Dodsley (1724–97), bookseller, brother and successor to Robert Dodsley.

6. Publication of *Letters of the Late Alexander Pope, Esq., to a Lady* was announced in *Daily Adv.* 8 May 1769. HW was mistaken in thinking that the letters were addressed to Martha Blount (1690–1762). They were actually written to Judith Cowper (ca 1701–81), who had won Pope's esteem by a poetical compliment to him. See Elwin and Courthope, *Works of Pope,* 1871–89, ix. 416. HW's copy of the *Letters* is now wsl; he has written 'Mrs Martha Blount' under 'a Lady' on the half-title.

7. *Ante* 8 May 1769.

8. See HW's verses to West on this subject (Gray i. 121–3).

From MASON, Wednesday 28 August 1771

Printed from MS now WSL.
Address: To the Honourable Mr Walpole.

York, August 28th, 1771.

Dear Sir,

I DEFERRED writing to you on the late melancholy occasion[1] till I heard you was upon your return from Paris.[2] I hope this will find you in perfect health after your journey, and I have sent it under Mr Stonhewer's cover that he may deliver it to you when he hears you are arrived in town.

You will be informed I presume before this that I am entrusted with all Mr Gray's papers 'to preserve or destroy at my own discretion,'[3] an important charge which I shall find myself unable to execute without the advice and assistance of his other friends, and therefore I do not doubt that if, amongst these, I apply to you you will think it no trouble to give me your opinion and counsel. Hitherto I have been able to do little more than to sort in parcels the letters of his living friends, that I may return them, or burn them, as the parties shall direct me to do. I do not find many of yours,[4] but those which I have found I have taken due care of, and shall wait your directions concerning them.

I do not believe that Mr Gray has left one finished poem,[5] but there are some considerable and beautiful fragments amongst which his 'Essay on Education'[6] is the principal, but at present I cannot speak with any certainty, as I have only examined his papers very transiently. When I am better informed I shall do myself the honour of

1. The death of Gray on 30 July 1771. Mason and Dr James Brown had been appointed his executors. See Mason to Wharton 18 Aug. 1771 in *Gray's Corr.* iii. 1275–6.

2. HW expected to set out on his return journey on 26 Aug. but was delayed until 2 Sept. He reached London 6 Sept. (COLE i. 229; DU DEFFAND v. 333–42).

3. 'I give to the Reverend William Mason, precentor of York, all my books, manuscripts, coins, music printed or written, and papers of all kinds to preserve or destroy at his own discretion' (Gray's will: see *Gray's Corr.* iii. 1285).

4. Only thirteen are now known (GRAY i. p. xxxiv).

5. Mason was mistaken. In his *Mem. Gray* ('Poems' 58–9, 60, and 62), he published for the first time three completed poems by Gray: 'The Death of Hoel,' the sonnet to West, and the epitaph for Sir William Williams.

6. The first part of this fragment, which Gray left untitled but described to Wharton as 'The Alliance of Education and Government,' was sent in Gray's letter to Wharton 19 Aug. 1748, and was printed by Mason with Gray's later continuation of the poem (*Mem. Gray* 192–200; see also *Gray's Corr.* i. 310–2).

writing to you more fully; in the mean time I thought it my duty to acquaint you with the above particulars, and to assure you that I am with the truest respect, dear Sir,

Your most obliged and faithful servant,

W. MASON

I have in my possession your printed letter to Dr Milles.⁷

To MASON, Monday 9 September 1771

Printed from Mitford i. 12–14.

Strawberry Hill, Sept. 9, 1771.

Dear Sir,

I JUDGE of your shock and concern at Mr Gray's [death] by my own.¹ I saw him the day before I left England;² he complained of the gout flying about him, and said he had been a month at Kensington for the air. I saw him changed and very low—yet I had not the least idea of any sudden misfortune. Three weeks after I read in the *Chronicle*³ at Paris, that he was dead! I would not believe it—not alas! from reason; but I could not bear to believe it—I wrote to Mr Cole to inquire—he has confirmed it,⁴ and I find it at my return but too true. I feel for you, Sir, and as I most heartily regret him, I would do anything to show my regard to his memory. If he has left anything for

7. Jeremiah Milles (1714–84), D.D., antiquary, Dean of Exeter 1762–84, president of the Society of Antiquaries 1768–84, had replied to HW's *Historic Doubts* (1768) in 'Observations on the Wardrobe Account for the Year 1483,' published in *Archæologia*, 1770, i. 361–83. Six copies of HW's 'Reply to the Observations of the Rev. Dr Milles' (*Works* ii. *221–*44) had been printed at SH in 1770 (Hazen, *SH Bibliography* 91, 95–6), one of which was doubtless this copy, which HW had sent to Gray. HW wrote to Cole 10 Jan. 1771, 'Mr Gray will show you my answer to Dr Milles' (COLE i. 212), and Gray did so (ibid. i. 213).

1. Written before HW received Mason's letter of 28 Aug. See HW to Stonhewer 16 Sept. 1771.

2. 7 July 1771. In his letter to Conway of 11 Aug., HW said Gray called on him 'two or three days' before he left; he told Cole it was 'four or five days' (COLE i. 228).

3. 'On Tuesday evening died of the gout in his stomach, at his rooms in Pembroke College, Cambridge, Thomas Gray, LL.B., professor of modern history and languages in that university; a gentleman well known in the literary world as author of the *Elegy in a Country Churchyard*, and many other much admired pieces. The professorship, worth upwards of £400 a year, is in the gift of the Crown' (*London Chronicle* 1–3 Aug. 1771, xxx. 120).

4. See HW to Cole 12 Aug. and Cole to HW 21 Aug. 1771, COLE i. 228–32.

the press, I flatter myself mine will be allowed to contribute to that office. I shall be very happy to bear all the expense—you, I am sure, Sir, will let his genius want no due honour—and it is not to interfere with anything that you design to say of him, and which you will say better than anybody, that I send you the following lines. They are not worthy of him, nor do I repeat them to you but as a proof of my sorrow, and a tribute to your friend, which is the only light in which they can please you. You will see that the lines suppose him buried among his real predecessors.

> Great shades of Shakspear, Milton, Dryden, hear;
> A genuine bard from Genius claims a tear.
> He, who in numbers, worthy of the lyre,
> Enshrined your names, now joins the mighty choir.
> Amidst your radiant urns his urn enclose,
> A spot more hallowed than where kings repose,
> Aloft let Pomp her Edwards, Henrys, keep;
> Near Homer's dust should Pindar's ashes sleep.[5]

If I could have greater contempt for the age than I have, it would be on observing that one single paragraph is all that has been said on our friend; but when there are columns in every paper on Sir Francis Delaval,[6] ought we not to be glad? Who would be the hero of these times?

Is there any chance, Sir, of your coming southwards? I long to pass a melancholy hour with you. Who has possession of the plate from my picture of Mr Gray?[7] I have many scraps and letters of his that show how very early his genius was ripe, and which will please you

---

5. This line is echoed in Mason's four-line epitaph later inscribed on the monument to Gray in Westminster Abbey (see *post* ca Nov. 1776 and n. 8). Gray is identified with Pindar because of his two Pindaric odes, 'The Bard' and 'The Progress of Poesy.' 'They are Greek, they are Pindaric, they are sublime!—consequently I fear a little obscure' (HW to Mann 4 Aug. 1757). HW's first four lines allude to 'The Progress of Poesy,' ll. 83–106.

6. Sir Francis Blake Delaval (ca 1727–7 Aug. 1771), K.B., 1761; M.P. Andover 1754–68 (GM 1771, xli. 378; see also MONTAGU i. 221 n. 2). Cole, who 'knew him from his birth,' wrote that he was 'the very soul of frolic and amusement' and 'overbalanced a few foibles by a thousand amiable qualities' (Nichols, *Lit. Illus.* viii. 574). 'Columns

in every paper' is an exaggeration, but besides the paragraph on his death in *London Chronicle* 6–8 Aug. 1771 (xxx. 134) there are additional paragraphs in the issues for 8–10, 10–13, and 13–15 Aug. (xxx. 143, 146, 154), in the last of which there is also a brief 'character' of Sir Francis contributed by a correspondent (xxx. 159).

7. The portrait of Gray by John Giles Eccardt, painted for HW in 1748 and now in the National Portrait Gallery. A plate engraved from it by J. S. Müller had been sent to Gray, and may have been destroyed by him. It was intended by Dodsley to serve as frontispiece to *Designs by Mr R. Bentley for Six Poems by Mr T. Gray*, 1753, but was suppressed on Gray's insistence. A good many copies of the engraving were preserved. See GRAY ii. 63 and *post* 5 Nov. 1772.

exceedingly. To collect the *reliques* of our friends is perhaps the sweetest employment of those moments that remain when we have lost them! It is a decent preparation too for our own fate. I am, dear Sir,

Your most obedient humble servant,

Hor. Walpole

From Mason, Saturday 21 September 1771

Printed from MS now WSL.

York, Sept. 21st, 1771.

Dear Sir,

YOUR favour of the 9th by being directed only to Aston and not *near Sheffeild* strayed I believe through all our three Ridings before it found me here. I had enclosed a letter[1] to Mr Stonhewer to deliver to you when you returned to England, which I hope you also have received ere this; and therefore will not think me deficient in point of respect to you on the melancholy occasion which led me to begin the correspondence. The lines which you have done me the honour to send me are excellently well turned and justly expressive of his poetical abilities, and I think with a little alteration might be inscribed on a monument in the Poets' Corner, Westminster Abbey. The alteration I mean is *bust,* for *urn;* in consequence of which the three latter lines would require a small change which might easily be made without altering the turn of thought. I know you will make me the same answer to this which you did when I talked of a certain alteration before in a greater work.[2] Yet I know you will excuse me for giving you my free sentiments—even when I add that the epitaph will still want something more, as it yet does not praise him for what I think he deserves more to be praised than for his poetical talents: I mean the qualities of his heart.

After thanking you for the very obliging offer you make of publishing his poems, etc., I will with the same freedom tell you my opinion upon that subject. I always thought Mr Gray blamable for letting the

1. *Ante* 28 Aug. 1771.   2. *The Mysterious Mother.*

booksellers have his MSS gratis. I never saw anything myself beneath the dignity of a gentleman in making a profit of the productions of one's own brain. I frequently had disputes with him on this matter, which generally ended in a laugh—he called me covetous and I called him proud. What you think upon this head I know not, yet I trust you do not carry your ideas of this kind so far as Monsieur de Nivernois,[3] because I remember what you said, when you gave me an anecdote about him and the French punctilio with regard to authorship.[4] Dodsley, however, has (I doubt not) got some hundred pounds by Mr Gray's suffering him to print his poems as he has hitherto done, and in my opinion Dodsley nor any of the great booksellers ought to have been an object of his beneficence. I should not wonder at present if Dodsley claims a right in the copies of such things as he has already printed, yet I fancy he can show no title to such a claim,[5] or at least his title cannot preclude mine, and therefore, it is not to be doubted that, if I prepared an edition of the poems in question with ever so little new in it, such an edition would stop the sale of his, and continue to bring in a considerable profit whether I kept the right or sold it to any other bookseller. My first business therefore will be to ascertain this right, and afterwards to make as much profit of the book as I possibly can. I hope you will do me the justice to believe that I shall dispose[6] of the money that may accrue in a way that will do honour to the memory of Mr Gray, and in so doing I flatter myself you will think that I shall do much better in this point than he did, who had certainly much better have taken the profits, and bestowed them on such benevolent purposes, for which his purse was never, till of late, sufficient to answer the demands of his heart and which might have been in some sort assisted by this means had he not thrown it away on the most undeserving of all objects, *printers and booksellers,* and those rich ones into the bargain.

What I have said does not in the least counteract your thought of an edition from your own press and I shall be happy to consult you

3. Louis-Jules-Barbon Mancini-Mazarini (1716–98), Duc de Nivernais; French writer and diplomat, and HW's friend and correspondent.

4. The anecdote has not been found, but *post* 15 May 1773 reaffirms Nivernais's 'punctilio' on the subject.

5. Dodsley could have produced a receipt for forty guineas, dated 29 June 1757

and signed by Gray, in which he assigned to 'Mr [Robert] Dodsley, his heirs, executors, administrators, and assigns,' the copyright of 'The Progress of Poesy' and 'The Bard' (Ralph Straus, *Robert Dodsley,* 1910, p. 164; see also Hazen, *SH Bibliography* 23–4).

6. Mason first wrote 'make a use.'

about it when we next meet. I only mean that the edition for public sale shall be contrived to be a lucrative one.

My ecclesiastical imprisonment[7] in this dullest of all provincial towns continues till the 11th of November. After a short stay at Aston I mean to go to Cambridge,[8] to assist Mr Brown[9] in settling affairs there, and think of being in town about Christmas[10] when I shall make it my first business to pay my respects to you in Arlington Street. I have the honour to be, dear Sir,

Your most obliged and faithful humble servant,

W. MASON

To MASON, Wednesday 25 September 1771

Printed from Mitford i. 17–20.

Strawberry Hill, Sept. 25, 1771.

I HAVE received both your letters, Sir, by Mr Stonhewer and by the post from York. I direct this to Aston rather than to York, for fear of any miscarriage, and will remember to insert *near Sheffield*.

I not only agree with your sentiments, but am flattered that they countenance my own practice. In some cases I have sold my works,[1] and sometimes have made the impressions at my own press pay themselves,[2] as I am not rich enough to treat the public with all I print there; nor do I know why I should; some editions have been given to charities, to the poor of Twickenham, etc.[3] Mr Spence's life of Maglia-

7. As a canon-residentiary of York Mason was required to reside there for three months annually (Davies, *York Press* 268).

8. Mason did not go to Aston, but went from York directly to Cambridge, whence he wrote to his curate, Christopher Alderson, on 3 Dec. For an account of Mason's unpublished letters to Alderson, see *ante*, Cue-Titles and Abbreviations, *sub* Alderson.

9. James Brown (see *ante* 1 Aug. 1756, n. 7) was joint executor, with Mason, of Gray's will (Venn, *Alumni Cantab.* and *Gray's Corr.* i. 222 n. 1, iii. 1285). His letters concerning Gray's last illness and death are printed in *Gray's Corr.* iii. 1270–5.

10. He was (*post* ?14 April 1772, n. 1).

1. I.e., the *Ædes Walpolianæ* (not the first edition, 1747, but the editions of 1752 and 1767), *The Castle of Otranto* (1765), *Historic Doubts* (1768), and numerous political pamphlets. Hentzner's *Journey into England* (1757), the *Catalogue of Royal and Noble Authors* (1758), and Lord Herbert's *Life* (1764) were first printed at SH and given away, but were later reprinted and published in London.

2. The *Anecdotes of Painting*, 1762–71 (Hazen, *SH Bibliography* 55–6).

3. Of Lord Whitworth's *Account of Russia as It Was in the Year 1710*, '700 copies

becchi was bestowed on the reading tailor.[4] I am neither ashamed of being an author, or a bookseller. My mother's father[5] was a timber-merchant, I have many reasons for thinking myself a worse man, and none for thinking myself better: consequently I shall never blush at doing anything he did. I print much better than I write, and love my trade, and hope I am not one of those *most undeserving of all objects*[6] printers and booksellers, whom I confess you lash with justice. In short, Sir, I have no notion of poor Mr Gray's delicacy; I would not sell my talents as orators and senators do, but I would keep a shop, and sell any of my own works that would gain me a livelihood, whether books or shoes, rather than be tempted to sell myself. 'Tis an honest vocation to be a scavenger—but I would not be Solicitor-General.[7] Whatever method you fix upon for the publication of Mr Gray's works, I dare answer I shall approve, and will, therefore, say no more on it till we meet. I will beg you, Sir, when you come to town to bring me what papers or letters he had preserved of mine—for the answer to

[were] printed, 600 sold, for the benefit of the poor of Twickenham, at 3s. a volume but deducting 3d. for binding in blue paper, and 3d. to the bookseller for selling them' (*Journal of the Printing-Office* 7). The profits from Lucan's *Pharsalia* (1760) went to Richard Bentley (Hazen, *SH Bibliography* 46–8); and Francis Hoyland's *Poems* (*ante* 5 April 1769 and n. 5) were printed for the author's benefit.

4. Joseph Spence's *A Parallel in the Manner of Plutarch: between a Most Celebrated Man of Florence* [Antonio Magliabechi, 1633–1714] *and One Scarce Ever Heard of in England* was printed at SH Oct.–Nov. 1758 and published by Dodsley 2 Feb. 1759 (Hazen, *SH Bibliography* 44). Robert Hill (1699–1777), the subject of the biography and in whose behalf it was published, was a self-educated tailor of Buckingham with a passion for reading. See Ronald Bayne's article in DNB, based chiefly on Spence's *Parallel*.

5. John Shorter (b. ca 1660) of Bybrook, Kent; a timber-merchant trading with the Baltic countries; eldest son of Sir John Shorter (d. 1688), K.B., goldsmith, lord mayor of London 1687–8, and his wife Isabella Birkett; married Elizabeth (living 1718), daughter of Sir Erasmus Philipps, 3d Bt; father of John, Erasmus, Arthur, Catherine, and Charlotte Shorter (Le

Neve's *Pedigrees of the Knights*, ed. G. W. Marshall, 1873, pp. 301–2; Edward Hasted, *History . . . of Kent*, 2d edn, 1797–1801, vii. 549–50; Cunningham v. 339 n. 1; A. B. Beaven, *Aldermen of the City of London*, 1908–1913, ii. 107, 191; Burke, *Peerage*, 1928, *sub* St Davids; see also Berry ii. 265–6 and *post* 13 April 1782).

6. Mason's phrase (*ante* 21 Sept. 1771).

7. An allusion to Alexander Wedderburn (1733–1805), who was solicitor-general from Jan. 1771 until June 1778. After succeeding to other high legal offices he became lord chancellor (1793–1801). Wedderburn was created Bn Loughborough in 1780 and E. of Rosslyn in 1801. HW's opinion of him is revealed in the following note in *Mem. Geo. III* iv. 69: 'Sprung from a Jacobite family (his uncle having been executed for the last rebellion), he had set out a courtly advocate, but being laid aside on the change of times, he had plunged into all the intemperance of opposition, and now [1770] appeared a warm partisan of liberty, and an accuser of his own immediate patrons. His mischievous abilities soon forced him again into employment, which as naturally led him back to his old monarchic principles to support which, he, so lately a champion of the constitution, was made attorney-general, and at length chief justice of the Common Pleas.'

Dr Milles it is not worth asking you to accept or to take the trouble of bringing me, and, therefore, you may fling it aside where you please.[8]

The epitaph[9] is very unworthy of the subject. I had rather anybody should correct my works than take the pains myself. I thank you very sincerely for criticizing it, but indeed I believe you would with much less trouble write a new one than mend that. I abandon it cheerfully to the fire, for surely bad verses on a great poet are the worst of panegyrics. The sensation of the moment dictated the epitaph, but though I was concerned, I was not inspired; your corrections of my play I remember with the greatest gratitude, because I confess I liked it enough to wish it corrected, and for that friendly act, Sir, I am obliged to you. For writing, I am quitting all thoughts of it—and for several reasons—the best is because it is time to remember that I must quit the world. Mr Gray was but a year older and he had much more the appearance of a man to whom several years were promised. A contemporary's death is the Ucalegon[10] of all sermons: in the next place his death has taught me another truth. Authors are said to labour for posterity; for my part I find I did not write even for the rising generation. Experience tells me it was all for those of my own, or near my own, time. The friends I have lost were I find more than half the public to me. It is as difficult to write for young people, as to talk to them; I never, I perceive, meant anything about them in what I have written, and cannot commence an acquaintance with them in print.

Mr Gray was far from an agreeable confidant to self-love, yet I had always more satisfaction in communicating anything to him, though sure to be mortified, than in being flattered by people whose judgment I do not respect. We had besides known each other's ideas from almost infancy, and I was certain he would *understand* precisely whatever I said, whether it was well or ill expressed. This is a kind of feeling that every hour of age increases. Mr Gray's death, I am persuaded, Sir, has already given you this sensation, and I make no excuse for talking seemingly so much of myself, but though I am the instance of these reflections, they are only part of the conversation, which that sad event occasions, and which I trust we shall renew. I shall sincerely

8. The present whereabouts of this copy is not known.

9. On Gray (*ante* 9 Sept. 1771).

10. Ucalegon was one of the elders of Troy, whose house stood next to that of Deiphobus and was burned with it ('Proximus ardet Ucalegon': *Æneid* ii. 311–2). HW uses the same allusion in his letter to Mann 22 June 1768 and to Mary Berry 29 Jan. 1791 (BERRY i. 183).

be a little consoled if our common regret draws us nearer together; you will find all possible esteem on my side; as there has been much similarity in some of our pursuits, it may make some amends for other defects. I have done with the business, the politics, the pleasures of the world, without turning hermit or morose. My object is to pass the remainder of my life tranquilly and agreeably, with all the amusements that will gild the evening, and are not subject to disappointment; with cheerfulness, for I have very good spirits, and with as much of the company, as I can obtain, of the few persons I value and like [value and like is one word].[11] If you have charity enough or inclination to contribute to such a system you will add much to the happiness of it, and if you have not, you will still allow me to say I shall be ever, with great regard, Sir,

> Your obedient humble servant,
>
> Hor. Walpole

From Mason, Tuesday ?14 April 1772

Printed from MS now wsl. The day and month are conjectural (see n. 1).
Address: To the Honourable Mr Walpole.

Curzon Street,[1] Tuesday morning, 1772.[2]

MR MASON presents his respects to Mr Walpole and desires his acceptance of the etchings which accompany this. He also desires that in the course of the summer he would let Mr Stonhewer have the perusal of those extracts of Mr Gray's out of the Cotton Library[3] etc., which Mr Mason left at Strawberry Hill, as Mr Stonhewer had not time to review them before.

11. So in Mitford. Cunningham and Toynbee omitted the brackets and the enclosed words, evidently believing that they were an interpolation of Mitford's; but HW habitually used brackets for parentheses. HW perhaps ran the words together, 'valueandlike.'

1. At Stonhewer's house (*Gray's Corr.* iii. 1177). Mason had reached London ca 13 Dec. 1771, and apparently left it to return to Aston 14 April 1772 (Mason to Al-

derson 13 Dec. 1771, 1 April and 10 April 1772). This appears to be a hasty note delivered by hand on the morning of Mason's departure.

2. Year added by HW.

3. I.e., the Cottonian Library, the collection of MSS formed by Sir Robert Bruce Cotton (1571–1631). In 1707 it had become a national possession when it was purchased from the Cotton family by the government, and in 1753 it was removed to the British Museum, which was opened

To Mason, Saturday 9 May 1772

Printed from Mitford i. 21–5.

Strawberry Hill, May 9, 1772.

I HAVE given up to Mr Stonhewer, as you desired, dear Sir, Mr Gray's volume of MSS, but shall be glad hereafter, if you do not dislike it, to print some of the most curious. He himself was to lend me the speech and letters of Sir Thomas Wyat.[1] At a leisure hour, would not it be amusing to you to draw up a little account of that poet?[2]

Dr Brown has sent me a very civil letter[3] of thanks for Gray's portrait;[4] he speaks too of the book[5] I intended for their college, and that he was to receive from you. I forget whether I troubled you with it or not.

I have selected for your use[6] such of Gray's letters, as will be intelligible without many notes: but though all his early letters have both wit and humour, they are so local, or so confined to private persons and stories, that it would be difficult even by the help of a comment to make them interesting to the public; some of the incidents alluded to have slipped out of my own memory; still there are about twenty of his juvenile letters that I think will please.[7] I will bring

---

to the public in 1759. Gray spent much of his time at the Museum during the next two years, studying and transcribing the MSS, chiefly those in the Harleian and Cottonian collections (W. P. Jones, *Thomas Gray, Scholar,* Cambridge, Mass., 1937, pp. 118–19).

1. Sir Thomas Wyatt (ca 1503–42), Kt, 1537. The speech, copied by Gray from BM MS Harl. 78, No. 7, was 'Sir Tho. Wyat's defence at his trial, when accused by Bishop Bonner of high treason,' printed by HW in *Miscellaneous Antiquities* No. 2, pp. 21–54. Wyatt's letters to Henry VIII were not printed by HW. See GRAY i. 147 n. 334, ii. 116 n. 62.

2. HW himself wrote Wyatt's 'Life,' which appears on pp. 3–20 of *Miscellaneous Antiquities* No. 2.

3. Missing.

4. Probably a print.

5. Perhaps a copy of *Royal and Noble Authors* (1759 edn) now in the Pembroke

College library, with the label 'Ex dono Jacobi Brown' (information from the late Sir Ellis Minns); or it may be the copy of *The Foundation of the Universitie of Cambridge,* 1621, 'collected' by John Scott and dedicated to Hierom Beale, Master of Pembroke, that HW gave the College.

6. In Mason's projected *Memoirs of Gray.*

7. 'Mr Walpole, on my informing him that it was my intention to publish the principal part of Mr Gray's correspondence with Mr West, very obligingly communicated to me the letters which he had also received from Mr Gray at the same period. From this collection I have selected such as I thought would be most likely to please the generality of readers; omitting, though with regret, many of the more sprightly and humorous sort, because either from their personality, or some other local circumstance, they did not seem so well adapted to hit the public taste' (Mason, *Mem. Gray* 16 n.). See also HW's introduc-

them with me[8] when I make you a visit in August. I have a great many more to the very end of his life;[9] but they are grave, and chiefly relative to questions in antiquity on which I consulted him, or begged him to consult the libraries at Cambridge; there are some criticisms on modern books and authors, either his own opinions or in answer to mine. These are certainly not proper for present publication: but I shall leave these and the rest behind me, and none of them will disgrace him; which ought to be our care, since it was so very much his own.

Mr Palgrave[10] is in town, and has promised to pass a day with me here, where I am continuing my immortal labours with those durable materials, painted glass, and carved wood and stone. The foundations of the Chapel[11] in the garden are to be dug on Monday. The State Bedchamber[12] advances rapidly, and will, I hope, be finished before my journey to Yorkshire. In short, this *old, old, very old castle,* as his prints called old Parr,[13] is so near being perfect, that it will certainly be ready by the time I die, to be improved with Indian paper;[13a] or to have the windows cut down to the ground by some travelled lady.

The newspapers tell me that Mr Chambers,[14] the architect, who

tory note to Gray's correspondence, GRAY i. 55. Mason printed only four of the thirty-eight early letters from Gray to Walpole; the rest were first printed by Paget Toynbee in *The Correspondence of Gray, Walpole, West, and Ashton,* Oxford, 1915.

8. HW apparently neglected to do so. See *post* 9 Sept. 1772.

9. See *post* 23 Feb. and 8 Dec. 1773.

10. William Palgrave (ca 1735–99), fellow of Pembroke College, Cambridge, 1764–99; Gray's friend and correspondent (*Gray's Corr.* ii. 576 n. 1).

11. Built by Thomas Gayfere (1720–1812), master mason to Westminster Abbey. 'The Chapel, in the south-west corner of the wood, is built of brick, with a beautiful front of Portland stone' ('Des. of SH,' *Works* ii. 507). See also COLE i. 243–4 and *passim,* and *SH Accounts* 151–4, 156–7.

12. Or Great North Bedchamber, the finest in the house. It was hung with crimson Norwich damask, and contained a chimney-piece designed by HW after the tomb of Bishop Dudley of Durham ('Des. of SH,' *Works* ii. 494). See also *post* i. 42, 446, COLE i. 256 and *SH Accounts* 145–7.

13. Thomas Parr (d. 1635), supposedly

born in 1483, was brought to London in 1635 by Lord Arundel and exhibited there as a curiosity. See Thomas Seccombe's article in DNB and W. J. Thoms, *Human Longevity,* 1873, pp. 85–94, 290–313. Two engravings of him entitled 'The old, old, very old man,' one by Cornelis van Dalen and the other anonymous, are listed in *BM Cat. of Engraved British Portraits* iii. 416. John Taylor's versified account of him, published in 1635 and reprinted by Thoms, op. cit. 291–308, is called *The Old, Old, Very Old Man: or the Age and Long Life of Thomas Parr.* HW owned a print of Parr, in a group with Jeffery Hudson the dwarf and William Evans, Charles I's tall porter, from a painting by Edward Bowers (or Bower): sold London 227.

13a. For this wall-paper see *Gray's Corr.* iii. 1006 and n. 9.

14. Sir William Chambers (1726–96) was born in Sweden of Scots parentage; visited China; studied architecture in Italy, whence he returned to England in 1755. From 1757 to 1762 he was employed by the Princess Dowager of Wales to erect various structures in Kew Gardens. His masterpiece was Somerset House, of which

has Sir-Williamized himself, by the desire as he says of the Knights of the Polar Star[15] his brethren, who were angry at his not assuming his proper title, is going to publish a treatise on ornamental gardening;[16] that is, I suppose considering a garden as a subject to be built upon. In that light it will not interfere with your verses[17] or my prose;[18] and we may both use the happiest expression in the world and

coldly declare him free.[19]

In truth our climate is so bad, that instead of filling our gardens

he was appointed architect in 1775. He was the author of *Designs of Chinese Buildings*, 1757 (HW's copy was sold London 960), *A Treatise on Civil Architecture*, 1759 (sold London 944), and *A Dissertation on Oriental Gardening*, 1772 (sold SH i. 161).

15. The Order of the Polar Star was instituted by Frederick I, King of Sweden, in 1748, supposedly as a revival of an earlier order, though under a new name. See Sir Levett Hanson, *An Accurate Historical Account of All the Orders of Knighthood at Present Existing in Europe*, [1802], ii. 66–9, and Nicholas Carlisle, *A Concise Account of the Several Foreign Orders of Knighthood*, 1839, pp. 458–60. The King of Sweden had conferred the order on Chambers in 1771, in return for a gift of some drawings of Kew Gardens. In that year Chambers is listed in the catalogue of the Royal Academy as 'William Chambers, Knight of the Polar Star, R.A.'; but in 1772, as HW says, he 'Sir-Williamized' himself (presumably with George III's permission, as Chambers claimed), and appears as 'Sir William Chambers, R.A.' (*The Exhibition of the Royal Academy*, 1771, p. 7; ibid., 1772, p. 7; see also Thomas Hardwick's 'Memoir' in Chambers's *Treatise on the Decorative Part of Civil Architecture*, 1862 edn, pp. 4–5; Mason's *Satirical Poems* 53). The exhibition in 1772 had opened on 24 April (*Daily Adv.*).

16. 'In a few days will be published, *A Dissertation on Ornamental Gardening*, by Sir William Chambers, Comptroller-General of his Majesty's Works' (*Daily Adv.* 7 May 1772). It was published on 25 May (ibid. 25 May: 'Ornamental' is corrected to 'Oriental'). For Mason's *Heroic Epistle to Sir William Chambers* (which begins

'Knight of the Polar Star!'), 1773, inspired by this treatise, see *post* 21 July 1772, 1 Dec. 1772, and *passim*.

17. That is, *The English Garden* (completed in 1781), Mason's most ambitious work in verse, of which the first book had been published on 10 Feb. 1772 (*Daily Adv.*); second edn 28 Feb. (ibid.). On 24 Feb. 1772 Mason wrote to Alderson: 'My muse . . . brings in her collection quick enough. . . . I must tell you that a thousand copies went off in a week and a new edition is now in the press. I have heard no objections to it yet of any consequence, and as to commendations, the generality of the world know me too well to venture to give them to my face.' On 10 April he wrote, 'I shall come home in a chaise of my own. Do not think me extravagant in so doing, as I can fairly say, *Hæc mihi musa dedit.*' That the first book may not have been as highly admired as Mason evidently supposed is shown in a letter from Gough to Tyson, 28 Feb. 1772: 'The town is disappointed by *The English Garden*, and thinks it prosaic and defective in the simplicity it means to recommend' (Nichols, *Lit. Anec.* viii. 584). See Draper, *Mason* 203–36, and Gaskell 12–13.

18. HW's 'On Modern Gardening,' first published in *Anecdotes of Painting* iv. 117–51. HW finished writing this volume in Dec. 1770 and the printing was completed 13 April 1771, but it was not published until 1780 (Hazen, *SH Bibliography* 63).

19.
'. . . Charles, the abject tool of France,
Came back to smile his subjects into slaves;
Or Belgic William, with his warrior frown,
Coldly declared them free . . .'
(*English Garden*, Bk I, ll. 468–71).

with buildings, we ought rather to fill our buildings with gardens, as the only way of enjoying the latter.

The dreaded East is all the wind that blows;[20]

and yet I am afraid to rail at it, lest the rain should make advantage of my plaints, and come and drown us till the end of July. I was lamenting the weather to M. de Guines,[21] the French ambassador. He said, 'In England you talk of nothing but the bad weather; I wonder you are not used to it.' Yet one must have seen such a thing, as spring, or one could not have invented the idea. I can swear to have formerly heard nightingales as I have been sitting in this very bow-window. If I was thirty years younger, I might fancy they are gone because *Phoebe is gone;* but I have certainly heard them long since my ballad-making days. I hope *your garden,*[22] which is not exposed to wayward seasons, but

will always flourish in immortal youth,[23]

advances a great pace; consider, you are to record what it was, when fashion and great lords shall have brought back square enclosures, walls, terraces and labyrinths and shall be told by the Le Nautre[24] of the day, that *their Lordships have invented a new taste;* and will never know to the contrary; for though beautiful poems preserve themselves, it is not by being read and known. Works of genius are like the Hermetic philosophers, none but adepts are acquainted with their existence; yet certainly nothing is ever lost—as you may find in Mr Wharton's new life of Sir Thomas Pope,[25] which has resuscitated more nothings, and more nobodies, than Birch's life of Tillotson or Louth's William of Wickham.[26]

20. Pope, *Rape of the Lock* iv. 20.

21. Adrien-Louis de Bonnières (1735–1806), Comte and (1776) Duc de Guines; ambassador to England 1770–76 (Marquis de Granges de Surgères, *Répertoire . . . de la Gazette de France,* 1902–6, ii. 620–1; DU DEFFAND ii. 416, iv. 263 and *passim*).

22. I.e., *The English Garden.*

23. 'But thou shalt flourish in immortal youth' (Addison, *Cato* V. i. 29).

24. André Le Nôtre (1613–1700), landscape architect, was patronized by Louis XIV, for whom he designed the park at Versailles and the Trianon gardens. He laid out also the gardens at Chantilly and the Tuileries, and in England designed Greenwich Park and St James's Park.

25. *The Life of Sir Thomas Pope, Founder of Trinity College, Oxford,* by Thomas Warton (1728–90), had just been published (*Critical Review* May 1772, xxxiii. 369–77).

26. *The Life of the Most Reverend Dr John Tillotson, Lord Archbishop of Canterbury,* 1752, by Thomas Birch (1705–66), D.D., and Robert Lowth's *Life of William of Wykeham,* 1758. HW's copies were sold SH iii. 88.

There has been a masquerade at the Pantheon,[27] which was so glorious a vision that I thought I was in the old Pantheon, or in the Temples of Delphi or Ephesus, amidst a crowd of various nations, and that formerly

Panthoides Euphorbus eram,[28]

and did but recollect what I had seen. All the friezes and niches were edged with alternate lamps of green and purple glass, that shed a most heathen light, and the dome was illuminated by a heaven of oiled paper, well painted with gods and goddesses. Mr Wyat,[29] the architect, has so much taste, that I think he must be descended from Sir Thomas. Even Henry VIII had so much taste, that were he alive he would visit the Pantheon. Adieu! dear Sir,

Yours most sincerely,

Hor. Walpole

27. The Pantheon, in Oxford Street, consisting of a rotunda and a suite of rooms on a plan similar to that of Ranelagh, was opened 27 Jan. 1772. See A. T. Bolton, 'The Pantheon in the Oxford Road,' in *London Topographical Record*, 1923, xiii. 55–67. The masquerade HW describes occurred on Thursday 30 April. In *London Chronicle* 5–7 May (xxxi. 434) appeared the following paragraph: 'The present luxury of the times may be easily estimated from the masquerade of last Thursday evening. Two thousand persons at two guineas each make four thousand guineas; and if we rate the price of all the various dresses at three guineas each (the money demanded at Tavistock Street for the use only of a domino) we shall immediately see that 10,-000 guineas, besides the expense of chair and coach-hire, were lavished on the entertainment of a single night, while our poor are absolutely perishing for bread in various parts of the kingdom.'

28. 'Morte carent animæ. . . .
     Ipse ego (nam memini) Troiani tempore belli
     Panthoides Euphorbus eram . . .'
     (Ovid, *Metamorphoses* xv. 158–61).
('Our souls are immortal. . . . I myself, for I remember it, at the time of the Trojan War, was Euphorbus, son of Panthoüs.')

29. James Wyatt (1746–1813). As a result of building the Pantheon, 1770–2, he received many commissions to build houses in the Græco-Italian style. Later he turned to Gothic, the style with which his name is usually associated, and designed, among many other buildings, Lee Priory (see Berry ii. 111, 136–7), Fonthill Abbey (1795), and the Royal Military College (now Academy) at Woolwich. HW commissioned him to build the offices (1790) at SH (see HW to Wyatt 31 Aug. 1789; Berry i. 74; *SH Accounts* 18, 176; 'Genesis of SH' 82 and fig. 29).

From MASON, Sunday 17 May 1772

Printed from MS now WSL.
Address: The Honourable Horace Walpole, Arlington Street, London.
Postmark: YORK 20 MA.

On the back of the letter HW wrote four lines in pencil containing about twenty words, of which only a few can be made out: 'They . . . ? tell me so . . . an honest man.'

York, May 17th, 1772.

Dear Sir,

MR STONHEWER only desired to look over the papers[1] in question, he will undoubtedly return you them very soon, and then I hope you will print whatever you think proper, for I am perfectly conscious that you are the fittest person to make such a selection, and it was from the hope that you would do so, that I gave them to you. Yet I think those that you reject should be preserved and I fancy you think so too.

I hear (for I have not seen the paper) that it has been printed as a piece of news that I have resigned my chaplainship,[2] and a cause assigned for it which I fear will offend Lord Hertford.[3] I could wish, therefore, if it came easily into conversation, that you would assure his Lordship that my intention of resigning (for it is at present only intention) arises merely from my resolution of not aiming at any further ecclesiastical preferment, but to sit down *uti conviva satur*[4] in a parsonage which I have built for that purpose; that as this parsonage is in Yorkshire and my temporal concerns also in Yorkshire, a London journey at a stated time[5] is often inconvenient and will be (when I advance more in years) constantly disagreeable. On this account and on this only I mean to relinquish the chaplainship, and would wish

1. Gray's transcripts of MSS in the Cottonian Library (*ante* ?14 April 1772, n. 4). See *post* 21 July 1772.
2. The newspaper paragraph has not been found. Mason had been 'appointed by the Duke of Devonshire chaplain in ordinary to the King, July 2, 1757,' and reappointed chaplain to George III 19 Sept. 1761 (Mason's 'Dates of the Principal Events Relative to Myself' printed in Mitford ii. 411–2). He resigned the chaplaincy in August 1772 (Draper, *Mason* 83 and n. 45; *Court and City Register*, 1772, p. 78; ibid. 1773, p. 78). For HW's account of the

resignation as reported by Pinkerton see *post* Appendix 1.
3. Francis Seymour Conway (1718–94), cr. (1750) E. and (1793) M. of Hertford; HW's cousin and correspondent. As lord chamberlain of the Household (1766–82) Lord Hertford controlled the appointment of royal chaplains.
4. 'Like a replete guest' (Horace, *Satires* I. i. 119).
5. Four chaplains in ordinary were assigned to serve each month. Mason's period of residence was the month of March (*Court and City Register*, 1772, p. 78).

to do it at any time when his Lordship thinks it most eligible, and I should imagine, that if you would please to intimate this to him, it would appear to him (as it is meant to be) a more civil way of proceeding than by an abrupt letter of resignation. Remember you have, once at least, asked for a chaplainship;[6] be assured if you ask for leave to resign one, you will find full as much gratitude from the person you do this latter favour for, as you did from the former. After all, if you do not like to concern yourself in state matters of such weighty moment, you have only to tell me so, and I will write a letter to my Lord Chamberlain in form and urge my own request. I could wish, however, that you would convince him that it is beneath me to be impertinent in a newspaper.

I mean to employ all the time that my frittered days will here allow in preparing Mr Gray's papers and my account of them for the press. As for gardens, etc., I leave them to the Knight of the Polish star[6a] and his modern Henry.[7] When I return to Aston and get into my own quiet garden I perhaps there may plan ideal ones. In the mean while I ⟨ple⟩as⟨e⟩[8] myself with the thoughts that you w⟨ill⟩ take your first glimpse of the bea⟨uties⟩ of the West Riding from my study ⟨?window⟩ before you advance to the centre of its beauties at Wentworth Castle.[9] Be assured of the most cordial welcome and believe me to be (with the truest sense of all your favours) dear Sir,

Most faithfully yours,

W. MASON

6. This implies that HW once asked for a chaplainship for Mason. In 1755, when Lord Hertford was proposed as ambassador to Paris, Mason asked Lord Holdernesse to request his appointment as Hertford's chaplain, and HW may have been approached for the same purpose.

6a. *Sic.* Mason may have thought that it was a Polish order, as HW at one time thought. The first draft of HW's note on 'Knight of the Polar Star' (see *ante* 9 May 1772, n. 15, and *post* May 1779, n. 1) begins, 'A Polish order appendant to a black ribband; given to artists and literati' (from MS now WSL).

7. See *ante* 9 May 1772, *ad fin.*

8. HW tore the writing when he broke the seal.

9. Lord Strafford's seat near Barnsley, Yorks; HW's 'favourite of all great seats' (BERRY i. 66). It was built ca 1730 by Thomas Wentworth, 1st E. of Strafford, n.c. (d. 1739), and remodelled ca 1768 by William (1722–91), 2d Earl (*Country Seats* 65; J. P. Neale, *Views of the Seats of Noblemen and Gentlemen,* 1st ser., 1818–23, vol. iv, No. 50). 'If a model is sought of the most perfect taste in architecture, where grace softens dignity, and lightness attempers magnificence; where proportion removes every part from peculiar observation, and delicacy of execution recalls every part to notice; where the position is the most

To Mason, Monday 25 May 1772

Printed from Mitford i. 27–9.

Strawberry Hill, May 25, 1772.

Dear Sir,

I HAVE told Lord Hertford of the injurious manner in which your thoughts of resigning the chaplainship have been represented in the newspapers, and of the obliging expressions you have used towards him in offering to give it up. He is extremely sensible of your civility, and desired I would thank you from him in the handsomest manner, and, as you permit him, will fill up your place, when you are willing to resign it. For myself, I assure you, dear Sir, that next to the pleasure I should have, if it was in my power to do you service, the greatest satisfaction I can enjoy, is to assist in delivering you from attendance on a court: a station below your sentiments and merit.

I have read Chambers's book. It is more extravagant than the worst Chinese paper,[1] and is written in wild revenge against Brown;[1a] the only surprising consequence is, that it is laughed at, and it is not likely to be adopted, as I expected; for nothing is so tempting to fools, as advice to deprave taste.

Lord Carlisle[2] has written and printed some copies of an ode on

happy, and even the colour of the stone the most harmonious; the virtuoso should be directed to the new front of Wentworth Castle: the result of the same elegant judgment that had before distributed so many beauties over that domain, and called from wood, water, hills, prospects and buildings, a compendium of picturesque nature, improved by the chastity of art' (HW, 'On Modern Gardening,' *Works* ii. 545).

———

1. Chinese wall-paper, which was first introduced into England in the seventeenth century, continued throughout the eighteenth century to be extensively imported and imitated by English papermakers. See Alan Victor Sugden and John Ludlam Edmondson, *A History of English Wall-Paper*, [ca 1925], pp. 97–108 and plates 51–64.
1a. 'In this island it [gardening] is abandoned to kitchen-gardeners, well skilled in the culture of salads, but little ac-

quainted with the principles of ornamental gardening. It cannot be expected that men uneducated, and doomed by their condition to waste the vigour of life in hard labour, should ever go far in so refined, so difficult a pursuit' (Sir William Chambers, *A Dissertation on Oriental Gardening*, 1772, p. iii). Lancelot Brown (1715–83), called 'Capability Brown,' landscapegardener and architect, began his career as kitchen-gardener to Lord Cobham, as HW notes in Mason's *Satirical Poems* 41. For Brown see Elizabeth W. Manwaring, *Italian Landscape in Eighteenth-Century England*, 1925, *passim*, Isabel W. U. Chase, *Horace Walpole, Gardenist*, Princeton, 1943, pp. 142–4, and Dorothy Stroud, *Capability Brown*, 1950.
2. Frederick Howard (1748–1825), 5th E. of Carlisle, 1758; friend of Charles Fox, and Byron's guardian. HW evidently saw a private printing of his *Poems*, which were first published in 1773 (reviewed in *Monthly Review* Feb. 1773, xlviii. 143–5).

Gray's death. There is a real spirit of poetry in it, but no invention; for it is only a description of Gray's descriptions.[3] There are also two epitaphs on Lady Carlisle's dog,[4] not bad, and a translation from Dante of the story of Count Ugolino,[5] which I like the least of the four pieces. Mrs Scott,[6] sister of Mrs Montague,[7] has written a life of Agrippa d'Aubigné,[8]—no—she has not written it, she has extracted it from his own account,[9] and no dentist at a fair could draw a tooth with less grace. It is only in a religious sense that she has made it a good book, for it seems she is very pious.[10] There is a Mr Jones[11] too, who has published imitations of Asiatic poets:[12] but as Chambers's book was advertised by the title of *ornamental* gardening,[13] instead of

See Mason's *Satirical Poems* 130, and Francis A. Yates, 'Transformations of Dante's Ugolino,' *Journal of the Warburg and Courtauld Institutes*, 1951, xiv. 94. See also Byron's attack on Carlisle in *English Bards and Scotch Reviewers*, ll. 725–40, and his apology in *Childe Harold* iii. 29.

3. Lord Carlisle's 'Ode Written upon the Death of Mr Gray' is largely made up of allusions to, and imitations of, Gray's five chief poems, to which references are given in footnotes.

4. 'For the Monument of Rose, a Favourite Spaniel' (Carlisle, *Poems*, pp. 9–10) and 'Another Inscription for the Same' (ibid. 11–12). Lady Carlisle was Lady Margaret Caroline Leveson-Gower (1753–1824); she married Lord Carlisle in 1770.

5. 'Translation from Dante, Canto XXXIII [lines 1–75]' (ibid. 13–17). It was also printed in the *Annual Register* for 1773, pt ii. 230–2. The translation was inspired by Reynolds's picture, 'Ugolino and his sons in the Hunger Tower,' begun in 1770 and exhibited at the Royal Academy in 1773. See Yates, loc. cit., and Paget Toynbee, *Dante in English Literature*, 1909, i. 333–8. For HW's opinion of Dante see *post* 25 June 1782.

6. Sarah Robinson (1723–95), dau. of Matthew Robinson of West Layton, Yorks; m. (1751) George Lewis Scott, the mathematician, but was separated from him soon afterwards; author of nine published works, fictional and historical (W. M. Crittenden, *Life and Writings of Mrs Sarah Scott*, Philadelphia, 1932, pp. 13, 26, 45).

7. Elizabeth Robinson (1720–1800), m.

(1742) Edward Montagu; 'queen of the Blues.'

8. Publication of the anonymously issued *Life of Theodore Agrippa d'Aubigné* [1552–1630], *Containing a Succinct Account of . . . the Civil Wars of France in the Reigns of Charles IX, Henry III, Henry IV, and in the Minority of Lewis XIII* was announced 19 May 1772 in *Daily Adv.* HW's copy was sold SH v. 125. D'Aubigné was a *littérateur* and the grandfather of Mme de Maintenon.

9. Most of Mrs Scott's material was drawn from D'Aubigné's own works—his *Histoire universelle* (1616–20) and *Mémoires* (posthumous, 1731)—but she also made use of the writings of other French memoirists. See Crittenden, op. cit. 91–2, and Bibl. Nat. Cat.

10. 'Good works are often performed by the Methodist ladies in the heat of enthusiasm, but thank God, my sister's is a calm and rational piety. . . . It has pleased God to lead her to truth by the road of affliction' (Elizabeth Montagu to Gilbert West 16 Oct. 1755, in *Letters of Mrs Elizabeth Montagu*, ed. Matthew Montagu, 1809–13, iii. 336–7).

11. William (later Sir William) Jones (1746–94); 'Persian Jones'; orientalist and jurist, and member of the Literary Club; F.R.S., 1772; K.B., 1783. See *post* ii. 35 n. 33.

12. Jones's *Poems Consisting Chiefly of Translations from the Asiatic Languages* had been recently published (reviewed in the *Critical Review* for April 1772, xxxiii. 314–8).

13. See *ante* 9 May 1772, n. 16.

oriental, I think Mr Jones's is a blunder of *oriental* for ornamental, for it is very flowery, and not at all Eastern.[13a]

Somebody, I fancy Dr Percy,[14] has produced a dismal dull ballad, called 'The Execution of Sir Charles Bawdin,'[15] and given it for one of the Bristol Poems, called Rowley's—but it is a still worse counterfeit, than those that were first sent to me;[16] it grows a hard case on our ancestors, who have every day bastards laid to them, five hundred or a thousand years after they are dead. Indeed Mr Macpherson,[17] etc., are so fair as to beget the fathers as well as the children. Adieu! dear Sir,

Yours most sincerely,

HOR. WALPOLE

To MASON, Monday 6 July 1772

Printed from Mitford 1. 29–30.

Strawberry Hill, July 6, 1772.

IT is with great pleasure, dear Sir, I see the time approach of making you my visit. The first of August I shall begin my progress, or very near that day:[1] but, as I do not travel on macaronic-wings,[2] it is

13a. Jones's 'flowery' imitations are written in the conventional metres and idiom of English verse of the time. HW might have considered them 'Eastern' if they had resembled Macpherson's Ossianic poems, which on first reading he found similar to the poetry 'of the East; that is, they contain natural images and natural sentiment elevated, before rules were invented to make poetry difficult and dull' (HW to Dalrymple 3 Feb. 1760, DALRYMPLE 61).

14. Thomas Percy (1729–1811), D.D., later (1782) Bp of Dromore; editor of the *Reliques of Ancient English Poetry* (1765).

15. Thomas Chatterton's *The Execution of Sir Charles Bawdin* (later called *Bristowe Tragedie*), the first of the Rowley poems to be printed separately. HW's reason for attributing the editorship to Percy was presumably the dedication to 'Elizabeth, Duchess of Northumberland . . . behind whose illustrious name the *Reliques of Ancient English Poetry* were with propriety

introduced into the world,' but the poem was edited by George Symes Catcott (1729–1802), Bristol pewterer, to whom Chatterton gave copies of several of his Rowley poems (Sir Ernest Clarke, 'New Lights on Chatterton,' *Transactions of the Bibliographical Society,* 1916, xiii. 236). See E. H. W. Meyerstein, *A Life of Thomas Chatterton,* 1930, pp. 132–41 and *passim.* HW's copy (in his 'Poems of George III' now in the Harvard Library) is dated by him 'May 15th.'

16. By Chatterton in 1769. See HW's correspondence with Chatterton and Lort.

17. James Macpherson (1736–96), author of the Ossianic poems. As were Chatterton's, Macpherson's fabrications were communicated to HW as genuine antiquities.

————

1. HW began his journey 3 Aug. (*post* 21 July 1772). The first town recorded in his itinerary is Stevenage, where he probably stopped the first night; on 5 Aug. he dined at Peterborough and supped at Slea-

uncertain how long I shall be before I reach Aston; but you shall know before, that I may not keep you waiting. You must be so good as to tell me my road, and if there is anything in my way worth stopping to see—I mean literally to *see*—for I do not love *guessing* whether a bump in the ground is Danish, British, or Saxon. Give me leave to consult you too on the rest of my journey. From you I shall go to Lord Strafford,[3] and thence wish to make excursions to York, Beverly, Castle Howard,[4] and Mr Aislabie's.[5] Will you draw me a map, and mark the distances? Consider I am lazy and not young; and do not weigh what can be done, but what I can do.

Mr Stonhewer has not returned me the book,[6] and unwilling to hurry him, I have forborne to send for it; if you write to him, will you mention it? I have printed King Edward's letters,[7] and will bring you a copy. I have since begun a kind of *Desiderata curiosa*,[8] and intend to publish it in numbers, as I get materials; it is to be an Hospital of Foundlings; and though I shall not take in all that offer, there will be no inquiry into the nobility of the parents; nor shall I care how heterogeneous the brats are.

Mr Cole tells me Dr Brown has given him a print of Mr Gray,[9] and that it is very like, which rejoices me, and makes me more impatient for one.

ford. For HW's account of his journey, which brought him back to London 20 Aug., see *Country Seats* 71–5.

2. Alluding to the foreign travels of 'macaronies' who flitted from place to place on the Grand Tour.

3. William Wentworth (1722–91), 2d E. of Strafford, 1739; HW's friend and correspondent.

4. Lord Carlisle's seat, about fifteen miles NE. of York.

5. William Aislabie (ca 1700–81), of Studley Royal, Yorks; M. P. Ripon 1721–81 (DNB *sub* John Aislabie; GM 1781, li. 243). Since HW does not mention Studley Royal in *Country Seats* he apparently did not go there.

6. I.e., Gray's transcripts (*ante* ?14 April and 9 May 1772).

7. Copies of *Seven Original Letters from King Edward VI to Barnaby Fitz-Patrick* was printed at SH, for private distribution, 1–13 June 1772, in an edition of 200 copies. The original MSS, copied for HW by Cole, belonged to Lord Ossory (Hazen, *SH Bib-*

liography 99–101; HW to Cole 29 May 1771, COLE i. 215; HW to Lord Ossory 23 June 1771).

8. The *Miscellaneous Antiquities*, which was 'in imitation of Peck's *Desiderata curiosa*, and is solely calculated for amusement' (HW's 'Advertisement' to *Miscellaneous Antiquities*). No. 1 (*post* 21 July 1772, n. 16) was printed 22–28 June 1772, and No. 2 (*ante* 9 May 1772, n. 1) 21 Sept.– 10 Dec. 1772. Each printing was of 500 copies on ordinary paper and 25 'on writing paper for presents.' The two numbers were published by John Bell, in the Strand, 1 Jan. 1773; but the sales were disappointing and HW printed no more numbers (Hazen, *SH Bibliography* 103–5; *Daily Adv.* 1 Jan. 1773). HW's copy of Peck's *Desiderata curiosa*, 1732, is now WSL.

9. See Cole to HW 22 June 1772, COLE i. 260. HW had misread Cole's letter; the print was of Mason. See Cole to HW 9 July 1772 (COLE i. 267) and *post* 21 July 1772.

I have a visitor just come in; you will lose nothing by it, for I do not know a syllable worth telling you, and am, dear Sir,

Yours most sincerely,

Hor. Walpole

From Mason, ca Saturday 18 July 1772

Missing.

To Mason, Tuesday 21 July 1772

Printed from Mitford i. 30–2.

Strawberry Hill, July 21, 1772.

Dear Sir,

I ANSWER your letter, as you bid me, the moment I receive it, though I can scarce write for laughing at Alma Mater and her nurslings.[1] I thank you a thousand times for so inestimable a present: I do not know where Lord R.[2] could get another bell[3] that would purchase it. It makes me very impatient to see the new poem[4] that is cast in the same mint.

You have chalked me out a noble route, but I have not courage to undertake so mighty a compass at once. I must besides be at Lord Strafford's earlier than such a tour would allow. I shall, therefore, set out on the third, go directly to him, and wait on you afterwards,[5] which will be soon after your return from York. A bad inn terrifies

1. Unexplained, in the absence of Mason's letter.

2. Charles Watson-Wentworth (1730–82), 2d M. of Rockingham, 1750; prime minister 1765–6 and again in 1782; leader of the 'Rockingham Whigs.'

3. Earlier in the year HW traded all his Roman medals 'of great brass' to Rockingham for an elaborately decorated silver bell, supposedly cast by Cellini for Pope Clement VII (HW to Mann 12 Feb. 1772; see also 'Des. of SH,' *Works* ii. 487, and *Walpoliana* i. 116). The bell was sold SH xv. 83 (a sketch appears on p. xix of the

sale catalogue). It was bequeathed in 1898 by Baron Ferdinand Rothschild to the BM, where it is now catalogued as 'German work of the School of Jamnitzer, late 16th century' (information from F. R. Goff; Eugène Plon, *Benvenuto Cellini*, Paris, 1883, pp. 316–7, plate facing p. 316; C. H. Read, *The Waddesdon Bequest*, 1902, p. 45).

4. Mason's *An Heroic Epistle to Sir William Chambers, Knight*. See *ante* 9 May 1772 and *post* 1 Dec. 1772, n. 17.

5. HW visited Mason at Aston 17–18 Aug. (*Country Seats* 74).

GREAT NORTH BED-CHAMBER.

THE TAPESTRY BED AT STRAWBERRY HILL

L. Vaslet ad vivum
delin: 1771.

C. Carter fecit
Aquaforti

Mr MASON.

WILLIAM MASON, BY LOUIS VASLET, 1771

me more than any antiquity of art or nature can invite me, and I have no taste for crossing washes and rivers: one should look so silly to be drowned at my age, and to be asked by Charon, *Qu'avais-tu à faire dans cette galère?*[6] I can pick up a few sights in a detached manner from Lord Strafford's, and the remainder I will consult with you at Aston.

Thank you for the account of the picture painted by Lambert.[7] The print of Mr Gray is the print of Mr Mason,[8] that is, either Mr Cole named one for the other, or I misunderstood him; one of those you was so good as to give me is framed, and installed in the chamber where I am writing; it is the Blue Room[9] where hang Madame du Deffand,[10] Grammont,[11] and Hamilton,[12] company that will tell you the value I set on your portrait.[13]

I shall bring you a copy of King Edward's letters and I hope my edition of Grammont,[14] if I can get Hamilton's print[15] from the engraver; by that time too I shall have the first number of my *Miscellaneous Antiquities* ready. The first essay is only a republication of some tilts and tournaments.[16] I have been at work on Sir Thomas Wyat's

6. An expression first used by Cyrano de Bergerac in *Le Pédant joué* (1654), II. iv, and popularized by Molière in *Les Fourberies de Scapin* (1671), II. vii, where it is repeated seven times.

7. Presumably George Lambert (1710–65), the landscape painter, of whom HW included a notice in the fourth volume of his *Anecdotes of Painting* (*Works* iii. 450–1).

8. See *ante* 6 July 1772 and n. 9. It was an etching by Mason's servant Charles Carter (see *post* 20 March 1773, n. 24, and 16 July 1773), after a portrait by the York miniaturist Louis Vaslet 'ad vivum delin. 1771.' It is listed in *BM Cat. of Engraved British Portraits* iii. 204. See illustration, and Cole i. 267. (The note on it in Cole i. 260, n. 3, is erroneous.)

9. Or the Breakfast-Room, which was 'furnished with blue paper, and blue and white linen' ('Des. of SH,' *Works* ii. 421).

10. Carmontelle's water-colour showing 'Mme la Marquise du Deffand, and the Duchesse de Choiseul giving her a doll, which the former, who was blind, holds out her hands to receive' ('Des. of SH,' *Works* ii. 425). It was sold SH xi. 111. See illustration in DU DEFFAND ii. 13.

11. HW's acquisition of this picture is described in GRAY ii. 157 n. 57. It was sold SH xi. 16.

12. Anthony Hamilton (ca 1645–1720), Gramont's brother-in-law and author of the *Mémoires du Comte de Grammont*. HW's engraving of him ('Des. of SH,' *Works* ii. 423) was sold SH xi. 4.

13. The 'Des. of SH' (*Works* ii. 427) mentions a 'print of Mr W. Mason, the poet' hanging as HW here states. A 'coloured drawing' of Mason in the Blue Breakfast-Room was sold SH xi. 109.

14. HW printed 100 copies of the *Mémoires* at SH April–May 1772 for private distribution (Hazen, *SH Bibliography* 96–9).

15. Made from HW's print (*Mémoires*, SH edn, 'Avis'; see also DU DEFFAND iii. 222). The plate was engraved by John Hall (1739–97).

16. *Miscellaneous Antiquities* No. 1 consists of extracts from the third book of *Honour Military and Civill* (1602) by Sir William Segar (d. 1633). Chap. V is entitled, 'Of Justs and Turneaments, how they were anciently judged by John Tiptoft Earle of Worcester, High Constable of England, in the reigne of King Edward the

life,[17] to prefix to his speech and letters, but it is not yet finished, so if you know anything more about him than is in Gray's papers, and in Leland[18] and our old biographers, I shall have ample room for it. Would it not be a pity to have so industrious a Caxton drowned? Mr Cole has told me of somebody else,[19] I forgot who it is, that is going to republish old historians à la Hearne.[20] This taste of digging up antiquated relics flourishes abundantly, unless Foote's last new piece[21] blows us up. He has introduced the learned society in Chancery Lane,[22] sitting as they really did, on Whittington and his cat;[23] and as I do not love to be answerable for any fooleries, but my own, I think I shall scratch my name out of their books.[24] Oxford has lately contributed to the mass *The Lives of Leland, Hearne, and Wood.*[25] In the latter's journal one of the most important entries is, *This day old Joan began to make my bed.*[26] What a figure will this our Augustan age make! Garrick's prologues, epilogues and verses, Sir W. Chambers's gardening, Dr Nowel's sermon,[27] Whittington and his cat, Sir

Fourth.' For Tiptoft see *post* 19 Sept 1772, n. 20.

17. See *ante* 9 May 1772 and n. 2.

18. John Leland (ca 1506–1552), appointed 'King's antiquary' by Henry VIII. His chief works were published posthumously by Thomas Hearne under the titles *Itinerary,* 1710–12, and *Collectanea,* 1715. In his letter of 22 June 1772 Cole gave HW several references to passages in Leland dealing with Wyatt (COLE i. 261–2).

19. James Nasmith (1740–1808), antiquary (COLE i. 185 n. 6, i. 267 and n. 3).

20. Thomas Hearne (1678–1735), the Oxford antiquary.

21. *The Nabob,* by Samuel Foote (1720–77), which was first performed at the Haymarket 29 June 1772 (Mary M. Belden, *Dramatic Work of Samuel Foote,* 1929, p. 195). It was not published until 1778; HW's copy is now WSL (see COLE i. 265 n. 8).

22. The Society of Antiquaries, which at this time had lodgings in Chancery Lane, removed to new quarters in Somerset House in 1781 (*London Past and Present* i. 53–4).

23. Sir Matthew Mite, the nabob, having been elected to the Antiquarian Society, is represented in Act III, scene i, as reading an inaugural address on Dick Whittington's cat. The scene is a burlesque of an

actual meeting of the society. See 'Short Notes,' GRAY i. 47.

24. HW resigned from the society before 28 July, using Foote's ridicule as an excuse, but actually because of attacks by members of the society upon his *Historic Doubts.* See COLE i. 265 n. 8; HW to Cole 28 July 1772, COLE i. 270.

25. Anthony à Wood (1632–95), Oxford antiquary and historian. *The Lives of Those Eminent Antiquaries John Leland, Thomas Hearne, and Anthony à Wood,* containing Wood's life 'written by himself and published by Mr Thomas Hearne,' was advertised 5 June 1772 as to be published 'on Tuesday the 16th instant' (*Daily Adv.* 5 June). It was printed at Oxford at the Clarendon Press. HW's copy was sold SH v. 124.

26. 'July 1 [1678]. Old Jone began to make my bed' (*Lives* ii. 276).

27. The sermon before the House of Commons preached on King Charles's day, 30 Jan. 1772, by Thomas Nowell (1730–1801), D.D., regius professor of modern history at Oxford. Dr Nowell attacked the Commons for their opposition to the King. The usual vote of thanks was passed, but on 25 Feb. the entry of thanks was voted to be expunged (Cobbett, *Parl. Hist.* xvii. 318).

John Dalrymple's history[28] and the *Life of Henry II*.[29] What a library of poetry, taste, good sense, veracity and vivacity! ungrateful Shebbear![30] indolent Smollet![31] trifling Johnson![32] piddling Goldsmith![33] how little have they contributed to the glory of a period in which all arts, all sciences are encouraged and rewarded. Guthrie[34] buried his mighty genius in a *Review*,[35] and Mallet died of the first effusions of his loyalty.[36] The retrospect makes one melancholy, but Ossian has appeared, and were Paradise once more lost, we should not want an epic poem. Adieu! dear Sir,

Yours ever,

H. W.

28. *Memoirs of Great Britain and Ireland,* 1771–90, by Sir John Dalrymple (1726–1810), 4th Bt. See *post* 2 March 1773 *bis.*

29. *The History of the Life of King Henry II* (1767–71), by George, Lord Lyttelton. 'No man so addicted to wisdom was less wise than Lord Lyttelton; no man so propense to art was less artful; no man staked his honesty to less purpose, for he was so awkward that honesty was the only quality that seemed natural to him' (HW in *Mem. Geo. III* ii. 19). When Lyttelton lent HW the MS of the *History* in 1758, HW returned it with expressions of admiration (HW to Lyttelton 20 June 1758); but see HW to Montagu 31 July 1767 (MONTAGU ii. 244–5), and to Lady Ossory 14 Dec. 1771. HW's copy of the *History* was sold SH v. 36. See *post* i. 104 n. 4.

30. John Shebbeare (1709–88), who as a result of his Jacobitical writings stood in the pillory in 1758, was granted a pension in 1764, and thenceforth became an apologist for the Court. See *Mem. Geo. III* i. 140 n. 2, and 262; *post* 27 July 1777.

31. Though Smollett's career as Court apologist was limited to his editorship of the short-lived *Briton* (1762–3), for which he was doubtless well paid, but not pensioned, HW never considered him in any light but that of another turncoat and mercenary like Shebbeare. See Mason's *Satirical Poems* 56–7 and *Mem. Geo. III* i. 140 nn. 1–2. HW called *Humphrey Clinker* 'a party novel, written by the profligate hireling Smollett, to vindicate the Scots and cry down juries' (ibid. iv. 218).

32. Johnson and Shebbeare, as two Court pensioners, were coupled in the Whig press as the He-bear and the She-bear (Boswell, *Johnson* iv. 113 n. 2). HW's severe remarks on Johnson in his commentary on the *Heroic Epistle* are capped by this sentence in the first draft of his notes: 'He was a prodigy of arrogance, brutality, partiality, bigotry, credulity, and bad taste—and to the disgrace of the age, its favourite author' (from MS now WSL). For a more temperate judgment of Johnson's style and character see HW's 'General Criticism on Dr Johnson's Writings,' *Works* iv. 361–2.

33. Goldsmith was neither a pensioner nor a Court supporter (HW himself praised him, in *Mem. Geo. III* iii. 119, for never having 'meddled with politics'), but HW considered him 'silly' though with 'bright gleams of parts' (HW to Cole 27 April 1773, COLE i. 310). See also *post* 27 March 1773, 7 April 1774, and 8 Oct. 1776.

34. William Guthrie (1708–70), a hack writer for the government. HW had engaged in a controversy with him over General Conway's dismissal in 1764 ('Short Notes,' GRAY i. 40).

35. HW is probably thinking particularly of Guthrie's criticisms of his *Historic Doubts* in the *Critical Review* Feb. 1768, xxv. 116–26. See GRAY ii. 180.

36. David Mallet (originally Malloch) (ca 1705–65) had expressed his 'loyalty' by his anonymously published *Truth in Rhyme,* 1761, addressed to Lord Chesterfield, in which he lavished praise on George III and Bute. In 1763 he was given a £300 sinecure. See Mason's *Satirical Poems* 47–8 n. and 57–8.

To Mason, Monday 24 August 1772

Printed from Mitford i. 33–4.

August 24, 1772.

I SHOULD be very ungrateful, dear Sir, after all your goodness to me, particularly for your kind request in asking an account of my journey, if I did not immediately thank you for all your favours. My journey was as agreeable as it could be after leaving so pleasant a place and such good company, and was attended by no accident, except an escape from being drowned in a torrent of whores and apprentices at Barnet races.[1] I passed through Clumber[2] and Thoresby[3] parks, and saw no one temptation to stop in either. Strawberry I found parched to the bone; it has rained for three days since, which has only brought down bushels of dead leaves, and advanced autumn without its change of hues. To make me amends, I found my new bedchamber[4] finished, and it is so charming that I have lost all envy of Castle Howard. The bed[5] would become Cleopatra on the Cydnus, or Venus if she was not past Cupid-bearing. In truth I fear I must call it Sardanapalus's,[6] who, Margaret[7] may, without breach of veracity, assure strangers lived still longer ago than the Goths.

Pray remember what I am going to tell you against you find yourself *en chapitre*.[7a] Your church of York enjoys an estate given by Queen Philippa[8] on the burial of her son William of Hatfield,[9] and yet you

1. In Hertfordshire. In 1772 they were run 18–20 Aug. (*Baily's Racing Register*, 1845, i. 356).

2. '[August] 19. . . . Passed through Clumber Park, belonging to the Duke of Newcastle, a dull dreary part of Sherwood, much planted lately with only evergreens. . . . There is a fictitious river, neither grand, natural, or beautiful' (*Country Seats* 74).

3. 'Close adjoining [Clumber] is Thoresby, the Duke of Kingston's, only preferable by having been longer planted, and by a much longer piece of water' (ibid.).

4. See *ante* 9 May 1772, n. 12.

5. 'The bed is of tapestry of Aubusson, festoons of flowers on a white ground, lined with crimson silk; plumes of ostrich feathers at the corners' ('Des. of SH,' *Works* ii. 494). See illustration *ante* p. 38.

6. According to Ctesias's mythical account, Sardanapalus was the last king who reigned over the Assyrian Empire of Nineveh, and died in its fall, 876 B.C., joining his wives, concubines, and treasure on an immense funeral pyre.

7. Margaret Young, HW's housekeeper at SH, one of whose duties was to show visitors through the house.

7a. In residence at York as prebendary.

8. Philippa of Hainault (ca 1314–69), queen of Edward III.

9. William of Hatfield (1336–44), second son of Edward III. 'This prince was born at Hatfield. . . . The queen Philippa, his mother, on this occasion, gave five marks *per annum* to the neighbouring abbey of Roch, and five nobles to the monks there; which sum[s], when he died, were transferred to the church of York, where the prince was buried, to pray for his soul;

have the conscience to let the poor prince's tomb be tossed about without a yard of earth it can call its own![9a] My compliments to Mr Alderson,[10] to *Argentile and Curan*,[11] etc.; nay to the old woman's picture[12] if you insist upon it.

Yours ever,

H. WALPOLE

Arlington Street.

I happened to come hither today[13] on business, and find Dr Brown has called twice, and left me in his own and your names a Goa stone[14] and a bloodstone seal, which both belonged to Mr Gray.[15] You know how really I shall value them, and I thank you very much, but I am greatly distressed how to thank Dr Brown; he has not left a direction where he lodges, and I am impatient to express how much I am obliged, of which I will beg you, dear Sir, to bear witness; I certainly would not neglect waiting on him directly, if I knew where to find him. If I do not, I will write to Cambridge.[16]

and are to this day paid to the dean and chapter, out of the impropriation of the rectory of Hatfield, as appears by the rolls' (Francis Drake, *Eboracum*, 1736, p. 490). See also HW to Cole 25 Aug. 1772 (COLE i. 275 and nn. 5–7) and *post* 12 May 1777.

9a. When HW visited York 11 Aug. 1772 he found the prince's tomb 'thrown aside into a hole' (HW to Cole 25 Aug. 1772, COLE i. 275 and n. 4).

10. Rev. Christopher Alderson (ca 1737–1814), Mason's curate, in 1797 succeeded him as rector of Aston on the presentation of the Duke of Leeds (to whom the manor had passed after Holdernesse sold the estate). Alderson was also rector of the near-by parish of Eckington in Derbyshire. He married a daughter of William Ball, steward to Lord Holdernesse. Mason, whose letters to Alderson show a paternal affection, appointed him one of his trustees and executor of his will (GM 1814, lxxxiv pt i. 418; 1852, n.s. xxxviii. 531;

Joseph Hunter, *Familiæ minorum gentium*, 1894–6, ii. 701; Draper, *Mason* 120).

11. 'A legendary drama in five acts, written on the old English model, about the year 1766' (Mason's *Works* ii. 207). It was never acted and was first published in Mason's *Poems*, 1796–7. See Draper, *Mason* 62 and 172–3, and Gaskell 37–8.

12. Possibly 'Alma Mater and her nurslings' (see *ante* 21 July 1772).

13. 25 August. See Brown to HW 25 Aug. 1772.

14. 'A fever medicine . . . consisting of various drugs made up in the form of a hard ball, from which a portion was scraped as required' (OED).

15. 'An agate puncheon with the arms of Mr Gray . . . and a Goa stone' ('Des. of SH,' *Works* ii. 499). They were sold SH xvi. 56.

16. HW's expressions of gratitude were conveyed to Brown by Cole (see COLE i. 278 n. 5).

From MASON, Wednesday 9 September 1772

Printed from MS now WSL.

Middleton Park,[1] Sept. 9th, 1772.

Dear Sir,

YOUR letter of August 24th after travelling to and fro all over Yorkshire (as your letters to me usually do) found me in Oxfordshire only yesterday. Let me, therefore, before I begin to answer it beg and pray that you would write these three words on the tablet of your memory, *Aston near Sheffeild,* and that you would never think either the village or the parson of it of consequence enough to be found out[2] without the neighbouring market town.

If you will take the pains to transcribe the anecdote you hint at about Queen Philippa I verily believe it will induce the Dean[3] to pay her son William the honours which he ought. If not, I will fit up a tomb myself if you will write the inscription.

Mr Stonhewer tells me that Dr Browne was at his house while in town, but that he is now at Cambridge, where I suppose you know he is now Vice-Chancellor.[4] I shall mention the obliging manner in which you receive the little memorials which we picked out for you.

Packets that come from the Secretary's office (though above weight)[5] are never charged at the post office. If, therefore, you would be pleased to make up those letters of Mr Gray's[6] which you mentioned either in one or two packets and send them to Mr Fraser[7] at Lord Suffolk's office[8] to be forwarded to me, you may be assured of their coming safe, for Fraser is punctuality and care itself.

I return to Aston tomorrow. The weather has not been so favourable to my tour as might have been wished. I have, however, seen Blen-

1. The seat of George Bussy Villiers, 4th E. of Jersey, built in 1756 on the site of a house that burned down in 1755 (J. C. Blomfield, *History of Middleton and Somerton,* Bristol, [1888], p. 54). 'Stonhewer has appointed me to meet him at Lord Jersey's in Oxfordshire the beginning of September' (Mason to Alderson 29 July 1772).

2. Mason first wrote 'known.'

3. John Fountayne (1714–1802), D.D., Dean of York 1747–1802.

4. Dr Brown was Vice-Chancellor of Cambridge 1771–2 (Venn, *Alumni Cantab.*).

5. The franking privilege was limited to letters not exceeding two ounces (Howard Robinson, *The British Post Office,* Princeton, 1948, pp. 114–5).

6. The early letters to HW (*ante* 9 May 1772 and n. 7).

7. William Fraser (ca 1727–1802), under-secretary of state for the northern department 1765–89, and writer of the *London Gazette* until 1802 (GM 1802, lxxii pt ii. 1171; *Royal Kalendar,* 1802, p. 131).

8. Henry Howard (1739–79), 12th E. of Suffolk, 1757, was secretary of state for the northern department 1771–9.

heim, Nuneham[9] and Rousham,[10] and if tomorrow is a tolerable day shall see Stowe[11] in my way homewards.

I have not time to add more at present than that I am with the truest esteem, dear Sir,

> Very sincerely yours,
>
> W. Mason

Addendum to the scenes of dalliance and delight:

> In some fair island will we turn to grass
> (With the Queen's leave) her elephant and ass;
> Giants from Africa, etc.[12]

To Mason, Saturday 19 September 1772

Printed from Mitford i. 36–9.

Strawberry Hill, Sept. 19, 1772.

I AM ashamed of having been so awkward about the direction, but in good truth I did not think it was necessary to specify what market town of Parnassus you lived near. For the future, I will remember that a letter to Governor Macdregs at Muxaduvad[1] would in this age find its way better than to Virgil, if he was living at Hampstead. I shall go to town next week, and will consign Gray's letters as you order, to Mr Fraser. I need not say that there are several things you will find it necessary to omit, and indeed, though to any one that knew him and me, they would be charming, I question whether you will

9. Or Nuneham Courtenay, Lord Harcourt's seat five miles SE of Oxford. Construction of the house was begun in 1755; the grounds were laid out by Lancelot Brown (*Harcourt Papers* iii. 91, 187, 199).

10. The seat of Sir Charles Cottrell-Dormer near Woodstock. See HW to Montagu 19 July 1760 (Montagu i. 290 and n. 14).

11. For HW's accounts of his visits to Stowe, Lord Temple's seat near Buckingham, see HW to Chute 4 Aug. 1753 and Montagu i. 122, ii. 44, 313–6.

12. Lines 75–7 of Mason's *Heroic Epistle*. The phrase 'dalliance and delight' occurs in l. 81. HW had evidently seen a draft of

the poem, which was not published until Feb. 1773. 'An elephant and a zebra were kept at Buckingham, now the Queen's house. A print of the latter animal was engraven by the title of the *Queen's Ass*: on which came out another print representing Lord Bute, and inscribed, *the King's Ass*' (HW, in Mason's *Satirical Poems* 60. For the prints mentioned see BM, *Satiric Prints* iv. 86–7, 89, Nos 3870, 3873).

1. Murshidabad (also spelled Maksudabad, Muxadavad) was the capital of Bengal until 1772. For another reference to Scots in India see *post* 28 March 1777 and n. 5.

find more than a very few proper for the public taste. That same public taste is the taste of the public, and it is a prodigious quantity of no tastes, generally governed by some very bad taste, that goes to the composition of a public: and it is much better to give them nothing, than what they do not comprehend and which they consequently misunderstand, because they will think they comprehend, and which, therefore, must mistake. I do not know whether it is not best that good writings should appear very late, for they who by being nearest in time are nearest to understanding them, are also nearest to misapprehending. At a distant period such writings are totally dark to most, but are clear to the only few that one should wish to enjoy them. It must be a comfort to great authors to reflect that in time they will be little read but by good judges.

Thank you for the new couplet; I have repeated it to myself forty times, and laughed as often; it is at least as good as any of the rest. The papers, alas! will tell you that I am doomed to sojourn in Egypt,[2] and must call cousins with Colonel Lutterel[3] who thinks it

—The sweetest of all earthly things,
To live with princes and to talk of kings![4]

Not that I am removing to the palace neither. No I hear the Five Mile Act[5] is drawing up against us too,[6] but I have a strange sangfroid, and

2. The marriage of Lady Waldegrave to the Duke of Gloucester, which HW feared might involve him in attendance at Court, had just been announced. HW had been formally notified of the marriage (which took place in 1766) on 19 May 1772; the King was notified 16 Sept. (Sir Edward Walpole to HW 19 May 1772; *Last Journals* i. 129–38).

3. Hon. Henry Lawes Luttrell (1737–1821), Lt-Col. in the 1st regiment of horse (*Court and City Register*, 1772, p. 182); later (1787) 2d E. of Carhampton; notorious for having been seated for Middlesex in the House of Commons, in 1769, against the wishes of the voters, who had elected Wilkes. Luttrell's sister, the Hon. Anne Luttrell, had married the Duke of Cumberland in November 1771. See HW to Mann 7 Nov. 1771; HW to Mme du Deffand 7 Nov. 1771 (DU DEFFAND iii. 131–2). The year of Luttrell's birth, wrongly given as 1743 in GEC and elsewhere, is in GM 1737, vii. 514;

and see G. F. Russell Barker and Alan H. Stenning, *The Record of Old Westminsters*, 1928, ii. 599.

4. 'Oh! 'tis the sweetest of all earthly things
   To gaze on princes, and to talk of kings'
   (Pope, *The Fourth Satire of Dr John Donne*, ll. 100–1).

5. The act of 17 Charles II (1665), c.2, forbidding nonconformist clergymen or schoolmasters to come within five miles of a city or corporate town without declaring that they would not 'at any time endeavour any alteration of government either in Church or State.'

6. At about this time the Duke and Duchess of Gloucester were prohibited from going to Court, as the Duke and Duchess of Cumberland had been; HW supposed himself included in the prohibition (*Last Journals* i. 136 and n. 1, 137; HW to Lady Ossory 4 Dec. 1771).

bear my honours and disgraces with equal temper: yet the former are showered upon me: but this very day, Mr Garrick, who has dropped me these three years, has been here by his own request, and told Mr Raftor[7] how happy he was at the reconciliation. I did not know we had quarrelled, and so omitted being happy too. He would not have been so much diverted, as I was the other day, I believe: Mr Granger[8] lent me a book, called *Sketches and Characters of the Most Eminent and Singular Persons Now Living*,[9] printed a year or two ago. My brother[10] is mentioned and said to be the only *surviving* son of a late great minister.[11] I was charmed with finding that though I have so often played the fool, I am still so fortunate as to be thought dead and gone. I will take care not to undeceive the kind person, who scorns to disturb my ashes. Apropos to Mr Granger, he is dying to have your print,[12] and swears as much as he loves a print of anybody only because it is a print of somebody, that he shall value yours for your own sake, and because he admires you infinitely. He has promised me an unique print, in return, of King Charles the First's chimney sweeper,[13] and I am sure you will not prevent my collection from being enriched with such a curiosity.

You are perfectly indifferent I hope about the revolution in Sweden,[14] and do not care whether the poor people are to be slaves to the King or House of Lords.

I intend to make a list of all that are going to shun me in public and

7. James Raftor (d. 1790), actor; brother of Kitty Clive, the actress, with whom he lived at Little Strawberry Hill.

8. James Granger (1723–76), vicar of Shiplake, Oxon; biographer and print collector.

9. A work published anonymously by Philip Thicknesse (1719–92), *Sketches and Characters of the Most Eminent and Most Singular Persons Now Living*, Bristol, 1770, vol. 1 (no more published). HW's copy was sold London 1046.

10. Sir Edward Walpole (ca 1706–84), K.B., 1753. The Duchess of Gloucester was one of four natural children of Sir Edward, who never married. For HW's characterization of him as a man of parts and merit who held himself aloof from society, see *Last Journals* i. 102–6.

11. 'Of Sir E—d W—p—e. This gentleman is the only surviving son of the greatest statesman this kingdom ever knew, and

he inherits all his father's private virtues' (*Sketches*, p. 83).

12. See *ante* 21 July 1772, n. 8, and *post* 9 Jan. 1773. On 29 May 1775 (possibly an error for 1773) Mason sent Granger a copy of the etching 'done by my servant, which is as good an impression as I can find, though not near so good as those which were first taken off' (James Granger, *Letters*, ed. J. P. Malcolm, 1805, p. 155).

13. The print has not been identified and there is no evidence that HW ever received it.

14. 'In the beginning of this month [Sept. 1772] came the first accounts of the revolution of Sweden, where the King had wrenched the power from the Senate' (*Last Journals* i. 129). Gustav III (1746–92), whose accession to the throne in 1771 was marked by widespread civil disorder, obtained French support for a *coup d'état* which effectively crushed all opposition.

squeeze my hand in private, assuring me how excessively glad they are of my niece's good fortune, and of all that will *not* squeeze my hand till they see me at St James's again, and then pinch half my fingers off with protestations of their joy. I have gone through all this farce in the former part of my life, therefore the repetition will divert me the more; when my father fell,[15] the good Bishop of Carlisle,[16] my old friend, came to condole with me, and to express his fears that we should all go to the Tower, though he could scarce contain his button-mouth from smiling. Even then I had the happy carelessness to be indifferent to what was passing, and it grievously offended Sir John Barnard.[17] I was sitting under him in the House of Commons; somebody asked me if I would go to Vauxhall one day in the next week— 'Vauxhall,' said I, 'bless me—*we* are all going to Siberia.' Well! one cannot help it if one's niece Dolgoruchi[18] marries the Czar, but at least one is not liable to have the knout, if there is a change of decoration. I am not at all desirous that Kirgate[19] my printer should, as no doubt he would, say like Caxton of Earl Tiptoft,[20] (I had rather it had been Earl Rivers for the royal marriage['s] sake)[21] 'O good blessed Lord God! what grete losse was it of that noble vertuous and well dispos'd lord! The axe then did at one blow cut off more learning, than was left in the heads of all the surviving nobility.'[22]—I hope he would

15. Sir Robert Walpole resigned the prime ministership in Feb. 1742.

16. Charles Lyttelton (1714–68), Bp of Carlisle 1762–8; friend and correspondent of HW.

17. Sir John Barnard (1685–1764), Kt, 1732; merchant and politician; M.P. London 1722–61; lord mayor of London 1736–7; opponent of Sir Robert Walpole.

18. Or Dolgorouky. The founder of the Romanoff dynasty, Czar Michael, married Princess Maria Dolgorouky in 1624 (Paul Dolgorouky, *Hand-Book of the Principal Families in Russia*, 1858, p. 52).

19. Thomas Kirgate (1734–1810), HW's printer and secretary 1768–97.

20. John Tiptoft (or Tibetot) (1427–70), Lord Tiptoft, cr. (1449) E. of Worcester; beheaded. He was a celebrated humanist, but because of his severity when constable of England and Lord-Lieutenant of Ireland in carrying out the orders of Edward IV, he came to be called 'the butcher of England.' R. J. Mitchell in *John Tiptoft*, 1938, has shown that many of the allegations

against him proceeded from partisan bias.

21. Anthony Woodville or Wydevill (ca 1440–83), 2d Earl Rivers, the brother of Elizabeth, 2d wife of Edward IV. His virtues were celebrated by Caxton, whose friend and patron he had been, especially in the epilogue to *Cordyale* (*The Prologues and Epilogues of William Caxton*, ed. W. J. B. Crotch, 1928, pp. 38–40).

22. 'O good . . . well dispos'd lord' is quoted from Caxton's epilogue to *The Declamacion of Noblesse*, translated by Tiptoft. HW could have read the epilogue in Joseph Ames's *Typographical Antiquities*, 1749, p. 27. The last sentence of the passage is not Caxton's, but one inaccurately recollected from Thomas Fuller's *History of the Worthies of England*, 1662, pp. 155–6. Both sentences had been quoted by HW in *Royal and Noble Authors* in the article on Tiptoft (*Works* i. 284), where their juxtaposition may have produced a mistaken recollection that they were part of the same quotation.

except my Lord Chancellor,[23] my Lord Rochford,[24] and the Bishop of London.[25]

From MASON, ca Thursday 1 October 1772

Missing. Mentioned in the following letter and *post* 13 Oct. 1772. Since the latter reference suggests that the letter may have been of a confidential nature, perhaps dealing with the *Heroic Epistle,* Mason may have asked HW to destroy it. For a similar injunction (which HW disregarded) concerning the *Heroic Postscript,* see *post* 23 Nov. 1773.

From MASON, Tuesday 6 October 1772

Printed from MS now WSL.
Address: To the Honourable Horace Walpole, Arlington Street, London.
Postmark: SHEFFIELD 8 OC.

Aston, Oct. 6th, 1772.

Dear Sir,

SINCE I had the honour of answering your last I have had an application from a young gentleman[1] now on his travels for a recommendatory letter or two to some person of fashion at Paris, that he may by that means be introduced into good company. When he went abroad about this time twelvemonth Lord Holdernesse[2] at my request gave him an introduction of this kind to some other places, but I cannot now with propriety repeat my application to him on this account.

23. Henry Bathurst (1714–94), cr. Bn Apsley, 1771; 2d E. Bathurst, 1775; lord chancellor 1771–8. 'By a universal consensus of opinion Earl Bathurst is pronounced to have been the least efficient lord chancellor of the last century' (W. P. Courtney in DNB).

24. William Henry Nassau de Zuylestein (1717–81), 4th E. of Rochford. For HW's opinion of him as 'an oaf' and 'a man of no abilities and of as little knowledge,' see MONTAGU i. 49 and *Mem. Geo. III* iii. 168.

25. Richard Terrick (1710–77), D.D.; Bp of Peterborough, 1757, of London, 1764. While Bp of Peterborough, Terrick was also vicar of Twickenham, and Cole comments on HW's rudeness in calling him

'Mr' or 'Dr' instead of 'my Lord' (COLE ii. 374). He secured his translation to the see of London by winning Bute's favour. HW says that he had a 'sonorous delivery' but 'no glimmering of parts or knowledge' (*Mem. Geo. III* i. 331).

1. Francis Ferrand Moore Foljambe (ca 1750–1814); entered as a fellow-commoner at St John's, Cambridge, 1768; M. P. Yorks 1784, Higham Ferrers, Northants, 1802–7 (*Gray's Corr.* iii. 1053, n. 10). See A. Gooder, 'The Parliamentary Representation of the County of York,' *The Yorkshire Archæological Society,* 1938, xcvi. 111–2.

2. Robert Darcy (1718–78), 4th E. of Holdernesse, diplomatist; Mason's patron.

Therefore I have written by this post[3] to Lord Nuneham[4] and I take also the liberty of writing to you to request the favour of a letter, but at the same time desire you not to comply with my request if it be in any sort disagreeable to you.

The gentleman's name is Mr Foljambe, of an ancient family and good fortune in this neighbourhood.[5] He is in company with a Mr Townshend,[6] and is now on his way from Vienna and I suppose will reach Paris in about a week or ten days from the date of this. He is not above three and twenty, consequently no *philosophe*, and who I suppose would therefore choose to be recommended to some person of the world, rather than a St Lambert[7] or a Marmontel.[8] All that I can say for him is that he is a genteel well-behaved young man with sense and accomplishments sufficient not to make your recommendation improper to any person you may choose to write. But (I repeat it again) if you dislike writing these kind of letters, I beg you will consider this letter as not written, and to assure yourself that I shall only be sorry for having made an improper request. It is necessary however for me to add that his address is 'À Monsieur Foljambe chez Messrs Tourton et Bauer, Banquiers, Place des Victoires,'[9] and I suppose a letter under cover to him sent thither would certainly reach him in time to be of the service desired.

Believe me to be, dear Sir,

Your much obliged and most sincere servant,

W. MASON

3. The letter is printed in *Harcourt Papers* vii. 36–7 (erroneously dated 'November 6th').

4. George Simon Harcourt (1736–1809), styled Vct Nuneham 1749–77; succeeded his father as 2d E. Harcourt, 1777; HW's and Mason's friend and correspondent.

5. Foljambe, who was the son of John Moore and Anne Foljambe, had assumed the name upon succeeding to the Foljambe estates on the death of his uncle, Thomas Foljambe, in 1758. The Foljambe seat was Aldwarke, near Aston (*Gray's Corr.* iii. 1053 n. 10 and Gooder, loc. cit.).

6. Not identified.

7. Jean-François de Saint-Lambert (1716–1803), poet, much admired by the *philosophes*. For HW's unfavourable opinion of his *Saisons* see DU DEFFAND ii. 213–4.

8. Jean-François Marmontel (1723–99), man of letters.

9. According to the *Almanach Royal*, 1772, p. xci, the address of the banking firm of Tourton et Bauer was 'rue des Deux Portes; vis-à-vis la rue Beaurepaire.'

To Mason, Tuesday 13 October 1772

Printed from Mitford i. 41–2. The first paragraph shows that the letter was dictated, probably to Kirgate.

Strawberry Hill, Oct. 13, 1772.

Dear Sir,

I DOUBT you will have thought me very inattentive to your orders, but, alas! it is far from being my fault. I have been in my bed this fortnight with the gout in every limb, and have not the use of either hand or foot.

Were I at liberty, I fear I could be but of little use to your friend. The acquaintance I had in the parliament have left Paris, and are retired into the provinces:[1] I have left off and had not seen in my three last journeys[2] the philosophers and literati; the house of Choiseul is dispersed:[3] the Président Hénaut,[4] where I used to sup frequently, is dead and the house broke up. In short I have no connection left at Paris, but with my old blind friend[5] and her society, which would not at all suit a young man of three and twenty. The best person to whom I could have recommended him, the Duchesse d'Aiguillon,[6] mother of the Duke,[7] is lately dead, and I have no more friends at Court. If the young gentleman goes into Italy I can be useful to him at Florence and Naples, and will give him letters thither very willingly.[8] I don't know whether anybody had had a curiosity about your last letter but one,[9] but I did not receive it till six days after it was dated.

I will not say any more, because I have no more to say, but about my

1. The struggle between Louis XV and his parliaments led early in 1771 to the dissolution and banishment of the parliament of Paris. See DU DEFFAND iii. 14, 17 and vi. 181–2.

2. Those made in 1767, 1769, and 1771.

3. Étienne-François de Choiseul-Stainville (1719–85), Duc de Choiseul, minister of foreign affairs 1758–70, fell from power through the enmity of Mme du Barry in 1770 and was exiled in 1771. He did not return to Paris until the accession of Louis XVI. See Gaston Maugras, *La Disgrâce du Duc et de la Duchesse de Choiseul*, 1903; John Fraser Ramsey, *Anglo-French Relations 1763–1770: A Study of Choiseul's Foreign Policy*, Berkeley, 1939, pp. 227–8.

4. Charles-Jean-François Hénault (1685–1770), président de la première chambre des enquêtes. See DU DEFFAND i. 3 n. 3 and *passim*.

5. Mme du Deffand.

6. Anne-Charlotte de Crussol de Florensac (1700–72), m. (1718) Armand-Louis Vignerot du Plessis-Richelieu, Duc d'Aiguillon (see DU DEFFAND, *passim*).

7. Emmanuel-Armand Vignerot du Plessis-Richelieu (1720–88), Duc d'Aiguillon.

8. That is, to his correspondents, the ministers, Sir Horace Mann and Sir William Hamilton.

9. *Ante* ca 1 Oct. 1772, missing. If the letter had to do with the *Heroic Epistle*, this hint that it might have been opened may have frightened Mason into taking the precautions suggested to HW *post* 1 Dec. 1772.

own sufferings, with which I do not wish to grieve anybody. I am, dear Sir,

Yours most sincerely,

Horace Walpole

From Mason, Thursday 5 November 1772

Printed from MS now WSL.
Address: The Honourable Horace Walpole, Arlington Street, London.
Postmark: SHEFFIELD 9 NO.

Aston, Nov. 5th, 1772.

Dear Sir,

LORD and Lady Strafford[1] called here about ten days ago and told me that they heard you was much better, but since that I have had a letter from his Lordship in which he tells me your gout still continues. I, therefore, cannot help troubling you with this, to beg you would order your servant to give me a line of information.

I found lately among Mr Gray's prints a proof of the unfinished head from your picture of Eckarts.[2] If you choose to have it I will send it you by the first opportunity. I will give you no more trouble at present than to assure you that I most sincerely wish you a speedy recovery and that I am

Most faithfully yours,

W. Mason

To Mason, Tuesday 10 November 1772

Printed from Mitford i. 43.

Strawberry Hill, Nov. 10, 1772.

Dear Sir,

HAVING from the shipwreck of all my limbs recovered the use of three fingers, I cannot employ them better than in thanking

---

1. Lady Anne Campbell (ca 1715–85), m. (1741) William Wentworth, 2d E. of Strafford.　　2. See *ante* 9 Sept. 1771, n. 7.

you for your kind letter and inquiry. Six weeks finish tomorrow, and I have not been yet out of my bedchamber, and little out of my bed, till lately, and in the middle of the day; the amendment is so slow, and so dispiriting, that I find it almost as difficult to recover of the recovery as of the gout; but I will not talk of it, though *I pay it off with thinking.*[1]

You will oblige me much with that print of Mr Gray—you may guess how much I have thought of him lately,[2] and how I have been weighing a shorter life against pain!

I see nobody; I know nothing; I cannot amuse you and will not tire you; the most pleasing thing that you could tell me, would be, that you had some thoughts of London. Adieu! dear Sir,

Yours very sincerely,

Hor. Walpole

To Mason, Thursday 26 November 1772

Printed from Mitford i. 44.

Strawberry Hill, Nov. 26, 1772.

THE papers, my only company at present, tell me that *Elfrida* is brought upon the stage, and pleases exceedingly.[1] I am rejoiced, and want to go and see it—but as I am not near being in a situation of going to plays, I trust I shall only wait to see it more agreeably, for you cannot be so unnatural a parent, as not to come and see Miss Mason in her glory, and then I flatter myself you will let me accompany you. Nothing could make me in cold blood expose myself to that fiery trial—yours was not so, for *Elfrida*'s character was established

1. 'Though he says nothing, he pays it off with thinking, like the Welshman's jackdaw' (*Oxford Dictionary of English Proverbs,* 2d edn, 1948, p. 564).
2. Because Gray also suffered from the gout.

———

1. Mason's *Elfrida,* with music by Thomas Augustine Arne (1710–78), was performed at Covent Garden 21 Nov. 1772. Mason had not been consulted about its adaptation for the stage, and was consequently angry. The play was performed twenty-seven times (Genest v. 360–1). A laudatory account appeared in the *London Chronicle* 21–4 Nov. 1772, xxxii. 501; the success was such that two new editions (the seventh and eighth) of the original text were published in Dec. 1772 (*London Chronicle* 12–15 and 24–6 Dec., xxxii. 571, 611).

long ago,² and you have had none of the plague and anxiety—but I
own I scarce conceive a greater pleasure than to see a dramatic work
of one's own crowned with success, and be witness to it, provided it
were well acted. Come, come, you must come and see it; do not deny
yourself so lawful a pleasure and that you deserve to enjoy—I mend so
slowly, that it seems to me that it will be supreme enjoyment to walk
cross my own room.

Yours ever,

Hor. Walpole

From Mason, Tuesday 1 December 1772

Printed from MS now wsl.
Address: To the Honourable Horace Walpole, Arlington Street, London.
Postmark: DONCASTER 3 DE.

Aston, Dec. 1st, 1772.

Dear Sir,

I WAS just going to give you some prudent cautions about locking
up your *Mother*¹ (who in conformity of character is your daughter
too) when I received your congratulations on the rape committed on
my illegitimate girl at Covent Garden.² Can you seriously think that
anything that old fumbler Dr Arne³ can do to her is likely to come
to good? No, surely; though little Mr Colman⁴ puts his finger into the

2. Although this was the first appearance
of *Elfrida* on the stage, it was first published
in 1752. See Gray to HW 3 March 1751,
Gray ii. 47. The reviewer in the *Monthly
Review* dared 'almost venture to predict,
that the author . . . may one day be esteemed the first tragic writer of the present
age, which this nation hath produced' (May
1752, vi. 387).

1. HW's *Mysterious Mother.*
2. In a letter to Lord Nuneham 2 Dec.
1772 Mason remarks that 'little Mr Colman and old fumbling Dr Arne have committed a rape on the body of my poor
daughter Friddy' (*Harcourt Papers* vii.
38). In 1778 Mason himself adapted *Elfrida*
for the stage. See *post* 6 Feb. 1778.

3. Arne's music for *Elfrida* has apparently not survived. Mason's animosity towards Arne vanished by 1776, when Arne,
with Mason's acquiescence, composed incidental music for *Caractacus* (*post* 8 Oct.
1776; Draper, *Mason* 331–3).
4. George Colman (1732–94), the elder,
dramatist, manager of Covent Garden 1767–
74, had adapted *Elfrida* for the stage. 'By
this alteration of *Elfrida,* in which the lyric
parts are both transposed and curtailed,
the author is said to have been much offended, and to have designed an angry address to Mr Colman . . . on the subject.
But that gentleman threatening him with
the introduction of a chorus of Grecian
washerwomen in some future stage entertainment, the bard was silenced, being per-

pie too. Depend upon it, if the play (or poem, call it which you will)
has any success it is owing to no intrinsic merit of its own but only
from its producing to the eye of the audience such a strange sight as
twenty British virgins. 'In England' (says Shakespeare) 'any strange
beast makes a man.'⁵ What then must twenty strange beasts do?

But do not you think it somewhat cavalier in Mr Colman to do
what he has done without any previous intimation of it to me? I should
have known nothing of the matter had not my bookseller⁶ heard of
it and demanded the property of the chorus books⁷ then printing off.
One of these he has sent me in which the odes are so lopped and
mangled that they are worse now than the productions of Handel's
poet Dr Morell.⁸ One instance I must give you because it is curious.
In my fourth ode I called the first man a *godlike* youth,⁹ authorized
so to do by the first chapter of Genesis.¹⁰ Dr Arne calls him a *royal*
youth,¹¹ an epithet which I fancy will be approved nowhere but at St
James's, for it carries the *jus divinum* higher than Sir Robert Filmer¹²
carried it. We have heard of a King Abraham and a King Noah, but
a King Adam is quite new. However, as the said King was no author
it will make no addition to your royal list.¹³

As I cannot think you serious in your congratulations, so I think
you still in jest when you say you can hardly conceive a greater pleasure than to see a dramatic work of one's own crowned with success,
etc. I conclude from this that your late fit of the gout has brought you
back to the age of five and twenty. But if you be really serious, pray
make Mr Colman a present of your *Mysterious Mother*. I will be answerable she procures you that pleasure provided you admit my alterations, for (*absit superbia*)¹⁴ I am confident they will do her more good

haps of opinion that his classical inter-
locutors would have suffered by the comparison' (David Erskine Baker, *Biographia
Dramatica*, 1782, ii. 101).

5. *The Tempest* II. ii.

6. I.e., Horsfield (*ante* 29 Dec. 1763, n. 1),
successor to the Knaptons, who had published *Elfrida* in 1752.

7. The *Chorus of the Dramatic Poem of
Elfrida* was advertised by Horsfield 23 Nov.
1772 (*Daily Adv.*).

8. Thomas Morell (1703–84), D.D., classical scholar and author of the libretti for
Handel's *Judas Maccabæus*, *Theodora*, and
other oratorios. See Nichols, *Lit. Anec.* i.
651–6 and ix. 789 (a friendly note by Cole).

Morell is perhaps best known for Hogarth's
portrait of him 'in the character of a Cynic
philosopher.'

9. Mason's *Works* ii. 51.

10. Genesis 1.27.

11. *Chorus of the Dramatic Poem of
Elfrida*, p. 13.

12. Sir Robert Filmer (d. 1653), author of
*Patriarcha, or the Natural Power of Kings
Asserted*, first published in 1680, which was
attacked by John Locke in the first of his
Two Treatises on Government as the manifesto of the absolutist party in contemporary political theory.

13. In HW's *Royal and Noble Authors*.

14. 'May pride be absent.'

than anything Mr Colman has done to *Elfrida,* and if so from the su
perior interest and novelty of the fable there is not the least doubt of
her being crowned with success. Yet I think you should stipulate for
Mrs Yates[15] instead of Mrs Hartley;[16] though I know neither of them.
I am informed that Garrick is in a fidget about *Elfrida,* which indeed
is the only thing that pleases me in the whole business; he says 'had
he thought it would have been agreeable to Mr Mason he would have
brought it on himself,' and adds 'surely Mr Colman acquainted him
with the design,' etc. This would almost lead me to forgive Colman,
was such a man worth one's forgiveness.

I conjecture that in a fortnight or three weeks you may find occasion
to write to me on a subject[17] we talked about when we were at the
Black Swan at York. Whatever news you send me on that head I must
desire you to write as of a third unknown person, as I suspect at that
time I shall find the seals of my correspondents not very firm. This
paragraph will convince you that I ought not hastily to come to town
even if *Elfrida* had more charms than Lady Pentweazle[18] to bring me
there, which indeed she has not.

I hope to have an opportunity soon of sending you safely Mr Gray's
print and also his catalogue of antiquities, scenes, etc.,[19] which is now

15. Mary Ann Graham (1728–87), tragic actress, m. (ca 1756) Richard Yates. She appeared at Drury Lane 1753–67, 1774–79, and at Covent Garden 1767–73, 1781–3.

16. Mrs Elizabeth Hartley (1751–1824), née Elizabeth White, at Covent Garden 1772–80. Mrs Hartley, who was distinguished more for her beauty than for her ability, created the rôle of Elfrida. According to an account in *London Magazine,* 1773, xlii. 471–2, she was not married, and her lover had merely assumed the name of Hartley when they began living together.

17. The *Heroic Epistle.* On 20 Jan. 1773 a letter, now WSL, not in Mason's hand, was sent to John Almon: 'Enclosed you have the poem which the author showed to you some time ago, which is now at your service; and he desires that you will print it immediately in the most correct and exact manner: and that you will, the day before it is published, send a copy to each of the persons whose names are enclosed: you will observe that there is now a preface added, which you will take care to insert correctly. I am, Sir' (signature cut off). HW's

name is not in the list of presentation copies, doubtless because of his close connection with the poem and both his and Mason's anxiety for secrecy. It is significant that Nuneham, Stonhewer, and Holdernesse are also not in the list, of which the MS (in another unidentified hand) is reproduced in the illustrated edition of *A Selection of the Letters of Horace Walpole,* ed. W. S. Lewis, New York, 1926, i. 214.

18. A hideously ugly lady in Samuel Foote's *Taste,* 1752. The play was revised in 1761 and produced at Drury Lane 6 April. See Edward H. Weatherly, 'Foote's Revenge on Churchill and Lloyd,' *The Huntington Library Quarterly,* Nov. 1945, ix. 49–60, where it is shown that Colman was also included in Foote's revenge, a circumstance that may have served to bring Lady Pentweazle to Mason's mind.

19. *A Catalogue of the Antiquities, Houses, Parks, Plantations, Scenes, and Situations in England and Wales,* of which Mason had printed privately 100 copies (C. S. Northup, *A Bibliography of Thomas Gray,* 1917, p. 69).

printed off, and also the Anglo-Indian clergyman[20] I formerly mentioned.

I am much interested that you should be at loo tables, etc., in three weeks' time to hear what people say and to keep your countenance at the same time; so pray get upon your legs, or I'll send Dr Caverhill[21] to you to make you, whether you will or no. Fine jesting! say you. But I hope you excuse it in a man that never had the gout, but who nevertheless can sympathize on occasion, and at present is sincerely sorry at your long illness, and heartily wishes your speedy recovery, being at all times, dear Sir,

Very sincerely yours,

W. Mason

To Mason, Saturday 9 January 1773

Printed from Mitford i. 47–9. At least one exchange of letters seems to be missing between this letter and Mason's last, in which he broached several matters calling for a reply.

Arlington Street, Jan. 9, 1773.

I WANT to send you my Grammont and two numbers of *Miscellaneous Antiquities;* how shall I convey them? The latter are published,[1] of the other there are only a hundred copies printed, and as a quarter of the number is gone to France, you must take it as a great present. I do not say it was printed *for my friends;* who would have an hundred? all I meant was not to make my favourite book common. For the *Antiquities,* I care not whether the *Critical Review,*[2] or Dr Milles, dislikes them. There is, I heard yesterday,[3] another man who

20. A coloured print (see *post* 14 Jan. 1773); not identified.

21. Dr John Caverhill (d. 1781), a Scots physician in London (*Royal Kalendar,* 1772, p. 223), author of *A Treatise on the Cause and Cure of the Gout,* 1769. 'From the nature of the disease, walking now appears to be the most rational way of treating the gout, when the pain is in the lower extremities. There are many living witnesses who have experienced this fact, and walked off a fit of the gout. When the pain is in the hands, elbows, or shoulders, mo-

tion must be distributed to them by other kinds of exercise' (ibid. 160).

——

1. On 1 Jan. (see *ante* 6 July 1772, n. 8).

2. The *Critical Review,* which was inclined to favour Tory authors, did not notice the *Antiquities* at all; the *Monthly,* which was partial to Whigs, devoted five pages of the April 1773 issue to résumés of the two numbers (xlviii. 263–7).

3. From Cole, in his letter of 6 Jan. (Cole i. 290).

wrote about some college in Cambridge,[4] that has printed a new pamphlet against my *Richard III;* it is to appear in the second volume of the Society's *discoveries.*[5] I shall wait with patience to see it then or never.

I have been here about three weeks, but have not yet arrived at more than taking the air, when there is a morsel of sun—As I have been fifty-five years in town, I find it extremely tolerable to see nothing but Piccadilly as I go to Hyde Park—You may comfort yourself, dear Sir, in *your* way too. If Mr Colman has violated *Elfrida,* Mr Garrick has cut out the scene of the grave-diggers in *Hamlet.*[6] I hope he will be rewarded with a place in the French Academy. I was indeed surprised at that play being revived[7] by so good a courtier.—*The adulterous Queen of Denmark* was certainly revived with great propriety just now.[8] I suppose *grave-diggers* shock Kings and Queens more than the gallantries of their relations. Obrien's *Duel,* translated from the *Philosophe sans le savoir,* was damned the first night.[9] I saw the original at Paris[10] when it was first acted, and though excessively

4. Rev. Robert Masters (1713–98), author of *The History of the College of Corpus Christi,* 1753–5; HW's copy was sold SH ii. 75.

5. *Some Remarks on Mr Walpole's Historic Doubts on the Life and Reign of King Richard III,* published separately, 1772, was included in *Archæologia,* 1773, ii. 198–215. The paper was read before the Society of Antiquaries 7 and 14 Jan. 1771 (ibid. 198).

6. The first performance of Garrick's altered *Hamlet* was given at Drury Lane 18 Dec. 1772. The changes (which were mainly in the fifth act) are summarized in G. C. D. Odell, *Shakespeare from Betterton to Irving,* New York, 1920, i. 385–9. Additional information appears in Percy Fitzgerald, *Life of Garrick,* 1868, ii. 288–94, and in David Erskine Baker, *Biographia Dramatica,* 1782, ii. 144, which begins, 'This alteration is made in the true spirit of Bottom the Weaver, who wishes to play not only the part assigned him, but all the rest in the piece.' HW in his copy of Baker (now WSL) has placed a mark of approval opposite this. Garrick's version was never printed. The MS of it is now in the Folger Library; it is discussed by George W. Stone, Jr, in 'Garrick's Long Lost Alteration of Hamlet,' *PMLA,* 1934, xlix. 890–921. See Appendix. 3.

7. 'Revived' is an odd word for HW to use: Garrick played Hamlet three times in the previous season (Genest v. 327), when it was also played twice at Covent Garden (ibid. 327, 334).

8. Caroline Matilda (1751–75), sister of George III and queen of Christian VII of Denmark, had been divorced in April 1772 and exiled from the court in consequence of her adulterous connection with John Frederick Struensee, a physician who had obtained absolute power as prime minister through Caroline's favour. Struensee was executed in 1772.

9. *The Duel,* by William O'Brien (d. 1815), adapted from *Le Philosophe sans le savoir* (1765) by Michel-Jean Sedaine (1719–97), was performed at Drury Lane 8 Dec. 1772 and was not repeated (Genest v. 342–3, who pronounces it 'unjustly condemned'). It was published shortly afterwards (*Critical Review,* Jan. 1773, xxxv. 71). HW's copy is now WSL. On the title-page he has inscribed, 'Acted but once, Dec. 2d [*sic*]. By Mr Obrien, formerly actor.' O'Brien's elopement with and marriage to Lady Susan Fox-Strangways, daughter of Lord Ilchester, occurred in 1764.

10. HW saw Sedaine's comedy 4 Dec. and 14 Dec. 1765 ('Paris Journals,' DU DEFFAND v. 280, 285).

touched with it, wondered how the audience came to have sense enough to taste it. I thought then it would not have succeeded here, the touches are so simple and delicate and natural. Accordingly it did not. I have been reading the translation, and cried over it heartily.

From Cambridge[11] I am told there is a very good print of Gray, done by one Henshaw,[12] as a companion to yours. Is it for your account of him? how does that work advance? you have forgot, but pray remember to send me one of your own prints for my friend Mr Granger.

Lord Newnham is come to town, and has been so good to visit my invalidity twice; what a meritorious pilgrimage it would be if you would too! I am perfectly reliques, I have nothing but dry bones left. You shall be rewarded with a shin-bone, which is of as much use to anybody as to the owner.

H. W.

PS. You know to be sure why I am exceedingly disappointed.[13]

From Mason, Thursday 14 January 1773

Printed from MS now WSL.
Address: The Honourable Horace Walpole, Arlington Street, London.
Postmark: SHEFFIELD 18 JA.

Aston, Jan. 14th, 1773.

Dear Sir,

I WAS meditating a how-do-ye letter to you, when yours came to give me the pleasure of knowing that your gout has not returned upon you. A friend of mine at York almost eight years older than you are, who was an absolute cripple five years, so as not to be able to move, and who took Le Febure's medicine[1] two years ago, has just now taken unto him a wife. I send you this anecdote to comfort you, though per-

---

11. In Cole's letter of 6 Jan. 1773 (COLE i. 291).

12. William Henshaw (ca 1753–75), a pupil of Bartolozzi. He exhibited two drawings at the Royal Academy in 1775 (Algernon Graves, *Royal Academy of Arts*, 1905–6, iv. 74). The print of Gray is reproduced in W. S. Lewis, *A Selection of the Letters of Horace Walpole*, 1926, i. 17.

13. Because of Almon's delay in pub-

lishing the *Heroic Epistle*. See the following letter, second paragraph *ad fin.*

1. A quack remedy for the gout. Mann had told HW about it 27 Oct. 1770, but HW was sceptical of its efficacy, and on 8 June 1771 wrote Mann that Le Fevre's reputation was 'quite exploded' both in London, which he had visited in 1770 (HW to Mann 26 Nov. 1770) and at Liége, where he usually practised.

haps you will think there is as little comfort in it as in Mrs Quickly's to Sir John Falstaffe, who bade him not think of God;[2] and will say in return, Heaven be thanked I am not yet so bad as to think of a wife. I must be cold upwards and upwards before I think of such a remedy.

I trust when you do me the honour to send me your Grammont, I shall value it as I ought to do, being proud to be ranked even amongst your hundred friends, though at the same time I have the vanity to believe I do not stand in the number of the last fifty, even if your French friends are in the first set. The carrier here is so very uncertain that I will not trust him with it, and therefore must desire you to keep it till I can get it by some private hand; but the second number of your *Antiquities* (for I have the first) if you would only send it to Mr Fraser at Lord Suffolk's office, he would enclose it in a couple of packets and send it me by the post. Colman and I have passed two pert letters to one another, in which I think I out-templar'd the templar.[3] I agree with you perfectly in the honours you think Garrick entitled to, and I trust he will have them. I am sure he would be pleased by them. Do not be disappointed. What is delayed is not laid aside. Wilful will do it,[4] *coûte que coûte;* but at present *non satis magnum theatrum mihi estis.*[5]

Yours is the first account I have heard of either Henshaw or his print. I shall be happy if it turns out so well as your account. I have this day sent off by a person going from hence to town a parcel which contains the print of Mr Gray done from your picture, and a Doctor and a Minerva à la indienne[6]—three uniques. What would Mr Grainger give for such a present? As to my own I believe Stonhewer has a few left. I will write to him for one when he returns ⟨from⟩[7] Euston. I am very glad Lord Nuneham ⟨visits⟩ you often, he is one of those very ⟨few who⟩ talk and think just as one likes. For myself I am absolutely tied down here for the winter, or else assure yourself, dear Sir, I would come to visit you without the reward you offer. Nay,

2. 'Now I, to comfort him, bid him 'a should not think of God . . . then I felt to his knees, and so upward, and upward, and all was as cold as any stone' (*Henry V* II. iii. 21–8).

3. Colman had been a law-student but not a 'templar,' having been called to the bar at Lincoln's Inn in 1757.

4. '*Wilfull:* Wilfull will do't, that's the word—Wilfull will do't, that's my crest—my motto I have forgot' (Congreve, *The Way of the World* IV. x).

5. 'You are not an audience large enough for me.' The source has not been found.

6. See *post* 1 and 23 Feb. 1773. The prints have not been further identified.

7. The defects in the MS were caused by the breaking of the seal.

if it would do you any good I would willingly part with half of my too-fat calves to dress up your shin-bones. Believe me to be

Very sincerely yours,

W. MASON

The life[8] goes on very slowly. There is so much transcription.

To MASON, Monday 1 February 1773

Printed from Mitford i. 51.

Arlington Street, Feb. 1, 1773.

I HAVE received and thank you much, dear Sir, for the print of Gray and the two Indian paintings—pray, tell me more about the latter: the Minerva is very curious, and both are prettily painted: I am sorry they are inseparable,[1] like Indamora and Lindamira.[2] You would have been thanked sooner, but I have had a relapse and kept my bed five days, nor can yet put on a shoe again. Mr Garrick, who has had both stone and gout, is still Ranger,[3] and dances a country dance! I do not envy his performances, but his *capabilities*.[4]

I agree with you heartily about Lord Nuneham; nor know anything so comfortable as one that talks and thinks, *just as one likes*, which I find a greater rarity than any print or picture in my collection, and to my sorrow I observe that the rareness increases every day: though unlike other curiosities, they are *not to be bought*. Your Elfrida, Mrs Hartley, I am told, is the most perfect beauty that was ever seen. I can neither go to see Mrs Hartley, nor *Elfrida;* but as I can read, I long for any of Elfrida's relations.

Have you heard of Mr Andrew Stuart's *Letters to Lord Mansfield?*[5]

8. Of Gray.

---

1. The painted prints were on opposite sides of a single leaf (*post* 23 Feb. 1773).

2. Conjoined twins, the heroines of Chapter xiv of Pope's and Arbuthnot's *Memoirs of Martinus Scriblerus.*

3. Garrick, who had acted the part in the first production of Benjamin Hoadly's comedy, *The Suspicious Husband,* in 1747,

played Ranger twice during the season of 1772–3 (Genest iv. 216 and v. 358).

4. As Lancelot Brown would say.

5. *Letters to Lord Mansfield,* 'printed and dispersed' in Jan. 1773 by the author, Andrew Stuart (d. 1801), M.P. Lanarkshire 1774–84, Weymouth and Melcombe Regis 1790–1801 (*Last Journals* i. 165; HW to Lady Ossory 25 Jan. 1773). HW's copy was sold SH vi. 52. Stuart, who had been

They will inform you how abominable abuse is, and how you may tear a man limb from limb with the greatest good-breeding. Alas! we are barbarians[6] and know nothing of these refinements.

Yours ever,

H. W.

From Mason, Tuesday 23 February 1773

Printed from MS now WSL.

Aston, Feb. 23d, 1773.

Dear Sir,

I SHOULD not have been so remiss in my inquiries after you, had not Lord Nuneham told me that you were a convalescent—I beg his pardon, he would not have used so pedantic a word for the world. However, he told me that notwithstanding so long and painful an illness he never saw you in better spirits or look more healthy, which account, I assure you, gave me very sincere satisfaction. That awkward business[1] which, being a deed without a name, one can hardly write intelligibly about, was another cause of my silence. I waited and waited—but in short I have now made up my mind about it. Expectation is over, and I verily believe *hush* money has been taken.[2] It would be wrong to enter into particulars, yet after a full month's time this suspicion surely is not without good grounds. O that I had Sir Andrew Steward's letters before me, they would I think produce something which in future might console one for the innocent sheep that is lost.[3] I am just this moment in an excellent humour for the undertaking because I am very much out of humour. Is it not possible to send it with the Count de Grammont?[4] (I heartily beg his pardon for putting him in such bad company, but his *politesse* I trust will excuse it.) If it be,

engaged in the famous Douglas cause to defend the claim of the Duke of Hamilton, in these letters charged Mansfield with partiality, as one of the judges when the case was decided in Douglas's favour in the House of Lords, Feb. 1769.

6. That is, not Scots.

1. The delayed publication of Mason's *Heroic Epistle*.

2. By Almon, the publisher; but Mason was mistaken. See *post* 20 March 1773.

3. That is, they would furnish Mason with material for a satire to replace the *Heroic Epistle*.

4. I.e., with the *Mémoires*, about the delivery of which HW had questioned Mason in his letter of 9 Jan. 1773.

and you would be pleased to send them to Mr Varelst's[5] in St James's Square with a message 'to desire them to send them to me with the first things they send by the wagon to Aston,' I should be sure of receiving them safe, though perhaps it would not be within a fortnight.

I can only say with respect to the Indian paintings that I found them in a book of Mr Varelst's among many others really Indian. He found me much struck with the red band, etc., of the clergyman, and Minerva happening to be on the other side the leaf, she also came to my share. He told me that he had in town several other English prints coloured by the Indians in the same fantastic manner.

I believe I have not yet thanked you for the second number of the *Antiquities*.[6] You have made the most (as you always do) of the little you had to do withal. And Sir Thomas's life will be read with pleasure, by people that cannot wade through his speech, amongst whom (pardon my *anti*antiquarian infirmity) is your humble servant, though I had the hippocricy[7] to scold my curate for owning the same defect of taste.

Pray do not entrust any of your *bon mots* to Lord Nuneham to send to me. He forgot every syllable you said about my negotiations with administration concerning Wolfe's epitaph,[8] for which I cannot forgive him.

I have altered my plan of Mr Gray's life very much from the manner I first intended and the sketch which you saw. I divide it into five or six sections, each of which introduces a distinct series of letters, poems, fragments, etc. The three first contain his correspondence with Mr West.[9] I have written almost all that I shall have occasion to write as his biographer, but as his editor I shall have many occasional notes to

5. Harry Verelst (1733–85), governor of Bengal 1767–9. After twenty years in India he returned to England in 1770, married, in 1771, Anne Wordsworth, one of Mason's cousins, and in 1774 purchased a fourth part of the Aston estates of Lord Holdernesse (*post* Mason to HW 28 June 1773; 2 Oct. 1774; 20 Nov. 1775). On Verelst's relations with Mason see Draper, *Mason, passim;* on his career in general, see DNB, and J. M. Holzman, *The Nabobs in England,* New York, 1926, p. 166.

6. See *ante* 9 May 1772 and nn. 1–2.

7. *Sic;* possibly a jocular archaism.

8. Lord North consulted Mason in the matter of the inscription for the projected monument to Gen. James Wolfe (1727–59) that was to be erected in Westminster Abbey. Mason advised 'a very short, plain classical inscription, either in English or Latin prose.' Later, at the request of Sir Grey Cooper, he drew up a specimen inscription; when it was not adopted he refused to submit another. See *Harcourt Papers* vii. 41–2 and 45–6.

9. Richard West (1716–42), intimate friend and correspondent of Gray and HW. The correspondence occupies more than half of the first three sections of *Mem. Gray.* The other correspondents are Gray's mother and father and HW.

insert, which perhaps will be done best as the work goes through the press. I believe I shall be able to send you soon by a private hand what I have written, but in the mean time I send you three or four paragraphs[10] where your name must necessarily be mentioned, which I would choose to alter entirely to your satisfaction, if you choose to have them altered. I could wish if you have any letters on literary matters which he writ latterly, i.e., from the year 1745 or '46 to his death, for I fancy I shall not make much use of the more juvenile ones which you sent me.[11] But as the latter collections will be miscellaneous, any letters of this sort would come in with a good grace. I have already some to Dr Wharton,[12] Stonhewer, Beattie[13] and myself that are excellent.

Pray (in the name of critical astonishment) what can be Macpherson's translation of Homer?[14] Has he Fingalized? has he Temoraized him? I'll lay my life he has. Homer à la Erse must be a curiosity with a vengeance. I hope it is printed *in usum Delphini*[15] and dedicated to my Lord of Chester.[16] But to release you from my epistolary longwindedness I will only add that I am, dear Sir,

Most truly yours,

W. MASON

10. Concerning HW's quarrel with Gray; see HW's reply 2 March 1773 *bis*.

11. See *ante* 9 May and 9 Sept. 1772.

12. Thomas Wharton (1717–94), M.D.; Gray's friend and correspondent (*Gray's Corr.* i. 141–2 and n. 8). See *post* ii. 16.

13. James Beattie (1735–1803), poet, philosopher, and divine.

14. The prose translation of the *Iliad* by James Macpherson, author of *Fingal* and *Temora*, was not published until 9 March 1773 (*Public Advertiser*), but an advertisement in *Public Advertiser* 19 Feb. announced that it would appear 'in the first week of March.'

15. 'For the use of the Dauphin.' The so-called Delphin edition of the classics, originally designed for the instruction of the son of Louis XIV, was published at inter-

vals from 1674 to 1730. The title-pages of each volume bore the words *Ad usum serenissimi Delphini*. Because the texts were expurgated the phrase *ad* or *in usum Delphini* acquired the meaning of 'bowdlerized.' Mason here, however, seems to be reverting to the primary significance of the phrase in a characteristic reference to the royal family. The phrase had come recently to his attention when he was editing Gray's letter to West 22 May 1739.

16. William Markham (1719–1807), classical scholar, educator, divine; Dean of Rochester 1765–7 and of Christ Church, Oxford, 1767–77; Bp of Chester 1771–7; Abp of York 1777–1807. He was appointed chaplain to George II in 1756 and from 1771 to 1776 he was preceptor to the Prince of Wales, hence Mason's ironical suggestion.

To Mason, Tuesday 2 March 1773

Printed from Mitford i. 62–3.

The letter which follows this one carries the same date and was printed by Mitford and Toynbee before this letter. But the first two sentences of the present letter make it quite clear that it is merely an acknowledgment of Mason's letter of 23 Feb. and that HW's answer to it will be delayed. Since the second letter has the same date, it is possible that HW began it before he wrote this one, but that on being interrupted by company he put it aside until he could finish it in the high style in which he began it. HW may have sent the longer letter with the parcel of books here mentioned.

Arlington Street, March 2, 1773.

I RECEIVED your letter so late yesterday, and had company all the evening, as I have had today, that there was no possibility for me to answer the particulars of it. Nay, I do not know whether you will receive my answer this week or fortnight, for I am at the mercy of everybody that pleases to visit me, and cannot be denied till I am able to visit too. You will receive the books as you directed. How you or your curate could want taste so much as not to go through Sir Thomas Wyat's oration,[1] is inconceivable. It is the finest piece that has been composed, as some pedant said, *since the Romans died*. To punish you, I will certainly send you Mr Home's new tragedy,[2] as soon as it is published—or one of his former; I dare to say it will be all the same;[3] though he says this is his best.

I do not wonder Lord Nuneham forgot my *bon mots*, for I am sure if I committed any, I have forgotten them myself.

Garrick has written a cantata for Millico's[4] benefit: a lyre tumbled

1. I.e., Wyatt's defence; see *ante* 9 May 1772, n. 1.

2. *Alonzo*, by John Home (1722–1808), author of *Douglas;* first acted at Drury Lane 27 Feb. 1773, published 6 March (*Public Advertiser*). HW's copy of *Alonzo* is now WSL. HW told Lady Ossory (11 and 16 March 1773) that he had read only the last three acts.

3. HW's low opinion of *Alonzo* was shared by contemporary reviewers. On its critical reception see Alice E. Gipson, *John Home: A Study of His Life and Works,* Caldwell, Idaho, 1916, pp. 149–58.

4. Giuseppe Millico (1739–1802), composer and singer. He visited England in the spring of 1772 and at first found little favour, but 'at the end of the next season, several who had boldly pronounced that . . . Millico [could not] sing, would have given a hundred pounds if they could have recalled their words' (Charles Burney, *A General History of Music*, 1776–89, iv. 498; see also Grove's *Dictionary of Music* and Gustav Schilling, *Encyclopädie der gesammten musikalischen Wissenschaften,* Stuttgart, 1840–1, iv. 702). The text of the cantata, not hitherto identified as Garrick's, was printed in *Lloyd's Evening Post* 26 Feb.–1 March 1773, xxxii. 204, under the heading: 'An English Cantata, sung at the Opera House by Signior Millico, on Thursday evening [25 Feb.], at his benefit. Being his farewell to England' (information from Miss Mary Etta Knapp).

out of heaven to play to it;[5] but it was so bad, the audience wished themselves at the devil. The only good thing I have seen this winter is an excellent *Papal* Bull[6]—I forgot to say above, that the town is so much of your and your curate's opinion about Sir T. Wyat's oration, that the *Miscellaneous Antiquities* have not sold above a fifth of them, so there will be no more.[7] If Sir Thomas had abused Cranmer and Latimer instead of Bonner,[8] he would have been more fashionable. Adieu! dear Sir,

Yours faithfully,

H. W.

To Mason, Tuesday 2 March 1773

Printed from Mitford i. 55–62. See preliminary note to preceding letter.

[Arlington Street,] March 2, 1773.

I AM not surprised, my dear Sir, that satire should be bought off,[1] when infamous scandals on the most virtuous characters[2] are printed at the Louvre[3] *in usum Delphini*. But shall the muse of retri-

5.   'Recitative.
But what is this that meets my eye?
A lyre! and sent me from the sky!
Some bounteous god, who knew my wants,
To me his heav'nly succour grants!
O may these strings my grateful heart reveal,
And sweetly breathe the transports that I feel.'

6. A *jeu d'esprit* by Mason occasioned by the publication of *Faldoni and Teresa* by Edward Jerningham (1737–1812), a friend and correspondent of HW and of Lord Nuneham. It was written 17 Feb. 1773. The text is printed in *Harcourt Papers* vii. 43–5.

7. 'He [HW] has already printed the speech of Sir Thomas Wyat . . . in the second number of his *Miscellaneous Antiquities*. The public must impute it to their own want of curiosity if more of them do not appear in print' (*Mem. Gray* 171 n.).

8. Edmund Bonner (ca 1500–69), Bp of London, was responsible for much of the Marian persecution.

———

1. See *ante* 23 Feb. 1773.

2. The second volume of Sir John Dalrymple's *Memoirs of Great Britain and Ireland* was published 24 Feb. 1773 (*Public Advertiser; Last Journals* i. 177). In it (pp. 255–64) was a letter of 14 Dec. 1679 from the French ambassador, Barillon (see *post* 20 March 1773, n. 21), to Louis XIV stating that Algernon Sidney, HW's hero, had taken bribes from the French. Two payments of 500 guineas are also given in Barillon's accounts (pp. 314–7). HW discusses the book at length in *Last Journals* i. 271–3. In a long note on this passage its first editor, John Doran, sums up the charge and concludes that Sidney 'undoubtedly accepted money, but for no selfish purpose of his own,' a conclusion HW half admits and condones to Lady Ossory 16 March 1773.

3. In *Last Journals* i. 272–3 HW states that the charge of bribery was 'pretended to be drawn from Barillon's papers at Versailles; a source shut up to others, and actually opened to Sir John by the intercession of even George III—a charge I would not make but on the best authority. Lord Nuneham, son of Lord Harcourt, then

bution be silent? shall a *censeur royal* clip her eagle wings? shall she
not dip her pen-feather in the blood of patriot martyrs, and write their
vindicias in crimson hues? you to whom the noble quill is descended,
must wield the weapon, and revenge Sidney and Russel[4]—probably,
deplore the sinking cause for which they fell in vain! Your writings
will outlive the laws of England—I scorn to say of *Britain* since it implies Scotland. *Her* laws will replace ours, though their most remarkable one is suspended in favour of him, whom you call Sir Andrew
Stuart; I mean, that against *leasing-making*.[5] You shall have the odious
book,[6] which is indeed as silly as it is detestable: nor does one know
whether the man is more malignant or absurd. He has given such
proofs of the villainy, folly and infamous treachery of Charles II,
James II and Louis XIV, as would make any nature but a royal one
shudder, nay laugh, if indignation did not harrow up the muscles.
Come, I will make *you* laugh even in your scornful mood. He justifies
James II against Burnet's charge of thinking only of saving his dogs,
when he was in danger of being shipwrecked.[7] How does he defend
him from the prelate's *lie?*[8]—it is Sir John's own word—why by a Scot's
letter which says the Duke of York insisted on preserving a trunk of
papers of such consequence to himself and his brother, that he would
as soon part with his life.[8a] The tenderness of a trunk's life is indeed

ambassador at Paris, told me his father
obtained licence for Sir John to search
those archives—amazing proof of all I
have said on the designs of this reign: what
must they be when George III encourages
a Jacobite wretch to hunt in France for
materials for blackening the heroes who
withstood the enemies of Protestantism
and liberty!' Dalrymple in the Preface to
his first volume (p. v), says that 'Lord Harcourt and Mr Walpole [presumably
Thomas Walpole, HW's cousin, the Paris
banker], considering the cause of letters
to be the cause of England, seconded my
request' to the Duc de Choiseul to let
Dalrymple have copies of the letters he
wanted. HW repeats his charges against
George III in Mason, *Satirical Poems* 115.
Dalrymple in the Preface to vol. 2 wrote
(p. iii): 'His Majesty gave orders that I
should have access to the cabinet of King
William's private papers at Kensington.'
By 'printed at the Louvre' HW means that
Dalrymple's book appeared under royal
patronage.

4. Algernon Sidney (1622–83) and William Russell (1639–83), styled Lord Russell,
were executed for complicity in the Rye
House plot, 1683.
5. 'Verbal sedition' (OED *sub* 'leasing').
6. That is, HW will send a copy of vol.
ii of Dalrymple's *Memoirs*. His own copy
was sold SH v. 62; when it was resold at
Sotheby's 20 Feb. 1854, lot 157, it was described as having notes by HW in pencil.
7. As stated by Bishop Burnet in his
History of His Own Time, 1724–34, i. 523.
8. *Memoirs*, appendix to pt i, p. 68.
8a. Dalrymple prints two letters (*Memoirs*, app. to pt i, pp. 68–72) concerning the
wreck of the *Gloucester* in 1682: the first
(9 May 1682) by Sir James Dick, a Scotsman,
and the second (25 Jan. 1724) by Lord
Dartmouth, whose father was on board the
Gloucester. It is not in the 'Scot's letter' that
the trunk is mentioned, but in Dart-
mouth's.

superlative proof of humanity. The dear trunk filled at least, I suppose, the place of one or two drowned men! and what damning papers
must that trunk have contained! Need I tell you at *whose* expense⁹
these treasures were transcribed? read the fond letters between their
most religious and Christian Majesties Charles II and Louis XIV, and
very few *mutatis mutandis* will suffice to open your ideas; need I tell
you that Sir John Dalrymple, the accuser of bribery, was turned out
of his place of solicitor of the customs for taking bribes from brew-
ers?¹⁰—*sed Jove nondum barbato.*¹¹—I will only wash my hands and
change the subject:¹² what shall I say? how shall I thank you for the
kind manner in which you submit your papers to my correction? but
if you are friendly I must be just. I am so far from being dissatisfied,
that I must beg leave to sharpen your pen, and in that light only, with
regard to myself, would make any alterations in your text. I am conscious that in the beginning of the differences between Gray and me,
the fault was mine. I was too young, too fond of my own diversions,
nay, I do not doubt, too much intoxicated by indulgence, vanity, and
the insolence of my situation, as a prime minister's son, not to have
been inattentive and insensible to the feelings of one I thought below
me; of one, I blush to say it, that I knew was obliged to me; of one
whom presumption and folly perhaps made me deem not my superior
then in parts, though I have since felt my infinite inferiority to him. I
treated him insolently: he loved me and I did not think he did. I reproached him with the difference between us, when he acted from conviction of knowing he was my superior; I often disregarded his wishes
of seeing places, which I would not quit other amusements to visit,
though I offered to send him to them without me. Forgive me, if I say
that his temper was not conciliating; at the same time that I will confess to you that he acted a more friendly part, had I had the sense to
take advantage of it; he freely told me of my faults. I declared I did not
desire to hear them, nor would correct them. You will not wonder that

9. That of George III.
10. See *post* Mason to HW 28 June and
HW to Mason 5 July 1773. In a note on
Mason's *Epistle to Dr Shebbeare* (1777)
HW remarked that Dalrymple 'incurred
the displeasure of the Marquis of Rockingham, then first lord of the Treasury, by
corruption' (Mason's *Satirical Poems* 115).
No further evidence of Dalrymple's acceptance of bribes has been found.
11. 'But that was when Jupiter was

still beardless' (Juvenal, *Satires* vi. 15–16).
12. HW seems to have exhausted it, for
on 16 March he wrote Lady Ossory: 'The
town and the newspapers have so fully
discussed the book that I neither listen to
the one nor read the other.'—The text of
this letter from this point to the end of
the paragraph was first printed by Mitford,
apparently very inaccurately, in his edition
of Gray's *Works*, 1835–6, iv. 216–7. See head-
note to *post* 27 March 1773.

with the dignity of his spirit, and the obstinate carelessness of mine, the breach must have grown wider, till we became incompatible. After this confession, I fear you will think I fall far short of the justice I promised him, in the words which I should wish to have substituted to some of yours. If you think them inadequate to the state of the case, as I own they are, preserve this letter, and let some future Sir John Dalrymple produce it to load my memory—but I own I do not desire that any ambiguity should aid his invention to forge an account for me. If you have no objection, I would propose your narrative should run thus, and contain no more, till a more proper time shall come for stating the truth, as I have related it to you. While I am living, it is not pleasant to read one's private quarrels discussed in magazines and newspapers.

In Section second.

'But I must here add in order to forewarn my readers of a disappointment that this correspondence (viz. during his travels) is defective towards the end, and includes no description either of Venice or its territory, the last places which Mr Gray visited. This defect was occasioned by an unfortunate disagreement between him and Mr W., which arising from the great difference of temper between the pensive, curious philosophy of the former, and the gay and youthful inconsideration of the latter, occasioned their separation at Reggio.'[13]

Note to be added. 'In justice to the memory of so respectable a friend, Mr W. enjoins me to charge him with the chief blame in their quarrel, confessing that more attention, complaisance and deference on his part to a warm friendship, and to a very superior understanding and judgment, might have prevented a rupture, that gave much uneasiness to both and a lasting concern to the survivor, though in the year 1744[14] a reconciliation was effected between them by a lady,[15] who wished well to them both.'

This note I think will specify all that is necessary, and though humiliating to me, it is due to my friend, and a vindication I owe him. It is also all that seems necessary either in section the second or fourth.

13. Mason printed this paragraph and the following note almost verbatim in *Mem. Gray* 40–1.

14. HW is in error. Gray's letter to Wharton in which the reconciliation is described has been dated on internal evidence 14 Nov. 1745 (*Gray's Corr.* i. 226).

15. In his copy of *Mem. Gray* (now in the Houghton Library, Harvard University) HW has written 'Mrs Kerr.' She has not been otherwise identified.

As to section third, it is far from accurate, and in one respect what I am sure you will have too much regard to me to mention, as it would hurt me in a very sensible part. You will I am sure sacrifice it to my entreaty, especially as it is to introduce nothing to the prejudice of Mr Gray: nay I think he would rather dislike the mention. I mean the place that I might have obtained for him from my father.[16] That I should have tried for such emolument for him, there is no doubt; at least have proposed it to him, though I am far from being clear he would have accepted it. I know that till he did accept the professorship from the Duke of Grafton,[17] it was my constant belief that he would scorn any place. My inclination to be serviceable to him was so intense, that when we went abroad together, I left a will behind, in which I gave him all I then possessed in the world—it was indeed a very trifling all! With regard to what my father would have done, let me recall the period to you or tell it to you, if you do not know it. I came over in the end of September; my father resigned in the beginning of the following February. Considering how unfavourable to him the new Parliament was, it would, I believe, with any partiality to me, have been impossible for him to have given away any place worth Gray's acceptance but to a member of Parliament during those four critical months; but this, my dear Sir, is not the part that touches me most. They are your kind words *favourite son.* Alas! if I ever was so, I was not so thus early! nor were I so, would I for the world have such a word dropped; it would stab my living brother to the soul, who I have often said, adored his father, and of all his children loved him the best.[18] You see I am making a pretty general confession, but can claim absolution on no foundation but that of repentance; you will at least, I am sure, not wound an innocent, meritorious brother from partiality to me. Do just as you think fit about his letters to me; I never thought above a very few proper for publication, but gave them up to you to prove my deference and unreserve. As I still think them charming, I beg to have them again; I have scarce any of his letters that I can call literary, for

16. *Mem. Gray* has nothing on this matter, indicating that Mason complied with HW's request. The suppressed passage doubtless occurred in the preamble of the third section at p. 120.

17. Augustus Henry Fitzroy (1735–1811), 3d D. of Grafton; statesman; chancellor of Cambridge 1768–1811. The letter offering Gray the regius professorship of modern history is not extant but its contents can be deduced from allusions to it in Gray's letters (*Gray's Corr.* iii. 1033).

18. See HW to Edward Walpole, May 1745.

they only relate to informations he gave me for my own trifling books; and I should be ashamed to show how ill I employed such time as his. Indeed they contain little more than the notices I have mentioned to have received from him; whatever I have of that sort are at Strawberry, and as I am but just able yet, after two and twenty weeks, to take the air in Hyde Park, God knows when I shall be able to go to Twickenham; life itself is grown far less dear to me, since I seem to see a prospect of surviving all that is worth living for. Mr Martin,[19] my reversionary heir, is ready in every sense to encourage me in these sentiments. Three months ago when the newspapers proclaimed me dying, he sent a Treasury-creature to my clerk[20] to know the worth of my place. The young man was shocked and asked why Mr Martin did not apply to me? No, said the agent, Mr Martin would think that too indelicate. However, not to be too delicate himself when his principal's interest was concerned, he threatened my clerk with Mr Martin's turning him out as soon as I should be dead. I recollect Martin's practising at the target for six months before he fought Wilkes,[21] and say if I am to blame in a resolution of never dining with my heir apparent.

I have written such a volume here, and so much on Dalrymples and Martins and kings, that my hand pretends to feel a little gout, and pleads that it is too hard to be forced to talk of Macpherson too. You may be sure, however, that I have not read nor shall read his Homer *travesti;* all I will add is, that the Scotch seem to be proving they are really descended from the Irish. Dalrymple has discovered humanity to a trunk; Macpherson, I suppose, has been proving by his version, how easy it was to make a Fingal out of Homer, after having tried to prove that *Fingal* was an original poem. But we live in an age of contradictions. Mr *Mac* Jenkinson,[22] the other day on the Thirty-Nine

19. Samuel Martin (1714–88), M.P. Camelford 1747–68, Hastings 1768–74; secretary to the Treasury 1758–63. In 1763 through Lord Bute he obtained the reversion of HW's ushership of the Exchequer. See Montagu ii. 65; *post* 20 and 27 March 1773; V. L. Oliver, *The History of the Island of Antigua,* 1894–9, ii. 240.

20. Charles Bedford (ca 1742–1814), at this time HW's clerk and later (1774) his deputy in the Exchequer (gm 1814, lxxxiv pt i. 701; *Royal Kalendars*).

21. HW gives an account of the duel in *Mem. Geo. III* i. 252. See *post* 20 March 1773, n. 18. In his later satire, the *Heroic Postscript* (1774), Mason gibed at Martin's preparations for the duel, but the lines, supplied by HW in his notes to the poem (Mason's *Satirical Poems* 83), were suppressed by the printer.

22. Charles Jenkinson (1729–1808), cr. (1786) Bn Hawkesbury, (1796) E. of Liverpool; favourite of Bute and George III.

Articles,[23] called Laud[24] a *very very great man*,[25] and in the same breath, stigmatized those apostles of the Stuarts, David Hume and Lord Bolinbroke.[26] Can a house divided against itself stand?[26a] did not Bolinbroke beget Lord Mansfield[27] and Andrew Stone?[28] Did not Mansfield and Stone beget the Bishop of Chester?[29] Are not atheism and bigotry first cousins? was not Charles II an atheist and a bigot? and does Mr Hume pluck a stone from a church but to raise an altar to tyranny? Thank God, if we have as great rogues as Buckingham,[30] Arlington[31] and Lauderdale,[32] at least they are as great fools as Father Petre[33]—for King James I find no parallel—he was sincere in his religion. Adieu: I leave my name out to be supplied by

Sir John Dalrymple.

From Mason, Saturday 20 March 1773

Printed from MS now WSL.

Aston, March 20th, 1773.

Dear Sir,

I DID not receive your parcel till two or three days ago, for which a thousand thanks. I was not so much a stranger to Sir John Dalrymple as you do me the honour to suspect. Five or six and twenty years

23. This was a motion in the House of Commons, 23 Feb. 1773, 'to reconsider the subscription to the Thirty-Nine Articles. The Archbishop of York had complained that Lord North had been too indifferent to them' (*Last Journals* i. 177; cf. *Journals of the House of Commons* xxxiv. 149).

24. William Laud (1573–1645), Abp of Canterbury.

25. Quoted by HW in *Last Journals* i. 177 n. In Cobbett, *Parl. Hist.* xvii. 752, Jenkinson's words are reported to have been: 'Yet candour must allow that Laud, with all his faults, was a very great man.'

26. Henry St John (1678–1751), 1st Vct Bolingbroke; statesman and orator; opponent of HW's father. Hume and he had been satirized by Mason in the *Heroic Epistle* within a few lines of each other (ll. 18–32).

26a. Matthew 12. 25.

27. William Murray (1705–93), cr. (1756)

Bn Mansfield, (1776) E. of Mansfield; chief justice of King's Bench, 1756. HW had a particular dislike for him.

28. Andrew Stone (1703–73), politician, who, as preceptor to George III before his accession to the throne, was suspected, along with his friend, Lord Mansfield, of instructing his pupil in Bolingbroke's Tory principles. See *Mem. Geo. III* i. 23 and iv. 91–2 and *Last Journals* i. 263; Montagu i. 144 and n. 4.

29. See *ante* 23 Feb. 1773 and n. 16.

30. George Villiers (1628–87), 2d D. of Buckingham, minister to Charles II.

31. Henry Bennet (1618–85), cr. (1672) E. of Arlington; influential adviser of Charles II.

32. John Maitland (1616–82), 2d E. of Lauderdale, cr. (1672) D. of Lauderdale; intimate associate of Charles II.

33. Edward Petre (1631–99), confessor of James II.

ago, I was acquainted with him at college,[1] travelled with him down into Yorkshire, lodged him and his Cambridge hack two or three days at my father's at Hull,[2] and in return for my civilities a year or two after he sent his brother-in-law to visit me at Pembroke Hall;[3] which said brother was a declared rebel, hight Wully Hamilton,[4] who writ 'The Tears of Scotland,' 1745,[5] and it was next to miracle that Bishop Keene[6] (with whom I was then very ill on account of his regulations)[7] did not take us both into custody. It was Andrew Steward's letters which I wanted, so I have only to be sorry that I knighted him. However, as I had the first part of Sir John amongst Mr Gray's books,[8] I am not displeased to have his second, though the little I have read in it has almost made me spew, I beg your pardon, and now as you wash your hands I'll take a clean pen.

This comes by my un-antiquarian curate who brings you also all the papers I have hitherto arranged relative to the *Memoirs*. I must beg you to revise them and to make your remarks on the blank pages with a pencil, and if you favour me with any additional notes, so much

1. Sir John Dalrymple was admitted fellow-commoner at Trinity Hall, Cambridge, 1746 (Venn, *Alumni Cantab.*).

2. William Mason (ca 1694–1753), father of the poet, was vicar of Holy Trinity, Hull, 1722–53 (Venn, *Alumni Cantab.*).

3. Where Mason had a fellowship. He was nominated in 1747 but was not elected until 1749 (*Mem. Gray* 172; Mason's 'Dates of the Principal Events Relative to Myself,' Mitford ii. 411; *Gray's Corr.* i. 314; Venn, *Alumni Cantab.*).

4. William Hamilton of Bangour (1704–54), poet, m. (ca 1751) Elizabeth, dau. of Sir William Dalrymple, the younger sister of Sir John Dalrymple (*The Poems and Songs of William Hamilton of Bangour. . . with Illustrative Notes and an Account of the Life of the Author*, ed. James Paterson, Edinburgh, 1850, pp. xxx and xxxiii; DNB; *Scots Peerage* viii. 123). Hamilton espoused the cause of the Stuarts and after Culloden (1746) was compelled to flee from Scotland to the Continent. He was permitted to return in 1749.

5. No poem with this title has been found in the writings attributed to Hamilton. Mason may be thinking of Smollett's 'The Tears of Scotland,' 1746.

6. Edmund Keene (1714–81); Master of Peterhouse 1748–54; Vice-Chancellor of Cambridge 1749–51; Bp of Chester 1752–71, of Ely 1771–81.

7. The Duke of Newcastle on becoming Chancellor of Cambridge instituted (1750) a reform program expressed in eighteen regulations of a disciplinary character that were intended to discourage 'such particular irregularities as call for a more immediate attention' (Newcastle's letter to the University, Add. MSS 35657 fol. 14, quoted in D. A. Winstanley, *The University of Cambridge in the Eighteenth Century*, 1922, p. 203 n.). They were bitterly resented and the attempts to enforce them were not successful. Concerning Keene's connection with the regulations, which as Vice-Chancellor he was charged with enforcing, HW wrote: 'He then was the Duke of Newcastle's tool at Cambridge, which university he has half turned Jacobite, by cramming down new ordinances to carry measures of that Duke' (HW to Mann 11 Dec. 1752). The regulations are printed in C. H. Cooper, *Annals of Cambridge*, 1842–52, iv. 278–81, and in GM 1750, xx. 311–2; for an account of them and their reception see Christopher Wordsworth, *Social Life at the English Universities in the Eighteenth Century*, 1874, pp. 64–75; D. A. Winstanley, op. cit. 199–200.

8. See *ante* 28 Aug. 1771 and n. 3.

the better. I flatter myself you will like the plan better than the execution. Yet as to the style, I hope to mend that as it goes through the press. I have already corrected the passages you objected to pretty exactly (except in a word or two) according to your letter. I have only to say further on this head, that the letter does your own heart infinite honour, and tenderly touches mine insomuch that nothing but your express order would prevail on me to print the note in question. You will find amongst these papers an Italian letter of West's and an answer to it in the same language;⁹ these relate to Mr G[ray]'s being about to settle in the Temple¹⁰ and to your going abroad. Something ought to be extracted from them to make the first series of letters complete, and some account given of your invitation to him to travel with you. Of this I have no materials to go upon and therefore wish you would fill the chasm. I also return you all the letters you favoured me with, except two or three which I shall use in the following sections. I must hint that (if you preserve these) it would be better to have them transcribed on account of the boyish beginnings and endings.¹¹ I send you also some of Mr Trollop's¹² letters, the author of the poem on the alphabet,¹³ from which and from Gray's a more perfect copy might be taken of that whimsical yet clever production.

Lord N[uneham] sent me above a week ago *An Heroic Epistle,*¹⁴

9. Both have been lost. They must have belonged to the winter of 1738–9, 'during which time a letter or two more passed between the two friends' which Mason thought it 'unnecessary to insert' (*Mem. Gray* 39).

10. West had chambers in the Inner Temple from Feb. 1738 to June 1740. Gray, who had been admitted to the society 22 Nov. 1735, planned to join West there, but no evidence has been found that he did so (*Gray's Corr.* i. pp. l, 79, 85, 95 n. 2, 164; Roger Martin, *Chronologie de . . . Thomas Gray*, 1931, p. 55).

11. Most of the salutations and signatures, 'Celadon' and 'Orosmades,' have been cut out with scissors, probably by HW.

12. William Trollope (ca 1707–49), fellow of Pembroke College 1731–49 (Venn, *Alumni Cantab.*).

13. HW was at one time inclined to believe that these verses were by Gray. 'Gray would never allow the . . . poem to be his, but it has too much merit, and the humour and versification are so much in

his style, that I cannot believe it to be written by any other hand' (HW's note printed in *The Correspondence of Thomas Gray and the Rev. Norton Nicholls,* ed. John Mitford, 1843, p. 218; see also *post* 27 March 1773 and GRAY ii. 27). It is likely, as Toynbee and Whibley suggest (*Gray's Corr.* i. 284), that Trollope wrote the verses and Gray corrected them. The verses are not included in recent editions of Gray.

14. According to a note by HW in his copy of the poem, the first edition appeared in February 1773, but the earliest advertisement that has been found is 11 March 1773 (*Public Advertiser*). For an account of the elaborate mystification that attended the publication see Mason's *Satirical Poems* 9–19 and 34. On 21 March Mason thanked Lord Nuneham for a 'curious poetical treat,' remarking 'I cannot help owning (though my loyalty crimsons my cheek while I own it), that I did frequently smile when I read that wicked poem' (*Harcourt Papers* vii. 46–7).

etc. I have heard nothing since about it, except that Mr Montagu[15] tells me he is assured by C. Fox[16] that Ansty[17] is the author of it, which is a probable conjecture. I was sorry to see a chasm in the 95th line;[18] 'tis a reflection upon the age we live in that it was not filled up. No name could be more proper than Martin's[19] now that Calcraft[20] is dead, and I adopt that reading in my own study. I am curious to hear more of the reception of the poem, because I think it is such a one as would make some little noise in the world at least for a day or two, and therefore I shall hope for some anecdotes concerning it when Mr Alderson returns, who will have my directions to call upon you for these papers in four or five days after he leaves them with you. My new pen is now dirty enough to resume Sir John Dalrymple's subject. I think there are evident internal marks of forgery in Barillon's memoir[21] relating to A. Sidney. He first gives the French King his character and then says, 'I have given him the sum you ordered and he wants

15. Frederick Montagu (1733–1800), of Papplewick, Notts; politician; friend of Gray and Mason; cousin and heir of George Montagu, HW's correspondent.

16. Charles James Fox (1749–1806), statesman.

17. Christopher Anstey (1724–1805), author of *The New Bath Guide*, 1766, which HW greatly admired.

18. The 'chasm' was caused by the printer's deletion of 'Martins,' an omission not indicated until the 13th edition (1776). In the first twelve editions the line reads, 'The R*g*ys, Mungos, B*ds*ws there,' the disguised names standing for Richard Rigby, Jeremiah Dyson, and Thomas Bradshaw. In some copies of the 13th edition the line reads as in the earlier editions, in other copies a blank has been inserted: 'The R*g*ys, ——'s, Mungos, B*ds*ws there.' In later editions the blank was filled with 'Calcrafts'; see below.

19. See *ante* 2 March 1773 *bis*. HW's note on l. 95 reads: 'In this blank stood the name of Martin, which the printer was probably bribed to omit, the person satirized having good cause to wish his name should forever be forgotten. This person was Mr Samuel Martin, secretary of the Treasury under Lord Bute. Being reproached in the *North Briton* with his baseness by the noted John Wilkes, he practised shooting at a target for six months, unwilling to challenge his accuser

till perfect in the science of manslaughter, and then fought and wounded him. For this great and other lesser services he was rewarded with the reversion of my place of usher of the Exchequer [this is inaccurate: the duel was in November 1763, six months after Martin had obtained the reversion]; and on my falling, as he flattered himself, dangerously ill not long after, he applied to my deputy, Mr Charles Bedford, to know the income of the post, and on being rebuffed, had the grosser indecency to threaten to discard him as soon as I should be dead; but on my recovery, his greediness was indemnified by an additional pension' (Mason's *Satirical Poems* 62–3).

20. John Calcraft (1726–72), politician. As deputy commissary-general of the army he amassed a considerable fortune. See Mason's *Satirical Poems* 13 and MONTAGU i. 233 n. 12.

21. Paul Barillon d'Amoncourt (ca 1630–91), Marquis de Branges, Seigneur de Mancy, de Morangis, and de Châtillon-sur-Marne; French ambassador to England 1677–89 (La Chenaye-Desbois and Badier, *Dictionnaire de la noblesse*, 1863–77, ii. 333; Anatole de Granges de Surgères, *Répertoire . . . de la Gazette de France*, 1902–6, i. 193). His 'memoir' was the letter to Louis XIV discussed *ante* 2 March 1773 *bis*, n. 2.

more.'[22] Could Louis have sent a specified sum to a man whose weight in Parliament he was unacquainted with? For my own part I will never believe it even if Sir John's employer should with his own royal mouth read to me the original paper. Adieu, my dear Sir, and, that you may live to see a thousand Martyns and Dalrymples kick the air, not 'in straw-stuffed effigy,'[23] but infamous reality, is the sincere wish of

Your affectionate servant,

W. MASON

I take the more pleasure in our present uncommonly fine weather because I hope it will tend to perfect your recovery. My amanuensis Charles[24] desires you to excuse his Greek and Latin.[25]

On looking out Mr Trollop's verses, I find on one of the papers a fragment of Mr Gray's of a History of Hell.[26] Pray take notice of the conclusion concerning *King-craft* and tell me whether he was not a prophet as well as poet.

To MASON, Saturday 27 March 1773

Printed from Mitford i. 74–9; collated with Mitford's first printing of portions of the letter in his edition of Gray's *Works*, 1835–6, iv. 218–9. The first printing was clearly very inaccurate, but corrects the 1851 text at certain points. The letter was misdated 'May' by Mitford in 1851; corrected from Gray's *Works*.

Strawberry Hill, [March] 27, 1773.

I RECEIVED your letter, dear Sir, your MS and Gray's letters to me, by Mr Alderson. Twenty things crowd about my pen and jostle and press to be said: as I came hither today (my first flight since my illness) for a little air and to read you undisturbed, they shall all have their place in good time; but having so safe a conveyance for my thoughts, I must begin with the uppermost of them, the *Heroic*

22. 'I gave him only what your Majesty permitted me. He would willingly have had more' (Dalrymple, *Memoirs* ii. 262).

23. *Heroic Epistle*, l. 96.

24. Charles Carter, Mason's 'painting servant.' He later went to London, where Mason reported him as 'half starving' in 1783. In 1787 he became insane and was

committed by Mason to the York Lunatic Asylum (*post* 4 May 1783; Mason to Alderson 26 Nov. 1787 and 20 Jan. 1788).

25. That is, in the papers relating to *Mem. Gray*.

26. Not printed in *Mem. Gray* and now presumably lost. See preliminary note to *post* 23 Aug. 1774.

Epistle. I have read it so very often that I have got it by heart, and as I am now master of all its beauties, I profess[1] I like it infinitely better than I did, and yet I thought I liked it infinitely before; there is more wit, ten times more delicacy of irony, as much poetry and greater facility than, and as, in the *Dunciad.*[2] But what signifies what I think? all the world thinks the same, except a dark corner,[3] where its being so much disliked is still better praise. No soul, as I have heard, has guessed within an hundred miles. I catched at Anstey's name and I believe contributed to spread that notion. It has since been called Temple Lutterel's,[4] and to my infinite honour mine. Lord Nuneham swears he should think so, if I did not commend it so excessively! oh how very vain I am! Sir William Chambers consoles himself with its having sold him three hundred copies of his book—I do not hear that the patron of arts consoles himself with anything, but is heartily sore[5] —He *would* read it insultingly to Chambers, but soon flung it down in a passion. It is already of the fourth edition.[6] Thank you for giving my impatient heir, Sam. Martin, a niche. There is published a defence of Negro slavery by his father.[7]

But now, my dear Sir, as you have tapped this mine of talent, and it runs so richly and easily, for Heaven's and England's sake do not let it rust. You have a vein of irony and satire that the best of causes bleeds for having wanted. Point all your lightnings at that wretch Dalrymple, and yet make him but the footstool to the throne as you made poor

1. Mitford's reading in Gray's *Works* is 'confess.'

2. 'It has as much poetry as the *Dunciad*, and more wit and greater facility' (HW to Lady Ossory 11 March 1773).

3. The Court.

4. Temple Simon Luttrell (ca 1739–1803), 2d son of Simon, 1st E. of Carhampton; M.P. Milborne Port 1775–80; turbulent member of the Opposition (G. F. Russell Barker and Alan H. Stenning, *The Record of Old Westminsters*, 1928, ii. 599; George Kearsley, *Complete Peerage*, 1802, ii. 432–3).

5. 'The King, expecting only an attack on Chambers, bought it [the *Heroic Epistle*] to tease, and began reading it to him; but finding it more bitter on himself, flung it down on the floor in a passion and would read no more' (*Last Journals* i. 179).

6. Published 23 March (*Public Advertiser*).

7. Samuel Martin (ca 1694–1776), planter. See V. L. Oliver, *The History of the Island of Antigua*, 1894–9, ii. 240; *The Diary of John Baker*, ed. Philip C. Yorke, 1931, p. 65. Martin's *Essay upon Plantership* was written and first published in Antigua ca 1755 (*Journal of a Lady of Quality*, ed. Evangeline W. and Charles M. Andrews, New Haven, 1921, p. 262). The third and subsequent editions were published in London. The fifth edition, 'with many additions and a preface upon the slavery of Negroes in the British colonies, showing that they are much happier than in their native country, much happier than the subjects of arbitrary governments, and at least as happy as the labourers of Great Britain,' was announced in *Daily Adv.* 12 Feb. 1773.

simple Chambers. We are acting the very same scene Dalrymple has brought to fuller light, sacrificing friends to stab heroes and martyrs. There are repeated informations from France that preliminaries of strict union are signed between that Court and ours;[8] Lord Stormont[9] is the negotiator, and Lord Mansfield, who has not courage enough even to be Chancellor,[10] hopes the Chancellor of France[11] has courage and villainy enough to assist him in enslaving us, as the French Chancellor has enslaved his own country![12] if you mind not me, depend upon it you will meet the indignant shade of Sidney in your moonlight walk by your cold bath, who will frown inspiration. You see what you can do, what Milton trusted to prose, what Pope had not principles elevated enough to do, and for doing what Gray's bards will bless you. In short you have seated yourself close to all three, and you must now remain in full display of your dignity. When Gray's life is finished, you are not permitted to write anything inferior to the *Dispensary*.[13] Thank you for your admirable remark on Barillon's letter; I will communicate it to Mrs Macaulay (without naming you); she will defend Sidney in her next volume[14]—but he demands a higher pen.

I am extremely pleased with the easy unaffected simplicity of your MS, nor have found anything scarce[15] I would wish added, much less retrenched—unless the paragraph on Lord Bute, which I do not think quite clearly expressed, and yet perhaps too clearly, while you choose to remain unknown for author of the *Epistle*. The paragraph I mean might lead to a suspicion: might it not look a little too, as if Gray,

8. That this was generally believed seems to be indicated by the following extract: 'In the French societies they speak with their usual indiscretion, say openly that 12,000 men are to be sent to Sweden to secure that country from any attacks from the neighbouring powers, and assert with their accustomed *étourderie* that a negotiation with us is now on foot for the free passage of their ships, and that an alliance with England will soon take place' (Col. Horace St Paul to Lord Rochford 10 Feb. 1773, in George Grey Butler, *Colonel St Paul of Ewart, Soldier and Diplomat*, 1911, i. 122). HW says much the same to Mann 12 March 1773.

9. David Murray (1727–96), 7th Vct Stormont; 2d E. of Mansfield, 1793; English ambassador to France 1772–8.

10. HW refers to his refusal to accept the seals in 1770 (*Mem. Geo. III* iv. 34; HW to Mann 18 Jan. 1770).

11. René-Nicolas-Charles-Augustin de Maupeou (1714–92), Chancellor, 1768.

12. See BERRY i. 28 and DU DEFFAND *passim*. Maupeou was the leading supporter of the absolutist policies of Louis XV.

13. By Sir Samuel Garth (1661–1719), Kt; M.D.; one of HW's favourite poems.

14. Which did not appear until 1781 (see *post* 3 Feb. 1781). She accepts Barillon's letter as genuine, but remarks that if Sidney accepted money from Louis XIV 'it was to procure the dissolution of a base and venal Parliament' (*History of England*, vii. 497).

15. Mitford in Gray's *Works* reads 'scarcely anything.'

at least his friends for him, had been disappointed?[16] especially as
he asked for the place, and accepted it afterwards from the Duke
of Grafton?[17] Since Gray (and I am sorry he did not) has left no marks
of indignation against the present times, I do not know whether it
were so well to mix politics with a life so unpolitical: but I only suggest this—you are sure I do not speak from disinclination to the censure, but from infinite regard both for him and you. The page and
reflections on poor West's death are new, most touching, most exquisitely worded.[18]

I send you Mr Andrew Stuart's book;[19] and as I had two given to me,
I beg you will accept that I send. It will be a great curiosity, for after
all his heroism, fear or nationality have preponderated, and it will
not be published.[20]

I can add nothing to your account of Gray's going abroad with me.
It was my own thought and offer, and was cheerfully accepted; thank
you for inserting my alteration; as I survive, any softening would be
unjust to the dead; and nobody can justify him so well as my confession and attestation. It must be believed that I was in the wrong,
not he, when I allow it; in things of that nature, the survivor has the
better chance of being justified: and for your sake, dear Sir, as well
as his, I choose you should do justice to your friend. I am sorry I had a
fault towards him; it does not wound me to own it.

I return you Mr Trollop's verses, of which many are excellent, and
yet I cannot help thinking the best were Gray's, not only as they appear in his writing, but as they are more nervous and less diffuse than
the others; when we meet, why should not we select the best, and make
a complete poem?

Dr Goldsmith has written a comedy[21]—no, it is the lowest of all
farces; it is not the subject I condemn, though very vulgar, but the
execution. The drift tends to no moral, no edification of any kind—the

16. The paragraph was removed. It was
probably a footnote on Gray's letter to
Wharton 4 Dec. 1762, in which Gray says
that on Shallet Turner's death 'I got my
name suggested to Lord B[ute]' to succeed
Turner as regius professor of modern history at Cambridge (*Mem. Gray* 293; *Gray's
Corr.* ii. 787).
17. In 1768.
18. *Mem. Gray* 156–7.
19. *Letters to Lord Mansfield*, 1773.
20. Although the book was issued privately (see *ante* 1 Feb. 1773, n. 5), it seems
to have been a large printing, and in 1775
an octavo edition appeared with a Dublin
imprint.
21. *She Stoops to Conquer*, first performed at Covent Garden 15 March 1773
(Genest v. 365); published 25 March (*Public Advertiser*). HW's copy was sold at the
American Art Association (Roderick Terry
sale) 2 May 1934, lot 103 (removed from
HW's 'Theatre of George III').

situations however are well imagined, and make one laugh in spite of the grossness of the dialogue, the forced witticisms, and total improbability of the whole plan and conduct. But what disgusts me most, is that though the characters are very low, and aim at low humour, not one of them says a sentence that is natural or marks any character at all.[22] It is set up in opposition to sentimental comedy, and is as bad as the worst of them. Garrick would not act it, but bought himself off by a poor prologue. I say nothing of the Home's *Alonzo*[23] and Murphy's *Alzuma,*[24] because as the latter is sense and poetry compared to the former, you cannot want an account of either.

Mr Nicoll[25] is returned, transported with Italy: I hope he will come hither with me next week,[26] Gothic ground may sober him a little from pictures and statues, which he will not meet with in his village, and which, I doubt, will at first be a little irksome. His friend Mr Barrett[27] stands for Dover, I suppose on the Court-interest, for Wilkes has sent down a remonstrating candidate.[28] I like the *Parliamentary right*[29] in his City remonstrance. I forgot to tell you too, that I believe the Scotch are heartily sick of their Dalrymplyan publication. It has

22. HW had stated his views on the use of low characters in his prefaces to the first and second editions of *The Castle of Otranto.*

23. See *ante* 2 March 1773 *bis.*

24. *Alzuma,* by Arthur Murphy (1727–1805), author and actor, was first performed at Covent Garden 23 Feb. 1773 (Genest v. 364), published 4 March 1773 (*Public Advertiser*). HW's copy, with a note 'Acted for the first time Feb. 23d,' is now WSL.

25. Rev. Norton Nicholls (ca 1742–1809), Gray's correspondent; rector of Lound and Bradwell in Suffolk. He left England 21 June 1771 (Nicholls to Gray 29 June 1771, *Gray's Corr.* iii. 1192, MS now WSL). It was the belief of Thomas James Mathias that Nicholls was second only to West in Gray's affections ('Memoir of the Rev. Norton Nicholls' in *Observations on the Writings and on the Character of Mr Gray,* 1815, p. 127).

26. It is not known if this visit took place. HW was much drawn to Nicholls at this time, but when in 1790 Nicholls moved to Richmond, HW tired of him. Although they must have corresponded, no letters between them have been discovered. Nicholls wrote his mother 17 May 1774 to ask for Gray's letters to him—'Mr Walpole is very anxious that Mr Mason should have ex-

tracts from them to publish in the life' (MS now WSL). Six of the letters were printed in *Mem. Gray.*

27. Thomas Barrett (1744–1803), of Lee, near Canterbury; HW's correspondent. He offered to take Nicholls with him to Italy in the status of a paid companion, but Nicholls declined (*Gray's Corr.* iii. 1040–2, 1045). They met abroad; Nicholls wrote his mother from Siena 9 April 1772, 'I found, too, a great resource in my friend *Barrett* (you saw him one afternoon on Cholmondeley Terrace with Mr Gray). He speaks to me, and to me only; he has exceeding good sense, well cultivated, and a good heart, and I believe a sincere esteem for me which I put among his good qualities. He has besides the accidental, but great advantage in this world of being very, very rich' (MS now WSL).

28. This by-election was occasioned by the death of Sir Thomas Pym Hales 18 March 1773 (GM 1773, xliii. 155), M.P. Dover. Barrett's opponent was John Trevanion (GM 1773, xliii. 198), a supporter of Wilkes's remonstrances to the King on what he regarded as abuses of civil liberties, especially the seating of Colonel Luttrell after his defeat by Wilkes in the 1768 Middlesex election. Barrett was elected.

29. 'Most Gracious Sovereign, We, your

reopened all the mouths of clamour; and the *Heroic Epistle* arrived in the critical minute to furnish clamour with quotations. You cannot imagine how I used it as fumigation. Whenever I was asked, have you read Sir J. Dalrymple? I replied, have *you* read the *Heroic Epistle*? Betty[30] is in raptures on being immortalized; the Elephant and Ass[31] are become constellations, and *he has stolen the Earl of Denbigh's handkerchief*[32] is the proverb in fashion—good night.

Pope—Garth—Boileau—you may guess whether I am or not

Your sincere admirer,

Hor. Walpole

From Mason, Friday 7 May 1773

Printed from MS now WSL.

Aston, May 7th, 1773.

Dear Sir,

THE very obliging, I had almost said flattering, letter which you sent me by Mr Alderson cannot on one of its subjects[1] be an-

Majesty's dutiful and loyal subjects, the Lord Mayor, Aldermen, and Livery of the City of London, beg leave to approach the Throne with the respect becoming a free people zealously attached to the laws and constitution of their country, and the Parliamentary right of your Majesty to the crown of these realms.' The text of the remonstrance is given in *Last Journals* i. 182–3 and in *Annual Register*, 1773, xvi. 209–10.

30. Elizabeth Munro (or Neale) (ca 1730–97):
'There at one glance, the royal eye shall meet
Each varied beauty of St James's Street;
Stout T*lb*t there shall ply with hackney-chair,
And Patriot Betty fix her fruitshop there'
(ll. 113–6).
HW's note on the last line reads: 'Elizabeth Munro was a celebrated fruit-woman in St James's Street, who took great liberties with the Court in her conversation—her shop was consequently much frequented by the Opposition' (Mason's *Satirical Poems* 66–7). Betty also seems to have been known as Mrs Elizabeth Neale (GM 1797, lxvii pt ii. 891; Montagu i. 109).

31. See *ante* 9 Sept. 1772 and n. 12.

32. 'See Jemmy Twitcher shambles; stop! stop thief!
He's stol'n the E* of D*nb*h's handkerchief'   (ll. 125–6).
Toynbee suggests that this is a reminiscence of Gray's *The Candidate*, especially of the lines 'Such a sheep-biting look, such a pickpocket air!' and 'Then he shambles and straddles so oddly.' 'Jemmy Twitcher,' the name of a pickpocket in Gay's *Beggar's Opera*, was applied to John Montagu (1718–92), 4th E. of Sandwich, after his betrayal of Wilkes in the affair of the *Essay on Woman*. Basil Feilding (1719–1800), 6th E. of Denbigh, was characterized by HW as 'a most worthless tool and spy of Lord Bute and the Court' (Mason's *Satirical Poems* 69).

1. The *Heroic Epistle*.

swered by me at present, which I am sorry for, because I have an excellent story to tell you relative to it. It is an account of a stratagem by which ten good golden guineas were obtained from a certain person, by another,[2] to which such a sum was of great service. This is all I can say, but the detail of the matter is highly comic, and you shall have it the first safe opportunity. In the mean time, you will perceive that this was not the primary end of the scheme, but that it served another excellent purpose.[3]

Lord Holdernesse has been here in his way to Hornby.[4] He did me the honour to dine with me and was wonderfully gracious, which astonished me much, as I thought my late resignation of the chaplainship[5] would have made him quite out of temper with me, and that he could hardly have concealed it, but he is a better courtier than I even ever thought him before, accordingly I strove to be as courtly as possible in return. Our talk was entirely on general subjects and literary matters, such as Sir John D[alrymple], and A. Steward's book, and the *Heroic Epistle;* I controverted none of his opinions, only, as he seemed to think that the *Epistle* had merit, I ventured to say that I thought it worthy of Soame Jennyns[6] had it suited his political sentiments. He replied, 'So it was, but S. J. would never have used that *harsh* kind of satire.' From his Lordship's account I find that it is generally supposed to be Temple Lutterell's,[7] although Almon declares it to be the work of a young man and his first work. After all, we live in an age of miracles that two such writers as he and Junius[8] should keep themselves concealed.

2. Presumably the payment by the publisher John Almon (1737–1805) to Mason for the *Heroic Epistle*. Almon seems never to have discovered that Mason wrote it or the *Heroic Postscript* (*Monthly Review* 1805, n.s., xlviii. 105). The 'stratagem' was accomplished through an unidentified young man (see ll. 8–12 of the *Heroic Postscript*, Mason's *Satirical Poems* 74–5; *post* 15 Jan. 1774). It is possible, as Draper conjectures (*Mason* 250 n. 103), that this was Mason's young friend John Baynes (1758–87), who acted as intermediary in the publication of some of Mason's later satires (see *post* 18 May 1782). But Baynes's youthfulness at this time, and HW's apparent ignorance of his identity in 1782 (*post* 7 May 1782), argue against the theory.

3. Possibly that of furthering Mason's design of secrecy.

4. Hornby Castle in the North Riding, the principal residence of Lord Holdernesse.

5. See *ante* 17 May 1772.

6. Soame Jenyns (1704–87), miscellaneous writer and M.P. 'Having seen . . . the causes and progress of the opposition to Sir Robert Walpole, . . . this gave him an early distaste to opposition in general; and nothing that passed afterwards in Parliament . . . ever tended to produce any alteration in his mind on that subject' ('Sketches of the Life of Soame Jenyns' in his *Works*, ed. C. N. Cole, 2d edn, 1793, i. p. xl).

7. See *ante* 27 March 1773 and n. 4.

8. The satirist, usually believed to be Sir Philip Francis (1740–1818), the first authorized edition of whose letters had appeared in 1772. Among those suspected

Next Monday I go to live at York for three whole calendar months. Hard as my fate is to quit the country for such a town, and though I now feel myself fastened for life to a piece of preferment attended with this annual inconveniency, yet I feel myself much more content than I should be with any exchange, which would put me under obligations to those persons who only could procure such exchange. And I trust you give me full credit for what I now say. I mean to put my *Memoirs of Mr Gray* to the press there,[9] and to print the work leisurely so that it may come out after next Christmas.[10] Accept my best thanks for the few strictures you have made, I wish they had been more numerous, all of them shall be attended to. Pray have you any letter relative to the *Long Story?*[11] I mean to introduce it in the fourth section and think that a letter and a note would be its best introduction. I beg my compliments to Mr Nicolls and congratulations on his return home. If he has any letters which he thinks proper to publish, you will inform him of my plan and he will send them or not as he chooses. Those which contain his sentiments of books, etc. will be the most eligible.[12]

Many thanks to you for Mr A. Steward's book. It is valuable on many accounts as containing the character of a Scotsman drawn by a Scotsman and as being able to rouse the indignation of an Englishman like me, which I confess it did when I read it, though, as I never dipped into the Douglas cause before, I am not sure how far I ought to have been indignant. I am told (by a friend of Lord M[ansfield]'s indeed) that it proves nothing against his Lordship. If so, I am sure nothing can be proved about anything.

I have seen none of the plays you mention. I always reserve these for my light lutestring[13] reading in my summer residence at York.

I fear you have no thoughts of a tour again this summer to Wentworth Castle. If so, I know not when I shall have the pleasure of seeing you. However, absent or present I hope you will always believe me to have the highest sense of your partiality to me and that you will believe me to be, dear Sir,

Very sincerely yours,

W. Mason

of having written the letters were Burke and HW. See references in Gray ii. 189 n. 8.

9. The first edition was printed at York at the press of Ann Ward.

10. It did not appear until the spring of 1775 (see *post* 3 April 1775).

11. Gray's humorous verses written in 1750. See *Mem. Gray* 211–20 and *Gray's Corr.* i. 330 n. 1.

12. Mason printed six (see *ante* 27 March 1773, n. 26).

13. A glossy silk fabric (OED).

I hope this late cold weather brings not with it any return of your complaint.

Since I writ the foregoing I have heard that the cathedral will be shut up till Whitsunday on account of repairing the roof, so that I have a reprieve of three weeks. Pray are these letters of Lady Rachel Russel[14] of consequence? Lord H. could tell me nothing about them, but he spoke high things of a certain poem[15] of the Duke de Nivernois. As you favour my obscurity sometimes with a literary journal, and, unlike other journalists, make the account more entertaining than the thing itself, pray in your next mention these two publications.

To MASON, Saturday 15 May 1773

Printed from Mitford i. 69–74.

Strawberry Hill, May 15, 1773.

YOU may imagine I am impatient to hear the history of the ten golden guineas. Though anybody will take such a sum, I thought few would fish for so little. We are in a higher style of cheating and plundering.[1]

What can I tell you of literary matters? Nothing of the poem you inquire after by Monsieur de Nivernois. He has written an hundred or two of fables,[2] and read some of them to the Academy,[3] but told me it was thought wrong for a nobleman in France to publish. How could he write, when he could be so far prejudiced? The fables are good, as far as anything can be so, that gives one no pleasure. There is I am told, a dialogue of Boileau and Horace written by the same nobleman and

14. Lady Rachel Wriothesley (ca 1637–1723), dau. of Thomas Wriothesley, 4th E. of Southampton; m. (1) (ca 1653) Francis, Lord Vaughan; m. (2) (1669) William, Lord Russell (GEC *sub* Bedford and Carbery; DNB *sub* William Russell). *Letters of Lady Rachel Russell* were published 21 May 1773 (*Public Advertiser*). Mason had apparently seen an advance announcement; the earliest that has been found is in *Daily Adv.* 7 May.
15. Not identified. See following letter.

1. HW apparently did not understand that Mason himself had received the guineas.
2. 250 were collected and published for the first time in Nivernais's works, 1796. A translation of a selection of them appeared in London in 1799.
3. Where they were well received (Lucien Perey, *La Fin du XVIIIe siècle: le Duc de Nivernais, 1763–1798*, 1891, pp. 58–64; É. A. Blampignon, *Le Duc de Nivernais ou un grand seigneur au XVIIIe siècle*, n.d., pp. 276–83).

even published,[4] not very lately. I have seen it formerly and thought I liked it.

Lady Russel's letters too I have seen formerly;[5] they are to and from her director,[6] a Jacobite clergyman, who triumphs on her husband's martyrdom, and whom with her sense and spirit I should have thought she would have kicked out of her house. I am much surprised in this our day that the Duchess[7] gives leave for the publication.[8] I should have expected that her conjugal piety, blended with *per*digious loyalty, would have concurred with her Lord's shade in calling Lord Russel *a very silly fellow,* as his Grace did in Ireland,[9] though he was pleased with the compliment of the mayor of Calais, who told him he hoped he was come with more pacific intentions than his great ancestor and namesake John Duke of Bedford, who had been their regent.[10] There are two other answers to Sir J. Dalrymple,[11] but not very good. The best answer is what he made himself to George Onslow,[12] whom he told on warning him for traducing the immortal Sid-

4. No copy or notice of this has been found.

5. 'I have now before me a volume of letters written by the widow of the beheaded Lord Russel, which are full of the most moving and expressive eloquence: I want to persuade the Duke of Bedford to let them be printed' (HW to Mann 14 Oct. 1751). HW's copy of the *Letters* was sold SH v. 74.

6. John Fitzwilliam (d. 1699), non-juring divine; chaplain in the household of Thomas Wriothesley, E. of Southampton, 1664–6. The letters to Fitzwilliam compose a little more than half of the published collection.

7. Hon. Gertrude Leveson-Gower (1715–94), m. (1737) John Russell, 4th D. of Bedford (Burke, *Peerage,* 1928, p. 2217).

8. The transcript of the letters was made in 1748 by Thomas Sellwood. The work was dedicated to the Duke of Bedford, who died in 1771.

9. The Duke of Bedford was Lord Lieutenant of Ireland 1756–61.

10. 'In France the Duke was received as their guardian angel. The most distinguished and unusual honours were paid to him; and the principal magistrate of Calais, thinking him descended from the other John, Duke of Bedford, brother of Henry V, complimented his Grace (and no

doubt felicitated himself on the comparison) on seeing him arrive with as salutary and pacific, as his great ancestor had formerly landed there with hostile, intentions' (*Mem. Geo. III* i. 151). This happened when the Duke went on the peace embassy to France, in 1762.

11. Prefixed to the *Letters of Lady Rachel Russell* was an Introduction vindicating the character of Lord Russell from the charges made by Sir John Dalrymple. In the 'Monthly Catalogue' for May in the *Critical Review* (1773, xxxv. 388–9) two rejoinders to Dalrymple's *Memoirs* are noticed: *Observations on a Late Publication Entitled, 'Memoirs of Great Britain, by Sir John Dalrymple,' in Which Some Errors, Misrepresentations, and the Design of That Compiler and His Associates Are Detected;* and Joseph Towers, *An Examination into the Nature and Evidence of the Charges Brought against Lord William Russel and Algernon Sidney, by Sir John Dalrymple, Bart.* In his copy of the latter (now wsl) HW has written 'April' below the date on the title-page. A scathing review of the first tract appeared in *Monthly Review,* 1773, xlviii. 505–6.

12. Two George Onslows were in the House of Commons at the time: George Onslow (1731–1814), 4th Bn Onslow, 1776, cr. (1801) E. of Onslow, son of Arthur On-

ney, that he had other papers which would have washed him as white as snow. With this Sir John has been publicly reproached in print[13] and has not gainsaid it. The upright soul!

Lord Holderness and you, who ought to be better judges than I am of the capabilities of Court-bards, must excuse me if I think Soame Jenyns could no more have written the *Heroic Epistle* than I could the best scene in Shakspeare. Please to point out any poetry in Jenyns's works: his best are humour rhymed; and sneers checked by the Court of Chancery from laughing out.[14] Pope is more likely to have written the *Heroic Epistle* since his death, than Soame Jenyns during his life.

So much for what we *have* been reading; at present our ears listen and our eyes are expecting East Indian affairs,[15] and Mr Banks's[16] voyage for which Dr Hawksworth[17] has received *d'avance* one thousand pounds from the voyager, and six thousand from the booksellers, Strahan and Co., who will take due care that we shall read nothing else till they meet with such another pennyworth.[18] Sir J. Dalrymple, over and above all his glory has gained toward four thousand. Our Scotch Alduses and Elzevirs keep down every publication they do not partake; and there is a society who contribute to every purchase they

slow who had been Speaker from **1728 to 1761**; and George Onslow (1731–92), M.P. Guildford 1760–83. HW entertained no high opinion of either (Mason's *Satirical Poems* 118), but probably here refers to the former, who was an occasional visitor at SH. See *post* 15 May 1778 and n. 7.

13. The reproach has not been found.

14. Probably an allusion to his most ambitious verses, 'The First Epistle of the Second Book of Horace Imitated,' 1748, which were dedicated to the Lord Chancellor, Hardwicke.

15. Under the date of 3 May HW wrote: 'Lord North moved for leave to bring in a bill to regulate the affairs of the [East India] Company at home and abroad, and he stated the chief correctives he had in view. Lord Clive then spoke for two hours and a half on his own case, and was heard with the utmost attention, and, though he did not convince, astonished and gained the admiration of all his audience' (*Last Journals* i. 197). There is a detailed account of the debates on East Indian affairs in Cobbett, *Parl. Hist.* xvii. 799–837 and 848–931.

16. Joseph (later Sir Joseph) Banks (1744–1820), cr. (1781) Bt; P.R.S. 1778–1820; accompanied Cook (at his own expense) on his first expedition around the world.

17. John Hawkesworth (ca 1715–73), LL.D., author; compiler of *An Account of the Voyages Undertaken . . . by Commodore Byron, Captain Wallis, Captain Carteret and Captain Cook . . . Drawn up from the Journals Which Were Kept by the Several Commanders and from the Papers of Joseph Banks, Esq.,* 3 vols, published 9 June 1773 (*Public Advertiser*). The 2d and 3d vols contain Banks's account of Cook's first voyage. HW's copy was sold SH v. 136.

18. Hawkesworth obtained an injunction that forestalled the prior publication of *A Journal of a Voyage to the South Seas,* by Sydney Parkinson, Banks's draughtsman (ibid. pp. xx–xxii; DNB *sub* Parkinson). Despite the hopes of Hawkesworth's publishers, the book was a financial failure (R. A. Austen-Leigh, 'William Strahan and His Ledgers,' *The Library,* 1923, 4th ser., iii. 285–6).

make of books, to keep the price at high-water mark.[19] Another club of print-sellers do the same. Woe be to those who do not deal with, and indeed enrich themselves by the monopolists!

The House of Commons has embarked itself in a wilderness of perplexities. Though Lord Clive[20] was so frank and high-spirited as to confess a whole folio of his Machiavellism,[21] they are so ungenerous as to have a mind to punish him for assassination, forgery, treachery and plunder, and it makes him very indignant. T'other night, because the House was very hot, and the young members thought it would melt their rouge and shrivel their nosegays, they all on a sudden, and the old folks too, voted violent resolutions, and determined the great question of the right of sovereignty,[22] though, till within half an hour of the decision, the whole House had agreed to weigh and modify the questions a little more; being so fickle, Lord Clive has reason to hope that after they have voted his head off, they will vote it on again the day after he has lost it.[23]

I have been looking over all Mr Gray's letters as you desired, but cannot find one relating to the *Long Story:* he therefore probably gave it me at some time that he was with me. I do not know where Mr Nicolls resides in the country, or would ask your question; he is gone out of town.

Though it will certainly be more convenient to you to have the life printed under your eye at York, I cannot but lament my press is not to be honoured with it, though in sooth two capital reasons are strong against it. The first, that the pace of my single printer,[24] who has not even an aide-de-camp or devil, is so wondrous slow that your

19. On the opposition to the monopolistic practices of the booksellers see Augustine Birrell, *Seven Lectures on the Law and History of Copyright in Books,* 1899, pp. 99–137; John W. Draper, 'Queen Anne's Act: A Note on English Copyright,' *Modern Language Notes,* 1921, xxxvi. 146–54; A. S. Collins, *Authorship in the Days of Johnson,* 1927, pp. 92–113; R. W. Chapman, 'Authors and Booksellers,' in *Johnson's England,* ed. A. S. Turberville, Oxford, 1933, ii. 317; Sir Frank MacKinnon, 'Notes on the History of English Copyright,' in Sir Paul Harvey, *Oxford Companion to English Literature,* 1937, App. ii.

20. Robert Clive (1725–74), cr. (1762) Bn Clive; K.B., 1764.

21. On 3 May (see n. 15).

22. One of the three 'violent resolutions' voted 10 May declared 'That all acquisitions made under the influence of a military force or by treaty with foreign princes do of right belong to the state' (*Journals of the House of Commons* xxxiv. 308).

23. Clive won his reprieve on 21 May: a motion 'That Robert Lord Clive did . . . abuse the power with which he was entrusted, to the evil example of the servants of the public' was defeated, and it was resolved 'That Robert Lord Clive did, at the same time, render great and meritorious services to this country' (ibid. xxxiv. 331).

24. Thomas Kirgate.

work would not be finished in this century; the other, is that I have
not the patience necessary for correcting the press. Gray was forever
reproaching me with it, and in one of the letters I have just turned
over, he says, 'Pray send me the proof sheets to correct, for you know
you are not capable of it.'[25] It is very true, and I hope future edition-
mongers will say of those of Strawberry Hill, they have all the beautiful negligence of a gentleman.[26] Mr Jerningham[27] has just desired my
consent to his dedicating a new poem[28] to me. I remonstrated, and advised him to Augustus,[29] the patron supreme; he would not be said
nay, and modesty, as it always does when folks are pressing, submitted;
but it was to be a homage to my *literary merit,* oh! that was too much,
I downright was rude. Sir, says I, literary merit I have none, literary
merit will be interpreted learning, science, and the Lord knows what,
that I have not a grain of. I have forgot half my Latin and all my
Greek. I never could learn mathematics; never had patience for natural philosophy or chess; I have read divinity, which taught me that no
two persons agree, and metaphysics which nobody understands: and
consequently I am little the wiser for either. I know a little modern
history of France and England, which those who wrote did not know;
and a good deal of genealogy, which could not be true unless it were
written by every mother in every family. If I have written anything
tolerable, it was to show I had common sense, not learning; I value
my writings very little and many others value them still less, which it
would be very unreasonable in me to resent, since nobody forgets
them so soon as myself, and, therefore, dear Sir, etc. Well he has consented, and I hope from his example, I never shall be called the
learned author again, as I have been by magazines, when magazines
were so cruel as to wish me well.

I should not have said, my pen is my witness, half so much of myself,
if I had had anything else to say—oh yes, I have. Mr Duncombe[30] has
published a volume of my good Lord of Corke's letters[31] to him[32] from

25. Apparently an imperfect recollection of Gray's letter of ca Aug. 1752: 'Pray, when the fine book is to be printed, let me revise the press, for you know you can't' (GRAY ii. 61 and *Gray's Corr.* i. 364). Gray was speaking of the *Designs by Mr R. Bentley for Six Poems by Mr T. Gray,* published by Dodsley in 1753.

26. HW is being unduly modest; the SH Press publications are not 'negligent.'

27. Edward Jerningham (1737–1812), poet and dramatist; HW's correspondent.

28. *The Swedish Curate, a Poem,* 1773. See *post* 12 and 17 Sept. 1773.

29. George III.

30. Rev. John Duncombe (1729–86), writer and editor.

31. *Letters from Italy in the Years 1754 and 1755 by the Late Right Honourable John Earl of Corke and Orrery,* 1773. The

Italy. I fear Pliny[33] would not give him his library for writing them, no more than his father did for thinking he could not write.[34] I am glad your Cathedral shuts its doors on you; you did not want that omen of your never wearing a mitre, the cap of liberty becomes such [a] head much better; though I believe you would be as singular as good Hoadley[35] and wear them together, 'tis, therefore, I am so much

And ever yours,

H. W.

From MASON, Monday 28 June 1773

Printed from MS now WSL.

York, June 28th, 1773.

THE strenuous idleness which always possesses me when I am here (the phrase is classical[1] though perhaps nonsensical) has prevented me, dear Sir, from answering your last most obliging letter sooner. In the mean time, you are become a great royal uncle or rather the great-uncle of royalty,[2] and all this while I have been deficient in point of congratulation. However, as I sincerely believe the only part of the matter which pleases you is the Duchess's safe recovery, I shall confine my congratulation to that point alone, which as her month is now about finished, I suppose will come at present with propriety; and I am not without hopes that you will in return, send me a curious anecdote or two relating to the part which the supreme Pattern of

letters were written by John Boyle (1707–62), 5th E. of Cork, 5th E. of Orrery, 2d Bn Boyle of Marston. HW's copy was sold SH v. 141.

32. The letters were written not to him but to his father, William Duncombe (1690–1769), miscellaneous writer and dramatist.

33. Pliny the Younger. Orrery translated his letters (1751) and prefaced the volume with an adulatory sketch of Pliny's life. See Duncombe's preface to the *Letters from Italy*, pp. xxxiv–vii.

34. The greater part of the library owned by Charles, Earl of Orrery, went, on the Earl's death, to Christ Church, Oxford. In the elder Orrery's will there is a reference

to his son's never having shown 'much taste or inclination for the knowledge which study and learning afford' (GEC iii. 422). Duncombe declares that the father intended to change his will but died before his lawyer arrived (*Letters from Italy*, p. iv).

35. Benjamin Hoadly (1676–1761), Bp of Bangor 1716–21, of Hereford 1721–3, of Salisbury 1723–34, and of Winchester 1734–61; leader of the latitudinarian party in church and state.

———

1. Horace's 'strenua inertia' (*Epistles* I. xi. 28).

2. Princess Sophia Matilda was born to the Duke and Duchess of Gloucester 29 May 1773.

fraternal affection has acted on this trying occasion. I wish also to know the real state of his R. Highness's health.[3]

I have printed the first section of the *Memoirs* and now am preparing the second, which, you may remember, is to include Mr G[ray]'s correspondence during his travels. I enclose two letters to Mr West written in French, which I think, in point of manner, are so very French, that they deserve to be printed; but whether they are so, in point of language, is a question which you must determine.[4] I fancy if they are not accurate, a few corrections of your pen would make them so, or perhaps if one letter was made out of them both, that would be a sufficient specimen of his excellence with respect to writing in a foreign language, which when he ever attempted, was it either in Latin, French or Italian, he became as it were a native and thought exactly in the national manner. 'Tis on this account that I wish to publish a specimen in each tongue, and have already given one in Latin[4a] in the first section. If you think as I do on this subject, I must beg you to revise the letters I now send, and to mark also in red ink what other passages, besides those which I have marked already, it would be right to omit. I shall stop the press till I am favoured with your answer.

This dull place affords me no news except that her Majesty's zebra[5] who, according to the advertisement in our *York Courant* of this day, it seems was lately the property of Mr Pinchy[6] and purchased by him of one of her domestics (though, as I rather suspect, given to him for the valuable consideration of his friendship) died the third day of April last at Long Billington[7] near Newark. This advertisement further adds 'that the proprietor has caused *her skin to be stuffed,* and that upon the whole *the outward structure* being so well executed, she is *as well* if not better *to be seen now* than *when alive,* as she was so *vicious* as not to suffer any stranger to come near her, and the curious may now have *a close inspection,* which could not be obtained before.'

3. On 23 June 1773 the *Public Advertiser* reported that 'the Duke of Gloucester was so ill on Monday night as gave his physicians little hopes (except an unexpected change) of their being able to re-establish him.' The Duke had a 'diseased constitution, nor was he ever above two years without some grievous crisis' (*Last Journals* ii. 51).

4. On HW's advice Mason omitted them (*post* 5 and 16 July 1773).

4a. To West, 22 Jan. 1738 (*Mem. Gray* 28–9).

5. See *ante* 9 Sept. 1772 and n. 12.

6. Christopher Pinchbeck the younger (ca 1710–83), inventor. As one of the 'King's friends' he was satirized by Mason in the *Ode to Mr Pinchbeck, upon His Newly-Invented Patent Candle Snuffers,* 1776 (Mason's *Satirical Poems* 87–93).

7. Almost certainly a mistake for Long Bennington, a village in Lincolnshire between Grantham and Newark-upon-Trent.

She is at present exhibited at the 'Blue Boar in this city with an oriental tiger, a magnanimous lion, a miraculous porcupine, a beautiful leopard and a voracious panther, etc., etc.' Pray do not you think the fate of this animal truly pitiable? who after having, as the same advertisement says, 'belonged to her Majesty full ten years,' should not only be exposed to the close inspection of every stable boy in the kingdom, but her immoralities while alive thus severely stigmatized in a country newspaper. I should think this anecdote might furnish the author of the *Heroic Epistle* with a series of moral reflections which might end with the following pathetic couplet:

> Ah beauteous beast! thy cruel fate evinces
> How vain the ass that puts its trust in Princes!

I am informed that Mr Cambridge,[8] instigated by the great fame of the forementioned author, has awakened his muse (who you may remember fell asleep in the Duchess of Norfolk's assembly room[9] fifteen years ago and never wakened since) and has added forty lines to the *H. Epistle*.[9a] I am promised a sight of them, but have not yet had that happiness. For my own part, I ought to employ myself in an epithalamium on the approaching nuptials in Hertford Street,[10] or rather in an elegy on the fate of Aston, whose sale is determined upon,[11] because it is too near the ducal seat at Kiveton.[12] I suspect that in the next reign the Irish[13] will take place of the Scots in point of favouritism.

I saw a *Scotchman* lately who averred to me that there was great

---

8. Richard Owen Cambridge (1717–1802), author of the *Scribleriad* and other satires and imitations. He had been a contemporary of HW's at Eton, and was his neighbour at Twickenham.

9. Cambridge's *Elegy Written in an Empty Assembly Room*, 1756, a parody of Pope's *Eloisa to Abelard*, represents Lady Townshend as lamenting not having been invited to a party at the Duchess of Norfolk's. In 1756 Cambridge also published *The Fakeer: A Tale*, but after this 'confined his poetic efforts to the production of witty trifles for his friends' (Richard D. Altick, *Richard Owen Cambridge: Belated Augustan*, Philadelphia, 1941, p. 126).

9a. The verses are not printed in Cambridge's *Works*, 1803.

10. The London residence of Lord Holdernesse, whose daughter, Lady Amelia Darcy, was to marry Francis Godolphin Osborne, Lord Carmarthen. See *post* 23 and 27 Nov. 1773.

11. I.e., the sale of part of the Holdernesse estates to Harry Verelst. See *ante* 23 Feb. 1773, n. 5.

12. Kiveton Park, one of the seats of the Duke of Leeds, was less than five miles east of Aston.

13. Possibly Mason alludes to HW's mention of the Duke of Bedford *ante* 15 May 1773. As Lord-Lieutenant of Ireland the Duke had pursued a policy of conciliation that was far from popular in some circles.

truth in the affair of Sir J. D[alrymple]'s bribery[15] and that the matter was hushed up, at the time, by Wheatly[16] now dead, who I know was Sir J.'s friend at college. I wonder that this thing, as well as his curious speech to Mr Onslow[17] is not fully sifted and authenticated, they would afford the best of all answers to his scandal.

I hope to have the great pleasure of hearing from you very soon, and beg you will believe me to be, dear Sir,

Most sincerely yours,

W. MASON

To MASON, Monday 28 June 1773

Printed from Mitford i. 79–81.

Strawberry Hill, June 28, 1773.

NOT that I have anything to say, but if I do not write to say [? so], when shall I have a minute's time? I have given myself two or three holidays, and must enjoy them by conversing with my friends. I am not going to India,[1] nor have been at Portsmouth.[2] It is not sure that I am not going to as unlikely a place, Newmarket.[3] All Lord Orford's affairs are devolved upon me because nobody else will undertake the office. I am selling his horses, and buying off his matches.[3a] I live in town to hear of mortgages and annuities, and do not wonder that Titus was called the delight of mankind, for he put *the Jews*[4] to

---

15. See *ante* 2 March 1773 *bis* and n. 10.
16. Thomas Whately (d. 1772), politician and writer. He had been admitted pensioner of Clare College, Cambridge, in 1745 (Venn, *Alumni Cantab.;* DNB).
17. See *ante* 15 May 1773 and n. 12.

1. Prominent in the newspapers because of the troubles of the East India Company and the Clive affair.
2. 'All the world are preparing for Portsmouth; whither the King is going to see the fleet' (HW to Mann 15 June 1773). For an account of the Portsmouth naval review see *Annual Register*, 1773, xvi. 202–7.
3. HW's nephew George Walpole (1730–91), 3d E. of Orford, after a severe illness

had for some months shown signs of insanity. The tangle of his affairs was for long a prime source of trouble to HW. Orford had left Houghton at this time and was living with his mistress, Mrs Turk, 'Patty,' at Eriswell, near Newmarket. More details appear in HW to Lady Ossory 26 June 1773 and to Thomas Walpole 1 July and 4 Sept. 1773. Thomas Walpole's letter to HW ca 11 Sept. 1773 expresses his gratitude 'as one of a family to whom you so generously sacrifice a long enjoyed and well employed retirement.'
3a. See HW to Lady Ossory 26 June and to Lord Ossory 7 July 1773.
4. That is, money-lenders.

the sword. Mr Manners,[5] who was the son of Lord William,[6] who was
the son of Beelzebub, deserves to be crucified. He was so obliging the
other day to make me a visit, and tell me he should seize the pictures
at Houghton—I sent for a lawyer to exorcise him. My dear Sir, what
vicissitudes have I seen in my family! I seem to live upon a chess-
board; every other step is black or white. A nephew mad and ruined,[6a]
a niece, a princess; Houghton, the envy of England—last week Mr
Vernon,[7] the jockey, offered to vouchsafe to live in it, if he might have
the care of the game: you do not think I believe that I need hear sermons. I have moralities enough at my elbow—The only shaft that
pierces deep, is the apprehension of losing the tranquillity I had so
sedulously planned for the close of my life. To be connected with
Courts or Inns of Courts is equally poison. To trifle here was my whole
wish, my little castle was finished,[8] I was out of Parliament, and
Temperance had given me her honour, that being as unsubstantial
as a sylph, I should be as immortal. I would as soon put my trust in
Lady St Huntingdon;[9] I have been six months in purgatory with the
gout, another's ambition has engrafted me upon Sandford's genealogical tree,[10] and I must converse with stewards and money-changers in
the Temple every term. Here is a Hieroglyphic Tale[11] with a witness.

You are fretting at being shut up in York, instead of sauntering and
piping to your sheep in your own grounds. I grieve for that as much
as you, yet you have whole evenings to loll in your chair as you do in

5. John Manners (ca 1730–92), illegitimate son of Lord William Manners by Cor-
betta Smith. His wife, Lady Louisa Tolle-
mache, was a sister-in-law of Lord Orford's
cousin, Lady Dysart. Lord Orford owed
him £9000. See GEC iv. 565–6; GM 1792,
lxii pt ii. 870; HW to Lady Ossory 11 and
26 June 1773 and 29 June 1777.

6. Lord William Manners (1697–1772),
2d son of John, 2d D. of Rutland (Irvin
Eller, *The History of Belvoir Castle*, 1841,
p. 113).

6a. HW wrote to Thomas Walpole 4
Sept. 1773 that he expected Orford's debts
to exceed £44,000 'independently of the
debts of his father and grandfather, which
leaves him infinitely poorer than a beggar.'

7. Richard Vernon (1726–1800), 'father
of the turf'; one of the original members of
the Jockey Club; M.P.

8. Except for the Beauclerk Tower (1776)
and Offices (1790).

9. Selina Shirley (1707–91), m. (1728)
Theophilus Hastings (1696–1746), 9th E. of
Huntingdon. She was a leader of the Meth-
odists.

10. *A Genealogical History of the Kings
of England*, 1677, by Francis Sandford
(1630–94). HW is alluding to the marriage
of his niece to the Duke of Gloucester.
HW's copy of Sandford is now WSL.

11. 'If I write any more Hieroglyphic
Tales, the scene will lie on Newmarket
Heath' (HW to Lady Ossory 26 June 1773).
HW wrote five 'Hieroglyphic Tales' in
1772 ('Short Notes,' GRAY i. 47) and printed
seven copies at SH in 1785. The MSS of four
of them and of an unpublished tale are
now WSL.

your print here.¹² Lay down that paper in your hand, and write me a letter upon it, I shall be transported to receive a line that is not upon business. Does *the life* increase? does it take up all your time? We have nothing new but what is as old as Paul's, the *Voyages* to the South Sea.¹³ The Admiralty have dragged the whole ocean, and caught nothing but the fry of ungrown islands, which had slipped through the meshes of the Spaniard's net.¹⁴ They fetched blood of a great whale called Terra Australis incognita, but saw nothing but its tail.¹⁵ However Lord Sandwich¹⁶ has given great ocean's King¹⁷ a taste for salt water, and we are to conquer the Atlantic, or let the sea into Richmond Garden, I forget which. Adieu; pray do not drop me, though I am got upon the *turf*.

To MASON, Monday 5 July 1773

Printed from Mitford i. 84–7.

Strawberry Hill, July 5, 1773.

THOUGH it was inconvenient, it looks like sympathy, that we wrote to each other at the same time. I resume my pen as yours requires an answer: mine contained nothing material.

The Duke of Gloucester has frequent returns of his asthma, but they are short. Dr Jebbe¹ is confident that there are no dangerous symptoms, still as there is a latent cause, for which he is not likely to be soon touched by either Pretender,² one must not be too sanguine. I hope you like *the Princess Sophia*. The history attending her birth is indeed curious, but fitter for a book³ than a letter. You must wait for it, dear Sir, till we meet, for as I told you in my last, I am too much

12. See *ante* 21 July 1772, n. 8, and illustration.

13. Hawkesworth's compilation (*ante* 15 May 1773).

14. The Admiralty and Society Islands, in particular.

15. That is, the east coast, named by Cook New South Wales. HW's figure was doubtless inspired by the map at the beginning of vol. i.

16. John Montagu (1718–92), 4th E. of Sandwich; first lord of the Admiralty 1771–82.

17. *Heroic Epistle*, l. 66.

1. Richard (later Sir Richard) Jebb (1729–87), cr. (1778) Bt; M.D. He attended the Duke when in Italy, was very successful in his practice, and was a favourite of George III.

2. An allusion to the Stuart practice of 'touching' for scrofula or the 'King's Evil.'

3. HW's suspicion that the King and his associates had attempted to cast doubt on the legitimacy of the Princess, by their efforts to have Lady Waldegrave and the Duke go through a second marriage ceremony, was reserved for *Last Journals* i. 203–29.

occupied by another nephew, to have time for being the historian of the royal one. I am not *the ass that puts its trust in Princes,*[4] nor that believes that Mr Cambridge can come within a thousand leagues of the *Epistle.* Indeed I should have thought him as little likely to attempt adopting that vein, as my Lord Bristol,[5] who vows he would as soon read blasphemy.

I firmly believe the story of Sir J. D[alrymple]'s bribery, it was palliated by the intercession of Charles Yorke,[6] but Lord Rockingham would not let it be totally suppressed. Onslow certainly told the other anecdote; but when I questioned him about it lately, he owned he had told it, but that Sir John had spoken to him since and explained away a good deal of the strength,—you will judge whether satisfactorily or not. I now come to Gray's letters. The first I well remember: the second you may be sure I never saw before. I cannot say that either of them satisfy me, nor do I know whether they would do him honour, though very well considering how young he was in French; but readers are more apt to criticize than excuse. The language is not correct, nor elegant; many of the idioms are downright English, and what gives them a French air chiefly, is a fault; I mean the phrases, which betray the tone of the provinces, not of the capital. Take them away, and you will not I think, find the spirit French. If you print them, I have no objection to your inserting the passage you have marked for reprobation, and which alludes to me. You see how easily[8] I had disgusted him; but my faults were very trifling, and I can bear their being known, and forgive his displeasure. I still think I was as much to blame as he was; and as the passage proves what I have told you, let it stand, if you publish the whole letter. I send it with some corrections most of which I am sure are necessary; but as I am a very imperfect Frenchman myself, a native of France I doubt would find several more, and deem the style very *baroque. Des ombres d'idées* may be Spanish, but I doubt the expression will be unintelligible to French ears. *Cela* is never *ça,* I believe. The beginning of the second letter is full of Anglicisms: I have endeavoured to make them a little more

4. Mason's line in his letter of 28 June.
5. George William Hervey (1721–75), 2d Bn Hervey, 1743; 2d E. of Bristol, 1751.
6. Hon. Charles Yorke (1722–70); politician.
8. Toynbee and Whibley suggest this is a misprint for 'early' (*Gray's Corr.* i. 111), a conjecture that is strengthened *post* 27 Nov. 1773: 'We had not got to Calais before Gray was dissatisfied. . . . I am sorry to find I disobliged Gray so very early.'

Académie, but you should not rely on my judgment: Madame du Deffand has told me, that I speak French worse than any Englishman she knows.⁹

I have almost waded through Dr Hawksworth's three volumes of the voyages to the South Sea. The entertaining matter would not fill half a volume; and at best is but an account of the fishermen on the coasts of forty islands.

I must conclude, that my letter may go by a private hand to town, and be delivered to Mr Fraser¹⁰ time enough for tomorrow's post. I use this method for the safety of Gray's letters, not for any secrets contained in this. Had I more leisure, I could tell you nothing but melancholy stories of my nephew, who is again grown furious, and has made several attempts lately to destroy himself, which keeps me in unceasing anxiety. Adieu, dear Sir; you do not send me a line, or a couple of lines, with which I am not charmed.

From Mason, Friday 16 July 1773

Printed from MS now WSL.

York, July 16th, 1773.

I HAVE followed your advice with respect to the two French letters, and instead of printing either of them have inserted one to his mother,¹ which will preserve the chain of correspondence. I ought to apologize for giving you fresh trouble at present, by desiring your opinion of two others, which I enclose, and I would do so did you not tell me that in your present situation (which I sincerely lament) an employment of this kind may serve for relaxation, and therefore I will take the liberty to chat with you as if there was not a nephew or a Houghton in existence. If I chat at an improper season you may throw down my letter here, and take it up again when you shall be at better leisure and spirits.

The first of these letters from Mr West,² though I think myself that there is good humour in it, will perhaps appear too bizarre for the

9. In her letters Mme du Deffand usually reassured HW about his French, once remarking that his mistakes 'ajoutent encore au naturel de votre style' (16 July 1766, DU DEFFAND i. 93).

10. See ante 9 Sept. 1772, n. 7.

1. *Mem. Gray* 50–2; *Gray's Corr.* i. 112–4.
2. Missing. Written in Feb. or March 1740 (*Gray's Corr.* i. 137).

public, but it is Mr Gray's Italian answer that I wish chiefly to be considered, because I suspect that the verses in it, *Te Dea,* etc., are his own,[3] and as far as I understand them, very beautiful; what he says, too, at the beginning about the Venus of Medicis occasioned a very pretty Latin elegy of West's[4] which he sent him in return and which I cannot print unless either an extract or a translation of this letter precedes it.[5] Now, I am far too unskilled in the language either to extract or translate it, or judge of its purity, and this illiterate place affords me no person to consult. I hear you say, 'I have forgot my Italian if I ever had any'; be it so, yet you can surely find out some proper person to review it, nay perhaps can find interest to lay it before the Cruscan or Tuscan eyes of Signore Baretti,[6] or some greater adept even than he. At all adventures I wish for a translation of it, if not an emendation of the original, and (in hopes that I shall obtain them either from you or by means of you soon) I shall leave a gap in the press till I receive your answer.

I have another favour also to beg of you. You must know that Mrs Dealtry the widow of our excellent physician[7] lately dead, has requested me to direct the two Fishers[8] here (who are very good statuaries) in designing a monument[9] to be put in our cathedral. My idea is a figure of Health with her old insignia of the serpent and staff in one hand, and a wreath falling out of the other, leaning in a pensive posture over the urn on which is inscribed his name and age, and upon the pedestal which supports the whole I think of writing the six following lines, if they meet with your approbation:

3. Gray's letter, with these verses, is also missing. Mason followed HW's advice (*post* 29 July 1773) and did not print it, even though Chute later agreed that the 'Te Dea' verses must be Gray's (*post* 17 Sept. 1773).

4. *Mem. Gray* 76–7; *Gray's Corr.* i. 151–2.

5. Mason interpolated in Gray's letter to West of 15 Jan. 1740 a reference to the Venus (*Gray's Corr.* i. 137–8).

6. Giuseppe Marc'Antonio Baretti (1719–89), writer; author of an Italian-English dictionary, 1760; friend of Johnson and the Thrales. 'Cruscan' refers to the dictionary of the Accademia della Crusca at Florence.

7. John Dealtry (ca 1708–73), M.D.; m. Elizabeth Langley of Wykeham Abbey,

Yorks (Venn, *Alumni Cantab.;* Mason's *Works* i. 139).

8. Richard Fisher (ca 1700–ca 1773) and his son, John Fisher (ca 1730–after 1802), monumental sculptors. See Katharine A. Esdaile, 'Sculptors and Sculpture in Yorkshire,' *The Yorkshire Archæological Journal,* 1944, xxxvi. 88–91.

9. 'A neat monument, the design of which was executed in statuary marble, by Messrs Fisher, of this city; it is a figure of Health in alto relievo, with her ancient insignia, bending over an urn, and dropping a chaplet' (Thomas Allen, *A New and Complete History of the County of York,* 1829–32, ii. 133). For a photograph of the monument see J. B. Morrell, *York Monuments,* [1944], pl. LXII.

> Here, bending o'er the tomb where Dealtry sleeps,
> Ambrosial Health in sculptured anguish weeps;
> Here drops her faded wreath. 'No more,' she cries,
> 'Let sickening mortals, with beseeching eyes,
> Invoke my feeble power; it failed to save
> My own and Nature's guardian from the grave.'[10]

I suspect they will be thought rather heathenish. I beg, however, you will give me your most impartial sentiments about them.

In like manner, and for the same purpose I send you a proof of an etching which my boy Charles has just done, from a drawing which I and a painter[11] made together from remembrance and a shade[12] of Mr Gray. If you think the medallion air of the head does not hurt the likeness too much I would adopt it for a frontispiece.[13] N.B. When the plate is worked off in a London press the etching will appear much finer.

I shall be happy to hear that you are more happy than you was in the situation when you favoured me with your two last letters, and beg you to believe that I sincerely sympathize with you, being with the truest esteem, dear Sir,

Your faithful servant,

W. MASON

10. Mason also sent these lines to Alderson (15 July 1773). As the lines now appear on the monument they read:
'Here, o'er the tomb where Dealtry's ashes sleep,
See Health, in emblematic anguish weep!
She drops her faded wreath: "No more," she cries,
"Let languid mortals, with beseeching eyes,
Implore my feeble aid: it failed to save
My own and Nature's guardian from the grave!"'
HW proposed one change (*post* 29 July 1773) and other revisions were made by Mason's friend, Edward Bedingfeld, to whom Mason wrote on 3 Oct. 1775, when the monument was being put in place, approving his alteration of the inscription (MS now in the Huntington Library).

11. Benjamin Wilson (1721–88), painter and scientist; friend and correspondent of Mason. The drawing seems to have been made in 1771 (Nichols, *Lit. Anec.* ix. 717–8).

12. 'There is a shadow of Mr Gray cut out, with the eyes, mouth, etc. drawn upon it in large, which you will find in the book of blue paper, amongst prints etc. lying on the table in the closet where my books are. Pray send it by Benjamin, for Wilson is making a picture of him and I would willingly give him all the helps in my power' (Mason to Alderson 13 Dec. 1771). This is presumably the silhouette by Francis Mapletoft, now at Pembroke College, Cambridge (reproduced in *Gray's Corr.* ii. 689; cf. ibid. p. xxxiii).

13. It was not adopted; see *post* 23 March 1774 and n. 9. HW's copy of what appears to be Carter's engraving, inscribed by HW 'from a drawing by Mr Mason when Mr Gray was about 40,' is in his copy of *Mem. Gray*, now in the Harvard Library. See illustration.

from a drawing by Mr. Mason, when Mr. Gray was about 40.

THOMAS GRAY, BY MASON AND WILSON,
CA 1756

WALPOLE'S GOLDFISH TUB

To MASON, Thursday 29 July 1773

Printed from Mitford i. 89–93.

Strawberry Hill, July 29, 1773.

YOUR letter, dear Sir, arrived here while I was at Ampthill,[1] which prevented my answering it as soon as I ought to have done. I do not know a soul in town at present that is acquainted with Baretti: but I expect to see Mr Chute[2] in a week, who lived seven years in Italy and is master of Italian. As far as I recollect that language, I cannot say I am at all pleased with the letter: it is made up of phrases and patches, and does not go off glibly at all—in short it seems to me totally unlike an Italian, and so very unlike Gray's sense, that I think it would discredit him as much as a boyish exercise could; surely you might mention his having spoken of the Venus of Medici [to][3] West, without producing the letter itself; and only as an introduction to the latter's verses.[4] Indeed as Gray's fragments will not add to the perfection of his reputation, I should be averse to inserting anything that might lower him to the level with others. He was not only great, but original. Forty young men that I have known, wrote French better than he did, and though few catch Italian so well, yet I would not publish the letter, as it has neither an Italian, nor an English understanding. You and I mean the same thing in different ways. You are for showing the universality of his talents; I, only the excellence of them, and there I think and feel, as he felt himself. Mr Chute will tell me whether the verses are Gray's or not—at least he knows where to find Martinelli,[5] who will do as well as Baretti.

I like the idea of West's letter, but not all the execution, which I think falls very short of what it might have been. As I loved and esteemed poor West very much too, I am glad you have condemned it.

Your design for the tomb, dear Sir, is as classic as I like those things should be, and the epitaph as Greek. You order me to object, and

1. Ampthill Park, Beds, the seat of Lord and Lady Ossory. See *Country Seats* 69–70.
2. John Chute (1701–76), friend and correspondent of HW, whose intimacy with him began in Florence in 1740 and continued until Chute's death.
3. Mitford reads 'in.'

4. See *ante* 16 July 1773, n. 5.
5. Vincenzo Martinelli (1702–85), Florentine writer who lived in England for many years and wrote the *Istoria d'Inghilterra*, 1770–3, which was paid for by HW's cousin, Thomas Walpole. See Boswell, *Johnson* ii. 220–2, 504, and *Enciclopedia italiana*.

therefore I do, but only to the epithet *ambrosial*,[6] which however proper to health, seems to clash with the sorrow in the end of the line. I do not believe I should have refined so much, if you had not invited me to be nice; so if you will retract the one, I will the other, as you may be sure I am pleased, when I have but a criticism so slight to make.

I shall go to Nuneham on Monday next for two or three days, and to Houghton not till the 20th of August: before which you will receive back the two letters.[7]

As the Fishers are at York, I wish they were inclined to take casts of the kings in the screen before the choir,[8] which struck me so much.[9] I am persuaded they might sell them well.[10] At least I should be glad to have exact drawings of Henry IV and Richard III,[11] if they would do them reasonably. Henry's is one of the most remarkable and characteristic countenances I ever saw, and totally unlike the common pictures of him, which have all but one dubious original.[12] Pray remember I do not desire James I, which ought to be changed, in the spirit it was put up, for every reigning king.

The etching of Gray has great resemblance, and I should approve it for the frontispiece, though with some corrections. The eye is too open and cheerful for his; and the eyebrow, towards the ear, rises too much from the end of the eyelid. The top of the head behind is too flat, and the dark shade from the ear to the chin is hard, too black and should be softened off. In general there is more vivacity than was in

6. Mason accepted this correction and later approved other changes in his epitaph, the finished version of which is given *ante* 16 July 1773, n. 10.

7. Of Gray and West.

8. 'On each side the choir-door of York Minster are the effigies of some of our English kings, in their regal ornaments, standing on pedestals, each of which has its particular inscription' (Thomas Gent, *The Ancient and Modern History of the Famous City of York*, 1730, p. 38). Originally the series represented the succession of kings from William the Conqueror to Henry VI, but the figure of Henry VI had long been missing, possibly removed during the reign of his successor, Edward IV. Its place was taken by an effigy of James I, placed there when he visited York. The choir-screen admired by HW was fifteenth-century work, made under the direction of the

mason William Hindley (Hyndley). In 1810 the original design was restored by the removal to Ripon Church (now Cathedral) of the statue of James and by the supplying of its place with a new figure of Henry VI. See *An Accurate Description and History of the Metropolitan and Cathedral Churches of Canterbury and York*, York, 1755, p. 123, and Frederick Harrison, *York Minster*, 1927, p. 101.

9. On his visit to York 11 Aug. 1772 (*Country Seats* 72).

10. The Fishers did not agree (*post* 12 Sept. 1773).

11. HW had forgotten that Richard was not represented on the choir-screen.

12. It was at Hampton Court in Herefordshire (*Anecdotes, Works* iii. 31, 34). In the first reference HW speaks of the picture as 'an undoubted original.'

his countenance; and yet I think it will be difficult now, to produce a more faithful likeness.

My poor nephew is now worse or better, according to the moon, all I mean is, periodically, for I have little faith in moons or physicians. These returns however renew my anxiety for his safety; and though every precaution is taken that can be, it is impossible not to be alarmed, as he has all the sullenness and cunning of people in that condition.

Have you got the *Annual Register?* you will like the article of Sweden,[13] which is remarkably well done; and so is that of Poland.[14]

Are not you escaping to your sensible house and agreeable garden? I have a pedestal making for the tub in which my cat was drowned:[15] the first stanza of the ode is to be written on it, beginning thus:—

'Twas on *this* lofty vase's side,[16] etc.

However as this and much of my collection is frail, I am printing the catalogue[17]—that is, like so many other men, I am pretending to step an inch beyond the grave into endless futurity, and record porcelain on paper. Apropos to such trifles, has not a Dr Berkenhout[18] sent to you for lists of your works and anecdotes of your life? I am sure he ought, for he thought even of me. I sent him word that the only merit I was conscious of, was having saved and published some valuable works of others; and that whenever he should write the lives of printers, I should have no repugnance to appear in the catalogue.

Mr Adam[19] has published the first number of his *Architecture*.[20]

13. *Annual Register,* 1772, xv. 46–70*.
14. Ibid. xv. 22–45.
15. The occasion of Gray's *Ode on the Death of a Favourite Cat.* The large blue and white tub and its pedestal were placed in the Little Cloister at the entrance to the house ('Des. of SH,' *Works* ii. 400). See Gray to HW 1 March 1747, GRAY ii. 23–4. The tub was sold SH xix. 32 and is now in the possession of Lord Derby at Knowsley. See illustration *ante* p. 99.
16. The label is missing from the vase, but it was reprinted by Kirgate, probably after 1781, in at least six copies (Hazen, *SH Bibliography* 209–10).
17. *A Description of the Villa of Horace Walpole . . . at Strawberry Hill (Journal of the Printing-Office* 17; Hazen, *SH Bib-*

liography 105–10). The printing was completed in 1774.
18. John Berkenhout (ca 1730–91), M.D., physician and writer. The first and only volume of his *Biographia Literaria, or a Biographical History of Literature,* extending to the end of the sixteenth century, appeared in 1777. HW's copy was sold SH v. 31. See HW to Berkenhout 6 July 1773. HW made notes on the book in his 'Book of Materials,' 1786 (now WSL), p. 18.
19. Robert Adam (1728–92), architect.
20. *The Works in Architecture of Robert and James Adam,* 3 vols, 1773–1822. The first volume appeared in five parts. Number 1, consisting of a preface and eight plates of Sion House with explanations, was published 24 July 1773 (*London Chron-*

In it is a magnificent gateway and screen for the Duke of Northumberland at Sion, which I see erecting every time I pass. It is all lace and embroidery, and as *croquant* as his frames for tables; consequently most improper to be exposed in the high road to Brentford. From Kent's[21] mahogany we are dwindled to Adam's filigree. Grandeur and simplicity are not yet in fashion. In his preface he seems to tax Wyat with stealing from him;[22] but Wyat has employed the antique with more judgment, and the Pantheon is still the most beautiful edifice in England.[23] What are the Adelphi buildings?[24] warehouses laced down the seams, like a soldier's trull in a regimental old coat.[25]

I will enliven the conclusion of a heavy letter with a riddle by George Selwyn,[26] the only verses I believe he ever made, and marked with all his wit:—

> The first thing is that thing without which we hold
> No very good bargain can ever be sold.
> The next is a soft white prim delicate thing,
> Which a parson has got 'twixt his knees and his chin.
> Then what at the playhouse we all strive to get,
> Or else are content to go in the pit.

icle 20–2 and 22–4 July 1773, xxxiv. 75, 83). HW's copy was sold London 922 (removed from SH viii. 73).

21. William Kent (1684–1748), architect and landscape-gardener. HW wrote in the *Anecdotes*, 'He had an excellent taste for ornaments, and gave designs for most of the furniture at Houghton [where it still is] as he did for several other persons. Yet chaste as these ornaments were, they were often unmeasurably ponderous,' etc. (*Works* iii. 489).

22. The preface contains no direct accusation, but Wyatt's Pantheon was executed in a style much like the Adams', and HW doubtless has in mind the underlying significance of the following remark: 'We have not trod in the paths of others, nor derived aid from their labours. In the works which we have had the honour to execute, we have not only met with the approbation of our employers, but, even with the imitation of other artists' (*Works in Architecture*, pt i, 1773, p. 3).

23. Mason apparently shared this opinion: 'The Pantheon was opened yesterday. I was not there myself, but Stonhewer says it was superb. I have seen it by daylight and think it the most astonishing and perfect piece of architecture that can possibly be conceived' (Mason to Alderson 28 Jan. 1772).

24. On the site of Old Durham House, bounded by the Strand, Ivy Bridge Lane, the Thames, and York Buildings, which was acquired by Robert Adam and his brothers in 1768 on a 99-year lease. They tore down the warehouses and other buildings on the site and built, in five years, the magnificent block of houses that formed their most notable work.

25. This much-quoted remark has been generally held to be unjust (see, e.g., John Summerson, *Georgian London*, 1945, p. 122). HW's attitude towards the Adams reflects the Whig anti-Scots bias, for the Adams were not only Scots, but were patronized by Bute. Doubtless, also, he was affected by their failure to design an acceptable cottage in the garden at SH after their success there with the Round Drawing-Room.

26. George Augustus Selwyn (1719–91), the wit, HW's friend and correspondent.

Then all this together will make an odd mess
Of something in something,—and that you must guess.

So you will,[27] and therefore I need not tell you the subject, nay nor
who writes this letter.

To Mason, Friday 3 September 1773

Printed from Mitford i. 94–6.

Strawberry Hill, Sept. 3, 1773.

DOES one break a promise, dear Sir, when one cannot perform
it? I have not seen Mr Chute yet, consequently could not show
him the two Italian letters: he is still at the Vine,[1] and I have been
learning to moralize in the land of mortification. In one word I am
just returned from Houghton, where I had an ample lecture on the
vanity of sublunary grandeur. If I had not suspected myself of being
too like Ananias and Sapphira, and of purloining a favourite miniature, I think I should have sold Strawberry the moment I came back,
and laid the purchase money at the feet of the first Methodist apostle
I met. This is telling you the havoc and spoil that my poor wretched
nephew and a gang of banditti[2] have made on the palace and estates
of my father. The pictures alone have escaped the devastation. Methinks I could write another sermon on them;[3] it would be crowded
with texts from the lamentations of Jeremiah. What can I say to you
but woe, woe, woe? I know nothing; I see nobody but lawyers, stewards and jockeys. I have given up every occupation and amusement
of my life, and think of nothing but saving my family, not that I have
any prospect of doing so, but merely because it is less uncomfortable
than totally to despair of re-establishing it. I know this is folly and
visionary pride: I am sensible that I sacrifice the remains of an agreeable life to disquiet and melancholy and trouble, but I cannot help

27. When he replied to this letter 12
Sept. 1773 Mason had apparently guessed
the riddle, and suggested an alternative
couplet for the third clue. The solution is
perhaps 'ribband-box,' suggested by several
readers of the *Johnsonian News-Letter*, in
which Dr James L. Clifford kindly inserted
our query; but how the 'first thing' can be
'rib' has not been convincingly explained.
Other possibilities are the slang phrase
'mine-arse-in-a-bandbox' (HW to Conway

15 Oct. 1784; Eric Partridge, *Dictionary of
Slang and Unconventional English*, sub
'bandbox'), and 'a bee in a bandbox,' suggested by a correspondent in N&Q 1919,
12th ser., v. 188.

———

1. The Vyne, Hants, Chute's seat.
2. See HW to Mann 2 Sept. 1773.
3. He had written one in 1742, which
was published in *Ædes Walpolianæ*, 1747.

it: the arrow is shot; it sticks in my breast, and I should not feel the pain of it the less for not trying to pluck it out: go and write a moral satire on me; I deserve it for I act with my eyes open.

You know Lord Lyttelton[4] is dead; the papers say Mr Garrick is to be the editor of his papers. I shall not be impatient to see the text or the comment, but truly I believe he left none.[5] He was [too] timid to write anything that he would have been afraid to publish, and was equally in dread of present and future critics, which made his works so insipid that he had better not have written them at all. His son[6] does not seem to have equal apprehensions of the world's censure. Though he was such a

Foe to the dryads of his father's groves,[7]

the shades of Hagley[8] are safe from his axe;[9] they are not liable to the fate of Houghton. When the forests of our old barons were nothing but dens of thieves, the law in its wisdom made them unalienable. Its wisdom now thinks it very fitting that they should be cut down to pay debts at Almack's[10] and Newmarket. I was saying this to the lawyer I carried down with me. He answered: 'The law hates a perpetuity'— 'Not all perpetuities,' said I; 'not those of lawsuits'—well, I will have done for I find every paragraph will close in the same way.

4. George Lyttelton (1709–73), 5th Bt, 1751; cr. (1756) Bn Lyttelton; politician and writer; 'the good Lord Lyttelton.' He died 22 Aug. 1773 (GM 1773, xliii. 414; Last Journals i. 244–5). For an account of his career see A. V. Rao, A Minor Augustan, Being the Life and Works of George, Lord Lyttelton, Calcutta, 1934. See also ante p. 41 n. 29.

5. Garrick was a close friend of Lyttelton's (Rao, op. cit. 119–20, 256–8), but he did not edit his papers. Lyttelton's collected Works, containing a few 'pieces never before printed' (title-page), were edited by his nephew, George Edward Ayscough, in 1774.

6. Thomas Lyttelton (1744–79), 2d Bn Lyttelton; politician, writer, and notorious libertine; 'the wicked Lord Lyttelton.' See Reginald Blunt, Thomas Lord Lyttelton: the Portrait of a Rake, 1936, and Last Journals i. 245.

7. Pope, Moral Essays iv. 94. In 1771

Thomas Lyttelton was thought to be trying to sell the reversion to his father's estate (Blunt, op. cit. 76).

8. Hagley Park, Worcs, the seat of the Lytteltons. See HW to Bentley Sept. 1753.

9. Thomas Lyttelton was in comparatively prosperous circumstances at the time of his father's death (Blunt, op. cit. 129).

10. A club in Pall Mall kept by William Almack (originally Macall) (d. 1781), founded in 1764 by a group of noblemen and gentlemen. In 1765 Almack established the assembly-rooms in King Street that bore his name for nearly a century, and by 1774 he had given up the management of the club, which was taken over by one Brooks or Brookes. In 1778 the club, then called Brooks's, was moved to St James's Street (E. B. Chancellor, Memorials of St James's Street, 1922, pp. 148–50; London Past and Present i. 37–9; DNB sub Almack).

By the way have I told you that I have been at Nuneham?[11] no I did not. I was strangely disappointed at my arrival and thought it very ugly. The next morning totally changed my ideas; it is capable of being made uncommonly beautiful. Lord Nuneham's garden[12] is the quintessence of nosegays; I wonder some macaroni does not offer ten thousand pounds for it—but indeed the flowers come in their natural season, and take care to bring their perfumes along with them. Do you know that the Muses have a little cabinet there? and a female votary[13] who writes with great facility and genteelly. I was trusted with the secret,[14] and mind I don't betray it. Adieu.

From MASON, Sunday 12 September 1773

Printed from MS now WSL.
Address: The Honourable Horace Walpole, Arlington Street, London.
Postmark: NOTTINGHAM 15 SE.

Aston, Sept. 12th, 1773.

Dear Sir,

PRAY give yourself no concern about the two Italian letters. I have printed the section without them, and your judgment about them in your former letter was sufficient to determine me that I did right in rejecting them. I should be glad, however, to have them returned at any convenient opportunity.

I am really sorry at the thoughts of your being so disagreeably employed, but I hope that self-satisfaction which always does and must

11. HW was at Nuneham 2–5 Aug. 1773 (HW to Lord Nuneham 27 July 1773 and to Lady Ossory 9 Aug. 1773).
12. The flower garden was designed by Mason, according to Lord Harcourt's account written in 1806 (*Harcourt Papers* iii. 201). That he had already begun his alterations is indicated by a letter from Mason to Nuneham of 14 Jan. 1773 (ibid. vii. 40–2), discussing a design for a garden seat. Two plates of the flower-garden, dated 1777, are in Paul Sandby's *Collection of One Hundred and Fifty Select Views*, 1781, i. pl. XXXIV–V.
13. Elizabeth Venables-Vernon (1746–

1826), dau. of George Venables-Vernon, 1st Bn Vernon of Kinderton, by Martha Harcourt, sister of 1st E. Harcourt; m. (1765) her first cousin, George Simon Harcourt (1736–1809), Vct Nuneham 1749–77, 2d E. Harcourt, 1777. Specimens of her verses, including some addressed to HW, August 1773, are given in *Harcourt Papers* xi. 122–42. HW's fruitless efforts to persuade Lady Nuneham to permit him to print her verses at SH are mentioned in later letters.
14. See HW to Nuneham 10 Aug. 1773. HW had already betrayed the secret to Lady Ossory (HW to Lady Ossory 9 Aug. 1773).

result from a consciousness of doing what is right will support your spirits and alleviate your present uneasiness. To say more about the matter would make my letter as unwelcome as the visit of an attorney or a jockey and, therefore, I'll change the subject.

I am very lately returned from a ramble of ten days with Mr Stonhewer round the Westmoreland lakes. We carried a journal of Mr Gray's[1] with us, and therefore seemed to see them with his eyes, yet when I saw them with my own I was sometimes a little disappointed. The great devastations which have been made about Keswick with regard to wood, and the dry season which had taken the principal feature from its cascades, or at least reduced it to a scanty rill, took away more than half the beauties of the scene. And I am not yet so confirmed a pupil of Sir William Chambers as to [be] pleased with the frightful and surprising only.

I wonder that you should ever, even for the first moment, be displeased with Nuneham. I am glad you were so soon reconciled to it, for I think it one of the most pleasing scenes I know. Your poetical news was indeed news to me. I hope the same muse that throws the oblation of its poesy[2] before the shrine of your *friendship*,[3] does not inspire the verses you speak of. If it does, be assured I never shall have candour enough to call them either facile or genteel. This I know, that if my Yorkshire curate was half so insipid as your Swedish one I would turn him off, and do all the duty of my parish myself.

I wish your former letter to York had come a month sooner, I would then have employed a person under my own eye to have copied the features of Henry IV and Richard III[4] as exact as possible. I will take care to have the drawings made during my next residence, till then that matter must sleep. As to casts, they would certainly never answer in point of sale, and the love of antiquity must certainly have *obfus-*

1. Now (1954) in the possession of Sir John Murray. Gray set out on his tour of the lakes and Yorkshire 29 Sept. 1769. Wharton began it with him, but was taken ill the first night and returned to Cambridge (*Gray's Corr.* iii. 1074). Gray later transcribed about half of the journal that he kept during the tour and sent it in a series of letters to Wharton; the second half was transcribed by Alderson and sent to Wharton 24 July 1770, after Gray and Wharton had met at Mason's house in June 1770. Doubtless the transcription was planned at that time. In *Mem. Gray* 350–79 Mason printed a garbled text of the letters. See *Gray's Corr.* iii. 1074–80, 1087–91, 1094–1110.

2. Jerningham's dedication to HW of *The Swedish Curate (ante* 15 May 1773).

3. The dedication is 'To the Honourable Horace Walpole (as a monument of friendship and esteem).'

4. Mason also was unaware that Richard III was not among the kings on the Minster choir-screen. See *post* 10 April 1776.

cated your reason when you thought so. The Fishers are of my opinion, but they do not express themselves either so pertly or pedantically upon your subject.

To show you that I have guessed the riddle you sent me, I give you what I think a great emendation of the 5th and 6th lines:

> What the hand of a lady (how prudish soe'er)
> Will give to a man if he presses her near.

But pray, for the sake of all clerical decency, don't say I suggested this various reading.

I have just seen the Adams's first number of *Architecture* and read their preface. Was there ever such a brace of self-puffing Scotch coxcombs? they almost deserve an Heroic Epistle. But I have scribbled out my paper and therefore must conclude myself, dear Sir,

Most truly yours,

W. MASON

To MASON, Friday 17 September 1773

Printed from Mitford i. 98–100.

Strawberry Hill, Sept. 17, 1773.

Dear Sir,

I HAVE been absent from home five days and found twelve letters:[1] after reading them and answering five on business,[1a] it is relaxation, dear Sir, to write to you. I will say no more on my occupation: I wish there were such mere merit in it, as to deserve what you say to me.

I enclose the two letters:[2] I kept them to show to Mr Chute, and am just come from him; he who is a much better Cruscan[3] than I am, dislikes the Italian letter still more; says it is not tolerably pure and composed of scraps of poetry; that the lines beginning *Te Dea,* are certainly Gray's, they are so incorrect; and yet more poetic than Sal-

---

1. Mason's of 12 Sept. and probably Thomas Walpole's of ca 11 Sept. (see *ante,* HW to Mason 28 June 1773, n. 3).

1a. Doubtless mainly relating to his nephew's affairs. His letter to Thomas Walpole of 4 Sept. includes a summary showing £1189 representing 'retrenchments' at Houghton, and an increase of £150 in rentals.

2. The Italian letters of Gray and West (*ante* 16 July 1773).

3. That is, a better judge of the Italian language; see *ante* 16 July 1773, n. 6.

vini's[4] lines—I do not wonder—but what would he have been if a Tuscan? you have found by your journey into Westmoreland that his inspired eyes even,

Made those bleak rocks and barren mountains smile.[5]

The Swedish curate certainly has not the same talent. With regard to the *friendship* of the dedication, I compounded for it in lieu of more pompous compliments—I might, had I so pleased, have been a patron of learning.

The drawings of the kings at York will be time enough next year for any leisure I shall have to bestow on them. I give up my idea of casts, and any thought that implies an opinion of real curiosity or taste in the present age. The nymphs holding necklaces on the outside of a bridge for Sion in Adams's first number, is a specimen of our productions in architecture, as the preface is of modesty and diffidence. The lottery[6] for the Adelphi buildings will, I suspect, be an example of rather more address. What patronage of arts in the Parliament, to vote the City's land[7] to those brothers, and then sanctify the sale of the houses by a bubble![8]

I have so totally forgotten what the riddle was I sent you, that I do not know whether your solution with all its humour is right; you may judge with what rubbish my head is filled.—I have learned so many new things of late, that I have lost my memory. I believe poor Lord

---

4. The loss of Gray's letter leaves the allusion obscure, but it is probably to Antonio Maria Salvini (1653–1729), poet, translator, and philologist. Gray may have imitated or paraphrased one of the 416 sonnets in his *Sonetti*, 1718.

5. Addison, *A Letter from Italy, to the Right Honourable Charles Lord Halifax in the Year MDCCI,* l. 140. Addison's line reads: 'And makes her barren rocks and her bleak mountains smile.'

6. In building the Adelphi the Adams got into financial difficulties, from which they were eased by an act of Parliament (13 Geo. III [1773], c. 75) permitting them to dispose of the unsold property by a lottery (*Survey of London,* vol. 18, *The Strand,* 1937, pp. 100, 141; Mason's *Satirical Poems* 65). The 'scheme of the Adelphi lottery' was printed in the *Public Advertiser* 26–31 July 1773.

7. 'In order to complete the design the brothers obtained an act of Parliament for enclosing and embanking the river (11 Geo. III [1771], c. 34), which left the rights of the Corporation, who claimed a right to the soil and bed of the Thames, to the decision of the Law Courts' (note by G. F. Russell Barker to the following passage in *Mem. Geo. III* iv. 215: 'Adam, the Scotch architect, was supported by the King and the Scots with success against the City of London, on whose territory and rights he had encroached with his new buildings at Durham Yard, to which he and his brothers gave the affected name of the Adelphi').

8. The lottery 'proved a notorious cheat, the fortunate finding their prizes some thousands short of the estimated value' (HW's note in Mason's *Satirical Poems* 65; see also *Survey of London,* vol. 18, *The Strand,* 1937, pp. 100–1).

Nuneham will return[9] in the same situation, you who have all your faculties in perfection may remember when I see you, which I long for, that I tell you of the success I have had in a contest, nay, in a money-contest with a mitre[10]—it will divert you, but is not proper for a letter. I know nothing of higher import, and must therefore bid you good night!

To Mason, Friday 19 November 1773

Printed from Mitford i. 100–1.

Arlington Street, Nov. 19, 1773.

I KNOW nothing of you; you have left me off. I know you are alive, for Lord Strafford has seen you twice.[1] Yet it is plain I am not out of charity with you, for I have been to see *Elfrida,*[2] don't think it was out of revenge, though it is wretchedly acted, and worse set to music. The virgins were so inarticulate, that I should have understood them as well if they had sung choruses of Sophocles. Orgar[3] had a broad Irish accent; I thought the first virgin, who is a lusty virago, called Miss Miller,[4] would have knocked him down and I hoped she would. Edgar[5] stared at his own crown, and seemed to fear it would tumble off. For Miss Catley,[6] she looked so impudent and was so big with child,

9. From Dublin. Lord and Lady Nuneham arrived there 7 Oct. 1773 on their visit to Lord Harcourt, Nuneham's father, who was then Lord-Lieutenant of Ireland (*Harcourt Papers* iii. 140). See HW to Nuneham 6 Nov. 1773.

10. Edmund Keene, Bp of Ely. The story of the money-contest, involving HW's illegitimate half-sister, Catherine Day, is told at length by Cole (Cole ii. 371–2). See *ante* 20 March 1773.

1. Meetings in Yorkshire reported to HW in missing letters from Lord Strafford.

2. On 16 Nov., when it was presented at Covent Garden with Mrs Hartley in the leading rôle (*Public Advertiser*). See also HW to Lady Ossory 18 Nov. 1773.

3. Played by Matthew Clarke (d. 1786) (*Public Advertiser;* Genest vi. 409; *European Magazine,* 1786, ix. 382).

4. Miss Miller, who was engaged at Covent Garden 1769–74, seems to have been involved in the beating Colman received at the hands of Rev. Richard Penneck, Keeper of the Reading Room of the British Museum, in Feb. 1773 (E. R. Page, *George Colman the Elder,* New York, 1935, pp. 197, 215). She is said to have been still living in 1807 (William Dunlap, *Memoirs of George Frederick Cooke,* 1813, i. 15; information from Mr C. B. Hogan).

5. Played by Robert Bensley (1742–1817) (*Public Advertiser;* C. B. Hogan, *Eighteenth-Century Actors in the* DNB: *Additions and Corrections* [reprinted from *Theatre Notebook,* 1952], p. 6).

6. Ann Catley (1745–89), actress and singer, played another 'British virgin' in the chorus. Many scandalous stories about her were current. See BM, *Satiric Prints* iv. 788–9.

you would have imagined she had been singing the 'Black Joke,'[7] only that she would then have been more intelligible. Smith[8] did not play Athelwold ill; Mrs Hartley is made for the part, if beauty and figure could suffice for what you write, but she has no one symptom of genius. Still it was very affecting and does admirably for the stage under all these disadvantages. The tears came into my eyes, and streamed down the Duchess of Richmond's[9] lovely cheeks. Mr Garrick has been wondrously jealous of the King's going twice together to Covent Garden,[10] and to lure him back, has crammed the town's maw with shows of the Portsmouth review[11] and interlarded every play with the most fulsome loyalties. He has new-written *The Fair Quaker of Deal*,[12] and made it ten times worse than it was originally, and all to the tune of Portsmouth and George forever;[13] not to mention a preface in which the Earl of Sandwich by name, is preferred to Drake, Blake and all the admirals that ever existed.[14]

7. The name of an air to which various songs were put, some of them indecent. A ballad-singer is represented as holding one such song in plate III of Hogarth's *Rake's Progress*. See Alexander Pope, *Imitations of Horace*, ed. John Butt, 1939, p. 220 n., and N&Q 1883, 6th ser., viii. 211; 1913, 11th ser., vii. 114–5.

8. William Smith (ca 1730–1819), called 'Gentleman' Smith because of his education at Eton and Cambridge; since 1753 one of the principal actors at Covent Garden; at Drury Lane 1774–88.

9. Lady Mary Bruce (1740–96), the daughter of Lady Ailesbury by her first marriage; m. (1757) Charles Lennox, 3d D. of Richmond. At the time of her marriage HW wrote Mann: 'It is the perfectest match in the world; youth, beauty, riches, alliances, and all the blood of all the kings from Robert Bruce to Charles II' (17 March 1757).

10. On 13 and 20 Oct. 1773 (*Lloyd's Evening Post* 11–13 and 18–20 Oct., xxxiii. 360, 384).

11. Garrick's revision of Thomson's and Mallet's masque, *Alfred*, first presented at Drury Lane 9 Oct. 1773 (Genest v. 394), ended with a scenic representation of the great review at Portsmouth in the preceding June. It was acted 'about eight times' during the 1773–4 season (Genest, loc. cit.). The royal review itself is described in GM 1773, xliii. 299–301.

12. The revision of Charles Shadwell's comedy (1710), first produced at Drury Lane 9 Nov. 1773 (Genest v. 397), was by Edward Thompson (ca 1738–86), naval officer and author and a friend of Garrick. Its new title was *The Fair Quaker, or the Humours of the Navy*; the first edition (1773) was published anonymously, but the second (1775) bears Thompson's name. Although Mason mistakenly concluded that Garrick himself had written both the revision and the preface, thus starting a chain of misunderstanding that runs through the next six letters, HW must have meant only to indicate Garrick's sponsorship of the author and close connection with the play, which is dedicated to him. In the 'Address to the Reader' Thompson says, 'In the alteration of this play, I boast of little merit; the first idea came from Mr Garrick,' etc. HW's copy of the 1773 edition is now wsl; on the title-page HW has written: 'Acted for the first time in November.'

13. 'Instead of *The Fair Quaker of Deal*, it may now properly be styled *The Fair Quaker of Portsmouth*, as the scene is removed to that seaport, and the time brought down to the late review of the British navy, a representation of which is introduced in this comedy' (*London Chronicle* 9–11 Nov. 1773, xxxiv. 457).

14. HW quotes Thompson's words in *post* 8 Dec. 1773.

Dr Hawksworth is dead,[15] out of luck not to have died a twelve-month ago.

Lady Holderness[16] has narrowly escaped with her life; she fell on the top of the stairs at Sion, against the edge of a door, which cut such a gash on her temple, that they were forced to sew it up; it was within half an inch of her eye, which is black all round, but not hurt, and her knee was much bruised.

This good town affords no other news, and is desolate; not that I make you any apologies for being so brief. I have ten times more business than you, and millions of letters of business, and sure you might always find as much to say as I had now.

From MASON, Tuesday 23 November 1773

Printed from MS now WSL.
Address: The Honourable Horace Walpole, Arlington Street, London.
Postmark: ROTHERHAM 26 NO.

Aston, Nov. 23d, 1773.

Dear Sir,

I WAS just going to make apologies to you for my late silence when I received your last, and to tell you that I had sent up a copy by Mr Stonhewer of the three first sections of the *Memoirs* for your perusal as to the matter, and for that of another friend as to the exact metre and Latinity of the Latin poems, that any page may be cancelled if necessary. I flatter myself that if you like what is sent, you will like the two following sections much better. I have only two letters to you yet uninserted; if you find more you will favour me with them. I think in one of your letters which I returned there were some marginal notes on a part of his poem on education and government. I should wish to have these, if you can find them,[1] as soon as possible and before you give me your opinion of these sections.

15. Hawkesworth died 17 Nov. 1773 (*London Chronicle* 16–18 Nov. 1773, xxxiv. 488). 'About this time he was severely attacked in the newspapers, particularly in letters signed "A Christian," for certain passages in the *Voyages*, from which it was inferred he did not believe in a Providence. These attacks affected him so much that from low spirits he was seized with a nervous fever, which on account of the high living he had indulged in had the more power on him; and he is supposed to have put an end to his life by intentionally taking an immoderate dose of opium' (from Malone's notes in Sir James Prior, *Life of Edmond Malone,* 1860, p. 441).

16. Mary Doublet (ca 1720–1801), m. (1743) Robert Darcy, 4th E. of Holdernesse.

1. No such letter to HW has been discovered. Fifty-seven lines of 'The Alliance

You are very good to give *Elfrida* so much countenance. Yet I think I should hardly go to see her even if old Macklin[3] was to play Athelwold. If I did it would be for the sake of a riot,[4] which I always loved as the only remaining vestige of English liberty, except that of the press, about which they say there is to be a message to Parliament.[5] Pray is there any grounds for this report? I ask for a very particular reason.[6] There are other folks besides Garrick that hope shortly to give the Portsmouth review due honour and pretend that they were the occasion of it.[7] I long to see Garrick's preface.[8] Mem: any packet how large soever will be sent me from Fraser at Lord Suffolk's office. Mem. also, I do not want to see the play.

I remember in one of your letters[9] that you told me the E. of Bristol said he would sooner read blasphemy than a certain poem. Did this come to your hands in such a manner that it might be ridiculed safely?[10]

I had heard before I received yours that Lady H. had broken her head, but I am yet to learn when Lord Carmarthen[11] is to break her daughter's head.[12] I wish it was fairly broken though my poor living and this goodly estate are to pay for it.[13]

I know not how to fill up my letter, and therefore I will transcribe

of Education and Government' are in Gray to Wharton 19 Aug. 1748 (*Gray's Corr.* i. 310–1).

3. Charles Macklin (ca 1697–1797), actor and dramatist. He was best known for his comic parts, but achieved a great success as Shylock. His last appearance on the stage was in 1789, when he was over ninety years old.

4. On 23 Oct. 1773 Macklin acted Macbeth in Scottish dress and was greeted with some hissing, which he accused two fellow-actors of starting. The quarrel attracted general attention and culminated in a riot at Covent Garden on 18 Nov. (*London Chronicle* 23–6, 26–8 Oct., 30 Oct.–2 Nov., 6–9, 18–20 Nov., xxxiv. 405, 415, 429, 452, 494; Edward Abbott Parry, *Charles Macklin*, 1891, pp. 159–77; Genest v. 427–30).

5. Such a message was not sent, but HW in *Last Journals* i. 289 remarks that there were rumours in the autumn of 1773 of the King's intention to send one.

6. His intention, not carried out (*post* 4 Jan. 1774), of introducing the rumoured message into the *Heroic Postscript*.

7. Mason alludes to his intention of

bringing the Portsmouth review into the *Heroic Postscript*, which he did in lines 42–8, quoted below.

8. To *The Fair Quaker*. See next letter.

9. *Ante* 5 July 1773.

10. It was, in the *Heroic Postscript*:
'If this its [the poem's] fate, let all the
       frippery things
Be-placed, be-pensioned, and be-starred by
       kings,
Frown on the page, and with fastidious eye,
Like old Young Fannius, call it blasphemy'
                            (ll. 59–62).
'The noble personage here alluded to, being asked to read the *Heroic Epistle*, said, "No, it was as bad as blasphemy" ' (Mason's note). Bristol is called 'Fannius' because he 'was a yet more effeminate figure than his father,' Lord Hervey, Pope's 'Lord Fanny' (HW's note in Mason's *Satirical Poems* 81).

11. Francis Godolphin Osborne (1751–99), styled M. of Carmarthen 1761–89; 5th D. of Leeds, 1789; F.R.S., 1773; F.S.A., 1776; politician and diplomatist.

12. That is, when he is to marry the Holdernesses' daughter and only surviving child, Lady Amelia Darcy (1754–84), who in 1778 became (*suo jure*) Bns Darcy, Bns

a part of an Heroic Postscript addressed to the public on their favourable reception of, etc.,[14] but you must promise to burn it instantly.

> For now, my Muse, thy fame is fixed as fate.
> Tremble ye fools I scorn, ye knaves I hate,
> I know the full-fledged vigour of thy wings,
> I know thy voice can pierce the ear of kings.
> Did China's monarch here in Britain doze,
> And was, like western kings, a king of prose,[15]
> Thy song could cure his Asiatic spleen,
> And make him wish to see, and to be seen;
> That solemn vein of irony so fine,[16]
> Which, even reviewers own, adorns each line,
> Would make him soon against his greatness sin,
> Desert his sofa, mount his palanquin,
> And post where'er the Goddess led the way,
> Perchance to proud Spithead's imperial bay;[17]
> There should he see, as others may have seen,
> That ships have anchors, and that seas are green,
> Should own the tackling trim, the streamers fine,
> With S—d—h prattle and with B—d—w dine,[18]
> And then sail back, amid the cannons roar,
> As safe, as sage as when he left the shore.

Conyers, and Countess of Mertola. They were married 29 Nov. 1773, and divorced by act of Parliament in May 1779. Lady Conyers m. (2) (1779) John Byron (GEC *sub* Leeds).

13. See *post* 20 Nov. 1775.

14. The title-page of the printed poem reads: *An Heroic Postscript to the Public Occasioned by Their Favourable Reception of a Late Heroic Epistle to Sir William Chambers, Knt, etc., by the Author of That Epistle.* The lines that follow appear as ll. 29–48 in the published *Heroic Postscript.*

15. 'The present Emperor of China is a poet, see Voltaire and Sir W. Chambers' (Mason's note in the MS, not published with the poem). Mason probably had in mind Voltaire's 'Épitre au roi de la Chine, sur son recueil de vers qu'il a fait imprimer,' 1770 (*Œuvres*, ed. Moland, x. 412 and n. 2). Chambers does not mention this in his *Dissertation on Oriental Gardening*, but Mason's lines about the monarch's 'Asiatic spleen' perhaps derive from Chambers's remark that the Chinese emperors 'are too much the slaves of their

greatness to appear in public' (*Dissertation*, p. 32).

16. '"A fine vein of solemn irony runs through this piece": *Monthly Review*' (Mason's note, incorporated in the printed poem: see Mason's *Satirical Poems* 76). The quotation appears in the account of the *Heroic Epistle* in *Monthly Review*, 1773, xlviii. 314.

17. 'The P[ortsmouth] review was two months after the publication of etc. *Facts are stubborn things*' (Mason's MS note, not in the published version). The second sentence is a quotation from Book X, ch. 1 of Smollett's translation of *Gil Blas* (ed. George Saintsbury, 1881, iii. 124). Mason's note is designed to call attention to the felicity of his phrase 'great Ocean's King' in the *Heroic Epistle* (l. 66).

18. The names of Sandwich and Bradshaw were printed in full in the published poem. The latter was Thomas Bradshaw (d. 1774), joint secretary to the Treasury. See HW to Mann 11 Nov. 1774, and *ante* 20 March 1773, n. 18.

To Mason, Saturday 27 November 1773

Printed from Mitford i. 104–8; possibly misdated, since the postscript is headed 'Saturday.'

Arlington Street, Nov. 27, 1773.

Dear Sir,

MR STONHEWER has sent me,[1] and I have read, your first part of Gray's life, which I was very sorry to part with so soon. Like everything of yours, I like it ten times better upon reading it again: you have with most singular art displayed the talents of my two departed friends to the fullest advantage; and yet there is a simplicity in your manner, which, like the frame of a fine picture, seems a frame only, and yet is gold. I should say much more in praise, if, as I have told Mr Stonhewer, I was not aware that I myself must be far more interested in the whole of the narrative, than any other living mortal, and therefore may suppose it will please the world still more than it will—And yet if wit, parts, learning, taste, sense, friendship, information can strike or amuse mankind, must not this work have that effect?—and yet, though *me* it may affect far more strongly, self-love certainly has no share in my affection to many parts. Of my two friends and me, I only make a most indifferent figure. I do not mean with regard to parts or talents. I never one instant of my life had the superlative vanity of ranking myself with them. They not only possessed genius, which I have not, great learning which is to be acquired, and which I never acquired; but both Gray and West had abilities marvellously premature; what wretched boyish stuff would my contemporary letters to them appear, if they existed; and which they both were so good-natured as to destroy![2]—what unpoetic things were mine at that age, some of which unfortunately do exist, and which I yet could never surpass; but it is not in that light I consider my own position. We had not got to Calais before Gray was dissatisfied, for I was a boy, and he, though infinitely more a man, was not enough so to make allowances. Hence am I never mentioned once with kindness in his letters to West. This hurts me for him, as well as myself. For the oblique censures on my want of curiosity, I have nothing to say. The fact was true; my eyes were not purely classic; and though I am now a dull antiquary, my age then made me taste pleasures and diversions

---

1. See HW to Stonhewer 27 Nov. 1773.
2. Twenty of HW's letters to West have been found, but only one to Gray (ca 15 Oct. 1735) before 1755. See GRAY.

merely modern:[3] I say this to you, and to you only, in confidence. I do not object to a syllable. I know how trifling, how useless, how blamable I have been, and submit to hear my faults, both because I have had faults, and because I hope I have corrected some of them; and though Gray hints at my unwillingness to be told them, I can say truly that to the end of his life, he neither spared the reprimand nor mollified the terms, as you and others know, and I believe have felt.

These reflections naturally arose on reading his letters again, and arose in spite of the pleasure they gave me, for self will intrude, even where self is not so much concerned. I am sorry to find I disobliged Gray so very early. I am sorry for him that it so totally obliterated all my friendship for him; a remark the world probably, and I hope, will not make, but which it is natural for me, dear Sir, to say to you. I am so sincerely zealous that all possible honour should be done to my two friends, that I care not a straw for serving as a foil to them. And as confession of faults is the only amendment I can now make to the one disobliged, I am pleased with myself for having consented and for consenting as I do, to that public reparation. I thank you for having revived West and his alas! stifled genius, and for having extended Gray's reputation. If the world admires them both as much as they deserved, I shall enjoy their fame—if it does not, I shall comfort myself for standing so prodigiously below them, as I do even without comparison.

There are a few false printings I could have corrected, but of no consequence, as 'Grotto del Cane,' for 'Grotta,'[4] and a few notes I could have added, but also of little consequence. Dodsley, who is printing Lord Chesterfield's letters,[5] will hate you for this publication. I was asked to write a preface[6]—*Sic notus Ulysses?*[7] I knew Ulysses too well. Besides, I have enough to burn without adding to the mass. Forgive me, if I differ with you, but I cannot think Gray's Latin poems inferior even to his English,[8] at least as I am not a Roman. I wish too that in a note you had referred to West's ode on the

3. That HW was being too hard on himself is clear from his letters to West.

4. Mason made the correction (*Mem. Gray* 102).

5. An advertisement in *Daily Adv.* 23 Nov. 1773 announced Dodsley's intention of publishing the letters, and the volumes appeared the following April. See *post* 7 April 1774.

6. See HW to Lady George Lennox 14 Oct. 1773.

7. Virgil, *Æneid* ii. 44.

8. 'Certain it is, that when I first knew him, he seemed to set a greater value on his Latin poetry, than on that which he had composed in his native language; and had almost the same foible then, which I have since known him laugh at in Petrarch . . .' (Mason, *Mem. Gray* 157).

Queen in Dodsley's miscellanies.⁹ Adieu! go on and prosper; my poor friends have an historian worthy of them, and who satisfies their and your friend

Hor. Walpole

PS. Since I wrote my letter which is not to go till tomorrow, I have received your letter, and most delightful lines—you are sure I think them so, and should if they were not yours. The subject prejudices me enough, without my affection for your writings. I cannot recollect now (for I lose my memory by having it over-stuffed with business) who told me the story of the blasphemy, and I will never affirm to you anything where I cannot quote my evidence. Perhaps I shall remember; the story however ought not to be lost, and may be reserved for even a twentieth edition; no I don't know whether there will be a twentieth. If what you tell me of a message¹⁰ be true, there will not be one. I had not heard it, but can easily believe it, and I could tell you exactly what it would cost, and will by word of mouth, if I ever see you again: for though I shall get some courtier to direct this, that it may pass safe, I cannot name my authority in writing. The fact is a secret yet, but will not be so long.

I will send for the life again to Mr Stonhewer, since the impression is not perfect, and will add two or three corrections and perhaps a note or two, which you may reject if you please. I do not recollect the notes on education, but will look for them, if I can get to Strawberry Hill next week, but I am demolished both in health and spirits by my poor nephew's affairs. I have neither strength nor understanding to go through them. I sometimes think of throwing them up and going to lay my bones in some free land, while there is such a country. This does not deserve to be so, but, *Qui vult tyrannizari tyrannizetur!*¹¹

I did not know the preface to the new Shakespeare¹² was Garrick's,¹³

9. *A Monody on the Death of Queen Caroline,* written in 1737 and printed in Dodsley's *Collection of Poems,* 1748, ii. 269–75. See *Gray's Corr.* i. 293, 299.

10. To Parliament on the freedom of the press (*ante* 23 Nov. 1773).

11. 'Let him who wishes it, be tyrannized,' a paraphrase of 'Qui vult decipi, decipiatur,' 'Let him who wishes it, be deceived.' The source of this is asked (and unanswered) in N&Q 1869, 4th ser., iii. 337.

It is there pointed out that Paracelsus and Thuanus are credited with the phrase. HW owned Thuanus, but apparently not Paracelsus.

12. The Johnson-Steevens edition, published 22 Oct. 1773 (*Public Advertiser*).

13. It was not; HW had misunderstood Mason, who had misunderstood HW. See *ante* 19 Nov. and n. 12, and 23 Nov. and n. 8.

which I suppose is what you mean. He is as fit to write it, as a country
curate to compose an excellent sermon from having preached one of
Tillotson's. I will send you the volume, and you will return it when
you have done with it.

I don't know when the young lady's head will be broken, they say
next week.[14] If her heart is not tough and Dutch,[15] that may be broken
too.

Saturday.

I cannot possibly recollect who told me the story above, but I am
certain it was related as an undoubted fact, nor does it sound at all
like invention.

To Mason, Wednesday 1 December 1773

Printed from Mitford i. 109–10.

Arlington Street, Dec. 1, 1773.

I HAVE again perused your sections very carefully, dear Sir, and
have made some slight but necessary corrections, and have added
a few still more inconsiderable notes. But there are two errors in point
of dates of more consequence. They relate to Crébillon's works and
the *Churchyard,* and I think you will alter them.[1] Crébillon's *Écumoire* was his first, and is perhaps his most known work, and is also
the most indecent.[2]

The *Churchyard* was, I am persuaded, posterior to West's death at
least three or four years,[3] as you will see by my note. At least I am sure

14. The marriage took place 29 Nov.
(*post* 1 Dec. 1773).
15. Lady Amelia Darcy's grandfather
was Francis Doublet, of Groeneveldt, Holland.

———

1. Mason did not make the recommended alterations.
2. Mason said in a note, 'As to Crébillon,
'twas his *Égarements du cœur et d'esprit*
that our author chiefly esteemed; he had
not, I believe, at this time published his
more licentious pieces' (*Mem. Gray* 139 n.).
L'Écumoire was published in 1733 (reprint,
Brussels 1884), nine years before the date of
Gray's letter (April 1742).

3. That is, in 1745 or 1746. Mason's reasons for dating it 1742 (*Mem. Gray* 157),
which were given in a later letter now
lost, apparently convinced HW (*post* 14
Dec. 1773). The point has been much discussed and is still unsettled; see especially
H. W. Garrod, 'Note on the Composition
of Gray's *Elegy*,' *Essays on the Eighteenth
Century Presented to David Nichol Smith*,
Oxford, 1945, pp. 111–6, and F. H. Ellis,
'Gray's *Elegy*: the Biographical Problem
in Literary Criticism,' *PMLA*, 1951, lxvi.
971–1008.

that I had the twelve or more[4] first lines from himself above three years after that period, and it was long before he finished it. As your work is to be a classic, I wish, therefore, that you would give me leave to see the rest before it is published. A dull but accurate commentator may be useful before publication, however contemptible afterwards; and I am so anxious for the fame of your book, that I wish you not to hurry it. It may have faults from precipitation, which it could have no other way.

I think you determined not to reprint the lines on Lord H[olland].[5] I hope it is now a resolution. He is in so deplorable a state, that they would aggravate the misery of his last hours,[6] and you yourself would be censured. I do not of all things suspect you of want of feeling, and know it is sufficient to give your heart a hint. As Gray too seems to have condemned all his own satirical works, that single one would not [? give] a high idea of his powers, though they were great in that walk; you and I know they were not inferior to his other styles; and I know, though perhaps you do not, that there never was but one pen as acute as his, with more delicacy and superior irony.

I have read today a pretty little drama called *Palladius and Irene*,[7] written by I know not whom. The beginning imitates Gray's runic fragments, the rest Shakespeare.

PS. Lady Emily was married last Monday.

From Mason, Friday 3 December 1773

Printed from MS now wsl.
Address: The Honourable Horace Walpole, Arlington Street, London.
Postmark: ROTHERHAM 6 DE.

4. Professor Garrod (op. cit. 113) suggests that HW wrote '72' and that Mitford transcribed it '12' in error. We believe HW wrote 12; HW's 1's and 7's are not at all similar, and it would have been unlike HW to count out the number of lines Gray sent him, or, if he had, to remember the total for a quarter of a century.

5. Gray's lines on Lord Holland's villa at Kingsgate, beginning 'Old and abandoned by each venal friend,' were written in 1768 and first printed in *The New Foundling Hospital for Wit*, 1769, iii. 34–5. See *Gray's Corr.* iii. 1259–62. Mason did not include them.

6. He lived until 1 July 1774.

7. Published 30 Nov. 1773 (*Daily Adv.*); never acted (Genest x. 189); author unidentified. HW's copy, with the note 'November' in his hand on the title-page, is now wsl.

Aston, Dec. 3d, 1773.

Dear Sir,

THIS is not an answer to your last. It only comes to tell you (in order to stop sending the book) that what I want is the thing, whatever it is, in which Garrick compares Lord S[andwich] to Blake, Drake, etc., which you said in your former letter he had done. When I am helping your memory, let me also correct my own which ought long ago to have told you that my friend Mr Palgrave would think himself highly obliged by a copy of Grammont.[1] I think he said you once gave him hopes of having one; however this be, you cannot bestow this favour better than on Palgrave, whose peculiar taste for writings of that kind, would make him infinitely obliged to you for such a present. I mean to write a longer letter very soon. In the mean time believe me, dear Sir,

Most sincerely yours,

W. MASON

The story[2] shall not be lost I assure you—I was only afraid it had been said to yourself, but I find to my comfort 'tis *publici juris*.

To MASON, Wednesday 8 December 1773

Printed from Mitford i. 111–3.

Arlington Street, Dec. 8, 1773.

I HAVE been to Strawberry Hill, but cannot find the notes you mention on education,[1] and which I do not remember ever to have seen. By Mr Fraser's assistance I send you four more of Gray's letters; all I can select that are printable yet. I mean that would not be too obscure without many notes, or that contain criticisms on living authors, very just, but, therefore, offensive. Your book will have future editions enough, and then they may appear. I have added an epitaph

1. HW's SH edition of the *Mémoires du Comte de Grammont*. See *ante* 21 July 1772, n. 14.
2. Concerning the Earl of Bristol's reception of the *Heroic Epistle*. See *ante* 27 Nov. 1773.

1. Gray's notes on his verses on education and government; see *ante* 23 Nov. 1773.

on West,[2] that he well merited, and nine of his letters to me,[3] that you may use if you have room, reject if you please, or if you please, reserve.

The passage you desire to see, is in the preface to the new *Fair Quaker of Deal*, or, as for the puppet-show's sake, it is now called, the *Fair Quaker of Portsmouth;*[4] take notice that you are not to suppose the corrections Garrick's, for they are dedicated to him, and he, you know, never flatters himself. You will not find Drake and Blake and Raleigh *totidem verbis*, but what you will find is a new mode of reasoning, viz. that a man, not bred to the sea, may draw a marine character in perfection, because Lord S[andwich], who was not bred there neither, is an excellent first lord of the Admiralty. Ergo, anybody that is dead, might have written the ghost in *Hamlet* as well as Shakespeare. But here is the passage itself: 'Perhaps some may say that none but a sailor could have made these alterations; the answer to that is simple and apposite; that many dramatic writers have drawn strong characters of professional men, without serving an apprenticeship to the trade. At present we have a strong instance to the contrary in the E. of S. who, [though] not bred a sailor, yet he governs the department in every minute sense of it, as well as any sailor that ever presided at the board!'[5]

There is another little misfortune in this passage, which is, that nobody could have made these alterations but a man who had picked up some sea-phrases, and had not the least idea of character at all. There is a rough sailor and a delicate one,[6] which, bating the terms, are Garrick's own Flash and Fribble[7] over again: I leave you to judge who was the author.

Mr Palgrave shall certainly have a Grammont,[8] but I told you that I forgot everything,—my mind is a chaos, and my life a scene of drudg-

---

2. The epitaph was by Thomas Ashton, a member of the 'Quadruple Alliance' with West, Gray, and HW at Eton. HW inserted it in his letter to Mann of 24 June 1742, q.v.

3. Mason did not print either the epitaph or the letters; see *post* 4 Jan. 1774.

4. So called, jocosely, in *London Chronicle;* see *ante* 19 Nov. 1773, n. 13.

5. *The Fair Quaker, or the Humours of the Navy*, 1773, p. v. Since the alterer, Edward Thompson, was a naval officer (*ante* 19 Nov. 1773, n. 12), this passage must have been intended to throw the reader off the

scent. In the 1775 edition, published with Thompson's name, the entire paragraph is omitted.

6. 'Flip, the Commodore,' and 'Mizen, a Sea-Fop.'

7. Characters in Garrick's *Miss in Her Teens, or the Medley of Lovers*, first acted 17 Jan. 1747 (Genest iv. 213).

8. HW also sent him a copy of *Modern Gardening* (BERRY ii. 260) and bequeathed him a copy of *Des. of SH*, 1784 (Charles Bedford's list in an interleaved copy at Chewton).

ery. I must now quit you to write letters on farming and game.⁹ I have quarrels with country gentlemen about manors. Mr Granger teases me to correct catalogues of prints,¹⁰ Dodsley for titles of Lord Chesterfield's works, and for a new edition of the *Noble Authors;*¹¹ at least I may take the liberty to refuse myself. My printer is turned into a secretary, and I myself into a pack-horse. I have elections of all sorts to manage,¹² and might as well be an acting justice of the peace; I could not know less of the matter. All my own business stands still; all my own amusements are at an end. Yet I have made one discovery that gives me great consolation, for the sake of the species. I see one may be a man of business and yet an honest man. I have cheated nobody yet; indeed, by the help of a lawyer, I was on the point of doing an unjust thing. I spend my own money, and there is no probability of my ever being the better for all my trouble. My family will, but they shall have no reason to be ashamed of their benefactor; that is, my vanity hopes that when the sexton shows my grave in the parish church at Houghton,¹³ he will say, 'Here lies old Mr Walpole, who was steward to my Lord's great-uncle.' Well; that is better than having played the fool all the rest of one's life, as I have done.

From Mason, ca Saturday 11 December 1773

Missing. This was the 'longer letter' promised *ante* 3 Dec. 1773. HW's reply, the date of which supplies the approximate date of this letter, shows that Mason was annoyed by HW's remarks on the sections of the *Memoirs of Gray* that had been submitted to him. That HW destroyed the letter would seem the most likely explanation of its absence.

9. These and the other communications mentioned in this paragraph have not been found.

10. Granger's *Supplement* to his *Biographical History of England* appeared in 1774. In it he acknowledged his 'particular' obligations to HW, to whom he had dedicated the original work.

11. HW's correspondence with the Dodsleys continued about forty years, but only three of HW's letters to them have been found. No new edition of *Royal and Noble Authors* was published until the Edinburgh reprint of 1792 (Hazen, *SH Bibliography* 36).

12. Lord Orford controlled four seats in the House of Commons: Callington (2), Castle Rising, and Ashburton (L. B. Namier, *The Structure of Politics at the Accession of George III*, 1929, i. 178). See *post* Oct. 1774. For HW's interest in a Cambridge election, see HW to Lady Ossory 28 Nov. 1773.

13. The sexton cannot do so, because HW's grave is sealed in the crypt.

To Mason, Tuesday 14 December 1773

Printed from Mitford i. 113–6.

Arlington Street, Dec. 14, 1773.

IF your aphorism and the inference you draw from it did not seem to include a compliment, I would thank you, dear Sir, for your letter as the kindest possible, for you reprove me like a friend, and nothing comes so welcome to me as to be told of my faults; the great business of my life being to mend as many, at least as much of them as I can. It is for this reason that though I have lived many useless years, yet I shall never think I have lived too long, since, if I do not flatter myself, I have fewer faults than I had. The consciousness of the number still humbles me, and causes the self-dissatisfaction you have perceived; and which I hope you will no longer call self-love, but a great desire of meriting my own esteem. When I have acquired that, I will eagerly claim the friendship you are so good as to offer me. At present I am in the predicament of devout persons, who sincerely reject all praise, and sigh if they are commended.

With the same spirit of verity I allow the force of all your arguments, nay I go farther. Whatever I feel on my own account, I had rather be mortified than subtract a [tittle][1] from the honour your pen is conferring on my two dead friends. It would be base to rob their graves, to save my own vanity; and give me leave to say, that were I capable of asking it, you would be scarce less culpable in granting it. I communicated to you the reflections that naturally arose to my mind on reading your work—but I prefer truth and justice to myself, and for a selfish reason too; I mean, I had rather exercise those virtues, than have my vanity gratified; for I doubt whether even you and La Rochefoucault will not find that the love of virtue itself is founded on self-love—at least I can say with the strictest veracity, that I never envied Gray or West their talents: I admired Gray's poetry as much as man ever did or will—I do wish that I had no more faults than they had! I must say too, that though I allow he loved me sincerely in the beginning of our friendship, I wish he had felt a little more patience for errors that were not meant to hurt him, and for that want of reflection in me which I regret as much as he condemned.—I have now done with that subject and will say no more on it. As I mean to be docile to your advice, whenever I have the pleasure of seeing you, we

1. Mitford (followed by Cunningham and Toynbee) reads 'little.'

will read over the remainder of the letters together, and burn such as you disapprove of my keeping. Several of them I own I think worth preserving. They have infinite humour and wit, are the best proofs of his early and genuine parts before he arrived at that perfection at which he aimed, and which thence appear to me the more natural. I have kept them long with pleasure, may have little time to enjoy them longer, but hereafter they may appear with less impropriety than they would in your work, which is to establish the rank of his reputation. At least I admire them so very much, that I should trust to the good taste of some few (were they mine) and despise any criticisms.

The note on Crébillon is certainly of no importance, if you, like me in what I have just said, repose on taste and laugh at tasteless criticisms. Your account of the *Elegy* puts an end to my other criticism.

I have sent you in the manner, and by the hand you pointed out,[2] a few more of Gray's and West's letters, and the extract from the dedication[3] you wot of. I hope all is arrived in safety—and you may swear, I pray as fervently for what you tell me. Adieu! I must answer three more letters, and in fact have nothing to tell you that deserves another paragraph.

Your much obliged

Hor. Walpole

PS. I have reason to think all letters to and from me, are opened since my relation to royalty. I know not what they will find that will answer but the blunders I make in letting farms.

From Mason, Tuesday 4 January 1774

Printed from MS now WSL.
Address: The Honourable Horace Walpole, Arlington Street.

Aston, Jan. 4th, 1774.

Dear Sir,

I HAVE at last found out an opportunity of sending you safely, what I have for some time wished you to see.[1] I shall now wish

2. William Fraser (*ante* 23 Nov. and 8 Dec. 1773).
3. Doubtless the extract from Thompson's 'Address to the Reader' sent *ante* 8 Dec. 1773.

1. The *Heroic Postscript*.

for your opinion of it, which you may send me too safely enough, if franked by some courtier and directed to me at the Reverend Mr Palgrave's, at Palgrave near Diss, Norfolk,[2] for I am going to Cambridge tomorrow and shall from thence make him a visit. I have led so sedentary a life of late that I think it necessary to jumble myself a little in a post-chaise before I go to York, where I shall be more sedentary still. If you know a dirtier and less considerable man than J[enkinso]n,[3] whose name consists of three syllables, you will do me a favour to mention him. Nay, I will not stand with you for a syllable.[4] I have laid my scheme so that the thing will come out soon after the meeting of Parliament,[5] *nisi tu docte dissentis.*[6]

And now to answer your two last obliging letters. Your packet came to me just in good time to insert the letter on the cat[7] and that on Polimetis.[8] Had I had Mr West's letters sooner they would have enriched my former sections, but at present they must rest. The epitaph on West I had before in Mr Gray's hand. But I did not think proper to publish it on account of the author and because, as you will find, I have intentionally avoided mention of that person, except on one occasion, viz. your verses to him,[9] about which verses I should have said more had they not been addressed to him. As I know you think very much the same concerning him that Mr Gray did,[10] I think you will believe my silence on his subject to be right.

2. Palgrave, of which William Palgrave was rector 1766–99 (*Gray's Corr.* ii. 576 n. 1), is in Suffolk, across the Waveney from Diss.

3. Charles Jenkinson had been a leader of the 'King's friends' and throughout Lord North's administration was thought to have considerable influence with the King. See the *Heroic Postscript* ll. 63–6 (Mason's *Satirical Poems* 77, 81–2).

4. Mason's 'J——n' may have brought to his mind Johnson, who is mentioned in the *Heroic Epistle* (l. 19) and, later, in the *Epistle to Dr Shebbeare* (l. 2).

5. Parliament convened 13 Jan. 1774; the *Heroic Postscript* was published 10 Feb. (Mason's *Satirical Poems* 72).

6. 'Nisi quid tu, docte Trebati, dissentis,' 'unless you, learned Trebatius, dissent' (Horace, *Satires* II. i. 78–9).

7. Mason printed two letters as one (*Mem. Gray* 188–9) and dated the composite 1 March 1747, the date actually only of the second (*Gray's Corr.* i. 271). The cat was 'the pensive Selima' whose death in

HW's 'lofty vase' Gray had commemorated. See *ante* 29 July 1773.

8. Gray to HW ca 19 Feb. 1747 (GRAY ii. 18–21), printed in *Mem. Gray* 185–7. The author of *Polymetis* was Joseph Spence (1699–1768), the elder Thomas Warton's successor as professor of poetry at Oxford 1728–38, and regius professor of modern history 1742–68, whom Gray and HW had met in Italy in 1739.

9. *An Epistle from Florence to Thomas Ashton, Esq.*, mentioned in a letter from Gray to West 16 July 1740 (*Mem. Gray* 102), was first published in Dodsley's *Collection of Poems*, 1748, ii. 305–20.

10. Ashton played a part, which is not clear, in the quarrel between Gray and HW. Gray's indifference to Ashton by 1745 is shown in his letter to Wharton on the reconciliation with HW (*Gray's Corr.* i. 226). Subsequent references in Gray's letters to Ashton are few and reveal an attitude that is cool if not contemptuous (see especially *Gray's Corr.* ii. 456, 461). HW broke with Ashton in 1750, when Ashton

As to your preserving Mr Gray's letters, I have only to say that I wish when you look them over again, you would only erase some passages, as for instance the *infantine* beginnings and conclusions of some of them, which are hardly fit for schoolboys and yet will not be considered as written by a schoolboy. This was a liberty I once thought of taking myself before I returned them.[11]

I must now return to the thing[12] you receive with this. You must know I have expunged a full third of it about the liberty of the press. I mean to make that a separate piece[13] for hereafter if there be occasion. It destroyed the unity of this, and it was in that rejected part that I meant to take notice of Garrick's *admirals*.[14] I mention this because you will perhaps wonder at the omission after what you writ concerning it. I think as it stands at present there is a proper mixture of the comic and serious. I do not expect it will *please* so much as the former, but I believe it will *frighten* some folks much more, and you'll own there is merit in doing that. However, as I said before, I shall depend entirely on your opinion as to publication, only give me your assent or dissent soon. I have many more letters to write so must excuse myself not only from writing longer, but for the haste in which this is written. Believe me to be, dear Sir,

Yours most sincerely,

W. MASON

Pray remember Grammont for Mr Palgrave.

To MASON, Friday 14 January 1774

Printed from Mitford i. 118–21.

Jan. 14, 1774.

Dear Sir—whom I respect and admire more and more—

DO not be surprised at my sending an express;[1] the subject of your letter is of too much consequence to venture the answer by

published a book against Conyers Middleton. See GRAY ii. 43 nn. 4–5.

11. See *ante* 20 March 1773 and n. 11.

12. The *Heroic Postscript*.

13. He did this in the *Epistle to Dr Shebbeare*, published in 1777.

14. That is, Thompson's remark about Lord Sandwich in the preface to *The Fair Quaker*; see *ante* 8 Dec. 1773.

1. A letter carried by special mounted messenger, for which the charge was 3d. a mile (Herbert Joyce, *The History of the Post Office*, 1893, pp. 63, 182). The express cost HW nearly £2.

the post, and I do not mind the expense, when it is to show my zeal for you and *the cause,* and enables me to speak more plainly.

Never was a man less fit to give advice than I, who want it myself to the highest degree. I am in all lights in the most difficult and delicate situation upon earth, and have half lost my senses myself with fatigue, plagues, anxiety and dread, for my nephew, my family, and my character. In short, Lord Orford is at once amazingly come to his senses, that is, to those he had or had not, before this time twelvemonth. The physicians,[1a] who must act by rules, declare they shall leave him this day month, because they dare not do otherwise by law.[1b] He will relapse, and perhaps kill himself, and I dare not stop them or him. My character is at stake and will suffer, whether I release or restrain him,—indeed I cannot restrain him. Judge of my situation without my tiring you with it! Judge too of my perplexity about what you have sent me. It is glorious, it is truth, has the noblest dignity of authoritative poetry, —must do good,—is wanted,—your country wants an avenger; you can do what a whole dirty nation will not do. Then what am I that would check your career a moment; yet hear me, Dr[1c] —— delivered it to me with great marks of apprehension, and protested he knew not what it contained; that he was ordered to deliver it to a person who was to call for it: this struck me extremely; the person I conclude is Almon, whom I know and have found to be a rogue.[2] He has already bragged, such a poem was coming out, and remember if he guesses the author, that you must manage him. Money will be offered him to tell, and he will take it and tell. Hence arises my first difficulty, and on your account, who I am sure would not for the world hurt Dr —— whom Almon will name. My next difficulty is relating to myself. If Dr ——, whom I cannot know, should name me, it would fall on one whom I am as tender of as myself, the Duchess of Gloucester. Do not imagine my paltry connection with royalty has changed me,—I despise it, lament it,—did my

1a. They included Drs Battie, Glynn, Plumptre, and Jebb (HW to Cole 12 Feb. 1773, COLE i. 298; correspondence between Thomas Walpole and William Moone, 1773, now in the possession of Mr David Holland).

1b. Dr Battie had set the period of a month as 'the term of test' (HW to Sir Edward Walpole 25 April 1777), but Sir Russell Brain and Professor Ralph S. Brown assure us that there was no 'law' setting such a period. See also HW to Mann 19 Jan. 1774.

1c. Not identified.

2. Almon, who published the *Heroic Epistle* and *Heroic Postscript,* also published HW's *Counter-Address to the Public,* 1764, at which time he was much patronized by the Opposition.

3. 'I had opposed the match till I had found it was to no purpose; and had continued steadfastly to avoid having any hand in it' (*Last Journals* i. 93–4). See HW to Mann 7 Nov. 1771.

utmost to prevent it,[3] and am hated both by those who are angry at it, and by *Him*[4] whom I would not humour in it. I have braved the King's resentment, and am ill used by the Duke, whom I would not encourage. It is not for him I fear, but for my poor niece; if her uncle could be proved to be privy to your piece,[5] she would be still more undone than she is; nay, what could I say, if the Doctor should name me? I never could tell a lie without colouring, and I trust you know that my heart is set on acting uprightly; that I lament my faults, and study to correct myself; in short I would give the world the poem had gone to the press without coming to me in the manner it did. Do not imagine that a man who thinks and tells you he should colour if he lied, would betray you to save his life. I give you my honour that I have not, to the dearest friend I have, named you for author of the other, nor would for this. I can answer for myself; I cannot for the Doctor, and I dare not hazard the Duchess. The result, therefore, of all is that I wish you could contrive to convey the poem to Almon without the intervention of Dr ———, whom I may mistake, but who seemed uneasy; and as he did not venture to trust me with his knowledge of the contents, I am not in the wrong to be unwilling to trust. I will keep it till I get your answer; and shall enjoy reading it over and over. If it is more serious than the former, though it has infinite humour too, the majesty of the bard, equal to that of the Welsh bards, more than compensates. If it appears, as I hope, I will write to you upon it, as a new poem, *in which I am much disappointed, and think it very unequal to the first.*[6] (This is the common style of little critics, who I remember said just so of the three last parts of the *Essay on Man*).[7] It will be hard if my letter is not opened at the post, when we wish it should. I am alone disappointed in not finding a hecatomb offered to Algernon Sidney,—that worst deed of the worst plan;[8] for what is so criminal as a settled plot to depreciate virtue? I hope it is in the part on the press.[9] I can give fifty additional motives and proofs

4. The Duke of Gloucester. HW has perhaps exaggerated the Duke's sentiments towards him. In his account of the royal marriage in *Last Journals* HW merely records that 'it was thought that I was in no favour with the Duke' (i. 136).

5. In which the King is severely satirized in the lines quoted *ante* 23 Nov. 1773.

6. Which HW did write *post* 14 Feb. 1774.

7. Dr Alured Clarke wrote to Lady Sundon 10 April 1733 that the second epistle was 'in many places . . . too hard to be understood' and 'not comparable to the first, though it has many beauties' (*Memoirs of Viscountess Sundon*, 1847, ii. 195, quoted in Pope's *Essay on Man*, ed. Maynard Mack, 1950, p. xvi n. 3).

8. See *ante* 2 March 1773 *bis* for HW's theory of the King's connection with the publication of Dalrymple's *Memoirs* and of the scheme to traduce the memory of the great Whig heroes.

9. The *Heroic Postscript* is chiefly de-

to whet your anger. How I wish I could see you but for a day: I am chained here by the foot to a madman; but can I avoid wishing you could steal to town for a day? It might be a secret; I would come to you wherever you would appoint. At least acquit me of royalty or Court-serving. I am not a tailor;[10] I am not corrupted: I am hated at Court and detest it. Keep my letter and print it in the Gazette either before or after my death, if I deceive you. Tell, show here, under my hand, that I exhorted you to publish both the *Heroic Epistle* and the *Postscript*.

I glory in having done so, but I own I would not have you risk hurting Dr ——, nor would I have my niece, who is ignorant and innocent, suffer for the participation of her uncle and your friend,

HOR. WALPOLE

From MASON, Saturday 15 January 1774

Printed from MS now WSL.

Palgrave, Jan. 15, 1774.

Dear Sir,

YOU are under much greater apprehensions than you need to be on this subject.[1] Hear a plain narrative. I sent up the packet to the Doctor by Mr Verelst's servant, desired him, the Doctor, to send it to you by some safe hand, and when he had received it back to keep it till called for. The person who was to call for it was not by any means him whom you suspect,[2] but the young man[3] who received the ten golden guineas for the last. He cannot come to town these ten days, and when he does I meant that he should negotiate this matter as he did the former. On his prudence and good management I can fully rely. As to the Doctor you may be quite as easy on his subject, and have nothing to do but to seal the packet up and send it to him by your

voted to praising 'the bulwark of the press' (l. 70). Mason's defence of Sidney is in the *Epistle to Dr Shebbeare*, ll. 14–15:
'Then Sydney's, Russel's patriot fame should fall,
Besmeared with mire, like black Dalrymple's gall.'
10. John Wilson Croker in the *Quarterly*

Review, 1851, lxxxix. 140 and Mrs Toynbee emend to 'traitor.'

———

1. The publication of the *Heroic Postscript*.
2. John Almon (*ante* 14 Jan. 1774).
3. Possibly John Baynes; see *ante* 7 May 1773, n. 2.

servant with charge to deliver it into his own hand. If after all you
have any fears as being made privy to it, I give you full liberty to burn
it instantly, and as there is no other copy extant you may be assured it
will perish completely. A[lmon] knows nothing about the matter yet,
and was it now in his hands would make no use of it till the beginning
of a new month for his own pecuniary reasons. And the apparent Marcellus[4] will vanish as soon as the interview is over, that is, if I permit
the interview, but this I shall not do till I hear from you again, which
I wish to do at my return to Cambridge, whither I mean to go from
hence on Monday the 24th; but for God's sake, no more expresses. I
have been at my wit's end to account for this to my present host,[5] but
have made a tolerable excuse. In your letter you need only say whether
or no you permit me to publish those letters of Mr Gray's which you
lately sent me and I shall understand you. Was I to come to town in
the present crisis and be seen by any person it would cause more suspicion than anything else, indeed in my own opinion it would be the
only dangerous step that could be taken in the whole transaction. I
cannot write more at present, except that I am

Extremely yours,

W. MASON

To MASON, Friday 21 January 1774

Printed from Mitford i. 123–5.

Jan. 21, 1774.

Dear Sir,

I HAVE returned those letters of Gray to your friend,[1] and earnestly
beg as well as consent myself, that they should be printed. I should
never forgive myself their being suppressed, as they will do him so
much honour, and you have perfectly satisfied me that the lady in
question[2] cannot be affected by them, which was my whole concern.

4. That is, the apparent author, Mason's
agent. Marcus Claudius Marcellus and his
brother Caius Claudius Marcellus were bitter enemies of Julius Cæsar.

5. Rev. William Palgrave (see *ante* 4
Jan. 1774).

1. HW is following the instructions given
him by Mason in the preceding letter. The
friend is the unidentified Doctor.

2. The Duchess of Gloucester.

I beg you will excuse all the trouble I have given you, but my mind was in such violent agitation about my nephew, that every object came magnified to my eyes; and my dread of doing wrong, when it is so difficult to do right in the variety of relations in which I stand, made me fearful that even so innocent a thing as Gray's letters might hurt a person[3] of whom I have no cause to complain. But I will say no more, than that I approve your reasons for omitting the epitaph on West,[4] and the author of it, and that I wish it may not be too late to desire your silence on my epistle[5] to the same person. Neither he nor my lines deserve notice in such a book. I no longer care about fame; I have done being an author, and above all, I should blush to have you stamp memory on anything that is not worthy of it. It is a sad place to offer you, especially considering that it has been self-filled, but you rise in my opinion as fast as I sink in my own. The spot however will be dignified by gratitude, of which I never can feel enough, considering the sacrifice you so generously offered to make,[6] and which nobody could make, but one that can do what he pleases. What a beast should I be, had I been capable of accepting it.

What can I tell you, I who for fifteen months have felt nothing but anguish in body and mind? Before I was delivered from the gout in every limb, my nephew's madness fell on me; since that, the burthen of his affairs; and for these last three weeks an anxious suspense between his recovery and fears of his relapse, all now heightened by the probability that the physicians will quit him in three weeks more, when he must be at full liberty—to destroy himself if he pleases! I neither dare restrain him, nor can approve his release, and shall probably be to answer for consequences that I foresee, without having power to prevent! In short my mind is broken, and where I am free enough to own it, sunk. I have spirits enough left to conceal my serious thoughts from the world, but I own them to you my confessor. I have found I have sense enough to learn many common things that I never believed myself capable of comprehending. I have found that better sense of acting as I ought, when it was necessary; for till this year I never really had anything to do. I shall be rejoiced to resume that

3. I.e., the Duchess.
4. HW here turns from his use of code to a genuine discussion of *Mem. Gray.*
5. The *Epistle from Florence to Thomas Ashton, Esq.* (see *ante* 4 Jan. 1774).

6. Mason's offer to permit HW to burn the MS of the *Heroic Postscript.*

happy idleness. I know not whether it will be my lot; I think I should
taste my old amusements again of books and *virtù*, yet with much less
eagerness, for I feel that even absolute idleness would be an enjoyment, though till eight months ago I never knew what it was to be
unemployed for a quarter of an hour. My ghostly father, tell me if
you can from this confession, what I really think, for I protest I do
not know; or if you will, laugh at me, and tell me anything of yourself, a much more interesting subject. I know nothing, but that politics are dead, literature obsolete, the stage lower than in the days of
mysteries, the actors as bad as the plays, the macaronies as poor as the
nabobs are rich, and nothing new upon earth, but coats and waist-
coats;[6a] as for the women, they think almost as little of their petticoats
as the men do. We are to have my Lord Chesterfield's works,[7] and my
Lord Lyttleton's works,[8] which will not much reanimate the age, the
Saturnia regna.[9] Adieu, when Gray can spare you, pray let me have a
line.

Yours most entirely,

H. W.

PS. Gen. Graeme[10] has resigned, and old Hermes of Salisbury[11] is
made secretary to the Queen; which I tell you, not as politics, which
you do not care about, but as an event in a title-page.

6a. Bought for the Queen's Birthday,
celebrated 18 Jan.

7. HW probably knew that Matthew
Maty was preparing an edition of Chesterfield's works, which finally appeared in
1777 (see *post* 13 March 1777 and n. 12), but
it is probable that he is here thinking of
Chesterfield's letters to his son, which
were published in April 1774 (*ante* 27 Nov.
1773 and n. 5, and *post* 7 April 1774).

8. *The Works of George, Lord Lyttelton*,
ed. G. E. Ayscough, were published early
in July 1774 (*London Chronicle* 5–7 July
1774, xxxvi. 21).

9. HW's belief that he was living in the
Golden Age died early in George III's
reign.

10. David Graeme (d. 1797: GM lxvii pt
i. 171), friend of Lord Bute, negotiator of
the marriage of George III and Charlotte,
to whom he became secretary and controller. 'This Graeme . . . was a notorious

Jacobite, and had been engaged in the
late rebellion. On a visit he made to Scotland, his native country, after this embassy [to Mecklenburg], David Hume, the
historian, said to him, "Colonel Graeme,
I congratulate you on having exchanged
the dangerous employment of making
Kings, for the more lucrative province of
making Queens"' (*Mem. Geo. III* i. 50).
According to HW, Graeme's resignation as
secretary was the result of pique at his
not obtaining the post of treasurer to the
Queen (*Last Journals* i. 282).

11. James Harris (1709–80), author of
*Hermes, or a Philosophical Inquiry Con-
cerning Universal Grammar*; M.P. Christ-
church 1761–80; secretary and controller to
Queen Charlotte 1774–80. He was born at
Salisbury, the eldest son of James Harris
by his second wife, Lady Elizabeth Ashley
Cooper, and was closely identified with
Salisbury throughout his life. 'Though a

From MASON, Thursday 3 February 1774

Printed from MS now WSL.
Address: The Honourable Horace Walpole, Arlington Street, London.
Postmark: ROTHERHAM 7 FE.

Aston, Feb. 3d, 1774.

Dear Sir,

I RECEIVED, while at Cambridge, your permission to print those letters of Mr Gray,[1] and have taken my measures accordingly. I have nothing therefore to say at present on that subject, only to repeat my firm belief that they cannot do any harm to the person you mentioned.

I should, if I had found time for it, have expressed my true concern for your present critical and affecting situation, in my last letter, but I was much hurried and writ in company. Permit me now to tell you that I sincerely sympathize with you in all your chagrins. I know by experience how impossible it is to do any effectual service in cases similar to that in which you have been of late so meritoriously employed. The poor man,[2] whom some years ago you so much befriended by printing his little poems at your press, has been on my hands ever since; and by the contributions I then raised, added to a small living which Mr Stonhewer procured for him, he and his wife and four children have been kept from starving, and this without much diminishing the little principal which I have kept in my hands. During all this time, he has been in such a state between madness and reason, that he is only capable at times of doing the common duties of his church but never of taking care of his own affairs; and now he has taken it into his head to send his children to York for education, which will of necessity run away presently with that money which I intended to have employed in setting up his wife and eldest daughter in some decent trade, in case of his death, which, from his apparently bad constitution, was long ago to be expected. I mention this merely to show how fruitless it is to hope to do real good in cases so deplorable as

student and an author, he was sociable, and especially encouraged concerts and the annual musical festival at Salisbury,' writes Leslie Stephen in DNB. Boswell also speaks of 'Harris of Salisbury' (*Johnson* iii. 256); Johnson said of him, 'Harris is a sound sullen scholar; he does not like interlopers.

Harris, however, is a prig, and a bad prig' (ibid. iii. 245).

————

1. I.e., the *Heroic Postscript* (*ante* 21 Jan. 1774).

2. Francis Hoyland (see *ante* 5 April 1769 and n. 5).

these. Yet I think at the same time it is our duty to act even without and against hope in such cases, but for our own ease we should always avoid laying any preconcerted scheme for our conduct, and only act as circumstances arise, otherwise we are sure of being disappointed.

You kindly pressed me to come to London in your former letter, and you may assure yourself I would readily have done so, could I have done it either with convenience or propriety, but I am obliged to begin my residence at York next week and to stay there till the middle of May. My only hope of seeing you, therefore, is at my Lord Strafford's in the summer, and to wait on you at Aston, both going and coming. But if you are resolved not to set your face northwards, I will contrive if possible to come southwards, provided always that I can do this without being necessitated to pay my compliments to a certain person in your Strawberry neighbourhood whose face (to tell you the truth) I wish never to see again, for he has of late behaved more shabbily than ever.[3]

Soon after I am settled at York, I mean to send you that fine lyrical fragment of Mr Gray's which I have had the *hardiesse* to complete, by the addition of two or three stanzas.[4] I mean to print it among some additional notes at the end of his poems. If it serves (as I think it will) to elucidate his design I shall not care how much it proves my lyrical inferiority. But more of this, when I send you the ode, of which I mean to print a few copies[5] for the sake of obtaining your judgment and that of a few other friends before I determine whether to insert it in the book or not. I shall hope to hear from you soon and let me beg you to remember to direct me at *York,* for you was always forgetful in points of this sort, even when you had not so good or rather so bad a cause to be forgetful. I hope I need not say how cordially I wish your mind to be more at ease, nor with what sincerity I am, dear Sir,

Your most obliged and faithful servant,

W. MASON

---

3. This was Lord Holdernesse, whose relations with Mason had become strained for reasons that are not clear. A letter from Mason to Alderson of 28 July 1773 suggests that Holdernesse may have behaved 'shabbily' to Mason's curate. If he did, he made up for it later; see *post* 26 Oct. 1777, n. 3.

4. The fragment written ca 1754–5, to which Mason gave the title 'Ode on the Pleasure Arising from Vicissitude.' Mason printed the fragment in *Mem. Gray* pp. 236–7, and again in pt ii ('Poems'), pp. 78–81, with his title and additions in italic.

5. See *post* 3 March 1774 and n. 3.

To Mason, Monday 14 February 1774

Printed from Mitford i. 128–31.

Feb. 14, 1774.

I AM most impatient for your lyric section[1] and the completion of the ode. Nay, I am glad to have lost so much of schoolboy and schoolmaster, as to be charmed with the fragment, though Dr Barnard frowns on it[2]—pray remember, however, that when you have so much piety for Mr Gray's remains, you are unpardonable in leaving your own works imperfect. I trust, as you will now enjoy your own garden in summer, and will have finished the life by your return from York, that you will perfect your *Essay on Modern Gardening:*[3] you have given a whole year to your friend[4] and are in debt to the public.

My troubles are at an end, my nephew is as well as ever *he* was, and is gone into the country either to complete his own ruin and his family's, or to relapse. I shall feel the former, I dread the latter—but I must decline the charge a second time. It half killed me, and would entirely have ruined my health. Indeed it has hurt me so much, that though my mind has recovered its tranquillity I cannot yet shake off the impressions and recall my spirits. Six months of gout and nine of stewardship and fears were too much for my time of life and want of strength. The villainy too that I have seen has shocked me; and memory predominates over cheerfulness. My inclination will certainly carry me this summer into Yorkshire, if dread of my biennial gout[5] does not restrain me. Sometimes, I have a mind to go to a warmer climate; but either at Aston or at Strawberry will insist on our meeting before winter; what signifies a neighbour you do not wish to see?[6] Are our enemies to deprive us of our best satisfaction, seeing our

1. That is, Mason's edition of Gray's poems appended to the *Memoirs.*

2. Presumably Edward Barnard (1717–81), D.D., headmaster of Eton, 1754; Provost, 1765. It is not certain when HW had seen the fragmentary ode, but probably it was in a missing letter with Mason's comment that Barnard did not admire it. HW is glad to find that he has outgrown his schoolboy awe of a Provost of Eton's opinion.

3. That is, *The English Garden.* See *ante* 9 May 1772 and n. 17.

4. Gray.

5. HW maintained that he suffered from gout only in alternate winters; see also *post* 7 April 1774, 6 Feb. 1776, and 10 Jan. 1782. Although the pattern of recurrence was perhaps not quite so uniform, the history of his gout that can be drawn from his letters during the decade 1766–75 shows that the severest attacks occurred in the winters of 1766–7, 1768–9, 1770–1, 1772–3, and 1774–5. The unscheduled attack in Feb. 1776 shook HW's confidence in his theory.

6. Lord Holdernesse (*ante* 3 Feb. 1774).

friends? I will presume to say you cannot have a warmer or more sincere one than myself, who never call myself so when I do not feel myself so, and who have few pleasures left but that of saying what I think. You are too wise and too good not to despise the dirtiness of fools, or to regret a man who came to years of discretion before he was past his childhood, and is superannuated before he is come to his understanding. He is decaying fast, and will soon exist but in his epitaph,[7] like those Poor Knights of Windsor who are recorded on their gravestones for their loyalty to Charles I.[8]

The House of Lords is busy on the question of literary property,[9] a question that lies between the integrity of Scotch authors and English booksellers. T'other House has got into a new scrape with the City and printers, which I suppose will end to the detriment of the press.[10] The ministers have a much tougher business on their hands in which even their factotum the Parliament may not be able to ensure success —I mean the rupture with America.[11] If all the black slaves were in

7. Holdernesse lived until May 1778.

8. And for nothing else. The Poor Knights are listed in Joseph Pote, *The History and Antiquities of Windsor Castle*, 1749, pp. 398–407, HW's copy of which is now WSL.

9. 'The occasion which brought this question before the public was as follows: certain booksellers had supposed that an author possessed by common law an exclusive right forever to the publication of his own works, and consequently could transfer that right. On this supposition, some of them had purchased copyrights, and had prosecuted others who published the same books. . . . A decree of chancery had been obtained in favour of Mr [Thomas] Becket, a prosecutor on these grounds, against Messrs Donaldsons, as pirates. . . . The defendants had appealed to the House of Peers' (Robert Bisset, *History of George III*, quoted in Cobbett, *Parl. Hist.* xvii. 955). The Lords reversed the decree 22 Feb. 1774 (Cobbett, op. cit. xvii. 1003). Boswell, who had acted as counsel for Donaldson in the case before the Scottish Court of Session, published its favourable decision in time to influence the English Lords. HW's copy of the second edition of that work, *Decision of the Court of Session upon the Question of Literary Property*, Edinburgh, 1774, is now WSL.

See F. A. Pottle, *The Literary Career of James Boswell*, Oxford, 1929, pp. 92–101, and the references there cited. Mr Pottle observes, 'This case (Donaldson *v.* Becket) is still the basis of all English and American copyright acts.'

10. On 11 Feb. 'appeared in the *Public Advertiser* a most daring attack on the Speaker, Sir Fletcher Norton, for notorious partiality in preventing the presentation of a memorial in behalf of one William Tooke' (*Last Journals* i. 289–90). The attack was written by 'Parson' John Horne (1736–1812), who later added to his name that of Tooke, whose heir he had become. He had been an intimate of Wilkes and had an active following among the City radicals. Horne and Henry Sampson Woodfall (1730–1805), the printer of the *Public Advertiser*, were brought before the House on an action of libel. The affair was taken up by the leaders of both parties, the freedom and 'insolence' of the press were debated, but Horne's connection with the libel could not be proved and Woodfall was soon released from custody. HW's prophecy was not fulfilled; the case strengthened the power of the press. See also HW to Mann 23 Feb. 1774; *Annual Register*, 1774, xvii. 92–4 and 97; Cobbett, *Parl. Hist.* xvii. 1003–50.

11. A reference to the Boston Tea Party,

rebellion, I should have no doubt in choosing my side, but I scarce wish perfect freedom to merchants who are the bloodiest of all tyrants. I should think the souls of the Africans would sit heavy on the swords of the Americans.

We are still expecting the works of Lord Chesterfield and Lord Lyttelton—on my part with no manner of impatience; one was an ape of the French, the other of the Greeks, and I like neither second-hand pertness or solemnity. There is published a *Postscript*[12] to the *Heroic Epistle* certainly by the same author, as is evident by some charming lines, but inferior to the former[13] as second parts are apt to be. The history of Charles Fox and Mrs Grieve is come out too in rhyme,[14] wretchedly done but minutely true. I think I have told you all I know and more than you will care whether you know or not. It is an insipid age. Even the macaronies degenerate; they have lost all their money and credit, and ruin nobody but their tailors. Adieu,

Yours most sincerely,

H. W.

From Mason, Thursday 3 March 1774

Printed from MS now WSL.

York, March 3d, 1774.

Dear Sir,

I COULD not with convenience get the ode[1] I mentioned to you printed before, as I was not come to the place in the *Memoirs*

16 Dec. 1773. See *Annual Register*, 1774, xvii. 86–8; HW to Mann 2 Feb. 1774; *Last Journals* i. 283, 286.

12. Published 10 Feb. 1774 (*Last Journals* i. 288; Mason's *Satirical Poems* 72).

13. The statement rehearsed by HW *ante* 14 Jan. 1774. But he expressed the same opinion of it to Lady Ossory 12 Feb.

14. Publication of *Female Artifice, or Charles F—— Outwitted* was announced in *Daily Adv.* 11 Feb. 1774. 'The Hon.' Mrs Elizabeth Harriet Grieve persuaded Fox that she 'could procure for him, as a wife, a Miss Phipps, with a fortune of £80,000' (*Last Journals* i. 269–70; see also HW to Lady Ossory 18 Nov. 1773 and 12 Feb. 1774; N&Q 1864, 3d ser., vi. 381–3; *Annual Register*, 1773, xvi. 147–8, and 1774, xvii.

158). This incident also provided Foote with material for *The Cozeners*, produced 15 July 1774; see Mary M. Belden, *The Dramatic Work of Samuel Foote*, New Haven, 1929, pp. 161–2; *Public Advertiser*. HW's copy of *Female Artifice* is bound in vol. 13 of his 'Poems of Geo. III' now in the Harvard Library. Above the date on the title-page he has written 'February.' It follows his copy of the *Heroic Postscript*. It is perhaps noteworthy that there is no reference to Mrs Grieve in G. O. Trevelyan, *The Early History of Charles James Fox*, 1880, or in Christopher Hobhouse, *Fox*, 1947.

1. 'On the Pleasure Arising from Vicissitude' (*ante* 3 Feb. 1774).

where the fragment is inserted. When that sheet was worked off I gave the printer my additions to print a dozen copies before the roman types were broken up.[2] One of these copies I send you,[3] and if you and a few other friends think that what I have added may serve to elucidate his general idea, I shall reprint it and publish it, but not among his odes, no not even in the *Memoirs,* but only among some additional notes which I mean to put at the end of his poems;[4] thrown in such a place perhaps I may escape censure for having had the vanity to make such an attempt.

We see nothing here but newspapers. If I send for a new pamphlet it is above a fortnight before it arrives. This was the case with the *Heroic Postscript* which you mentioned in your last. But you did not tell me that I had the honour of being placed in the same line with Dr Goldsmith.[5] If you had, I should hardly have sent for it. However, I am more contented with my company than Garrick will be with his. I think much the same about the piece itself as you do, and as there is certainly less comic humour in it than in the former, I should think neither its reputation nor its sale would be so great—but here I find from the last paper, ministry steps in as usual, and by the voice of Col. Onslow[6] stamps the reputation it might want upon it, and hereby enhances Almon's profit. Were it not for this I'll be bound to say not three persons in York would have read it; now it will spread through the county.

You gave me in your last (expressed in a line and a half) all the sense that has or can be spoken on the subject of literary property. But much more may be said and I hope you will say it on the result of the debate.[7] I think Lord Mansfeild has finessed the matter[8] far beyond all his

2. That is, the completed ode was to be printed from the same setting of roman type that appears in sheet Gg in the *Memoirs,* with Mason's additions set in italic.

3. It has disappeared. Only one of these copies is now known, the copy in the William Andrews Clark Memorial Library, Los Angeles. It was reproduced in facsimile, with an introduction by Leonard Whibley, in a privately printed edition of 200 copies in 1933.

4. See *ante* 3 Feb. 1774, n. 4.

5. 'Admit him then your candidate for fame,
    Pleased if in your review he read his name,
    Though not with Mason and with Goldsmith put,

Yet cheek by jowl with Garrick, Colman, Foote'   (ll. 77–80).

6. The M.P. for Guildford of this name (see *ante* 15 May 1773, n. 12) was a Lt-Col., 1759. Mason alludes to this attack on the *Heroic Postscript* in his *Epistle to Dr Shebbeare,* ll. 96–9; HW added in his note that Onslow had 'declaimed in the House of Commons' against the poem (Mason's *Satirical Poems* 108, 118). No newspaper notice of the attack has been found.

7. Mason probably means in HW's memoirs. See also *ante* 5 July 1773, n. 3, and *post* 2 April 1782.

8. 'The judges . . . all delivered their opinions except Lord Mansfield, who declined speaking as a judge' (Cobbett, *Parl.*

former finesses. His silence—the palinodia[9] of my Lord Chancellor—all, all are equally admirable. I must insist on another paragraph from you on this interesting subject.

I heartily rejoice that your family *concerns* are at least *actively* at an end, *passively* your heart will never suffer them to be, and perhaps it ought not. But I beg and entreat that same heart not to be too solicitous in future, for the sake of itself and for the sake of its friends, amongst which number (as it lately permitted me so to do) I have both the pleasure and honour to rank, dear Sir,

Your faithful servant,

W. MASON

To MASON, Saturday 19 March 1774

Printed from Mitford i. 133.

Arlington Street, March 19, 1774.

Dear Sir,

I ARRIVED here but four hours ago from Houghton, where I have been this fortnight with my nephew: I find your letter, your printed ode, and messages from Mr Stonhewer, to whom I have not yet had an instant's time to send, nor have, but to say one syllable to you, as I approve your additions exceedingly, and would not delay saying so; that if my taste or judgment can have any weight, you may be determined to print what Gray might envy—I am fond of modesty even in the flower of authors, but not carried too far, as you do now, by degrading Gray to an appendix,[1] because you, though unworthy, will not sit by him in his Works. You have finished him as well as he himself, with all his love of polishing, could have done, and I think

---

Hist. xvii. 992). In 1766 Mansfield had rendered a decision in a similar case (Millar *v.* Taylor) in the King's Bench that was the reverse of the Lords' decision in Donaldson *v.* Becket. In Mansfield's defence see C. H. S. Fifoot, *Lord Mansfield,* Oxford, 1936, pp. 223–7.

9. I.e., recantation. Lord Apsley, speaking in the House of Lords 22 Feb., said that although as Lord Chancellor he had granted the decree, he was not biased in its favour, and 'concluded with declaring that he was clearly of opinion with the appellants' (ibid. xvii. 1001–2).

---

1. Mason left the ode in the fourth section of the *Memoirs,* however (pp. 236–7), and repeated it with his additions in his notes to part ii ('Poems'), pp. 78–81.

truly that yours have more harmony than some of his lines. I wonder at it, for I dislike the metre, which in the fourth line has a sudden sink, like a man with one leg shorter than the other²—but I have not time for a word more, you shall have a longer letter in a post or two. Adieu,

Yours most devotedly,

HOR. WALPOLE

To Mason, Wednesday 23 March 1774

Printed from Mitford i. 134–7.

Strawberry Hill, March 23, 1774.

Dear Sir,

I WROTE my last in a great hurry, and not much knowing what I said, being just lighted from my chaise after being a fortnight at Houghton with my nephew, where my head was filled with business, and my heart with anxiety and grief and twenty other passions, for (not to return to the subject) if he is recovered I doubt it will not be for a long season. He is neither temperate in his regimen nor conduct, and if I have chased away seven evil spirits, as many are ready to enter. In short, the rest of my life, I find, and they will shorten it, is to be spent in contests with lawyers, the worst sort of lawyers, attorneys, stewards, farmers, mortgagees and toad-eaters. I do not advance and cannot retreat, I wished to live only for my friends and myself, I must now, I find, live for my relations—or die for them; you are very kind in pitying, and advising me to consult my ease and health, but if you knew my whole story and it was not too long, even for a series of letters like Clarissa's, you would encourage me to proceed, for I flatter myself that my duty is the incentive to my conduct, and you, whose life is blameless, would I am sure advise your friend to sacrifice his happiness at last to his family, and to the memory of a father to whom he owes everything,—but no more on this, though it has and does occupy my mind so much, that I am absolutely ignorant of the affairs of the world and of all political and literary news, though the latter are the only comforts of the few moments I have to myself.

2. The fourth line in each of the 8-line stanzas is a trimeter, the rest tetrameters.

I began Mr Bryant's—what shall I call it?—pre-existent History of the World,[1] but had not time to finish the first volume. It put me in mind of Prior's Madam, who

To cut things [short] came down to Adam.[2]

There are two pages[3] under the radical Macar, that will divert you; an absolute account of Μακαρωνες, though I dare to swear the good man never dreamt that he was writing the history of Almack's.[4] I have just got Mr Wharton's *Life* of poetry,[5] and it seems delightfully full of things I love, but not a minute to begin it; nor Campbell's long expected work on commerce,[6] which he told me twenty years ago should be the basis on which he meant to build his reputation.[7] Lord Lyttleton and Lord Chesterfield are coming forth, and one must run them over in self-defence, still I say to you, *O quando ego te aspiciam*[8] —yes, *te*, both you and your Gray! I am impatient for the remainder, though I would not have it hurried. Mr Stonhewer will have told you what I said on the print; but if he could make sense of it I shall wonder, for I was on both sides; for your print, as the more agreeable;[9]

1. *A New System, or an Analysis of Ancient Mythology*, 1774–6, by Jacob Bryant (1715–1804), antiquary and philologist. HW's copy was sold SH v. 39.
2. 'And lest I should be wearied, Madam, To cut things short, came down to Adam'
(Prior, *Alma* ii. 373–4).
3. In the first chapter, on radicals, the roots of names in ancient mythology.
4. The club to which the macaronies belonged. 'It is remarkable that a very grave and very learned author, Mr Bryant, has described them in his *Analysis*, without intending it. Under his radical word, Macar, he says, *the Macaronis were a happy people, and lived in an island*' (HW's note in Mason's *Satirical Poems* 70). 'The Grecians supposed the term Macar to signify happy. . . . This term is often found compounded, Macar-On: from whence people were denominated Μακαρωνες . . . and places were called Μακρων. This probably was the original of the name given to islands' (Bryant, op. cit. i. 68–9).
5. The first volume of Thomas Warton's *History of English Poetry* was published 21 March (*Public Advertiser*). HW's jocular title *Life* is explained *post* 7 April 1774. His copy was sold SH v. 63.

6. *A Political Survey of Britain*, 1774, by John Campbell (1708–75), was published 15 March (*Daily Adv.*). No copy of this book appears in the SH records. This is the only reference we have found to HW's acquaintance with Campbell.
7. 'Johnson, though he valued him highly, was of opinion that there was not so much in his great work, "A Political Survey of Great Britain," as the world had been taught to expect; and had said to me, that he believed Campbell's disappointment, on account of the bad success of that work, had killed him. He this evening observed of it, "That work was his death." Mr Warton, not adverting to his meaning, answered "I believe so; from the great attention he bestowed on it." Johnson. "Nay, Sir, he died of *want* of attention, if he died at all by that book"' (Boswell, *Johnson* ii. 447).
8. 'Oh, when shall I look upon thee?' (Horace, *Satires* II. ii. 60).
9. This is probably Charles Carter's engraving (*ante* 16 July 1773 and n. 13), which HW describes *ante* 29 July 1773 as too 'cheerful' and showing too much 'vivacity.' However it is possible that Mason considered using his own portrait of Gray, engraved by Mason 'with his own hand'

for Wilson's picture[10] as extremely like, though a likeness that shocks one; there are marks, evident marks of its being painted after Gray's death—I would not hang it up in my house for the world; I think I am now come to know my own mind, it is to have prints of both;[11] from yours at the beginning to front his juvenilia; from Wilson's, at or towards the end, as the exact representation of him in his last years of life. The delay will not signify, as your book[12] is a lasting one, no matter if it comes out in the middle of summer; it does not depend for its sale on a full London, it will be sent for into the country, and will always continue to be sold. Were I to write anything that I could hope to have minded, I would publish in summer. The first ball, duel, divorce, new prologue of Garrick, or debate in the House of Commons makes everything forgotten in a minute in winter. Wedderburn's philippic on Franklyn,[13] that was cried up to the skies, Chief Justice de Grey's on literary property,[14] Lord Sandwich's honourable behaviour to Miller the printer[15] are already at the bottom of Lethe. Made-

in 1760 (Gray to Brown 23 Oct. 1760, *Gray's Corr.* ii. 706 and n. 7).

10. The plate of the frontispiece that Mason decided on is inscribed 'W. Mason et B. Wilson vivi memores delineavere.' The engraver was James Basire. On the plate in his own copy HW has written, 'From a picture painted after Mr Gray's death by Mr Wilson, partly by memory and partly from a drawing by Mr Mason. It is very like Mr Gray towards his death.' This painting (1774) is now at Pembroke College, Cambridge, and Wilson's drawing that was probably the immediate source of the print is in the National Portrait Gallery (*Gray's Corr.* iii. p. xxxiii; George Scharf in *The Athenæum* 24 Feb. 1894, pp. 251–2). HW's dislike of the portrait is expressed more strongly in a letter to Cole 25 April 1775 (COLE i. 367).

11. Mason disregarded HW's advice and used only the Basire engraving, which is the only plate in the volume.

12. Mitford reads 'look.'

13. The occasion was Benjamin Franklin's appearance before the Privy Council in the course of the investigation of the Hutchinson and Oliver letters. On 29 Jan. 1774 'Wedderburn, solicitor-general, made a most bitter and abusive speech against him, which was much admired' (*Last Jour-*

nals i. 284; see also ibid. i. 243, 276–80). The speech was printed in *The Letters of Governor Hutchinson and Lieut.-Governor Oliver . . . together with the Substance of Mr Wedderburn's Speech Relating to Those Letters,* ed. Israel Mauduit, 1774, pp. 77–113. HW's copy of the second edition is now WSL.

14. William de Grey (1719–81), cr. (1780) Bn Walsingham of Walsingham, Norfolk, solicitor-general 1763–6, attorney-general 1766–71, lord chief justice of the Common Pleas 1771–80, spoke in the House of Commons 21 Feb. 1774 against the theory of a perpetual copyright (Cobbett, *Parl. Hist.* xvii. 988–92).

15. John Miller, the printer of the *London Evening Post,* was indicted for libel by Lord Sandwich because of letters he had printed that accused Sandwich of offering to sell a position on the navy board (GM 1773, xliii. 347–9; *Annual Register,* 1773, xvi. 178–82; *Last Journals* i. 241 and 275). In *London Chronicle* 12–15 March 1774 (xxxv. 252) is Miller's letter describing his dealings with Sandwich after the decision. Sandwich was awarded damages of £2000, and, according to Miller, later agreed to accept £500 and costs, but repented of this decision and insisted on the original award of the court.

moiselle Heinel[16] dances tomorrow, and Wedderburn and Lord Sandwich will catch their deaths if they wait in either of the temples of fame or infamy in expectation of admirers.

I know not a word more than I told you, or you have heard, of the affair of literary property. Lord Mansfield's finesse as you call it, was christened by its true names, pitiful and paltry. Poor Mrs Macaulay has written a very bad pamphlet on the subject.[17] It marks dejection and sickness. In truth, anybody that has principles must feel. Half of the King's opposition at least are hurrying to Court. Sir William Meredith[18] has ridden thither on a white stick;[19] Colonel Barré[20] on the necks of the Bostonians, his old friends; Mr Burke, who has a tolerable stake in St Vincent's,[21] seems to think it worth all the rest of America. Still, I do not know how, an amazing bill of an amazing parent, has slipped through the ten thousand fingers of venality, and gives the constitution some chance of rousing itself—I mean Grenville's bill for trying elections.[22] It passed as rapidly as if it had been

16. Anne-Frédérique Heinel (or Heynel) (1753–1808), m. (1792) G. A. B. Vestris. She made her début as a dancer in Paris in 1768 and came to London in 1771. See DU DEFFAND iii. 154 n. 13, and Gaston Capon, *Les Vestris*, 1908, *passim*.

17. *A Modest Plea for the Property of Copyright* was published 16 March 1774 (*Public Advertiser*). HW has inserted 'March' below the date in his copy (now WSL).

18. Sir William Meredith (ca 1725–90), Bt; politician. HW describes him as 'that fluctuating patriot, who had broken with all parties, and at last had dropped anchor at his own interest, as controller' (*Last Journals* i. 311).

19. His badge of office as controller.

20. Isaac Barré (1726–1802), soldier and politician. 'Colonel Barré said, if the Bostonians were so guilty as they had been represented, we ought to make war on them; there could be no middle measures' (*Last Journals* i. 313). Barré's remarks were made during the debate on the bill requested by the King that measures be taken against America and especially against 'the violent and outrageous proceedings at the town and port of Boston.' Barré's remarks on the bill as reported in Cobbett show him disposed to demand a policy of control over Boston, but they do not have the uncompromising character that HW attributes to them. See Cobbett, *Parl. Hist.* xvii. 1159, 1163, 1169–70, 1178.

21. Edmund Burke's younger brother, Richard, had speculated in land on the island of St Vincent in the West Indies in 1770. The legality of his purchases was questioned, and for many years he was engaged in various schemes designed to urge his claim. The loyal support of Edmund Burke had as early as 1771 aroused the suspicion that he was involved in the speculation. See Dixon Wecter, 'Edmund Burke and His Kinsmen,' *University of Colorado Studies, Series B, Studies in the Humanities*, 1939, i. 49–68. HW's copy of *Authentic Papers Relating to the Expedition against the Charibbs and the Sale of Lands in the Island of St Vincent*, 1773 (now WSL) has numerous marginalia. HW's interest arose from his strong feelings against slavery.

22. The bill had originally been introduced in 1770 by George Grenville (1712–70). It transferred the trial of petitions involving controversial elections from the House of Commons at large to a select committee empowered to examine witnesses upon oath. The bill was made perpetual 25 Feb. 1774 (Cobbett, *Parl. Hist.* xvii. 1061–77).

for a repeal of Magna Charta, brought in by Mr Cofferer Dyson.[23]
Well! it is one o'clock in the morning, and I must go to bed. I have
passed one calm evening here alone, and have concluded it most agreeably by chatting with you. Tomorrow I must return into the bustle—
but I carry everywhere with me the melancholy impression of my life's
tranquillity being at an end. I see no prospect of peace for me, whether
my nephew lives, dies, relapses, or remains as he is at present. I love to
be occupied, but in my own way, unobserved and unconnected; my
joy is to read or write what I please: not letters of business, accounts
or applications; but good night; I have tired you and myself; my sole
excuse is, if you will take it for one, that I had other things to do that
I should have liked doing—but writing to you was the greatest pleasure, and according to my former habits I preferred what amused me
best.

Yours ever,

H. W.

To Mason, Thursday 7 April 1774

Printed from Mitford i. 137–41.

Strawberry Hill, April 7, 1774.

WELL, I have read Mr Warton's book;[1] and shall I tell you what
I think of it? I never saw so many entertaining particulars
crowded together with so little entertainment and vivacity. The facts
are overwhelmed by one another, as Johnstone's[2] sense is by words;
they are all equally strong. Mr Warton has amassed all the parts and
learning of four centuries, and all the impression that remains is, that
those four ages had no parts or learning at all. There is not a gleam
of poetry in their compositions between the scalds and Chaucer: nay
I question whether they took their metres for anything more than
rules for writing prose. In short, it may be the genealogy of versifica-

---

23. Jeremiah Dyson (1722–76), politician
and civil servant; 'a most useful tool of
Lord Bute, and of every succeeding ad-
ministration—but Lord Rockingham's'
(HW's note in Mason's *Satirical Poems* 63).
'Mr Dyson is appointed cofferer of the
Household in the room of Mr [Hans]

Stanley' (*London Chronicle* 1–3 March
1774, xxxv. 210).

---

1. *The History of English Poetry*. See
ante 23 March 1774.
2. *Sic* in Mitford, though Dr Johnson is
clearly meant.

tion with all its intermarriages and anecdotes of the family—but Gray's and your plan[3] might still be executed. I am sorry Mr Warton has contracted such an affection for his materials, that he seems almost to think that not only Pope, but Dryden himself have added few beauties to Chaucer.[4] The republic of Parnassus has lost a member; Dr Goldsmith is dead[5] of a purple fever,[6] and I think might have been saved if he had continued James's powder,[7] which had had much effect, but his physician[8] interposed. His numerous friends neglected him shamefully at last, as if they had no business with him when it was too serious to laugh.[9] He had lately written epitaphs[10] for them all, some of which hurt, and perhaps made them not sorry that his own was the first necessary. The poor soul had sometimes parts though never common sense.

I shall go to town tomorrow and send for my Lord Chesterfield's letters, though I know all I wished to see is suppressed.[11] The Stanhopes applied to the Chancellor for an injunction, and it was granted.[12] At last his Lordship permitted the publication on two con-

---

3. Gray collected materials for their collaborative history of English poetry, which seems to have been initiated by Mason. They abandoned it on learning of Warton's projected work (HW to Montagu 5 May 1761, Montagu i. 364 and n. 5; Gray's Corr. ii. 517 n. 4; William Powell Jones, Thomas Gray, Scholar, Cambridge, Mass., 1937, pp. 84–107, 180). Mason's MS commonplace book now in the Cathedral library at York contains many notes and extracts apparently intended for the history (information from Mr Robert A. Smith).

4. Warton says that Pope in his imitation of the 'House of Fame' has 'not only misrepresented the story, but marred the character of the poem' (History, i. 396). Of the 'Knight's Tale' he writes, 'We are surprised to find, in a poet of such antiquity, numbers so nervous and flowing: a circumstance which greatly contributed to render Dryden's paraphrase of this poem the most animated and harmonious piece of versification in the English language' (ibid. i. 367). Despite this compliment HW apparently felt that Warton had placed Chaucer too close to Dryden's throne. HW's preference of Dryden to Chaucer is even more marked post 14 April 1775 and 13 Nov. 1781.

5. Goldsmith died 4 April 1774.

6. 'An old name for purpura; but also applied vaguely to other fevers attended with purplish cutaneous eruptions' (OED). On the cause of Goldsmith's death, which was probably Bright's disease, see F. A. Pottle in N&Q 1925, 13th ser., cxlix. 11–12.

7. A widely used fever powder consisting of antimony and phosphate of lime. See ibid. and Cole i. 337 n. 1.

8. William Hawes (1736–1808), founder of the Royal Humane Society and author of several pamphlets on medical subjects, including An Account of the Late Dr Goldsmith's Illness, So Far as Relates to the Exhibition of Dr James's Powders, 1774.

9. This is untrue.

10. Retaliation, probably written in Feb. 1774, but not published until after Goldsmith's death.

11. For a full discussion of the circumstances of the publication of Chesterfield's letters by Eugenia Stanhope, widow of Chesterfield's son, who had kept the originals, see Sidney L. Gulick, Jr, 'The Publication of Chesterfield's Letters to His Son,' PMLA 1936, li. 165–77.

12. No record of this has been found (Gulick, op. cit. 168).

ditions,[13] that I own were reasonable, though I am sorry for them. The first, that the family might expunge what passages they pleased: the second, that Mrs Stanhope[14] should give up to them, without reserving a copy, Lord Chesterfield's portraits of his contemporaries, which he had lent to his son, and re-demanded of the widow, who gave them up, but had copied them. He burnt the originals himself,[15] just before he died, on disgust with Sir John Dalrymple's book, a new crime in that sycophant's libel.

Campbell's book[16] I have not looked into, and am told is very heavy —thus I have given you an account of my reading as my confessor in literature. I know nothing else, and am happy to have time for thinking of my amusement.

Your old friend[17] passes by here very often airing, and I am told looks ghastly and going.[18] It has been so much expected, that his post of governor[19] was destined, I hear, to Lord Bristol, and his Cinque Ports[20] I know were offered to Lord [George] Germaine,[21] for there seems to be a general comprehension, and nobody is to remain discontented, but those who see their reversions promised.

I don't ask about your own books, for I wish you to have a whole summer of readers to yourself, as I told you in my last. I do inquire when I shall see you, and hope it will be in the summer too, for in autumn I expect the gout, my biennial tyrant. If he is as severe as last time, he will be soon like the woman who killed her hen that laid golden eggs.

13. Actually the Chancellor advised the executors to make these conditions (ibid. 172).

14. Eugenia Peters (d. 1783), illegitimate dau. of ——Domville, m. (ante 1757) Philip Stanhope, Chesterfield's illegitimate son, to whom the letters were addressed. See Samuel Shellabarger, *Lord Chesterfield*, 1935, pp. 353–4 and *passim*; Gulick, op. cit. 165 n. 2; HW to Lady George Lennox 14 Oct. 1773.

15. HW was misinformed; they were not burnt, and are now in the possession of Mr Arthur A. Houghton (*A Checklist of Literary Manuscripts in the Library of Arthur A. Houghton, Jr*, compiled by Robert F. Metzdorf, privately printed, New York, 1953, pp. 27–8). For the publication of the *Characters* see *post* 18 April 1777.

16. *A Political Survey of Great Britain* (*ante* 23 March 1774).

17. Lord Holdernesse. See *ante* 3 Feb. 1774 and n. 3.

18. On 23 March 1774 Mason had written to Alderson, 'Here is news here in York, though I know not to [? from] whom it comes, that Lord H. is so ill that he cannot continue many days.' Five days later, however, he wrote again, 'I must tell you that my letter from Stonhewer dated 21st said Lord H. was growing better and one from him today of the 24th says nothing about him; I therefore fancy as the spring is coming on he may weather this bout.'

19. To the Prince of Wales.

20. He was lord warden of the Cinque Ports 1765–78.

21. Lord George Sackville (after 1770 Sackville-Germain) (1716–85), 3d and youngest son of 1st D. of Dorset; cr. (1782) Vct Sackville; army officer and politician. See also *post* i. 235 n. 8.

I forgot in my confession, to say that I have gone through half of Mr Bryant's first volume.[22] Lord John[23] has read both, and likes them, and thinks there is a great deal made out. I got far enough to see that the Tower of Babel might have been finished, if you would allow the workmen to begin at the top and bottom at once—but this was not my reason for mentioning the book. If you have it or it is in your neighbourhood, pray in the radicals read the article of Macar. You will find that there was a happy people, a favourite name, who lived in an island and were called Μακαρωνες. Mr Bryant is no joker, and I dare to swear never thought on our macaronies, when he was talking of Cushites and Ammonians. But I forgot that you are not as idle as I am, nor are bound to hear of every book I read. I can only say in excuse that when one is alone, one is apt to think of those one loves, and wishes to converse with them on common pursuits; is not it natural too, to wish to engage them in a little conversation? One tells them news, and wants them to care for it, in hopes of an answer. In short, you have won my affection, and must sometimes be troubled with it; but you are at liberty to treat it coolly or kindly, as you please.[24] The mass will remain, though you should not encourage me to send you papers full of it at a time. Adieu.

9th. I was too late for the post on Thursday and have since got Lord Chesterfield's letters,[25] which, without being well entertained, I sat up reading last night till between one and two, and devoured above 140.[26] To my great surprise they seem really written from the heart, not for the honour of his head, and in truth do no great honour to the last, nor show much feeling in the first, except in wishing for his son's fine gentlemanhood. He was sensible what a cub he had to work on, and whom two quartos of licking could not mould, for cub he re-

22. Of *Ancient Mythology,* which HW had already discussed *ante* 23 March 1774 in much the same terms as here.

23. Lord John Cavendish (1732–96), 4th son of the 3d D. of Devonshire; twice chancellor of the Exchequer, 1782, 1783. Mason had been Lord John's private tutor at Cambridge, and it was from his father that Mason had obtained his royal chaplaincy (*Gray's Corr.* i. 424 n. 5; Mitford ii. 411).

24. Mason had not answered HW's last two letters.

25. *Letters Written by the Late Right*

Honourable Philip Dormer Stanhope, Earl of Chesterfield, to His Son, Philip Stanhope, Esq., was published 7 April 1774 (Gulick, op. cit. 176). HW's copy, now WSL, contains some 500 marginalia in HW's hand. His great interest in the letters is reflected in his parody of them, 'The New Whole Duty of Woman, in a series of letters from a mother to a daughter,' written in May 1774 ('Short Notes,' GRAY i. 49; *Works* iv. 355–60).

26. Which fill 382 pages.

mained to his death. The repetitions are endless and tiresome. The
next volume, I see, promises more amusement, for in turning it
over, I spied many political names. The more curious part of all is
that one perceives by what infinite assiduity and attention his Lordship's own great character was raised and supported,—and yet in all
that great character what was there worth remembering but his *bon
mots;* his few fugitive pieces that remain show his genteel turn for
songs and his wit;—from politics he rather escaped well, than succeeded by them. In short, the diamond owed more to being brillianted
and polished, and well set, than to any intrinsic worth or solidity.

From MASON, ca Wednesday 13 April 1774

Printed from MS now WSL. This letter is dated, in HW's hand, 'York 1777.' That
this notation is wrong is shown by the following considerations: in the letter
Mason speaks of the fifth section of his life of Gray as just written, which makes
it evident that the letter was sent before 1775; Warton's *History of English Poetry,*
spoken of by Mason as recently received by him, was published 21 March 1774.
The letter is placed ca 13 April 1774 by HW's answer, 17 April 1774, where he
censures Mason for signing himself 'with perfect respect.'

THOUGH I have had the pleasure of receiving three letters from
you, I have not been so long in your debt as you may imagine,
for two of them travelled about the county as your letters usually do,
and, by being misdirected, saw Wakefeild, Rotherham, Aston, etc.,
before they reached me at York, where I have now been two months,
and must stay another before I am released from presiding over the
diurnal devotions of decayed tradesmen and card-playing old gentlewomen. I beg their pardon for not giving these latter the precedence
in my period, they would pull my surplice over my head, and un-
cover my shame if they knew it. So much for apology (if it can be called
by that name). Let me now thank you, which I do most cordially, for
the great entertainment these letters have given me, because they
treat precisely of those very topics which I cannot learn here and
which of all others I love to have news about. Continue them I beseech
you for sweet Saint Charity. I assure you my situation here in point
of literary matters is just as awkward as if I had lived in the 12th century when all the books in Oxford, as Mr Warton says, were contained

in a few chests in St Mary's Church.[1] 'Tis true, however, if I subscribe my half crown a quarter to the bookseller,[2] I can read all the Jemmy Jessamies[3] that come out, and at the middle of a month can have the high treat of that *Review* which was published on the first day of it. But this is the utmost York affords me. Yet by writing to Stonhewer I did get Tom Warton down by the coach in due time, but have yet only had time to get through his two preliminary dissertations[4] and to own the truth thought it more like wading than reading, but I intend to wade on whenever opportunity offers.

If I had really that papistical supremacy over letters that I once pretended to have to Mr Jerningham[5] I would prohibit everybody from studying antiquities except those very few that had from nature more wit than they knew what to do with. I think when you was young you were one of this class and therefore you would have escaped my prohibition. I know not whether this be a compliment to you or not. However, I mean to say that your antiquarian studies have done you (and you only of all I know) more good than harm. They have left you with as much of your wits about you as any man ought to be trusted with, and I dare say (if you would own it) you find those wits more tractable and manageable now, than before you was an antiquarian. I doubt when I have gone through the huge quarto now before me, I shall not judge thus favourably of what antiquities have done to its author.[6] I am already much displeased at what he says about the works of Ossian.[7] He does not seem by any means to believe them genuine, and yet either his rage for antiquity or his fear of Macpherson makes him pretend to think them so and yet in so weakly a way does he say the little he does in their defence that he will rather heighten the suspicion against them. By the way, I have been very

1. 'The library of that university, before the year 1300, consisted only of a few tracts, chained or kept in chests in the choir of St Mary's Church' (Thomas Warton, *History of English Poetry*, 1774–81, i, Dissertation II, sig. b₁v).

2. For the privilege of borrowing books from the local circulating library. On the institution see A. S. Collins, *Authorship in the Days of Johnson*, 1927, pp. 245–6; Alan Dugald McKillop, 'English Circulating Libraries, 1725–50,' *The Library*, 1934, 4th ser., xiv. 477–85.

3. That is, fashionable books of little importance.

4. I. On the origin of romantic fiction in Europe. II. On the introduction of learning into England.

5. See *ante* 2 March 1773 and n. 6.

6. This scepticism is remarkable in the light of Warton's reference, in his Preface, to Mason's 'liberality which ever accompanies true genius' (*History of English Poetry*, i. p. iv).

7. Ibid., Dissertation I, sig. g₂v–g₃v.

petulant and pert in some of my notes[8] on this subject to a few of Mr Gray's letters, and expect not only to have Macpherson himself but all the Mac's in Scotland upon my back. I had an opportunity of sending by a private hand (only the other day) the greatest part of my fourth section to Mr Stonhewer, from whom you may have a sight of it whenever you please. You will there read forty letters, and the twenty more which complete the section are now in the press, and I shall send them to him as they come from it. Two sheets more will go by this post.

I am in no haste about publication, and for the same reason that you withhold your last volume of *Anecdotes*[9] from the world, I am certain my notes, etc., will create me many enemies; and yet for my life I cannot help writing what I think the truth. Pray is the study of antiquities as useful towards checking a redundancy of truth as of wit? If so, I think that I too must commence antiquarian.

They tell me that my name has been mentioned in the House of Commons about literary property and that it was said 'I did not think it worth my while now to print the work I had in hand.'[10] I certainly never said this. I believe I might say that it would be well for me to wait and see whether anything would be done to secure one's property.[11] The truth is, as you know, that I wish to make the publication lucrative, and for what I think a good purpose.[12] Now as it was difficult to do this before the Lords' decision it is ten times more difficult to do it now, for what way have the booksellers now left to make themselves

---

8. HW advised against publishing these notes and Mason followed the advice, at least in part. See *post* 17 April, 23 April and n. 2.

9. The fourth volume of HW's *Anecdotes of Painting* was printed at SH in 1771 but not published until 1780. In a copy (now WSL) appears this note, written in an unidentified hand: 'This completion Mr Walpole told me he had no design of publishing himself—perhaps he might leave it behind him. "Truth," said he, "which I am determined to adhere to, might offend the near relations and friends of some of the artists that are dead, and prejudice those that are living"' (Hazen, *SH Bibliography* 63). It was chiefly Hogarth's widow whose feelings HW wished to spare; see his letter to her of 4 Oct. 1780.

10. No other record of this remark has been found. It was presumably made in

the course of the committee hearings on the petition of the booksellers to the House of Commons for relief against the adverse decision rendered in the House of Lords, a petition ultimately tabled. See *ante* 14 Feb. 1774 and A. S. Collins, *Authorship in the Days of Johnson*, 1927, pp. 103–5.

11. That is, Mason intended to wait for the decision of the House of Commons. He was planning to print in the *Memoirs* 'some fifty lines of hitherto unpublished poetry, which he believed would make him the legal owner of Gray's collected poems, as well as of the *Memoirs*. The matter was soon tested; John Murray I published in 1776 an edition of Gray's poems which incorporated Mason's new material' (Gaskell 17). For the sequel see *post* 26 May 1777.

12. A charitable fund in honour of Gray (*ante* 21 Sept. 1771 and *post* 17 April 1774).

atonement for their loss of copyright, but the easy and effectual way of pirating salable books? I verily believe they did this before the decision, and therefore I am sure they will do it now. One way that I thought of preventing this was by means of the head you saw, which I thought they could not so easily pirate, and whether I use this or no I mean to write my name in every copy,[13] for which I have the respectable authorities of Churchill[14] and Tristram Shandy.[15]—It does not appear to me that the case of authors, i.e., of those few writers who like me have published by means of a bookseller and have yet reserved their right of copy in themselves, has ever yet been considered in either of the debates. At present I have lost all right and title in all my own things merely because my bookseller neglected to enter them in Stationers' Hall.—But enough and more than enough on so dull a subject.

I saw near three weeks ago the advertisement of a *Familiar Epistle to the Author of the Heroic E[pistle] and Postscript*.[16] If it had been good for anything I imagine you would have mentioned it, as you know I liked those publications. Is not their author yet found out?

I will say nothing of my meditated visit to you and a very few other friends in town and its environs till I hear from my curate Mr Alderson, who is now at Syon Hill and who will soon give me an account not only of his Lordship's present state of health, but his intended motions. If either a journey to Bath or Yorkshire leaves me the Middlesex coast clear, I shall seize on that moment to visit you, for with this view I keep myself quite disengaged after I am free from my present confinement, which ends the 11th of next month, till which time I beg you to *remember* that I am *at York* and nowhere but at York.

Believe me to be with the most perfect respect, dear Sir,

Yours very sincerely,

W. MASON

13. Mason did not do this.
14. Charles Churchill (1731–64), the satirist, author of *The Rosciad*. Copies of *The Times*, 1764, and *Independence*, 1764, bear his autograph signature (Iolo A. Williams, *Seven XVIIIth-Century Bibliographies*, 1924, p. 202).

15. On Sterne's signatures in early editions of *Tristram Shandy* see W. L. Cross, *The Life and Times of Laurence Sterne*, New York, 1909, pp. 532–3.
16. Publication was announced in the *London Chronicle* 15–17 March 1774, xxxv. 263. The author has not been identified.

To Mason, Sunday 17 April 1774

Printed from Mitford i. 141–8.

April 17, 1774.

YOU may say what you please, my dear Sir, but, yes you will be tired with the sight of my letters; and this perhaps will be still less welcome than any of its predecessors. They, poor souls, had no excuse for their gossiping. This is written more seriously, and from good will prepense. In one word, my admiration has been ripened into warm friendship; and I do not see why friendship should be debarred of the privilege of telling one's friend his merits, when ill nature may so cheaply borrow its mask to reprove him for his faults. Mr Stonhewer brought me your section[1] yesterday, before I received your letter—and do you know, I am exceedingly discontent with it? [not][2] for its faults, for there is not a single blemish—but for your honesty and rashness—what can provoke you to be so imprudent? or do you think I love you so little, as to enjoy your free spirit and not tell you what a nest of hornets—nay of hyenas[3] you are incensing! I do beseech you to repress your indignation and cancel the papers in question. They will enrage, and you will have a life of warfare to lead to your dying day. Martyrdom itself might be delightful, if good could spring from the drops of blood. In the present case what benefit could arise? to yourself endless disquiet must be the consequence—well, but if I cannot touch your own intrepidity, I know I can stagger it, when your friend's memory is at stake. In Gray's own letters there is enough to offend; your notes added, will involve him in the quarrel, every silly story will be revived and his ashes will be disturbed to vex you. You know my idea was that your work should consecrate his name. To ensure that end, nothing should be blended with it that might make your work a book of party and controversy. By raising enemies to it, you will defeat in part your own benevolent purpose of a charitable fund;[4] when so numerous a host are banded against it, the sale will be clogged; reflect how many buyers you will exclude. At least

1. *Ante* ca 13 April and HW's comments below show that he had received from Stonhewer at least 'the greatest part' of the fourth section, that is, the forty-seven letters comprising *Memoirs* 170–303.

2. Mitford, 'nor.'
3. That is, the believers in Ossian.
4. See *ante* 21 Sept. 1771.

as there is no loving-kindness in my mercy, reserve the objectionable letters and your own notes to a future edition—nay it will be policy; if the book appears without its sting, Gray's character will be established, and unimpeached. Hereafter let them decry him if they can. I will dwell no longer on the subject; your letter tells me you are not in haste. One Mr Stonhewer will write, will tell you that the *neighbouring inconvenience*[5] will soon be removed one way,[6] and my last that it is likely to be removed every way.[7] I hope to see you at Strawberry Hill on the first dislodgment, and then we shall have time to squabble on the several articles I object to.

I have a few other difficulties, not of much consequence. I would omit every passage that hints at the cause of his removal from Peterhouse.[8] Don't you or do you know that that and other idle stories were printed in an absurd book called *Lexiphanes*?[9] I would be as wary as the Church of Rome is before they canonize a saint. They wait till he has been dead an hundred years, that no old woman may exist to tell a tale of the frailtie[s] of his youth, as a beldame did when Charles Borromée was to be sainted. ['I am glad of it,' said she, 'for he had my maidenhead.']¹⁰ Now I descend to verbal criticism. In p. 234, line 17 of the note, there is an *he* that is obscure. It means Gray, but by the construction refers to Akenside. 'He would tire of it as soon as *he* did.' The second *he* should be *Mr Gray*.¹¹ I have slight faults to find when

5. Lord Holdernesse (*ante* 3 Feb. 1774).

6. 'Pigot, who is now with the Eglins, says that he [Lord Holdernesse] is expected at Hornby in about three weeks' (Mason to Alderson 23 March 1774).

7. Lord Holdernesse rallied unexpectedly and on 3 June 1774 Mason wrote to Alderson: 'The news from the Continent is that your Lord is surprisingly better for his journey.'

8. Presumably following HW's advice, Mason gave in the published *Memoirs* (p. 241 n.) a vague and colourless account of Gray's removal from Peterhouse to Pembroke, attributing the action merely to the 'riots' and 'ill-behaviour' of 'two or three young men of fortune,' of whose conduct Gray had complained without avail. There is a more circumstantial account of the affair in a letter from John Sharp to John Denne, 12 March 1756, in Nichols, *Lit. Illus.* vi. 805; the incident is fully discussed in *Gray's Corr.* iii. 1216–20. Mitford's note on the removal from Peter-

house is supplemented in his own copy of his edition by a marginal MS note: 'In a catalogue of his goods that he moved from Peterhouse Gray has mentioned in one of his MS pocket books—rope ladders and fire bags' (i. 426).

9. *Lexiphanes,* a satire directed against Johnson, published anonymously in 1767, was written by Archibald Campbell (ca 1726–80). The story of Gray's troubles at Peterhouse does not appear in it, but is in another satire by Campbell, published, also anonymously, in the same year, *The Sale of Authors, A Dialogue, in Imitation of Lucian's Sale of Philosophers.* The pertinent passage, with notes and comment, is given in *Gray's Corr.* iii. 1217–9.

10. Her remark is omitted by Mitford, but Mrs Toynbee supplied it from Mitford's transcripts of passages omitted from the letters (Add. MSS 32563 fol. 49). The source of the story has not been found.

11. This went uncorrected in the first edition, the sheet being no doubt already

this is a big one; here is one still more diminutive: p. 239, for *d'ont* read *dont*.[12] In p. 241, note 1, Gray was not mistaken.[13] Before the Duc de Choiseul was disgraced,[14] I was privy to many abject solicitations made by Voltaire to both the Duke and Duchess for leave to go to Paris,[15]—but the Duke did not think it worth his while to quarrel with the clergy and parliament upon his account. The moment the Duke was out, Voltaire renewed the battery of flattery to the breast of the Duc d'Aiguillon,[16] but as the first part of the transaction was communicated to me in confidence, I would not have it made public while the parties are living. His letters on that occasion are extant, and some time or other I suppose will appear.[17]

In Algarotti's[18] letter are two false printings, for *quan io porso* it should be *quanto io porrò*, or rather I believe *potrò*, and for *sottescrivam* read *sottoscrivermi*.[19]

In defiance of my Lord Chesterfield, who holds it vulgar to laugh, and who says wit never makes one laugh,[20] I declare I laughed aloud,

printed off; in the second edition Mason changed the second 'he' to 'our author.'

12. I.e., the French word *dont*. The correction was made in the second edition.

13. Gray had written to Stonhewer: 'I am much obliged to you also for Voltaire's performance; it is very unequal . . . and looks like the work of a man that will admire his retreat and his Leman Lake no longer than till he finds an opportunity to leave it.' On this Mason wrote a note: 'I do not recollect the title of this poem, but it was a small one which M. de Voltaire wrote when he first settled at Ferney. By the long residence he has since made there, it appears either that our author was mistaken in his conjecture, or that an opportunity of leaving it had not yet happened.' The note is unchanged in the second edition. The poem was the *Épître de Monsieur de V—— en arrivant dans sa terre près du lac de Genève, en mars, 1755.* See *Gray's Corr.* i. 419, 432. In his own copy of *Mem. Gray* (now in the Harvard Library) HW has written after Mason's note: 'It proved a prophecy at last. Voltaire had sued to the Duc de Choiseul for leave to come to Paris in vain.'

14. See *ante* 13 Oct. 1772, n. 3.

15. HW noted in his 'Paris Journals,' 13 Sept. 1769: 'To Mme du Deffand. Many persons there, and Mme Denis, Voltaire's

niece, to solicit permission for him to come to Paris. Mme du Deffand said she would not enter into it till she had seen Mme de Choiseul. . . . She [Mme de Choiseul] bade Mme du Deffand say, she admired Voltaire, but loved her husband better, and as it might hurt him, especially at this crisis, she would not interfere' (du Deffand v. 329).

16. The Duc d'Aiguillon, Choiseul's chief enemy, was instrumental in his downfall.

17. They have never appeared. The published correspondence of Voltaire includes many flattering letters to the Duc and the Duchesse de Choiseul, but none that explicitly ask for help in obtaining permission to visit Paris.

18. Francesco Algarotti (1712–64), man of letters. His correspondence with Gray is discussed in *Gray's Corr.* iii. 1235–6.

19. Mason was able to alter these readings in the first edition, but they are still wrong: 'quanto io porrò' and 'sottoscrivermi.'

20. His objection to laughter appears in several of the letters, but HW doubtless has in mind i. 268 (1774 edn), where Chesterfield says, 'True wit or sense never yet made anybody laugh.' On this and the following page HW has made four marginalia in his copy. 'Chesterfield's Objection to

though alone, when I read of the professor[21] who died of turbot *and
made a good end.*[22] If this is not wit, I do not know what is. I am much
more in doubt of his Lordship's wit, since I have finished his letters.
Half of the last volume has many pretty or prettyish ones,[23] but sure
no professor of wit ever sowed so little in two such ample fields! He
seems to have been determined to indemnify himself for the falsehood
and constraint of his whole life by owning what an impostor he had
been. The work is a most proper book of laws for the generation in
which it is published, and has reduced the folly and worthlessness of
the age to a regular system, in which nothing but the outside of the
body and the superficies of the mind are considered. If a semblance of
morality is recommended, it is to be painted and curled, and Hippolytus himself may keep a w——,[24] provided she is married and a woman
of quality. In short if the idea were not an old one, I would write on
the back of this code, *The whole duty of man, adapted to the meanest
capacities.*[25]

If you like my telling you literary news, I will whenever I have any.
I now have time to read and enjoy myself. Your observation on Mr
Warton's civility to Macpherson is very just. It is like Protestants who
in Catholic countries bow to the sacrament, but do not kneel, and I
do not doubt but both the priests and the Scot would burn the
heretics if they could. I wish I could satisfy you about the Parliament's
intention on literary property, but as a bill is ordered in,[26] you will

Laughter' is discussed by Sprague Allen
in *Modern Language Notes*, 1923, xxxviii.
279–87.

21. Thomas Chapman (1717–60), D.D.,
master of Magdalene College, Cambridge,
1746–60.

22. *Hamlet* IV. v. 185. 'Our friend
Dr—— . . . is not expected here again in
a hurry. He is gone to his grave with five
fine mackerel (large and full of roe) in his
belly. He ate them all at one dinner; but his
fate was a turbot on Trinity Sunday, of
which he left little for the company besides
bones. He had not been hearty all the
week; but after this sixth fish he never held
up his head more, and a violent looseness
carried him off.—They say he made a very
good end' (Gray to Dr John Clerke 12 Aug.
1760, in *Mem. Gray* 282–3). See *Gray's Corr.*
ii. 693.

23. HW's marks of approval in the margin are more numerous in this portion of

the work than elsewhere. He singled out
for special notice the letter of 4 Oct. 1752,
apparently for its remarks on Voltaire and
epic poetry. Next after this he seems to
have liked the letters of 19 Oct. 1753 and
1 Feb. 1754.

24. Hippolytus became a type of the
continent male by resisting the advances
of his stepmother, Phædra.

25. A seventeenth-century devotional
work that remained popular throughout
the next century was *The Whole Duty of
Man, Laid Down in a Plain and Familiar
Way, for the Use of All, but Especially the
Meanest Reader*, 1658. It is now generally
attributed to Richard Allestree (1619–81).
HW's copy, the 1727 edition, was sold SH
iii. 39.

26. The House of Commons had voted
24 March that leave be granted to bring in
a bill on behalf of the booksellers who protested the decision of the House of Lords

know more of the event before you think of publishing. I scarce know more of the Parliament's transactions than what I read in the papers. When I was at Rome, I never pried into the actions of the Senatore di Roma. All I know of our senate is, that it is held in the Temple of Concord.

I inquire so little after their transactions, that I did not hear your name had been mentioned on that bill. I was told that a name of much less consequence, my own, was quoted by Mr Wedderburne,[27] I protest I did not ask whether in approbation or dislike, or to what end. Apropos, I did hear that the other day Lord North declaiming against the Opposition (I don't guess where he found them) , and saying they meant nothing but pensions and places,[28] turned to his right, and there sat Cornwall[29] blushing up to the eyes; turning short from a crimson conscience, on the right sat Wedderburne, pale as death;[30] come, there is some merit in crimson.

You ask about answers to books: in good sooth I never read such matters, nor can tell who does but their authors. At least I never heard of the one you mention,[31] nor disturb the departed. I must now say a word about that insignificant personage myself. I will not quarrel with you about what you say of my wit. Whether I have it, or have had it, I neither know nor care. It was none of my doing; and even if I had it, I am guilty of never having improved it, and of putting it to very trifling uses. Whatever it was, it is gone with my spirits, or passed off with my youth—which I bear the loss of too with patience, though a better possession. But I am seriously hurt with those two words at the conclusion of your letter, *perfect respect.* Jesus! my dear Sir, to me, and from you, *perfect respect!* on what grounds, on what title?—what is there in me respectable? To have flung away so many advantages in so

on copyright. The bill was presented 22 April (Cobbett, *Parl. Hist.* xvii. 1089).

27. Wedderburn's remarks on HW have not been found.

28. The text of this speech also has not been found.

29. Charles Wolfran Cornwall (1735–89); M. P. Grampound 1768–74, Winchelsea 1774–84, Rye 1784–9: Speaker 1780–9. He was assisted in his political career by his marriage to Elizabeth Jenkinson (1730–1809), sister of Charles Jenkinson, later Earl of Liverpool. In 1772 HW had described Cornwall as 'a comely sensible man, decent in his manner and matter, but of no

vivacity' (*Last Journals* i. 80). But in 1774, when Cornwall became one of the lords of the Treasury, HW referred to him (ibid. i. 311) as 'the late patriot, Mr Cornwall (who had taken a pension for life only as a retaining fee).' He had received his £1500 pension in 1763, after acting as a commissioner for liquidating the German accounts (GM 1789, lix pt i. 87).

30. For HW's opinion of Wedderburn and his time-serving see *ante* 25 Sept. 1771, n. 7.

31. The *Familiar Epistle to the Author of the Heroic Epistle and Postscript* (see *ante* ca 13 April 1774).

foolish a manner as I have done, is that respectable? to have done nothing in my life that is praiseworthy, not to have done as much good as I might; does this deserve respect from so good a man as you are? have I turned even my ruling passion, that preservative I call it, pride to account? No—yet hear my sincere confession; I had rather be unknown, and have the pride of virtue, than be Shakespeare, which is all I can say of mortal wit. Nay I would rather accept that pride of virtue preferably to all earthly blessings, for its own comfortable insolence, though I were sure to be annihilated the moment I die; so far am I from thinking with the saint, that suffering virtue without a future reward, would of all conditions be the most miserable. There are none, or few real evils, but pain and guilt. The dignity of virtue makes everything else a trifle, or very tolerable. Penury itself may flatter one, for it may be inflicted on a man for his virtue, by that paltry thing [of] ermine and velvet a king. Pray, therefore, never respect me any more, till my virtues have made me a beggar. I am not melancholy, nor going to write *divine poems*. I have a more manly resolution, which is to mend myself as much as I can, and not let my age be as absurd as my youth. I want to respect myself, the person in the world whose approbation I desire most. The next title I aspire to, but not till that person is content with me, is that of being

Your sincere friend,

H. W.

PS. You will be diverted to hear that a man who thought of nothing so much as the purity of his language, I mean Lord Chesterfield, says, 'You and *me* shall not be well together,' and this not once, but on every such occasion. A friend of mine says, it was certainly to avoid that female inaccuracy of *they don't mind you and I,* and yet the latter is the least bad of the two.[32] He says too, Lord Chesterfield does, that for forty years of his life he never used a word without stopping a moment to think if he could not find a better.[33] How agreeably he passed his time!

32. For a discussion of eighteenth-century usage in expressions involving the cases of personal pronouns see Sterling Andrus Leonard, *The Doctrine of Correctness in English Usage,* Madison, Wisconsin, 1929, pp. 186–8.

33. 'It is now above forty years since I have never spoken, nor written one single word, without giving myself at least one moment's time to consider, whether it was a good one or a bad one, and whether I could not find out a better in its place'

From MASON, Saturday 23 April 1774

Printed from MS now WSL.

York, April 23d, 1774.

Dear Sir,

I HAVE cried *peccavi* in so many and long periphrases to Stonhewer and Dr Hurd[1] that I have no more words left to express my contrition. I will, therefore, only say to you that only have patience with me and I will cancel every syllable that can offend either Mr Macpherson or the most itchy Highlander that ever came to a register office in search of perfarment.[2] I now know and feel my own old English nothingness and I never speak to my Scotch printer's[3] Scotch devil without rising from my writing-desk and desiring him to be seated.—But as I have said before, you must have patience with me, and having stopped the press, you must suffer me to let it remain quiet for some months, before I open it again with my fifth section. In the mean while be assured I will not be idle, but will try to improve myself under the tuition of that great master of urbanity my Lord Chesterfield, who being dead yet speaketh. I will prove by my own example that his work which Mrs Eugenia says will improve the youth, shall also improve the grown gentlemen of these kingdoms.[4] I have already under his tuition begun to treat my conscience as Jack and Martin in

(letter of 9 Dec. 1749, Chesterfield's *Letters*, 1774, i. 510). HW has placed a large exclamation point opposite this passage in his copy, and in the Introduction to his parody of the letters (*ante* 7 April 1774, n. 25) he wrote, 'He, who in forty years never uttered a word without stopping to search for a better, could not have been so indolent as not to cultivate the duties of humanity, had he discovered that they tended to recommend the possessor' (*Works* iv. 355–6).

———

1. Richard Hurd (1720–1808), D.D.; Bp of Lichfield, 1774, of Worcester, 1781. Mason's letter on this subject is not in their printed correspondence (ed. Whibley, 1932).

2. Mason seems to have reconsidered this offer to 'cancel every syllable' offensive to Macpherson, for not only do uncomplimentary remarks by Gray about Macpherson

appear in the *Memoirs* but also several sardonic footnotes by Mason on the passages. That some of the footnotes were removed is shown by Mason's later references (*post* 9 Aug. and 2 Oct. 1774) to 'chasms.' Leonard Whibley, in his Appendix 'Gray and James Macpherson' in *Gray's Corr.* iii. 1223–6, remarks, 'The "objectionable notes" which he [Mason] took out must have stated his doubts more plainly and more forcibly' (ibid. iii. 1226).

3. The superintendent of Ann Ward's press in York was David Russell (Davies, *York Press* 261). Mason spoke of Russell as the printer of *Mem. Gray* (Mason-Bedingfeld correspondence in the Huntington Library).

4. Eugenia Stanhope in the Advertisement (i. p. vii) to the 1774 edition expressed a hope that the letters would prove 'of as much utility to the youth of these kingdoms' as they were to Chesterfield's son.

the *Tale of the Tub* did their old coats.[5] The first pluck I gave was at the tag of my sincerity. I pulled hard and found the operation painful, nay it still hangs by two or three strong threads, but I hope in time to get fairly quit of it. I will next have a bout with my simplicity. This tag I know will occasion a great rent, but I will piece it up with any French frippery that comes to hand. When this is over there will remain only a little religion and morality which will drop of themselves. Indeed, they are so sewed to the first tag that if one comes fairly off the two others will come with it. And so, when all of them are detached, I will devoutly consume them in one great *Sacrifice to the Graces*.[6] If I succeed in this operation what have you not to expect from me when I come in my regenerated state to visit you in your Gothic castle of Strawberry? I on my part expect you will think of no personages of less *monde* fit to invite to our *partie carré* than Lord Carlisle and Mr James.[7] The former, one would hope, cannot offend me by laughing, even if the latter should be guilty of a *bon mot*. Take care, however, that I never see anything like *mauvaise honte,* for I die at the sight of it. Apropos to *mauvaise honte,* pray does not the last page of your last letter smell terribly of its asafœtida? You seem ashamed that I should respect you, and give this fine reason for it, that you do not deserve respect. *Homme sauvage et vulgaire!* Who ever had respect that deserved it? Who ever was without it that did not deserve it? Was I writing in my old character, I should say that a penitent of all other persons deserved the most respect, but penitence is not now in my catechism. Besides this I have another quarrel with you. You call me somewhere or other 'so good a man.' *Mon dieu! Bon!* the phrase is barbarous. It is now never applied except in the feminine to a *gouvernante.* In your next I suppose you will call me *ma bonne,* and make a Mademoiselle Kromm[8] of me. These strictures, my dear Sir, I hope

---

5. Peter, Martin, and Jack in Swift's satire represent the Roman, Anglican, and Dissenting churches. They disobey their father's injunctions not to alter or repair their coats.

6. Which was what Chesterfield constantly urged his son to do.

7. Probably the 'Mr James' mentioned as a typical macaroni in HW to Strafford 3 July 1769, who may be the West Indies proprietor whose losses are described in HW to Lady Ossory 4 and 9 Jan. 1781. Mitford identifies him (i. 427) as 'Haughton James, a West-India proprietor,' and says that he

'formed two libraries, sold the first to Robert Heathcote, Esq., and the second to Mr Thomas Payne, the bookseller.' In *Caribbeana,* 1912, ii. 1, Vere L. Oliver reproduces the bookplate of Haughton James (ca 1738–1813), son of Haughton James of Jamaica (GM 1813, lxxxiii pt ii. 508).

8. Mademoiselle Krohme (d. 1777), French teacher in the royal nursery 1768–77. Mason was probably acquainted with her, for when she died she was living at Lord Holdernesse's London house (*London Chronicle* 29 March–1 April 1777, xli. 307; *Court and City Registers*).

will have a good effect upon you and make the style of your next a little more *décrotté;* in the mean while you must own that the friend of Madame du Deffand has lived to a fine time, when he sees himself the pupil (in point of *politesse*) of a Yorkshire parson.

One word of serious and I have done. I am much more sorry to find you object to the manner I have treated Gray's removal to Pembroke, than for other matters which you think of more consequence. I had read *Lexiphanes* in its lifetime; it has been dead long, and I hardly think what I say will revive it. In a life so void of events, how is it possible to omit this? would not the omission make the world believe him more wrong than he really was? I think they would supply the omission from *Lexiphanes,* which would be the means of his resuscitation. But this and everything else shall be altered to all your minds if you give me time for it, but indeed and indeed I am at present heartily tired of the work itself, and if you knew the pains and the thought it has taken me to arrange the letters in order to form that variety which I aimed at to make it read pleasantly you would not wonder I was tired. I believe I have seldom written a sprightly note but with a view of enlivening a less sprightly letter. All these, therefore, I can easily give up, for I would much sooner be guilty of publishing even a dull book than by a lively one hurt any deserving friend, or create him an enemy. I have filled my paper so full that I have now no room for *respect* even if I durst use it.

W. M.

To Mason, ca May 1774

Printed from HW's *Works,* v. 653–5, where it is undated. Mrs Toynbee, following Cunningham, placed it among the letters for 1782, but in Toynbee *Supp.* ii. 163 it is correctly dated with reference to HW's letter to Mme du Deffand 1 May 1774, which contains similar references to Pliny and Jupiter (DU DEFFAND iv. 47). Miss Berry must have printed from a draft, or possibly HW did not send the letter. Since Mason did not refer to it, the latter possibility is the more likely.

I HAVE been reading a new French translation of the elder Pliny,[1] of whom I never read but scraps before; because, in the poetical

1. The first volume of the *Histoire natu-relle de Pline,* trans. Louis Poinsinet de   Sivry, 12 vols, 1771–82. HW's set of six volumes was sold SH v. 184.

manner in which we learn Latin at Eton, we never become acquainted with the names of the commonest things, too undignified to be admitted into verse; and therefore I never had patience to search in a dictionary for the meaning of every substantive. I find I shall not have a great deal less trouble with the translation, as I am not more familiar with their common *drogues* than with the Latin. However, the beginning goes off very glibly, as I am not yet arrived below the planets. But do you know that this study, of which I have never thought since I learnt astronomy at Cambridge, has furnished me with some very entertaining ideas! I have long been weary of the common jargon of poetry. You bards have exhausted all the nature we are acquainted with; you have treated us with the sun, moon, and stars, the earth and the ocean, mountains and valleys, etc., etc., under every possible aspect. In short, I have longed for some American poetry, in which I might find new appearances of nature, and consequently of art. But my present excursion into the sky has afforded me more entertaining prospects, and newer phenomena. If I was as good a poet as you are, I would immediately compose an idyll, or an elegy, the scene of which should be laid in Saturn or Jupiter; and then, instead of a niggardly soliloquy by the light of a single moon, I would describe a night illuminated by four or five moons at least, and they should be all in a perpendicular or horizontal line, according as Celia's eyes (who probably in that country has at least two pair) are disposed in longitude or latitude. You must allow that this system would diversify poetry amazingly.—And then Saturn's belt! which the translator says in his notes, is not round the planet's waist, like the shingles, but is a globe of crystal that encloses the whole orb, as you may have seen an enamelled watch in a case of glass.[2] If you do not perceive what infinitely pretty things may be said, either in poetry or romance, on a brittle heaven of crystal, and what furbelowed rainbows they must have in that country, you are neither the Ovid nor natural philosopher I take you for. Pray send me an eclogue directly upon this plan—and I give you leave to adopt my idea of Saturnian Celias having their everything quadrupled—which would form a much more entertaining rhapsody than Swift's thought of magnifying or diminishing the species in his *Gulliver*. How much more execution a fine woman

2. 'Telle est mon opinion, à ne considérer cet anneau que comme une simple bande; car je pense, au reste, que cette prétendue bande est une véritable bulle ou globe concave, continu et transparent, que sert en tout sens d'enveloppe et de coque à Saturne' (*Histoire naturelle de Pline*, vol. i, 1771, Bk ii, p. 34 n.).

would do with two pair of *piercers!* or four! and how much longer the
honeymoon would last, if both the sexes have (as no doubt they have)
four times the passions, and four times the means of gratifying them!
—I have opened new worlds to you—You must be four times the poet
you are, and then you will be above Milton, and equal to Shakespeare,
the only two mortals I am acquainted with, who ventured beyond the
visible diurnal sphere, and preserved their intellects. Dryden himself
would have talked nonsense, and, I fear, bawdy, on my plan; but you
are too good a divine, I am sure, to treat my quadruple love but Pla-
tonically. In Saturn, notwithstanding their glass case, they are supposed to be very cold; but Platonic love of itself produces frigid con-
ceits enough, and you need not augment the dose—But I will not
dictate. The subject is new; and you, who have so much imagination,
will shoot far beyond me. Fontenelle would have made something of
the idea even in prose; but Algarotti would dishearten anybody from
attempting to meddle with the system of the universe a second time
in genteel dialogue. Good night! I am going to bed.—Mercy on me!
if I should dream of Celia with four times the usual attractions!

To Mason, Tuesday 19 July 1774

Printed from Mitford i. 153–4.

Strawberry Hill, July 19, 1774.

I SEND you by the Fraser Mercury[1] the itinerary of Mr Gray[2] with
my manuscript additions.[3] I don't know whether I have made
them too long or too short, but as you are entirely at liberty to curtail

1. I.e., William Fraser in the secretary of state's office. See *ante* 9 Sept. 1772.

2. This was *A Catalogue of the Antiquities, Houses, Parks, Plantations, Scenes, and Situations in England and Wales*, printed by Mason in 1773 in an edition of 100 copies (C. S. Northup, *A Bibliography of Thomas Gray*, New Haven, 1917, p. 69). See next letter. Gray wrote to Wharton 21 Feb. 1758: 'The drift of my present studies is to know, wherever I am, what lies within reach that may be worth seeing, whether it be building, ruin, park, garden, prospect, picture, or monument; to whom it does or has belonged, and what has been the characteristic and taste of different ages. . . .

I am persuaded whenever my list is finished you will approve it' (*Gray's Corr.* ii. 564–5). Mason's note on the catalogue reads: 'He wrote it, under its several divisions, on the blank pages of a pocket atlas. I printed lately a few copies of this catalogue for the use of some friends curious in such matters; and when I am sufficiently furnished with their observations and improvements upon it, shall perhaps reprint it and give it to the public, as a shorter and more useful pocket companion to the English traveller than has hitherto appeared' (*Mem. Gray* 260).

3. These were apparently never printed and their present whereabouts is unknown.

or lengthen, or omit such as you disapprove, it does not signify what
they are. They have indeed a fault I cannot mend, unless by time, and
which yet I probably shall not mend. I mean they are not complete,
for there are some considerable places that I never saw, and I am
grown too lazy since I can walk but little, to think of visiting them
now.

I shall take care how I wish earnestly again for your coming southward, you gave me so little of your time and was so much in request,
that I was only tantalized.[4] I like your fixed stars that one can pore
at when one pleases; but there is such a fuss with you comets, that even
women and children must know all about them.

I know nothing but that we have deplorable weather; the sun like
you has called but once at Strawberry. To make amends the cold has
brought on the winter fruits so fast, that I had a codlin tart today, and
expect pears and apples ripe before peaches and nectarines. I wish we
had never imported those southern delicacies, unless we had brought
their climate over too. We should have been very happy with our hips
and haws and rainy days, and *called it luxury*.[5] I cannot afford to have
hot-houses, and glass-houses, and acres of tanner's bark, as every trade-
man has at his villa, or at his mistress's villa. I kill my own strawberries
and cream, and can aim no higher.

Do you know that it would be charity to send me something to
print, or to tell me what I shall print? My press is at a dead stand, and
I would fain employ it while I may, without permission of a licenser,
for though it has always been as harmless as if it was under the canon[6]
of Sion Hill, it would be *vocal no more*,[7] if it might only utter Dutch
Bibles[8] or editions *in usum Delphini*.[9] I know you have twenty things
in your *portefeuille*. I will print as few copies as you please. I have
no ambition of serving or amusing the public, and think of nothing
but diverting myself and the few I love. What signifies taking the

4. The date and duration of Mason's
visit to SH are not known. He was in
Curzon Street by 23 May and remained until 8 July, as we know from his letters to
Alderson.

5. A reminiscence and development of
the fifth paragraph of *Spectator* No. 69.
'Called it luxury' is probably an imperfect recollection of a line from Addison's
Cato (I. iv. 71), 'Blesses his stars and thinks
it luxury.' HW quotes the line in a letter
to Mann 3 Oct. 1743.

6. Cunningham and Toynbee read 'cannon,' but Mitford was right: HW means
under the direction of Lord Holdernesse,
the owner of Syon.

7. 'Vocal no more, since Cambria's fatal
day' (Gray, *The Bard*, l. 27).

8. An allusion to Lady Holdernesse's
Dutch birth.

9. I.e., for the Prince of Wales, to whom
Holdernesse was governor.

trouble to be put I don't know how soon, into an Index Expurgatorius! today is ours, let us enjoy it.

Yours ever,

H. W.

From Mason, Tuesday 9 August 1774

Printed from MS now WSL.
Address: The Honourable Horace Walpole, Arlington Street, London.
Postmark: ROTHERHAM.

Aston, August 9th, 1774.

Dear Sir,

I OUGHT to have thanked you much sooner for your notes on Mr Gray's itinerary and your obliging letter. These additions will be extremely useful to the public, if ever the public deserves well enough of any person to reprint the catalogue in question.[1] Whether I shall take that pains is at present very doubtful. If I do, it will not be for the sake of that public, but only to get its money, to make a better use of than it usually makes of it itself.

I have employed myself since I came down in endeavouring to supply the chasms in the sheets where the objectable notes,[2] etc., occurred, and I purpose to call at York the latter end of this week in my way to Scarbrough and shall leave the altered copy with Mr Bedinfeld[3] that my printer and he may settle the text. When this is done I mean on my return hither to proceed as speedily as I can to a conclusion, for I begin now to be very desirous of having it finished.

1. Gray's *Catalogue* was reprinted in *A Supplement to the Tour through Great Britain*, published in London by G. Kearsley in 1787, without HW's notes. Though the title-page announces 'several additions by another hand' (unidentified), the text of the catalogue is identical with that printed by Mason in 1773 (C. S. Northup, *A Bibliography of Thomas Gray*, New Haven, 1917, p. 69; BM Cat.).

2. That is, the deleted matter relating to Macpherson (*ante* 23 April 1774, n. 2, and *post* 2 Oct. 1774, n. 2). This form of 'objectionable,' now obsolete, is recorded by the OED in quotations dated 1775 and 1776.

3. Edward Bedingfeld (1730–*post* 1795), York acquaintance and correspondent of Mason who helped to see some of his works through the press. Mason wrote of him to Gray 28 June 1763, 'Of all the admirers I have had in my time, I think he would tire me the most was I to have much of him' (*Gray's Corr.* ii. 801). On Bedingfeld see Joseph Gillow, *A Literary and Biographical History, or Bibliographical Dictionary of the English Catholics*, [1885–1902], i. 165–6; *Catholic Record Society: Miscellanea VI, Bedingfeld Papers, etc.*, 1909, *passim*, especially Bedingfeld's journal (pp. 208–10) and p. 236.

I paid a visit the other day at Wentworth Castle[4] where I found the noble owners very solitary,[5] but to all appearance perfectly happy. They had been that morning at Wortley[6] on a visit to Lady Bute,[7] who is now there settling accounts with her stewards from morning to night. Lady Mary Coke[8] is expected at Wentworth Castle next week and they wish much for you *per trastullarsi coll' istessa Principessa*,[9] neither do they think the excuse you make of waiting at Strawberry for a much less entertaining biennial companion[10] a very good or even a rational one. I must own I have the honour to think precisely as they do on this occasion and I heartily hope you will be disappointed of your company even if you expect him or her (for I know not of which sex the creature is of) ever so impatiently. Lucian I know makes her female and a goddess,[11] but Lucian was a heathen and wrote heathen Greek.

You flatter me much by offering to open your Strawberry press for me, but I have nothing by me that in any sort merits such an honour. Scraps I have and fragments, dramatic and lyric, in plenty, but nothing in any sort finished or capable of being finished at present. Why not return again to your *Miscellaneous Antiquities?* Why should the neglect of the public prevent you from proceeding?[12] There may come a public hereafter who will not neglect them and if such a public never comes, your private amusement is still secured. Try them if you please

4. The Yorkshire seat of William Wentworth (1722–91), 2d E. of Strafford, HW's correspondent.

5. Lady Louisa Stuart wrote of Lord and Lady Strafford: 'They had few neighbours, fewer visitors; he was too stiff to make new acquaintances; he hated humble companions; and, in short, Wentworth Castle became a magnificent hermitage. . . . Both of them bitterly deplored their ill-fate in being childless' ('Some Account of John Duke of Argyll and his Family,' *The Letters and Journals of Lady Mary Coke, 1756–74*, 1889–96, i. p. xlviii).

6. The Yorkshire seat of John Stuart (1713–92), 3d E. of Bute. Lady Strafford's sister, Elizabeth, had married the Hon. James Stuart Mackenzie of Rosehaugh, brother of Lord Bute.

7. Mary Wortley Montagu (1718–94), dau. of Edward and Lady Mary Wortley Montagu; m. (1736) Lord Bute; cr. (1761) Bns Mount Stuart of Wortley.

8. Lady Mary Campbell (1727–1811),

dau. of John, 2d D. of Argyll, and sister of Lady Strafford; m. (1747) Edward, Vct Coke; HW's correspondent, noted for her delusions of grandeur and persecution.

9. 'To sport with that same Princess.' Mason had originally written 'Contessa,' but emended it to 'Principessa' to point up Lady Mary Coke's weakness for Royalties, or perhaps as a specific allusion to her fancy that she was the widow of Edward Augustus, Duke of York (see BERRY ii. 11 n. 6 and *post* 31 May 1778).

10. The gout (see *ante* 14 Feb. 1774, n. 5).

11. The goddess Podagra in the burlesque poem *Tragopodagra*, attributed to Lucian. See J. D. Rolleston, 'Lucian and Medicine,' *Janus: Archives internationales pour l'histoire de la médecine et la géographie médicale*, 1915, xx. 99–101.

12. HW had announced *ante* 2 March 1773 that he was giving up *Miscellaneous Antiquities*. See also HW to Cole 18 Feb. 1773, COLE i. 300.

with the more modern parts of Mr Gray's transcripts, my Lord Rochester's letters,[13] for instance. I'll lay my life they will devour them greedily. You know that neither I nor my curate perfectly relished Sir Thomas Wyat's eloquence,[14] and yet my curate and I are neither of us the dupes of fashion, but speak what we think in all simplicity. Treat us therefore with something more to *our* goût, and the world, even the great world, will not disdain to follow our plain Yorkshire taste.

I believe Mr Palgrave and I shall stay about a fortnight or three weeks at Scarbro, in the mean while a letter directed to me here NEAR ROTHERHAM (I write it in capitals to impress it on your memory) will be forwarded to me. Mr Palgrave begs his best compliments; as to myself I hope I need not say how truly and sincerely I am

Yours,

W. MASON

To MASON, Tuesday 23 August 1774

Printed from Mitford i. 154–6.

At the end of the letter Mitford printed the list of titles given below, with this note: 'N.B. This catalogue of Gray's MS poetry is in Mason's writing at the end of Walpole's letter. Ed.' But the list includes transcripts and original prose as well as verse. Several of the titles do not occur elsewhere, and are unexplained.

'Proposals for printing his own travels.[1]
Duke of Newcastle's Journal going to Hanover.[2]
History of the Devil, a Fragment.[3]

13. Gray's transcript of Rochester's letters has not been found (see the register of Gray manuscripts in William Powell Jones, *Thomas Gray, Scholar*, Cambridge, Mass., 1937, pp. 175–81).

14. In the introductory life of Wyatt in *Miscellaneous Antiquities* No. 2 (see *ante* 9 May 1772, and nn. 1–2). HW wrote, 'His soul was vigorous, his genius manly . . . his employments, his letters, his orations, speak how able a statesman he was, how acute an orator' (p. 9).

1. A *jeu d'esprit* sent to Wharton from

Florence 12 March 1740 (*Gray's Corr.* i. 138–40). In his copy of the correspondence Mitford has marked this item 'P.' (as also the 4th, 5th, and 6th items below), probably standing for 'printed.' Mitford had printed the 'proposals' in his 1816 edn of Gray's *Works*, ii. 71–7.

2. This may refer to the Duke of Newcastle's journey to Hanover in June 1748 (see HW to Mann 7 June 1748 and n. 3).

3. Probably the 'History of Hell' mentioned *ante* 20 March 1773. Nothing more is known of it.

Jemmy Twitcher's Courtship.4
Inscription on the villa of a decayed statesman.5
Shakespeare to Mr M[ason]'s housekeeper.6
Fragments of an act of Parliament relating to monuments erected in Westminster
    Abbey.7
The Mob Grammar.
Character of the Scotch.'

EXCUSE me, but I cannot take your advice nor intend to print any more for the public; when I offer you my press it is most selfishly, and to possess your writings, for I would only print a few copies for your friends and mine. My last volume of the *Anecdotes of Painting* has long been finished,8 and as a debt shall some time or other be published, but there I take my leave of Messieurs the readers. Let Dr Johnson please this age with the fustian of his style and the meanness of his spirit! both are good and great enough for the taste and practice predominant. I think this country sinking fast into ruin; and when it is become an absolute monarchy and thence insignificant, I do not desire to be remembered by slaves and in a French province. I would not be Virgil or Boileau on such conditions; present amusement is all my object in reading, writing or printing. To gratify the first especially, I wish to see your poem9 finished. You, 'who erewhile the happy garden sung,' continue to 'sing recovered Paradise'!10 I am less impatient for Gray's life, being sure of seeing it, whether published or not: and as I conclude neither his letters nor Latin poems will be admired to the height they deserve, I am jealous of his fame, and do not like its being cast before swine. In short I wish his and your writings to meet with a fate that not many years ago was reckoned an ignominy, that they may be sent to the colonies! for

Arts and sciences will travel west11

and

4. I.e., 'The Candidate.' See *post* 16 Sept. 1774.
5. The lines on Lord Holland; see *ante* 1 Dec. 1773 and n. 5.
6. Verses sent by Gray to Mason in July 1765; see *Gray's Corr.* ii. 879–80.
7. Apparently an unidentified transcript. Gray's notes on English cathedrals in his commonplace-books (now at Pembroke College) include notes on Westminster Ab-

bey (Roger Martin, *Chronologie de . . . Thomas Gray*, 1931, p. 146).
8. As already noted, the volume was not published until 1780.
9. *The English Garden.*
10. *Paradise Regained*, ll. 1–3.
11. A favourite quotation—or invention —of HW's. He used it in his letter to Mann 13 May 1752 and to Montagu 23 Dec. 1759.

The sad Nine in Britain's evil hour[12]

will embark for America.

I have been in Gloucestershire[13] and can add a little to the catalogue,[14] having seen Berkeley Castle, Thornbury Castle, and a charming small old house of the Abbots of Gloucester. Indeed I could not enjoy the first, for the Earl[15] was in it with all his militia,[16] and dispelled visions. To Wentworth Castle I shall certainly make no visit this year. If I went any journey it would be to Paris; but indolence persisting in her apprehensions of the gout, though I have had no symptoms of it for some time, will fix me here and hereabouts. I discover charms in idleness that I never had a notion of before, and perceive that age brings pleasures as well as takes away. There is serenity in having nothing to do, that is delicious: I am persuaded that little princes assumed the title of Serene Highness from that sensation.

Your assured friend,

HORACE LE FAINÉANT

Given at our Castle of Nonsuch,[17] Aug. 23, 1774.

Salute our trusty and well beloved The Palsgrave on our part.

To Mason, Friday 16 September 1774

Printed from Mitford i. 159–60, *Gray's Corr.* iii. 1241–2, and Add. MSS 32563 fol. 49. See nn. 7 and 9 below.

Strawberry Hill, Sept. 16, 1774.

WHAT is the commonest thing in the world?—Lord! how can you be so dull as not to guess? why to be sure, to hunt for a

12. Adapted from 'The sad Nine in Greece's evil hour' (Gray, 'The Progress of Poesy,' l. 77).

13. HW wrote a long descriptive account of his Gloucestershire visit to Cole 15 Aug. 1774 (COLE i. 340–5). See also *Country Seats* 75–6.

14. Gray's *Catalogue* (see *ante* 19 July 1774, n. 2).

15. Frederick Augustus Berkeley (1745–1810), 5th E. of Berkeley.

16. Berkeley was lord-lieutenant of the county. 'Lord-lieutenants, when first in-

troduced in the 16th century, were to take an active part in the defence of the realm, and down to 1871 they had extensive powers with regard to the militia' (OED).

17. HW's fantasy of a do-nothing prince is heightened by his adopting the name of Henry VIII's palace at Cheam in Surrey. He was partial to it because of Hentzner's account—'One would imagine everything that architecture can perform to have been employed in this one work' (Paul Hentzner, *Journey into England*, SH, 1757, pp. 82–4).

thing forty times, and give it over, and then find it when you did not look for it, exactly where you had hunted forty times. This happened to me this very morning, and overjoyed I am; I suppose you don't guess what I have found; really Mr Mason you great poets are so absent, and so unlike the rest of the world! Why what should I have found, but the thing in the world that was most worth finding? a hidden treasure?—a hidden fig—no, Sir, nor the certificate of the Duchess of Kingston's first marriage,[1] nor the lost books of Livy,[2] nor the longitude, nor the philosophers' stone, nor all Charles Fox has lost.[3] I tell you it is, what I have searched for a thousand times, and had rather have found than the longitude, if it was a thousand times longer—oh! you do guess, do you! I thought I never lost anything in my life; I was sure I had them, and so I had, and now am I not a good soul, to sit down and send you a copy[4] incontinently? Don't be too much obliged to me neither. I am in a panic till there are more copies than mine, and as the post does not go till tomorrow, I am in terror lest the house should be burnt tonight. I have a mind to go and bury a transcript in the field—but then if I should be burnt too! nobody would know where to look for it; well here it is! I think your decorum will not hold it proper to be printed in the life,[5] nor would I have it. We will preserve copies, and the devil is in it, if some time or other it don't find its way to the press. My copy is in his own handwriting, but who could doubt it; I know but one man[6] upon earth who could have written it but Gray.[7]

1. Elizabeth Chudleigh (ca 1720–88), maid of honour to Queen Caroline, had married privately in 1744 the Hon. Augustus John Hervey, later 3d E. of Bristol. When in 1759 it seemed likely that Hervey was about to succeed his brother as Earl of Bristol she had her marriage entered in the register-book of Lainston Chapel at Lainston, Hants. In 1769 she obtained a decree from the consistory court declaring her a spinster, and in the same year married Evelyn Pierrepont (1711–73), 2d D. of Kingston. After the death of the Duke of Kingston the legitimacy of his marriage to Elizabeth Chudleigh was a favourite topic of speculation. She was brought to trial, and in 1776 the House of Lords found her guilty of bigamy. But she claimed and was allowed her peerage as Countess of Bristol, and escaped punishment.

2. For a note on the missing books of Livy's *Annals* see Gray i. 131 n. 29.

3. The gaming losses of Charles James Fox were notorious; in the winter of 1773–4 his debts amounted to £140,000, which his father paid. HW's account of Holland's negotiations in raising the money, which was suppressed by Henry, 3d Lord Holland, was printed by Lord Ilchester in *Studies in Art and Literature for Belle da Costa Greene*, ed. Dorothy Miner, Princeton, New Jersey, 1954, pp. 449–58, under the title 'Some Pages Torn from the Last Journals of Horace Walpole.'

4. Of Gray's 'Candidate,' which HW enclosed.

5. The verses were not printed in *Mem. Gray*.

6. I.e., Mason himself.

7. The subject of the following verses by

When sly Jemmy Twitcher had smugged up his face
With a lick of Court whitewash, and pious grimace,
A-wooing he went, where three sisters of old
In harmless society guttle and scold.

Lord! sister, says Physic to Law, I declare
Such a sheep-biting look, such a pickpocket air!
Not I, for the Indies! you know I'm no prude;
But his nose is a shame, and his eyes are so lewd!
Then he shambles and straddles so oddly, I fear—
No; at our time of life, 'twould be silly, my dear.

I don't know, says Law, now methinks, for his look,
'Tis just like the picture in Rochester's book.[8]
But his character, Phyzzy, his morals, his life!
When she died, I can't tell, but he once had a wife.[9]
They say he's no Christian, loves drinking and whoring,
And all the town rings of his swearing and roaring,
His lying, and filching, and Newgate-bird tricks:—
Not I,—for a coronet, chariot and six.

Divinity heard, between waking and dozing,
Her sisters denying, and Jemmy proposing;
From dinner she rose with her bumper in hand,
She stroked up her belly, and stroked down her band.

What a pother is here about wenching and roaring!
Why David loved catches,[10] and Solomon whoring.
Did not Israel filch from th'Egyptians of old
Their jewels of silver, and jewels of gold?
The prophet of Bethel, we read, told a lie:
He drinks; so did Noah: he swears; so do I.
To refuse him for such peccadillos, were odd;
Besides, he repents, and he talks about God.

Gray was Lord Sandwich's candidacy in 1764 for the High Stewardship of Cambridge. Gray had apparently given HW a MS copy, and possibly circulated other copies among his friends. On the early printings of the verses see Hazen, SH Bibliography 212, and see also post Appendix 7. A MS copy in HW's hand, 'The Candidate. By Mr T. Gray,' is in the Morgan Library; a second copy in HW's hand, 'The Candidate. On Lord Sandwich standing for High Steward of Cambridge. By Mr Th. Gray,' endorsed by Miss Berry 'Gray's Verses upon Lord Sandwich, from L. Orf. 1794,' is now WSL. Mitford did not print the poem, which is printed here from HW's MS copies.

8. 'Lord Sandwich was [great-]grandson of Lord Rochester and resembled his portraits' (HW's note in copy now WSL).

9. 'Lady Sandwich was confined for lunacy, but Lord S.'s enemies said she was still shut up after she recovered her senses—at least she never appeared again in the world' (HW). Lady Sandwich separated from her husband in 1755, became insane, and did not die until 1797 (GEC).

10. 'Lord S. instituted the Catch Club' (HW).

Never hang down your head, you poor penitent elf;
Come, buss me, I'll be Mrs Twitcher myself.
Damn ye both for a couple of Puritan bitches!
He's Christian enough, that repents, and that stitches.[11]

Methinks I wish you could alter the end of the last line, which is too gross to be read by any females, but such cock bawds as the three dames in the verses—and that single word is the only one that could possibly be minded.

PS. Might it not do thus?

Damn you both! I know each for a Puritan punk.
He is Christian enough that repents when he's drunk.[12]

From Mason, Sunday 2 October 1774

Printed from MS now WSL.
Address (in unidentified hand): To the Honourable Horace Walpole, Arlington Street, London.
Postmark: ROTHERHAM 6 OC.

Aston, Oct. 2d, 1774.

I MAY be ashamed of myself and in sober sadness am horribly ashamed of myself for having neglected to answer your two last letters, but I know not how it is, I grow as lazy, as lolloping as—a king; and as little inclined to keep on good terms with my correspondents as he with his subjects. After making a simile so humiliating to myself, and feeling, as Mr Ansty has it, *The conscious blush of self-condemning—*not *praise*[1] but truth, I hope you will acquit me without further apology.

A million of thanks to you for finding and sending what you have

11. 'A term for lying with a woman' (Eric Partridge, *A Dictionary of Slang and Unconventional English*, 1950, quoted from Grose, 1785). The final couplet is omitted from HW's MS now WSL.
12. The passage 'Methinks . . . he's drunk,' here first printed, has been supplied from Mitford's MS notes, Add. MSS 32563 fol. 49, where it is also recorded that Mason wrote on this letter an alternative to HW's alternative:

'Damn ye both for a couple of Puritan saints,
He's Christian enough that both whores and repents.'
Under 'whores,' Mason added 'drinks.' See next letter.

1. Christopher Anstey, *The Priest Dissected*, Bath, 1774, p. 19: 'The conscious pang of self-condemning praise.'

found and sent. The couplet which you wish me to alter is one of those that can only be altered, not improved; the utmost one can hope is a passable alteration. However I think with you (and always did) that the lines ought to be altered. I read (somewhat nearer his idea than yours)

> Damn ye both for two prim puritanical saints!
> He's Christian enough that both whores and repents!
> (or) that drinks, whores and repents.

The rhymes here are not quite perfect, yet in this sort of verse I believe they are permissible. I remember when he repeated them to me (for I never before saw them in writing) that the epithet in the fourth line was *awkward* society, which I think better than *harmless*.

I have been employed of late in filling up those chasms in the *Memoirs* which the cancelled pages[2] required. I hope I have made them more innocent, but you shall see the whole when it is printed, and have as many more cancels as you please, whatever pains it costs me. For as to obstinacy and self-will, I flatter myself I am not similar to any great personage in the universe, 'tis the passive, not the active vices of majesty that I emulate.

A relation of mine,[3] now abroad, has sent me an Italian translation of *Elfrida*, lately published at Florence by Abbé Pillori.[4] I am not

2. Mr Hazen, *Bibliography of HW* 141, describes Kk₂, Pp₂, Pp₃, and h₄ as cancels. Of these only Pp₃ (*Mem. Gray* 301–2) relates to Macpherson (see *ante* 23 April and 9 Aug. 1774); it contains a paragraph in a letter from Gray to Brown dated by Mason 17 Feb. 1763 in which Gray remarks that in 'Ossian, the son of Fingal' one finds that 'Imagination dwelt many hundred years ago, in all her pomp, on the cold and barren mountains of Scotland,' etc. In the cancel leaf in the first edition of *Mem. Gray* there is no note on this paragraph, but in the second edition Mason inserted a note that may represent at least a partial salvage of his original comment: 'One is led to think from this paragraph that the scepticism, which Mr Gray had expressed before, concerning these works of Ossian, was now entirely removed. I know no way of accounting for this (as he had certainly received no stronger evidence of their authenticity) but from the turn of his studies at the time. He had of late much

busied himself in antiquities, and consequently had imbibed too much of the spirit of a professed antiquarian; now we know, from a thousand instances, that no set of men are more willingly duped than these, especially by anything that comes to them under the fascinating form of a new discovery' (quoted from *Gray's Corr.* ii. 798 n. 6).

3. Not identified.

4. *Elfrida. Poema drammatico scritto sopra il modello dell' antica tragedia greca, tradotto in versi italiani dall' Abate A. Pillori*, Florence, 1774 (BM Cat.; *Novelle letterarie pubblicate in Firenze*, 1774, v. 403–5). Abate Antonio Pillori also translated Pope's *Essay on Criticism* (1759) and Robertson's *History of America* (1777) (Bibl. Nat. Cat.). He may have been Niccolò Antonio Pillori (d. 1782), chaplain of the Florentine cathedral and member of the Accademia degli Apatisti (information from Dott. Ferdinando Sartini).

sufficiently master of the language to know whether it be well or ill done, but it flatters me much to find it dedicated to Lord Mansfeild's nephew, my Lord Stormont. It seems the Abbé is now about *Caractacus*.[5] I hope he will dedicate it to Lord Mansfeild himself.

At last the fate of Aston is decided and my nabob cousin[6] is in possession of the house, manor, etc., and last night the boys of the village having dragged a cart of coals from the pits made a bonfire on the occasion. This goodly estate which came into the D'Arcy family by a marriage with an heiress of the Meltons,[7] *temp*. Prin. Eliz., now goes from it because a broken Scots quartermaster (steward to the Duke of Leeds) would not suffer him to redeem it.[8] Take physic, Pomp![9] As I see nothing new in the book way for ages after publication, I beg you will give me some account of Dr Johnson's tour into Scotland when it is published.[10] You will perhaps wonder at my curiosity, but I have heard he has gone far in detecting Macpherson's plagiaries with respect to Ossian[11] and 'tis on this account only that I want to be informed about it. Pray tell me how this horrid rainy season[12] agrees with you and whether you do not repent your not having gone into France with Lord Mansfeild[13] merely for better weather.

Believe me to be, dear Sir, both in rain and sunshine,

Most faithfully yours,

W. MASON

5. If Pillori did translate *Caractacus*, his version has not been found.

6. Harry Verelst.

7. Apparently the marriage of George, Lord Darcy (d. 1558) to Dorothy Melton (1509–57) (*Yorkshire Pedigrees*, ed. J. W. Walker, 1942–4, ii. 286; *The Visitation of Yorkshire Made in the Years 1584–5 by Robert Glover*, ed. Joseph Foster, 1875, p. 47).

8. The purchase of the Aston estates was attended by legal difficulties. In a letter to Alderson (25 Jan. 1775) Mason speaks of the examination of a title that is being made for Verelst, and in the same letter says that Verelst is reported to have advanced £40,000 on the purchase, presumably of Aston manor.

9. *King Lear* III. iv. 33.

10. Johnson's *Journey to the Western Islands of Scotland* appeared 18 Jan. 1775 (*Daily Adv.*).

11. Johnson did not accuse Macpherson of plagiarism but of fabrication. See R. W. Chapman's edition of the *Journey* and Boswell's *Tour*, Oxford, 1924, pp. 106–8.

12. 'September, commonly the dryest month of the year, had been incessantly raining. The floods were out, and though most of the wheat was in, the barley and oats were rotting on the ground' (*Last Journals* i. 378–9).

13. 'Lord Mansfield, who has been here some weeks, intends to return to England in about a fortnight's time' (dispatch from Paris, 23 Sept., *London Chronicle* 1–4 Oct. 1774, xxxvi. 326).

To Mason, October 1774

Printed from Mitford i. 160–2. Dated by the allusions to the general elections of 1774.

I HAVE not imitated your silence from irony, but convenience,— not from want of forgiveness, but of matter. In a time of general elections[1] I have no more ideas than in Newmarket season, when everybody is talking of matches and bets. I do not know who has been distanced, or thrown or won a cup. I have only observed in the papers, that Lord John[2] has been hard run,[3] though he has got the plate; and as the race was at York, I suppose you was on the course. The new senate, they tell me, will be a curious assemblage of patricians and plebeians and knights—of the post.[4] An *old clothes man,* who, George Selwyn says, certainly stood for *Monmouth,*[5] was a candidate, but unsuccessful. Bob,[6] formerly a waiter at White's, was set up by my nephew[7] for two boroughs[8] and actually is returned for Castle Rising with Mr Wedderburne;[9]

Servus curru portatur eodem;[10]

which I suppose will offend the Scottish consul,[11] as much as his coun-

1. Parliament was dissolved 30 Sept. 1774 and writs for a new Parliament to meet 29 Nov. were issued (Cobbett, *Parl. Hist.* xvii. 1408).

2. Lord John Cavendish had sat for Weymouth and Melcombe Regis 1754–61 and Knaresborough 1761–8. He was first elected for York in 1768.

3. The York candidates in 1774 were Charles Turner, Lord John Cavendish, and Martin Bladen Hawke. Turner received 828 votes, Cavendish 807, and Hawke 674 (of which 537 were plumpers, that is, votes for one candidate only cast by voters empowered to cast more than one vote). The polling at York lasted five days. See Godfrey R. Park, *Parliamentary Representation of Yorkshire,* Hull, 1886, p. 57.

4. I.e., perjurers (OED *sub* 'Knight of the post').

5. Monmouth Street in London was noted for its second-hand clothing shops (*London Past and Present* ii. 554). Since the elections both for Monmouth town and Monmouthshire appear to have been uncontested (GM 1775, xlv. 383), Selwyn's joke must refer to an unidentified old-clothes man who was defeated elsewhere.

6. Robert (later Sir Robert) Mackreth (1726–1819), M.P. Castle Rising 1774–84, Ashburton 1784–1802. He began his career as a billiard-marker and waiter at White's, but subsequently set up in business for himself. Through his marriage in 1761 to Mary Arthur, daughter of the owner of White's, he became its proprietor. Notorious as a usurer and book-maker, he was nevertheless knighted by George III in 1795 for services he had rendered the Crown while serving in Parliament.

7. Mackreth was brought into Parliament by HW's nephew George, 3d Earl of Orford, who was in debt to him. See HW to Mann 22 Oct. 1774.

8. See *ante* 8 Dec. 1773 and n. 12.

9. Alexander Wedderburn, who was also returned for Okehampton, for which he chose to sit rather than for Castle Rising.

10. 'The slave rides in the same chariot [with his master]' (Juvenal, *Satires* x. 42).

11. I.e., Wedderburn.

trymen resent an Irishman[12] standing for Westminster, which the
former reckon a borough of their own. For my part, waiter for waiter,
I see little difference; they are all equally ready to cry, 'Coming, coming, Sir.'

I have heard nothing but what you tell me of Johnson's detection,[13]
nor shall believe it till I see it; I have been likewise told that Macpherson is to publish the papers of James II,[14] and detect Sir John Dalrymple.[15] *Credat Judæus!*[16] Is that house[17] so divided against itself? I
should have as soon believe[d] Lord Mansfield had been to Paris for
materials to prove the assassination plot.[18] Really, Mr Mason, you people who live in the country are strangely credulous! We are ignorant
enough at Twickenham, *mais point jusqu'à ce point-là.*

Your Life may as well have patience a little longer still. If it comes
out in the midst of contested elections, flatter yourself as much as you
will, no soul will read it. Alas, Sir! the history of a dead poet will make
no more impression now than the battle of Agincourt. If you can tell
us any news of the assembly of the Colonies, we shall listen to you with
avidity.—If you have any private intelligence that Boston is levelled
to the ground, and sown with salt, better and better; but, dear Sir, Mr
Gray never set his foot in the Massachusets. He and Pindar might sing
very pretty catches for aught we know, but nobody cares about such
things nowadays. You lose your time, indeed you do. The *belles
lettres* were in fashion once, and so were fardingales. But this is a
grave nation, and soon grows weary of trifles; for one while we were

12. Wilkes set up Hervey Redmond
Morres (ca 1743–97), 2d Vct Mountmorres
of Castlemorres, as a candidate for Westminster in this general election. Morres was
not successful. See HW to Mann 22 Oct.
1774.

13. Of the Ossianic forgeries.

14. *Original Papers, Containing the
Secret History of Great Britain, from the
Restoration to the Accession of the House
of Hanover.* The work did not appear until
10 March 1775. See *post* 14 April 1775, n.
10.

15. The source of this rumour has not
been discovered. When HW saw the Macpherson volumes he promptly associated
the author with Dalrymple in the plot that
he believed the 'Scotch Jacobites now
countenanced at Court' had concocted to
defame 'the most spotless characters' (*Last
Journals* i. 445).

16. 'Credat Judæus Apella', 'Let Apella
the Jew believe that!' (Horace, *Satires* I. v.
100).

17. The supporters of George III, especially his Scottish supporters.

18. The Jacobite plot against the life
of William III, discovered in Feb. 1696.
Lord Mansfield was of a Jacobite family
and retained an affection for the idea of
royal prerogative. On Mansfield's visit to
France HW wrote: 'I mention it only as a
conjecture; but who can doubt but Lord
Mansfield went to endeavour to persuade
the French Court not to interfere in our
differences with America? to procure which
he might promise all submission on our
part to other views of France. It was the
very conduct which Charles II and James
II had held' (*Last Journals* i. 373).

mad about commerce, but that bubble is over too; we have at last found out that fleets do more good by destroying trade than by protecting it;[19] for if we have no trade, we are not vulnerable by an enemy. Spain enjoys Peru and Mexico by extirpating the inhabitants. She found that her natives migrated thither. What did she do? Laid waste the New World; and the Spaniards stayed at home—to be sure, and we are going to be as wise. I wish you would turn your mind to these things as I do. There is some good in fathoming the arcana of government, but poetry and writing lives is an occupation only fit for a schoolboy,—

> Non sic fortis Etruria crevit,
> Scilicet et rerum facta est pulcherrima Roma.[20]

No, she conquered the world and plundered her provinces, and then was blessed with those demigods, Caligula, Domitian and Heliogabalus, who were always sent to heaven as soon as they were ripe for it. Adieu!

From Mason, Sunday 29 January 1775

Printed from MS now wsl. Mason dated the letter merely 'The Eve of the Martyrdom.' HW at a later time wrote on the letter '1772,' but the reference to HW's Epilogue for *Braganza* determines the year.
Address: The Honourable Horace Walpole.

Curzon Street, the Eve of the Martyrdom.[1]

Dear Sir,

I REALLY see nothing to object to in your Epilogue,[2] but many things to approve, only in general I think it more in the style of a prologue; but perhaps the author would not have liked one more

19. A reference to the reprisals against America, especially the dispatching of fresh troops thither. See HW to Conway 7 Sept. 1774.

20. 'Not thus did Etruria grow strong, nor, indeed, thus did Rome become the fairest of all things' (altered from Virgil, *Georgics* ii. 533–4).

1. The anniversary of the execution of Charles I. On 26 Jan. 1775 there 'was a debate in the Commons against observing the 30th of January, but it was maintained by 136 to 50. Wilkes said he should certainly vote against keeping that day as a fast, having always observed it as a festival' (*Last Journals* i. 423).

2. To *Braganza*, by Robert Jephson (1736–1803), Irish poet and dramatist. In addition to this Epilogue (*Works* iv. 400–1) HW also addressed to Jephson three letters on this occasion, later printed in *Works* (ii. 305–14) as 'Thoughts on Tragedy.' Jephson in 1781 wrote *The Count of Narbonne,*

comic,³ and yet (comic being out of the case) it seems introductory to the Duchess's⁴ character, and therefore rather of the prologue cast. Two lines occur to me which perhaps would mark who you mean by *a wit* more strongly, yet perhaps too comically.

> No, says a wit, made up of French grimaces,
> Yet, self-ordained, the high priest of the Graces.⁵

This is really all that occurs to me on the perusal of it. Believe me, dear Sir,

Most sincerely yours,

W. Mason

To Mason, Saturday 18 February 1775

Printed from Mitford i. 165–7.

Arlington Street, Feb. 18, 1775.

BRAGANZA was acted last night¹ with prodigious success.² The audience, the most impartial I ever saw, sat mute for two acts, and seemed determined to judge for themselves, and not be the dupes of the encomiums that had been so lavishly trumpeted. At the third act, they grew pleased, and interested: at the fourth they were cooled and deadened by two unnecessary scenes,³ but at the catastrophe in

based on *The Castle of Otranto*. In the printed version of *Braganza*, published early in 1775, the Epilogue does not carry the name of its author, but is simply said to be 'By a friend.' In his own copy (now WSL) HW has annotated this, 'Mr H. Walpole.' The composition of the Epilogue is shown by this letter, and by HW to Mme du Deffand 31 Jan. 1775 to belong to January, in spite of the fact that in his 'Short Notes' HW places it in Feb. 1775 (GRAY i. 49). It is not known when he sent a copy to Mason.

3. Epilogues to serious dramas were by convention usually humorous. See HW to Mme du Deffand 31 Jan. 1775 (DU DEFFAND iv. 151–2), and *Johnson's England*, ed. A. S. Turberville, Oxford, 1933, ii. 176. HW's Epilogue is easy and sentimental rather than 'comic.'

4. Louisa, Duchess of Braganza, the res-

olute heroine of the play. Mrs Yates, who spoke the Epilogue, played this part.

5. HW accepted these lines and they are so printed. In his copy of the Epilogue HW has added 'Lord Chesterfield' as a note to 'wit,' and it is so printed in *Works* iv. 401.

————

1. At Drury Lane. HW has noted in his copy of the play, 'Acted for the first time Feb. 17th,' the date given in Genest v. 448.

2. 'No play was ever more attended to in the getting up,—Mr Garrick spared no pains nor expense,—the dresses are superb, —the scenery quite in a new taste.—It was received with very great applause' (William Hopkins, prompter at Drury Lane, quoted in Dougald MacMillan, *Drury Lane Calendar 1747–1776*, Oxford, 1938, p. 184).

3. The fourth act as printed contains only two scenes.

the fifth, they were transported; they clapped, shouted, huzzaed, cried bravo, and thundered out applause both at the end, and when given out again;[4] yet the action was not worthy of the poet. Mrs Yates shone in the dignified scenes, but had not variety[5] enough; Smith,[6] recalling Garrick in *Richard III*, played the Viceroy with great spirit; but Reddish[7] was pitiful and whining in the Duke; Aikin[8] ridiculous in the first old conspirator, and the Friar[9] totally insignificant, though engaged in the principal scene[10] in the play where indeed he has too little to say. The charming beauties of the poetry were not yet discovered, and the faults in the conduct may be easily mended. In short, I trust if this tragedy does not inspire better writers, that it will at least preserve the town from hearing with patience the stuff we have had for these fifty years. There was an excellent Prologue written by Murphy;[11] for my poor Epilogue,[12] though well delivered by Mrs Yates, it appeared to me the flattest thing I ever heard, and the audience were very good in not groaning at it. I wish it could be spoken no more. The boxes are all taken for five and twenty nights, which are more than it can be acted this season.[13] I went to the rehearsal with all the eagerness of eighteen, and was delighted to feel myself so young again. The actors diverted me with their dissatisfactions and complaints, and, though I said all I could, committed some of what they called proprieties, that were very improper, as seating the Duke and Duchess on a high throne, in the second act, which made the spectators conclude that the revolution, as I knew they would, had happened. The scenes and dresses were well imagined, and the stage handsomely crowded. All this was wanted, for, from the defect in

4. That is, when a performance of the play on the following night was announced. 'The new tragedy of *Braganza* . . . was received with general approbation and uncommon applause' (*Public Advertiser* 18 Feb. 1775).

5. 'For, through the regions of that
        beauteous face,
   We no variety of passions trace'
        (Churchill, *The Rosciad*, ll. 735–6).

6. After the 1773–4 season Smith had announced his retirement from the stage, but in Sept. 1774 he joined Garrick's company at Drury Lane. See *Poems of Charles Churchill*, ed. James Laver, 1933, i. 27.

7. Samuel Reddish (1735–85), for ten

years (1767–77) with the Drury Lane company, then at Covent Garden until 1779, when he became insane.

8. James Aikin (Aickin) (d. 1803).

9. Ramirez, played by John Hayman Packer (1730–1806).

10. The first scene of the third act.

11. Arthur Murphy, the dramatist and actor.

12. HW's lines were characterized by the *London Chronicle* (16–18 Feb. 1775, xxxvii. 167) as 'a sing-song kind of epilogue, written by Mr Horace Walpole.'

13. *Braganza* was played fifteen times during the 1774–5 season (MacMillan, op. cit. 214).

the subject, which calls for but two acts,[14] several scenes languished. A little more knowledge of the stage in the author may prevent this in his future plays; for his poetry, it is beautiful to the highest degree. He has another fault, which is a want of quick dialogue; there is scarce ever a short speech, so that it will please more on reading, than in representation. I will send it to you the moment it is published.[15]

There is nothing else new, nor do I hear of anything coming. The war with America goes on briskly, that is as far as voting goes.[16] A great majority in both Houses is as brave as a mob ducking a pickpocket. They flatter themselves they shall terrify the Colonies into submission in three months, and are amazed to hear that there is no such probability. They might as well have excommunicated them, and left it to the devil to put the sentence in execution.

Good night, and write to me; you are an idle creature, and I am very jealous of your harpsico-violin[17]—it is your interleaved Linnæus.[18]

14. 'The subject in reality demands but two acts, for the conspiracy and the revolution' (HW to Lady Ossory 1 Feb. 1775).

15. It was published by 27 Feb. 1775 (*Public Advertiser*). An excerpt from the printed play appeared in the *London Chronicle* 4–7 March, xxxvii. 217–8. HW sent it to Mason 7 March; see *post*.

16. Both Houses had consistently voted for strong measures against America. In February an Address to the King urging the use of force against the colonies, and bills to increase the size of the army and navy, were voted. See HW to Mann 15 Feb. 1775.

17. 'I heard a sweet new instrument called the *celestinet*, the improvement, *if not* the invention of Mr Mason the poet. . . . The shape is that of a short harpsichord, with the same sort of keys, and played on only with the right hand in the same manner; and at the same time you draw with your left hand a bow like the bow of a fiddle, that runs in a groove under the keys, and by proper management presses on the wires and brings out a delicate, exquisite sound, something between the finest notes of a fiddle and the [musical] glasses. It is not above two feet long and one foot and a half in the broadest part, where the keys are, which are placed on the top of the instrument' (*Delany Correspondence* v. 90–1, with a rough sketch). Mitford (i. 432) quotes the beginning of a ten-page manuscript description of the celestinette in Mason's handwriting dated 30 March 1761: '. . . The clearness of the tone of the instrument, the facility of its touch, . . . all depends principally on that part of it which is employed in making it sound; namely, the single horsehair attached to the movable ruler or bow, which is drawn backwards and forwards over the strings by the left hand of the performer, while his right is employed in pushing down the keys.'

18. That is, it took up as much of Mason's time as Gray's habit of annotating his interleaved copy of the *Systema naturæ* took up of his. 'Mr Gray often vexed me by finding him heaping notes on an interleaved Linnæus, instead of pranking on his lyre' (HW to Lady Ossory 8 Sept. 1791).

To Mason, Tuesday 28 February 1775

Printed from Mitford i. 167–9. It was addressed to Mason in Suffolk (*post* 7 May 1775).

Arlington Street, Feb. 28, 1775.

THOU recreant clerk—I do not mean for not replying to my last missive, but for changing thy mind,[1] thou unhallowed relapse, which I did not know when I wrote to thee last, or I would not have cockered thee up with a promise of *Braganza,* yet to show thee that I keep faith even with heretics, thou shalt have it when thou sayest how it may be sent. Thy sin is too foul to name, but thy conscience tells thee what I mean. 'Tis an Omission worse than any of the tribe of *Com;* and though posterity will be so selfish as to forgive it, there is not a Christian in being that ever can—oh yes, there are some that could, though I trust they cannot. I suppose you will be glad to hear that I have got a codicil to my last gout. I had an inflammation in my face, and yesterday was blooded for it. It sunk in two hours, but baited[2] and gave me a sore throat; this morning I waked lame, and cannot walk without a stick; so the whole is gouty, for that devil can act any distemper, like a fine lady. It has hindered my going to Strawberry, whither the fine weather invited me. I wish we ever had such in summer.

The gates of Janus's temple are opened and shut every other day; the porter has a sad time of it, and deserves a reversion for three lives. We are sending the Americans a sprig of olive,[3] lapped up in an Act for a famine next year,[4] for we are as merciful as we are stout. However, as the two Houses do not much reckon upon bonfires to come,[5] each is treating itself with one at present, and have ordered a weekly

1. Mason's reply (*post* p. 182) suggests that he had decided not to complete or to publish an unidentified satire.

2. Made a short stay (OED).

3. On 20 Feb. 1775 Lord North carried a resolution to permit the American colonies to tax themselves, though the tax would be subject to revision in England.

4. '10th [Feb.]. Lord North moved for leave to bring in a bill for putting the trade of America with England, Ireland, and the West Indies under temporary restrictions,

and for restricting the refractory provinces from fishing on the banks of Newfoundland' (*Last Journals* i. 433). Since the bill, even if passed, could not reach America before the end of the current fishing season, its effect would not be felt until the following year. Having passed both Houses the bill received the royal assent 30 March 1775 (*Journals of the House of Commons* xxxv. 241).

5. In celebration of military victories.

paper[6] and a pamphlet,[7] each called *The Crisis,* to be burnt by the common hangman;[8] and as contradictions[9] now go hand in hand, each party has its victim. I have seen neither of the sacrifices,[10] both they say are very stupid; the first is too free with his Majesty: the second compliments him with the sole right of taxation; methinks all parliaments have a mortal aversion to the word *crisis.*

Since you left town, I have made another considerable purchase, for which I have been long haggling, the rest of the Digby miniatures.[11] They had been divided into two shares. There is one superb piece of Sir Kenelm, his wife,[12] and two sons,[13] by Peter Oliver,[14] after Vandyck,[15] in the highest preservation, and certainly the capital miniature[16] of the world. I am not quite sure whether you did not see them two years ago; but why do I tell you anything? you are twiddling your instrument of the composite order,[17] and care no more than Orpheus

6. *The Crisis,* printed by T. W. Shaw. Ninety-two numbers were issued in 1775–6. It was Number 3 that caused the trouble here described. See Paul Leicester Ford, 'The Crisis,' *The Bibliographer,* 1902, i. 139–52.

7. *The Present Crisis with Respect to America Considered,* published by Thomas Becket. The author has not been identified.

8. For an account of the burning of the papers see GM 1775, xlv. 148, and *Annual Register,* 1775, xviii. 95.

9. 'The principles of these offensive publications were diametrically opposite to each other' (*Annual Register,* 1775, xviii. 94).

10. Neither appears in the records of the SH library.

11. In 1771 HW had bought nine miniatures of the Digby family ('Des. of SH,' *Works* ii. 421–2; James Granger, *Letters,* ed. J. P. Malcolm, 1805, p. 308) from a descendant of Watkin Williams, who was 'probably descended from Sir Kenelm. . . . This set of pictures, with a few more less fine, cost Mr Walpole three hundred guineas' (*Works* ii. 422). The second purchase from 'the lady who shared them with the other heir' completed the set (*Works* ii. 423). The names of these heirs have not been found, nor the price HW paid for the second set.

12. Sir Kenelm Digby (1603–65) m. (1625) Venetia Anastasia Stanley (1600–33).

13. Probably Kenelm (1625–48) and John (b. 1627), the eldest sons of Sir Kenelm and Lady Digby. Two other sons, Everard and George, died young.

14. (1594–1648), miniature-painter, especially celebrated for his copies in water-colour of works of old masters.

15. The original Van Dyck was then in Lord Oxford's collection. A water-colour drawing of it by Vertue is in Vertue's Harleian collections bought by HW from his widow. It is now WSL.

16. HW wrote to Cole in similar words 11 April 1775 (COLE i. 358). He had previously nominated the portrait of Lady Lucy Percy, the mother of Venetia Lady Digby, as 'perhaps the finest and most perfect miniature in the world' ('Des. of SH,' 1774; *Works* ii. 422). The miniature of the family was sold SH xi. 56. It was exhibited at South Kensington, 1862; at the Burlington Fine Arts Club, 1889; sold Christie's (Bns Burdett-Coutts sale) 11 May 1922, lot 361; *penes* (1923) Hjalmar Wicanders (see *The Connoisseur,* Sept.–Dec. 1923, lxvii. 18). It is now in the National Museum at Stockholm (*Nationalmusei Mästerverk,* ed. Sixten Strömbom, Stockholm, 1949, No. 51, with reproduction: information from Mr J. M. Osborn and Mr F. B. Adams, Jr). It is reproduced also in J. J. Foster, *British Miniature Painters,* 1898, plate XI.

17. The celestinette.

whether anybody but beasts listens to you. You now owe me two
letters, and paid I will be, or I am

Your most obedient humble servant,

H. W.

From MASON, Friday 3 March 1775

Printed from MS now WSL.

York, March 3d, 1775.

THIRTY years ago when I was turned twenty I used to leave
Cambridge for London whenever I had five guineas to spare, on
what they then called a scheme.[1] *My* scheme was to dine every day at
a chop-house behind St Clement's at two, in order to be in the middle
of the pit at four, there to remain with all the impatience of expectation till the curtain drew up.[2] And this I continued to do daily while
my money lasted,[3] and with as much regularity as I at present go morning and afternoon to see the ancient maiden gentlewomen and decayed tradesmen of this famous city of York mumble their matins and
their vespers. Now, Sir, if your former letter had been written thirty
years before its present date there is no question but I should have
had both talents and spirit to answer it. The reading, it is true, put
me, like Hezekiah's sundial,[4] several degrees backward, and I felt myself for a few moments adolescent. But the effect was, as I say, but
momentary. The Minster bell tinkled me to prayers and the effect
vanished. However, when you send me the tragedy itself, perhaps I
shall be able to fill a page with *closet* criticism, for that power has not
quite left me, and I distinguish it from *theatrical* criticism widely.
Expect then to hear whether your favourite poet has observed his
unities so well as a certain person who wrote *The Mysterious Mother*
and despised himself for having observed them; whether the Duchess
of the one has as much of the *sibi constet*[4a] as the Countess of the other;

---

1. 'An escapade of a humorous character,
a "spree"' (OED *sub* 'scheme' sb.1 5d).

2. Plays began at six o'clock in the evening. See Dougald MacMillan, *Drury Lane
Calendar 1747–1776*, Oxford, 1938, p. xix.

3. Seats in the pit sold for three shillings
(ibid.).

4. 2 Kings 20. 8–11.

4a. Consistent with itself: cf. Horace, *Ars
Poetica* 127.

and which has the best hand at preserving the *costume*[5] when he delineates a friar. In the mean time I quit your former letter like the first head of one of my sermons and proceed secondly to that which I received this morning.

It begins, 'Thou recreant clerk! thou unhallowed relapse! thou heretic!' and it begins well. I take every one of the titles to myself and bow beneath the scourge. There may come a time, however, when I may wash my Ethiopianism white, but that time I never wish to live to see, because if I do I must survive the majority of my friends. In the meanwhile here I sit with my pen in my hand muzzled like a mastiff wishing to bite and yet unable even to bark, convinced of this melancholy truth, that no situation however independent, no desires or ambition however moderated, nay even (as I can truly say) annihilated, will authorize a man in these days to do what he thinks right, unless he is as callous as a prime minister and as unfeeling as his master.[6] You, though you are the son of a prime minister, have not this callousness about you and therefore from you I not only expect but demand forgiveness.

As to the two *Crisis*'s you mention, I can only say I envy their fate. To be burnt by the common hangman is a thing devoutly to be wished. No fate except that of the pillory exceeds it. I would be content with even an unpensioned pillory.[7] And yet this stern fate denies me. However, that you may run no risk of either from receiving this letter, I shall prudently put it under a secretary of state's cover.[8]

I congratulate you on your new miniatures, though I know they will one day become Court property and dangle under the crimson-coloured shop glasses of our gracious Queen Charlotte. I never saw the piece you mention, though I burn to see it.

I condole with you on your gout, though I would almost bear its pain for you, if I could also possess your spirits. I hope it will be but a short fit, yet might not a little care of cold afterwards—I say no more, for I know it is in vain—and yet an under-waistcoat—don't throw my

5. That is, the character and custom proper to the period (*ante* 8 May 1769, n. 2).

6. The King.

7. Both Mason and HW liked to believe that many who received pensions in the reign of George III were men who had been put in the pillory in the previous reign. See Mason's *Satirical Poems* 32 and 55. Here Mason is probably alluding to John Shebbeare, who was pilloried in 1758 and pensioned in 1762.

8. I.e., through William Fraser. See *ante* 9 Sept. 1772.

letter in the fire till it has told you how much and how sincerely I am

Yours,

W. MASON

Pray don't flirt at my musical instrument, it and Fidget[9] are my only comforts at present. Tell Lord Nuneham that I have finished the translation of Rousseau's *Pigmalion*,[10] which he set me about three years ago, purely to keep myself innocently employed and out of harm's way. He shall have it for writing for. You, I know, will despise it. No matter, could an actor be found to act it (but for this the soul of Pritchard,[11] the voice of Mrs Cibber,[12] and the eye of Garrick must all unite in the form of a male figure as young and beautiful as Mrs Hartley) I say it would pit, box, and gallery[13] with *Braganza*.

To MASON, Tuesday 7 March 1775

Printed from Mitford i. 172–3.

March 7, 1775.

IF your contempt for your contemporaries extended to total silence, perhaps I should not disagree with you. There is dignity in indignation that refuses wholesome food to a stupid age, that is content

9. Mason's dog. 'Pray tell Benjamin of my intended motions and if Fidget is in the straw let all possible care be taken of her and her young ones' (Mason to Alderson 25 Jan. 1775).

10. Rousseau's dramatic scene, designed to be presented with music, first appeared in print in the *Mercure de France* Jan. 1771 (pp. 200–9). The first edition, possibly published without Rousseau's knowledge or consent, was issued in Geneva in 1771. See Théophile Dufour, *Récherches bibliographiques sur les œuvres imprimées de J.-J. Rousseau*, 1925, i. 219–21. Mason's translation was first printed in his *Works*, 1811, ii. 363–77.

11. Hannah Vaughan (1711–68), actress, m. (*ante* 1733) William Pritchard, later treasurer of Drury Lane Theatre (C. B. Hogan, *Eighteenth-Century Actors in the* DNB: *Additions and Corrections* [reprinted from *Theatre Notebook*, 1952], p. 15). Churchill praised her in *The Rosciad*: 'Pritchard, by Nature for the stage designed, In person graceful, and in sense refined; Her art as much as Nature's friend became, Her voice as free from blemish as her fame' (ll. 803–6). HW wrote an Epilogue to Rowe's *Tamerlane* for her to speak 4 and 5 Nov. 1746 ('Short Notes,' GRAY i. 16).

12. Susannah Maria Arne (1714–66), actress and singer; m. (1734) Theophilus Cibber, son of Colley Cibber. She first achieved fame at Covent Garden, but from 1753 until her death she was associated with Garrick at Drury Lane.

13. 'In fine, it shall read, and write, and act, and plot, and show; ay, and pit, box, and gallery, egad, with any play in Europe' (Buckingham, *The Rehearsal*, I. i).

with carrion. But why then publish Gray's life? Keep it back till you like to publish it with the original notes. Leave the Johnsons and Macphersons to worry one another for the diversion of a rabble that desires and deserves no better sport.

Here is *Braganza;* I do not say that either the subject or conduct are interesting. The language is good, the poetry charming. Read any tragedy written within these thirty years, and then wonder that I was delighted to see even a cousin of Melpomene.

If you have *translated* Pygmalion, I shall be very glad to see him too; if you have only translated the music, I shall not be much the wiser, yet do not think my ignorance makes me supercilious. I admire all your talents, though not a judge of all. Your writings, your composite instrument, your drawings are dear to me according to my degrees of capacity; and when I seize every opportunity of drawing you into a correspondence, does not it say that I love your letters, and do my utmost to cultivate your friendship? Yes, I do; let all the prime ministers since my father, whom you name, say as much if they can![1] To my great sorrow we live at a distance, and when I wish to see you most, I have seen you least; yet Strawberry, where you scarce ever was in summer, is pleasant then. If you would at any time give me a week I should think it no trouble to fetch you. Time grows precious to me, and, therefore, I would employ it in the way most agreeable to me. Don't think me importunate, but it shall not be my own fault, if I do not please myself.

Yours most sincerely,

H. W.

To Mason, Monday 3 April 1775

Printed from Mitford i. 173–7.

Arlington Street, April 3, 1775.

WELL! your book[1] is walking the town in mid-day. How it is liked, I do not yet know. Were I to judge from my own feelings,

1. 'I was *once,* forty years ago, at the late Duke of Newcastle's levee, the only minister's levee at which I ever was present except my own father's' (HW's 'Account of My Conduct Relative to the Places I Hold under Government,' 1782, *Works* ii. 369).

1. The *Memoirs of Gray,* published 30 March 1775 (*Public Advertiser*).

I should say there never was so entertaining or interesting a work: that it is the most perfect model of biography;[2] and must make Tacitus, and Agricola too, detest you. But as the world and simple I are not often of the same opinion, it will perhaps be thought very dull. If it is, all we can do, is to appeal to that undutiful urchin, posterity, who commonly treats the judgment of its parents with contempt, though it has so profound a veneration for its most distant ancestors. As you have neither imitated the teeth-breaking diction of Johnson, nor coined slanders against the most virtuous names in story, like modern historians,[3] you cannot expect to please the *reigning* taste. Few persons have had time, from their politics, diversions and gaming, to have read much of so large a volume, which they will keep for the summer, when they have full as much of nothing to do. Such as love poetry, or think themselves poets, will have hurried to the verses and been disappointed at not finding half a dozen more Elegies in a Churchyard. A few fine gentlemen will have read one or two of the shortest letters, which not being exactly such as they write themselves, they will dislike or copy next post; they who wish or intend to find fault with Gray, you, or even me, have, to be sure, skimmed over the whole, except the Latin, for even spite, *non est tanti—*. The reviewers no doubt are already writing against you; not because they have read the whole, but because one's own name[4] is always the first thing that strikes one in a book. The Scotch will be more deliberate, but not less angry; and if not less angry, not more merciful. Every Hume, however spelt, will I don't know what do;[5] I should be sorry to be able to guess what. I have already been asked, why I did not prevent publication of the censure on David?[5a] The truth is (as you know) I never saw the whole together till now, and not that part; and if I had, why ought I to have

2. It was Boswell's model: 'Instead of melting down my materials into one mass, and constantly speaking in my own person, by which I might have appeared to have more merit in the execution of the work, I have resolved to adopt and enlarge upon the excellent plan of Mr Mason, in his *Memoirs of Gray*' (Boswell, *Johnson* i. 29).

3. In *Last Journals* i. 445 HW speaks of 'the infamous characters of Dalrymple and Macpherson, the two chief aspersers.'

4. No reviewers are mentioned by name, but in a letter to Mason [23] July 1756 Gray wrote: 'Sure I . . . am something a better judge than all the man-midwives and

Presbyterian parsons [Mason's footnote observes that 'the reviewers, at the time, were supposed to be of these professions'] that ever were born. Pray give me leave to ask you, do you find yourself tickled with the commendations of such people? . . . And can then the censure of such critics move you?' (*Mem. Gray* 246; cf. *Gray's Corr.* ii. 466–7).

5. An allusion to the censure of John Home's *Agis* in Gray to Wharton 8 March 1758 (*Mem. Gray* 261, where it is spliced to the letter of 21 Feb. 1758).

5a. In Gray's letter to Beattie 2 July 1770 (*Mem. Gray* 384–5).

prevented it: Voltaire will cast an *imbelle* javelin *sine ictu*[6] at Gray, for he loves to depreciate a *dead* great author, even when unprovoked,—even when he has commended him alive, or before he was so vain and so envious as he is now. The Rousseaurians will imagine that I interpolated the condemnation of his *Eloïse*.[7] In short, we shall have many sins laid to our charge, of which we are innocent; but what can the malicious say against the innocent, but what is not true? I am here in brunt to the storm; you sit serenely aloof and smile at its sputtering. So should I too, were I out of sight, but I hate to be stared at, and the object of whispers before my face. The macaronies will laugh out, for you say I am still in the fashionable world.—What! they will cry, as they read while their hair is curling,—that old soul;—for old and old-fashioned are synonymous in the vocabulary of mode, alas! Nobody is so sorry as I to be in the world's fashionable purlieus; still, in truth, all this is a joke and touches me little. I seem to myself a Stralbrug,[8] who have lived past my time, and see almost my own life written before my face while I am yet upon earth, and as it were the only one of my contemporaries with whom I began the world. Well; in a month's time there will be little question of Gray, and less of me. America and feathers[9] and masquerades will drive us into libraries, and there I am well content to live as an humble companion to Gray and you; and, thank my stars, not on the same shelf with the Macphersons and Dalrymples.

One omission I have found, at which I wonder; you do not mention Gray's study of physic,[10] of which he had read much, and I doubt to his hurt.[11] I had not seen till now that delightful encomium on

---

6. 'Telumque imbelle sine ictu coniecit' '—and hurled his weak and useless spear' (Virgil, *Æneid* ii. 544–5).

7. Gray wrote Mason 22 Jan. 1761: 'There is no one event in it [the *Nouvelle Héloïse*] that might not happen any day of the week . . . in any private family; yet these events are so put together, that the series of them is more absurd and more improbable than *Amadis de Gaul*. The *dramatis personæ* (as the author says) are all of them good characters; I am sorry to hear it: for had they been all hanged at the end of the third volume, nobody (I believe) would have cared' (*Mem. Gray* 289). The 'Rousseaurians' would suspect HW because of his letter to Rousseau (1765) in the name of the King of Prussia.

8. I.e., Struldbrug, one of the immortals encountered by Gulliver during his visit to Luggnagg in the third part of *Gulliver's Travels*.

9. 'Our young ladies are covered with more plumes than any nation that has no other covering' (HW to Mann 20 March 1775). Satirical poems and prints on the fashion were appearing in great numbers.

10. Robert Antrobus, Gray's uncle, had encouraged him in the study of medicine. Gray never took up the study formally, but his notes on various learned journals betray an interest in curious features of medical history. See William Powell Jones, *Thomas Gray, Scholar*, Cambridge, Mass., 1937, pp. 164–74.

11. Gray's letters show him unmistak-

Cambridge, when empty of its inhabitants.[12] It is as good as anything in the book, and has that true humour, which I think equal to any of his excellencies. So has the apostrophe to Nicols, 'Why, you monster, I shall never be dirty and amused as long as I live,'[13] but I will not quote any more, though I shall be reading it and reading it for the rest of my life.[14]

But come, here is a task you must perform, and forthwith, and if you will not write to me, you shall *transcribble*[15] to me, or I will *combustle*[16] you. Send me incontinently all the proper names that are omitted. You know how I love writing marginal notes in my books,[17] and there is not a word in or out of the book of which I will be ignorant. To save you trouble, here is a list of who is's.[18] Page 152, fill up the asterisks;[19] ditto p. 174;[20] ditto 206;[21] ditto 232;[22] 249, Peer, who is

---

ably hypochondriac, which is doubtless all that HW means.

12. 'Cambridge is a delight of a place, now there is nobody in it. I do believe you would like it, if you knew what it was without inhabitants. It is they, I assure you, that get it an ill name and spoil all' (Gray to Dr Clerke, 12 Aug. 1760, *Mem. Gray* 282).

13. Ibid. 346, letter of 24 June 1769 (paraphrased).

14. HW had his copy (now in the Harvard Library) bound in full-grain morocco with his arms on the sides, the binding he reserved for contemporary books he held in highest esteem. From time to time HW inserted illustrations and marginal notes. For example, on page 291 he has identified 'Lord * * * *' as Lord John Cavendish, and has described him as 'afterwards Chancellor of the Exchequer in 1782, and again in 1783.' On page 118 he has pasted a clipping from the *Morning Herald*, an English translation of Gray's Latin lines written at the Grande Chartreuse, and has dated it 18 Oct. 1788.

15. Gray to Wharton 11 [Sept.] 1746: 'Thirdly, he [Aristotle] has suffered vastly [by] the transcribblers, as all authors of great brevity necessarily must' (*Mem. Gray* 182; cf. *Gray's Corr.* i. 241).

16. Gray to Mason [7 June] 1760: 'So if you have any mind to *combustle* about it well and good; for me, I am neither so literary nor so combustible' (*Mem. Gray* 284; cf. *Gray's Corr.* ii. 312).

17. Perhaps one in four of HW's books has marginalia.

18. Mason's reply to this letter is missing. The following notes are based on HW's marginalia in the Harvard copy of *Mem. Gray*.

19. 'I shall see Mr * * and his wife, nay, and his child too, for he has got a boy. . . . There is my Lords * * and * * *, they are statesmen: do not you remember them dirty boys playing at cricket?' (Gray to West 27 May 1742, *Mem. Gray* 152). HW's marginalia, presumably given him by Mason, identify the suppressed names as 'Mr Cambridge,' 'John Earl of Sandwich,' and 'George Earl of Halifax.' This identification of the Earls is made in *Gray's Corr.* i. 210, but the identification of Richard Owen Cambridge in this letter is now first printed. Cambridge's first son, Richard Owen, was baptized 8 Dec. 1741 (R. D. Altick, *Richard Owen Cambridge: Belated Augustan*, Philadelphia, 1941, p. 31).

20. 'Methinks I see Dr * * , . . . lost in admiration of your goodly person and parts, cramming down his envy (for it will rise) with the wing of a pheasant and drowning it in neat burgundy' (Gray to Wharton 27 Dec. [1743], *Mem. Gray* 174). HW's marginal note: 'Dr Askew, who proposed to give an edition of Æschylus, but did not.' For Anthony Askew (1722–74) and his projected Æschylus, see DNB.

21. 'Our friend * * 's zeal and eloquence surpassed all power of description' (Gray to Wharton 8 Aug. 1749, *Mem. Gray* 206).

it?[23] 250, ditto, the Lady of quality?[24] 251, the leader;[25] 275, who the asterisk?[26] 282, the Doctor, who;[27] 283, ditto;[28] 284, the B's and [C]'s;[29] 288, where, whose is Stratton?[30] 290, Lord?[31]

You see my queries are not very numerous. If you do not answer them I will not tell you a syllable of what the *fashionable* say of your book, and I do not believe you have another correspondent amongst

HW's marginal note: 'In the original it is *Chappy*, and means Dr Chapman, fellow of Christ's College, afterwards Master of Magdalen, and when this letter was written, vice-chancellor. See an account of his death p. 282.' Dr Thomas Chapman (see below, n. 27, and *ante* 17 April 1774, n. 21) was a fellow of Christ's College, Cambridge, 1741–6, and vice-chancellor 1748–9 (Venn, *Alumni Cantab.*).

22. 'I dare say that Mason, though some years younger than I, was as little elevated with the approbation of Lord * and Lord * , as I am mortified by their silence' (Gray to Wharton [26 Dec. 1754], *Mem. Gray* 232). HW wrote no marginalia here; Gray's MS reads only 'Lord D. and Lord M.' The former may have been Lord De La Warr (*Gray's Corr.* i. 416 and n. 3).

23. 'Another (a Peer) believes that the last stanza of the second Ode ['The Bard'] relates to King Charles the First and Oliver Cromwell' (Gray to Hurd 25 Aug. 1757, *Mem. Gray* 249). HW wrote no note on the 'peer,' who however can be identified from two letters to Wharton (not printed by Mason) as Lord Barrington (*Gray's Corr.* ii. 518 and n. 1, 526 and n. 9).

24. 'Oh yes, a Lady of quality (a friend of Mason's) who is a great reader [esteems the *Odes*]' (same letter, *Mem. Gray* 250). HW's marginal note: 'Caroline Marchioness of Lothian, sister of Lord Holderness.' This identification is now first printed (Toynbee and Whibley, *Gray's Corr.* ii. 520 n. 6, guessed Lady Holdernesse). Lady Caroline Darcy (d. 1778) m. (1735) William Henry Kerr, 4th M. of Lothian, 1767.

25. This refers to Mason's note on Gray's letter to him of 28 Sept. 1757, in which Gray placed *Caractacus* above *Elfrida* (*Mem. Gray* 251). Mason remarked that 'the world' was of a different opinion, and added that 'one of its leaders went so far as to declare that he never knew a second work fall so much below a first from the

same hand.' HW's marginal note: 'Dr Hayter, Bishop of London' (Thomas Hayter, 1702–62, D.D.; Bp of Norwich, 1749, of London, 1761).

26. 'Do you remember Mr * * 's account of it [Clarendon's continuation of his *History*] before it came out? How well he recollected all the faults, and how utterly he forgot all the beauties' (Gray to Palgrave 24 July 1759, *Mem. Gray* 275). HW's note: 'Mr Cambridge.'

27. 'Our friend Dr * * . . . is gone to his grave with five fine mackerel . . . in his belly' (Gray to Clerke 12 Aug. 1760, *Mem. Gray* 282–3). HW's note: 'Dr Chapman.' See *ante* 17 April 1774.

28. Mason seems to have omitted this identification in his reply, and HW repeated the query *post* 14 April (q.v., and n. 16).

29. (Previously printed 'E'.) 'I will never believe the B * * s and the C * * s are dead, though I smelt them' (Gray to Mason [27 June] 1760, *Mem. Gray* 284). HW's note: 'The Blascows and Chapmans. Dr Blascow was canon of Windsor.' Richard Blacow, of Brasenose College, Oxford, canon of Windsor 1754–60, died 13 May 1760; Dr Chapman died 9 June (*Gray's Corr.* ii. 673 n. 5, 678 n. 6). These identifications are now first printed, Mason having cut the names out of Gray's MS (ibid. ii. 683 and n. 7).

30. 'You are to observe . . . whether Old Park most resembles Upsal or Stratton' (Gray to Wharton [31 Jan.] 1761, *Mem. Gray* 288). HW has no note on Stratton; Toynbee and Whibley identify it as 'Stratton-Strawless, near Aylsham, in Norfolk, where was the ancient seat of the Marsham family' (*Gray's Corr.* ii. 725 n. 4).

31. 'Pray, ask Lord * [about the opera]; for I think I have seen him there once or twice, as much pleased as I was' (Gray to Mason 22 Jan. 1761, *Mem. Gray* 290). HW's note: 'Lord Holderness.'

them. At present they are labouring through a very short work,[32] more peculiarly addressed to them, at least to a respectable part of them, the Jockey Club,[33] who to the latter's extreme surprise have been consulted on a point of honour by Mr Fitzgerald, which however he has already decided himself[34] with as little conscience as they could do in their most punctilious moments.

If you satisfy me, I will tell you the following *bon mot* of Foote, but be sure you don't read what follows till you have obeyed my commands. Foote was at Paris in October, when *Dr Murray*[35] was, who *admiring* or *dreading* his wit (for commentators dispute on the true reading) often invited him to dinner with his nephew.[36] The ambassador produced a very small bottle of Tokay, and dispensed it in very small glasses. The uncle to prove how precious every drop, said it was of the most exquisite growth, and very old. Foote taking up the diminutive glass, and examining it, replied, 'It is very little of its age.' Return me my story if you don't perform the conditions. I wish I could send you anybody's else life to write!

From MASON, ca Monday 10 April 1775

Missing. Evidence of its existence is HW's letter of 14 April, in which he thanks Mason for replying to his queries concerning the *Memoirs of Gray,* included in his letter to Mason of 3 April 1775.

32. *An Appeal to the Jockey Club; or, a True Narrative of the Late Affair between Mr Fitzgerald and Mr Walker,* by George Robert Fitzgerald (ca 1748–86), noted chiefly for his quarrelsome disposition and many duels. His stormy career was terminated by hanging. For a lively picture of this 'Mohawk' see *The Memoirs of William Hickey,* ed. Alfred Spencer, 1913–25, i. 287–97. The *Appeal* was published 20 March 1775 (*Public Advertiser*); HW has written on the title-page of his copy (now WSL) 'March 1775.' HW's copies of Walker's *Answer to Mr Fitzgerald's Appeal* and Fitzgerald's *Reply to Thomas Walker, Esq.* are also WSL.

33. Founded about 1750. For the history of this organization, the chief purpose of which was the establishment and maintenance of high standards in the conduct of

horse racing, see Robert Black, *The Jockey Club and Its Founders,* 1891.

34. Fitzgerald's appeal involved a sum of money allegedly owed him by a Thomas Walker, not otherwise identified, who maintained that he had already compounded the debt. Fitzgerald had caned Walker at the Ascot races and had subsequently fought a duel with him in which Walker was injured slightly.

35. 'Lord Mansfield certainly set out very privately, and tried both at Dover and Calais to pass by the name of Dr Murray, but so many persons knew him that he found it impossible' (*Last Journals* i. 373). On Lord Mansfield's visit to France in the autumn of 1774 see *ante* Oct. 1774, n. 18.

36. Lord Stormont, English ambassador to France 1772–8.

TO MASON, Friday 14 April 1775

Printed from Mitford i. 177–81.

Arlington Street, April 14, 1775.

WHAT is the perfection of ingratitude? silence; what is the perfection of gratitude? silence. Obedience is better than sacrifice but obedience may be sacrifice too: judge.

We are both a little disappointed, are not we? how could we imagine that a quarto, that contained nothing but wit, humour, sentiment, truth, morality, reflection, genuine and original poetry, and the memoirs of two poets, of which one was a youth without guile or gall, and the other a good man through life, should interest the present age? especially when such ingredients were arranged with exquisite taste and judgment, and compose the most pleasing work, the standard of biography? no, my good friend, unless folks spare their praises because it would charm me to hear them, I have been forced to ask what is thought of Gray's life. Indeed nobody, without my avidity, could read it at once, and as it has been published a fortnight, it was impossible it could keep its station amidst the torrent of unlively follies that overflow each day. Well the best books were certainly never calculated for the plurality of readers; or, which is wondrous rare, some very good judge must be the dictator of the age. Still it is a comfort that works of genius are indestructible. They can neither be overlaid by the dullness of co-temporaries, nor escape the penetration of subsequent taste in all centuries, who, like the adepts in chemistry, transmit the secret to the brotherhood, and preserve the nostrum of the elixir for those who are worthy of it.[1]

For me, though I recur once or twice a day to *the volume*, I have had time to read other things too, as a journey to Spain and Portugal,

1. Posterity's view has not been flattering. As Leonard Whibley put it, 'Boswell . . . did Mason too much honour in thinking that he was following "his excellent plan" [see *ante* 3 April 1775, n. 2]. . . . The first charge against Mason, as the author of Gray's *Memoirs,* is that he did not attempt to perform, even in a perfunctory way, the ordinary duty of a biographer. If the letters and the notes appended to them are taken out, what is left is little more than a meagre chronicle of Gray's birth and death, and of some few events between. . . . He committed a worse sin in his treatment of the letters, which he intended to supply the place of the biography. With a wealth of admirable letters at his disposal, he chose such parts of them as suited the purpose that he had of depicting Gray as a decorous man of letters. These parts he falsified by omissions and transpositions and garblings of his own; and from the parts thus corrupted he fabricated letters which Gray did not write' ('William Mason, Poet and Biographer,' *Blackwood's Magazine,* 1927, ccxxii, 526–7).

by a Mr Twiss,[2] who tells one nothing in vulgar aims at wit but what Baretti[3] and others have told, that those kingdoms contain nothing but muleteers and bad inns, and are as dull and depopulated as countries must be, where the Inquisition has reigned so long, and despotism reigns still. I have waded through Mr Tyrrwhit's most tedious notes to the *Canterbury Tales*,[4] for a true antiquary can still be zealous to settle the genuine shape of a lump of mineral from which Dryden extracted all the gold, and converted into beautiful medals.[5] I was paid for my trouble by lighting on this couplet so applicable to her Grace of Kingston,—

> I graunt it well, I have of non envie,
> Who maidenhed preferre to bigamie.[6]

I have dipped into the second volume of *Nugæ antiquæ*,[7] and was lucky there too, finding a madrigal, not at all despicable, by the Viscount Rochford,[8] Anne Boleyn's brother, of whom I had never been able to discover a single distich.[9] For Macpherson, I stopped dead

2. Richard Twiss (1747–1821), traveller and author. His *Travels through Portugal and Spain in 1772 and 1773* was published 7 April 1775 (*Public Advertiser*). HW's copy was sold SH v. 153. See HW to Robertson 30 May 1777, DALRYMPLE 137 and n. 12.

3. In 1770 Baretti had published his *Journey from London to Genoa through England, Portugal, Spain and France*. HW's copy was sold SH v. 145.

4. *The Canterbury Tales of Chaucer, to which are Added an Essay upon His Language and Versification, an Introductory Discourse and Notes*, 4 vols, published 27 Feb. 1775 (*Daily Adv.*). A fifth volume, consisting of a glossary for the *Tales*, appeared in 1778. The editor, Thomas Tyrwhitt (1730–86), rediscovered the principles of Chaucer's versification. HW's copy was sold SH iii. 36.

5. Dryden in the Preface to his *Fables, Ancient and Modern, Translated into Verse from Homer, Ovid, Boccace and Chaucer* (1700) had written: 'Chaucer, I confess, is a rough diamond, and must first be polished e'er he shines.' See also *ante* 7 April 1774 and n. 4.

6. Lines 95–6 of the Prologue to the *Wife of Bath's Tale* (Tyrwhitt i. 226).

7. The first volume of *Nugæ antiquæ*, a collection of papers chiefly relating to Sir John Harington (1561–1612), had appeared in 1769, the second in late March or early April 1775 (*Lloyd's Evening Post* 31 March–3 April 1775, xxxvi. 320). A three-volume enlarged reprint appeared in 1779. The work is a collection of miscellaneous papers dating from the time of Henry VIII to that of James I. The first volume was published anonymously, but the title-page of the second gives the name of the editor, Henry Harington (ca 1755–91), in whose family the collection of papers had been preserved. One of HW's sets was sold SH i. 83; the other, sold London 995 (removed from SH vii. 120).

8. George Boleyn (d. 1536), 2d Vct Rochford, involved in his sister's fall from royal favour and executed two days before her. The madrigal here attributed to him (*Nugæ antiquæ* ii. 252–3) is the well-known lyric 'My lute, awake,' first printed in *Tottel's Miscellany* and generally believed to be by Sir Thomas Wyatt. Hyder Rollins in his edition of *Tottel's Miscellany* (Cambridge, Mass., 1928–9) dismisses Harington's ascription of the poem to Rochford as without substantiation (ii. 189).

9. HW had included the name of Viscount Rochford in his *Royal and Noble Authors*, 1758, i. 72–5, although 'none of his works are come down to us, unless any of the anonymous pieces, published along with the Earl of Surrey's poems, be

short in the first volume;[10] never was such a heap of insignificant trash and lies—one instance shall suffice; in a letter from a spy to James II there is a blank for a name: a note without the smallest ground to build the conjecture on, says 'probably the Earl of Devonshire,'[11] pretty well! yet not content, the honest gentleman says in the index, 'The Earl of Devonshire is suspected of favouring the excluded family.'[12] Can you suspect such a worthy person of forgery? could he forge Ossian?—I forgot in excuse for the town, to tell you that it is very busy about a history of two Perriaus and a Mrs Rudd,[13] who are likely to be hanged for misapplying their ingenuity. They drew bills, instead of rising from the pillory to pensions by coining anecdotes against the author and friends of the Revolution. As Mrs Rudd has turned evidence, I suppose as soon as her husband is executed she will have eight hundred a year to educate her children.[14]

To return to Ossian; is not it evident that the Scots are of Irish parentage? hurt at the charge of having never produced a *poet*, they forge an epic in *prose*.

of his composition.' HW was therefore delighted to find this ascription to Rochford in the *Nugæ antiquæ*. His admiration for the 'melancholy simplicity and harmony in the lines' and for the elegance of 'the measure and general expression' tempted him to make a few alterations that would permit the poem to 'pass for the production of a more refined age.' HW's modernization appears in *Works* i. 528–9.

10. James Macpherson's *History of Great Britain from the Restoration to the Accession of the House of Hanover*, 2 vols, and *Original Papers, Containing the Secret History of Great Britain, from the Restoration to the Accession of the House of Hanover*, 2 vols, were both published 10 March 1775 (*Public Advertiser*). It was the first volume of the *Original Papers* that occasioned HW's displeasure. HW's copies of the *Original Papers* and the *History* were sold SH v. 65.

11. William Cavendish (1641–1707), 4th E. (later 1st D.) of Devonshire, an early Whig leader. No such note on a letter to James II has been found, but there is a note to this effect on a letter of 13 May 1695 from the Jacobite Earl of Middleton to one Mordaunt (*Original Papers*, 2d edn, 1776, i. 514).

12. This refers to a different passage and is in the index to the *History*.

13. The approaching trial of the Perreau brothers and of their accomplice, Mrs Rudd, was attracting much attention (see, for example, *Public Advertiser* 30 March 1775; *Lloyd's Evening Post* 27–9 March, 5–7 April, xxxvi. 300, 332; *London Chronicle* 4–6 April, xxxvii. 321–2). Robert Perreau was believed to be a respectable apothecary, but his twin brother Daniel had a dubious reputation. Mrs Rudd was Margaret Caroline Young, or Youngson (ca 1745–97), who had married (ca 1762) Valentine Rudd, but soon left him, and, after rumoured liaisons with Wilkes and the Duke of Cumberland, became in 1770 the mistress of Daniel Perreau. For the series of forgeries in which the three were involved the brothers were ultimately hanged; in her subsequent separate trial Mrs Rudd was acquitted. Opinion on the trials was sharply divided. Mrs Rudd later became the mistress of James Boswell (*Boswell Papers* xi. 297–300, xvi. *passim*; BERRY i. 208). HW's copies of *The Female Forgery*, 1775, and *Mr Daniel Perreau's Narrative*, 1775, are now WSL.

14. Mrs Rudd had three children by Daniel Perreau.

Thank you for answering my queries.[15] I have one more; who was the person Gray suspected of writing Colman's and Loyd's satire?[16] I imagine the person mentioned in the next page.[17] Mr Chute says, posterity will not believe that such a book as yours could be written in this age, which has so totally lost sight of taste and common sense; pray, did you write it now, or when *somehow or other* (as women and the French say) you lived in the Augustan age?

Since I wrote this, I have gone farther into the *Nugæ antiquæ,* and have found three invaluable letters[18] with admirable pictures of the Courts of that time. They show clearly what a sad dog Queen Bess was, and K. James what a silly bitch. There is a *bon mot* to the latter of Sir John Harrington's, translator of Ariosto, who had a great deal of wit. The son of David *did much presse for my opinion touchinge the power [of] Satane in matter of witchcraft, and askede me with much gravitie if I did truelie understande why the devil did worke more with anciente women than others. I did not refraine from a scurvey jeste and even saide (notwithstandinge to whom it was saide) that we were taughte hereof in scripture, where it is tolde that the devil walketh in dry places.*[19] Was it possible to make a better answer to such a foolish question? Is not this worthy of being hung up as a companion to Foote's?[20] bad as the ages we wot of, they furnish *bon mots* at least.

Lord Nuneham has just been here, and says everybody he has heard

15. *Ante* 3 April 1775, answered in a missing letter.

16. *Two Odes,* parodies of the odes of Gray and of Mason, published anonymously ca 1 June 1760 (*Lloyd's Evening Post* 30 May–2 June 1760). The authors were George Colman the elder and Robert Lloyd (1733–64), as Mason states in a note on p. 283. Mason printed: 'I concluded at first it was Mr * * *' (*Mem. Gray* 283). HW wrote 'Mr Pottinger' in his copy of the *Memoirs,* on hearing from Mason (*post* 18 May 1775). The ungarbled and uncut text of Gray's letter to Mason 7 June 1760 is in *Gray's Corr.* ii. 672–6. Toynbee and Whibley identify Pottinger as Richard Pottinger (1724–94), secretary to Lord Holdernesse at The Hague, under-secretary of state (south) 1751–4, (north) 1754–61, and later one of the four clerks to the privy seal (*Gray's Corr.* ii. 674; R. A. Austen-Leigh, *Eton College Register 1698–1752,* Eton, 1927, pp. 275–6). The composition of the

Two Odes is discussed by Robert Halsband, 'A Parody of Thomas Gray,' *Philological Quarterly,* 1943, xxii. 255–66.

17. David Garrick. Colman is mentioned on p. 284 of the *Memoirs* as 'a particular acquaintance of Mr Garrick.' It is odd that HW should have thought that Gray suspected Garrick of being the author, since HW had printed at SH Garrick's consolatory verses to Gray, 'Repine not, Gray,' on the failure of the public to appreciate Gray's *Odes* in 1757.

18. 'In that very curious repository [*Nugæ antiquæ*] are particularly three letters, which exhibit more faithful portraits of Queen Elizabeth and James I than are to be found in our most voluminous historians. *Vide* vol. ii. pp. 116, 132, 271, 2d edit. 1779' (*Royal and Noble Authors, Works* i. 526).

19. *Nugæ antiquæ* ii. 105.

20. HW means the *bon mot* quoted *ante* 3 April 1775, *ad fin.*

speak of it likes your book; that does not content me; they must say as Mr Chute and I do, that we will read it for the rest of our lives. Adieu.

Your constant reader,

H. W.

PS. I forgot to put my letter into the post on Saturday.

To Mason, Sunday 7 May 1775

Printed from Mitford i. 181–4.

Strawberry Hill, May 7, 1775.

OF all the birds in the air, I like a Freemason best, and next a physician that gives one pills to purge melancholy.[1] I am content to be sick, when my medicines are palatable. I remember the first words of a letter I wrote to you into Suffolk,[2] and if you do too, repeat them if possible with exaggeration.

You are the idlest of beings, and never set pen to paper, or I am an indefatigable correspondent, and plague you with my letters. I cannot help it. Not that I have anything to say, or any reason for not waiting to hear from you. The reviews do not know yet what to say to your book,[3] and so have not mentioned it; probably they are afraid of stumbling over the Æolian harp[4] again, and are weighing every word they write in a pair of lexicon-scales. Lord Nuneham, who maintained to me at first that everybody was charmed with your work, does own now that some folks begin to carp at it, had cause to dislike it, have had time to whisper their prejudices; no matter. Its merit does not de-

1. The point of this is obscure. Mason had presumably sent HW a *jeu d'esprit* (see *post* 18 May 1775), but a copy has not been found. The phrase 'pills to purge melancholy' seems to be an allusion to *Wit and Mirth: or Pills to Purge Melancholy*, 1698–1720, in which Tom D'Urfey's songs were printed. The pun on Mason's name is repeated *post* 12 and 17 June 1775.

2. Doubtless 'Thou recreant clerk,' etc. (*ante* 28 Feb. 1775).

3. The first reviews appeared in the May issues of the magazines, published ca 1 June (*Critical Review* May 1775, xxxix. 378–88; *Monthly Review* May 1775, lii. 377–87).

4. An unidentified writer (not Thomas Francklin, as Gray mistakenly supposed) in the *Critical Review* (1757, iv. 167) mistook the 'Æolian lyre' in the first line of 'The Progress of Poesy' for the Æolian harp that had been invented in the sixteenth or seventeenth century. See Grove's *Dictionary of Music*; *Mem. Gray* 250; *Gray's Corr.* ii. 523.

pend on the competence of the present age, you have fixed the method of biography, and whoever will write a life well must imitate you.

You have done another service that you are not aware of. I who, simpleton as I was, loved to be an author, am so ashamed of my own stuff, and so convinced that nobody but you and Gray could write, have taken shame to myself, and forsworn the press; yet as I cannot be idle, it is impossible. I have invented a new and very harmless way of *making books,* which diverts me as well, and brings me to no disgrace. I have just made a *new book,* which costs me only money, which I don't value, and time which I love to employ. It is a volume of etchings by *noble authors.* They are bound in robes of crimson and gold; the titles are printed at my own press, and the pasting is *by my own hand.*[5] What I shall *compose* next I do not know. As you too seem to have given over writing, I wish you would draw for me, or etch, but with your variety of talents, perhaps you are making another match between two musical instruments. Is Mynheer Drum contracted with Signora Flageolet? or are you contriving how to make one mouth blow a trumpet, and sing at the same time? Mr Bentley[6] was always inventing new dishes by compounding heterogeneous ingredients and called it cultivating the *materia edica,* for you geniuses hate the beaten road. He never would draw with common colours, or Indian ink, but being purely indolent too, always dipped his brush in the first thing he met, no matter whether the ashes, or the oil and vinegar, or all together, and ten to one but he tasted too, whether they would not make a good sauce, for cleanliness was not one of his delicacies.

I have been at all the exhibitions,[7] and do not find that we are got

5. The book, a portfolio, was sold London 1126 (removed from SH viii. 56) and is now WSL. It is bound in crimson morocco, is elaborately tooled, has HW's arms on the sides in gilt cartouches, and silk ties. The spine is lettered 'Etchings by Amateurs, Vol. I.' There are four title-pages, the first of which is 'A Collection of Prints Engraved by Various Persons of Quality,' a more accurate description than 'noble authors.' HW has annotated the prints freely.

6. Richard Bentley (1708–82), son of the classical scholar and critic; HW's close friend and correspondent until they quarrelled in 1760.

7. The Royal Academy exhibition opened 25 April 1775, but there had been a private showing and dinner on 22 April which HW had attended (HW to Mann 17 April; *Public Advertiser* 25 April). HW's annotated set of the catalogues of the Academy's exhibitions are now (1953) in the possession of Lady Sybil Grant. HW's notes were printed by Algernon Graves in *The Royal Academy of Arts,* 1905–6. Other exhibitions opening at this time were those of the Incorporated Society of Artists of Great Britain on 25 April, and of the Society of Artists Associated for the Relief of Their Distressed Brethren, Their Widows and Children (the Free Society). HW's notes in his catalogues of these exhibitions (now WSL) are printed in the 27th Walpole Society volume, 1938–1939, pp. 55–88: 'Notes by Horace Walpole . . . on the Exhibitions of the Society of Artists and the

an inch nearer Raphael than we were. Sir Joshua[8] has indeed produced the best portrait he ever painted, that of the Primate of Ireland,[9] whom age has softened into a beauty: all the painters are beg-
ging to draw him, as they did from Reynolds's beggar-man.[10] My
brother has given me the view of Gray's tomb and churchyard,[11] very
prettily done, and inspired by Gray's own melancholy. I have hung it
here in my favourite blue room,[12] as a companion to Madame de
Sévigny's Hôtel de Carnavalet,[13] and call them my *Penseroso* and
Allegro. Sir Edward was disappointed at your not revisiting his pentachord,[14] for you inventors are jealous gods; but I assured him you had
left town in a very few days after you were with him.

I am to dine on Monday at the Hôtel d'Harcourt.[15] The town says
the father's kingdom[16] is soon to be invaded by the Spaniards;[17] but

Free Society of Artists, 1760–1791,' ed. Hugh
Gatty.

8. Sir Joshua Reynolds (1723–92), Kt,
1769; President of the Royal Academy
1768–92.

9. Richard Robinson (ca 1708–94), Bp
of Killala, 1752, of Leighlin and Ferns,
1759, of Kildare, 1761; Abp of Armagh,
1765; cr. (1777) Bn Rokeby. The portrait
is described in Algernon Graves and William Vine Cronin, *A History of the Works
of Sir Joshua Reynolds*, 1899–1901, ii. 828.

10. George White, an Irishman. He had
been a paver, and was a beggar when he
was discovered by Sir Joshua. A half-length
portrait of White as an old man had been
shown at the Royal Academy exhibition in
1771. HW's note in his catalogue reads:
'Very fine, an old beggar man. This was an
old beggar, who had so fine a head that Sir
Joshua chose him for the father of his picture from Dante, and painted him several
times, as did others in imitation of Reynolds. There were even busts and cameos of
him' (Algernon Graves, *The Royal Academy of Arts*, vi. 271).

11. 'A view of the church of Stokepogeys
in Buckinghamshire; the moon shining on
Mr Gray's tomb in the churchyard; by
Baron: a present from Sir Edward Walpole' ('Des. of SH,' *Works* ii. 425). The picture was sold SH xviii. 91; it is now in
the Master's Lodge, Pembroke College,
Cambridge. It was painted by William Augustus Barron (living 1813), landscape
painter and protégé of Sir Edward Walpole, through whom he obtained a post in

the Exchequer (DNB; *Royal Kalendar* 1813,
p. 255).

12. The Breakfast-Room, 'furnished with
blue paper and blue and white linen'
(*Works* ii. 421).

13. 'View of the Hôtel de Carnavelet,
where Madame de Sévigné lived, in la rue
Coulture St Catherine, at Paris; built by
Du Cerceau; painted by Raguenet' (ibid.
ii. 426). See DU DEFFAND v. 304 and n. 267.
It was sold SH xi. 18.

14. Of his brother HW wrote: 'He drew
well, but seldom, was a profound musician,
and even invented a most touching instrument, which, from the number of its
strings, he called a *pentachord*' (*Last Journals* i. 102).

15. Harcourt House in Cavendish
Square, at this time the London residence
of Viscount Nuneham. It later became the
Duke of Rutland's town house, and was
torn down early in the twentieth century.
Nuneham had a 'decided preference to
French manners and fashions' (Collins,
Peerage, 1812, iv. 450).

16. Ireland. Simon Harcourt (1714–77),
1st E. Harcourt, was Lord Lieutenant
1772–7.

17. Spanish military preparations, allegedly against the piratical Barbary States,
seemed to England and other countries
somewhat excessive for their purported object (*Annual Register*, 1775, xviii. 142*–3*).
In April and early May 1775 England was
particularly apprehensive of Spanish ac-
tivities (*Calendar of Home Office Papers of
the Reign of George III, 1773–1775*, ed.

the ministers, who certainly ought to know best, swear it is not true,[18] so to be sure it is not.

I forgot to tell you that our friend Mrs D.[19] is one of the warmest admirers of Gray's life;[20] but then she is equally charmed with Mrs Chapone's[21] writings, and thinks they will go a great way towards making the Bible fashionable.[22] She lent them to me, but alas! they could not have so much effect on me, had I wanted it, for I could not read the Madam's works themselves.

Have you had your summer, as we have? the fine ladies did not dare to ride on the causeway from Wednesday was sennight till last Friday, for fear of being tanned. We are now relapsed to fires. Adieu,

Yours most devotedly,

H. W.

PS. I like the Hôtel d'Harcourt, it has *grand air* and a kind of Louis XIV old-fashionhood that pleases me. There is a large garden and new *parterre,* and we want some *treillage* if the Irish Exchequer would

Richard Arthur Roberts, 1899, p. 342; *Last Journals* i. 459). The same rumour mentioned here by HW is echoed in a terse newspaper story: 'A letter from Dublin says, "We are under no apprehensions from the report of a Spanish invasion; as it is not material to whom we are slaves"' (*London Chronicle* 30 May–1 June 1775, xxxvii. 520).

18. The denials to which HW alludes may not have been made publicly; none have been found. Ten days after this letter, however, in a debate in the House of Lords, the subject of the Spanish preparations arose and assurances were given by Lord Rochford as spokesman for the ministers that Spain had no hostile intentions against England (*Last Journals* i. 462–3; Cobbett, *Parl. Hist.* xviii. 666–75).

19. Mary Granville (1700–88), m. (1) (1718) Alexander Pendarves; m. (2) (1743) Patrick Delany, Dean of Down. HW saw her frequently in London and so did Mason until he offended her in 1784 by changing his politics (*Delany Correspondence* vi. 232 n. 2). Mrs Delany bequeathed Mason 'Sacharissa's portrait copied after the original by Vandyke' (ibid. 487). She made several such bequests, including one to HW (a miniature of Liotard by himself,

now WSL), so that 'these much esteemed friends may sometimes recollect a person who was so sensible of the honour of their friendship and who delighted so much in their conversation and works' (ibid.).

20. 'I have amused myself lately with Mr Mason's publication of Mr Gray's *Memoirs,* and liked them extremely. Mr Mason's zeal for his friend is very amiable' (Mrs Delany to Bernard Granville 29 ?April 1775, ibid. v. 109).

21. Hester Mulso (1727–1801), m. (1760) John Chapone. Her *Letters on the Improvement of the Mind, Addressed to a Young Lady,* 1773, was very popular, and new editions continued to appear throughout the eighteenth century and the first half of the nineteenth. At the time of this letter the fifth edition had recently appeared (*London Chronicle* 1–4 April 1775, xxxvii. 319), as well as a second edition of her *Miscellanies in Prose and Verse.*

22. In Nov. 1774, in a set of maxims composed for a young lady, Mrs Delany said of Mrs Chapone's *Letters,* 'I know no book for a young person (next to the Bible) more entertaining and edifying if read with due attention' (*Delany Correspondence* v. 55).

afford it. Lord N[uneham] says, Oxford pouts at you as well as Cambridge. Lord Lyttelton does not admire. Mr Palgrave, who was here this morning, says all the world admires, which is more than I demand. Pray, because you have written *the book,* do you never design to write anything else? Is *The English Garden* to be a fragment, and do you expect that anybody should finish it and write your life, as well as you have done both for Gray?

From MASON, Thursday 18 May 1775

Printed from MS now WSL.
Address: The Honourable Horace Walpole, Arlington Street, London.
Postmark: ROTHERHAM 23 MA.

Aston, May 18th, 1775.

Dear Sir,

I AM at last released from my York residence and am returned from a disagreeable journey to Hull on *landed* business[1] of which I made nothing. I sit down quietly now for the first moment at Aston *near Rotherham* (pray remember that) and apply myself to the answering two of your letters, which before I could not possibly do, so pray forgive me, for I assure you I have behaved worse to the Delegates of the Press of the University of Oxford and a Mr Falconer[2] (the, is to be, editor of Strabo) who want me to transcribe all Mr Gray's geographical lucubrations,[3] which, as near as I can compute, would make a book half as large as the *Memoirs.*

The person you inquire after as the person G. suspected of writing Colman's satire, is neither more nor less than the lively and spirit*u*el (not spiritual) Mr Potenger,[4] and as such pray book him.[5]

What you say about my *Memoirs* does not flatter me half so much

1. Probably in connection with an estate (unidentified) in the East Riding that came to Mason by reversion in 1768 (Mitford ii. 412).

2. Thomas Falconer (1738–92), classical scholar and antiquary. He never completed his edition of Strabo. His materials were left to his nephew, Thomas Falconer (1772–1839), who published the Oxford edition of Strabo in 1807.

3. For Gray's life-long interest in geography and the literature of travel see William Powell Jones, *Thomas Gray, Scholar,* Cambridge, Mass., 1937, pp. 70–83, and Roger Martin, *Essai sur Thomas Gray,* 1934, pp. 215–8.

4. See *ante* 14 April 1775, n. 16.

5. That is, HW is to write the name in his copy of *Mem. Gray,* which he did.

as what you say about my pills. I think in time I shall rival Dr Hill[6] with his tincture of spleenwort. 'Tis pity, however, that my medicine is not vendible, do you think his Majesty would grant me a patent for it?

You say the University of Oxford pouts at me. I know not for why, but in revenge I'll tell you a story about them which I think you cannot have heard. Last year a young Irish gentleman, Mr Burgh, who has for some time lived at York,[7] writ a book called a scriptural confutation of Mr Lindsey's apology,[8] defending the doctrine of the Trinity in a new and (as we orthodox divines say) masterly manner. To the second edition[9] he set his name, and the University of Oxford met to consider of the propriety of giving him an honorary degree of Master of Arts. After much debate the intention was put off, *sine die,* at the very meeting when they gave Dr Johnson a degree of Doctor of Laws.[10] They said he had not laid sufficient stress on natural religion, but the true reason was that he had in a note abused David Hume[11] and in a

6. John Hill (ca 1716–75), apothecary, quack, and miscellaneous writer. The King of Sweden gave him the Order of Vasa for his *Vegetable System,* 26 vols, 1759–75, after which he called himself Sir John Hill. HW and Mason both disliked him because of his political connections, which gave him a place in the *Heroic Epistle* (l. 19) and in HW's commentary: 'He was a physician, quack, botanist, author of a paper called *The Inspector,* and of various other things, especially of many folios of natural history, and above all, at the head of the plagiaries of the age. He wrote easily, and in a good style; and all these superficial merits, particularly his skill in botany, recommended him to Lord Bute, in comparison of whom Dr Hill was profoundly learned in anything that either pretended to' (Mason's *Satirical Poems* 54).

7. William Burgh (1741–1808), writer and politician; M.P. Athy, Kildare, in the Irish Parliament 1769–76; friend of Mason and admirer of his writings. He contributed commentary and notes to the 1783 edition of Mason's *English Garden* (*post* 10 March 1782). Burgh moved to York while still a young man and for many years lived in a house on the north side of Bootham Street (Davies, *York Press* 299).

8. *A Scriptural Confutation of the Argu-*

ments against the One Godhead . . . Produced by the Rev. Mr Lindsey in His Late Apology, published anonymously 2 June 1774 (*Daily Adv.*). The *Apology,* 1774, by Theophilus Lindsey (1723–1808), a Church of England divine who adopted Unitarianism in 1773, was designed as a justification of Lindsey's change of faith. Burgh appears to have had the assistance of Mason in the preparation of his confutation, for Mason told Lindsey that he had revised some of Burgh's proof-sheets (Thomas Belsham, *Memoirs of the Late Reverend Theophilus Lindsey, M.A.,* 1820, p. 95).

9. The second edition of Burgh's *Scriptural Confutation* was noticed in the *Critical Review* for May 1775, xxxix. 427.

10. Johnson's degree of Doctor of Laws was dated 30 March 1775 (Boswell, *Johnson* ii. 332). In 1788 Oxford made Burgh a Doctor of Civil Law.

11. 'David Hume . . . is excellently qualified to abet Mr Lindsey's tenets, having undertaken to subvert the religion and liberties of this country. Whenever the bonds of religion are loosed, and the restrictions of conscience taken away, a substitute must be found to control mankind, and an earthly tyrant be established on the throne of a deposed God' (*A Scriptural Confutation,* 1775, 2d edn, p. 197).

dedication to Edmund Burke doubted a little whether the *royal* fountain of honour was much purer than ditch water.[12] I wish you would look into this dedication and also page 197[13] of his second edition. I think you would be pleased—*au reste* I can only say that had he writ on any other subject, you would also have been more pleased; for he is a young man of the quickest parts and most general knowledge I ever met with. He is of the Irish House of Commons, brother-in-law to Mr Hussey[14]—and *one of us*[15] *au merveil*. But is it not curious, that, on a doctrinal point in which the Oxonians in particular so much interest themselves, they will not suffer a man to defend their cause who has the misfortune to be a Whig?

I take shame to myself for not having waited on Sir Edward Walpole before I left town and am much obliged to you for having told a civil lie upon the occasion. But don't go to flirt at our pentachords and our celestinettes, mind your noble etchings and your print shearings, and suffer us as well as yourself to ride our own hobby horses quietly and discreetly. I am now in the very act of making an electrical machine[16] by the help of our village wheelwright. Go to! If I choose to amuse myself with electrifying mice instead of writing second books of English Gardens, who shall control me?

I mean to write to Lord Nuneham soon to get me from France Watelet's *Essay on Gardening*[17] and M. Chabanon *Sur la manie des jardins anglais*.[18] Perhaps you will deign to assist in procuring me these two brochures, the sillier they are I shall like them the better. Believe me, dear Sir,

Most sincerely yours,

W. MASON

---

12. '. . . Though I have not much to boast of any approbation personally addressed to myself, from those who have drawn their honours from the royal fountain, yet I was not unnoticed by others, who derive theirs from the clear and unpolluted spring of merit' (ibid. p. ii).

13. I.e., the note on David Hume. HW apparently did not own the pamphlet and did not look at it.

14. Walter Hussey (later Hussey Burgh) (1742–83), Irish statesman, orator, and jurist; m. (1767) Anne Burgh, sister of William Burgh.

15. Burgh later altered his political views (Davies, *York Press* 299).

16. No further reference to Mason's electrical machine has been found.

17. The *Essai sur les jardins*, 1774, by Claude-Henri Watelet (1718–86).

18. *Épître sur la manie des jardins anglais*, 1775, by Michel-Paul-Gui de Chabanon (1730–92).

To Mason, Saturday 27 May 1775

Printed from Mitford i. 187–90.

May 27, 1775.

To Mrs Crewe,[1]

By the Honourable Charles Fox.

Where the loveliest expression to feature is joined,
By Nature's most delicate pencil designed,
Where blushes unbidden and smiles without art,
Speak the sweetness and feeling that dwell in the heart;
Where in manners enchanting no blemish we trace,
But the soul keeps the promise we had from the face,
Sure philosophy, reason and coldness must prove
Defences unequal to shield us from love.
Then tell me, mysterious enchanter, O tell
By what wonderful art or by what magic spell,
My heart is so fenced, that for once I am wise
And gaze without madness on Amoret's eyes:
That my wishes which never were bounded before,
Are here bounded by friendship and ask for no more.
Is it reason? No, that my whole life will belie,
For who so at variance as reason and I.
Is't ambition that fills up each chink of my heart,
Nor allows to one softer sensation a part?
Ah! no, for in this all the world must agree
That one folly was never sufficient for me.
Is my mind on distress so intensely employed?
Or by pleasure relaxed or variety cloyed?
For alike in this only enjoyment and pain
Both slacken the springs of the nerves which they strain.
That I've felt each reverse that from fortune can flow,
That I've tasted each bliss which the happiest know,
Has still been the whimsical fate of my life,
Where anguish and joy have been ever at strife.

1. Frances Anne Greville (d. 1818), m. (1766) John Crewe, who was cr. (1806) Bn Crewe. 'She is certainly, in my eyes, the most completely a beauty of any woman I ever saw. I know not, even now, any female in her first youth who could bear the comparison. She uglifies everything near her' (*The Diary and Letters of Madame d'Arblay, 1778–1840*, ed. Charlotte Barrett and Austin Dobson, 1904–5, v. 89, 18 June 1792). HW printed the verses at SH in June 1775, and issued the sheet with Fitzpatrick's *Dorinda* (*Journal of the Printing Office* 18; Hazen, *SH Bibliography* 217).

But though versed in th' extremes both of pleasure and pain
I am still but too ready to feel them again.
If then for this once in my life I am free,
And escape from a snare might catch wiser than me;
'Tis that beauty alone but imperfectly charms,
For though brightness may dazzle, 'tis kindness that warms.
As on suns in the winter with pleasure we gaze,
But feel not their force, though their splendour we praise;
So beauty our just admiration may claim,
But love and love only our hearts can inflame.

As I design to be very temperate in writing to you, you would not receive so sudden a return to yours, were it not to send you the foregoing verses, which though current, are not yet got into the papers or magazines. I think you will like the ease and frankness of the lines, though they are not poetic; in that light and as characteristic, they are pretty original, so they are for being love-verses without love, the author's reason for not having which, is the worst part, and if poetry was peremptory logic, the inference would be that you must be in love with a woman before you can desire her: at least she must be in love with you, which I take to be seldom the case.

I am to have a longer copy of verses by Fitzpatrick,[2] which I expect to like much, since he writes as easily as his friend, and is a more genuine poet. Lord Carlisle has written some too,[3] to his wife's sister, Lady Louisa Leveson:[4] I shall have them too, as a *noble* author's[5]— but I have seen them and they are not worth sending; no more than some by Lord Palmerston,[6] occasioned by others written some time

2. Hon. Richard Fitzpatrick (1748–1813), general, politician, and wit; brother of HW's friend Lord Ossory; intimate friend of Charles James Fox. The poem referred to was *Dorinda, a Town Eclogue,* also addressed to Mrs Crewe and printed at SH June 1775. See G. O. Trevelyan, *The Early History of Charles James Fox,* 1928 edn, p. 306; Hazen, *SH Bibliography* 112–4. See also Appendix 6.

3. These verses have not been found.

4. Lady Louisa Leveson-Gower (1749–1827), eldest dau. of the 2d E. Gower; m. (1777) Archibald Macdonald, the jurist, cr. (1788) Kt and (1813) Bt.

5. Lord Carlisle's grandfather, Charles Howard, the 3d E. of Carlisle, was later in-

cluded by HW in the 'Noble Authors Omitted in Former Editions' of *Royal and Noble Authors,* and there compared unfavourably with his grandson: 'His lessons of experience and virtue he bequeathed in verse, composed few hours before his death, to his son and successor; and it is pity that such wholesome precepts were not couched in more harmonious numbers—It was not from his Lordship that his grandson inherited a genuine talent for poetry' (*Royal and Noble Authors, Works* i. 534–5).

6. Henry Temple (1739–1802), 2d Vct Palmerston. Palmerston is noticed in Thomas Park's augmented edition of *Royal and Noble Authors,* 1806, v. 327–8.

ago by the Duchess of Devonshire[7] when a girl to her father.[8] These
are a greater rarity, and I am laying out for them. Thank my stars I
have done both with authorship and noble authors, for my Lord
Lyttelton has printed a speech,[9] though I thought we should not have
had his till his execution.[10] It is a poor affair, void of argument and
grossly abusive on Lord Camden.[11] It will be as difficult for the court
to uphold his oratory as his character, if he has recourse to the press.

Burke has printed a second speech,[12] which I prefer much to his
first.[13] It is grave, solid, temperate and chaster from exuberant imagination. If his fancy breaks out, it does not soar above the third heaven
and come tumbling down flat. Apropos to authors, the husband[14] of
Mrs Montagu of Shakespeareshire[15] is dead, and has left her an estate
of seven thousand pounds a year in her own power. Will you come
and be a candidate for her hand? I conclude it will be given to a

7. Lady Georgiana Spencer (1757–1806),
m. (1774) William Cavendish, 5th D. of
Devonshire. In HW's list of 'Ladies and
gentlemen distinguished by their writings,
learning, or talents in 1783' appears
'Georgiana, Duchess of Devonshire, some
poems' ('Book of Materials' 1771, p. 90).
For an account of the Duchess's verses see
Hugh Stokes, *The Devonshire House Circle,*
1917, pp. 272–9 and *passim.*

8. John Spencer (1734–83), cr. (1761) Bn
Spencer of Althorp and Vct Spencer, (1765)
Vct Althorp and Earl Spencer. Georgiana's
verses to him have not been found, but
what appear to be Lord Palmerston's are
preserved with other verses by Georgiana
in BM Add. MSS 37728, fol. 79. The sixteen
lines are headed 'On Reading Some Poetry
of Lady Georgiana Spencer's, Wrote at Al-
thorp—1774,' and begin:
'In groves oft haunted by the tuneful choir
When sweet Georgiana waked the Muse's
    lyre
And wildly warbling as she roved along
Poured the soft music of her artless song—'
The lines conclude with an allusion to
Waller and Sacharissa, and a note identifies
Sacharissa as Georgiana's ancestress, the
Countess of Sunderland.

9. *The Speech of Lord Lyttelton, on a
Motion Made in the House of Lords for a
Repeal of the Canada Bill, May 17, 1775.*
HW's copy is now WSL.

10. For HW's low opinion of Thomas,
Lord Lyttelton see *ante* 3 Sept. 1773.

11. Charles Pratt (1714–94), cr. (1765) Bn
Camden, (1786) Earl Camden; jurist and
politician; lord chancellor 1766–70. 'On the
17th Lord Camden moved for a repeal of
the Quebec Bill, and made a great figure,
as Lord Mansfield, who defended it, made
an artful one. . . . Lord Shelburne spoke
finely too, and Lord Lyttelton with applause, and . . . with most indecent abuse
of Lord Camden, whom he taxed with Re-
publicanism and Jacobitism; but printing
his speech immediately afterwards, as was
grown a custom, it was so wordy and void
of argument, that he fell greatly in the
public opinion' (*Last Journals* i. 462).

12. *The Speech of Edmund Burke, Esq.,
on Moving His Resolutions for Conciliation with the Colonies.* The speech had
been delivered 22 March 1775 and was published 22 May (*Public Advertiser*). HW's
copy is now WSL.

13. *The Speech of Edmund Burke, Esq.,
on American Taxation, April 19, 1774,*
published 10 Jan. 1775 (*Public Advertiser*).
HW's copy is now WSL. HW has noted
beneath the date on the title-page, 'January
10th,' and has made numerous marginalia
on the text.

14. Edward Montagu (1692–1775), grandson of Edward, 1st E. of Sandwich, died 20
May 1775 (Venn, *Alumni Cantab.*).

15. Because of her *Essay on the Writings
and Genius of Shakespeare,* 1769. Elizabeth
Robinson (1720–1800), m. (1742) Edward
Montagu; bluestocking.

champion at some Olympic games, and were I she, I would sooner marry you than Pindar.

The history of the heroine Kingstone,[16] as registered in our daily chronicles,[17] is literally authentic, and so is the respect paid to her in the King's Bench, though I suppose, penned by herself,

> For little brimstones[18] oft submit to fate
> That great ones may enjoy the world in state.[19]

The intrepidity of her countenance, while her indictment was reading, was worthy of Joan of Arc. I'm persuaded she will avoid any further trial.

Thank you for your Oxonian anecdotes, but alas! they may be paralleled all over the kingdom. In return I will write next week to France for the two tracts you wot of;[20] you shall not be idle for want of anything I can pimp for.

I am happily embarked on two vast folios of the History of [Dorsetshire],[21] which I prefer to every author of the age but one. I have picked up some excellent narratives of Mr Bruce,[22] but have not room for them; but here is what is better. He was asked before G. Selwyn if the Abyssinians have any music? he replied they have one *lyre*. Selwyn

16. Elizabeth Chudleigh, *soi-disant* Duchess of Kingston (*ante* 16 Sept. 1774 and n. 1).

17. 'On Wednesday morning the Duchess of K[ingston] came through the back door of the Duke of Newcastle's house, and went up the stairs which lead to Lord Mansfield's room, behind the Court of King's Bench. . . . The counsel on the other side, by the advice of the Chief Justice, agreed to dispense with some legal ceremony. . . . The court was very full upon the occasion, which her Grace saluted at her entrance, and repeated the same as she withdrew; the business was finished in about ten minutes, during which time her Grace received the utmost respect from the court and the auditors' (*Daily Adv.* 26 May 1775).

18. Viragos, spit-fires (OED sub 'brimstone' 4).

19. 'Where little villains must submit to fate,
That great ones may enjoy the world in state'

(Sir Samuel Garth, *The Dispensary,* Canto i, ll. 9–10).
HW quotes these lines in his letter to Lady Ossory 10 June 1780.

20. Watelet's *Essai sur les jardins* and Chabanon's *Épître sur la manie des jardins anglais.* HW wrote to Mme du Deffand for them immediately, and she promised in her letter of 4 June 1775 to send them to him (see DU DEFFAND iv. 196).

21. Cunningham and Mrs Toynbee thus emend Mitford's 'Devonshire.' The book was doubtless John Hutchins, *The History and Antiquities of the County of Dorset,* 2 vols, 1774. WH's copy was sold SH i. 75.

22. James Bruce (1730–94), African traveller and author, who had returned to England in 1774. His accounts of his adventures were soon widely circulated, although he did not publish his *Travels* until 1790.

whispered his neighbour, 'They have one less since he left their country.'[23] Adieu! I remove to Strawberry tomorrow.

Yours ever,

H. W.

To Mason, Monday 12 June 1775

Printed from Mitford i. 151–2, where it is dated 1774, incorrectly, as its contents
show. Cunningham also misplaced it, but it is correctly dated in Toynbee.

Arlington Street, June 12, 177[5].

I RECOMMEND this with your two tracts on gardening to Mr
Fraser; you see I hasten to send you straw, that your brick-kiln
may blaze.[1] I shall send you soon Fitzpatrick's *Town Eclogue,* from
my own furnace. The verses are charmingly smooth and easy, but I
am much mistaken if you like them so well as Charles Fox's, as the
former have certainly no novelty to recommend them, though there
is one line about *squeezing* that is delightful.[2]

The *Manie des jardins anglais* is very silly, and unpoetic even for
French verse. T'other author[3] has stolen all his ideas from us, and is
ungrateful,[4] is very French too, absurd and superficial, meaning to
be philosophic; has no idea of situation, but thinks it can be made;[5]
and in reality does not conceive helping or improving nature, but
would make puppet-shows, for different ranks.[6] He puts me in mind of

---

23. The same story is told *post* 29 Feb.
1776 and in *Walpoliana* ii. 2–3. On the
general scepticism that greeted Bruce's
stories of his travels see BERRY i. 239 and
n. 23.

---

1. And produce another book of Mason's
English Garden. See *ante* 7 and 18 May
1775.
2. 'And oh! what bliss, when each alike
    is pleased,
    The hand that squeezes, and the hand
      that's squeezed'
                    (*Dorinda,* ll. 97–8).
3. Claude-Henri Watelet.
4. 'Les parcs qu'on dispose sur les nou-

veaux principes, sont désignés par le nom
d'une nation que nous imitons dans quelques usages assez peu intéressants, avec une
affectation souvent ridicule' (Claude-Henri
Watelet, *Essai sur les jardins,* p. 50. HW's
copy was sold SH v. 169).
5. For Watelet's insistence that nature
should be controlled by art see his *Essai,*
pp. 60–1, 75–7.
6. 'Les lieux de plaisance, faits pour
n'être qu'agréables, sont la plupart imités
les uns des autres; ils se distinguent cepen-
dant aussi par quelques traits, ou quelques
nuances du caractère, et de l'état de ceux
qui en ont ordonné les dispositions et les
ornements' (ibid. 91).

one of his countrymen, who seeing some of ours hang up their hats on a row of pegs at a tavern, said, *On voit bien que c'est une nation qui pense.* I think they are ten times more foolish since they took to thinking.

By the waters of Babylon we sit down and weep, when we think of thee O America![7] Tribulation on tribulation! since Gage's defeat,[8] eighteen, some say twenty-eight thousand men have invested Boston; ten thousand more are on their march from Rhode Island. Two ships laden with provisions for him have been destroyed at New York, and all his Majesty's friends turned out thence.[9] *Nous ne savons plus à quel saint nous vouer.* The City says there must be a pacification and a change of actors.[10] Much good may it do those who will read their parts! Old *Garrick*[11] perhaps will return to the stage,[12] because he has no time to lose—however the manager's company[13] talks of a troop of Hessians, etc.[14]

7. Paraphrased from Psalm 137.1; HW's favourite quotation from the Bible.

8. The defeat of British troops sent out by Gen. Thomas Gage (1721–87), governor of Massachusetts, in the battle of Lexington on 19 April. HW's account, apparently based on the first unofficial dispatches printed in the newspapers at the end of May, but roughly accurate as to the relative strength of the forces and the numbers killed, was entered in his journal for 28 May: 'Arrived a light sloop sent by the Americans from Salem, with an account of their having defeated the King's troops. General Gage had sent a party to seize a magazine belonging to the provincials at Concord, which was guarded by militia of the province in arms. The regulars, about 1000, attacked the provincials, not half so many, who repulsed them, and the latter retired to Lexington. Gage sent another party under Lord Percy to support the former; he, finding himself likely to be attacked, sent for fresh orders, which were to retreat to Boston. The country came in to support the provincials, who lost about 50 men, and the regulars 150' (*Last Journals* i. 463–4).

9. 'The action at Concord flew like wildfire, and threw the whole continent into a flame. The mob rose at New York, seized, unloaded, and destroyed the cargoes of two ships lying there with provisions for Gage.

. . . Troops from every quarter marched towards Boston, and 18,000 men invested the town. Ten thousand more were said to be on the march from Rhode Island. The King's friends were driven out of New York' (*Last Journals* i. 465). The source of HW's figures has not been found. *Daily Adv.* for 5 June, the same issue that contains the story of the seizure of the two ships in New York harbour, reports 24,000 provincials at Boston. William Ellery, writing from Newport 25 April, gave the number as 'not less than twenty thousand,' formed in a semicircle from Charlestown to Roxbury (*American Archives*, ed. Peter Force, Washington, 1837–53, 4th ser., ii. 381–2).

10. 'It was yesterday reported, that a change in the administration will soon take place' (*Daily Adv.* 20 June 1775).

11. William Pitt the elder (1708–78), cr. (1766) E. of Chatham. 'I think my winter will be very well amused, whether Mr Garrick and Mr Pitt act or not' (HW to George Selwyn 2 Dec. 1765).

12. 'The Duke of Richmond, thinking the ministers could not stand it, had gone to Lord Chatham, and told him that, as it was likely they should be sent for, it would be necessary to settle some plan of administration' (*Last Journals* i. 467).

13. Supporters of the King.

14. 'The ministers were aground: they

I have got another noble author, Lord Mahon;[15] he writes on the gold coin;[16] if he can make gold as well as coin, he will be of great use to his father-in-law *Garrick*, and a very good prop to his administration. Your old Pollio[17] is returned very lean and very deaf. Considering all things, methinks you might now hold a lodge,[18] Mr Mason. Adieu.

PS. Here is the *Eclogue*.

From MASON, Saturday 17 June 1775

Printed from MS now WSL.
Address: The Honourable Horace Walpole, Arlington Street, London.
Postmark: ROTHERHAM 20 JU.

Aston, June 17th, 1775.

YOU are goodness itself for sending me what you have sent me.[1] I thank you for the French before I read it. Let the books be as bad as you say, they may, perhaps, lead one to think of something better; if they don't, you know, there is no harm done. With respect to the English, I think much the same about them as you do. The young cub's[2] is certainly the best, it has something of character and originality about it. The other is the most old-fashioned thing to be

first thought of sending Hessians, Hanoverians, and even a large body of Russians—but found it would be too expensive or too unpopular' (*Last Journals* i. 467). In a letter sent from Boston 12 June 1775 Gage wrote: 'Nothing is to be neglected of which we can avail ourselves. Hanoverians, Hessians, perhaps Russians may be hired' (*The Correspondence of General Thomas Gage*, ed. Clarence E. Carter, New Haven, 1931–3, ii. 684). That HW's information was accurate is also indicated by a manuscript letter of 20 June cited by Allen French, *The First Year of the American Revolution*, Boston, 1934, p. 316, which is concerned with the opening stages of negotiations with Russia.

15. Charles Stanhope (1753–1816), styled Vct Mahon 1763–86; 3d E. Stanhope, 1786; scientist and politician; m. (1774) Hester Pitt, dau. of 1st E. of Chatham.

16. *Considerations on the Means of Pre-* venting Fraudulent Practices on the Gold Coin, published 6 June 1775 (*Daily Adv.*). HW's copy is now WSL. The pamphlet did not win him a place among the 'Noble Authors Omitted in Former Editions' (see ante 27 May 1775, n. 5).

17. Gaius Asinius Pollio (76 B.C.–A.D. 5), protector and patron of Virgil. 'On Tuesday night the Earl of Holdernesse . . . arrived in town from Paris, having been absent upwards of fifteen months in Italy and France, for the recovery of his health' (*London Chronicle* 6–8 June 1775, xxxvii. 542).

18. Still another pun on Mason's name occurs in *post* 17 June 1775.

1. The two French essays on gardening requested in the letter of 18 May 1775 and the two sets of verses on Mrs Crewe by Fox and Fitzpatrick (*ante* 27 May 1775).

2. I.e., Charles James Fox's.

written by a young man of fashion that I ever read. He might have writ it in a full-bottomed wig, a cravat and roll-ups.[3] And Sir Conyers Darcy[4] had he been alive might have admired it and carried it to Lady Betty Germaine[5] as a *jeu d'esprit* of my Lord Lansdown's.[6] If my friend Mr Kirgate had not dated it, I should have thought it printed somewhere about the four last years of Queen Anne.[7] *Explicit* my criticism.

You are always telling me of your additional Noble Authors and do not mention one worth all the rest of the bunch. I mean my neighbour here Lord Effingham.[8] Was there ever anything ancient or modern better either in sentiment or language than his late speech?[9] I have one miserable defect in my constitution which is that I never could bear above one pint of port at a sitting, a bottle was always too much for me, else I would incontinently introduce myself to his Lordship by an ode and he should be my Pollio. I would hope to be one of his club at Boston Castle[10] and try to leap a five-barred gate with his

3. After 1720 bag-wigs, bob-wigs, and pigtails became more popular than the old full wig that covered the shoulders. Cravats continued to be worn, but the long, wide neck-cloth that had been fashionable early in the century yielded to several rival modes, notably the solitaire. Roll-ups, or stockings worn outside the breeches and drawn up over the knee, ceased to be fashionable in France around 1730 and in England a few years later. See Iris Brooke and James Laver, *English Costume of the Eighteenth Century*, 1931, pp. 22, 34, 64.

4. Sir Conyers Darcy (ca 1685–1758), K.B., 1725, uncle of Lord Holdernesse; M.P. co. York 1707–8, 1747–58, Newark 1715–22, Richmond 1722–47; master of the King's household, 1720, controller, 1730 (Arthur Gooder, *The Parliamentary Representation of the County of York*, vol. ii, 1938, pp. 101–2; *Members of Parliament*, pt ii, 1878, pp. 42, 54).

5. Lady Elizabeth Berkeley (1680–1769), m. (1706) Sir John Germain, cr. (1698) Bt, from whom she inherited a large fortune. She was a friend and correspondent of Swift and of Lady Suffolk.

6. George Granville (1666–1735), cr. (1712) Bn Lansdown of Biddeford; poet-aster and patron of Pope. HW wrote of him: 'Imitated Waller; but as that poet has been much excelled since, a faint copy of

a faint master must strike still less' (*Royal and Noble Authors, Works* i. 441).

7. Doubtless Mason has in mind Swift's *History of the Four Last Years of the Queen*.

8. Thomas Howard (1747–91), 3d E. of Effingham. His chief seats were Holmes and 'the Grange,' both near Rotherham (Collins, *Peerage*, 1812, iv. 283; John Guest, *Historic Notices of Rotherham*, Worksop, 1879, pp. 558–9).

9. In the debate on the admissibility in the House of Lords of the 'memorial' of the General Assembly of New York, 18 May 1775. In his speech Lord Effingham explained that his recent resignation from the army was caused by his unwillingness to bear arms in America against his fellow-subjects (Cobbett, *Parl. Hist.* xviii. 688). He returned to the army in Rockingham's administration with the rank of Lt-Col. (1782).

10. 'A room which he built about two years ago on a fine brow of a hill between this place and Rotherham, which commands much the best prospect in this country. He christened it Boston Castle because no tea was ever to be drank in it. The statute is religiously observed' (Mason's note in the MS). For an account and engraving of this castellated shooting-box see John Guest, op. cit. 558–61 and 564.

lady.[11] Seriously though, is it not a pity that a man of such integrity and ability should be what he is?[12]

A man who styles himself Philo-Gray of Salisbury has twitted me in the newspaper for not publishing a complete edition of Gray, because I have omitted the stanzas on a decayed statesman.[13] You must take this sin of mine upon your own back. I suspect it is Almon in order to sell his own *Foundling Hospital of Wit* where those verses are printed.

Mr James Boswell, the friend of Paoli and Dr Johnson, has writ me a very Scotch letter about Gray's character, to tell me it was written by a friend of his, Mr Temple, and that he put it into the *London Magazine* without his leave.[14] I writ him a very plain English answer[15] which I hope will quit me of this correspondent. My Oxonian correspondence about Strabo is also at an end, which I rejoice at, for I have had so many letters to answer which these *Memoirs* have oc-

11. Lord Effingham had married (1765) Catherine Proctor (1746–91), dau. of Metcalfe Proctor of Thorpe, near Leeds.

12. HW speaks of Lord Effingham as 'a rough soldier, of no sound sense' and 'a wild sort of head' (*Last Journals* i. 439, 466).

13. The verses on Lord Holland's villa at Kingsgate, which HW had urged Mason not to print (*ante* 1 Dec. 1773). The newspaper item has not been found.

14. Boswell's draft of this letter is among his papers now at Yale. '. . . Amidst many gratifications which your *Memoirs* of Mr Gray have afforded me, I . . . received a very high one, from finding a character of him published in the *London Magazine* stamped with your approbation. That character, Sir, was written by a very particular friend of mine, Mr Temple, rector of Mamhead in Devonshire, formerly of Trinity Hall, Cambridge, a learned, ingenious, and most worthy man. It was never intended for publication, for it made part of a letter to me about the time of Mr Gray's death. I liked it so much that I copied it out and sent it to the magazine, which Mr Temple never knew till now that his composition and my taste have been impartially honoured' (from the unpublished draft of Boswell's letter to Mason, 30 May 1775, quoted by permission of the Yale Editorial Committee on the Boswell Papers and the McGraw-Hill Book Co., Inc.). The character,

by the Rev. William Johnson Temple (1739–96), was printed in the *London Magazine* for March 1772. Mason inserted his extract from it at the close of *Mem. Gray* (402–4), prefacing it with the remark that 'as it comes from an anonymous pen, I choose the rather to insert it, as it will, on that account, be less suspected of particularity.'

15. 'There was some truth in the character and it was well written; what I thought exceptionable in it I endeavoured to obviate in my notes. . . . [Mr Temple] knows best how far he is obliged to you for publishing it at first, without his leave, through so very ordinary a vehicle. In my poor opinion, had you meant to do him credit, it would have been better to have communicated it in MS to the person who you *then* knew was preparing the memoirs of Mr Gray for the press' (from Mason's unpublished letter, 14 June 1775, quoted by permission of the Yale Editorial Committee on the Boswell Papers and the McGraw-Hill Book Co., Inc.). Boswell wrote to Temple, to whom he submitted both letters, 'Observe with what arrogance he talks of his *strictures* on your character of Gray. When I published it, I *did not* know that he was preparing memoirs. I fancy he is of a sour temper' (Boswell to Temple 19 June 1775, *Letters of James Boswell*, ed. C. B. Tinker, Oxford, 1924, i. 234).

casioned that I have hardly had time to write to those whom I love to write to.

Though I am a free Mason I am not a grand master and therefore cannot myself call the lodge you wish me to call.

Pray send me all the news you can ab⟨out Ame⟩ri⟨ca.⟩[16] I take for granted that by this time Gage ⟨must⟩ be on shipboard. Is there no chance of your coming down to Wentworth Castle this summer? I hear Lord Strafford is now there. I hope the present warm weather contents you and that you begin to think our good planet has not been pushed so far out of its former orbit as some philosophers have suspected. Everything here gives us the prospect of plenty and we are not in the least burnt up. Believe me, dear Sir,

Most truly yours,

W. MASON

Is Lord Nuneham still in town? I have not yet written to him. Shame! Shame!

To MASON, Monday 10 July 1775

Printed from Mitford i. 190–3.

Strawberry Hill, July 10, 1775.

I HAVE been so constantly here and know so little, that if I told you what I do know, it would be but a transcript of the newspapers. The general opinion is that the war is to be pursued: and so far we and the Americans agree, that the news in the meadows (our Mall) last night was, that the Congress has taken the same resolution,[1] and as they have not quite so far to send troops, will probably be a little more alert in putting their resolutions in execution. The Admiral,[2] I was told too, thinks he shall be desired to convey the garrison

16. The MS has been slightly damaged by the breaking of the seal.

———

1. 'From some accounts there is reason to fear that the Congress now sitting at Philadelphia will publish a manifesto, in which they will proclaim to all the world the reasons of their separation from Great Britain, and an invitation to all Europe to trade with them, and to assist them in their determined resolutions never more to submit to the Parliament of England' (*Lloyd's Evening Post* 7–10 July 1775, xxxvii. 29).

2. Samuel Graves (1713–87), Vice-Adm., 1770; commander-in-chief on the North American station from Oct. 1774 to Jan. 1776; Adm., 1778.

of Boston, not into the heart of the Colonies, but home. I am amazed the Parliament does not meet and vote that this will be a breach of the Act of Navigation. The Colonies are really so cowardly,[3] that they go on like the old song,[4] beating those who never beat them in their lives, and have driven away all the cattle from General Gage's Smithfield,[5] and burnt a schooner[6] that he sent to defend them. As the stocks have shown no sensibility till now,[7] I suppose some rich *butcher* has sold out. This is all I can tell you of politics.

To your other question, I doubt, I doubt I shall not see Yorkshire this summer. I am actually thinking of a tour to Paris; and if I do go, it will be before the end of August. Shall I bring you a slice of their English gardens? or a whole one second-hand? they may be out of fashion by this time, and the moment anything is, they sell it.

Has a little book called *The Correspondents*[8] strolled so far north? It is a singular publication, and an abominable one, at least I suspect the motive to be so; they are letters between a late grave noble author and his daughter-in-law, before she married his son,[9] they are perfectly innocent, and very good and very wise—but the spirit was not always entirely uppermost. They seem to be genuine, but if they are, one must guess and abhor the publisher.[10]

3. In the House of Lords 16 March 1775 the Earl of Sandwich had said: 'Suppose the Colonies do abound in men, what does that signify? they are raw, undisciplined, cowardly men' (Cobbett, *Parl. Hist.* xviii. 446).

4. Not identified.

5. On 26–7 May the Americans raided General Gage's livestock on Hog and Noddle's islands in Boston harbour. A circumstantial account is given in *Lloyd's Evening Post* 5–7 July 1775 (xxxvii. 17).

6. The *Diana*, commanded by Gage's nephew, Thomas Gage. For several hours the schooner and the raiders exchanged fire, but at length the British abandoned the ship. 'The schooner being thus left, drove ashore; about break of day the provincials carried some hay under her stern, set fire to it, and burnt her to ashes' (*Lloyd's*, loc. cit.).

7. The stocks declined slightly between 29 May and 28 June, but during July there was little change (GM 1775, xlv. 303, 352).

8. *The Correspondents, an Original Novel, in a Series of Letters,* noticed in the *Monthly Review* for May 1775 (lii. 430–7). Four editions were published. HW's copy is not certainly identifiable in the SH records.

9. *The Correspondents* was meant to be taken as a series of authentic letters between the first Lord Lyttelton and the woman who became his daughter-in-law, Apphia Witts (1743–1840), m. (1) Joseph Peach; m. (2) (1772) Thomas 2d Bn Lyttelton. 'The letters illustrate too well the current literary fashion to be genuine documents. Furthermore, a close similarity of style between the two sets of letters makes it fairly evident that both were written by the same hand' (Rose M. Davis, 'The Correspondents,' *PMLA*, 1936, li. 215–6). The executors of Lord Lyttelton's estate denied the authenticity of the letters, and HW concluded they were spurious (HW to Lady Ossory 3 Aug. 1775). See also CHATTERTON 293 n. 7.

10. That is, the person responsible for having the book published. Had the letters been authentic, this would presumably have been the second Lord Lyttelton.

Mrs Wood[11] publishes an essay,[12] which her husband showed me and I liked,[13] on Homer's country. My late brethren, the Antiquaries,[14] have given a third volume,[15] with some pretty plates of horns,[16] and some trifling trinkets, dissertations on cockfighting and shoeing horses, and half a volume on their print of the interview in the Vale of Cloth of Gold,[17] and the room at Cowdry,[18] in which I am censured for liking it only as a curiosity and not as a picture,[19] though there is

11. Ann, widow of Robert Wood (ca 1717–71), politician and antiquary. In 1773 she had applied to HW for advice on a monument for her husband and their deceased son, Thomas, and accepted his suggestions and the epitaph that he composed. See HW's correspondence with her.

12. *An Essay on the Original Genius and Writings of Homer: with a Comparative View of the Ancient and Present State of the Troade*. It had been prepared for the press by the antiquarian Jacob Bryant (Nichols, *Lit. Anec.* viii. 427), and was published 7 July 1775 (*Public Advertiser*). HW wrote to Mrs Wood 7 July acknowledging her gift of the volume, which was sold SH i. 54, 'splendidly bound in green morocco,' with HW's arms on the sides. Its last appearance in the sale room was in the Hoe sale, Anderson Galleries, New York, 24 April 1911, lot 3509, when it was sold to George D. Smith.

13. Wood had sent HW a copy of the 1769 edition of his *Essay on the Original Genius of Homer* (HW to Wood 23 Nov. 1769), of which only seven copies were printed (Nichols, *Lit. Anec.* iii. 81–2; Wood to J. D. Michaelis 27 April 1770, in Hans Hecht, *T. Percy, R. Wood, und J. D. Michaelis*, Stuttgart, 1933, p. 25). HW's letter of acknowledgment contains a detailed criticism, undoubtedly made at the author's request. There also seems to exist a 1767 edition of the *Essay*, published with the title, *A Comparative View of the Ancient and Present State of the Troade. To Which is Prefixed an Essay on the Original Genius of Homer*. A copy that was in the Grenville Library (John Thomas Payne and Henry Foss in *Bibliotheca Grenvilliana; or Bibliographical Notices of Rare and Curious Books forming Part of the Library of the Rt Hon. Thomas Grenville*, 1842–72, ii. 812, erroneously give the date as 1768) is now in the British Museum

(BM Cat.). It contains only the *Essay on Homer*. W. P. Courtney believed that it was this edition that was limited to seven copies (DNB *sub* Wood), but the letter to Michaelis and the account in Nichols show him to have been mistaken. HW's copy of the 1769 edition does not appear in the SH records.

14. HW had been elected a fellow of the Society of Antiquaries 19 April 1753 and resigned in July 1772 (see 'Short Notes,' GRAY i. 28 and 47).

15. The third volume of *Archæologia: or Miscellaneous Tracts Relating to Antiquity*, published 28 June 1775 (*Daily Adv.*). HW's set is now WSL.

16. Prints of hunting horns engraved by Basire.

17. 'An Historical Description of an ancient picture in Windsor Castle, representing the interview between King Henry VIII and the French King Francis I between Guines and Ardres, in the year 1520. By Sir Joseph Ayloffe, Baronet, V.P.A.S. and F.R.S.' (*Archæologia* iii. 185–229).

18. 'An Account of some ancient English historical paintings at Cowdry, in Sussex,' also by Ayloffe (*Archæologia* iii. 239–72). The two articles fill less than a fifth of the volume. Cowdray, near Midhurst, Sussex, was the seat of Anthony Joseph Browne (ca 1728–87), Vct Montagu. It was built ca 1535–45 and was destroyed by fire in 1793; see Julia Anne Elizabeth Roundell, *Cowdray: the History of a Great English House*, 1884, pp. 7–10, 126.

19. HW visited Cowdray in 1749 and again in 1774 (MONTAGU i. 98; *Country Seats* 76). Of the so-called Holbein Room and its frescoes (lost in the 1793 fire) he wrote: 'Though the histories represented there, the habits and customs of the times, make that room a singular curiosity, they are its only merit. There is nothing good either in the designs, disposition, or colour-

no more perspective or drawing than in an Indian screen. To stamp
my doom, in the index is said, *the Cowdry picture defended against
Mr W.*[20]—see what it is to try to teach owls to be singing birds! I was
the first soul that ever endeavoured to introduce a little taste into
English antiquities, and had persuaded the world not to laugh at our
Hearnes and Hollingsheds, and the graceless loggerheads fly in my
face! but I have left them to themselves and could not have left them
in worse hands.

This letter is only chaperon to a parcel that I must beg you to convey to Peckitt[21] at York, and which I send open to save troubling you
with the purport (is not this an *Iricism?*); when you have read it or
not, as you please, you will be so good as to seal it.

July 12th.

Since I began my letter two days ago, I have taken my resolution;
and shall set out on the 14th of next month, to be back in the beginning of October,[22] by which time I suppose you will have frightened
the Americans out of their senses, or the Americans the ministers into
theirs.

I have not yet seen the reviews for this month; those of the last were
exceedingly civil to you. One piece of service you have rendered me.
The proprietor of the asterisk[23] on Lord Clarendon's history has certainly reconnoitred himself, for he has not called on me since the publication, though very civil when we meet, yet never opening his mouth

ing' (*Anecdotes, Works* iii. 83). Ayloffe
quotes the last sentence and adds, 'I must
dissent from him in that opinion' (*Archæologia* iii. 271). He also criticizes HW in
his paper on 'An Ancient Picture in Windsor Castle': 'Mr Walpole, who barely mentions this picture [in *Anecdotes of Painting*
i. 57], says, that it is commonly supposed to
be painted by Holbein, but is beneath his
excellence' (*Archæologia* iii. 227).

20. The index reads under Cowdray,
'paintings . . . observations on, and defence of, against Mr Walpole, 271, 272.' Under Walpole the index reads, 'his stricture
on the Cowdry paintings.'

21. William Peckitt (1731–95), glass-
painter of York (see J. A. Knowles, 'William
Peckitt, Glass-Painter,' *Walpole Society*
1928–9, xvii. 45–60). HW employed Peckitt
in 1762 'for the five painted tops of the
gallery windows and the yellow star in the

ceiling of the Cabinet' and in 1773 'for ten
panes of arms for windows of Great Bedchamber' and 'for window of Chapel etc.'
(*SH Accounts* 9, 13, 111, 114). In the following letter Mason says he forwarded this
'armorial parcel to Peckitt.' It may be that
this was a pane of painted glass broken by
the explosion of the powder mills on
Hounslow Heath 6 Jan. 1772 (see HW to
Conway 7 Jan. 1772). Four were destroyed
and four others broken (HW to Mann 14
Jan. 1772). The *Description of SH* and SH
sale catalogue mention several panes
painted with the Walpole arms; one of
them, broken and repaired and broken
again, is now WSL.

22. HW set out for Paris 16 Aug. and
returned to London 17 Oct. 1775 ('Paris
Journals,' DU DEFFAND v. 342, 353).

23. Richard Owen Cambridge. See *ante*
3 April 1775, n. 26.

on that subject. I bear this misfortune with great philosophy, as I always do everything I do not care about.

My Lord of Rochester[24] has consulted me for an altar-piece for the choir of Westminster. I have suggested[25] an octagon canopy of open arches, like Chichester Cross,[26] to be elevated on a flight of steps, with the altar in the middle, and semicircular arcades to join the stalls, so that the Confessor's chapel and tombs may be seen through in perspective. His Lordship, indeed, wanted to remove that whole chapel, but his chapter luckily opposed.[27] Here is the ground plot[28] of my idea; if you approve it you may draw the elevation as beautifully as you please.

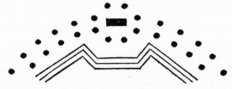

From MASON, Monday 31 July 1775

Printed from MS now WSL.

Aston, July 31st, 1775.

I AM glad that you are going to France, not because you are going to France, but because the intention indicates that you are in good health and spirits, and since you will not come into Yorkshire you may as well be in France as at Strawberry as to my particular interest in the

24. John Thomas (1712–93), D.C.L.; Dean of Westminster 1768–93; Bp of Rochester, 1774.

25. HW's correspondence with Dr Thomas has not been found. He breakfasted at SH in Oct. 1773 (HW to Lady Ossory 7 Oct. 1773) at which time he may have heard of HW's disapproval of the changes made by his predecessor in the Abbey, as set forth by HW in his letter to Conway of 5 Aug. 1761, and solicited HW's advice on his own proposed changes. He may also have heard of HW's 'directing the east window at Ely' (HW to Cole 15 July 1769, COLE i. 178).

26. It was erected ca 1500 by Bp Edward

Story and extensively repaired in 1746. HW had already persuaded the Earl of Strafford to model a 'little Gothic building' on it (MONTAGU i. 295).

27. 'It was during the time of this Dean that the choir was fitted up in its present improved state of simple, elegant, and appropriate decoration' (Rudolph Ackermann, The History of the Abbey Church of St Peter's, Westminster, 1812, i. 289).

28. HW made another rough sketch of this, with a slightly different ground plot and a very elementary sketch of the elevation, on the back of the letter from Mme du Deffand of 1 July 1775. His advice was not followed (COLE ii. 185).

matter. Besides I look upon myself as having a kind of hereditary right in your correspondence while abroad, which may make me amends for certain excellent letters I returned you heretofore,[1] and which had I retained I should have read at least once a year with fresh delight, and not have envied people who relish Madame Sévigné, who you know is beyond my taste, to my shame be it spoken.

I have no commission to give you, except, peradventure, you could smuggle me over Monsieur Watelet's twelve little boats that support his bridge, with all the *caisses garnies de fleurs* and his *treillages en lozange peints en blanc.*[2] I have lately dug a horse-pond to which I think such a bridge would make a good accompaniment. I wish you would go see his Laurentin[3] and describe it to me in your English, for I do not well comprehend his French. He says it is but a *une heure de distance de la ville;*[4] if by *ville* he means Paris as we say town, surely you might easily take the expedition.

But before you go I wish you would inquire amongst my brethren of the Church whether the Archbishop of Canterbury[5] has prepared a form of prayer with thanksgiving for our late victory.[6] I want to know this that I may sit down to write my Fast Sermon, and be in readiness for that solemnity. I take for granted his Majesty will go to Paul's and I am sorry I resigned my chaplainship,[7] else I might have got my Lord Holdernesse's interest to preach before him on the occasion. If the bishops sit down in good earnest to write a proper form I think they should mix thanksgiving and fasting together; there would be something new in the idea, it would be like a supper of hot and cold, which I believe the French cooks call an *ambigu.*[8]

You did not see the *London Review* by Dr Kenrick,[9] else you would

1. Apparently HW had asked Mason to return some of his letters.

2. The bridge is described by Claude-Henri Watelet in his *Essai sur les jardins,* 1774, pp. 151–2.

3. That is, Watelet's villa on the Seine near Argenteuil, the *Moulin Joli.* In the *Essai* he refers to it as 'Laurentin' (pp. 138, 160) by analogy with the younger Pliny's villa at Laurentum.

4. *Essai,* p. 138.

5. Hon. Frederick Cornwallis (1713–83), Bp of Lichfield, 1750; Abp of Canterbury, 1768.

6. Gage's official report of the 'victory' at Bunker Hill on 17 June 1775 was re-

leased in London 25 July, having been preceded by many rumours (*Public Advertiser* 25–6 July; *Last Journals* i. 471). The casualty lists showed a total of over 200 killed and over 800 wounded. The actual number, about 1150, represented the loss of 46 per cent of the British forces engaged (Henry Belcher, *The First American Civil War,* 1911, i. 175).

7. Which he did in 1772 (*ante* 17 May 1772 and n. 2).

8. An informal meal in which all the dishes are put on the table at once. The word had been naturalized in England nearly a century before (see OED).

9. William Kenrick (ca 1725–79), miscel-

have been convinced what a very mediocre poet Gray was, and what a bold panegyrist I am to dare to commend his poetry. The world, I believe, are of the Doctor's opinion, for the 2d edition[10] is not half sold. No matter; if they will but continue to buy my Lord Chesterfield's letters, Dodsley and I shall be satisfied.[11]

I like your idea for the high altar at Westminster so prodigiously that I am sure it will never be executed, at least not in our day. When our Popish sons of Canada shall have helped us to conquer our Puritan sons of Boston,[12] they will perhaps choose to conquer their heretical mother of England, and then Chicester Cross will walk to Westminster Abbey. When I began to write this sentence I never thought it would conclude so like a prophecy. Therefore I do believe it will be a true prophecy, for it certainly flowed from an unpremeditated pen.

I will not wish you a good voyage because I hope to hear from you again before you embark. I mean to visit my Lord Strafford tomorrow where I fancy we shall be unfashionable enough to drink your health.

I forwarded your armorial parcel to Peckitt immediately, and am, dear Sir,

Very sincerely yours,

W. MASON

To MASON, Monday 7 August 1775

Printed from Mitford i. 199–202.

Strawberry Hill, Aug. 7, 1775.

LET me tell you you have no more taste than Dr Kenrick, if you do not like Madame de Sévigné's letters. Read them again; they

laneous writer; awarded an honorary degree of Doctor of Laws by Marischal College and the University of Aberdeen for his translation of Rousseau's *Nouvelle Héloïse*, 1761. He founded the *London Review* in Jan. 1775. His unsympathetic review of *Mem. Gray* appeared in June (*London Review* 1775, i. 406–14).

10. Published 5 May 1775 (*Daily Adv.*). Mason nevertheless was planning in 1776 a 3d edition in 3 vols (Mason to James

Dodsley 30 Jan. 1776, kindly lent us by Prof. F. W. Hilles).

11. Dodsley printed four editions of the letters in 1774.

12. 'It is said that clothing for three thousand troops, Canadians, was sent off yesterday; and that the same contractor has orders for fitting up seven thousand more with all possible dispatch' (*London Chronicle* 27–9 July 1775, xxxviii. 103). Efforts to raise a Canadian army proved unavailing.

are one of the very few books that, like Gray's life, improve upon one every time one reads them. You have still less taste if you like my letters, which have nothing original, and if they have anything good, so much the worse, for it can only be from having read her letters, and his. He came perfect out of the egg-shell, and wrote as well at eighteen as ever he did—nay, letters better, for his natural humour was in its bloom, and not wrinkled by low spirits, dissatisfaction, or the character he had assumed.[1] I do not care a straw whether Dr Kenrick and Scotland can persuade England, that he was no poet. There is no common sense left in this country; with arts and sciences it has travelled west.[2] The Americans will admire him and you, and they are the only people by whom one would wish to be admired. The world is divided into two nations, men of sense that *will* be free, and fools that like to be slaves. What a figure do two great empires make at this moment! Spain, mistress of Peru and Mexico, amazes Europe with an invincible armada; at last it sails to Algiers, and disbarks its whole contents, even to the provisions of the fleet. It is beaten shamefully, loses all its stores, and has scarce bread left to last till it gets back into its own ports![3]

Mrs Britannia orders her senate to proclaim America a continent of cowards, and vote it should be starved unless it will drink tea with her. She sends her only army to be besieged in one of their towns, and half her fleet to besiege the *terra firma,* but orders her army to do nothing, in hopes that the American senate at Philadelphia will be so frightened at the British army being besieged in Boston, that it will sue for peace. At last she gives her army leave to sally out, but being twice defeated,[4] she determines to carry on the war so vigorously till she has not a man left, that all England will be satisfied with the total loss of America; and if everybody is satisfied, who can be blamed? Besides

1. Presumably HW has in mind the description of Gray by Temple with which Mason concluded the *Memoir:* 'There is no character without some speck, some imperfection; and I think the greatest defect in his was an affectation in delicacy, or rather effeminacy, and a visible fastidiousness, or contempt and disdain of his inferiors in science' (*Mem. Gray* 403). On 'effeminacy' Mason notes: 'This is rightly put; it was rather an affectation in delicacy and effeminacy than the things themselves; and he chose to put on this appearance chiefly before persons whom he did not wish to please.'

2. HW is paraphrasing the unidentified line quoted *ante* 23 Aug. 1774.

3. 'The great Spanish armament, on which attention had hung so long, had at last attacked Algiers and were repulsed with great loss and retired' (*Last Journals* i. 472). News of this Spanish defeat early in July appeared in *Lloyd's Evening Post* 28–31 July and 4–7 Aug. 1775 (xxxvii. 101, 127), and *Daily Adv.* 5 Aug. 1775.

4. At Lexington and Bunker Hill.

is not our dignity maintained? have not we carried our majesty beyond all example? when did you ever read before of a besieged army
threatening military execution on the country of the besiegers! *car
tel est notre plaisir!* but alack! we are like the Mock Doctor; we have
made the heart and the liver change sides; *cela était autrefois ainsi,
mais nous avons changé tout cela!*[5]

I will certainly visit Monsieur Watelet's garden that he has curled
and powdered *à l'anglaise.* I shall like to be amused with less serious
follies than our own, though I doubt I shall find they laugh a little
more at us than we can at them. Well! I will wrap myself up in my
Robinhood! They cannot say the good old man my father did it.[6]
Have you heard the history of Foote and her Grace of Kingston? She
applied to the Lord Chamberlain,[7] and prevented the piece[8] being
licensed, though Foote had an audience, and with his usual modesty
assured her he had not had her Grace in view. The dame, as if he had
been a member of Parliament, offered to buy him off.[9] Aristophanes's
Grecian virtue was not to be corrupted; but he offered to read the
piece, and blot out whatever passages she would mark, that she thought
applicable to her case. She was too cunning to bite at this; and they
parted. He swears he will not only print his comedy,[10] but act her
in Lady Brumpton.[11] He has already printed his letter to Lord Hertford,[12] and not content with that, being asked why it was not licensed,
replied, 'Why my Lord Hertford desired me to make his youngest
son[13] a box-keeper, and because I would not, he stopped my play.'
Upon my word, if the stage and the press are not checked, we shall
have the army, on its return from Boston, besieged in the Haymarket

5. Molière, *Le Médecin malgré lui,* II. iv.

6. The sense seems to be that HW would
shrug off any criticism of England and the
American war by reminding the critics
that he was the son of Robert Walpole who
always strove for peace.

7. Lord Hertford.

8. *A Trip to Calais,* in which the Duchess
was to have been lampooned as 'Lady Kitty
Crocodile' (*London Chronicle* 1–3 Aug.
1775, xxxviii. 120).

9. 'Foote [was] in great spirits but bitter
against the Lord Chamberlain. He will
bully 'em into a license. The Duchess has
had him in her closet and offered to bribe
him; but Cato himself, though he had
one more leg than our friend, was not

more stoically virtuous than he has been'
(Garrick to Colman 25 [July] 1775 in *Posthumous Letters . . . to Francis Colman
and George Colman the Elder,* ed. George
Colman the younger, 1820, p. 316–7).

10. It was altered and acted in 1776 as
The Capuchin, but *A Trip to Calais* was
not printed in its original form until 1778,
after Foote's death.

11. A bigamous lady in Steele's *The
Funeral.*

12. It was printed in the newspapers, e.g.
London Chronicle 1–3 Aug., xxxviii. 120,
and *Lloyd's Evening Post* 2–4 Aug. 1775,
xxxvii. 118.

13. George Seymour-Conway (later Lord
George Seymour) (1763–1848).

itself: what are we come to, if maids of honour[14] cannot marry two husbands in quiet! Well General Gage is recalled,[15] and is to be hanged;[16] we had conquered America by this time, they say, if he had not betrayed us, and desired the provincials to block him up—so *en attendant* Hancock and Adams, and Putnam and Washington, you may divert yourselves with executing your own General. Voltaire will abuse you, as he did about poor Byng;[17] but really a government must condemn somebody, or the mob—but I am going to Paris, and leave you to your own devices. Don't finish your *Essay on Gardening* till I bring you the newest improvements from the Opera, where to be sure the Elysian fields will be laid out *naturally*. If anything strikes me particularly, you shall hear from me, but as my stay will be short, I don't promise, for I have been so often at Paris, that my staring is extremely *émoussé*, and one must travel to Abyssinia,[18] to find anything very new. Adieu.

Yours entirely,

H. W.

To Mason, Wednesday 6 September 1775

Printed from Mitford i. 202–6.

Paris, Sept. 6, 1775.

I HAVE made very little progress yet towards the account I am to give you of the propagation of the faith in this kingdom, but stay, this is a little too metaphoric; and lest I should be taken for an ex-

14. The Duchess of Kingston had married Hervey while she was maid of honour to Augusta, Princess of Wales.

15. George III's decision to recall Gage had been made in July (George III to Lord North 28 July 1775 in *Corr. Geo. III* iii. 236). Lord North wrote the letter of recall 2 Aug., and Gage sailed for England 10 Oct. 1775.

16. Gage was brought home on the pretext that the administration desired to consult him on the situation in America, but it had already been decided that his services were no longer required, and in

April 1776 he was formally relieved of his command (J. R. Alden, *General Gage in America*, Baton Rouge, 1948, p. 286).

17. Admiral Hon. John Byng (1704–57), court-martialled and executed for neglect of duty in his encounter with the French fleet at Port Mahon 20 May 1756. Voltaire believed the sentence unjust and before the execution sent the court-martial a letter written on behalf of Byng by his adversary, Marshal Richelieu. Voltaire also refers to Byng's execution in *Candide*.

18. Like James Bruce. See *ante* 27 May 1775.

Jesuit or a spy, I declare, like the writer of an opera, that I neither believe in the gods of old Rome or new, excepting Vertumnus, Flora and Pomona, and that I am going to write to you, my provincial,[1] on the conversion of the French to English gardening. I have begun my observation as methodically as if I was to draw up an article for the Encyclopedia; I have laid the axe to the root of the tree, for I have begun by visiting M. Watelet's isle, called *le Moulin Joli*.[2] If he has laid the axe to the root and even to the branches, he has used it nowhere else. Instead of finding, as I expected, a windmill made of ivory and inlaid with false stones; instead of dryads and hamadryads gathering acorns in baskets of gauze, M. Watelet has jumped back into nature, when she was not above five hundred years old—in one word his *island* differs in nothing from a French garden into which no mortal has set his foot for the last century, it is an *ate*[3] (I don't know whether I spell well) joined to his *terra firma,* by two bridges, one of which he calls Dutch and the other Chinese, and which are as unlike either as two peas, and which is pierced and divided into straight narrow walks *en berceau*[4] and surrounded by a rude path quite round. To give this *étoile*[5] an air *champêtre,* a plenary indulgence has been granted to every nettle, thistle and bramble *that grew in the garden, and they seem good in his sight.*[6] The receipt is as follows: take an *ate* full of willows, cram it full of small elms and poplar pines,[7] strip them into cradles, and cut them into paths, and leave all the rest as rough as you found it, and you will have a *Moulin Joli.* You must know this effort of genius is the more provoking, as the situation is charming, besides that the isle is in the middle of the Seine, every peep-hole (though so small that you seem to look through the diminishing end of a spying-glass) besides terminating on one real windmill, is bounded by a *château,*

1. 'The ecclesiastical head of a province; the chief of a religious order in a district or province' (OED).

2. HW went with the Neckers 2 Sept. 1775 (DU DEFFAND v. 346). Though one of the early examples of the so-called 'English' garden, Watelet's was not the first; Ermenonville, the seat of the Marquis de Girardin, laid out about 1770, is said to have been the first notable example of the new fashion (John C. Loudon, *An Encyclopedia of Gardening,* [1835], i. 85). For a description of Watelet's garden see his own *Essai sur les jardins* and Daniel Mornet, *Le Sentiment de la nature en France de J.-J.*

Rousseau à Bernardin de Saint-Pierre, 1907, pp. 378–81.

3. 'Ait . . . An islet or small isle; especially one in a river, as the aits or eyots of the Thames' (OED). The spellings 'ayte' and 'aight' were also common in the 18th century. There are several aits near SH.

4. Arched with foliage.

5. I.e., a star-shaped planting design crossed by paths.

6. HW is freely paraphrasing Genesis 1.11 and 2.9.

7. Lombardy poplars (OED *sub* 'poplar' 3).

a *clocher,* a village, a *couvent,* a villa where Henrietta Maria was educated, or hermitage to which Bossuet retired, not to mortify himself but Fénelon. It is true, you catch these points of view over wide fields of chalk, which would produce frankincense as soon as grass, and which if they had symptoms of verdure, were waving ranks of fennel. I always perceive here, when I am out of Paris; but I never can think myself in the country. I shall next week see some more English essays.

But they are imitating us in better things, their King is of an excellent disposition, he has driven away the Chancellor,[8] the Duc d'Aiguillon,[9] and those wretches who had given perfection to despotism in the last reign. Monsieur de Maurepas[9a] restored the old parliament, and Monsieur Turgot,[10] the Controller-General, has destroyed *corvées,*[11] that most execrable oppression, and is every day planning and attempting acts for public happiness. The *éloges* of the Academy roll on maxims of virtue and patriotism, and the King publicly applauds them,[12] you may judge whether they do not stare at all we are doing! they will not believe me when I tell them that the American war is *fashionable,* for one is forced to use that word to convey to them an idea of the majority. A great lady asked me t'other day, if I was not a Bostonian? and I have not met with a single Frenchman who does not express indignation or sneer contempt at all our late acts

8. Maupeou. At the demand of the new King, Louis XVI, Maupeou had surrendered his seal of office 24 Aug. 1774, but refused to relinquish the chancellorship. He withdrew, however, from active participation in politics, taking up residence at his seat at Roncherolles (DU DEFFAND iv. 87; Charles Lacretelle, *Histoire de France pendant le dix-huitième siècle,* 1819–26, iv. 347).

9. The Duc d'Aiguillon had been minister of foreign affairs and of war. Realizing that Louis XVI was not friendly, he resigned 2 June 1774 (DU DEFFAND iv. 60; *Mémoires du ministère du Duc d'Aiguillon,* 1792, p. 58). A year later the Queen's hostility brought about his exile to Aiguillon (Louis Petit de Bachaumont, *Mémoires secrets pour servir à l'histoire de la république des lettres en France,* 1784–9, viii. 72–4; *Colonel St Paul of Ewart,* ed. George C. Butler, 1911, ii. 165).

9a. Jean-Frédéric Phélypeaux (1701–81), Comte de Maurepas, secretary of state 1715–49, minister of the marine 1723–49.

In 1749 an epigram against Mme de Pompadour was attributed to him and he was banished from Court. He was recalled by Louis XVI in 1774, and in November restored the Parlement de Paris (NBG).

10. Anne-Robert-Jacques Turgot (1727–81), Baron de l'Aulne; contributor to the *Encyclopédie;* intendant of Limoges 1761–74; minister of the marine, 1774; controller-general 1774–6.

11. Unpaid services given by the peasants to their masters or the state. On 6 May 1775, at a time when the domestic economy of France was upset by corn riots, Turgot suspended the *corvées* temporarily.

12. As when, on 2 July 1775, the Academy formally waited on Louis XVI at Versailles to offer congratulations on his consecration (*Les Registres de l'Académie Française,* 1895, iii. 375). On the amicable relations between the Academy and the new King see D. Maclaren Robertson, *A History of the French Academy,* 1910, pp. 108–9.

of Parliament.[13] Monsieur de Castries[14] being told that Lord North has the Garter, was surprised and said for what? for having lost America?[15]—Upon these subjects, as I have not a vast deal to say on behalf of my dear country, I choose to shift the conversation to her Grace of Kingston, whose history seems as strange to them as our politics. What a *chef-d'œuvre* is Foote's answer![16]

Sept. 10.

Chap. II

On Anglo-Franco gardens,

which by the by they call Anglo-Chinois gardens, as they say that by the help of Sir William Chambers's lunettes[17] they have detected us for having stolen our gardens from the Chinese.[18] I shall tell them another tale when I publish my last volume.[19] Yesterday I went to see the Countess de Boufflers'[20] English garden at Auteuil, and it is strictly English, and begotten on her by[21] an English gardener.[22] There are

13. HW gives an example of these remarks in 'Paris Journals' 31 Aug. 1775. The Bishop of Mirepoix 'said to me on America, "Vous êtes devenus nous, et nous vous, et vous y perdrez"' (DU DEFFAND v. 346).

14. Charles-Eugène-Gabriel de la Croix (1727–1801), Marquis de Castries; minister of the marine, 1780; Maréchal de France, 1783.

15. 'At Metz, where the troops were reviewed for them [the Duke and Duchess of Gloucester], M. de Castries, the commanding officer, asking the Duchess who were Knights of the Garter, and she naming Lord North, he said, "Pourquoi l'a-t-il, lui? est-ce pour avoir perdu l'Amérique?"' (*Last Journals* i. 525–6).

16. On 13 Aug. 1775 Foote wrote to the Duchess of Kingston that he would abandon *A Trip to Calais* if she stopped her public attacks on him. She sent him an insolent reply that read in part: 'I am writing to the descendant of a merry-andrew, and prostitute the term of manhood by applying it to Mr Foote.' The correspondence appeared in the newspapers (e.g., *London Chronicle* 12–15 Aug. 1775, xxxviii. 159–60, and *Public Advertiser* 16 Aug.), as did Foote's second letter, which contained unmistakable references to the Duchess's career: 'Prostitutes and players too must live by pleasing the public; not

but your Grace may have heard of ladies who, by private practice, have accumulated amazing great fortunes. . . . My mother . . . was upwards of fourscore years old when she died, and, what will surprise your Grace, was never married but once in her life' (*London Chronicle* 15–17 Aug., xxxviii. 168).

17. His *Dissertation on Oriental Gardening*, 1772.

18. See, e.g., Watelet's *Essai sur les jardins*, p. 50.

19. Of his *Anecdotes of Painting in England*. HW's essay on *Modern Gardening* concludes the volume. It was in print at this time, but was not published until 1780. HW disparages the Chinese taste in gardening (*Anecdotes* iv. 133–5). In the 1782 edition of the *Anecdotes* (iv. 283; *Works* ii. 533), he added a long note on 'Le goût Anglo-Chinois,' the material for which he doubtless assembled at this time.

20. Marie-Charlotte-Hippolyte de Camps de Saujon (1725–1800), m. (1746) Édouard, Comte (later Marquis) de Boufflers-Rouverel. HW recorded this visit in 'Paris Journals' (DU DEFFAND v. 347).

21. Previously printed 'by her on.'

22. His name was Prescott (Thomas Blaikie, *Diary of a Scotch Gardener at the French Court at the End of the Eighteenth Century*, ed. Francis Birrell, 1931, p. 194).

fifty-two acres, which ascend from the house up a hill that is laid out in fields with a sunk fence and loose trees and shrubs, and has tolerable turf, except that it is coarse and of a green seldom worn by a gentleman's garden in England. All along the summit reigns a noble terrace surrounded by the Bois de Boulogne into which a grille opens upon a lofty avenue bounded by a sugar-loaf hill. The terrace looks over the lawn upon a glorious prospect, which begins from the left with one of the King's houses,[23] is joined by a wood out of which juts Passy, the Duc de Penthièvre's,[24] that forms the side-scene and flings a rich view of hills and towns to a great distance. The middle of the landscape advances again; on the foreground are villages and villas, over which is extended all Paris with the horizon broken by the towers and domes of Notre Dame, St Sulpice, the Invalides, the Val de Grâce, etc.; the whole height of the semicircle goes off in hills decked with villages and country-houses that are closed by Meudon, and forests on higher hills. In this sumptuous prospect nothing is wanting but verdure and water of which you do not see a drop.[25] In short, they can never have as beautiful landscapes as ours, till they have as bad a climate.

I think I shall stay here a month longer. If you send me a line, direct it to Arlington [Street]; it will be conveyed or kept for me.

Yours ever,

H. W.

From Mason, Sunday 22 October 1775

Printed from MS now WSL.
Address: The Honourable Horace Walpole, Arlington Street, London.
Postmark: ROTHERHAM 26 OC.

Aston, Oct. 22d, 1775.

Dear Sir,

MY newspaper has this day announced your arrival.[1] I will not therefore defer a moment to answer your most agreeable letter from Paris of the 6th of last month, which I should have answered

23. La Muette. See Gustave Pessard, *Nouveau dictionnaire historique de Paris,* 1904, pp. 1013–4.
24. Louis-Jean-Marie de Bourbon (1725–93), Duc de Penthièvre, grandson of Louis XIV.
25. The dryness of the region made it necessary to water the garden with a specially constructed hydraulic machine (P. E. Schazmann, *La Comtesse de Boufflers,* 1933, p. 136).

———

1. In London 17 Oct.

immediately after I received it, had there been a chance of its reach-ing you while in France. But I got it late, being absent on a visit in Staffordshire. All this, however, is idle apology. Let me hasten to in-quire how you do after your tour, and that before the meeting of Parliament, when nobody will be well,[2] either those in Parliament or out (if I have the gift of prophecy) except peradventure the new-made Lords[3] who will choose to be in good spirits till the novelty of their nobility ceases.—But as for me, *il faut cultiver mon jardin*,[4] and there-fore I'll only talk to you at present on the theme of your last letter, and tell you that I am as well acquainted now with Mr Watelet's *Moulin Joli* as if I had seen it with my own eyes, such are your de-scriptive powers, when you please to make use of them, not that I wish you often to make use of them on such a subject; and yet to describe bad taste well, requires as much the powers of a master as to describe good, and the description is perhaps full as useful, always more enter-taining. Once more therefore I thank you for the treat you have given me. I have nothing to send you in return except a story which I picked up the other day from a country squire who had the honour to dine with her Grace of Kingston at Grantham[5] in her way from Thoresby[6] to town. She was attended by three elderly personages dressed in black, one of which he found was her lawyer, the second her chaplain,[7] and the third a German physician by name Dr Falke.[8] After dinner her Grace retired, and the lawyer began a very high encomium on her

2. Parliament opened its session 26 Oct. (*Daily Adv.* 27 Oct. 1775). 'As the Parlia-ment grew near, the inferior ministers be-gan to apprehend that so much money and lives wasted, so much money to be asked, so little done, and such total miscarriage of all their schemes, must begin to open the eyes of men' (*Last Journals* i. 478).

3. 'Yesterday the Lord Chancellor or-dered a writ of summons to be issued out for calling to Parliament Lord Viscount Maynard, in the room of his father, de-ceased. And another for calling to Parlia-ment, Lord Willoughby of Parham, in the room of his uncle deceased' (*Daily Adv.* 21 Oct. 1775). The new peers were Charles Maynard (1752–1824), 2d Vct Maynard, and George Willoughby (1742–79), 14th Bn Willoughby.

4. 'Cela est bien dit, répondit Candide, mais il faut cultiver notre jardin' (the con-cluding sentence of Voltaire's *Candide*).

Mason was at work on the continuation of *The English Garden* (*post* 20 Nov. 1775).

5. A market town in Lincolnshire at which the Duke of Kingston occasionally broke his journeys to and from London (C. E. Pearce, *The Amazing Duchess*, [1911], ii. 101–2).

6. Thoresby Park, the Duke of Kings-ton's seat in Nottinghamshire, near Sher-wood Forest.

7. William Field (d. 1783), attorney, of the Inner Temple, and the Rev. John For-ster, M.A., who had been tutor to Edward Wortley Montagu (*Trial of the Duchess of Kingston*, ed. Lewis Melville, 1927, p. 75; GM 1783, liii pt ii. 717; Nichols, *Lit. Anec.* iv. 626; *London Chronicle* 17–19 Aug. 1775, xxxviii. 176; C. E. Pearce, op. cit. ii. 174).

8. Nicholaus Detleff Falck (d. 1798), author of several treatises on medical and other subjects (Wilhelm Haberling *et al.*,

understanding, of which he gave many specimens in his own way relative to her late manœuvres in the courts of law. The squire heard him
with attention, and when he had finished his panegyric, replied very
bluntly: 'Mr Lawyer, this may be all very true. I believe the Duchess
is a clever sort of woman, but by G— she never was so much out in
her life as when she ventured to write a letter to Foote.' The lawyer
owned she had better have let that alone, upon which Dr Falke got
up, ran to the squire and taking him by the button said in very broken
English: 'O sire, me give you letel piece of advice; pray no mention
such matter to her Grace, her Grace no bear to hear of it.'

This story I think carries its own marks of authenticity about it.
I will not answer for another he told, which was, that, when she was
in deep mourning she eat *black* puddings and drank *black* cherry
brandy, not being able to bear to eat or drink anything of a gayer
colour. This latter I only give you as *ben trovato*. I agree with you in
thinking Foote's answer one of the very best things in the English
language and perfect in its kind. Mr Pope's letter to Lord Hervey[9] is
nothing to it.

This letter being only to ask you how you do after your voyage, and
having nothing to say about myself worth your hearing, ought to conclude soon and perhaps the sooner the better. It shall not, however,
conclude without expressing how very much and how sincerely I am,
dear Sir,

Your faithful servant,

W. MASON

To MASON, Wednesday 25 October 1775

Printed from Mitford i. 208–10.

Strawberry Hill, Oct. 25, 1775.

I AM returned to my own Lares and Penates,—to my dogs and cats;
and was not a little edified by my journey. I saw a King who ac-

*Biographisches Lexikon der hervorragen-
den Ärzte aller Zeiten und Völker,* Berlin
and Vienna, 2d edn, 1929–35, ii. 471; *Journals of the House of Lords* xxxiv. 531). See
post 16 Dec. 1775.

9. The *Letter to a Noble Lord,* printed

in 1733 but not published until its appearance in Warburton's edition of *The
Works of Alexander Pope,* 1751, viii. 253–
80. The 'Noble Lord' was John Hervey
(1696–1743), Bn Hervey of Ickworth, father of Augustus John Hervey, 3d E. of

cords everything that is asked for the good of his people,[1] and I saw two ministers, Messieurs de Malherbes[2] and Turgot, who do not let their master's benevolent disposition rust. The latter is attempting to take off *corvées,* that quintesse[nce] of cruel and ostentatious despotism, but the *country gentlemen,* that race of interested stupidity, will baffle him.[3] Monsieur de Malesherbes, in the most simple and unaffected manner, gave me an account[4] of his visitation of the Bastille,[5] whence he released the prisoners, half of whom were mad with their misfortunes, and of many of whom he could not find even the causes of their commitment. One man refused his liberty; he said he had been prisoner fifteen years, and had nothing in the world left; that the King lodged and fed him, and he would not quit the Bastille unless they would give him half his pension. M. de Malesherbes reported it to the King, who replied, *C'est juste,* and the man has fifteen hundred livres a year and his freedom. This excellent magistrate, who made my tears run down my cheeks, added that what the prisoners complained of most was the want of pen and ink. He ordered it. The demons remonstrated and said the prisoners would only make use of the pen to write memorials against the ministers; he replied, *Tant mieux.* He is going to erect a court of six masters of request to examine the petitions of those who demand *lettres de cachet* for their relations.[6] Under the late Duc de la Vrillière,[7] his mistress, Madame Saba-

---

Bristol and lawful husband of Elizabeth Chudleigh.

---

1. An observation that is repeated by HW in his letter to Lady Ossory 3 Oct. 1775 and to Mann 10 Oct. 1775.

2. Chrétien-Guillaume de Lamoignon de Malesherbes (1721–94). With the return of the Parlement de Paris in Nov. 1774 he had resumed his presidency of the Cour des Aides. On 28 July 1775 he relinquished this office, somewhat reluctantly, and became minister of the King's Household (Anatole, Marquis de Granges de Surgères, *Répertoire . . . de la Gazette de France,* 1902–6, iii. 130). See DU DEFFAND iv. 207.

3. HW was right. On Turgot's difficulties see Douglas Dakin, *Turgot and the Ancien Régime in France,* 1939, pp. 239–44, 264.

4. HW and Malesherbes dined at Mme de Villegagnon's 7 Oct. ('Paris Journals,' DU DEFFAND v. 352).

5. As minister of the King's Household Malesherbes had among his duties the administration of prisons and of *lettres de cachet.* He had visited the Bastille 9 Sept. 1775 (John M. S. Allison, *Lamoignon de Malesherbes: Defender and Reformer of the French Monarchy 1721–1794,* New Haven, 1938, pp. 90–2).

6. *Lettres de cachet* (royal orders of exile or imprisonment) were often sought by the relatives of someone whose conduct was considered inimical to family honour. This kind of *lettre de cachet* is discussed by Frantz Funck-Brentano in *Les Lettres de cachet à Paris: étude suivie d'une liste des prisonniers de la Bastille (1659–1789),* 1903, pp. xxii–xxx.

7. Louis Phélypeaux (1705–77), Comte de Saint-Florentin, and, after 1770, Duc de la Vrillière. He succeeded Choiseul as minister of foreign affairs 1770–1. From 1749 to 1775 he had been minister of the King's

tin, had a bureau of printed *lettres de cachet* with blanks, which she sold for twenty-five louis apiece. When a great Scotch judge[8] was last in France, at the restoration of the old parliament,[9] he said, 'If the ministers mean the good of the people, they are doing right, but if they regard the prerogative of the Crown, very wrong'; what a diabolical 'but'! Do not imagine these ministers will hold their places long; they will soon be epigrammatized out of them. The first event since my return, after hearing of this jail-delivery, is Mr Sayer[10] being sent to the Bastille, but it is not the prisoners in this country that are mad, but the ministers. They have committed him for designing to steal the Tower and the King, he and one more,[11] and I suppose send them to New York; not to Halifax, for that is gone, and Quebec[12] too, and Boston by this time,[13] so now we know what we have to do; only retake all America, which is very easy from three hundred thousand cowards.

26th, Arlington Street.

I had written thus far last night as you perceive, and find your letter on my return, for which I would thank you more if you did not say such fine things to me; pray never do any more, I have no talent, nor anything else but taste for those who have: and that taste is almost a sinecure. If I had time I could increase your Kingstoniana with still better stories, but she is not worth one's while. I have but just a moment to ask if there is any chance of seeing you this winter, which would be a great comfort, and I am not young enough to put off my pleasures. Adieu.

Pray did you pay Mr Peckitt?[14] tell me that I may pay you or him.

Household, and had become notorious for his zeal in the interests of royal prerogative, especially through his use of *lettres de cachet*. See du Deffand i. 262 n. 7; NBG.

8. Lord Mansfield.

9. In Nov. 1774 (*ante* 6 Sept. 1775, n. 9a).

10. Stephen Sayre (1736–1818), banker and former sheriff of London; arrested 23 Oct. at the instance of Lord Rochford and committed to the Tower on a charge of high treason brought against him by Francis Richardson, an American, adjutant of the Guards. Sayre was accused of trying to bribe Richardson to assist him in his plans of capturing George III (du Deffand iv. 230; *Dictionary of American Biography; Daily Adv.* 25 Oct. 1775). See *post* 18 Feb. 1776 and n. 39.

11. 'Labelic, a poor mad enthusiast to liberty' (*Last Journals* i. 482). Not further identified.

12. False reports of the taking of Halifax and the imminent capture of Quebec appeared in *Daily Adv.* 23 Oct. 1775.

13. The British evacuation of Boston did not occur until 17 March 1776.

14. For the commission mentioned *ante* 10 July and 31 July 1775.

To Mason, Friday 27 October 1775

Printed from Mitford i. 211–3. The repetitions from the preceding letter may have been caused by HW's hurry in posting it, and consequent failure to reread or remember what he had written.

Arlington Street, Oct. 27, 1775.

I WAS at Strawberry Hill when your letter arrived, and could not thank you for it so early as I should have done if I had received it sooner. If my description of the *Moulin Joli* pleased you, it was from the circumstances of the place, for I neither describe well nor recount well, nor have any original talent. I pretend to nothing, but taste for talents, and that taste is almost a sinecure. I am returned because I wanted to be *at home;* not that I was particularly charmed with France, or impatient to be in England, but when one is old and has no particular business anywhere, methinks one is *déplacé* anywhere but *chez soi*. The *amor patriæ* burns in me no fiercer than love for my wife would, if I had one and she proved a shrew. I love the free constitution of England more than the acres, and should wish better to California if it had the better form of government; not but I can feel the pride of patriotism when my country is worth being proud of; when it sinks by its own folly, I content myself with my citizenship of the world, and pray for that part that is most reasonable.

I could improve your Kingstoniana if I had leisure; the subject in truth is little worth it, but as superlative in its kind. My chief business with you is to know if I am likely to see you this winter. My pleasures grow dear to me because I have no long time to enjoy them, and cannot live on hopes. Though I still live in the world, most of my hours are passed alone, because they are not passed with the few I love, and all the rest are perfectly indifferent to me; old people are thought to have little affection—how is that possible, for they seem to like company to the last? I should as soon think of taking leave of everybody if I was dying. Of my cotemporaries for whom I do not care, I have seen or known enough, or too much, and to converse with young people, is like asking for the beginning of a story of which one is never to hear the end. With you I can never pass time enough, and alas pass very little; you are not, ought not to be so indifferent to the world as I am, and as you live more out [of] it, why should not you keep up a little acquaintance with it? Your chief reason against coming[1] is worn out by length of time, and other circumstances are such as to dispense with the reiteration of the grievance. It would not be expected, and probably not desired; I dare to say the coolness is sufficiently established.

As I am in town you may expect [? me] to talk of what you will see so much in the newspapers, the commitment of Mr Sayer; but it appears to me so nonsensical a business, that I charitably conclude the ministers have some deeper scheme in view; they can never have sent a man to the Tower that they should have sent to Bedlam, if they do not want a pretence for greater strokes; or choose to be laughed at for this, rather than have the people find fault with something else. However they have brought themselves into such difficulties that I shall not wonder if they are puzzled which to prefer, and as it certainly is not genius that has led them into the scrape, it is not likely to help them out.

Tell me what is more to my purpose, what you have been doing? I am going to read Sterne's letters.[2] From Paris I have absolutely brought nothing at all: my good friend, Europe is worn out, perhaps genius may rekindle in America, but what is that to me? Adieu.

PS. I have run through a volume of Sterne's letters, and have [?never][3] read more unentertaining stuff. The D. of Grafton, Lord Lyttelton and the Bishop of Peterborough[4] divided yesterday with the Opposition.[5] Don't you think the ship is sinking? come and see.

1. Mason's resentment against Lord Holdernesse, whom he might meet in the neighbourhood of SH.

2. *Letters of the Late Rev. Mr Laurence Sterne to His Most Intimate Friends*, published 25 Oct. 1775 (*Public Advertiser*). The letters were edited by Sterne's daughter. See Wilbur L. Cross, *The Life and Times of Laurence Sterne*, New Haven, 1925, ii. 194–8, and Lewis P. Curtis, 'Forged Letters of Laurence Sterne,' *PMLA* 1935, l. 1076–1106. The *Letters* do not appear in the SH records.

3. See *post* 27 Nov. 1775.

4. John Hinchliffe (1731–94), Master of Trinity College, Cambridge, 1768–88; Bp of Peterborough 1769–94.

5. After the King's speech to Parliament, addresses of thanks were moved in both Houses. The three lords here mentioned had been supporters of the administration's earlier measures against America, but now voted against the King's policy. For their remarks see Cobbett, *Parl. Hist.* xviii. 710–18; *Last Journals* i. 483–5. It was not long before Lyttelton again reversed his position and rejoined the administration. The Duke of Grafton relinquished the Privy Seal 9 Nov. 1775 (*Last Journals* i. 491; *Daily Adv.* 11 Nov.).

From MASON, Monday 20 November 1775

Printed from MS now WSL.

Wentworth Castle, Nov. 20, 1775.

Dear Sir,

I HAVE had your fashionable London influenza[1] for above a fortnight (fresh imported to Aston by Mr Verelst and kindly communicated to me in a post-chaise). Upon my getting a little better I
came hither to pay my respects to Lord and Lady Strafford, to whom
I had long owed a visit, and who have long been particularly civil to
me, much of which civility I have always imputed to the partiality of
your friendship for me. Be this as it may, here I am, and much better
for my journey, and a long walk which I took yesterday in a clear frosty
morning with his Lordship. All this, if you can make an apology out
of it, for I hardly can, is meant for one to you for my silence, certain
it is my cold and the having nothing to say prevented my writing at
home; and as I meditated then a visit here, I thought I should perhaps
find something more to say from hence. In this, however, I am mistaken, for except condoling with you for that you have lately lost £40
at loo to Mrs Howe[2] (which latter circumstance only is our topic of
condolence, for if you had flung it into the Thames we should not have
cared a whit about the matter), I find little more to put into my letter.
One thing, however, may be necessary to hint, that you are not quite
in the odour of sanctity here for your long silence, but this I only
gather from half-dropped expressions, and these always accompanied
with sentiments of great kindness, so that if you was to write a line or
two soon, and before you see them in town, I think it would be well
taken.[3]

You are very kind to me in your last by expressing so great a desire

---

1. The epidemic first manifested itself
in London early in November and seems to
have spread thence to other parts of the
country. The contemporary accounts of the
epidemic by several physicians are given
in *Medical Observations and Inquiries by
a Society of Physicians in London*, 1757–84,
vi. 340–406, and in *Annals of Influenza*, ed.
Theophilus Thompson, 1852, pp. 86–116.
Dr William White of York reported that
the epidemic had become general there 'in
the beginning of November, at which time

many whole families were indisposed' (ibid.
105).

2. Hon. Caroline Howe (ca 1721–1814),
m. (1742) John Howe of Hanslope, Bucks.
HW's brother, Edward, had at one time
thought of marrying her (HW to Mann 23
Nov. 1741); she was regarded by HW as a
'virago' (BERRY ii. 90).

3. Only one letter from HW to Lord
Strafford between 15 Nov. 1773 and 2 Nov.
1776 has been found; it was written 11 Nov.
1774.

of seeing me soon in town, and I feel I assure you as I ought on the subject and wish as much to be with you, as you can wish it. But my reasons for staying in Yorkshire at present are very urgent. The manner in which Lord Holdernesse has disposed of his Aston estate, of which Mr Verelst has bought only a fourth part,[4] and the rest sold in small parcels, will occasion so much difficulty in regulating my tithes, with the new proprietors, that it is absolutely necessary I should be on the spot till after New Year's day. And though this matter will in fact be all settled not by me, but my curate Mr Alderson, on whose judgment and honesty I can fully depend upon, yet I must appear to do it myself to prevent any odium that might fall upon him from the parish, and indeed without my personal assent to every new contract they would not be valid. Early in February I must repair to my York residence. Therefore, till the beginning of May I cannot possibly think of setting my face southward, but then I fully intend it. The Hertford Street reason[5] against my coming, which you call, and which was once my chief reason, is now none at all.[6]

Political matters seem now to be in such a state as to resemble the reign of chaos and old night, nay to be the identical thing, but as that state was not without its deity, therefore in order to keep myself out of an uncomfortable atheistical way of thinking, I intend to worship *Old Night* in the form of that brazen image commonly called the Duchess of Bedford.[7] I hope you will join with me in my devotions.

You ask me what I am doing. I am very innocently and very leisurely printing in the York Press[8] a few copies of my *English Garden;*[9] *il faut cultiver le jardin,* but this, God be thanked! I do not say in the spirit or meaning of Voltaire. In this way of printing I copy my betters, and have the thoughts of publishing as far from me, as that very ingenious writer had who printed five years ago a history of the same

4. See *ante* 23 Feb. 1773 and n. 5.

5. Lord Holdernesse. See *ante* 3 Feb. 1774.

6. This perhaps points to a partial reconciliation, which had occurred before June 1776 (see *post* 7 June 1776, n. 3). Or it may mean that with the sale of the Aston estate Mason would no longer be expected to call on Holdernesse.

7. Hon. Gertrude Leveson-Gower (1715–94), dau. of 1st E. Gower; m. (1737), as his 2d wife, John Russell, 4th D. of Bed-

ford. Her husband died in 1771, but as Dowager Duchess she continued to play a part in society. As early as 1759 Mrs Delany had described her as looking 'as yellow as a kite's foot' (*Delany Correspondence* iii. 572). See also HW to Montagu 24 Sept. 1761, MONTAGU i. 388.

8. I.e., Ann Ward's (Davies, *York Press* 288).

9. The second book, published in 1777. Mason distributed this private printing in May 1776; see *post* 20 May 1776 and n. 5.

art.[10] I question whether either production will be *publici juris* till they are reprinted at Philadelphia with the *imprimatur* of John Handcock[11] Americæ Septentrionalis R.P. Protector, and that I suppose can hardly happen this current year. The Lord and Lady of this place send all sorts of good wishes to you. Believe me to be, dear Sir, with perfect sincerity,

Yours,

W. MASON

To MASON, Monday 27 November 1775

Printed from Mitford i. 216–8.

Nov. 27, 1775.

I THOUGHT it long since I heard from you; it is plain you did not forget me, for the first moment of an opportunity to show me kindness, made you show it; fortunately I had written to Lord Strafford[1] the very day you wrote to me, and our letters passed each other, though without bowing. I think it still more fortunate that I had not written sooner, because I like to be obliged to you; I had delayed because in truth I had nothing to say but what I thought; and when my friends and I do not think alike,[2] I prefer silence to contradiction or disputes, for I cannot say what I do not think, especially to my friends; to other people one can talk a good deal of nonsense which serves instead of thinking.

Your delay of coming displeases me, because what I wish, I wish for immediately; when spring comes, I shall be glad my joy was postponed, and I like better to see you at Strawberry than in town, especially when Strawberry is in its beauty; and as you and it are two chiefs of the few pleasures I have left, or to come, I am luxurious and love a complete banquet.

What shall I say more? talk politics? no; we think too much alike.

10. HW's *Modern Gardening.*
11. Hancock had been elected (24 May 1775) President of the Second Continental Congress.

1. HW's letter is missing.
2. The subject on which HW and Straf- ford differed was the American war. A year later he wrote Strafford, 'I will say no more on a subject on which I fear I am so unlucky as to differ very much with your Lordship, having always fundamentally disapproved our conduct with America' (HW to Lord Strafford 2 Nov. 1776).

England was, Scotland is—indeed by the blunders the latter has made one sees its Irish origin,—but I had rather talk of anything else. I see nothing but ruin whatever shall happen, and what idle solicitude is that of childless old people, who are anxious about the first fifty years after their death, and do not reflect that in the eternity to follow, fifty or five hundred years are a moment, and that all countries fall sooner or later.

Naturally I fly to books, there is a finis too, for I cannot read Dean Tucker,[3] nor newspapers. We have had nothing at all this winter but Sterne's letters, and what are almost as nothingly,—Lady Luxborough's.[4] She does not write ill, or, as I expected affectedly, like a woman, but talks of *scrawls*,[5] and of her letters being *stupid*.[6] She had no spirit, no wit, knew no events; she idolizes poor Shenstone, who was scarce above her,[7] and flatters him, to be flattered. A stronger proof of her having no taste is, that she says coldly, she likes Gray's Churchyard *well*;[8] in good truth the productions of this country and age are suited to its natives. Mr Cumberland,[9] the maker of plays, told me lately, it *was pity Gray's letters were printed; they had disappointed him much;*[10] no doubt he likes Sterne's, and Shenstone's, and Lady Luxborough's. Oh! Dodsley, print away: you will never want authors

3. Josiah Tucker (1712–99), economist and divine; Dean of Gloucester, 1758. One of his tracts on the American war, *An Humble Address and Earnest Appeal*, advocating separation from the Colonies, was published 15 Nov. 1775 (*Public Advertiser*). HW wrote on the title-page of his copy (now WSL), 'November.'

4. *Letters Written by the Late Right Honourable Lady Luxborough to William Shenstone*, published 24 Nov. 1775 (*Public Advertiser*). The writer of the letters was Henrietta St John (1699–1756), m. (1727) Robert Knight, cr. (1745) Bn Luxborough of Shannon, from whom she separated within a few years of their marriage. She lived on his estate, Barrells, in Warwickshire, where she was a neighbour of William Shenstone, the poet. For HW's annotated copy of the book (sold London 1055, removed from SH vii. 37), see Lord Rothschild's catalogue No. 1338, p. 342. A selection of HW's notes was printed in 'Bibliomania,' by John Taylor Brown, in John

Brown's *Spare Hours*, 2d ser., Boston, 1866, pp. 374–7.

5. Lady Luxborough, op. cit. 97, 111, 297.

6. Ibid. 78, 252.

7. HW thought Shenstone's letters amusing 'though containing nothing but trifles' (HW to Cole 14 June 1769, COLE i. 165).

8. 'I cannot tell who wrote the Verses in a Country Churchyard, but I like them well' (Lady Luxborough, op. cit. 266). HW noted on this in his copy of the *Letters*: 'Excellent taste to admire the *Scribleriad* and Shenstone, and like Gray only *well*.'

9. Richard Cumberland (1732–1811), dramatist; nephew of HW's correspondent, Richard Bentley.

10. HW repeats Cumberland's remark about Gray *post* 30 Jan. 1780 and to Miss Berry 29 July 1790 (BERRY i. 103). In his *Memoirs* Cumberland characterized Gray as 'the most costive of poets' (*Memoirs of Richard Cumberland Written by Himself*, 1806, p. 17).

or readers, unless a classic work like Gray's life should, as Richardson[11] said of Milton, be born two thousand years after its time![12]

I approve your printing in manuscript, that is, not for the public, for who knows how long the public will be able, or be permitted to read? Bury a few copies against this island is rediscovered, some American versed in the old English language will translate it, and revive the true taste in gardening; though he will smile at the diminutive scenes on the little Thames when he is planting a forest on the banks of the Oroonoko. I love to skip into futurity and imagine what will be done on the giant scale of a new hemisphere; but I am in little London, and must go and dress for a dinner with some of the inhabitants of that ancient metropolis, now in ruins, which was really for a moment the capital of a large empire, but the poor man[13] who made it so, outlived himself and the duration of the empire.

From Mason, Saturday 16 December 1775

Printed from MS now wsl.
Address: The Honourable Horace Walpole, Arlington Street, London.
Postmark: ROTHERHAM 19 DE.

Aston, Dec. 16, 1775.

I AM much entertained with the newspaper account of the evidence of the three physicians[1] before the House of Lords. I want to know whether it struck you in the same way. One talks of her Grace being in a kind of *stupor*—and *at intervals* much affected in her understanding;[2] a second of her being *seemingly* deprived of her *recollection*[3]

---

11. Jonathan Richardson the elder (1665–1745), portrait-painter and author.

12. 'Milton's true character as a writer is that he is an ancient, but born two thousand years after his time' (Jonathan Richardson the elder and Jonathan Richardson the younger, *Explanatory Notes and Remarks on Milton's Paradise Lost*, 1734, p. cxlvii). The observation appears in the Introduction, written by the elder Richardson. HW's copy of *Explanatory Notes* was sold SH iii. 160.

13. Chatham.

---

1. Isaac Schomberg (1714–80), Richard Warren (1731–97), and N. D. Falck (*Jour-nals of the House of Lords* xxxiv. 530–1; see *ante* 22 Oct. 1775, n. 8), attending the Duchess of Kingston.

2. 'Doctor Schombergh . . . understood that she had been attacked with a kind of fit in St James's Chapel on the Sunday sennight preceding; this produced a kind of stupor which had greatly affected her, as he was informed previous to his seeing her; that she was, at intervals, much affected in her understanding' (*Lloyd's Evening Post* 11–13 Dec. 1775, xxxvii. 567).

3. 'Doctor Warren confirmed the testimony of everything advanced by Doctor Schombergh; said he was called in for the first time the day preceding; that the

and a third (her body physician)[4] says that if she continued to mend as she had done *the last twenty-four hours* she would soon be well enough, etc.[5] Now this seems to me to be a description of a person in her cups rather than in the palsy. If I am uncharitable in my censure, pray check me, although the subject be the person who calls herself Duchess of Kingston, for even in this case I will kiss the rod.

I admire Mr Cumberland's rudeness to you exceedingly, for to condemn Gray's letters to *you*, who had contributed so much to the collection, was worse than if he had condemned them to the editor. The editor might be excused in printing bad letters out of deference and respect to those who furnished him with them. The contributors to such a collection could have no such plea. But more than enough of this poor man, let him go on with his sentimental comedies, this anecdote shows he is qualified for the task because it shows he can have no feeling. Taste in all cases is out of the question.

Pray is it certain that a Great Personage in his treaty for foreign troops styled himself Sovereign of the Grand American Empire?[6] If it be, what an excellent moment he took for assuming such a title!

I have lately learned a very different doctrine about personal identity than Mr Locke[7] taught me at the University. He said, I think, that it consisted in consciousness of a man's knowing himself to be the same man today that he was yesterday, etc. Now, I say it depends merely upon the alphabet. Every man has from his father and his godfather a certain quota of letters given him at his birth and his baptism, by which he is what he is. Let him but contrive to change these and the coward of Minden becomes the secretary militant against America,[8] and everybody instantly loses their recollection about him as if

lady was seemingly deprived of her recollection, and her understanding was apparently much impaired' (ibid.).

4. Dr Falck, who 'had attended the Duchess of Kingston for some months past' (*Journals of the House of Lords* xxxiv. 531).

5. 'The last witness said, indeed, that if she continued to mend, as she did within the last twenty-four hours, it was probable she would be soon well enough to come out, but not so early as Monday next' (*Lloyd's Evening Post*, loc. cit.).

6. The source of this gossip about George III has not been found. See the following letter.

7. John Locke (1632–1704), in his *Essay concerning Human Understanding*.

8. Lord George Sackville had commanded the British forces in Germany in 1758–9 in the allied army under Prince Ferdinand of Brunswick. Having refused in the battle of Minden to follow Ferdinand's orders and advance, Sackville was court-martialled at his own request and dismissed from the service. His name was erased from the books of the Privy Council, but in 1765 restored by George III. In 1769 he inherited the estate of Drayton and a considerable fortune from Lady Elizabeth Germain, and in 1770 was empowered by an

they were in the same deplorable way with her Grace of Kingston. Nay, I would wager that his own recollection is lost too. If this be not a complete change of identity I know not what is; and yet it is all done by the power of the alphabet. Q. E. D.

I wish in your next favour, which I hope to have soon, you would be pleased to seal with a very clear impression of your antique sacrifice,[9] for I have been painting from a very bad one, a figure in chiaroscuro for one of my book presses, and I have succeeded so tolerably that I think it will do when finished from a better original.

Lord Strafford left Yorkshire I believe yesterday, but I have heard that he had received and was much pleased with your remembrance of him. We talked little about politics when I was with him, yet what I said of that sort (which was by no means of the neutral kind) did not seem to displease him.

Believe me, dear Sir,

Most truly yours,

W. MASON

To MASON, Thursday 21 December 1775

Printed from Mitford i. 221–4.

Arlington Street, Dec. 21, 1775.

I SHALL make the impression of the seal to this letter as perfect as I can; yet probably it will ill answer your purpose for it is only one of Wedgwood's antiques, and they are not very sharp; you exercise, I find, all your various talents but the one I love the best *in you.* I should not say so much to everybody: a thousand pictures give me pleasure for one poem.

Foote and you agree in convicting the Duchess of ebriety,[1] and

act of Parliament to adopt the name of Germain. He was secretary of state for the American colonies 1775–82 (GEC).

9. We learn from the next letter that this was 'one of Wedgwood's antiques,' but Messrs Josiah Wedgwood and Sons have been unable to identify it. 'The year which elapsed between 1773–1774 saw the production of the largest number of small intaglios, 414 appearing in a special cata-

logue of that year; of these 183 were from antiques generously lent to Wedgwood by Sir Watkin Williams Wynne' (Eliza Meteyard, *The Wedgwood Handbook,* 1875, p. 111).

---

1. Foote had written in his second letter to the Duchess of Kingston (*ante* 6 Sept. 1775): 'I can't help thinking but it would have been prudent in your Grace to have

you both prove it equally well in different ways. Nay, she seems to allow it herself, for she abandons insanity; intends, I hear, to rest her safety on pleading guilty,[2] lest standing on her spotless innocence should drag to light too many crimes. Lord Mansfield has added one more to his own list: his shameless protection of her.[3]

I never heard of the imperial title you mention, nor believe it, indeed I know of no treaty. That foreign troops have been treated for, is certain; if any are obtained, I am not in the secret.[4] In the mean time, the empire is shrunk to as narrow limits as that of the Holy Roman Empire; which when it had nothing left but one eagle, made it into two, by splitting it, as cooks serve a pigeon. By this time Canada probably is no part of the imperial dominions unless Lord Dunmore[5] has transported it on board his own government and ship, where he pretends to have imprisoned one of the provincial deputies, who to-day's papers say never existed[6]—unless by your hypothesis of alphabetic identity, one man may become another. That many men do become other men, I see every day, and so entirely other men, that they retain none of the blushing shame of their original nymphhood,[7] when they become butterflies.

I felt Mr Cumberland's folly so much, that his impertinence was lost on me. He has written an ode,[8] as he modestly calls it, in praise of Gray's odes—charitably no doubt to make the latter taken notice of. Garrick read it t'other night at Mr Beauclerc's,[9] who comprehended so

answered my letter before dinner, or at least postponed it to the cool hour of the morning' (*Public Advertiser* 18 Aug. 1775).

2. HW was misinformed.

3. In the debate (11 Dec. 1775) on procedure in the coming trial, Lord Mansfield showed a desire to give every possible consideration to the accused (Cobbett, *Parl. Hist.* xviii. 1111–4). When the Duchess of Kingston had first returned to England to stand trial, he had been helpful and courteous (*ante* 27 May 1775).

4. The treaties for the Hessian troops were not drawn up until January and February 1776 (Cobbett, *Parl. Hist.* xviii. 1155–67).

5. John Murray (1730–1809), 4th E. of Dunmore; Governor of New York 1769–70 and of Virginia 1770–6.

6. On 5 June 1775 Lord Dunmore had fled from his province and had taken refuge on shipboard. He collected a small fleet

and began a series of raids on Virginia towns. The story of his successes was published in the newspapers (e.g., *London Chronicle* 16–19 Dec. 1775, xxxviii. 585), but the *Public Advertiser* 21 Dec. 1775 questioned his exploits and pointed out that one of Dunmore's prisoners, a certain Robinson, could not be a delegate to the provincial convention, as Dunmore claimed, because his name was not on the list of delegates.

7. Nymph: 'An insect in that stage of development which intervenes between the larva and the imago' (OED *sub* 'nymph' 3).

8. 'To the Sun,' later published with an ode to Dr James (*post* 11 March 1776 and nn. 6–7).

9. Topham Beauclerk (1739–80), m. (1768) Lady Diana Spencer; friend of Johnson.

little what it was about, that he desired Garrick to read it backwards,[10] and try if it would not be equally good; he did and it was. I came in just afterwards; and the conversation continuing, Garrick said, with all the candour he could affect, 'I wonder at it, but people cry down Mr Mason's life of Gray extremely; I really think it very ingenious.' I made him no more answer than he deserved. I broke through this rule two days ago on a new impertinence to myself. In the paper-office[11] there is a wight, called Thomas Astle,[12] who lives like moths on old parchments. It was he who lent me the coronation roll,[13] and to whom I communicated my book on Richard III, to every tittle of which he agreed. Some of the moths his *commensales*[14] remonstrated to him I suppose, that he had fouled his own chrysalis by helping to unravel an intricate web. From that time I never saw him; on Monday he sent me a printed copy of the act of attainder of George, Duke of Clarence[15] (which corroborates remarkably one of my arguments), but which he not perceiving, very impertinently added a *quære*, which implied I had been in the wrong. The *quære* itself was so absurd that I could not deny myself the pleasure of laughing at him and his council. I send you a copy of my letter[16] as the shortest way of explaining

10. The incident was alluded to by Thomas Barnard, then Dean of Derry, in his verses addressed to 'Sir Joshua Reynolds and Co.'
'The art of pleasing, teach me, Garrick,
Thou who reversest odes Pindaric.'
Johnson's comment on the odes is given in Boswell, *Johnson* iii. 43–4.

11. The State Paper Office, first established, under the Great Seal, in 1578. Ultimately it was consolidated with the Public Record Office (*The Thirtieth Annual Report of the Deputy Keeper of the Public Records*, 1869, pp. 212–23).

12. Thomas Astle (1735–1803), antiquary and paleographer; one of the three commissioners appointed in 1763 for 'methodizing and digesting' the State Papers ('Calendar of Documents relating to the History of the State Paper Office to the Year 1800' in *The Thirtieth Annual Report*, p. 259); HW's occasional correspondent.

13. 'I do not wonder you could not guess the discovery I have made. . . . It is the original Coronation Roll of Richard III by which it appears that very magnificent robes were ordered for Edward V and that he did, or was to have walked at his uncle's

coronation' (HW to Dalrymple 17 Jan. 1768, DALRYMPLE 117). 'This singular curiosity was first mentioned to me by the Lord Bishop of Carlisle. Mr Astle lent me an extract of it, with other useful assistances; and Mr Chamberlain of the Great Wardrobe obliged me with the perusal of the original' (*Historic Doubts on the Life and Reign of King Richard the Third*, 1768, p. 65). When challenged by Milles, HW agreed that the document was a wardrobe account and not a coronation roll (*Works* ii. 231*–2*; GRAY i. 46 n. 318).

14. The other members of the commission were Sir Joseph Ayloffe (1709–81) and Andrew Coltee Ducarel (1713–85), both prominent members of the Society of Antiquaries ('Calendar of Documents,' loc. cit.).

15. 'The Attainder of George, Duke of Clarence' was printed in *Rotuli parliamentorum*, 1767–77, vi 193–5. Astle, one of the editors of the *Rotuli*, probably sent HW only the sheets containing the copy of the attainder (COLE ii. 2 n. 9).

16. Of 19 Dec. 1775. HW also sent a copy to Cole in his letter of 26 Jan. 1776.

what I have told you, and because I conclude the foolish Society of
Antiquaries will be convinced he has guessed happily, and that we
shall have a new dissertation against me in the next volume of the *old
women's logic,* as I call the *Archæologia.*[17] I have reserved two or three
more arguments,[18] with which they shall be treated if they do attack
me again, but with which I would not trust Astle, lest any one of the
body should have sense enough to see their folly and stop them. You
must excuse me, but some time or other I am determined to publish
all my answers.[19] I am offended for the honour of Richard's understanding, that all they charge him with tends to represent him as a
drivelling fool, though indeed such are their understandings that
they mean to prove he was an able knave.

Fools! yes, I think all the world is turned fool, or was born so, *cette
tête à perruque,* that wig-block the Chancellor,[20] what do you think
he has done? Burnt all his father's[21] correspondence with Pope, Swift,
Arbuthnot, etc.[22]—why do you think? because several of the letters
were indiscreet. To be sure he thought they would go and publish
themselves, if not burnt, but indeed I suspect the indiscretion was that
there were some truths which it was not proper to preserve, considering *considerandis.* That is just what I should like to have seen. There
was otherwise so much discretion, and so little of anything else except
hypocrisy in all the letters of those men that have appeared, that I
should not so much regret what discreet folly has now burnt. Apropos, did I ever tell you a most admirable *bon mot* of Mr Bentley? he
was talking to me of an old devout Lady St John,[23] who burnt a whole

17. Instances are in Cole i. 218–9, 270,
304. HW's set of the first twelve volumes
of *Archæologia* (now wsl) contains numerous marginalia.
18. See Cole ii. 3 and n. 13.
19. They are in *Works* ii. 185–252*.
20. Lord Bathurst, who was lord chancellor 1771–8. Sir Nicholas Wraxall said of
him that he 'may probably be considered as
the least able lawyer to whom the Great
Seal of this country was confided, in the
course of the eighteenth century' (*Historical Memoirs of His Own Time,* 1836, ii.
203).
21. Allen Bathurst (1684–1775), cr. (1712)
Bn and (1772) E. Bathurst.
22. HW's informant has not been identified. Twenty-six letters between Pope and
Bathurst are included in the Elwin and

Courthope edition of Pope's works, 1871–
89 (viii. 321–65). Elwin remarks: 'Some of
his [Pope's] letters to Lord Bathurst have
been dispersed, and many more than are
printed here may still exist.' About half the
letters in Elwin and Courthope were
printed from autographs found among the
papers of the Bathurst family. Several of
the missing letters have since been found
(Helen S. Hughes, 'Pope to Lord Bathurst:
An Unpublished Letter,' *Studies in Philol-
ogy* 1928, xxv. 462–7; information kindly
supplied by Dr George Sherburn). Eleven
letters between Bathurst and Swift are
printed in *The Correspondence of Jonathan
Swift, D.D.,* ed. F. Elrington Ball, 1910–4.
23. Johanna St John (d. ca 1704), dau.
of Oliver St John, Lord Chief Justice of
the Common Pleas, m. (ca 1651) Sir Walter

trunk of letters of the famous Lord Rochester, 'for which,' said Mr Bentley, 'her soul is now burning in heaven.' The oddness, confusion, and wit of the idea struck me of all things. I wish you good night.

From Mason, ca Thursday 1 February 1776

Missing. It may have been written in verse. See *post* 18 Feb.

To Mason, Tuesday 6 February 1776

Printed from Mitford i. 226–7. Dictated by HW to Kirgate (see the opening of Mason's reply).

Arlington Street, Feb. 6.

Dear Sir,

I SEND you word as soon as I can that I received your charming letter very safe, but that is all I can do or say, and God knows when I shall be able to send you any other answer for I am, and have been this week confined to my bed with the gout in six or seven different places. As I never had it before in my leap year,[1] I would suppose that it is owing now to the late bitter weather,[2] for you see that even in my condition one can be fool enough to flatter oneself with some straw to the last. Adieu. I heartily wish you all I want, without envying you what I want.

Yours ever,

H. W.

St John of Lydiard Tregoze (GEC, *Complete Baronetage* i. 25). He was a younger brother of Anne, Countess of Rochester, mother of the poet. Five pious letters from the Countess to her sister-in-law on the subject of the death-bed repentance of the profligate Earl suggest that Lady St John shared the Countess's piety. See Gilbert Burnet, *Lives, Characters, and an Address to Posterity,* ed. John Jebb, 1833, pp. 262–71.

1. That is, the alternate winters during which HW believed himself to be immune to his 'biennial visitor.' See *ante* 14 Feb. 1774, n. 5.
2. 'The year [1776] began with a remarkable snow and frost that lasted a month' (*Last Journals* i. 516). The newspapers in January and February contained many stories of the cold and heavy storms, which in the eighteenth century were believed to induce attacks of gout.

From MASON, Thursday 15 February 1776

Printed from MS now WSL.
Address: The Honourable Horace Walpole, Arlington Street, London.
Postmark: YORK ⟨? 17⟩ FE.

York, Feb. 15th, 1776.

Dear Sir,

I WAS extremely sorry to receive an answer to my last written by your amanuensis, yet I beg you would employ him immediately again just to tell me how you do, if you are not by this time able to use your own hand, which I heartily hope may be the case.

As to this very troublesome and unwelcome guest visiting you a year sooner than you expected him, I can easily account for that from the late severe weather, especially when I consider that had it been twice as severe it would never have prompted you to button a single button the closer.[1]

I most cordially wish for a good account of you soon, and am, dear Sir,

Most truly yours,

W. MASON

To MASON, Sunday 18 February 1776

Printed from Mitford i. 228–32.

Feb. 18, 1776.

AS my illness prevented my answering your delightful letter[1] I do not see why the leisure and solitude of convalescence should not be employed in replying to it, not poetically; for the current of the blood, frozen by age and chalk-stoned by the gout, does not, though loosened from disease, flow over the smooth pebbles of Helicon; mine at best were factitious rills that, like the artificial cascatelle of Hagley,[2] played for moments to entertain visitors, and were not the natural

1. HW prided himself on taking no precautions against cold and wet.

1. The missing letter of ca 1 Feb. 1776.

2. For an account of the cascades at Lord Lyttelton's seat see HW to Bentley Sept. 1753.

bounty of the soil;[3] *you* are forced to restrain your torrent and the dikes of prudence must be borne down before it overflows the country. Not so Mr Anstey; because his muddy mill-pool had in one point of view, the roar and lustre of a cascade when it fell over a proper wheel,[4] he thinks every pail full of its water, though soused down by a ploughman, has the same effect. His Somersetshire dialogue[5] is stupidity itself, you described it prophetically[6] before you saw it.

Somebody or other has given us an epistle of another kind by the late Lord Melcombe;[7] not different from having more meaning, for Phœbus knows it has none at all, but so civil, so harmless, and so harmonious, that it is the ghost of one of Pope's tunes. How the puffy Peer[8] must have sweated when learning to sing of Pope, whom he could have strangled![9] The whole and sole drift of this cantata is to call Lord Bute Pollio, and to beg to be his vicegerent upon earth. I should like to have heard Lord Bute asking Sir Harry Erskine[10] who Pollio was.

3. Nearly forty years earlier HW had written to another poet,
'Seeds of poetry and rhyme
  Nature in my soul implanted;
But the genial hand of Time,
  Still to ripen 'em is wanted:
Or soon as they begin to blow,
My cold soil nips the buds with snow.'
    (To West 3 Jan. 1737, GRAY i. 121.)

4. *The New Bath Guide*, 1766, which HW greatly admired.

5. *An Election Ball, in Poetical Letters in the Zomerzetshire Dialect, from Mr Inkle, a Freeman of Bath, to His Wife at Glocester. With a Poetical Address to John Miller, Esq. By the Author of the New Bath Guide*, 1776. Publication was first announced in *Daily Adv.* 31 Jan. 1776. HW's copy is in the Harvard Library.

6. Presumably in the missing letter of ca 1 Feb. 1776. Mason satirized Anstey later in the *Epistle to Dr Shebbeare*, 1777 (Mason's *Satirical Poems* 104).

7. George Bubb-Dodington (1691–1762), cr. (1761) Bn Melcombe; politician. The verses here referred to are *A Poetical Epistle from the Late Lord Melcombe to the Earl of Bute: with Corrections by the Author of the Night Thoughts*, published 13 Feb. 1776 (*Public Advertiser*). The Advertisement prefixed to the poem reads: 'The distinguished names on the title-page can excite no expectations in the public which the poetical merit of the following epistle is not capable of gratifying. It bears date the 26th of October 1761. To preclude every doubt concerning its authenticity, the original manuscript in Lord Melcombe's handwriting, with the corrections in that of Dr Young, is left for inspection at the shop of the publisher.' An early MS copy of the verses, dated (?by HW) '1760,' made before Young had corrected them, is now WSL and is described (inaccurately as 'the original manuscript') in *A Selection of the Letters of Horace Walpole*, ed. W. S. Lewis, 1926, i. pp. xx–xxi. The first page is reproduced at ii. 291. HW's copy of the printed poem, in the Harvard Library, has his (erroneous) note on the title, 'April 8.'

8. Lord Melcombe's 'bulk and corpulency' and somnolent habits are described by Cumberland (*Memoirs*, 1806, pp. 142, 145).

9. Because of Pope's satirical jibes at him in *Moral Essays* iv. 19–22, *Epistle to Dr Arbuthnot* ll. 279–80, and elsewhere. Pope wrote to Swift 6 Jan. 1734, 'I hope, and I think, he [Dodington] hates me, too, and I will do my best to make him' (Elwin and Courthope, *Works of Pope*, 1871–89, vii. 319).

10. Sir Henry (or Harry) Erskine (d. 1765), 5th Bt, of Alva and Cambuskenneth, Clackmannanshire; Lt-Gen.; M.P. Ayr

Mr Whitehed[11] has just published a pretty poem called *Variety*,[12] in which there is humour and ingenuity, but not more poetry than is necessary for a laureate; however the plan is one [*sic*], and is well wound up.[13] I now pass to prose.

Lo, there is just appeared a truly classic work: a history, not majestic like Livy, nor compressed like Tacitus; not stamped with character like Clarendon; perhaps not so deep as Robertson's[14] *Scotland,* but a thousand degrees above his *Charles;* not pointed like Voltaire, but as accurate as he is inexact; modest as he is *tranchant* and sly as Montesquieu without being so *recherché.* The style is as smooth as a Flemish picture, and the muscles are concealed and only for natural uses, not exaggerated like Michael Angelo's to show the painter's skill in anatomy; nor composed of the limbs of clowns of different nations, like Dr Johnson's heterogeneous monsters. This book is Mr Gibbon's *History of the Decline and Fall of the Roman Empire.*[15] He is son of a late foolish alderman,[16] is a member of Parliament,[17] and called a

burghs 1749–54, Anstruther Easter burghs 1754–65. He had been useful to Bute in preventing the publication of certain letters of Lady Mary Wortley Montagu's (Bute's mother-in-law). HW owned (and annotated) *A Narrative of What Passed between General Sir Harry Erskine and Philip Thicknesse, Esq., in Consequence of a Letter to the Earl of B—, Relative to the Publication of Some Original Letters and Poetry of Lady Mary Wortley Montague's, Then in Mr Thicknesse's Possession,* 1766; it is now WSL.

11. William Whitehead (1715–85) accepted the laureateship in 1757, succeeding Colley Cibber, after Gray had declined it. Whitehead, like Mason, was an intimate friend of Lord Harcourt; Whitehead's letters to him are in the seventh volume of the *Harcourt Papers.* After Whitehead's death Mason wrote an account of him that was published as the preface to the third volume (1788) of Whitehead's collected works.

12. *Variety: A Tale for Married People,* published 15 Feb. 1776 (*Daily Adv.*). HW's copy with his note 'February' above the date is at Harvard.

13. The *Critical Review* summarized the story of the two young lovers 'who by leading a rural life totally secluded from society, contracted a mutual disgust, which destroyed their conjugal happiness.' They

removed to London, 'where they entered into every scene of polite dissipation.' Impaired in health and repentant they 'resolved to live afterwards in a moderate intercourse with the world, as the only means of securing domestic comfort' (xli. 153).

14. William Robertson (1721–93), D.D., historian and HW's occasional correspondent. HW greatly admired his *History of Scotland during the Reigns of Queen Mary and of King James VI till His Accession to the Crown of England,* 1759 (HW to Robertson 4 Feb. and to Dalrymple 25 Feb. 1759, DALRYMPLE 41–5, 46–7), but liked only the first volume of his *History of the Reign of the Emperor Charles V,* 1769 (HW to Robertson 7 March 1769, DALRYMPLE 125 and n. 9, and *post* April 1778).

15. The first volume was published 17 Feb. (*Public Advertiser;* Jane E. Norton, *A Bibliography of the Works of Edward Gibbon,* Oxford, 1940, p. 37). Gibbon sent HW a presentation copy (HW to Gibbon Feb. 1776). It was sold SH v. 64 and is in Lord Rothschild's catalogue, No. 942, pp. 231–2.

16. Edward Gibbon (1707–70), alderman of the Vintry Ward 1743–5. The elder Gibbon's Tory and Jacobite leanings explain HW's 'foolish.' See D. M. Low, *Edward Gibbon 1737–1794,* 1937, pp. 10, 23, 207.

17. Gibbon was M.P. for Liskeard 1774–80, and in 1781 was returned for Lymington.

whimsical one because he votes variously as his opinion leads him; and his first production[18] was in French, in which language he shines too. I know him a little, never suspected the extent of his talents, for he is perfectly modest, or I want penetration, which I know too, but I intend to know him a great deal more[19]—there! there is food for your residence at York.

Do I know nothing superior to Mr Gibbon? yes, but not what will entertain you at York. Mr Gibbon's[20] are good sense and polished art. I talk of great original genius. Lady Di Beauclerc[21] has made seven large drawings in soot-water[22] (her first attempt of the kind) for scenes of my *Mysterious Mother*.[23] Oh! such drawings! Guido's grace,[24] Albano's children,[25] Poussin's expression,[26] Salvator's boldness in landscape[27] and Andrea Sacchi's simplicity of composition[28] might perhaps have equalled them had they wrought all together very fine; how an author's vanity can bestow bombast panegyric on his flatterers! Pray, Sir, when did I take myself for an original genius! Did not Shakespeare draw Hamlet from Olaus Ostrogothus,[29] or some such name?

18. *Essai sur l'étude de la littérature,* 1761. HW's copy, which was presented to him by Gibbon, was sold SH iii. 73. He owned another copy, sold SH v. 171, now WSL. In return for this book HW sent Gibbon the first two volumes of *Anecdotes of Painting,* 1762 (D. M. Low, *Gibbon's Journal to January 28th, 1763,* 1929, p. 63).

19. See HW to Gibbon 14 Feb. 1776.

20. A word such as 'virtues' seems to be omitted.

21. Lady Diana Spencer (1734–1808), m. (1) (1757) Frederick St John, 2d Vct Bolingbroke, who divorced her in 1768; m. (2) (1768) Topham Beauclerk. She was a Twickenham neighbour of HW's, at Little Marble Hill.

22. A kind of India ink.

23. The drawings were begun in the preceding December (HW to Lady Ossory 27 Dec. 1775) and all seven are said to have been 'conceived and executed in a fortnight' ('Des. of SH,' *Works* ii. 504). HW added the Beauclerk Tower at SH to contain them (*post* 17 Sept. 1776; 'Genesis of SH' 82). The drawings, which were in 'ebonized and gold frames,' were sold SH xvii. 32 to the Hon. Lionel Dawson-Damer, 3d son of the 1st E. of Portarlington. Their present whereabouts is unknown.

24. Guido Reni (1575–1642). 'In Guido were the grace and delicacy of Coreggio, and colouring as natural as Titian's' (*Ædes Walpolianæ, Works* ii. 235).

25. Francesco Albani or Albano (1578–1660) was noted for the cupids in his allegorical paintings.

26. Nicholas Poussin (1594–1665). 'Nicolo Poussin was a perfect master of expression and drawing, though the proportion of his figures is rather too long' (ibid. ii. 234).

27. 'The greatest genius Naples ever produced resided generally at Rome; a genius equal to any that city itself ever bore. This was the great Salvator Rosa [1615–73]. His thoughts, his expression, his landscapes, his knowledge of the force of shade, and his masterly management of horror and distress, have placed him in the first class of painters' (ibid. ii. 233).

28. Andrea Sacchi (1599–1661) 'did not, indeed, shun the elegant, though he seems born for the grand style–grave miens, majestic attitudes, draperies folded with care and simplicity' (Luigi Lanzi, *The History of Painting in Italy,* trans. Thomas Roscoe, 1828, ii. 218).

29. Both Sir Thomas Hanmer and Johnson note that the story of *Hamlet* may be found in Saxo Grammaticus. HW owned both editions of Shakespeare; his copy of Hanmer's is now WSL.

did Le Sœur[30] conceive the Chartreuse[31] from any merit in the legend of St Bruno?[32] seeing is believing, miracles are not ceased; I know how prejudiced I am apt to be; some time or other you will see whether I am so in this instance.[33]

Now for specific answers to your queries—many of which answers will not be specific, for I know little more than if I were at York. I know nothing of Garrick's sale of patent,[34] but I know forty stories of his envy and jealousy, that are too long to tell you by mouth of pen —of a Monsieur Le Texier,[35] another real prodigy, who acts whole plays, in which every character is perfect—and pray observe he has not read *my* play.[36] In sum, Garrick says when he quits the stage, he will read plays too, but they will be better than Monsieur Texier's (who only reads those of other authors) for he shall write them himself. This I know he has said twice. *Ex pede Herculem.*

The Duchess of Kingston only knows whether she will be tried.[37] The Earl's[38] zeal against her was as marvellous to me as to you; I know

30. Eustache Le Sueur (1617–55), French painter; one of the founders of the Académie de Peinture.

31. That is, the twenty-two paintings of the life of St Bruno that Le Sueur executed for the Carthusian monastery in Paris. They were purchased from the monastery by Louis XVI in 1776, and have been in the Louvre since 1793. See HW to West ca 15 May 1739 NS, GRAY i. 169 and n. 17.

32. (ca 1030–1101), the founder of the Carthusian order.

33. In his 'Advertisement' (dated 1 Oct. 1780) to the fourth volume of *Anecdotes of Painting*, p. viii, HW has this to say of Lady Di: 'Has any painter ever executed a scene, a character of Shakespeare, that approached to the prototype so near as Shakespeare himself attained to nature? Yet is there a pencil in a living hand as capable of pronouncing the passions as our unequalled poet; a pencil not only inspired by his insight into nature, but by the graces and taste of Grecian artists. . . . Whoever has seen the drawings, and bas-reliefs, designed and executed by Lady Diana Beauclerc, is sensible that these imperfect encomiums are far short of the excellence of her works.' See also the fifth volume of the *Anecdotes,* ed. Frederick W. Hilles and Philip B. Daghlian, New Haven, 1937, pp. 233–4.

34. 'The purchasers of Mr Garrick's share of the patent of Drury Lane Theatre, we hear, are Dr Ford, Mr Ewart, Mr Linley, and Mr Richard Sheridan. The purchase money is £35,000' (*Lloyd's Evening Post* 19–22 Jan. 1776, xxxviii. 74).

35. A.-A. Le Texier (d. ca 1814). 'Monsieur Tessier, of whom I have heard much in France, acted an entire play of ten characters, and varied his voice and countenance, and manner, for each so perfectly, that he did not name the persons that spoke, nor was it necessary' (HW to Lady Ossory 23 Nov. 1775). See DU DEFFAND iv. 32, 41, and *passim*.

36. In 1772 and 1773 Mme du Deffand had talked of having *The Mysterious Mother* translated, but nothing ever came of her plans. In 1776 she was still hoping for a translation and a performance of it by Le Texier (DU DEFFAND iv. 365).

37. The trial had finally been set for 15 April (*London Chronicle* 25–7 Jan. 1776, xxxix. 96) and Earl Bathurst, the Lord Chancellor, had been named High Steward of Great Britain for the conduct of the proceedings (ibid. 10–13 Feb.). Without Mason's letter one can only guess what question HW was here answering, but he seems to be saying that the Duchess of Kingston was still trying to have the trial abandoned or postponed.

38. Elizabeth Chudleigh's husband, Augustus John Hervey (1724–79), who suc-

reasons why he should have done the reverse, and cannot reconcile contradictions. Why should not Sayre's affair sleep?[39] what, who is awake? For your hundred other queries which you have not put to me, I shall not attempt to guess them, not from idleness, but from the probable incapacity of my being able to answer them. The womb of time is big; we shall see, whether she is delivered of mice or mountains.

One word about myself and I have done. I know you disliked my answer to Dr Milles,[40] and I know I was angry both at him and Mr Hume. The latter had acted very treacherously by the story I have hinted at of the Swiss reviewer.[41] Dr Milles is a fool, who had been set on by Lord Hardwicke[42] and that set, and at whom I have glanced.[43] I have received many indirect little mischiefs from the Earl,[44] who has of late courted me as much,[45] and I have been civil to him.[46] But my answers shall some time or other appear when I only shall be blamed and my antagonists will be dead, and not hurt by them. For Mr Mas-

ceeded his brother in the Earldom of Bristol in March 1775. See *post* 14 April 1776, n. 4.

39. See *ante* 25 Oct. 1775. In June 1776 Sayre brought a successful action in the Court of Common Pleas against Rochford for false arrest (DNB *sub* Zuylestein, W. H. Nassau de, E. of Rochford).

40. See *ante* 28 Aug. 1771.

41. Jacques-Georges Deyverdun (ca 1734–89), Gibbon's intimate friend and collaborator in the *Mémoires littéraires de la Grande Bretagne*. HW believed that the review of *Historic Doubts* in the *Mémoires* for 1768, pp. 1–25, actually by Gibbon, was by Deyverdun. Hume's treachery in HW's eyes lay in his having persuaded HW to send a copy of the *Life of Lord Herbert of Cherbury* to Deyverdun for review in the *Mémoires* and then contributing critical notes to the review of *Historic Doubts*. See 'Short Notes,' GRAY i. 44–5. HW's comments upon the review and Hume's hand in it are in 'Supplement to the *Historic Doubts*,' *Works* ii. 193–4.

42. Philip Yorke (1720–90), 2d E. of Hardwicke; F.S.A., 1744. HW lost few opportunities to express his dislike of Hardwicke, which was inspired by his belief that the elder Hardwicke had 'basely betrayed' Sir Robert Walpole (COLE ii. 116).

43. In the *Reply to the Observations of the Rev. Dr Milles*. 'I now and then heard that some persons, who had wished my doubts could be answered, and who would have been more glad if they had been able to answer them themselves, affected to pronounce the Dean's work a full confutation of my book' (*Works* ii. 222*).

44. I.e., Hardwicke. In 1757 Hardwicke issued a privately printed edition of the *Letters from and to Sir Dudley Carleton, Knight, during His Embassy in Holland*. HW spoke with gratitude of the 'munificence' of the editor in giving it to the public and said that it was not the fault of the editor that Carleton's negotiations 'turned chiefly on the Synod of Dort' (*Royal and Noble Authors, Works* i. 349). In his second edition (1775) Hardwicke denied this and claimed 'a right to rank this correspondence amongst the materials for no uninteresting period of civil history' (pp. xxv–xxxvi). See COLE i. 380, 386; HW to Dalrymple 23 Feb. 1764, DALRYMPLE 98–9 and n. 37.

45. Hardwicke had requested HW to reprint the Carleton letters at the SH Press (COLE ii. 109).

46. As HW's letters to him of this time prove.

ters,[47] he is a dirty simpleton,[48] who began by flattering me,[49] and because I neglected him joined the pack. The arguments in the answers are very essential to the question, and I shall not give myself the trouble of extracting the ridicule on the answerers, as they deserved it.

My hands you see are well, but I could not have written so long an epistle with my feet, which are still in their flannels. As my spirits always revive in proportion as pain subsides, I shall take the liberty, Sir Residentiary, to trespass on your decorum by sending you an impromptu I wrote yesterday, to pretty Lady Craven,[50] who sent me an eclogue of her own,[51] every stanza of which ended with *January*, and which she desired me not to criticize, as some of the rhymes were incorrect, a license I adopted in my second line:

> Though lame and old, I do not burn
> With fretfulness to scare ye;
> And charms and wit like yours would turn
> To May my January.
>
> The God who can inspire and heal
> Sure breathed your lines, sweet fairy;
> For as I read, I feel, I feel,
> I am not quite January.

Probably you would have liked better to have the eclogue, but I had not leave to send it.

47. Robert Masters (see *ante* i. 58 n. 4) read a paper entitled *Some Remarks on Mr Walpole's Historic Doubts* at the Society of Antiquaries on 7 and 14 Jan. 1771. It was published in *Archæologia* ii. 198–215. HW's reply, *Short Observations on the Remarks of the Rev. Mr Masters*, referred to in a letter to Cole of 27 April 1773, was printed in 1794 but not published until 1798, when it appeared in *Works* ii. 245*–51*.

48. HW's low opinion of Masters was instigated at least in part by Cole's stories of his sharp practices (COLE i. 218, 268 and *passim*).

49. See his letter of Aug. 1762 to HW on the *Anecdotes of Painting* (COLE i. 22–4).

50. Lady Elizabeth Berkeley (1750–1828), m. (1) (1767) William, 6th Bn Craven (from whom she separated in 1780), and (2) (1791) Christian Karl Alexander Friedrich, Margrave of Brandenburg-Anspach. HW grew tired of her ultimately (HW to Harcourt 1 Sept. 1787), but at this time he was on excellent terms with her. He had printed verses to her at SH in 1775 (Hazen, *SH Bibliography* 214–7) and in 1778 printed her translation of Pont-de-Veyle's *La Somnambule* (ibid. 114 and *post* 17 Sept. 1778).

51. The text of the verses is in her letter to HW of 17 Feb. 1776 (now WSL).

To Mason, Thursday 29 February 1776

Printed from Mitford i. 232–5.

Feb. 29, 1776.

MY confinement has made me a great devourer of quartos; I am impatient to tell you what I have found in one as large as Mr Gibbon's, not quite so excellent a work, nor so compressed, but which is not barren of entertainment, though the first sections to be sure are to me absolute Hebrew. This is Dr Burney's *History of Music*,[1] a volume that I fear will a little interfere with my friend Sir John Hawkins's[2] on the same subject.

I must begin with telling you that in page 168 the Doctor says, he holds it impossible to be a great poet and a great musician too.[3] Now not to mention Gray, who (I believe, though I know nothing of music) was a great musician,[4] how could he forget you whom he has not forgotten, for he has celebrated your harmonic knowledge in his notes,[5] though I perceive he did not know that you are an *inventor* in the science, and have begotten a new instrument by the marriage of two others:—but to the point.

Would you believe that the great Abyssinian, Mr Bruce, whom Dr B. made me laugh by seriously calling the *intrepid traveller*,[6] has had the intrepidity to write a letter to the Doctor, which the latter has printed in his book,[7] and in which he intrepidly tells lies of almost as

---

1. *A General History of Music from the Earliest Ages to the Present Period*, 4 vols, 1776–89. The first volume only was 'ready to deliver to the subscribers' 31 Jan. 1776 (*London Chronicle* 30 Jan.–1 Feb., xxxix. 108). The author was Charles Burney (1726–1814), Mus.D. and F.R.S., friend of Johnson and father of the novelist, Fanny Burney. HW appears in the list of subscribers; his four volumes were sold SH v. 32. The first ten sections comprise the 'Dissertation' and are on technical matters. Presumably HW's interest began at p. 195 with the 'History.'

2. Sir John Hawkins (1719–89), Kt, 1772. From 1759 to 1771 he had been a Twickenham neighbour of HW's. His *General History of the Science and Practice of Music*, 5 vols, on which he had been working since 1759, appeared late in 1776. HW 'it was who first suggested to my father the idea

of the *History of Music*' (Lætitia-Matilda Hawkins, *Anecdotes*, 1822, i. 101; see also COLE ii. 28 and HW to Mann 2 Jan. 1761). HW's copy of Hawkins is now WSL.

3. 'This is not the place to discuss the point; but it appears to me as if the being at once a great poet, and a great musician, were utterly impossible' (i. 168).

4. 'His taste in this art was equal to his skill in any more important science' (Mason, *Mem. Gray* 342). See GRAY i. 233 and n. 21.

5. 'Mr Mason . . . has not been able to conceal from his friends how little his genius and taste have been confined to poetry, or how great a progress he has made in the knowledge and practice of music' (i. 499). Burney then quotes definitions of harmony communicated to him by Mason.

6. *General History of Music*, i. 214.

7. Ibid. i. 214–24*.

large a magnitude as his story of the bramble, into which his Majesty of Abyssinia and his whole army were led by the fault of his general, and which bramble was so tenacious, that his Majesty could not disentangle himself without stripping to the skin and leaving his robes in it, and it being death in that country to procure or compass the Sovereign's nudity, the general lost his head for the error of his march.[8]

In short Mr Bruce has not only described six Abyssinian musical instruments, and given their names in the ancient Ethiopic and in the court language, but contributed a Theban harp,[9] as beautifully and gracefully designed as if Mr Adam had drawn it for Lady Mansfield's[10] dressing-room,[11] with a sphinx, masks, a patera, and a running foliage of leaves. This harp, Mr Bruce says, he copied from a painting in fresco on the inside of a cavern[12] near the ancient Thebes, and that it was painted there by the order of Sesostris;[13] and he is not at all astonished at the miracle of its preservation, though he treats poor accurate Dr Pococke[14] with great contempt for having been in the cave without seeing this prodigy,[15] which however, graceful as its form is, Mr Bruce

8. The story is in Bruce's *Travels to Discover the Source of the Nile*, Edinburgh, 1790, iv. 66–7 and v. 50. That version differs from HW's. Only the King had the unlucky accident of riding into the bramble (called 'kantuffa' by Bruce), and the punishment was meted out to the local 'shum,' the official in charge of the district in which the event happened, and his son. Bruce claims to have been an eyewitness of the episode, which is said to have occurred in 1770 during the early years of the reign of Tecla Haimanout II. The official and his son were executed not because of a tactical error, but because Abyssinian law made it the responsibility of the subjects always to see to it that the King's progress was never impeded by the 'kantuffa.'

9. Burney, op. cit. pl. VIII (facing i. 222*). A list of later copies of the wall-painting is given in Bertha Porter and Rosalind L. B. Moss, *Topographical Bibliography of Ancient Egyptian Hieroglyphic Texts, Reliefs, and Paintings*, 1927–51, i. 15.

10. Lady Elizabeth Finch (1704–84), m. (1738) William Murray, later E. of Mansfield.

11. Ken Wood (or Caen Wood), Lord Mansfield's seat in the neighbourhood of Hampstead, was redecorated and enlarged

by the Adam brothers ca 1767–71. See John Swarbrick, *Robert Adam and His Brothers*, [1915], pp. 173–81.

12. The sepulchre of Ramses III in the Theban necropolis, styled as a result of this discovery communicated to Burney 'Bruce's Tomb' or 'the Harper's Tomb.' See Porter and Moss, op. cit. i. 13.

13. 'I look upon this instrument, then, as the Theban harp, before and at the time of Sesostris, who adorned Thebes, and probably caused it to be painted there' (Burney, op. cit. i. 222*). 'To the name Sesostris . . . tradition attached the first foreign conquests of the Pharaohs. . . . In Greek times Sesostris had long since become but a legendary figure which cannot be identified with any particular king' (James Henry Breasted, *A History of Egypt from the Earliest Times to the Persian Conquest*, New York, 1905, p. 189). The painting actually belongs to the tomb of Ramses III, who reigned ca 1198–ca 1167 B.C. (Porter and Moss, op. cit. i. 13–5).

14. Richard Pococke (1704–65), D.C.L.; Bp of Ossory, 1756, of Meath, 1765; traveller and numismatist. HW owned his *Description of the East and Some Other Countries*, 1743–5, which was sold SH iv. 72.

15. 'Pococke, I think (for though I have sometimes looked into him, I never could

thinks was not executed by any artist superior to a sign-painter,[16] yet so high was the perfection of the arts in the time of *Sesac*,[17] that a common mechanic could not help rendering faithfully a common instrument. I am sorry our Apelles, Sir Joshua, has not the sign-painter's secret of making his colours last in an open cave for thousands of years.[18]

It is unlucky that Mr Bruce does not possess another secret reckoned very essential to intrepid travellers, a good memory. Last spring he dined at Mr Crauford's,[19] George Selwyn was one of the company; after relating the story of the bramble and several other curious particulars, somebody asked Mr Bruce, if the Abyssinians had any musical instruments? 'Musical instruments,' said he, and paused—'Yes I think I remember one lyre'; George Selwyn whispered his neighbour, 'I am sure there is one less since he came out of the country.'[20] There are now six instruments there.

Remember this letter is only for your own private eye, I do not desire to be engaged in a controversy or a duel.

My gout is waning, and my ambition looks down to getting on a shoe in a few days. Mr Stonhewer called on me yesterday, and I diverted him with what had just happened. Mr Cambridge had been with me, and asked me if I knew the famous Beaumarchais, who is in England.[21] I said, 'No, Sir, nor ever intend it.'[22] 'Well now,' said he,

read him), was in this grotto, and slept here, I suppose, for he takes no notice of one of the few monuments from which we may guess at the former state of arts in Europe' (Burney, op. cit. i. 220*).

16. 'To guess by the detail of the figure, the painter should have had about the same degree of merit with a good sign-painter in Europe' (ibid. i. 221*).

17. Sir Isaac Newton believed that Sesostris and Sesac were one and the same man (*Chronology of Ancient Kingdoms Amended*, 1728, pp. 68–9), and Bruce accepted this identification (Burney, op. cit. i. 223*). Sesac, the Biblical Shishak, was actually Sheshonk I, the founder of the twenty-second dynasty, who ruled from ca 945 to ca 920 B.C.

18. The tomb of Ramses III was open from the time of the Ptolemies (Sir J. Gardner Wilkinson, *Topography of Thebes and General View of Egypt*, 1835, p. 114).

19. John ('Fish') Craufurd (d. 1814),

HW's friend and correspondent. See DU DEFFAND i. 6 n. 21.

20. HW had already told this story to Mason (*ante* 27 May 1775).

21. Pierre-Augustin Caron de Beaumarchais (1732–99), dramatist, controversialist, and man of affairs. His legal contest with Mme Goëzmann in 1774 and his *Barbier de Seville*, acted 23 Feb. 1775, had recently served to keep him before the public. See DU DEFFAND iv. *passim*. Beaumarchais visited England frequently in 1775 and 1776 as a secret agent of the French crown. He had arrived on one of these visits in the preceding January. See Louis de Loménie, *Beaumarchais et son temps*, 1856, ii. 83–112, and P. P. Gudin de la Brenellerie, *Histoire de Beaumarchais*, 1888, p. 183.

22. On 15 May 1774 Mme du Deffand wrote HW: 'Je doute que le Beaumarchais vous fasse autant de plaisir à voir, qu'il vous en a fait à le lire; avant ses mémoires,

'that is exactly my way; I made a resolution early never to be acquainted with authors, they are so vain and so *troublesome.*' I am persuaded he has got acquainted with Beaumarchais by this time. Adieu.

PS. When you read Dr Burney, pray observe in p. 256 in the notes, a quotation from Huet[23] that exactly describes Bryant's *Ancient Mythology.*[24]

From MASON, ca Thursday 7 March 1776

Missing.

To MASON, Monday 11 March 1776

Printed from Mitford i. 235–7.

Arlington Street, March 11, 1776.

VENISTI, vidi, vicisti,[1] your letter arrived on Saturday, General Conway[2] came yesterday; Sir John Legard[3] will have ample credentials to Brunswic, for Mr Conway is in friendship and correspondence with Prince Ferdinand,[4] and Sir John will certainly have leave to go *after the review*[5] if officers are allowed to go abroad *at this time.* Thank you heartily for giving me this opportunity.

il passait pour un homme de mauvaise compagnie' (DU DEFFAND iv. 53).

23. Pierre-Daniel Huet (1630–1721), Bp of Avranches.

24. 'Le véritable usage de la connaissance des langues étant perdu, l'abus y a succédé. . . . Par cet art, un allemand que j'ai connu prouvait que Priam avait été le même qu' Abraham: et Æneas le même que Jonas' (letter from Huet to Bochart, quoted by Warburton, *Divine Legation of Moses,* 4th edn, 1765, iii. 240).

1. Unexplained in the absence of Mason's letter, but presumably Mason had asked HW to procure letters of introduction from Conway for Sir John Legard.

2. Hon. Henry Seymour Conway (1719–95), general and (1793) field marshal; HW's cousin and correspondent.

3. Sir John Legard (ca 1758–1807), 6th Bt, 1773. His commission as cornet in the Royal Horse Guards, of which Conway was colonel, is dated 20 March 1775 (*Army List* 1777, p. 21).

4. Prince Ferdinand of Brunswick (1721–92), one of Frederick the Great's field marshals; after 1757 commander of the Westphalian army in the Seven Years' War, during which command Conway served under him with the British troops.

5. Presumably the elaborate review on 19 March of the Foot Guards selected for duty in America. It was attended by the King, many dignitaries of state, and important visitors (*Public Advertiser* 20 March). Legard's regiment, the Royal Horse Guards, took part.

Mr Cumberland has published two odes[6] in which he has been so bountiful as to secure immortality for Gray,[7] for Dr James's powder,[8] and indeed for his own odes, for Father Time would fall asleep before he could read them through. There is a dedication to Romney the painter,[9] that hisses with the pertness of a dull man.

Bishop Keene wrote to me t'other day[10] to know if I knew anything of a whole length of my father,[11] that was to be sold by auction,[12] and if I had any objection to his buying it; was this folly? or is it repentance, and he wants a memento to remind him that he cheated my father's daughter of a living and of marriage?[13]

I mentioned this to my nephew the Bishop of Exeter[14] just now, who told me that when Mr Grenville was turned out,[15] who had offered my Lord of Ely[16] the primacy of Ireland,[17] he sent for the person who had brought him the offer, and desired him to tell Mr Grenville, that he should always acknowledge the obligation, but that as Mr Grenville was now out, he thought it right (perhaps he said honest)

6. Cumberland's two *Odes* were published 5 March 1776 (*Public Advertiser*). HW's copy is now in the Harvard Library.

7. The first ode (pp. 11–20), 'To the Sun,' celebrating a tour by the author through Westmorland and Cumberland, contains the lines:
'Ah! where is he that swept the sounding lyre,
And while he touched the master string,
Bade *Ruin seize the ruthless King*
With all a prophet's fire?' (p. 17.)
In the dedicatory epistle to Romney, Cumberland writes: 'Mr Gray, whose faculty of describing can give life to scenes which I should have conceived nothing but the pencil could convey, hath left behind him a journal, for which we are indebted to his candid friend and editor. This journal refers to all the scenes hinted at in the following ode' (p. 4). The 'journal' is the series of letters to Wharton 1769–70 printed in *Mem. Gray* 350–80.

8. The second ode (pp. 21–7), 'To Dr Robert James,' 'was suggested by the recovery of my second son from a dangerous fever, effected under Providence by his celebrated powders' (Cumberland's *Memoirs*, 1806, pp. 280–1).

9. George Romney (1734–1802), life-long friend of Cumberland. The dedicatory epistle pp. [3]–10) begins, 'Whilst you was

engaged in contemplating those wonderful productions of ancient art, which Italy is enriched with, I was tracing the ruder beauties of Nature in a domestic tour through the mountainous parts of Westmoreland and Cumberland.'

10. The letter is missing.

11. The full-length portrait by Jean-Baptiste Vanloo (1684–1746), painted for Henry Bromley (1705–55), cr. (1741) Bn Montfort.

12. The auction of Lord Montfort's pictures was conducted by James Christie 16–17 Feb. 1776 (*Daily Adv.*; Frits Lugt, *Répertoire des catalogues de ventes, 1600–1825*, The Hague, 1938). Keene lost the picture to Lord Hertford (Cole to HW 12 Sept. 1777, Cole ii. 57).

13. See *ante* 17 Sept. 1773 and n. 10.

14. Hon. Frederick Keppel (1729–77), Bp of Exeter, 1762; m. (1758) Laura Walpole, eldest daughter of HW's brother Edward.

15. George Grenville (1712–70) on 10 July 1765 was succeeded as first lord of the Treasury and prime minister by the Marquess of Rockingham.

16. Bishop Keene.

17. The archbishopric of Armagh had become vacant on the death of George Stone 19 Dec. 1764. See Montagu ii. 145 and *Gray's Corr.* ii. 871–2.

to tell him that his Lordship must look up to the King, and to *whomever* his Majesty should make his minister.

The Duke of Wirtemburg[18] is arrived with a mistress,[19] whom he got made Countess of the Empire. The Queen of France would not receive her; she has been received at Court here;[20] the man who keeps the *hôtel garni*[21] in Covent Garden would not lodge her for the reputation of his house.

Here is a new epigram[22] from France.

> Quelqu'un, dit-on, a peint Voltaire
> Entre La Beaumelle,[23] et Fréron;[24]
> Cela ferait un vrai Calvaire
> S'il n'y manquait le bon larron.

Voltaire himself has written a little poem called *Sésostris*,[25] which I do not send you, for it is only the worn-out choice of Hercules.[26]

PS. I have often thought of a thing, and which, as you are now at York I will mention, and beg you to suggest to Peckitt. You know he and all the modern glass-painters cannot recover the fine ancient reds and greens; how is that possible, when every necklace-shop sells false

18. Karl Eugen (1728–93), D. of Württemberg 1737–93.

19. Franziska von Bernardin (1748–1811), m. (1) Baron Friedrich von Leutrum; m. (2) (1785) Karl Eugen, Duke of Württemberg. She was created (1774) Reichsgräfin von Hohenheim by Emperor Joseph II (*Allgemeine deutsche Biographie*, Leipzig, 1875–1912, xv. 390–1).

20. 'Thursday [7 March] the Lady of the Duke of Wirtenburgh, and another foreign Lady of their suite, were presented to their Majesties at St James's, being introduced by Lady North' (*Public Advertiser* 9 March 1776).

21. Opened by David Low in 1774; described by Cunningham and Wheatley as 'the first family hotel . . . established in London' (*London Past and Present* i. 463).

22. Sent to HW by Mme du Deffand in her letter of 3 March 1776. On the following day she wrote (but did not immediately post) a second letter, in which she said: 'L'épigramme que je vous ai envoyée, que je croyais nouvelle, est ancienne.' See DU DEFFAND iv. 274, 277. The occasion of the epigram was the appearance in 1775 of the

second edition of La Beaumelle's *Commentaire sur la Henriade*, with corrections by Fréron, the engraved title-page of which shows Voltaire flanked by La Beaumelle and Fréron. Another version of the epigram is printed in Voltaire's *Œuvres*, ed. Moland, x. 593.

23. Laurent Angliviel de la Beaumelle (1726–73), one of the bitterest enemies of Voltaire, whom he had offended in his early work, *Mes Pensées* (Copenhagen, 1751), by stating that Voltaire's rewards from Frederick the Great were out of proportion to his deserts.

24. Elie-Catherine Fréron (1718–76), another of Voltaire's literary foes.

25. The poem was being circulated in Paris in early March 1776. HW's copy was sent to him by Mme du Deffand in her letter of 3 March. See DU DEFFAND iv. 275 and n. 6. It is an allegory in honour of Louis XVI.

26. Xenophon's story, in which Hercules has to choose between Pleasure and Virtue. Sésostris is required to make a similar choice between La Volupté and La Sagesse.

rubies and emeralds, which jewellers must take out of the setting, to be sure they are not true! and what are those counterfeits but coloured glass? pray too, could not Peckitt sketch the exact faces of Henry IV and Richard III from their statues on the screen of your cathedral?²⁷ I would pay him for them.

From Mason, Monday 25 March 1776

Printed from MS now wsl.
Address: The Honourable Mr Walpole, Arlington Street.

March 25th, 1776.

WHAT I here send you was written yesterday *currente calamo,* as you will see, and might be much improved, if you would please to retouch it. The idea I think is a good one and I could wish it might appear in the papers,¹ for some personal reasons of my own.² If any use is made of it, it must be transcribed by some person who does *not know my hand* and the original burnt. I fear after all the usual fate that attends my squibs will fall on this, and it will be *still-born.* I question much whether every news printer be not in her pay at present and yet you see all mention of her trial is for that account avoided in the letter. I will say no more, but burn it, or otherwise, as you think best. I send it through the Secretary's office to you for safety.

[Enclosure.]

To Her Grace the Duchess of Kingston.

Madam,

I have just now seen in the public papers that your Grace with a spirit of Christian benevolence, which exceeds that of our two metropolitans in the proportion of somewhat more than three to two, has contributed the

27. HW had asked Mason in 1773 to have these drawings made from the York choir screen. Mason received the letter too late to attend to the request, but promised to do so at his next residence in the following year. He seems to have forgotten or ignored the commission. See *ante* 29 July and 12 Sept. 1773 and *post* 10 and 14 April 1776.

1. The enclosure was apparently not published. See *post* 10 April 1776.

2. 'You will hear a horrible story of your humble servant when you get to town, for my rebellious spirit has produced such a card to Marsden, who has sent it to the Archbishop, about the subscription to the American clergy, that his Grace and I, nay and the whole bench, are all at daggers drawing' (Mason to Alderson 9 March 1776).

sum of fifty pounds towards alleviating the distresses of the clergy in North America.[3] This emboldens me to ask you a few questions concerning that charity and to state an objection or two relative to it, not doubting but that your Grace before you thought it prudent to honour the list of subscribers with a name that would undoubtedly make both the clergy and laity proud of following so illustrious an example, demanded to see those authentic accounts of the distresses in question, which have hitherto been withheld from the world, though the press daily afforded so ready a method of communication.

I beg therefore to learn from your Grace whether these misfortunes affect the parochial clergy only in North America, or extend also to the missionaries sent out for the propagation of the gospel in foreign parts, by the Society instituted for that purpose.[4]

If the parochial clergy be the only sufferers, it must be by deprivation, or loss, of their tithes and oblations. Now I should conceive that the best way to relieve them in this point would be to take them home (for the Congress I presume would readily part with them) and to place them immediately under the patronage of those diocesans from whom they received their letters of orders, for it cannot be doubted but that many of their Lordships who have shown so much alacrity to provide for their nephews, daughters' husbands, etc., etc., might in a very short space of time put these their distressed brethren more at their ease than they were even before the American troubles broke out. Of this fact we are very sure, that the annual income of the dignities and pluralities held by two relatives of one opulent prelate, more than trebles the sum that the whole bench have subscribed on this occasion, with your Grace's fifty pounds into the bargain.

If these distresses extend to the missionaries, the same mode of recalling them is more peculiarly necessary; indeed it would be now necessary even if they were not distressed. At least they should have orders from administration to look upon their missions as sinecures: for while the Indians remain in their heathen state, they will surely be better allies to us, and answer our present political purposes with greater *energy*, than if they were previously converted to Christianity. Except indeed these missionaries were gifted enough to regenerate them in a moment into such good Christians as

3. Early in 1776 the Archbishops and Bishops opened a subscription for the relief of the clergy in North America. The Archbishops of York and Canterbury each subscribed thirty pounds to the fund, and the Duchess of Kingston fifty pounds (*London Chronicle* 24–7 Feb., 19–21 March, xxxix. 197, 276).

4. The Society for the Propagation of the Gospel in Foreign Parts, founded in 1701 (J. S. M. Anderson, *The History of the Church of England in the Colonies and Foreign Dependencies of the British Empire*, 1845–56, iii. 81).

your Grace, Lord Sandwich and Lord G. Germaine, a species of conversion, which, as miracles have ceased, is rather to be wished than to be expected.

But perhaps your Grace will say, 'Who are you that ask these impertinent questions?' 'Madam, I am a country clergyman.' 'Go then to your diocesan to satisfy your scruples of conscience.' No, Madam, I choose to apply myself to you and for these three cogent reasons. First, I believe from my soul that you write letters with more ease than my diocesan, and that your epistolary style is much more spirited and poignant, especially after dinner.[5] Secondly, because you have much more Christian humility and obliging condescension than my diocesan. He, I know, would flout my tattered crape and disdain to give me an answer. But when I tell your Grace that I can bring my college certificate that I had an university education, and my parochial register that I was born of honest parents, I am morally certain that you will not be too haughty to become my correspondent. No, you will never deny that honour to a clergyman of the Church of England which you so lately bestowed on a reptile whom you believed to be the son of a merry-andrew.[6] Thirdly and lastly, your Grace has by this your late superb donation taken this charity into your immediate and personal protection. You are by this act and deed of yours become *the head of the clergy*, and therefore, though I am the lowest member of that body, I have the ambition on this occasion to treat with *principals only*. Beholding your Grace in this most respectable light, I subscribe myself with the truest devotion, Madam,

Your Grace's most dutiful son and servant,

A COUNTRY CLERGYMAN

Isle of Ely,[7] March 22d, 1776.

To MASON, ca Monday 1 April 1776

Missing; indicated by the final paragraph of *post* 10 April.

From MASON, ca 4 April 1776

Missing; indicated by the first words of the following letter.

---

5. An allusion to Foote's remark in his published letter to the Duchess of Kingston (*ante* 21 Dec. 1775, n. 1).

6. Alluding to the Duchess's letter to Foote (*ante* 6 Sept. 1775, n. 16).

7. Struck out in MS.

To Mason, Monday 8 April 1776

Printed from Mitford i. 241–3.

April 8, 1776.

YOU find Circe and Alma Mater are too powerful, perhaps they are in alliance; *il faut cultiver son jardin:* you must stick to your garden.[1]

There is Dr Chandler who was sent by the Dilettanti to, and has just published his travels in, Greece.[2] They are rather travels in Pausanias, for he does little but tell us what Pausanias found worth seeing there. Except that, which is no merit, the book is ill-written and unsatisfactory; and yet he revived my visions towards Athens, and made me wish I was a great king and could purchase to restore it; a great king probably would hold it cheaper to conquer it. This Dr Chandler, as if to avenge his namesake,[3] flirts at Gray[4] for having clothed Delphi's barren steep with woods, and converted Meander's muddy waves into amber, as if amber did not poetically imply the same.[5] I don't wonder with so little taste he has written no better.

I bought yesterday a poem in blank verse called *Amwell,*[6] by a John Scott, Esq.;[7] it is a pious design to immortalize a village in which John

1. In this disguised reference to Mason's anonymous letter to the Duchess of Kingston, Circe is the Duchess, Alma Mater the Church. Mason, HW says, must get on with his *English Garden,* and it would seem that he is telling Mason that his letter is not going to be published.

2. *Travels in Greece, or an Account of a Tour Made at the Expense of the Society of Dilettanti* was published 3 April 1776 (*Daily Adv.*). The author was Richard Chandler (1738–1810), D.D., antiquary and traveller. HW's copy of this book was sold SH v. 134. The Society of Dilettanti, founded ca 1732, was originally a convivial society of gentlemen who had made the Grand Tour. Its interests in time became more serious, and the Society sponsored much important work in classical archæology. See Lionel H. Cust, *History of the Society of Dilettanti,* ed. Sidney Colvin, 1898. HW was never a member.

3. See HW's postscript for the explanation of this confusion.

4. Chandler does not name Gray, but writes: 'And here it may be remarked, that the poets who celebrate the Ilissus as a stream laving the fields, cool, lucid, and the like, have both conceived and conveyed a false idea of this renowned water-course. They may bestow a willow fringe on its naked banks, amber waves on the muddy Meander, and hanging woods on the bare steeps of Delphi, if they please; but the foundation in nature will be wanting' (*Travels in Greece,* 1776, p. 79).

5. 'Woods, that wave o'er Delphi's steep . . .
Or where Meander's amber waves
In lingering lab'rinths creep'
(Gray, 'Progress of Poesy,' ll. 66–70).

6. Published 5 April 1776 (*Public Advertiser*). HW's copy is now in the Harvard Library and bears his note, 'April 5.'

7. John Scott (1730–83) of Amwell, Herts; Quaker poet.

Scott, Esq., lives. I only mention it for one grand and beautiful image which struck me extremely—

> —oft Fancy's ear
> Deep in the gloom of evening woods, has heard
> The last sad sigh of Autumn, when his throne
> To Winter he resigned.[8]

It puts me in mind of that sublime passage in Dyer's *Ruins of Rome,*

> hears the voice of Time
> Disparting towers.[9]

I don't know whether you are much acquainted with my Swiss footman, David;[10] well! he does not think there is so great a prince in the world as I. Yesterday as I came to breakfast, he told me coolly the Duke of Wirtemburg had called at eight o'clock and wanted a ticket for Strawberry Hill. 'Bless me,' said I, 'and what did you say?' 'I told his Grace you was not awake, and bade him come again at ten.' 'Good God,' said I, 'tell him to call again! don't you know he is a Sovereign Prince?' 'No I did think he was only a common Duke'—I could not help laughing, though I was so shocked. In short he had called again, and had again been sent away, nor can David yet conceive that I was to be waked. I was forced to write a thousand lies and excuses,[10a] and swear I was bedrid with the gout, and could not pay my duty to his Serene Highness, and upon the whole was very glad for being reduced to plead the gout. I sent Philip[11] to show my house, and persist in my crippletude, which in truth is still so fresh, that it would all have revived, if I must have walked or stood two hours to show his Serenity the tombs.

They are translating Shakespeare in France,[12] and *Othello* is so well done, that it has incredible success. The Abbé Barthélemi,[13] a very

8. Ll. 431–4.
9.   '. . . The pilgrim oft
    At dead of night, 'mid his oraison hears
    Aghast the voice of Time, disparting towers'
                (*Ruins of Rome*, ll. 38–40).
10. David Monnerat (d. 1785).
10a. The letter is missing.
11. Philip Colomb (d. 1799), HW's Swiss valet.
12. The first two of the twenty volumes

of *Shakespeare traduit de l'anglais*, by Pierre-Prime-Félicien le Tourneur (1737–88) and others, appeared early in 1776 and were presented to Louis XVI 18 March 1776 (DU DEFFAND iv. 289). The first play in the first volume is *Othello.*

13. Jean-Jacques Barthélemy (1716–95), antiquary, numismatist, and writer, was an intimate friend of Mme de Choiseul, at whose house HW first met him in 1766 (see DU DEFFAND i. 21).

good judge and no partialist to England, desired Mad. du Deffand to tell me,[14] he finds Shakespeare *supérieur à tout et qu'il me priait de ne regarder que le dieu et de ne pas faire attention à l'homme.* This is a strong proof that both the Abbé and the translators understand Shakespeare, but what will they do with Falstaffe?—impossible—unless they are as able as Townley,[15] who translated *Hudibras* so admirably, which before seemed the most impracticable of all achievements.

Is not your residence[16] nearly exhausted, and don't you intend coming southward? Am not I to harbour you? you shall be troubled with no Serene Highnesses, nor have I wasted all my budget in my letters; Lady Di's drawings alone are worth a pilgrimage,—ask Mr Palgrave who has seen them.

PS. I have made a blunder, which will have puzzled you, I recollect it was a Dr Chapman, not Dr Chandler, who made so good an end by choking himself with mackerel.[17]

From MASON, Wednesday 10 April 1776

Printed from MS now WSL.
Address: The Honourable Mr Horace Walpole, Arlington Street, London.
Postmark: YORK 12 AP.

York, April 10th 1776.

I HAD formed a scheme by means of an artist here to get you the exact masks in plaster of the two heads which you wanted[1] out of our screen, which I thought would be infinitely more satisfactory to you than any drawing, but upon examination I find no King Richard III amongst them. The sequence ends with Henry V, then comes Jammy, who turned out Henry VI to make room for his own sweet person,[2] and whom Time in revenge has more mutilated and pitted than any of his more ancient predecessors; but I am sorry for your sake that the

---

14. In her letter to HW of 21 March 1776, DU DEFFAND iv. 288–9.

15. John Towneley (1697–1782), a Catholic Jacobite who resided in France most of his life. His translation of *Hudibras,* originally undertaken to show that Voltaire was wrong in describing it as untranslatable, was first published anonymously in 1757.

16. At York.

17. A reference to the story told by Gray in his letter to Clerke 12 August 1760. See *ante* 17 April 1774 and n. 22.

1. Of Henry IV and Richard III (*ante* 11 March 1776).

2. See *ante* 29 July 1773 and n. 8. The figure of Henry VI was removed long before the accession of James I.

said Time has made very free with the mouth and chin of your friend
Harry IV, insomuch that I hardly think any mask or drawing can be
depended upon if taken from it, for there is plainly a circle about the
size of a crown piece fallen off round the mouth of the monarch. You
may now see indeed where his lips were, but the shape of those lips
are quite obliterated. I am sorry that I am obliged to give you so sad
an account of his Majesty, but the truth is too glaring to be concealed.
If after all you will have either a mask or drawing of it, I will do my
best to serve you. It may perhaps serve future antiquaries to demonstrate from it that the King's Evil was inherent in English royalty from
Temp. Hen. Quart.

The event you talked of in the *Public Advertiser*[3] has not reached
York. Indeed the *P. Advertiser* never comes to York. Mercy on me,
cry you, York is in the Orcades; but I can say no more, only that if I
have not an account of the D[uchess] of Kingston's trial[4] every day
from you I shall die of the pip. The post is just going.

Yours, etc., etc.

W. MASON

To MASON, Sunday 14 April 1776

Printed from Mitford i. 244–6.

Strawberry Hill, Eve of St Elizabeth of Kingston.

I WILL not trouble you for a cast of King Richard's face, since
there is no such thing; nor of King Henry's, since it has lost its
mouth. I am grown such an antiquity myself, and have so little time
left to satisfy my fancies, that I willingly contract them within as narrow a compass as I can; yet you commission me to send you journals
of the Duchess's trial, as if I was to be there! My curiosity would certainly carry me thither sooner almost than to any show upon earth. I
have known her from five years old,[1] and seen her in all her stages, but

3. Presumably in the missing letter of ca
1 April. HW had apparently sent Mason's
'Country Clergyman' letter to the *Public
Advertiser,* and Mason was awaiting its
publication. It did not appear, however,
nor did Woodfall, in his customary manner, print in his notes to correspondents
his reasons for rejecting it.

4. The trial was to open 15 April.

1. HW had known Elizabeth Chudleigh when he lived in Chelsea next to the
Hospital of which her father was deputy-
governor (HW to Mann 24 April 1776).

I am not well enough to attend this last act of her drama—possibly may never go to a public place again, having a strong notion of the propriety of seceding, and not trailing one's weaknesses into the world, when age and illness have told one to retire. Thus you must expect no ocular accounts from me, perhaps nothing better than the newspapers would tell you, except with a little more authenticity.

Tuesday, April 16.

The Duchess-Countess has raised my opinion of her understanding, which was always but at low ebb, for she has behaved so sensibly and with so little affectation, that her auditory are loud in applause of her. She did not once squall, scream or faint, was not impudent, nor gorgeous, looked well though pale and trembling; was dressed all in black, yet in silk, not crape; with no pennon hoisted but a widow's peak. She spoke of her innocence and of her awe of so venerable an assembly;[2] yesterday passed in the pleading of her counsel[3] against a second trial, urging the finality of the ecclesiastic sentence.[4] I should think no more would be done today than hearing the reply of the prosecutor's counsel.[5]

A previous incident was more entertaining than any part of the

2. 'My Lords, I, the unfortunate widow of your late brother, the most noble Evelyn Pierrepont, Duke of Kingston, am brought to the bar of this right honourable House without a shadow of fear, but infinitely awed by the respect that is due to you, my most honourable judges' (*The Trial of Elizabeth Duchess Dowager of Kingston for Bigamy . . . Published by Order of the House of Peers*, 1776, p. 8; *The Whole of the Evidence on the Trial of Her Grace Elizabeth, Duchess Dowager of Kingston . . . Published by the Order of Her Grace, from the Short Hand Notes of Mr Gurney*, [1776], p. ix).
3. James Wallace (d. 1783), solicitor-general, 1778–80, attorney-general, 1783 (GM 1783, liii pt ii. 982; R. C. Mitchell and L. W. Morse, *Chronicle of English Judges, Chancellors, Attorneys General, and Solicitors General*, Oswego, N.Y., 1937, p. 82); James (later Sir James) Mansfield (1733–1821), solicitor-general 1780–82, Chief Justice of the Court of Common Pleas, 1804 (Venn, *Alumni Cantab.*; GM 1821, xci pt ii. 572); Peter Calvert (d. 1788), LL.D., F.R.S., Dean of the Arches, 1778 (Venn, op. cit.; GM 1788,

lviii pt ii. 757); William (later Sir William) Wynne (d. 1815), LL.D., advocate-general, 1778, Dean of the Arches 1788–1809, Judge of the Prerogative Court of Canterbury 1788–1809 (Venn, op. cit.); and the Duchess's attorney, William Field (*ante* 22 Oct. 1775, n. 7). See *The Whole of the Evidence*, p. [v].
4. The sentence of the Consistory Court of the Right Reverend Lord Bishop of London, which tried the claim of Augustus John Hervey that Elizabeth Chudleigh was his wife. The court pronounced 10 Feb. 1769 that Elizabeth Chudleigh 'was and now is a spinster, and free from all matrimonial contracts or espousals.' The arguments of the defendant's counsel for the validity of the sentence and its decisiveness on the question of her bigamy are printed in the *Trial*, pp. 20–51.
5. Counsel for the prosecution were Edward Thurlow (1731–1806), cr. (1778) Bn Thurlow, attorney-general 1771–8, lord chancellor 1778–92; Alexander Wedderburn, solicitor-general 1771–8; John Dunning (1731–83), cr. (1782) Bn Ashburton; and George Harris (1722–96), D.C.L.

piece; the *Grand Seneschal*[6] invited the Duke of Wirtemburg to dinner by a card, and translated it neither into law Latin nor Norman
French. By the help of Boyer's dictionary[7] it began *'Le haut Intendant
envoie ses compliments,'* etc. He ordered everybody to be uncovered
while the King's commission was reading, and then sat down himself
and put on his hat.

Lord Nuneham has just been here,[8] not attending his friend
through all her course. She lay at home[9] (or according to the chaste
modern phrase, *slept* there), and the Usher of Black Rod[10] slept in the
next room. My journals are short, but you shall have the sequel.
Adieu.

PS. I this minute receive a letter from poor Mr Granger's nephew
to tell me his uncle was seized, at the communion table, on Sunday
with an apoplectic fit, and died yesterday morning at five o'clock.[11]
He was a good man as ever lived.

2nd PS. Thurloe, Wedderburn and Dunning[12] have answered the
Duchess's counsel, and then the Lords adjourned till Friday, so at
soonest you will hear again by Saturday's post.

To Mason, Saturday 20 April 1776

Printed from Mitford i. 247–8.

April 20, 1776.

YOUR obedient journalist proceeds. He might plead a headache;
but as that is generally pleaded when not felt, a real one must not

6. Lord Bathurst, who had been named
Lord High Steward for the trial.

7. *Dictionnaire royal français et anglais*,
by Abel Boyer (Pierre Abel de Boyer) (1667–
1729), French Huguenot who came to London in 1689. His dictionary, first published
in 1702, was the standard French-English
dictionary of the eighteenth century.

8. When he doubtless communicated the
details given by HW above.

9. According to the newspapers she 'retired in the custody of the Black Rod to
an apartment at the Duke of Newcastle's,
adjoining to the Hall' (*London Chronicle*
16–18 April 1776, xxxix. 374).

10. Sir Francis Molyneux (ca 1737–1812),
Kt; 7th Bt, 1781; Gentleman Usher of the

Black Rod 1765–1812 (GEC, *Complete
Baronetage* i. 48; GM 1812, lxxxii pt i.
604–5). His office was that of 'chief Gentleman Usher of the Lord Chamberlain's
department of the royal household, who
is also usher to the House of Lords and to
the Chapter of the Garter'(OED). His sym-
bol of office is a black wand surmounted by
a golden lion.

11. For accounts of his death see GM 1776,
xlvi. 313, and James Granger, *A Biographical History of England*, 5th edn, 1824, i.
p. xxvii; see also HW to Cole 16 April
1776, COLE ii. 9. The letter from Granger's
nephew (unidentified) is missing.

12. Their speeches are printed in full in
the *Trial*, pp. 51–85.

be disgraced by being turned into an excuse, especially by so sacred a minister of truth—as a newswriter.

The plot thickens, or rather opens; yesterday the judges were called on for their opinions, and *una voce* dismantled the ecclesiastic court, which has not been treated with much respect by the common law. The Attorney-General then detailed the life and adventures of Elizabeth Chudleigh, alias Hervey, alias the most high and puissant Princess the Duchess of Kingston. Her Grace bore the narration with a front worthy of her exalted rank. Then was produced the capital witness,[1] the ancient damsel who was present at her first marriage and tucked her up for consummation.[2] To this witness the Duchess was benign, but had a transitory swoon at the mention of her dear Duke's name; and at intervals has been blooded enough to have supplied her execution if necessary. Two babes were likewise proved to have blessed her first nuptials, one of which for aught that appears may exist and become Earl of Bristol.[3] The gallant and faithful Earl of Hilsborough[4] used all his prowess to cross-question and browbeat the deponent,[5] but her Grace's other champion Lord Mansfield did not enter the lists. The court is now hearing the other witnesses. I have forsworn prophecy and therefore tell you no particulars of what is to come. If I hear anything in time this evening of the events of the day, you shall know, if not, good night.

PS. It is near seven and the trial is not over, I must go out and learn

1. Ann Cradock, who at the time of Elizabeth Chudleigh's marriage to Hervey was the servant of Mrs Ann Hanmer, an aunt of the accused. Ann Cradock later married a servant of Hervey's. See *Trial,* pp. 108–16.

2. As she testified at the trial (ibid. 109–10; *Whole Evidence,* p. 1). The last six words, not in Mitford, were first printed by Mrs Toynbee from Mitford's MS transcripts (Add. MSS 32563 fol. 50) of passages omitted from the letters.

3. The birth of only one child (in 1747), a son who died within a few months, was alleged at the trial (*Trial,* pp. 105, 110–1), but Ann Cradock's testimony was not altogether clear and HW's informant may have been misled. At one point Ann Cradock expressed her belief that the defendant had had but one child by Hervey, and she declared that she first heard of its existence after the father's first return from sea

duty. But she had previously said, 'After his return the second time I believe the child to have been begotten' (*Trial,* p. 111). Later in her testimony (ibid.) she seemed to imply that the Duchess was with child about 1768. That gossip had for some time attributed two children to the defendant is indicated by HW's letter to Mann 28 Feb. 1769.

4. Wills Hill (1718–93), 2d Vct Hillsborough, 1742; cr. (1751) E. of Hillsborough and (1789) M. of Downshire.

5. Hillsborough tried to discredit Ann Cradock's testimony by eliciting from her the admission that she hoped for reward for giving it (*Trial,* pp. 115–6). She acknowledged that she had been promised a sinecure by some unknown friend of one of her acquaintances, one Mr Fozard, but she maintained that the offer was not accompanied by a request for her testimony.

anecdotes, and cannot come home before the post goes out; so you must have patience till next week.

To Mason, Sunday 21 April 1776

Printed from Mitford i. 248–9.

Sunday, April 21, 1776.

I HAVE an half-hour to spare and employ it to continue the trial which will not be finished before Tuesday evening, when I shall certainly neither have collected the sequel, nor have time to write it, as I am to dine at the Royal Academy.[1]

Friday and Saturday have produced so much against the Duchess-Countess, that she must have been distracted to have sought the trial, or not poisoned the witnesses. The judges quashed the ecclesiastic court, as summarily as Luther could have done; and Thurloe has given an Atalantis[2] of her Grace's adventures, confirmed by evidence. A maid has appeared who was present at her first marriage and almost at its consummation. Sergeant Hawkins[3] has authenticated the birth of at least one child; and the widow of the parson[4] who married her, and on whom she forced a fictitious register when she expected the late Lord Bristol's death and had a mind to be a Countess,[5] has deposed, that though privy to all these circumstances, visiting the new *Duchess,* the latter said to her, 'Mrs Phillips, was not the Duke very good to marry an old maid?'[6] Both these women, her avarice had

1. This was the annual dinner and private showing of the pictures on the eve of the opening of the public exhibition. A list of the guests at the dinner printed in *Public Advertiser* 26 April 1776 shows that HW attended.

2. 'A secret or scandalous history' (OED).

3. Cæsar (later Sir Cæsar) Hawkins (1711–86), sergeant-surgeon to George II and George III; cr. (1778) Bt. His testimony appears in *Trial*, pp. 119–26.

4. Judith, the widow of Rev. Thomas Amis, who performed the secret marriage of Elizabeth Chudleigh and the Hon. Augustus John Hervey at Lainston, Hants, in 1744. After the death of her husband (1759), Mrs Amis married a Mr Phillips, steward to the Duke of Kingston (*Trial,* pp. 130–3).

5. Amis had apparently made no record of the marriage. In 1759 George, 2d E. of Bristol, was believed to be dying; his brother was next in line for the earldom, and Elizabeth Chudleigh was therefore very anxious that her position be safeguarded. She went to Amis, then on his death-bed, and persuaded him to manufacture a marriage-register so that there would be no doubt of her rights as Hervey's wife.

6. 'Mrs Phillips [testified,] "I waited upon her in Arlington Street, after her marriage with the Duke of Kingston. She said to me, Was it not very good-natured of the Duke to marry an old maid? I looked her in the face and smiled, but said nothing then" ' (*Trial,* p. 132).

turned against her. Lord Barrington,[7] subpœnaed against her, after taking the oath, declared he would betray no confidential secrets.[8] The Lords were going to hang him for perjury,[9] but thought better on it, lest a quarrel between the two Houses[9a] should prove favourable to America. His Lordship faltered[10] as well as they did; told more than he had declared he would not tell,[11] and yet prevaricated;[12] but for this interlude you must wait for the printed trial, as I cannot relate it accurately.

Tomorrow the Duchess makes her defence; and on Tuesday the Lords give sentence. She has not preserved the philosophy of the first day, but abused the first female evidence while giving testimony. Lord Mansfield left the ecclesiastical court in the lurch;[13] his cowardice always supplanting his knavery. Adieu, you shall know the sequel by Wednesday or Thursday's post.

PS. When does your residence conclude? and when do you come to Strawberry Hill?

7. William Wildman Barrington-Shute (1717–93), 2d Vct Barrington.

8. 'My Lords, . . . if anything has been confided to my honour, or confidentially told me, I do hold, with humble submission to your Lordships, that as a man of honour, as a man regardful of the laws of society, I cannot reveal it' (*Trial*, p. 127).

9. The propriety of Lord Barrington's withholding information was hotly debated, and it was decided that he ought to answer all questions put to him (ibid. 129–30).

9a. Barrington (an Irish peer) was M.P. for Plymouth 1754–78.

10. 'My memory I have found by long experience to be a very erroneous one, and especially with relation to things past long ago. To the best of my memory and belief, the Duchess has never honoured me with any conversation on the subject [of her marriage to Hervey] for many, many years past; I believe I might say for above twenty years past. And, my Lords, that being the case I must answer . . . very doubtfully' (ibid. 130).

11. 'The Duchess of Kingston . . . did

entrust me with a circumstance in her life relative to an engagement of a matrimonial kind with the Earl of Bristol, then Mr Hervey' (ibid.).

12. HW apparently found it difficult to believe Lord Barrington's statement that 'The Duchess of Kingston has never communicated to me, in the course of her life, to the best of my memory or belief, anything which was, at the time she was pleased to communicate it to me, in the least a deviation from the strictest rules of virtue and religion' (ibid.).

13. Lord Mansfield was on friendly terms with the defendant and HW expected him to act in her defence. Her strongest argument was that she had received a decree of nullity from an ecclesiastical court and therefore could not be accused of bigamy. Lord Mansfield failed to uphold the finality of the ecclesiastical decision, and at no time took an active part in the trial beyond interjecting occasional remarks or questions. He joined in the unanimous vote of guilty (*Trial*, p. 154).

To MASON, Tuesday 23 April 1776

Printed from Mitford i. 250.

April 23, 1776.

IF you expect a long letter, you will be disappointed, if you are tired of my letters you will be released. The wisdom of the land has been exerted five days in turning a Duchess into a Countess, and does not think it a punishable crime[1] for a Countess to convert herself into a Duchess. After a paltry defence and an oration of fifty pages, which she herself had written and pronounced well, the sages in spite of the Attorney-General, who brandished a hot iron,[2] dismissed her with the simple injunction of paying her fees; all voting her guilty, the Duke of Newcastle[2a] softening his vote with *erroneously, not intentionally.*[3] So ends that solemn farce! which may be indifferently bound up with the State Trials and the *History of Moll Flanders*. If you write to her you must direct to the Countess of Bristol. The Earl they say does not intend to leave her that title, nor the House of Meadows[4] a shilling, but there will be quæres to both designs. The ecclesiastic court, full as guilty as the culprit, I dare to say, will escape as well. Adieu! allow that I have obeyed you implicitly. I am glad to have done with her.

From MASON, Wednesday 1 May 1776

Printed from MS now WSL.
Address: The Honourable Mr Horace Walpole, Arlington Street, London.
Postmark: YORK 3 MA.

York, May 1st, 1776.

Dear Sir,

I FEAR you will think me less susceptible of gratitude than his Grace of N[ewcastle][1] and less punctilious in point of honour than

1. The Duchess of Kingston was found guilty of bigamy, but she claimed benefit of clergy, a right of members of the peerage, and her plea was accepted (*Trial*, pp. 156–66).

2. 'Mr Attorney-General objected to claim of the prisoner, insisting that she was not entitled to the privilege of a peer, and that she was liable to be imprisoned and marked by fire as a common felon' (*London Chronicle* 20–23 April 1776, xxxix. 392). See *Trial*, pp. 163–6.

2a. Henry Fiennes-Clinton (later Pelham-Clinton) (1720–94), 9th E. of Lincoln, 1730; 2d D. of Newcastle-under-Lyne, 1768.

3. *Trial*, p. 155.

4. The prosecution of the Duchess of Kingston had been initiated by Evelyn Philip Medows whose mother, Lady Frances Pierrepont, was the Duke's only sister. See GEC *sub* Kingston.

1. The bracketed names have been expanded by HW in the MS.

Lord Viscount B[arrington] for not having thanked you sooner for your four exquisite journals. I have, however, prepared something[2] for you which I have the vanity to think will amply recompense you for your trouble, but whether you will receive it two posts after this or not receive it at all I am not able to say. I would not, however, hang you on the tenter of expectation longer than for the space of two posts, and therefore, if you do not receive it in that time, rest in the philosophical reflection that all is for the best, and that your loss will be the public gain,[3] which is a patriotic as well as philosophical sentiment.

In an age whose motto ought to be *squibimus docti indoctique*[4] it is very hard you should forbid me to squib, and turn me to work in my garden. But I have obeyed you, and I hope you will soon see my second book[5] in print, if you do not see its author with it; the last sheet is now in the press. I leave York for Aston on Monday the 13th, but hope to hear from you here before I leave it.

Our spiritual courtiers here say, that the sentence of their court binds the parties themselves, though it does not bind other persons. Ergo B is not married to C because they were proved not to be married there, and though C has been proved to be married to B in another court, B is not married to C notwithstanding. Therefore, B cannot sue for a divorce, because he has not been proved in their court to be married to C. I hope you understand me right, *si quid novisti rectius, candidus imperti.*[6]

If I come to town I shall certainly for my own happiness spend as much of my time at Strawberry as possible, but I can say nothing about my journey till I get to Aston.

I am, dear Sir,

Very sincerely yours,

W. MASON

---

2. A drawing for Gray's *Fatal Sisters* (*post* 20 May 1776).

3. Mason seems to have been weighing the alternatives of sending the drawing to HW or to a public exhibition. See *post* 14 May.

4. A play on Horace's 'scribimus indocti doctique poemata passim' (*Epistles* II. i. 117), 'skilled or unskilled, we scribble poetry at random.'

5. Of *The English Garden.*

6. 'Si quid novisti rectius istis, candidus imperti,' 'If you know something better than these precepts, be generous and impart it' (Horace, *Epistles* I. vi. 67–8).

To Mason, Saturday 4 May 1776

Printed from Mitford i. 252–4.

Strawberry Hill, May 4, 1776.

DO you think I have a duchess to deplume every day that you bid me write to you again already? unconscionable divine, voracious appetite! think of my poor swelled fingers that sigh after repose, think of my quivering ankles, that will carry me to no mart of news. I am here these two days smelling my lilacs, and listening to my nightingales, and leaving the wicked town to the young and healthy. I did not *utinam* that *sedes senectæ*[1] should be my fate, that I should be able to do nothing but *sit* in my garden; but I am content hitherto, though I doubt the rest of my days will be still less comfortable; you might gild them if you would, but your letter hesitates whether you shall come southward or not this summer; remember, I must not calculate without my host the gout. Well, let me see the drawing you talk of, and which yet I must wait two posts before I know whether I am to see or not. You must have a mighty opinion of my patience or indifference, when you put it to so tantalizing a trial; be assured I have neither; neither the virtue of commanding my desires, nor the apathy that looks like commanding them. Those same desires of mine it is true, are exceedingly contracted of late years, but then I *valde volo* what I do *volo*. My curiosity about anything you draw or write, is augmented in proportion as it is decayed in general: my eyes are grown stronger, as my other utensils are enfeebled. They twinkle with eagerness when you tell me of your drawing, or your *Garden* being finished.

The Countess of Bristol retired to Calais incontinently. A *ne exeat regno* came forth the night she was gone![2] a strange neglect in her adversaries! Don't let us talk of her any more. Yes, I will tell you what the droll caustic Lord Abercorn[3] said. Somebody hoped his Lordship had not suffered by the trial; he replied, 'Nobody suffered by it.'

They write to me from London that the provincial army, having been reinforced, had prepared to storm Boston, and had begun to can-

1. 'Tibur Argeo positum colono
        sit meæ sedes utinam senectæ'
                (Horace, *Odes* II. vi. 5–6).
'May Tibur, founded by Argive settlers, be the home of my old age.'
    2. HW's information was correct. See the letter written from Calais by the

Duchess on 26 April, a copy of which HW sent to Lady Ossory with his letter of 25 June 1776.
    3. James Hamilton (1712–89), 8th E. of Abercorn, 1744; cr. (1786) Vct Hamilton. For stories of his tartness and arrogance see GM 1789, lix pt ii. 961.

nonade it, and that General Howe[4] unable to maintain his post had withdrawn with all his forces to Halifax.[5] I had heard this on Thursday before I came out of town, but did not believe it, for the Americans have done nothing yet that has given me a high opinion of their generalship. And that Halifax was left for Howe to retreat to is hitherto incomprehensible, not to me, for I am ignorance itself; but everybody says so, and you know everybody is always in the right.

Soame Jenyns has published a confirmation of the Christian religion from internal evidence.[6] Pray was not his *Origin of Evil*[7] a little heterodox? I have dipped a little into this new piece, and thought I saw something like irony,[8] but to be sure I am wrong, for the *ecclesiastical court* are quite satisfied. I must seal my letter, and leave my blue room to be seen by *Prince Yuzupoff*,[9] who sent for a card of admission. We have a torrent of foreigners in England, and unfortunately they are all sent hither, but then they comprehend nothing, and are gone in half an hour. I have read an account of Strawberry in a book called *Londres*,[10] in which my name is Robert, my house lives at Putney, the bookcases in the library are of inlaid woods, and I have not a window but is *entirely* of painted glass;[11] this is called seeing and describing. Adieu,

                                         Yours ever,

                                              H. W.

4. William Howe (1729–1814), 5th Vct Howe, 1799. On 10 Oct. 1775 he had succeeded Gage in the command of the British forces south of Canada.

5. *London Chronicle* 2–4 May 1776, xxxix. 430. The story was confirmed in the *London Gazette* 30 April–4 May 1776. The evacuation of Boston began 6 March.

6. Publication of *A View of the Internal Evidence of the Christian Religion* was announced in *Daily Adv.* 5 April 1776. HW's copy was probably sold SH v. 141 as 'View of the Christian Religion.'

7. *A Free Inquiry into the Nature and Origin of Evil*, 1757. Johnson wrote a severe review of the book in *The Literary Magazine* (1757, ii. 171–5, 251–3, 301–6), and Gray, in a letter to Mason, called it 'the little wicked book about evil' (*Gray's Corr.* ii. 499). HW's copy was sold SH iii. 20.

8. HW was not the only reader to sus-

pect irony. The reviewer for the *Monthly Review*, Dr Abraham Rees, wrote that 'the perusal of this book . . . excited at first some suspicions and apprehensions as to its general tendency' (1776, liv. 472; B. C. Nangle, *The Monthly Review . . . Indexes*, Oxford, 1934, p. 215), and the reviewer for the *Critical* also spoke of the prevalent doubts concerning Jenyns's sincerity (1776, xli. 475).

9. Prince Nikolai Yusupov (1750–1831), diplomatist and art collector (*Grand dictionnaire universel du XIXe siècle*). He arrived in London 19 March and was presented at Court on 20 March (*Public Advertiser* 22 March 1776).

10. By Pierre-Jean Grosley (1718–85), Lausanne, 1770. HW's copy, which was the second edition, 4 vols, Lausanne, 1774, was sold SH iv. 92.

11. 'M. Robert Walpole, plus recommandable et plus connu par son goût pour

From MASON, ca Thursday 9 May 1776

Missing; indicated by the first sentence of the following letter.

To MASON, Tuesday 14 May 1776

Printed from Mitford i. 254–5.

May 14, 1776.

YOU are not apt to express yourself unintelligibly nor I, I hope, to misunderstand you; I did not expect a drawing in colour, but with the pen, in chiaroscuro, which I like better on some subjects than in oil. I am still sorry it is not to be in the Exhibition.[1]

I am but this minute come to town, and know nothing but from the papers, which say everything prospers with the Americans. As they are driving out all the Scotch,[2] I conclude the Duchess of Kingston will contribute another bank-note.[3]

Do you, or do you not, ever come to town again? do not be enigmatic in a reply to this question.

Yours ever,

H. W.

les sciences et pour les arts, que par un nom qu'immortaliseront les annales du XVIII siècle, s'est bâti a Patney, au milieu d'une agréable solitude, une maison délicieuse. . . . Les livres sont enfermés dans une continuité d'armoires dont les battants formés en vitraux d'église, sont des bois les plus précieux. . . . Enfin cette bibliothèque n'a de jour que celui qu'elle reçoit par d'anciennes vîtres peintes' (Londres, 2d edn, 1774, iii. 250–1).

1. Unexplained. No exhibition opening in London in May has been found, although three that opened in April were still in progress: the Royal Academy, the Incorporated Society of Artists, and the Free Society of Artists (Public Advertiser, 18, 23, 25 April 1776). Perhaps there was an exhibition at York, mentioned in a missing letter.

2. HW had probably seen the following 'intelligence from America' in the Public Advertiser for 13 May: 'The Scotchmen in the Colonies have universally taken up arms or otherwise assisted in attempting to destroy the liberties of America. Notwithstanding they . . . pledged their faith not to aid or assist the King's troops by any means whatever, they have supplied them as far as was in their power with provisions and intelligence; have taken up arms with them, and have stimulated the Negroes to rise upon the families in which they live. . . . After these atrocious instances of treachery and cruelty, the Americans have determined to drive them all out of the country. . . .'

3. An allusion to the Duchess of Kingston's contribution for the relief of the loyalist clergy in North America (ante 25 March 1776).

BENTLEY'S SKETCH FOR *THE BARD*

To Mason, Monday 20 May 1776

Printed from Mitford i. 255–6.

Strawberry Hill, May 20, 1776.

BY my being here for some days I did not receive your drawing[1] so soon as I ought to have done, nor even knew it was arrived. I thank you for it and like it excessively; you have done full justice to Gray; I am sorry he cannot see it, for it is as fine as Mr Bentley's drawings for the rest of his odes.[2] I admire particularly the figure of

Mista, black terrific maid,[3]

who has a masculine gait that put me in mind of old Leveridge,[4] when he used to act Hecate in *Macbeth*. I hope you will draw *The Descent of Odin*, too, which I love as much as any of Gray's works. I never was fond of *The Triumphs of Owen*.

Tonight I have received (here in town) from Mr Stonhewer your second *Garden;*[5] it has my fullest imprimatur. I thought the beginning a little cold, but it soon rises into charming poetry, and from the 210th line is more beautiful than the first book. I like the *sheep devouring the lawn into verdure*,[6] and from thence all is quite to my taste. The *dusty Sabbath*[7] is admirable, but above all I am touched with the scene of cottage children,[8] which is equal to anything you

1. Illustrating Gray's *Fatal Sisters*. It has not been found.
2. Bentley's original drawings for *The Bard* are now WSL; those for *The Progress of Poesy*, if made, have not been found.
3. *The Fatal Sisters*, l. 17.
4. Richard Leveridge (ca 1670–1758), singer and composer. Hawkins says that at Lincoln's Inn Fields 'he made himself very useful by performing such characters as Pluto, Faustus, Merlin, or . . . any part in which a long beard was necessary.' It was rumoured that he arranged the music in Rowe's edition of *Macbeth* (*History of Music*, 1776, v. 182–3).
5. The second book of *The English Garden*, a few copies of which Mason had privately printed for distribution among his friends. He planned to defer publication until the poem was completed, but in the following year he learned that there was danger of piracy and therefore had

the volume reprinted for public sale (Gaskell 21–2). See *post* 18 April 1777. HW's copy of the private printing of Book 2 is in vol. 14 of his 'Poems of George III' in the Harvard Library (note by Philip Gaskell in *Transactions of the Cambridge Bibliographical Society*, i pt iv, 1952, p. 360).

6.   '. . . for if there
   Sheep feed, or dappled deer, their wandering teeth
   Will, smoothly as the scythe, the herbage shave,
   And leave a kindred verdure' (ll. 262–5).
7. 'Let those, who weekly, from the city's smoke,
   Crowd to each neighb'ring hamlet, there to hold
   Their dusty Sabbath . . .' (ll. 355–7).
8. Ll. 406–47.

ever wrote; so are the lines on their sorrow and smiles.[9] The story of Abdolonimus[10] finishes the whole nobly. Write away, write away and if you will not come to town—write away; yet I do wish now and then to see such a priest of Apollo. Adieu.

PS. This was not sent so soon as it ought to have been by an accident.

From Mason, Tuesday 28 May 1776

Printed from MS now wsl.
Address: The Honourable Horace Walpole, Arlington Street, London.
Postmark: ROTHERHAM 31 MA.

Aston, May 28th, 1776.

Dear Sir,

YOU are wondrous partial both to my drawing and my didactic poem, but I want to hear what worse, yet more impartial, judges say to them—at present I know nothing—but don't tell me by letter, for I mean to see you speedily. I have agreed with Mr Montagu[1] to accompany him to town next week. Be assured after my arrival I shall make you a speedy visit at Strawberry where I fancy this will find you. I mean to fly about from place to place a good deal, to make amends to my constitution for the last half-year of my life which has been very sedentary and pick-toothish—more of my schemes when we meet. At present excuse this hasty scribble which is merely to tell you that I am coming and that I am

Most truly yours,

W. Mason

I shall be to be heard of after Wednesday or Thursday at mine host's of Curzon Street.[2]

9.   '. . . As the cloud
That weeps its moment from thy
   sapphire heav'n,
They frown with causeless sorrow; as
   the beam,
Gilding that cloud, with causeless
   mirth they smile!'
                          (ll. 450–3).
10. The story of the humble gardener raised to the throne of Sidon by Alexander the Great. A note by Mason reads: 'The fact, on which this episode is founded, is recorded by Diodorus Siculus, Plutarch, Justin, and Q. Curtius; the last is here chiefly followed. M. de Fontenelle and the Abbé Metastasio have both of them treated the subject dramatically' (Mason's *Works* i. 402). Quintus Curtius Rufus tells the story in the fourth book of *De rebus Alexandris Magni.*

1. Frederick Montagu.
2. Stonhewer (see *ante* ?14 April 1772).

From MASON, Friday 7 June 1776

Printed from MS now WSL. The date is conjectured from the postscript to the preceding letter.
Address: The Honourable Horace Walpole, Strawberry Hill.

Curzon Street, Friday evening, 1776.[1]

I WAS ready here either to drink coffee with you today or to dine on *apple-pie* and *cheese* with you, two things that I think make a better union than many governors and preceptors[2] do, however unfashionable it may be to think so. I am sorry you could not come, but whenever you let me know you are in town, I will take the first moment to wait on you, and to attend you to Strawberry Hill,[3] if I can get all my necessary visits of punctilio paid before, but I find infinitely more *good* company left in town, than either I expected or wished.

FROM MASON, n. d.

Printed for the first time from MS now WSL, found among the Bentley papers. It appears to be Mason's reply to a question from HW, and was probably delivered by hand during one of Mason's visits to London.
Address: The Honourable Mr Walpole.

The breast-plate on which were twelve stones seems to have been an ornament which bound the ephod on the shoulders, etc.; it may therefore I think be properly called the breast-plate of the ephod. The stones on this breast-plate were in four rows, and set in this order:

Sardius	Topaze	Carbuncle
Emerald	Sapphire	Diamond
Ligure	Agate	Amethyst
Beryl	Onyx	Jasper

See Exodus, Chap. 39, 1st ver. to 27th.

1. Year added by HW.
2. Lord Holdernesse, governor to the Prince of Wales and Prince Frederick, was in a violent disagreement with the preceptor to the princes, William Markham, then Bishop of Chester. Educational policy was the point at issue, and the immediate cause of the storm was the dismissal of Cyril Jackson, the sub-preceptor, who was supported by Markham. The quarrel led to the resignation of Holdernesse, the Bishop, and Leonard Smelt, the sub-governor (HW to Mann 5 June 1776; Mason to Alderson 16 June 1776; *Last Journals* i. 554-8).
3. On 10 June Mason wrote Alderson that he was to go to SH 'tomorrow.' From SH he proceeded to Syon Hill where he paid a duty call of condolence on the occasion of Holdernesse's resignation. 'My dinner at Sion Hill passed off exactly to

To Mason, Tuesday 17 September 1776

Printed from Mitford i. 257–9.

Strawberry Hill, Sept. 17, 1776.

I WAS exceedingly rejoiced the other day to hear by a letter from Lord Strafford[1] that you are alive, which I doubted. I had some thoughts of looking into the *Annual Register* to see if your preferments were given away; but as I find you have only been in a lethargy, and that now I shall not disturb your nap, I venture to put you in mind of a person of whom you have not dreamt these four or five months. This has not been my case, though I have given you no more signs of life. I have been going to write to you fifty times, and only waited for that *small peculiar*[2] of a letter, something to say. I hope you have had no other reason for silence. My want is not yet removed, but though a good excuse for a letter's being short, is not above half a reason for not writing at all. Swinny[3] used to tell a story of two old companions, who sitting together one evening till it was quite dark without speaking, one called to t'other, 'Tom, Tom.' 'Well,' said his friend, 'what do you say?' 'Oh,' said t'other, 'are you there?' 'Ay,' said the friend. 'Why then don't you say "humph"?' said the first; if I had been in Parliament, and could have franked 'humph,' I really should have written it before now, though General Howe, who like his family never wastes a monosyllable,[4] does not think such little amities necessary. Perhaps he reflects that even that symptom of life would not be communicated to the public, who it seems, have no business to know anything that happens out of their own island. Master Froissart says, 'By the famous wrytyng of auncient auctours all thynges ben knowen in one place or other,'[5] which is a great comfort, and the present age seems to be satisfied with what their posterity will know.

I have lately met with a famous auncient auctour, who did not think that everybody ought to know everything. He is a classic, Sir,

my wish. His Lordship's afternoon nap took him away from us most of the time' (Mason to Alderson 16 June 1776).

1. Missing.
2. 'By tincture or reflection they augment Their small peculiar . . .'
    (*Paradise Lost* vii. 367–8).

3. Owen Mac Swinny (d. 1754), dramatist and manager of the Haymarket Theatre.
4. Both Admiral Howe and his brother, General Howe, were dilatory in sending dispatches. See *post* i. 327 and n. 6.
5. Bk I, chap. i of Lord Berners's translation of Froissart's *Chronicles*. HW owned the original Pynson black-letter edition, 1523–5, sold SH iii. 197.

with whom you ought to be acquainted; his very name is expressive of his vocation and science; he was called *Sir Hugh Plat*,[6] and has written a tractate on gardening, called *The Garden of Eden*,[7] a very proper title, for though he has planted a tree of knowledge, he forbids it to be tasted, having concealed his principal secret in a figurative description in imitation of Baptista Porta[8] in his *Natural Magic*, so that you might as soon understand a book of alchemy, as Sir Hugh's treatise, at least his secret.[9] This deep volume is not quite to your purpose, not being an essay on landscape-gardens, but rules to improve fruit and flowers, which being still more the fashionable rage at present than laying out ground, I think you would do well, Mr Mason, to add a book on that subject. One very great secret Sir Hugh has deigned to disclose; it is a receipt for making a peach-tree bring forth pomegranates; the process is very simple, and consists in nothing but watering (or strictly speaking milking) the peach-tree with goat's milk for three days together.[10]

To be sure you want to know a great deal about me myself, though you forgot you did. My whole history consists in having built a new tower, which is a vast deal higher, but very little larger in diameter than an extinguisher; however it fully answers the founder's intention, which is to hold Lady Di's drawings.[11] Have you done as much in your way, or any way? I could send you a paltry scurrilous letter

6. Sir Hugh Plat (or Platt) (1552–1608), inventor, and author of works on agriculture.

7. Plat's chief work on gardening. It was published in 1608 with the title *Floraes Paradise*. Charles Billingham, a relative of Plat, brought out a revised edition in 1653, entitled *The Garden of Eden*. A fifth edition, with a continuation of the work based on Plat's unpublished notes, appeared in 1660, and a sixth in 1675. HW owned two copies, one sold SH v. 118 and the other sold London 1062 (removed from SH vii. 111).

8. Giovanni Battista della Porta (ca 1538–1615), natural scientist, best known for his *Magia naturalis*, 1589.

9. 'In a little tract in my possession called *The Garden of Eden* or a description of flowers and fruits and how to improve them, by Sir Hugh Plat, Kt, Lond. 1660, he avows in his Epistle to the Reader p. 14 having concealed his principal secret in a figurative description, in imitation of

Bapt. Porta in his *Natural Magic*. This nonsensical way of telling something without telling it, was borrowed from the Hermetic philosophers, who however were more in the right, for they had nothing to tell, but passed for men of wonderful knowledge the less sense they uttered. Sir Hugh has borrowed their dialect for his secret in his first part, p. 167' (HW, 'Book of Materials' 1771, p. 54).

10. 'But another secret, in which he is more explicit, is so absurd that it is not worth while to search for the meaning of his riddle. His receipt for making a peach-tree bring forth pomegranates is to water it, when it begins to flower, with goat's milk for three days together, pt 2d p. 147' (ibid.).

11. See *ante* 18 Feb. 1776 and n. 23. The Tower bears some resemblance to a candle-snuffer. It contained 'an hexagon closet of seven feet diameter' (HW to Conway 30 June 1776).

against Shakespeare, by Voltaire,[12] but it is not worth sending;[13] if it did, you don't deserve it at my hands, so adieu.

From MASON, ca Saturday 5 October 1776

Missing.

To MASON, Tuesday 8 October 1776

Printed from Mitford i. 263–5.

Arlington Street, Oct. 8, 1776.

I ANSWER your letter incontinently, because I am charmed with your idea of the cenotaph for Gray,[1] and would not have it wait a moment for my approbation. I do not know what my lines were, for I gave them to you,[2] or have burnt or lost them, but I am sure yours are ten times better, as anything must naturally be when you and I write on the same subject. I prefer Westminster Abbey to Stoke, or Pembroke chapel; not because due to Gray, whose genius does not want any such distinction, but as due to Westminster Abbey, which would miss him, and to humble the French, who have never had a Homer or a Pindar,[3] nor probably will have, since Voltaire could make nothing more like an epic poem than the *Henriade,* and Boileau and Rousseau have succeeded so little in odes, that the French still think that ballad-wright Quinault[4] their best lyric poet—which shows how much they understand lyric poetry! Voltaire has lately written a letter against Shakespeare (occasioned by the new paltry translation, which still has discovered his miraculous powers), and it is as downright billingsgate as an apple-woman would utter if you overturned

12. Voltaire to Charles-Augustin Ferriol (1700–88), Comte d'Argental, 19 July 1776 (*Œuvres,* ed. Moland, l. 57–9). Mme du Deffand sent a copy to HW in her letter of 4 Aug. 1776 (DU DEFFAND iv. 345). The occasion of the letter was the publication of the first two volumes of Le Tourneur's Shakespeare (*ante* 8 April 1776).

13. HW later sent Mason a copy of the letter (*post* ?Nov. 1776).

1. Presumably communicated to HW in the missing letter of ca 5 Oct. 1776.

2. HW sent them *ante* 9 Sept. 1771.

3. See Mason's epitaph on Gray (*post* ?Nov. 1776, n. 8).

4. Philippe Quinault (1635–88), dramatist and librettist. His work was held in high regard by Mme du Deffand (DU DEFFAND i. 58 and *passim*).

her wheelbarrow. Poor old wretch! how envy disgraces the brightest talents! how Gray adored Shakespeare! Partridge the almanac-maker,[5] perhaps, was jealous of Sir Isaac Newton. Dr Goldsmith told me he himself envied Shakespeare, but Goldsmith was an idiot,[6] with once or twice a fit of parts. It hurts one when a real genius like Voltaire can feel more spite than admiration, though I am persuaded that his rancour is grounded on his conscious inferiority. I wish you would lash this old scorpion a little, and teach him awe of English poets.

I can tell you nothing more than you see in the common newspapers; impatience is open-mouthed and open-eared for accounts from New York, on which the attack was to be made on the 26th of August;[7] success there is more necessary to keep up credit than likely to do more. Should it fail, there is an end of America for England; and if it succeeds, it is at most ground for another campaign—but we choose not to see till we feel, though they who have done the mischief, do not disguise their apprehensions. The Colonies have an agent[8] openly at Versailles, and their ships are as openly received into their ports—but I had rather talk of *Caractacus*,[9] I agree that he will not suffer by not being sputtered by Barry,[10] who has lost all his teeth. Covent Garden is rather above Drury Lane in actors, though both sets are exceedingly bad, so bad that I almost wish *Caractacus* was not to appear. Very seldom do I go to the play for there is no bearing such strollers. I saw *Lear* the last time Garrick played it,[11] and as I told him I was more shocked at the rest of the company than pleased with him, which I believe was not just what he desired; but to give a greater brilliancy to his own setting, he had selected the very worst performers

5. John Partridge (1644–1715), the astrologer and almanac-maker whose predictions inspired Swift's Isaac Bickerstaff satires.

6. See *ante* 21 July 1772 and n. 33.

7. A *London Gazette Extraordinary* on 10 Oct. published the news of the British victory in the battle of Long Island 27 Aug. (*Public Advertiser* 11 Oct.; HW to Mann 13 Oct.). The *Gazette* of 4 Nov. carried the official announcement of the British advance into New York on 15 Sept. and the evacuation of the city by the American forces (*Public Advertiser* 5 Nov. 1776).

8. Silas Deane (1737–89), the first American to represent the united Colonies abroad.

9. 'I am employed at present in altering *Caractacus* for the stage. The Covent Garden manager [Thomas Harris] asked me to do this so very civilly that ⟨I⟩ think it right to oblige him. 'Tis to be acted next winter' (Mason to Alderson 5 July 1776). The first performance of the alteration, for which Thomas Arne wrote incidental music, was given at Covent Garden 6 Dec. 1776 (Genest v. 563; Gaskell 20–1).

10. Spranger Barry (1719–77), actor, for many years Garrick's chief rival for public favour. From Oct. 1774 until his death Barry was at Covent Garden, but during that time was partially disabled by gout. The rôle of Caractacus at the first performance was played by Matthew Clarke (*ante* 19 Nov. 1773, n. 3).

11. 8 June 1776 (Genest v. 497).

of his troop; just as Voltaire would wish there were no better poets than Thompson and Akenside. However, as *Caractacus* has already been read,[12] I do not doubt but it will succeed. It would be a horrible injury to let him be first announced by such unhallowed mouths. In truth the present taste is in general so vile, that I don't know whether it is not necessary to blunt real merit before it can be applauded.

I have not time to say more—I can say nothing about law, but that I always avoid it if I can, that and everything else wants reformation, and I believe we shall have it from that only reformer, Adversity. I wish I were with you and the good *Palsgrave* and I always wish you was with me. Adieu,

Yours ever,

H. W.

To Mason, ?November 1776

Printed from Mitford i. 259–63, where it is mistakenly appended to HW's letter of 17 Sept. 1776, although it was clearly not sent until after that of 8 Oct. Mrs Toynbee tentatively assigned it to November (see N&Q 1900, 9th ser., vi. 82).

LETTRE DE VOLTAIRE À M. D'ARGENTAL[1]

Fernet, 19 juillet, 1776.

Mon cher ami,

J'apprends que Monsieur de St Julien[2] arrive dans mon désert avec Le Kain.[3] Si la chose est vraie, j'en suis tout étonné et tout joyeux; mais il faut que je vous dise combien je suis fâché pour l'honneur du tripot contre un nommé Tourneur, qu'on dit Secrétaire de la Librairie,[4] et qui ne me parait pas le Secrétaire du bon goût. Auriez-vous lu deux volumes misérables dans lesquels il veut faire regarder Shakespear comme le seul modèle de la

---

12. The first edition of *Caractacus* was published 30 May 1759 (Gaskell 7). HW's copy of the 1777 edition is now WSL.

---

1. This is the letter sent to HW by Mme du Deffand 4 Aug. 1776. See *ante* 17 Sept. 1776 and n. 12. The text as printed by Moland (*Œuvres* l. 57–9) contains several additional sentences not relating to Shakespeare, and numerous verbal differences.

2. Properly Mme de St Julien (Voltaire, *Œuvres*, ed. Moland, l. 57), Anne-Madeleine-Louise-Charlotte-Auguste de la Tour (ca 1730–1820), m. (1748) François-David

Bollioud, Seigneur de St Julien, was a friend and correspondent of Voltaire; she helped him build his model village at Ferney, where she was a frequent visitor. See La Chenaye-Desbois and Badier, *Dictionnaire de la noblesse*, 1863–76, xix. 98; Voltaire, *Œuvres* x. 392.

3. Henri-Louis Cain (called Lekain) (1728–78), actor, especially celebrated as a tragedian.

4. Le Tourneur was the librarian of the Comte de Provence, brother of Louis XVI (NBG). See *ante* p. 258 n. 12.

véritable tragédie? Il l'appelle le Dieu du Théâtre; il sacrifie tous les français sans exception à son idole, comme on sacrifiait des cochons à Cérès: il ne daigne pas nommer Corneille ou Racine: ces deux grands hommes sont seulement enveloppés dans la proscription générale sans que leurs noms soient prononcés: il y a déjà deux tomes d'imprimés de ce Shakespeare, qu'on prendrait pour des pièces de la foire, faites il y a deux cents ans; ce maraud a trouvé le secret de faire engager le Roi et la Reine et toute la famille royale à souscrire à son ouvrage. Avez-vous lu son abominable grimoire dont il y aura encore cinq volumes? Avez-vous une haine assez vigoureuse contre cet impudent imbécile? Souffrirez-vous l'affront qu'il fait à la France? Vous et Monsieur de Thibouville[5] vous êtes trop doux. Il n'y a pas en France assez de camouflets, assez de bonnets d'ânes, assez de pilories[5a] contre un pareil facquin? Le sang petille dans mes vieilles veines en parlant de lui. S'il ne vous a pas mis en colère, je vous tiens pour un homme impassible. Ce qu'il y a d'affreux c'est que le monstre a un parti en France, et pour comble de calamités, et d'horreur, c'est moi qui autrefois parlai le premier de ce Shakespeare; c'est moi qui le premier montrai aux français quelques perles que j'avais trouvées dans son énorme fumier. Je ne m'attendais pas que je servirais à fouler aux pieds les couronnes de Racine et de Corneille, pour en orner le front d'un histrion barbare.

Tachez je vous prie d'être aussi en colère que moi, sans quoi je me sens capable de faire un mauvais coup. Quant à mon ami M. le cocher Gilbert,[6] je souhaite qu'il aille au carcan à bride abattue, etc. etc.

I have a mind to provoke you, and so I send you this silly torrent of ribaldry; may the spirit of Pope that dictated your *Musæus*[7] animate you to punish this worst of dunces, a genius turned fool with envy. I have a mind to be a dunce too and alter one line of your epitaph, the last. I think *She heard* should not be repeated twice; *heard* is an inharmonious word and the elision between *she* and *heard,* adds to the cacophony. I would read,—

> She heard thy Homer in her Milton's strains,
> *And* Pindar's music from the lyre of Gray[8]—

5. Henri Lambert d'Herbigny (1710–84), Marquis de Thibouville; soldier, writer, and friend of Voltaire.

5a. *Sic;* Moland reads 'piloris.'

6. A former coachman of the Comte de Morangiès, who had testified against his master during a suit for the non-payment of a debt. See DU DEFFAND iii. 364 n. 13. In 1772 and 1773 Voltaire had taken an active interest in the case on the side of Morangiès. He had recently heard that Gilbert had been arrested for thievery. See Voltaire, *Œuvres*, l. 45 and 48–50.

7. Mason's *Musæus, a Monody to the Memory of Mr Pope*, was written in 1744 and published by Dodsley in April 1747 (Gaskell 1).

8. In its final form the epitaph reads: 'No more the Grecian Muse unrivalled reigns,

To Britain let the nations homage pay; She felt a Homer's fire in Milton's strains,

Or *thy*. It is very impertinent in me who have no ear and am no poet to correct you, who are a musician, and a poet if ever there was one, but then, I will submit if you do not approve my emendation.

Having nothing new to read, I have been tumbling over my old books, and there I found what I had never read nor heard mentioned, and which I think has a vast deal more of wit than the ancients used in their writings. Mind, I say used, for no doubt all times and all countries have produced men of wit, and I know Julius Cæsar had a collection of Cicero's *bon mots*. Diogenes Laertius too has recorded those of the philosophers, very few of which I allow to have any wit in them. The piece I mean is Seneca's *De morte Claudii Cæsaris*.[9] There is a good deal of Greek in it, and I have forgotten my Greek, and some of my Latin too, and do not understand many passages in this satire—but let me give you an instance of great wit: speaking of his death and the astrologers, who had not foretold it rightly, he says, *horam ejus nemo novit, nemo enim illum unquam natum putavit.*[10]

Last night, I took up Pope's letters to Mr Digby,[11] and finding Lady Suffolk's name,[12] I regretted having never questioned her about the latter. This is a sort of pleasure I lose every day. I came into the world long enough ago to have informed myself from elder persons of many things I should now like to know; and there is much more satisfaction in inquiring into old stories than in telling them. Formerly I was so foolish, like most young people, as to despise them. I don't mean by this to invite the young to apply to me; I am not over fond of their company. Recollection is more agreeable than observation at the end of life. Will Dr Johnson, and I know not most of the rest by name, interest the next age like Addison, Prior, Pope and Congreve? will General Gage or Sir Peter Parker[13] succeed to the renown of the Duke

A Pindar's rapture in the lyre of Gray.' See *post* 28 Aug. 1778 and illustration.

9. HW owned an Elzevir edition of Seneca, Amsterdam, 1672 (sold SH iii. 181).

10. Seneca, *Apocolocyntosis*, 3: 'No one knew his hour, for no one knew he had ever been born.' A proverbial expression; other occurrences are listed in *The Satire of Seneca on the Apotheosis of Claudius*, ed. A. P. Ball, New York, 1902, p. 166.

11. Hon. Robert Digby (d. 1726), second son of William, Bn Digby of Geashill (Collins, *Peerage*, 1812, v. 381).

12. 'You say you propose much pleasure in seeing some new faces about town, of my acquaintance. I guess you mean Mrs Howard's and Mrs Blount's' (Elwin and Courthope, *Works of Pope* ix. 83). The letter appears in Pope's *Works*, vi, 1739, p. 92. (HW's copy of this volume is now WSL.) Henrietta Hobart (ca 1688–1767), m. (1) (1706) Charles Howard, 9th E. of Suffolk, 1731; m. (2) (1735) Hon. George Berkeley; mistress of George II. In her old age she became the friend and correspondent of HW and was the source of his *Reminiscences* and *Notes of Conversations with Lady Suffolk*, ed. Paget Toynbee, Oxford, 1924. Her house, Marble Hill, was near SH.

13. Sir Peter Parker (1721–1811), Kt,

of Marlborough, even had the last had no more merit than Macpherson will allow him?[14] Oh! there is another of our authors, Macpherson! when one's pen can sink to him, it is time to seal one's letter.

To Mason, Monday 17 February 1777

Printed from Mitford i. 265–7.

Feb. 17, 1777.

I DO not know whether you will value the execution of a promise, when the letter is observed and not the spirit. I write only because you desired it, and that I said I would; neither the literary nor political world furnish much matter. I have read *The Goat's Beard*[1]—the lines on Charles II[2] are very good, and there is true humour here and there: but the humour is often missed, and I think the whole much too long—it is far inferior to *Variety*.[3] Mr Tyrrwhit has at last published the Bristol poems.[4] He does not give up the antiquity,[5] yet fairly leaves everybody to ascribe them to Chatterton if they please,[6] which I think the internal evidence must force every one to do, unless the amazing prodigy of Chatterton's producing them should not seem a larger miracle than Rowley's and Canning's[7] anticipation of the style

1772; cr. (1783) Bt; Rear-Adm., 1777, Adm. of the Fleet, 1799; associated with Howe in the attack on Long Island.

14. 'All his passions . . . were either subdued or extinguished by the love of money; and to that unhappy circumstance must be ascribed the ruin of his reputation. Upon the whole, if Marlborough is less to be admired than some other distinguished statesmen and generals, it is perhaps because his secret intrigues and actions are better known' (James Macpherson, *The History of Great Britain from the Restoration to the Accession of the House of Hannover*, 1775, ii. 517).

1. By William Whitehead; published anonymously 12 Feb. 1777 (*Public Advertiser*). HW's annotated copy is in his 'Poems of Geo. III,' vol. 15, at Harvard.

2. *The Goat's Beard*, 1777, pp. 28–9.

3. See *ante* 18 Feb. 1776.

4. *Poems, Supposed to have been Written at Bristol, by Thomas Rowley, and*

Others, in the Fifteenth Century appeared 8 Feb. 1777 (E. H. W. Meyerstein, *A Life of Thomas Chatterton*, 1930, p. 461). HW's annotated copy is now WSL (see CHATTERTON 344–5).

5. In his edition of the *Canterbury Tales*, 1775, iv. 87, Tyrwhitt indicated his belief in the existence of the poet Rowley. For his change of mind see *post* 24 July 1778 and n. 29.

6. On the authenticity of the poems Tyrwhitt wrote: 'It may be expected perhaps that the editor should give an opinion upon this important question; but he rather chooses, for many reasons, to leave it to the determination of the unprejudiced and intelligent reader' (*Poems, Supposed to have been Written at Bristol*, p. xii).

7. Thomas Rowley, priest of Bristol, was Chatterton's invention. William Canynges (ca 1399–1474) was a Bristol merchant who in Chatterton's fiction is a friend and patron of Rowley (see Meyerstein, op. cit. 156–249).

1ᵒ

of very modern poetry. Psalmanazaar[8] alone seems to have surpassed the genius of Chatterton, and when that lad could perform such feats, as he certainly did, what difficulty is there in believing that Macpherson forged the cold skeleton of an epic poem, that is more insipid than *Leonidas*.[9] Mr Tyrrwhit seems to have dreaded drawing himself into a controversy, which joys me, who dreaded being drawn into one too.

The news from America are as usual, difficult to be fathomed; the Court denies being certain of the discomfit of the Hessians,[10] yet their runners pretend that the Hessian prisoners have been retaken.[11] It is fact that the royalists have neither yet taken Providence nor the Americans' ships;[12] the other side believe that Lord Cornwallis[13] has received a check at the Jerseys.[14] Lee is certainly taken[15] by the poltroonery of

8. George Psalmanazar (b. ca 1679–84, d. 1763), literary impostor, author of *An Historical and Geographical Description of Formosa*, 1704. See Boswell, *Johnson* iii. 443–9.

9. Richard Glover's epic, first published (in nine books) in 1737, expanded (twelve books) in 1770.

10. 'A New York paper is said to be received, from which the following paragraph is taken, dated the 30th of December, 1776: "Wednesday morning last one of the Hessian brigades stationed at Trenton, was surprised by a large body of rebels, and after an engagement which lasted for a little time, between 300 and 400 made good their retreat, and the whole loss is about 900 men." The matter, however, is little credited' (*Lloyd's Evening Post* 7–10 Feb. 1777, xl. 143). The unwillingness of the administration to believe in the American victory at Trenton is again mentioned in the same newspaper 10–12 Feb., but it was not long before corroboration of the report was received in England. See *post* 27 Feb. 1777, n. 23, and William S. Stryker, *The Battles of Trenton and Princeton*, Boston, 1898, pp. 219–26.

11. It was so reported in the *Public Advertiser* 15 Feb. 1777.

12. 'A letter from on board the *Asia* man-of-war has the following article: "It is imagined by some, that the American ships in Providence River will certainly be taken; but you may be assured that it will not only be a very difficult work, but hazardous to take any part of them; for they have built such strong batteries that our men-of-war cannot get up the river without being sunk; and they are daily adding new works"' (*London Chronicle* 18–20 Feb. 1777, xli. 170).

13. Charles Cornwallis (1738–1805), 2d E. Cornwallis, cr. (1792) M. Cornwallis. On 1 Jan. 1776 he was given the local rank of Lt-Gen. in America and the command of seven regiments of infantry. His troops followed the retreating American army across New Jersey after the British victories at Brooklyn and White Plains (*Correspondence of Charles, First Marquis Cornwallis*, ed. Charles Ross, 1859, i. 21, 24).

14. On Howe's orders Cornwallis halted for a time at Brunswick, New Jersey. Shortly thereafter he received his superior's permission to advance to Philadelphia, but in the attempt to do this found the crossing of the Delaware impracticable because of the inclement weather and the scarcity of boats (ibid. 24–5).

15. Charles Lee (1731–82), British army officer who in 1774 resigned his commission and on 17 June 1775 was appointed Maj.-Gen. in the American army. He was second in command to Washington during the winter campaign of 1776–7, but was an intractable subordinate. He was captured 13 Dec. 1776 at his quarters at Basking Ridge, N.J., by a patrol of light dragoons under Col. Harcourt. At this time Lee was regarded in England as the most skilful of the American generals, and his capture excited hopes of a capitulation of the rebels. The English intended to send Lee to England to be treated as a deserter, but

his own men, of whom he had eighteen to Col. Harcourt's fourteen.[16] He has written a short letter in which he himself says so, and adds, that he submits to his fate, only regretting that liberty will no longer enjoy a foot of earth.[17]

The Habeas Corpus bill you see has appeared, though nobody would believe it.[18] Lord Rockingham and his ingenious band have contrived to make a more ridiculous figure by doing nothing, than they ever did by anything they attempted.[19] They are sure of not being taken up during the suspension on the suspicion of a plot. You have seen in the papers, I suppose, that John the Painter[20] is a Scot, and that

fear of reprisals kept him in America as a prisoner of war. In 1778 an exchange of prisoners returned him to the American forces (DNB; *Dictionary of American Biography*).

16. Hon. William Harcourt (1743–1830), son of Lord Harcourt and younger brother of Vct Nuneham, whom he succeeded in the earldom in 1809. He commanded the 16th regiment of light dragoons in the 1776–7 campaign. A brief memoir of his life and a selection of his letters are in *Harcourt Papers* xi. 145–249. The story of this raid was variously reported in the British press. Harcourt himself describes his patrol as 'a party of three officers and thirty men' (ibid. xi. 182). No authoritative account of the size of Lee's detachment has been found.

17. 'The following is said to be a copy of a letter sent by General Lee, after he was taken by Colonel Harcourt, to his old friend, Captain Kennedy, in our army: "The amazing alertness of Colonel Harcourt, and the poltroonery of my guard, have thrown me into the hands of your army; whatever may be my fate, I hope to sustain it with fortitude; sure no man was ever engaged in a better cause; but fate seems determined there shall be no freedom, and a horrid, gloomy slavery universal"' (*Lloyd's Evening Post* 17–19 Feb. 1777, xl. 174). It is true that Lee's guard had left their arms and their posts 'and were sunning themselves on the south side of a house about 200 yards from the tavern' (General James Wilkinson, *Memoirs of My Own Times*, Philadelphia, 1816, i. 107), but it is also true that Lee's capture was partly due to his exceptional carelessness (ibid.).

18. A bill to suspend the Habeas Corpus act was presented to the House of Commons 7 Feb. 1777. It was formally called 'a bill to empower his Majesty to secure and detain persons charged with, or suspected of, the crime of high treason committed in North America, or on the high seas, or the crime of piracy' (Cobbett, *Parl. Hist.* xix. 4). 'I communicated my intelligence [of the bill] to Charles Fox, the Duke of Grafton, and Lord Camden too, but neither they nor the Rockinghams would believe there could be such a design, till the bill itself came into Parliament' (*Last Journals* ii. 6).

19. 'Lord Rockingham held a meeting to consider whether they should return and oppose, and they had great divisions. Lord Rockingham, the Cavendishes, and Burke adhered to their stupid retreat, but Charles Fox would not; and even Sir George Saville, though more attached to Lord Rockingham, was so honest as to attend the House on the third reading, and spoke against the bill' (ibid. ii. 7). Rockingham and his followers had at first absented themselves from Parliament at the first appearance of the bill on the grounds that opposition would be futile and would only increase the national confusion. See Edmund Burke, *A Letter . . . to John Farr and John Harris*, 1777 (*post* 16 May 1777).

20. James Aitken (also known as James Hill, James Hind, James Actzen, and John the Painter) (1752–77), itinerant painter. He was an enthusiastic supporter of the American Revolution, and hoped to win fame by a series of fires directed at English shipping. On 7 Dec. 1776 he set fire to the docks at Portsmouth; on 16 Jan.

he dated the conflagration at Bristol from an American merchant's house,[21] and committed a burglary,[22] which it is not even pretended to have been directed by the orders of the Congress.

The Landgrave of Hesse[23] on the strength of our subsidy[24] is gone to Rome,[25] to make a solemn renunciation of the Protestant religion at the feet of the Pope,[26]—who ought to declare him vice-defender of the faith against the heretics and Quakers of Philadelphia.

Mr Palgrave is in town, and so is a third inundation of snow, yet I have gone about these three weeks and had no return of my disorder. Give me as good an account of yourself.

To Mason, Thursday 27 February 1777

Printed from Mitford i. 267–70.

Feb. 27, 1777.

I WAS very wise in never advertising retirement. I knew well how difficult it is to quit the world, and yet have done with it. The love of fame has its colt's tooth as well as old ladies. Alas! my good friend,

1777 he started fires at Bristol. His arrest was announced in the *London Chronicle* 6–8 Feb. 1777, xli. 134–5. He was brought to trial at Winchester 6 March 1777, condemned, and executed 10 March. See Mary E. Knapp, 'John the Painter and Silas Deane,' *Yale University Library Gazette*, 1955, xxix. 137–47; *Annual Register*, 1777, xx. 28–31 and 166.

21. John Latimer, in *The Annals of Bristol in the Eighteenth Century*, 1893, p. 427, says that the fire started in 'the warehouses of Messrs Lewsley and Co., in Bell Lane. . . . Some of the principal merchants were Americans, and . . . an American was the chief sufferer by the fire.'

22. Aitken's robbery of a certain 'Mr Brothers of Fairfield, near Gloucestershire' was described in the *London Chronicle* 11–13 Feb. 1777, xli. 151.

23. Friedrich Wilhelm (1720–85), Landgraf of Hesse-Cassel (1760) as Friedrich II (*Allgemeine deutsche Biographie*, Leipzig, 1875–1912, vii. 524).

24. The treaty between England and Hesse-Cassel, dated 15 Jan. 1776, allowed the Landgraf 30 crowns (£7 4s.) for every

man furnished for the American war, and an annual subsidy of 450,000 crowns (£108,-281 5s.), to be continued for one year after the actual return of the troops to Hesse-Cassel. The Landgraf agreed to send 12,000 men, but as a result of later treaties nearly 17,000 Hessians served in America (Cobbett, *Parl. Hist.* xviii. 1162; Edward J. Lowell, *The Hessians and the Other German Auxiliaries of Great Britain in the Revolutionary War*, New York, 1884, pp. 19 and 299).

25. References to the Landgraf's presence in Rome during Jan. 1777 were appearing at this time in the public press (see *Lloyd's Evening Post* 17–19 Feb., xl. 173, and *Public Advertiser* 26 Feb. 1777).

26. HW may be indulging in irony, for it was well known in England that the Landgraf had abjured Protestantism in 1749. The Landgraf had married Princess Mary, daughter of George II, in 1740; she separated from him in 1754 as a result of his conversion. See Theodor Hartwig, *Der Übertritt des Erbprinzen, Friedrich von Hessen-Cassel zum Katholicismus*, Cassel, 1870, p. 4; DNB *sub* Mary, Princess of Hesse.

heroes, philosophers, statesmen, have their itchings left, though all their needs have been fully satisfied. Poor Mr Garrick labours under this infirmity of age;[1] he has complained of Monsieur Le Texier for thinking of bringing over Caillaud[2] the French actor in the Opéra-Comique, as a mortal prejudice to his reputation; and no doubt would be glad of an act of Parliament that should prohibit there ever being a good actor again in any country or century; but this is not all, he has solicited King George to solicit him to read a play.[3] The piece was quite new, *Lethe*,[4] which their Majesties have not seen above ten times every year for the last ten years. He added three new characters equally novel, as a Lady Featherby, because the Queen dislikes feathers. The piece was introduced by a prologue *en fable;*[5] a blackbird grown grey-haired, as blackbirds are wont to do, had retired from the world, but was called out again by the Eagle. Mr Hare[6] asked Garrick, if his Majesty looked very like an Eagle? The audience was composed of King, Queen, Princess Royal,[7] Duchess of Argyll,[8] Lady

1. He had retired in 1776.

2. Joseph Caillot (1732–1816), celebrated singer and actor in the Opéra-Comique. In 1764 Garrick had given him a few lessons in acting. See Frank A. Hedgcock, *A Cosmopolitan Actor: David Garrick and His French Friends*, [1912], p. 267.

3. On 2 Feb. 1777 Garrick wrote to William Woodfall: 'Their Majesties have employed me every minute—I have written within these last two days three scenes and two fables' (*Some Unpublished Correspondence of David Garrick*, ed. George Pierce Baker, Boston, 1907, p. 85). 'We hear that on Saturday evening [15 Feb.] David Garrick, Esq., had the honour to recite a dramatic performance, and to speak a prologue, written by himself for the occasion, before their Majesties, at the Queen's Palace' (*London Chronicle* 15–18 Feb. 1777, xli. 166).

4. Garrick's first play, first presented at Drury Lane 15 April 1740 (Genest iii. 609). It was frequently acted. Garrick kept it up to date by several revisions (Mary E. Knapp, 'Garrick's Last Command Performance,' *The Age of Johnson*, New Haven, 1949, pp. 61–71).

5. The 'Occasional Prologue, written and spoken by Mr Garrick on reading his farce of *Lethe* to their Majesties after he had quitted the stage,' survives in several MS copies, and there is a cutting of it (kindly called to our attention by Miss Knapp) in the Yale Library ('Folio Pamphlets' 10, p. 54), from an unidentified newspaper. Among the 77 lines, of which the last 61 are headed 'The Mimic Blackbird, a Fable,' are the following:

'The Blackbird saw, one fatal day,
His jetty feathers changing grey. . . .
The Eagle saw with piercing sight,
What the old Blackbird would delight,
  Perhaps might yield some sport;
  So sent for him to Court. . . .
He never felt before such pride;
  Though crippled, old, and cracked his note,
The royal smile each want supplied,
  Gave him a new melodious throat,
And youth, and health, and fame;
  Gave spirit, voice, and art,
  Gave rapture to his loyal heart,
Years to his life, and honour to his name.'

6. James Hare (1747–1804); M. P. Stockbridge 1772–4, Knaresborough, 1781–1804 (G. P. Judd, *Members of Parliament* 222).

7. Charlotte Augusta Matilda (1766–1828), m. (1797) Friedrich Wilhelm Karl (1754–1816), D. of Württemberg (1797), K. of Württemberg (1805) as Friedrich I.

8. Elizabeth Gunning (1733–90), the celebrated beauty; m. (1) (1752) James Hamilton (1724–58), 6th D. of Hamilton;

Egremont,[9] Lady Charlotte Finch;[10] the Prince of Wales was not present; and all went off perfectly ill, with no exclamations of applause and two or three formal compliments at the end. Bayes[11] is dying of chagrin, and swears he will read no more.

My second moral example is in higher life. That old ruinous fragment of faction, Lord Temple,[12] has had an aching gum too; become by his separation from Lord Chatham,[13] and by the death of his brother George,[14] too insignificant and too impotent to overturn, awe or even alarm the administration, he has been attempting to wriggle into a little favour by a mongrel mixture of treachery, spying and *informing*, below a gentleman, and even below any Lord, but one.[15] Affecting to be shocked at the attempt on Bristol, he employed one of his own old incendiaries to resort to the prison where John the Painter lies,[16] and his worthy agent by worming himself into that

m. (2) (1759) Col. John Campbell, 5th D. of Argyll, 1770. She was one of the Ladies of the Bedchamber to Queen Charlotte 1761–84.

9. Alicia Maria Carpenter (d. 1794), m. (1) (1751) Charles Wyndham (1710–63), 2d E. of Egremont; m. (2) (1767) Hans Moritz (ca 1737–1809), Graf von Brühl, Saxon ambassador to Great Britain. She also was a Lady of the Bedchamber to the Queen.

10. Lady Charlotte Fermor (1725–1813), m. (1746), as his 2d wife, Hon. William Finch. She was governess to the children of George III (Collins, *Peerage*, 1812, iv. 207; Burke, *Peerage, sub* Winchilsea; GM 1813, lxxxiii pt ii. 93).

11. I.e., Garrick. Bayes is the bombastic dramatist in Buckingham's *The Rehearsal;* the part satirizes Dryden. Garrick not only played this part (Thomas Davies, *Memoirs of the Life of David Garrick*, 1780, ii. 417), but also borrowed the name of the character for his one-act play, *The Meeting of the Company, or Bayes's Art of Acting* (first acted 17 Sept. 1774). See *Three Plays by David Garrick*, ed. Elizabeth P. Stein, New York, 1926, pp. 113–51.

12. Richard Grenville (afterwards Grenville-Temple) (1711–79), 1st E. Temple. His person in 1776 is thus described by Sir N. W. Wraxall: 'A disorder, the seat of which lay in his ribs, bending him almost double, compelled him, in walking,

to make use of a sort of crutch' (*Historical Memoirs of His Own Time*, 1836, i. 127). HW elsewhere speaks of him as 'the old decrepit Lord Temple, whose crippled body was still agitated by the smothered flames of ambition' (*Last Journals* ii. 12). Temple's political career had been notorious. 'Opposition to his factious views,' wrote HW, 'seemed to let him loose from all ties, all restraint of principles' (*Mem. Geo. III* i. 234).

13. Temple was for many years intimately associated with Pitt, who had married Hester Grenville, Temple's only sister, in 1754. His quarrel with his brother-in-law began in July 1766 over the formation of a cabinet (*Mem. Geo. III* ii. 243–4). There was a reconciliation in Nov. 1768, but coolness again developed in 1770 (ibid. iv. 126).

14. George Grenville died 13 Nov. 1770. Temple's motive in the action described in this letter is said by HW to have been the indulgence of 'his late brother George's rancour to America' (*Last Journals* ii. 12).

15. HW may be alluding to Lord Sandwich, whose treachery to Wilkes in the affair of the *Essay on Woman* would come to mind in connection with Temple, an old supporter of Wilkes. See *Last Journals* ii. 12.

16. A certain John Baldwin, whose earlier services to Temple have not been discovered, testified that at the instigation

man's confidence, pretends to have learnt from him that the said John had received £300 from Silas Deane[17] for the purpose of burning, not only Bristol, Portsmouth, and Plymouth, but the Bank of England, for stone and gold are wonderfully combustible. The natural philosophers in power believe that Dr Franklin has invented a machine of the size of a toothpick-case, and materials, that would reduce St Paul's to a handful of ashes.[18] I know a very pious Seigneur that firmly believes in this revival of the nostrum of the Old Man of the Mountain[19] —though I do not think he would like this destructibility of gold, if he did believe in it.

The capture of the Hessians is confirmed with circumstances somewhat untoward, for they were not surprised,[20] and yet all laid down their arms as if they liked lands in America better than the wretched pittance they are to receive out of the Landgrave's dole.[21]

It is now the fashion to cry up the manœuvre of General Washington in this action,[22] who has beaten two English regiments too,[23] and obliged General Howe to contract his quarters—in short the campaign has by no means been wound up to content.

There is a great breach in the house of Holderness. Dayrolles'

of Temple he visited John the Painter in the New Prison, Clerkenwell, several times in Feb. 1777, won his confidence, and elicited from him an acknowledgment of his guilt (*The Trial of James Hill*, 1777, p. 13).

17. The American agent in France (*ante* 8 Oct. 1776, n. 8). Despite Baldwin's testimony (*The Trial of James Hill*, p. 15), John the Painter denied that he had received this money (*London Chronicle* 8–11 and 15–18 March 1777, xli. 237, 262).

18. 'Dr Franklin, too, was involved in the charge; the ministers, to decry him, pretending to believe that he had invented a new and most destructive machine for burning towns' (*Last Journals* ii. 12).

19. The leader of the Assassins, the fiercest of the fanatical sects of the Islamic world. The founder and first master was Hassan Sabbah (d. 1124). The leader's title was translated as 'Old Man of the Mountain' by the European Crusaders. See Charles E. Nowell, 'The Old Man of the Mountain,' *Speculum*, 1947, xxii. 497–519.

20. It was reported in the papers that 'the affair of the Hessians was rather a re-

volt than a surrender. On the appearance of the provincials, they made no resistance, but laid down their arms' (*Lloyd's Evening Post* 26–8 Feb. 1777, xl. 202). 'Many people suspect, that there is more meant than meets the ear in the capture of the Hessian brigade in the Jerseys. . . . When a strict discipline was attempted to be introduced by the Howes . . . the inferior auxiliaries began to listen to the large offers of lands given by the Congress, by the means of the German natives of America' (*Public Advertiser* 27 Feb. 1777).

21. See *ante* 17 Feb. 1777, n. 24.

22. The battles of Trenton and Princeton. Washington crossed the Delaware on Christmas night, 1776, and the following day defeated the Hessian regiments at Trenton. On 3 Jan. 1777 the American troops again encountered the enemy, consisting of both English and auxiliary forces, and were again victorious. Howe's letter of 5 Jan., relating Washington's victory, was published in the *Public Advertiser* 26 Feb. 1777.

23. The seventeenth and fifty-fifth (*Public Advertiser* 26 Feb. 1777).

daughter[24] has eloped to *Leonidas* Glover's youngest son,[25] who is friend of Lord Carmarthen: Lady Carmarthen has harboured, and the Countess her mother has forbidden the daughter her court. This is my second letter; mem. I have not had a line from you.

From MASON, ca Sunday 9 March 1777

Missing; indicated by HW's letters *post* 13 March and 5 April 1777.

To MASON, Thursday 13 March 1777

Printed from Mitford i. 270–4.

March 13, 1777.

SO you think I have always something to say because I live in London? If I have, I am sure novelty does not constitute my cargo; the present world seems composed of forgery and informers,[1] and the peers dignify the latter list,[2] and may perhaps the former; I am not ambitious of being their historian. One Dignam,[3] a candidate for the borough of Hindon,[4] and Parliament,[5] had given information of a

24. Solomon Dayrolles (d. 1786), diplomatist, godson and friend of Lord Chesterfield, had three daughters (*Miscellanea genealogica et heraldica*, 1898, 3d ser., ii. 293), but which of them eloped has not been discovered.

25. Glover had two sons by his first wife, of which one, Richard, was M.P. for Penryn 1790–6 (Leslie Stephen in DNB; *Members of Parliament*, pt ii, 1878, pp. 188, 201). It has not been ascertained which of them was concerned in this affair.

1. An allusion to the trial 22 Feb. 1777 of Rev. William Dodd (1729–77), for forging the signature of his patron, Lord Chesterfield, and to the testimony of John Baldwin in the trial of John the Painter (*ante* 27 Feb. 1777).

2. Lord Temple gathered evidence against John the Painter (*ante* 27 Feb. 1777).

3. 'David Brown Dignam was tried before Sir John Fielding at the session at Guildhall, Westminster, for defrauding Mr

Clarke of upwards of £700 under pretence of appointing him clerk of the minutes in the custom-house, at Dublin, by means of a forged warrant, pretended to be signed by Lord Weymouth and Mr Daw. The jury, without going out of court, found him guilty, and the magistrates, after consulting together, sentenced him to work five years upon the river Thames. . . . Some little time before his detection he had the audacity to wait upon a nobleman in high office, and charge some gentlemen of fortune and character with a conspiracy against the life of the King, in which, he said, he had been so fortunate as to discover their haunts' (GM 1777, xlvii. 191, *sub* 5 April).

4. In Wiltshire. 'When Mr Dignam was apprehended, he had lodgings in Delahaye Street, Westminster. He gave himself out for a member of the Irish Parliament, and was lately a candidate to represent the *immaculate* borough of Hindon' (*Public Advertiser* 12 March 1777). Hindon was notorious for its corrupt elections; in 1775

plot against the King's life, which he had invented, and it neither producing a place for him nor Lord Temple, he took to selling places to others, which all his merit could not obtain for himself, and so he is only in Newgate. This is a specimen of town-news; it is better to be at York, than write memoirs of Mrs Grieve,[6] Mrs Rudd,[7] Dr Dodd, Mr Dignam, and Lord Temple.

Hume's life written by himself is just published.[8] It is a nothing, a brief account of his disappointments on his irreligious works making no noise at first, and his historic making some. He boasts that in the latter he dared to revive the cause of despotism[9]—a great honour truly to a philosopher, and he speaks of your friend Bishop Hurd with a freedom, that I dare to say the whole Court will profess to his Lordship they think monstrous rudeness.[10] My Lord H[ertford] whose piety could swallow Hume's infidelity, will be shocked now that he should have employed such a brute.[11]

The *Memoirs* and *Miscellaneous Works* of Lord Chesterfield are come out too;[12] they are in two huge quartos, drawn up by Dr Maty[13] and his son,[14] and compiled chiefly from pamphlets. I am got but a

a bill to disfranchise it had been presented, but was quashed (*Last Journals* i. 451–2). There is no evidence that Dignam actually stood for Hindon, and his name does not appear in the official list of members of the Irish Parliament.

5. Mitford's text seems to be corrupt. It is probable that HW, following the *Public Advertiser* story cited in the preceding note, had mentioned Dignam's alleged membership in the Irish Parliament.

6. See ante 14 Feb. 1774.

7. See ante 14 April 1775.

8. *The Life of David Hume, Esq., Written by Himself,* published 11 March (*London Chronicle* 8–11 March 1777, xli. 239).

9. Hume merely spoke of himself as one 'who had presumed to shed a generous tear for the fate of Charles I and the Earl of Strafford' (Hume's *Life,* p. 19). Also see pp. 22–3.

10. 'In this interval, I published at London my *Natural History of Religion,* along with some other small pieces; its public entry was rather obscure, except only that Dr Hurd wrote a pamphlet against it, with all the illiberal petulance, arrogance, and scurrility, which distinguish the Warburtonian school' (ibid. 21).

11. Hume was secretary to the embassy

when Hertford was ambassador at Paris (1763–5). Cole remarked on the 'great virtue and strict morality' of Hertford (COLE i. 237); Chesterfield described him as 'in my opinion, the honestest and most religious man in the world' (*The Letters of Philip Dormer Stanhope, 4th Earl of Chesterfield,* ed. Bonamy Dobrée, 1932, vi. 2667); HW thought him 'a little of the prude' (MONTAGU i. 235).

12. *Miscellaneous Works of the Late Philip Dormer Stanhope, Earl of Chesterfield,* containing 'Memoirs' by Matthew Maty, was advertised as published 14 March (*Public Advertiser* 13–14 March), but as this letter shows, some copies at least must have been issued before the publication date. See Sidney L. Gulick, Jr, *A Chesterfield Bibliography to 1800,* 1935, p. 75. HW's copy was sold London 1056 (removed from SH vii. 40) and is now in the BM. See n. 17 below.

13. Matthew Maty (1718–76), M.D.; physician, writer, and principal librarian of the BM. Chesterfield had been Maty's patron.

14. Maty's edition was completed after his death by his son-in-law, John Obadiah Justamond (d. 1786), surgeon and F.R.S. (GM 1786, lvi pt i. 270).

little way into them with small edification, yet I have found a new anecdote or two, that are curious, and there are some of his *bon mots* that will be new to others. In the second volume are several of his French letters to a Madame de Monconseil,[15] whom I know; she was married to a French officer,[16] and when I was first recommended to her above thirty years ago, her mother kept a gaming-house,[17] and the daughter has ever since dealt in intrigues of all sorts, which latterly, you may be sure, have been chiefly political;[18] and of both sorts I believe interest was generally the motive. Towards the end of the Duke of Choiseul's power, her house was the rendezvous of all his enemies; I have seen Madame de Mirepoix[19] there with Marshal Richelieu,[20] whom, till faction reunited them, she would never be in a room with (but at Court) as he killed her first husband.[21] She married her nephew[22] to Madame de Monconseil's daughter,[23] and that made a quarrel between Mad. de Mirepoix and the Prime Minister,[24] and was the true cause of his fall; for the Princess de Beauvau,[25] her sister-in-law and enemy, to hurt Mad. de Mirepoix, drove the Duchess de Grammont[26] into all the violence against Madame du Barry,[27] and

15. Claire-Cécile-Thérèse-Pauline Rioult de Douilly (1706–87). See HW's correspondence with Mme du Deffand for references to her and the other French mentioned in this letter.

16. In 1725 she married Étienne-Louis-Antoine Guignot (1695–1782), Marquis de Monconseil, Lt-Gen. in the army, 1748 (Henri de Woelmont de Brumagne, *Notices généalogiques*, 1923–35, vi. 629–30).

17. In the marginal notes written in his copy of Chesterfield's *Miscellaneous Works* and published in *Philobiblon Society Miscellanies*, 1867–8, vol. xi, HW wrote: 'I was introduced to her in 1739, when her mother kept a gaming-house' ('Marginal Notes,' p. 63).

18. 'Madame de Monconseil . . . was a most intriguing and interested woman, and dipped in all kinds of cabals' (ibid. 62).

19. Anne-Marguerite-Gabrielle de Beauvau-Craon (1707–91), m. (1) (1721) Jacques-Henri de Lorraine (1698–1734), Prince de Lixin; m. (2) (1739) Charles-Pierre-Gaston-François de Lévis de Lomagne, Duc de Mirepoix, Maréchal de France.

20. Louis-François-Armand Vignerot du Plessis (1696–1788), Duc and Maréchal de Richelieu.

21. Richelieu killed the Prince de Lixin in a duel in 1734 ('Marginal Notes,' p. 63; *Mem. Geo. III* iv. 13; La Chenaye-Desbois and Badier, *Dictionnaire de la noblesse*, 1863–76, xii. 439).

22. Charles - Alexandre - Marc - Marcellin d'Alsace-Hénin-Liétard (1744–94), Prince d'Hénin.

23. Étiennette Guignot de Monconseil (ca 1750–1824). In 1766 she married the Prince d'Hénin.

24. The Duc de Choiseul. The marriage offended him because Madame de Monconseil was one of his enemies (*Mem. Geo. III* iv. 12).

25. Marie-Sylvie de Rohan-Chabot (1729–1807), m. (1) (1749) Jean-Baptiste-Louis de Clermont d'Amboise, Marquis de Renel; m. (2) (1764) Charles-Juste de Beauvau-Craon, Prince de Beauvau.

26. Béatrix de Choiseul-Stainville (1730–94), sister of the Duc de Choiseul; m. (1759) Antoine-Antonin, Duc de Gramont.

27. Jeanne Bécu (1743–93), m. (1768) Guillaume, Comte du Barry; at the time of which HW speaks, the new favourite of Louis XV.

the Duke[28] was so weak as to let those two women embroil him with the mistress.[29] I was an eye-witness of those scenes, and at the Duke's three or four nights in a week, and heard all their indiscretions.

There are I see besides, a letter or two to Madame de Tencin,[30] a most horrid woman, sister of the Cardinal.[31] She had great parts and so little principle that she was supposed to have murdered and robbed one of her lovers,[32] a scrape out of which Lord Harrington,[33] another of them, saved her; she had levees from eight in the morning till night, from the lowest tools to the highest. Dalembert[34] was her natural son, Madame Geoffrin her pupil,[35] and Pontdevesle[36] her nephew, who was supposed to have only adopted [sic] her novels,[37] the *Comte de Cominges,* and the *Mémoires de Philippe Auguste.*[38] This acquaintance with the personages, English and French, makes me eager about these

28. The Duc de Choiseul.

29. HW describes in some detail the intrigues and factions of the Court at the time of Mme du Barry's ascendancy, in *Mem. Geo. III* iv. 4–20.

30. Claudine-Alexandrine Guérin (1682–1749), Marquise de Tencin. HW's note on her, repeating what he says here, is printed in 'Marginal Notes,' p. 60.

31. Pierre Guérin de Tencin (1680–1758), Abp of Embrun, 1724, of Lyon, 1740; cardinal, 1739. For an account of his career see Maurice Boutry, *Une Créature du Cardinal Dubois: intrigues et missions du Cardinal de Tencin,* 1902.

32. HW doubtless had in mind Mme de Tencin's involvement in the death of Charles-Joseph de la Fresnais, one of the Seigneurs du Grand Conseil, who committed suicide in Mme de Tencin's house in 1726, leaving a will in which he accused her of having robbed him and of plotting his death. She was imprisoned, but was released in two months by order of the King. See Pierre-Maurice Masson, *Une Vie de femme au XVIIIᵉ siècle: Madame de Tencin (1682–1749),* 1909, pp. 47–58, 253–6.

33. William Stanhope (ca 1683–1756), cr. (1742) E. of Harrington. Nothing further has been found about his intervention in the La Fresnais affair.

34. Jean le Rond d'Alembert (1717–83), 'philosophe' and encyclopædist. His father was the Chevalier Destouches-Canon, lieutenant-général de l'artillerie. His mother, Mme de Tencin, is said to have abandoned the child on the steps of the

Church of St Jean-le-Rond. His father sought him out, had him educated, and left him a small fortune. See Masson, op. cit. 22–3.

35. Marie-Thérèse Rodet (1699–1777), m. (1713) François Geoffrin. 'J'ai dit que, du vivant Mme de Tencin, Mme Geoffrin l'allait voir, et la vieille rusée pénétrait si bien le motif de ces visites qu'elle disait à ses convives: "Savez-vous ce que la Geoffrin vient faire ici? elle vient voir ce qu'elle pourra recueillir de mon inventaire" ' (*Mémoires de Marmontel,* ed. Maurice Tourneux, 1891, ii. 82). After Mme de Tencin's death, her coterie drifted to Mme Geoffrin (ibid. ii. 83; Masson, op. cit. 188).

36. Antoine Ferriol (1697–1774), Comte de Pont-de-Veyle. His mother was Angélique Guérin, youngest sister of Mme de Tencin.

37. Not clear; perhaps Mitford's text is corrupt. Mme du Deffand believed that Pont-de-Veyle collaborated with his aunt in her *Siège de Calais* and *Malheurs de l'amour* (DU DEFFAND iii. 218); HW states elsewhere that Pont-de-Veyle was 'the author of some pieces that passed for hers' (ibid. vi. 77). Mme de Tencin's authorship of the *Mémoires du Comte de Comminges* (1735) and *Le Siège de Calais* (1739) has been affirmed by Masson (op. cit. 132–3).

38. Not identified; apparently not by Mme de Tencin or Pont-de-Veyle. HW may have been thinking of Marguerite de Lussan's *Anecdotes de la cour de Philippe-Auguste,* 1733–8; his copy (2 vols, 1734) was sold SH ii. 134.

memoirs, and as I love nothing so much now as writing notes in my books, this will furnish me with employment.

I am extremely of your opinion about the new old poems;[39] indeed you talk *en connaissance de cause,* who can dispute with the author of the *Monody?*[40] As I already have *your Garden*[41] I am less interested about its publication; I almost grudge the swine your pearls; yet write the third and the fourth, and sometimes to me, for I must be encouraged, or I cannot write even newspapers. There is nothing pleases me so much as humbling myself to the level of my talents. Writing notes in my books, as it requires only truth and memory, and no parts, suits me exactly; and had I always known myself as well as I do now, I should never have soared out of my sphere, and my works would have been highly valued, as I should have never had above one reader to each, the person who buys my books at my auction. Don't tell me you have nothing to say; you see how easy it is to make a long letter; one might have written this in the Isle of Sky, but you are a poet and a tragic author, and will not condescend to write anything lest your letters should rise in judgment against you. It is a mercy to have no character to maintain. Your predecessor Mr Pope laboured his letters as much as the *Essay on Man,* and as they were written to everybody, they do not look as if they had been written to anybody; however as I expect to be indemnified for your silence, I will consent to send you three letters for one, provided you give me a satisfactory account hereafter of your having been better employed than in answering mine. I certainly shall do nothing better than writing to you, and therefore whenever I have anything worth telling you, you shall hear it, and I shall not consider whether it is worth posterity's knowing or not,—posterity must deserve my favour a little better than their ancestors now living, or I shall [? not] care a straw for their suffrage.

39. Presumably Chatterton's. See *ante* 17 Feb. 1777.

40. Mason's *Musæus, a Monody* (*ante* ? Nov. 1776, n. 7) was written 'in imitation of Milton's *Lycidas,*' as was stated on the title-page. Perhaps Mason had said that Chatterton, or Tyrwhitt, should have described the Rowley poems as imitations.

41. That is, a copy of the private printing of the second book of *The English Garden.* See *ante* 20 May 1776 and n. 5.

To Mason, Friday 28 March 1777

Printed from Mitford i. 274–5 and Add. MSS 32563 fol. 50; see n. 16 below.

Strawberry Hill, March 28, 1777.

I HAVE been here these six days alone, enjoying the bounty of March, which has laid aside its old dry winds and behaved with a warmth, a heat that June seldom condescends to bestow. I have had every door and window all day open for these three days, and in the garden the sun was even too hot. I wonder that in this pious age there is no fear of an earthquake,[1] and that my Lord of London[2] has not threatened us with one in his pastoral letter on Good Friday![3] I left the town in a buzz about Lord Pigot's arrest,[4] in which the Scots are said to have acted an ungentle part,[5] nay one of guile, if they could be suspected of any unfair dealings. We have fancied that this little isle could hold both the east and the west *in commendam*,[6] and supply the places of Montezuma and Aurenzebe. I doubt France will soon present to both those cures of souls.[7] Caius Manlius Washingtonius Americanus, the dictator,[8] has got together a large army, larger than that our ally the Duke of Wirtemburg was to have sold us,[9] and Gen-

1. 'Long dry hot seasons . . . are usually the preparatory forerunners of earthquakes' (Stephen Hales, *Some Considerations on the Causes of Earthquakes, Which were Read before the Royal Society, April 5, 1750*, 1750, p. 19).

2. Richard Terrick. See *ante* p. 49 n. 25.

3. The Bishop of London's pastoral letter calling for a more strict observance of Good Friday, dated 19 March 1777, was printed in most of the newspapers and journals. See, e.g., *London Chronicle* 22–25 March, xli. 286; *Public Advertiser* 25 March; GM 1777, xlvii. 104. After the earthquakes of 1750 HW wrote Mann, 'We have swarmed with sermons, essays, relations, poems, and exhortations on that subject' (19 May 1750).

4. George Pigot (1719–77), cr. (1766) Bn Pigot; governor of Madras. On his refusal to recognize the claims of the Nawab of Arcot against the Raja of Tanjore, the members of the Council of Madras repudiated his authority and put him under arrest 24 Aug. 1776. See *post* 4 Feb. 1778 and Lucy S. Sutherland, *The East India Company in Eighteenth-Century Politics*, Oxford, 1952, pp. 317–28.

5. Pigot's arrest was planned by John Macpherson whom Pigot had dismissed from the Company on the grounds of disloyalty.

6. An ecclesiastical phrase referring to a benefice held by a dignitary along with his own.

7. That is, France threatened British possessions in both India and the New World.

8. Unusual powers were granted Washington 27 Dec. 1776 by the Continental Congress (*Journals of Congress Containing the Proceedings from January 1, 1776 to January 1, 1777*, Yorktown, 1778, p. 515). *Public Advertiser* 24 March reported that 'the Congress, after declaring General Washington dictator of the American states for six months, had withdrawn to Baltimore in Maryland.'

9. 'When the D— of W— was last summer in England, a treaty was agreed upon between our Court and him for the use of six thousand of his troops; but whether from the late defeat of the Hessians, or what other cause, not above two thousand can be procured, and they not in a position to march till perhaps we shall not want

eral Howe who has nothing but salt provisions in our metropolis, New York, has not twenty thousand pounds' worth of pickles as he had at Boston;[10] but I do not understand military matters, and therefore will say no more of them. Have you read Hume's life, and did you observe that he thought of retiring to France and changing his name, because his works had not got him a name?[11] Lord Bute called himself Sir John Stewart in Italy[12] to shroud the beams of a title too gorgeous; but it is new to conceal a name that nobody had heard of. Have you got Lord Chesterfield? I have read his letters and like them, but Dr Maty is no *Mason* at biography; you will be charmed with his *Common Senses* and *Fogs,* if you never read them, and with his *Worlds,* which you have read.[13] They are the best of his works. Mr Jephson has sent me his *Vitellia,* which Garrick rejected last year[14] with as much judgment as he acted all the wretched pieces that appeared at Drury Lane for so many years; it has beautiful poetry as *Braganza* had, and more action and more opportunities for good actors, if there were any.

There has been a young gentlewoman overturned and terribly bruised by her *Vulcanian stays.* They now wear a steel busk down their middle, and a rail of the same metal across their breasts. If a hero attempts to storm such strong lines, and comes to a close engagement, he must lie as ill at his ease as St Laurence on his gridiron.[15]

This is my second since my promise of three, of which I repent al-

them' (*Public Advertiser* 8 March 1777).

10. In the House of Commons 12 March 1776 'Mr Tuffnal complained of an extravagant article for pickles and vinegar for 6000 men at Boston for three months, and said, that if they had lived upon nothing else the whole time, it could not have come to half the money' (*Lloyd's Evening Post* 11–13 March 1776, xxxviii. 255).

11. 'I was, however, I confess, discouraged; and had not the war been at that time breaking out between France and England, I had certainly retired to some provincial town of the former kingdom, have changed my name, and never more have returned to my native country' (*The Life of David Hume,* 1777, p. 20).

12. When Bute was in Italy in 1769 'he received very few visits anywhere, never wore his Garter, and left cards under the name of Mr Stuart' (Mann to HW 25 March 1769).

13. Chesterfield's essays, which had originally appeared in *Fog's Journal, Common Sense,* and *The World,* were printed in the first volume of the *Miscellaneous Works.* On the authorship of these essays see Roger Coxon, *Chesterfield and His Critics,* 1925, pp. 213–20. The essays in *The World* were both the most numerous (twenty-three were printed by Maty) and the best known.

14. *Vitellia* was rejected by Garrick in Dec. 1775 (*Private Correspondence of David Garrick,* 1831–2, i. 530, ii. 113–4). HW commented on it in his letter to Jephson 13 July 1777. It was ultimately produced, under the title of *The Conspiracy,* in 1796. It is described in Genest vii. 286–7.

15. This paragraph was first printed by Mrs Toynbee from Mitford's transcripts of omitted passages, Add. MSS 32563 fol. 50. Mitford indicated only the page on which the paragraph belonged; Mrs Toynbee placed it at the end of the letter.

ready as I have no satisfaction in writing but to hear from you; but I can make all three as short as I please, for the spirit and the letter of a promise are two very different things, *vide* Sanchez,[16] Escobar,[17] Mansfield, and other casuists on coronation oaths.

To Mason, Saturday 5 April 1777

Printed from Mitford i. 276–9.

Strawberry Hill, April 5, 1777.

YOUNG folks may fancy what they will of such antiques as I am, having no original pleasures, or only scraps and ends. Lord Holland was always whining on the miseries of old age,[1] now I can tell both the one and the other, that there are very cordial enjoyments, which only the old can have. I have just tasted two great raptures of the sort I mean,—but indeed they do not happen very often. The transports I allude to, are living to see the *private* works, sentiments and anecdotes of one's own time come to light. The two last folios of Lord Chesterfield delighted me upon that score, but there is still a fresher work of the same kind, and by far one of the most curious and authentic that ever was published. It is a history of many interesting parts of the latter end of Louis Quatorze, of the Regent, and of the late King of France, taken from an immense collection of state papers amassed by the two last Maréchaux de Noailles,[2] furnished by the family, and though of dates so recent, and though published at Paris, written with a freedom and impartiality that are stupendous. I will give you an instance that is striking; one of the Maréchals[3] congratulates Louis on

16. Tomás Sánchez (1550–1610), Spanish Jesuit; author of theological treatises, in one of which, the *Opus morale in præcepta decalogi,* 1613, he expounds a theory of mental reservation.

17. Antonio de Escobar y Mendoza (1589–1669), Spanish Jesuit, author of *Summula casuum conscientiæ,* 1627, and other works dealing with purity of intention.

1. See *ante* 1 Dec. 1773.
2. *Mémoires politiques et militaires, pour servir à l'histoire de Louis XIV et de Louis XV, composés sur les pièces originales recueillies par Adrien-Maurice, Duc de Noailles, Maréchal de France et ministre d'état,* ed. Claude-François-Xavier Millot, 6 vols, 1776–7. The first volume was especially concerned with the career of Anne-Jules (1650–1708), Duc de Noailles, the first Marshal of that name. Most of the remaining material had to do with the first Marshal's son, Adrien-Maurice (1678–1766). HW's copy (sold SH v. 194) was sent him by Louis de Noailles (1713–93), Duc d'Ayen, 1737, and de Noailles, 1766; Maréchal de France, 1775. See DU DEFFAND iv. 420.
3. Anne-Jules, in a letter of 7 July 1692.

the taking of Namur, and says it is a conquest that he alone could achieve. King William, says the author, took it with much more deserved applause two years afterwards.[4] There are six duodecimos, pretty thick; the first relates chiefly to the persecution of the Protestants on the revocation of the edict of Nantes: is severe on the King, but unsatisfactory, because the Marshal being recalled, the author follows him and not the war, and this is almost the only kind of fault I find in the work, which ought to have been called memoirs of the two Marshals, instead of memoirs of two reigns. But the invaluable part, and that pretty perfect, is the genuine and secret history of Spain on the establishment of Philip V.[5] Nothing ever was more curious—you will even see the pains Louis XIV took to persuade his grandson to give up Spain and content himself with Sardinia,[6] and you cannot doubt it. The two last volumes are not less interesting to me, who have the very minute of time before my eyes. I remember how I trembled, as Lord Chesterfield did[7] (for these memoirs are the counterpart of his) just before the peace of Aix-la-Chapelle,[8] and yet you will see that the court of France was in as great a panic as we had reason to be.[9] I remember saying often, that a little thing saved us as ruined us, and that if France had not as incapable ministers as we had, we must be undone. Perhaps, when more memoirs of the family of Noailles appear, somebody or other will make this reflection again.

The second Marshal had (luckily for posterity, though probably a little wearisome at the time) a rage of drawing up memorials; but he was a good and a prudent man; and the latter quality made his courage a little doubted, as the author fairly owns. I remember a *bon mot* of his son, the present Marshal, on that topic. The old gentleman had like to have been drowned by going in a boat on the water; his son, the Duc d'Ayen, a great *bon-mot*ist, scolded the servants for not hindering his father, and said, 'Ne savez-vous pas que mon père craint l'eau comme le feu?'

4. 'Cette conquête était bien digne de V.M. et n'appartenait qu'à votre seule personne. [Le roi Guillaume prouva le contraire en 1695.]' (*Mémoires politiques et militaires*, i. 205).

5. Philip V (1683–1746), King of Spain, grandson of Louis XIV; second son of Louis, Dauphin of France, and of Marie-Anne of Bavaria. While Duke of Anjou he became King of Spain in 1700 by the will of his grand-uncle, Charles II of Spain, an event that precipitated the War of the Spanish Succession.

6. *Mémoires politiques et militaires*, iv. 137–9.

7. See, e.g., *Miscellaneous Works*, ii. 328.

8. These fears are not expressed in HW's published letters of Sept. and early Oct. 1748.

9. See *Mémoires politiques et militaires*, vi. 251.

You cannot conceive the avidity with which I devoured these volumes; one cannot be more vigorous at eighteen, but alas! one cannot go to Drury Lane and pick up two Noailleses every night! It is vexatious too, that as these papers will spread the taste of hoarding state papers (which the old Marshal had retained from the taste of memoir-writing that was rife in his youth) I shall not live to see those collections. We are indeed likely to have an immense collection ere long, but not quite so important. It seems by a note of Dr Maty,[10] that Lord Chesterfield, who I thought had used him only as a butt to shoot wit at, had kept up a correspondence with long Sir Thomas Robinson[11] for fifty years. Well; Sir Thomas is dead too;[12] and lest the public should sigh for his answers, as they did for Madame de Grignan's,[13] he was so industrious as to keep copies of his, nay, he had preserved every letter he ever received, nay, and he had kept copies of all his answers to all them too; and he has left all, letters and answers, to the Roman people; that is, to an apothecary who married his natural daughter,[14] with injunctions to publish all,[15] which will last me my life. Oh, but stay, the Primate of Ireland,[16] Sir Thomas's brother, is not quite so indulgent as the House of Noailles, who have suffered a letter of a bishop, their uncle,[17] who teases the Marshal for promotion,

10. 'I have been informed that an intimate acquaintance subsisted between the writer of the following letters [Lord Chesterfield], and the gentleman [Sir Thomas Robinson] to whom they are addressed, for above half a century, which gave rise to a very voluminous correspondence. Should these letters, together with the answers that have been carefully preserved, ever appear in print, as possibly they may, they must prove an agreeable acquisition, and furnish a very striking and progressive picture of modern times' (*Miscellaneous Works*, ii. 449).

11. Sir Thomas Robinson (ca 1702–77), Bt, 1731, of Rokeby, Yorks; F.R.S.; M.P.; governor of Barbados 1742–7; called 'long Sir Thomas' to distinguish him from his contemporary, Sir Thomas Robinson, cr. (1761) Bn Grantham.

12. He died 3 March 1777 (*London Chronicle* 1–4 March, xli. 215).

13. Françoise-Marguerite de Sévigné (1648–1705), m. (1669) François de Castellane-Adhémar de Monteil, Comte de Grignan; dau. of Madame de Sévigné and recipient of most of her letters. Mme de Grignan's letters are lost, presumably destroyed by her daughter, Mme de Simiane. See *Lettres de Madame de Sévigné*, ed. Monmerqué, 1862–6, i. 314–6; Janet M. Murbach, *Le Vrai visage de la Comtesse de Grignan*, Toulouse, 1939, pp. 9–15.

14. Anne (d. 1824), m. William Pirner or Pirnor (living 1824), of Arlington Street, 'joint apothecary with Mr Brande to their Majesties' (Robinson's will at Somerset House, information from Mr Robert A. Smith; GM 1824, xciv pt ii. 189).

15. HW's information was inaccurate. Robinson left his papers to Pirner and three other executors jointly, 'leaving it to them at their discretion to dispose of and publish the same in such manner as they shall think proper, as I am fully persuaded they will make no other use of them but what is suitable to the nature of such a trust and perfectly consistent with a sincere regard for my memory and the reputation of my family and connections.'

16. Richard Robinson. See *ante* p. 196 n. 9.

17. Jean-Gaston de Noailles (1669–1720),

to be published.[18] My Lord of Armagh is consulting lawyers whether he cannot stop the publication,[19] and in truth it is an abominable thing that private letters of living persons should be printed.

I do not know a tittle of what has happened in Europe (or America) since Lord Chesterfield and Monsieur de Noailles died, but I shall go to town on Monday, recollect the living, and tell you what they have been doing; but then you must take care to answer this, which is *the third*,[20] or if Lord Temple should find a plot in a meal-tub or a flower-pot, I shall not be able to tell you till I am empowered to write a first letter.

8th, Lond.

The Bishop of London is dead,[21] and Mlle Khrome.[22] I thought your friend Dr Hurd would have succeeded them both.[23] The message for the debts and civil list[24] is to be delivered tomorrow. Somebody knocks, and I must finish.

From Mason, Monday 14 April 1777

Printed from MS now WSL.
Address: The Honourable Horace Walpole, Arlington Street, London.
Postmark: YORK 17 AP.

York, April 14th, 1777.

SHAME upon me, I have indeed now three unanswered letters of yours, and such letters too as every one of them deserve three answers apiece for the entertainment which they severally afforded; but if these nine letters were all of them written from this place and in

Bishop of Châlons-sur-Marne (P. B. Gams, *Series episcoporum*, Ratisbon, 1873, p. 535).

18. HW apparently was thinking of a letter from the second Maréchal to the Bishop of Châlons in which the prelate's importunity is reprimanded. See *Mémoires politiques et militaires*, v. 409–10.

19. The Bishop's efforts apparently succeeded, for the correspondence has never been published.

20. That is, HW's third letter without a return (see *ante* 13 March 1777).

21. Terrick died 31 March 1777 (*London Chronicle* 29 March–1 April, xli. 311).

22. Mademoiselle Krohme (see *ante* 23 April 1774, n. 8) died 29 March 1777 (GM 1777, xlvii. 195).

23. On 5 June 1776 Hurd succeeded Bishop Markham as preceptor to the Prince of Wales and to Prince Frederick, Bishop of Osnaburgh. It was reported in the newspapers that Hurd would be translated to the see of London (*London Chronicle* 29 March–1 April 1777, xli. 312), but the appointment actually was given to Robert Lowth, at the time Bishop of Oxford.

24. The King's message was read 9 April. See *post* 14 April 1777 and n. 16.

my present monotonous situation, they would, I am convinced, not make one equal sufficient answer or be deemed fair and full payment by any person conversant in the course of epistolary exchange, so I must content myself with resting in a state of insolvency and continuing your poor debtor to the end of my residentiarial days, if not to the end of my natural life. But pray (say you), Mr Residentiary, what is a monotonous situation? is it not a phrase similar to 'a spontaneous coat' which puzzled a wit at White's so much that in order to get rid of it he laid a bet that there was no such word as 'spontaneous' in Johnson's Dictionary?[1] No, Sir, I assure you there is the strictest propriety in the epithet, for my hours are all regulated by a certain tinkling monotonous machine called the Minster prayer-bell, which even now (while I am writing) begins to move its clapper and will hardly let me finish my sentence, with an adieu to you till I have obeyed its summons and have gone to my matins* * * *

And now, Sir, my matins are finished and I resume my pen, but the singing boys have bawled so horridly out of tune, that I have lost all the good temper I was possessed of after my breakfast when I first sat down to write to you; and this is every day the case, and as the post goes off every day at noon, every letter I attempt to write is liable to the same mischance, so that nothing *suivie*, nothing that your critics would call a composition can possibly fall from my pen. Well, reply you, but are my letters compositions? No, but they are better things than compositions, and therefore when a man cannot write such better things than compositions, he must either compose or not write at all. Q.E.D.

I saw lately in a review,[2] the only species of literary beings (and you will allow them to be of the true Drury Lane stamp)[3] on which one can here be vigorous, an account of a work of Marmontel's[4] called, I think, *Les Incas*,[5] which seemed to be a sort of historical novel on the conquest of Peru. Perhaps it might give one some hint for a drama similar to that which you once recommended to me.[6] Marmontel is

1. The wit lost his bet, which is not recorded in the Betting Book of White's (ed. W. B. Boulton, 1892). Johnson defined 'spontaneous' as 'voluntary; not compelled; acting without compulsion or restraint,' etc., and gave quotations from Milton, Prior, and Pope. A 'spontaneous coat' would seem to be one selected at random, without regard to the rest of the costume.

2. Probably *Monthly Review* March 1777, lvi. 216–7.

3. That is, 'wretched' (*ante* 28 March 1777).

4. Jean-François Marmontel (1723–99), French poet, novelist, and critic.

5. *Les Incas, ou la destruction de l'empire du Pérou*, 1777.

6. Possibly in conversation. No such rec-

no favourite writer of mine, but he has invention, and, sometimes, traits of character. Have you seen the work and is it worth sending for to town? I could get it perhaps in a fortnight if the wagoner pleases.

O! for the Muse of Lord Lyttleton or of Mrs Montagu[7] that I might finish the imperfect dialogue which David Hume has left us between himself and Charon,[8] and O for the dedicatorial powers of Sir John Hawkins that I might dedicate it either to the King[9] or my Lord Hertford![10]

A friend of mine here who is an excellent scholar[11] has examined Pliny with the greatest accuracy concerning all he has left relative to encaustic painting[12] and gone much further than Count Caylus[13] or any French scholar I believe could possibly do, on such a subject; in short he has found out the precise colours and mode of operation which Protogenes[14] used, and from the single specimen he has produced has made it very clear to me that the art is capable of being carried to absolute perfection, and is equally excellent for its simplicity, and promise of durability. And I have reason to think that as the tints employed are fixed and permanent, pictures might be copied in this

ommendation is found in the correspondence, nor did *Les Incas* (which HW sent *post* 2 May 1777) inspire Mason to write a drama, as far as is known. Later, however, he wrote one on an Indian subject; see *post* 8 Nov. 1783 and n. 13, and 25 Dec. 1783 and n. 3.

7. An allusion to the first Lord Lyttelton's *Dialogues of the Dead* (1760), the last three of which were by Mrs Elizabeth Montagu.

8. In the 'Letter from Adam Smith, LL.D., to William Strahan, Esq.,' printed as a supplement to the *Life of David Hume Written by Himself*, Smith tells how his friend diverted himself during his last days 'with inventing several jocular excuses, which he supposed he might make to Charon, and with imagining the very surly answers which it might suit the character of Charon to return to them' (*Life*, p. 49).

9. To whom Hawkins wrote the fulsome dedication of his *General History of the Science and Practice of Music* (1776).

10. Alluding to Lord Hertford's piety that 'could swallow Hume's infidelity' (*ante* 13 March 1777).

11. Perhaps Thomas Beckwith: see *post* 9 Nov. 1781 and n. 6.

12. There are scattered allusions to encaustic painting throughout Bk xxxv of the *Natural History*. The *locus classicus* is Chapter 149. See *The Elder Pliny's Chapters on the History of Art*, trans. K. Jex-Blake, with notes by Eugénie Sellers, 1896, p. 172; *The Elder Pliny's Chapters on Chemical Subjects*, ed. K. C. Bailey, 1929–32, ii. 222–3.

13. Anne-Claude-Philippe de Thubières de Grimoard de Pestel de Lévis (1692–1765), Comte Caylus; French archæologist, collector, and art patron. His theories on the encaustic painting of the ancients were given currency in England by the publication in 1760 of *Encaustic: or Count Caylus's Method of Painting in the Manner of the Ancients*, by Johann Heinrich Müntz (1727–98), whom HW had employed at SH 1755–9. HW had planned to write and publish a book on encaustic, but lost interest in it after dismissing Müntz in November 1759. See 'Short Notes,' GRAY i. 34.

14. The Greek painter (d. 300 B.C.), whose work is described by Pliny in *Natural History*, Bk xxxv *passim*.

way by persons no better skilled in drawing than the workmen in mosaic at Rome, or the tapestry weavers at the Gobelins. And now, Sir, by the time this reaches you the budget will be opened,[15] the increase of the civil list moved for,[16] and everything that can make the felicity of this nation as permanent as the most genuine encaustic painting secured to us and our posterity. Let me not, I beseech you, owe all my intelligence of these blessed events to a newspaper, but indulge me (*pro more*) with a speedy account from your own pen, to which I will give no other epithet than that it is to me a most charitable pen, and shall have my prayers for its preservation both at matins and vespers, good creature as it is.

                                                                Amen.

To MASON, Friday 18 April 1777

Printed from Mitford i. 282–6.

                                                        April 18, 1777.

I HAVE *seen* but not read one syllable of Marmontel's *Yncas*, nor ever will. History is romance enough, without purposely perverting it. I could not wade through a quarter of his *Belisarius*.[1] I hope the Peruvians will have better masters to teach them liberty than French *philosophes,* and not be obliged to go to Paris on their way to Thermopylæ. However, as you can strike fire from a flint, I am disposed to send you the book, and shall be delighted if you beget a Pandora on a cloud.

It is easy to me to believe your friend's discoveries in encaustic. Müntz went far enough to prove the facility, use and durability, but not far enough to get the method adopted; not from any defect or difficulty in the practice, but from the stupidity and obstinacy and John-trot-plodding-in-the-same-wayness of the professors. If you think, because it talks more of the arts, that the age is grown more

---

15. Consideration of the budget did not begin until 13 May (*London Chronicle* 13–15 May 1777, xli. 464).

16. A message from the King, read to both Houses 9 April, acquainted Parliament with his debts and requested more adequate provisions in the future. Consideration of the message was postponed to 16 April so that there might be more opportunity to prepare the accounts and present the details to the members of Parliament (Cobbett, *Parl. Hist.* xix. 103).

1. *Bélisaire,* 1767. An English translation with the title of *Belisarius* was published in the same year.

sensible and docile, I shall not agree with you. In truth, I have made up my mind in a superb contempt of everything present, not because I am old and prefer the days of my youth; I go much further back. Except yours, which can produce adamants that will resist time and live to be dug up in a brighter century, I am for totally discouraging genius. The soil in which it could shoot and flourish vigorously is worn out, at least in this island. It is a reprobated land in every sense, and if I were twenty years younger, I would seek a wiser country; for there is a joy in looking up to great men and admiring them; there is none to a generous mind in looking down on anybody, much less on all, and without any of the pride of virtue. I trust one may, without vanity, despise a world that respects nothing but gold, whether to hoard or squander. The contempt of money is no more a virtue than to wash one's hands is one; but one does not willingly shake hands with a man that never washes his.

Lord Chesterfield's *Characters* are published,[2] and are not even prettily written, as might have been expected. They are not so much as terse and quaint, which would not indeed have made them better, but they are even vulgar and ill expressed; one would think he did not know the personages well with whom he had been so conversant. This is not from prejudice that I speak, for my father's is tolerably impartial, and in some parts just, yet as it was preserved by his Lordship, so many years after the confutation was notorious, it shows old prejudice to tax him with having sacrificed everything to the purpose of making a great fortune.[3] He was born to £2500 a year, left a nominal estate of £8000, and died fifty thousand in debt.[4] Tom Windham[5] was more ingenuous, even though in opposition, and in the height of the clamour; going to see Longleat,[6] built by Sir John Thynne,[7]

2. *Characters of Eminent Personages of His Own Time, Written by the Late Earl of Chesterfield,* 1777. The first edition was apparently not advertised, and this letter is the earliest reference to it that has been found (Sidney L. Gulick, Jr, *A Chesterfield Bibliography to 1800,* 1935, p. 79). The second edition was published ca 24 April (*Public Advertiser* 21 and 24 April). The book may have been one of the three 'tracts relative to Lord Chesterfield' listed in the SH sale catalogue vii. 40.

3. 'Profuse and appetent, his ambition was subservient to his design of making a great fortune' (*Characters,* pp. 17–18).

4. For an account of Sir Robert's estate

and legacies see HW to Mann 15 April 1745, n. 3.

5. Probably Thomas Wyndham (1686–1752) of Clearwell, Glos, and Cromer, Norfolk; M. P. Truro 1721–7, Dunwich (Suffolk) 1727–34 (genealogical table in R. W. Ketton-Cremer, *Country Neighbourhood,* 1951, p. 224; *Members of Parliament,* pt ii, 1878, pp. 38, 51, 67, 79; information from Mr Ketton-Cremer).

6. Longleat, Wilts, the seat of Thomas Thynne, Vct Weymouth, 1st M. (1789) of Bath. HW's most extensive account of Longleat appears in *Country Seats* 45.

7. Sir John Thynne (d. 1580), Kt.

steward to the Protector Somerset,[8] and the man who showed the house (which by the way is a town in comparison) saying, 'It is a large house, but we don't pretend that it rivals Houghton,' Windham replied, 'No—yet I believe Mr Jenkins'[9] (my father's steward) 'has not built such an one.' The character of the Queen[10] is equally unjust: avarice was by no means her failing.[11] Lord Hardwicke is as ridiculously exalted.[12] More, Bacon, Clarendon were nothing to that mirrour of magistrates; you would think that Lord Chatham could have out-reasoned Lord Mansfield,[13] as easily as his thunder shook that aspen leaf. I do not recommend to your friend to copy these portraits in encaustic.

There is another scurrilous poem[14] by the author of *The Diaboliad*,[15] it is particularly hurled at the heads of the Hertfords.[16] The writer is supposed to be a Captain Coombes,[17] whose title to the office of censor-general, is having been guilty of forgery;[18] and to be executioner, to having married a common woman, who was kept by Lord

8. Edward Seymour (ca 1500–52), brother of Jane Seymour; cr. (1537) E. of Hertford and (1547) D. of Somerset; governor to his nephew, Edward VI, on his accession to the throne, and Protector of the realm 1547–9.

9. Who died in 1736 (GM 1736, vi. 55).

10. Caroline.

11. 'She loved money, but could occasionally part with it, especially to men of learning, whose patronage she affected' (*Characters*, p. 13).

12. Philip Yorke (1690–1764), cr. (1733) Bn and (1754) E. of Hardwicke; lord chancellor. See *Characters*, p. 33.

13. 'His [Chatham's] eloquence was of every kind, and he excelled in the argumentative, as well as in the declamatory way' (ibid. 46–7).

14. *The First of April; or the Triumphs of Folly: a Poem, Dedicated to a Celebrated Duchess* [Ds of Devonshire], *by the Author of the Diaboliad*, published 14 April 1777 (*Public Advertiser*). HW's copy is in his 'Poems of Geo. III' in the Harvard Library. The author was William Combe (1742–1823), satirist and editor, best known for his *Tours of Doctor Syntax*, illustrated by Thomas Rowlandson. The year of Combe's birth is established by Franz Montgomery, 'The Birth and Parentage of William Combe,' N&Q 1941, clxxx. 254–7.

15. Published earlier in 1777 (reviewed in *Monthly Review* Feb. 1777, lvi. 155); a satire directed chiefly against Lord Beauchamp (see nn. 19 and 21 below) and Lord Irnham. HW's annotated copy is now in the Harvard Library.

16. In a passage alluding to the marriage of Lady Frances Seymour-Conway to Lord Lincoln in May 1775:

'There H[ertford]'s Countess views the
          ducal heir,
With silent caution does the toils prepare,
And with her raw-boned daughters baits
          the snare.
The wretched B[eauchamp] sneaks behind
          to wait
The doubtful progress of his s[iste]r's fate,'
          etc. (p. 18).

A note on the passage charges the Hertfords with religious hypocrisy and adds that 'in the midst of affluence' they 'grasp at every means of domestic emolument.'

17. Combe's name does not appear in the *Army Lists*, but according to Thomas Campbell 'at one time he was driven for a morsel of bread to enlist as a private in the British army, and at another time in a similar exigency he went into the French service' (*Life of Mrs Siddons*, 1834, i. 42).

18. Combe's debts kept him for many years within the precincts of the King's Bench, but substantiation of this charge of forgery has not been found.

Beauchamp,[19] and dismissed by him for having *made him a present*[20] that she cannot pardon his not having pardoned, though he gave her £500 at parting.[21] Are not we an exemplary people?

The payment of the King's debts was gratefully accorded yesterday by those who had contributed to cause his necessities. Charles Fox made a great figure in behalf of Lord John's motion for a committee.[22] The latter apologized for the secession of his friends, on their finding they could do no good. Wilkes made a panegyric on the real King of France[23] for his tenderness to his brothers, unlike the gloomy tyrant —and then he paused—Louis XI.[24] In the Lords, Lord Rockingham and the Duke of Grafton differed on one motion, and agreed on another. I know nothing of the budget, but I am charmed with a new mode of government, which everybody else laughs at; I mean the decision of the directors of the East India Company, by tossing up heads and tails, whether Lord Pigot should be a prisoner or a nabob.[25] If

19. Francis Seymour-Conway (later Ingram-Seymour-Conway) (1743–1822), styled Vct Beauchamp 1750–93, E. of Yarmouth 1793–4; M. of Hertford, 1794; HW's first cousin once removed and his correspondent.

20. A venereal one, presumably.

21. This passage, beginning with 'and dismissed,' is now first printed from Mitford's transcripts of omitted passages, Add. MS. 32563 fol. 50. In his 'Book of Materials' 1771, p. 62, HW says that Beauchamp 'dismissed her for boundless infidelities, yet settled £300 a year on her. This creature egged on her husband, Combe, to satirize Lord Beauchamp and all his family, which he did in various satires with unbounded malice and virulence, but with some good poetry.' According to Thomas Campbell (op. cit. i. 42) Combe 'married the mistress of a noble Lord, who promised him an annuity with her, but cheated him, and in revenge he wrote a spirited satire entitled *The Diaboliad*.' Other satires in which Combe attacked Beauchamp and his family are *The Diabo-Lady*, 1777, in which Lady Augustus Fitzroy, Beauchamp's aunt, is crowned Queen of Hell; *The Diaboliad, Part II*, 1778, in which one of the candidates for the hellish throne is Mrs Damer, Beauchamp's cousin; and *The Justification*, 1777, directed chiefly against Beauchamp, of whom Combe says,

'While I can write, each winter shall afford

Its lashings for that mean, unpitied Lord.'
HW's copies of these, with many notes identifying the suppressed or disguised names, are among his 'Poems of Geo. III' in the Harvard Library.

22. On 16 April 1777 Lord John Cavendish moved that the King's request for money with which to pay his debts and to augment the civil list be referred to a committee of supply. Charles James Fox spoke for the motion, pointing out that evidence of the necessity of the requested money had not been shown. A brief account of the speech is in Cobbett, *Parl. Hist.* xix. 136–9.

23. That is, Louis XVI, not George III, whose title was 'King of Great Britain, France, and Ireland, Defender of the Faith,' etc.

24. 'Wilkes . . . mentioned the Duke of Gloucester, and said he was not abroad by choice; nor had the Duke of Cumberland, an amiable young prince, an income to live like a prince;—and then he extolled the King of France for his affection for his two brothers ['Monsieur' and the Comte d'Artois], who find in him an affectionate brother, not a gloomy tyrant—like Louis XI' (*Last Journals* ii. 21). The panegyric on Louis XVI is similarly worded in the full report of Wilkes's speech in Cobbett, *Parl. Hist.* xix. 108–22.

25. 'On Friday last the Court of Directors [of the East India Company] came to a

every nation was to be ruled by this compendious and impartial method, the people would on every occasion have an equal chance for happiness from every measure; and I beg to know where it is not three to one against them by every other mode. I would be content to live under the most despotic monarchy that could be devised, provided King Heads-and-Tails were the sovereign.

You wonder I say nothing on your second *Garden*.[26] No you don't. It is not upon any of the topics of the week, and the silent few that read from taste, come seldom in my way, who live half the week stark alone at Strawberry, and the rest of it with folks whose reading is the last thing I desire to hear them talk of; yet they do talk of it, for it is the *Morning Post*.[27] Lord Nuneham indeed told me tonight that a Lord of his acquaintance had taken your *Garden* for Gray's and did not like it. We were both very glad of both, and I am sure you agree with us. Adieu.

To Mason, Friday 2 May 1777

Printed from Mitford i. 291.

Arlington Street, May 2, 1777.

I ASK Mr Fraser to send you the *Incas:* I wish they may produce a thousandfold.

You must not expect news nor anything from me. I have been again involved in a sea of troubles; my nephew Lord Orford is relapsed and

ballot on the question, whether the majority of the Council of Madras should be suspended for having removed Lord Pigot from the government, when the numbers being equal, viz. eleven on each side, the Treasurer was brought in to decide by lot, and the lot falling upon the affirmative of the question, the whole Council of Madras was removed' (*London Chronicle* 12–15 April 1777, xli. 358).

26. Publication of the second book of Mason's *English Garden* was announced in the *London Chronicle* 10–12 April 1777, xli. 349.

27. The *Morning Post* was founded in 1772 by a group of business men as a 'daily advertising pamphlet,' but it was 'soon re-shaped as a regular newspaper and a shameless organ of the King's party and the ministry' (H. R. Fox Bourne, *English Newspapers*, 1887, i. 220). From 1775 to 1780 it was edited by Henry Bate (later Sir Henry Bate Dudley; see *post* 23 March 1782 and n. 15), who during that time 'was a very constant, diligent, zealous, and able, though perhaps too warm a writer on the part of government' (Lord North's memorandum to the King, ca 1782, *Corr. Geo. III* v. 471; cf. Bourne, loc. cit.). The *Morning Post* survived until 1937, when it was merged with the *Daily Telegraph*. See Wilfrid Hindle, *The Morning Post 1772–1937: Portrait of a Newspaper*, 1937.

I have passed the last ten days between the inn[1] at Barton Mills, and the hovel where he is five miles thence.[2] He is so far come to himself, that when he will speak, which is only in a whisper, his answers are rational. I will not tire you with the variety of my distresses which are manifold; doctors, lawyers, stewards, rogues and relations, take up my whole time.[3] I stole one day to walk through [Cambridge] and dine with old Cole;[4] I sighed to take the vows at the former. I think I could pass my last days there with great comfort. King's Chapel is more beautiful than Strawberry Hill. A bookish monk is a happy being, he is neither disposed to laugh, nor to feel, and scarce knows that the other two divisions are fools and villains. Adieu.

From MASON, Monday 12 May 1777

Printed from MS now WSL.
Address: The Honourable Horace Walpole, Arlington Street, London.
Postmark: YORK 14 MA.

York, May 12th, 1777.

I HAD heard of the melancholy account of your nephew's relapse only a day or two before I received your last favour, dated on the 2d, with the *Incas,* which I am obliged to you for and will take care to return safely at some convenient opportunity. But as I received them only yesterday cannot look into them till I get to Aston, where I hope to be next Saturday after taking a tour eastward to look after some *improved* farms of mine[1] which grow no corn and on which my tenants break, and which keep exact pace with all other improvements in this improving age of ours. Your journey to Barton Mills, melancholy as it must have been and which I sincerely condole with you for the cause of, could hardly be more comfortless than mine which I am about to take, but *parlons d'autres choses.*

I have found out an empty Gothic shrine in a conspicuous part of the Minster, which on measurement will exactly fit William de Hatfeild, in which I mean to place him (the Dean willing) at my next

1. The Bull, about eight miles north of Newmarket.
2. Lord Orford was living in the Rev. Dr Ball's parsonage at Eriswell, Suffolk.
3. For a more detailed account of HW's attendance upon his nephew see HW to Sir Edward Walpole 21, 22, and 25 April and HW to Mann 28 April 1777.

4. HW dined with Cole at his house at Milton, near Cambridge, 27 April 1777. See COLE ii. 43–4.

1. See *ante* p. 198 n. 1.

residence.[2] But I must do it at my own expense, I suspect; for though we have received five marks a year ever since the Reformation for *not* praying for the said William's soul, I do not think we shall be grateful enough to his alabaster body to place him in the said shrine, by expense of chapter. However, I think I can achieve this work for three or four guineas, and if you will go halves with me and write an inscription in right good classical-Gotho Latin you shall be heartily welcome. I think we cannot get or secure fame for our joint love of dead princes at a cheaper rate, than by this restoration of the said Prince William. You must send me also an exact blazon of his arms,[3] which my encaustic friend, who goes on very prosperously, has promised to encausticate gratis.

I am so over head and ears in epistolary debts that I must apply to my correspondents to pay them, and as I can safely say they brought me into this debt they cannot in conscience refuse the grant. You stand highest creditor in this letter-list and therefore my first application is to you. We expect and demand therefore that you take this short and dull scrawl for full payment of all the long and most entertaining letters we have received from you during our precentorial residence, and we promise to be more economical when we are found at Aston near Rotherham, where please to remember we are forthwith going, and so we heartily bid you

Farewell.

To MASON, Friday 16 May 1777

Printed from Mitford i. 371–3, where it is misdated 1778; date corrected by Mrs Toynbee.

May 16, 177[7].

AS a Goth, as a respecter of princes of the name of William[1] and as uncle of one of that name,[2] I certainly shall not refuse my mite to the re-enshrinement of the bones of poor William of Hatfield. I will

2. See *ante* 24 Aug. 1772 and n. 9. The statue was restored, through Mason's and HW's efforts. See *post* 16 and 26 May, and HW to Cole 25 Aug. 1772 and 22 May 1777 (COLE i. 275 and n. 7, ii. 46); see also J. B. Morrell, *York Monuments*, [1944], p. 5.

3. HW sought this information from Cole (COLE ii. 46 and 49).

1. HW considered William III 'the greatest man of modern times since his ancestor William Prince of Orange' (*post* ca 18 April 1778).

2. That is, William Henry, D. of Gloucester, married to HW's niece, Maria; and their son, William Frederick (1776–1834), D. of Gloucester, 1805.

willingly be at the whole expense if you will take care I shall have no honour from it, as I hate crowding one's name into Fame's account book, by bringing her in a bill for stone and mortar; you shall have his Royal Highness's arms too, and anything but the epitaph. I have neither time nor understanding left for writing anything. My nephew's situation will employ and poison all my leisure; and were it not my way to occupy every minute, I could not go through half I have to do, and all I wish to do I leave undone. If I forget Prince William's arms, you must put me in mind.

In all my trouble I cannot be forgetful of you. Here is come out a paltry supplement to Hume's *Life*,[3] with his will, a supplement to his vanity. He modestly orders only his name to be mentioned on his tomb, but appoints posterity his executors, and requires them to write an epitaph setting forth his great abilities according to the high opinion they will have of them.[4] *Voilà un philosophe*. The editor[5] grossly abuses you for what I hope you glory in, the publication of Gray's letters, in particular that which censures Hume,[5a] which the fool calls illiberal.[6] By Hume's own account of himself he attacked all religion in order to be talked of.[7] It is *illiberal* in a very moral man to be shocked at atheism! This is Scotch morality! The condemnation of Gray's letters is Scotch taste! The whole nation hitherto has been void of wit and humour, and even incapable of relishing it. The dull editor says Gray never thought his letters would see the light.[8] He does not perceive how much that circumstance enhances their merit; I do not

---

3. *A Supplement to the Life of David Hume, Esq.* Publication was announced in the *London Chronicle* 10–13 May 1777, xli. 455.

4. 'I also ordain, that if I shall die anywhere in Scotland, I shall be buried in a private manner in the Calton churchyard, the south side of it, and a monument be built over my body, at an expense not exceeding a hundred pounds, with an inscription containing only my name, with the year of my birth and death, leaving it to posterity to add the rest' (*Supplement*, 1789 edn, pp. 61–2).

5. Probably Samuel Jackson Pratt (1749–1814), actor and hack writer. See DNB, and T. E. Jessop, *A Bibliography of David Hume and of Scottish Philosophy from Francis Hutcheson to Lord Balfour*, 1938, p. 44; Samuel Halkett and John Laing,

Dictionary of Anonymous and Pseudonymous English Literature, 1926–34, v. 395.

5a. Gray to Beattie 2 July 1770. See *ante* 3 April 1775 and n. 5a.

6. 'The illiberal criticisms which Mr Gray threw out against him, in his epistolary correspondence, gave him much concern' (*Supplement*, pp. 8–10). To this the editor of the *Supplement* has added a footnote that begins: 'Perhaps the mercenary Mason is more deserving of this censure than Mr Gray.'

7. HW may be thinking of Hume's statement that a pamphlet which Bishop Hurd had written against his *Natural History of Religion* 'gave me some consolation for the otherwise indifferent reception of my performance' (*Life*, p. 21).

8. *Supplement*, p. 9.

wonder he is insensible of their charming beauties. Nobody yet ever wrote letters so well and his earliest have more marks of genius than his latest. Your crime does not lie in what you have given of Gray but of yourself. The Scots like to wound with another man's dagger; you will only smile at their impotence. I wish they could only stab with their pens,—

> The grey-goose quill that is thereon,
> In no man's blood will be wet.[9]

I know no news. You have seen the Speaker's remonstrance,[10] and how ably Charles Fox made the House adopt it, and consequently the condemnation of their own act.

I have seen Sheridan's new comedy,[11] and liked it much better than any I have seen since *The Provoked Husband*.[12] There is a great deal of wit and good situations; but it is too long, has two or three bad scenes that might easily be omitted, and seemed to me to want nature and truth of character; but I have not read it, and sat too high to hear it well. It is admirably acted. Burke has published a pamphlet on the American war, and an apology for his own secession and that of his friends.[13] I have not had time to look at it, but I do not believe I shall

9. HW has 'Chevy Chase' in mind:
'The grey-goose wing that was thereon
In his heart's blood was wet.'
See *The English and Scottish Popular Ballads*, ed. F. J. Child, Boston, 1883–98, iii. 313. The lines are quoted in *Spectator* No. 74. HW may possibly have been reminded of them by his perusal of Tyrwhitt's edition of Chatterton's Rowley poems (see *ante* 17 Feb. 1777), for Chatterton was clearly indebted to the ballad when he wrote, in his 'Battle of Hastings' (No. 1), ll. 199–200:
'The grey-goose pynion, that thereon was sett,
Eftsoons wyth smokyng crymson bloud was wett.'
10. On 7 May 1777 Sir Fletcher Norton (1716–89), cr. (1782) Bn Grantley, Speaker of the House of Commons 1770–80, presented to the King 'an act for the better support of his Majesty's household, and of the honour and dignity of the Crown of Great Britain.' In a speech commenting on what he considered to be the excessive generosity of the act, Norton observed that the House had 'not only granted to your Majesty a large present supply, but

also a very great additional revenue; great beyond example; great beyond your Majesty's highest expense.' On 9 May, in a debate on the income of the Dukes of Gloucester and Cumberland, Richard Rigby accused Norton of misrepresenting the state of affairs and of not expressing the sentiments of the House. Fox spoke against Rigby, and persuaded the House that Norton had honestly presented the views of the majority. See Cobbett, *Parl. Hist.* xix. 213 and 224–6.
11. *The School for Scandal*, first acted at Drury Lane 8 May 1777 (Genest v. 555).
12. Colley Cibber's completion (first acted 1728) of Vanbrugh's fragment, *A Journey to London*. See HW to Lord Strafford 11 Nov. 1774.
13. *A Letter from Edmund Burke, Esq., One of the Representatives in Parliament for the City of Bristol, to John Farr and John Harris, Esqrs, Sheriffs of that City, on the Affairs of America*. Publication was announced in the *London Chronicle* 15–17 May, xli. 467. In the letter Burke explains that his silence in the debate proceeded from his belief that 'it would

agree with him on the latter part so much as on the first.[14] Do not return me the *Incas;*[15] I shall never read it. I hear your *Garden* was criticized in the *Morning Post.*[16] Continue to plant

Flowers worthy of paradise,[17]

and do not mind their being trampled on in such a soil as this. Adieu! I wish I had leisure to chat with you longer.

From Mason, Monday 26 May 1777

Printed from MS now WSL.
Address: The Honourable Horace Walpole, Arlington Street, London.
Postmark: ROTHERHAM 29 MA.

Aston, May 26th, 1777.

I FOUND your obliging letter of the 16th when I returned hither out of the East Riding, enclosed in the supplement to David Hume's *Life,* which came safe and speedily by the Leeds coach; but how you came to find out that mode of conveyance puzzles me, 'tis however a very good one and drops any parcel at my door most conveniently and therefore *occasionally*[1] it may be a safer conveyance than the post. This same supplement I suspect is written by Murray,[1a] a Scotch bookseller with whom I have a chancery suit at present on account of his pirating Gray's poems.[2] About a fortnight ago he sent me

have been vain to oppose, and impossible to correct' the bill for suspending the Habeas Corpus Act (see *ante* 17 Feb. 1777), for he feared that active controversy would inflame 'the distemper of the public counsels' (*Letter,* pp. 17–19). HW's copy is now WSL.

14. I.e., HW was in substantial agreement with Burke in opposing the American war, but deplored Burke's silence on the suspension of the Habeas Corpus Act.

15. Apparently Mason did not return it, for it does not appear among the SH books.

16. Mason's strained poetic diction in *The English Garden* was ridiculed in a letter to the editor of the *Morning Post* 2 May 1777.

17. *Paradise Lost* iv. 241.

1. That is, when HW wants to comment on one of Mason's satires.

1a. John Murray (1745–93). He was born in Edinburgh, served as a lieutenant in the Marines, then settled in London, where, in 1768, he bought William Sandby's shop in Fleet Street (H. R. Plomer *et al., A Dictionary of the Printers and Booksellers . . . in England . . . from 1726 to 1775,* Oxford, 1932, pp. 177–8). The editor of the *Supplement,* however, is generally believed to have been Samuel Jackson Pratt.

2. In 1776 Murray published an edition of Gray incorporating three poems first printed by Mason in *Mem. Gray.* Mason obtained an injunction against him, granted 13 Feb. 1777, stopping the sale of the edition. Murray offered to settle out of court, but Mason professed himself chiefly interested in the establishment of a legal precedent (Gaskell 17 and n. 2). The case was decided in Mason's favour 11 July (*post* 27 July 1777). Samuel Smiles gives an

a printed letter[3] which he said, in a MS letter which accompanied it, that he should publish on the 21st instant,[4] but sent it me before, 'that he might not treat me with ill manners.' I suppose therefore the letter is now published, and I hope you have either read it or will read it immediately. I have nothing to say to it, but that I have got by it what Job wished for, when he said, 'O that my adversary had written a book, surely I would take it upon my shoulder and bind it as a crown to me,'[5] for the abuse is so gross and illiberal that I think it will tend greatly to give a right issue to the cause, and lead to the end for which I first instituted it, which you know was to procure an act in favour of authors, and prevent the piracy of booksellers. You will say I know that in times like these when there is no author fit to be read that cares whether his works be pirated or no, it is little worth while to aim at such a thing, but perhaps it may benefit posterity, and on that perhaps I mean to proceed.

I have waded through almost a volume of the *Incas*, but it was pain and grief to me. Your French *philosophes* think it incumbent upon them to turn preachers themselves after they think they have demolished preaching. But they turn out the dullest *prôneurs* in the world, insomuch that I should not wonder if a fine French *belle esprit* laid down her Diderot or her Marmontel and took up old Père Bourdaloue[6] merely *pour se désennuyer*. I am sure I can read my friend Jeremy Taylor[7] with great contentation after the most eloquent of them.

You must not expect the great honour of re-enshrining (not the bones but) the alabaster figure of William of Hatfeild unless you will share it with me and join your name to mine on the occasion. But as nothing can be done in this matter till my next residence, I hope to talk the thing over with you in London before that time.

account of the affair that is marked by obvious hostility to Mason (*A Publisher and His Friends: Memoir and Correspondence of the Late John Murray*, 1891, i. 15–7); in Mason's defence see John W. Draper, 'Queen Anne's Act: A Note on English Copyright,' *Modern Language Notes*, 1921, xxxvi. 146–54.

3. *A Letter to W. Mason, A. M., Precentor of York, Concerning His Edition of Mr Gray's Poems, and the Practices of Booksellers*.

4. It was published 21 June 1777 (*Public Advertiser*). The copy in the Yale Library contains on the fly-leaf the following MS note: 'A copy of this pamphlet was transmitted to Mr Mason three weeks before publication, and every reasonable expedient used by the author to suppress it, but without success.' A second note in an unidentified hand reads: 'The above is the handwriting of John Murray I.'

5. Job 31. 35–6.

6. Louis Bourdaloue (1632–1704), Jesuit preacher, author of several volumes of sermons.

7. Jeremy Taylor (1613–67), author of *Holy Living* and *Holy Dying*.

I hear our Archbishop[8] has preached a fine Tory-rory sermon about propagating the gospel,[9] and seems inclined rather to propagate popery than Presbyterianism,[10] but I cannot get a sight of it though I writ a month ago to Montagu[11] to send it to me. This is unlucky, because as I am catechizing my parish in order to prepare them for his Grace's confirmation, I ought to learn the proper way of expounding to them what is meant by that spiritual grace which his archiepiscopal palm is to convey to them.

I suppose Burke's pamphlet is made out of the paper which he drew up in the beginning of last winter for the use of his friends in the minority and which they had not the courage to make use of. I had a sight of it, and thought it in many parts excellently written. I have no chance of seeing it till the Parliament breaks up and Mr Montagu returns into my neighbourhood.[12]

I am anxious to have better accounts of Lord Orford for your sake, but would not wish you till then to pain yourself on so melancholy a subject. Believe that I interest myself most cordially in your concerns and that I am, dear Sir,

Most truly yours,

W. MASON

To MASON, Tuesday 10 June 1777

Printed from Mitford i. 380–3, where it is misdated 1778; date corrected by Mrs Toynbee.

Strawberry Hill, June 10, 177[7].

IF you wonder you have not heard from me *voici pourquoi*. I might plead business, but though I have enough, that was not the impedi-

8. William Markham, translated from Chester to the archiepiscopal see of York in January 1777.

9. *A Serman Preached before the Incorporated Society for the Propagation of the Gospel in Foreign Parts . . . in the Parish Church of St Mary-le-Bow on Friday, February 21, 1777*. It was printed, but was not offered for public sale until interest in it was aroused by a violent debate on its sentiments in the House of Lords 30 May 1777 (*Monthly Review* May 1777, lvi. 404; *Last Journals* ii. 29–30). Markham's theme

was the necessity of employing the machinery of the state in spreading Christianity. He devoted a considerable part of the sermon to a condemnation of the Americans.

10. Markham declared that 'the laws enacted against papists have been extremely severe; but they were not founded on any difference in religious sentiments' (*Sermon*, p. 17). He expressed his approval of a tolerant policy towards the Catholic clergy of Canada (ibid. 23–4).

11. Frederick Montagu.

12. Montagu lived at Papplewick, Notts.

ment. The true reason why I have not written was, because I have. I wrote to you above a week agone intending Mr Montagu should be the bearer, and gave it to Mr Stonhewer, but lo! his friend was set out, and the former returned my epistle to me. As the news it contained would be still-born, instead of being so lazy as to send it, I begin anew.

You now know all the history of your warlike metropolitan Archbishop Turpin.[1] I hope he made his entrance into his capital by beat of drum; if he attains what he deserves, and perhaps ambitions, a red hat, I shall beg to present him with that of his predecessor, Wolsey, out of my own museum;[2] but I hope he will never be able to say with that son of a butcher, and with equal foundation from his pulpit, *Ego et Rex meus*. My brother, who is no American, is exceedingly scandalized at this champion of high church. This vulture has been so plumed in both his flights,[3] that I fancy his successor will learn to mix the prudence of the serpent with the timidity of the dove, and creep on his belly instead of soaring.

Your adversary Murray is a blackguard; you may bear to have filth thrown at you, when it is at the Duchess of Devonshire[4] and at the youngest and handsomest women in town. It is a polished, sweet-tempered age.

What care you about all the new promotions?[5] or what cares any-

1. William Markham (alluding to the warlike Archbishop in the *Chanson de Roland*). 'Lord Shelburne was still more severe on the Archbishop of York, who rose with most intemperate pride and fury, and said, that though, as a Christian and bishop, he ought to bear wrongs, there were injuries that would provoke any patience, and that he, if insulted, *should know how to chastise any petulance*' (*Last Journals* ii. 29). For a fuller account of Markham's speech in the House of Lords 30 May 1777, see Cobbett, *Parl. Hist.* xix. 347–8.

2. 'The red hat of Cardinal Wolsey, found in the Great Wardrobe by Bishop Burnet when Clerk of the Closet. From his son the Judge [Sir Thomas Burnet] it came to the Countess Dowager of Albemarle, who gave it to Mr Walpole' ('Des. of SH,' *Works* ii. 455). The early history of the hat was given by Lady Albemarle in the letter she sent to HW with it: 'This hat was Cardinal Wolsey's, and when Bishop Burnet was Clerk of the Closet to Queen Anne, he took it *or stole it* out of the Wardrobe, and left it to his son

Judge Burnet. He gave it to his house-keeper, and she gave it to Gerrard my butler, who gave it to me who beg Mr Walpole's acceptance of it. Sunday, Nov. 28, 1776.' The hat was sold SH xvii. 73 to Charles Kean for £21, and is now in the library of Christ Church, Oxford.

3. The sermon and the Archbishop's speech in the House of Lords were subjected to severe criticism.

4. William Combe's *A Letter to the Duchess of Devonshire* and *A Second Letter to the Duchess of Devonshire,* charging her with frivolity and irresponsibility, had recently been published (*Critical Review* May 1777, xliii. 397). Combe had also lampooned her in several satirical poems: *The Duchess of Devonshire's Cow, a Poem; An Heroic Epistle to the Noble Author of the Duchess of Devonshire's Cow;* and *The Duchess of Devonshire's Bull to the Duchess's Cow, a Poetical Epistle (Public Advertiser* 20 May, 3 June 1777). HW is perhaps also thinking of Combe's *First of April (ante* 18 April 1777, n. 14), dedicated to the Duchess.

5. A list of new appointments by the

body but the promoted and the disappointed? one of the latter, Lord Howe, is the only one worth naming. He expected to be treasurer of the navy,[6] because the appointments of commanders-in-chief and ambassadors,[7] are not sufficient to content that family. Their sister[8] declares the quarrel[9] is irreconcilable. It is a disinterested age.

I send you six *Gazettes littéraires;*[10] you needed not to celebrate the conveyance.[11] Mr S[tonhewer] and I do not reckon you the pink of discretion.

I have almost finished the first volume of Dr Robertson.[12] The materials are well put together, and it is a book that must please anybody to whom the matter is new. In short, it is not all so, and though the arrangement is good, I see no genius nor shrewdness, none of that penetration that shone in the *History of Scotland* and totally left him in his *Charles V.*[13] Two expressions have shocked me: speaking of that indefatigable good man Las Casas,[14] who laboured to rescue the poor Americans from the tyranny of their conquerors, the Doctor calls it a *bustling* activity,[15] and says he was ashamed to show his face after the fatal termination of his *splendid* schemes;[16] what epithets for so humane a design! Could Archbishop Markham in a sermon before

King is given in the *Public Advertiser* 7 June 1777.

6. The post was given instead to the Hon. Welbore Ellis (ibid.).

7. The British army in America was commanded by Sir William Howe, the navy by his brother, Richard (1726–99), 4th Vct Howe, 1758; cr. (1788) E. Howe. A commission empowering the Howes to treat for peace with the Colonies had been given them early in May 1776. 'The pay and emoluments of Lord Howe and his brother are said to be greater than those ever received by any two officers on the public service before. As commissioners for accommodating matters with the Congress only, they have twenty pounds each *per diem*' (*Public Advertiser* 19 June 1777).

8. Mrs John Howe (*ante* 20 Nov. 1775, n. 2).

9. Between her brothers and the administration.

10. *Gazette littéraire de l'Europe, par une société de gens de lettres,* published monthly at Amsterdam 1764–85 (A.-A. Barbier, *Dictionnaire des ouvrages anonymes,* 1872–9, ii. 525).

11. That is, since HW had sent his letter of 16 May by the Leeds coach to avoid the possibility of its being opened in the post, it was reckless of Mason to mention it. See *ante* 26 May 1777.

12. William Robertson's *History of America,* published 28 May 1777 (*Public Advertiser*). Robertson sent HW a copy, which HW acknowledged 30 May (Dalrymple 136 and n. 1).

13. See *ante* 18 Feb. 1776.

14. Bartolomé de las Casas (1474–1566), Spanish theologian, historian, and missionary in the new world, called the 'Apostle of the Indians.'

15. 'Las Casas . . . possessed a bustling indefatigable activity, which sometimes accomplishes its purposes with greater success, than the most exquisite discernment and address' (*The History of America,* i. 224).

16. 'Astonished at such a succession of disasters, Las Casas was ashamed to show his face after the fatal termination of all his splendid schemes' (ibid. i. 236).

the society for propagation of the gospel by fire and sword, paint charity in more contemptuous terms? It is a Christian age.

I retract saying I have found nothing new; I did not know that great part of the Spanish clergy adopted the compassion of Las Casas.[17] I did not know that Las Casas, and there he was culpably bustling indeed! suggested the idea of supplying the Spanish settlements with African slaves.[18] This was guilt with a witness, for any lucrative mischief has fifty times more chance of being adopted, than a humane plan that combats interest. What contradictions we are! Las Casas had reason not to show [his] face, not because the one scheme failed, but because the other succeeded.[19] Is not he a fine historian who insinuates that a virtuous man ought to blush if the perversity of the age defeats his efforts to correct it? The doctrine no doubt will be applauded by all who have rendered *patriots* an opprobrious term for those who laboured to prevent the effusion of English and American blood. It is a tender-hearted age.

My nephew continues sullen and calm. This saves me alarms though not business and fatigue, yet I can get repose here, and now and then a moment to amuse myself; my Beauclerc Tower is almost finished. Adieu.

17. 'The missionaries, in conformity to the mild spirit of that religion which they were employed to publish, early remonstrated against the maxims of their countrymen with respect to the Americans, and condemned the *repartimientos,* or *distributions,* by which they were given up as slaves to their conquerors, as no less contrary to natural justice and the precepts of Christianity, than to sound policy' (ibid. i. 215).

18. Ibid. i. 225. Las Casas 'once, early in his career, advised that Negroes born as slaves in Spain should be brought to work in America to spare the Indians, but soon after declared that, since learning that the Portuguese had captured and enslaved them unjustly, he now believed "that it is as unjust to enslave Negroes as it is to enslave Indians, and for the same

reasons"' (Lewis Hanke, *The Spanish Struggle for Justice in the Conquest of America,* Philadelphia, 1949, p. 125, quoting from Las Casas, *Historia de las Indias,* Book iii, c. 102; see also George Edward Ellis, 'Las Casas and the Relations of the Spaniards to the Indians,' in *Narrative and Critical History of America,* ed. Justin Winsor, Boston, 1884–9, ii. 312).

19. In his copy of Robertson (now in the Dyce Collection, Victoria and Albert Museum) HW notes on i. 236, 'Las Casas had no reason for not showing his face, because his virtuous views were defeated; but he had, because his abominable project for sending African slaves to America was adopted. In that he was a bustling projector, and a lamentable instance of the contradictions in human nature!'

From MASON, Saturday 21 June 1777

Printed from MS now WSL.
Address: The Honourable Horace Walpole, Arlington Street, London.
Postmark: ROTHERHAM 24 JU.

Aston, June 21st, 1777.

I FOUND your favour of the 10th with the *Gazettes littéraires* (for both which many thanks) at Sheffeild on the 18th just after I had taken my leave of my diocesan[1] at his visitation,[2] who was then setting out for Wentworth Castle, on the invitation of its noble owner;[3] except from him and the Duke of Newcastle I do not find he has received any civilities hitherto on his progress. I, indeed, the day before, treated him with a stinking turbot at Aston. But I and my stinking turbot are nothing. The papers will tell you how he puffed his predecessor Robin Goodfellow[4] in his charge.[5] And except this, which gave great offence to everybody who knew Robin's real character,[6] that is to say the whole body of the clergy who heard him, save one unprovided-for chaplain who wept bitterly—except this I say, all other matters went off quietly and dully enough in conscience. Though naturally very ungracious in his manner, dry, reserved, and absent, he put on his most benign aspect to your humble servant, and invited both me and my portmanteau to Bishopthorpe,[7] which I returned with two bows, one for my portmanteau and another for myself.—I feel no little comfort in finding his Grace now northward of me, for almost all my time the fortnight before was taken up in parochial preparations, such as

1. The Archbishop of York.
2. To Nottingham, where he confirmed 7000 persons (*Lloyd's Evening Post* 16–18 June 1777, xl. 580).
3. Lord Strafford.
4. Robert Hay Drummond (1711–76), Bp of St Asaph, 1748, of Salisbury, 1761, Abp of York 1761–76. HW describes him as 'a sensible, worldly man, but much addicted to his bottle' (*Last Journals* i. 593). To Mason, who also called him 'Robin Goodfellow' in a letter to Alderson 3 June 1774, he was something less forgivable than 'a knavish sprite.'
5. 'His Grace went to the chancel, and after the clergy were called over, addressed them in a short but pathetic charge, when he began with lamenting the loss to the clergy in the late Archbishop, and which

he himself particularly felt, who had had a long and intimate acquaintance with him in the early part of his life, by which he had frequent opportunities of observing his great virtues and abilities, both natural and acquired' (*Lloyd's Evening Post* 16–18 June 1777, xl. 580).
6. Some months before Archbishop Drummond's death Mason had written: 'As a fracas which I have just had with Parson Evans will, I imagine, set the Archbishop and me at absolute daggers drawing, we must expect he will revenge himself as a Christian prelate should do, on everybody that I am a friend to' (Mason to Alderson 6 April 1776).
7. The Archbishop's palace, a few miles south of York.

THE OLD RECTORY AND CHURCH AT ASTON

making out terriers,[7a] catechizing children, writing them confirmation tickets, etc., etc., preaching on the subject, etc., etc., all which you have no conception of, and would think it, if you had, my curate's business. Yet I had my reasons for taking it upon myself as much as possible on the present occasion. Nevertheless, I have done something else; 'Are you advised of that?' as Mrs Quickly says.[8] No; but I trust you will ere long. But the conveyance though safe is so uncertain in point of time, witness your *Gazettes littéraires* (which ought to have been dropped at my door five days before I found them ten miles off at Sheffeild) that I shall find another method of giving you a sight of the drawings to which I allude,[9] therefore you must wait with patience till they arrive.

I must tell you one speech which I made to his Grace, as I have no speeches of other folks to send you. He praised my house and said it must have cost me a good deal of money.[10] I said it did, and perhaps I was imprudent to lay out so much, but it gave me consolation to think I had by doing so, made a pretty adequate return to Lord H[oldernesse] for his patronage, especially as the living was retained in the family; and as to the situation I thought it so pleasant that a man might very well preserve his independency in it, the only thing which I thought worth preserving. His Grace was silent, but whether his silence gave consent to the opinion, I pretend not to determine.

I will add no more till you receive my drawings, which as they are done in a pretty free way will, I hope, please you well enough to excuse my writing you a longer letter. I do not expect you to put them up in the Beauclerk Tower which, by the way, I long much to see, but I find no possibility of coming southward this year.

Believe me, dear Sir,

Very sincerely yours,

W. Mason

7a. Parish records of lands.

8. 'Are you avised o' that? You shall find it a great charge. . . . To tell you in your ear,—I would have no words of it . . .' (*The Merry Wives of Windsor* I. iv. 105).

9. Mason's anxiety over the safety of the conveyance suggests fear of censorship and that the 'drawings' are his *Epistle to Dr Shebbeare* and *Ode to Sir Fletcher Norton*. See *post* 27 July 1777.

10. 'Mason pulled down the old rectory [at Aston] and built another very commodious house, changing the site, so as from his windows to command a beautiful and extensive prospect, bounded by the Derbyshire hills' (Mitford's note in his edition of *The Correspondence of Thomas Gray and William Mason*, 1853, p. 210).

To Mason, Sunday 6 July 1777

Printed from Mitford i. 298–300.

Strawberry Hill, July 6, 1777.

I DON'T know anybody so much in the wrong as you are for not coming to me this summer; you would see such a marvellous closet, so small, so perfect, so respectable, you would swear it came out of Havering in the Bower,[1] and that Catherine de Valois[2] used to retire into it to write to Owen Tudor.[3] Lady Di's drawings[4]—no offence to yours, are hung on Indian blue damask,[5] the ceiling, door and surbase are gilt, and in the window are two brave fleurs-de-lis and a lion of England, all royally crowned in painted glass,[6] which as Queen Catherine never did happen to write a *billet doux* in this closet, signify Beauclerc, the denomination of the Tower. This cabinet is to be sacred and not shown to the profane, as the drawings are not for the eyes of the vulgar. Yours shall have a place, which is the greatest honour I can do them.[7] Miss Pope[8] the actress, who is at Mrs Clive's,[9] dined here yesterday, and literally shed tears, though she did not know the story.[10] I think this is more to Lady Di's credit, than a tomtit pecking at painted fruit. The ceiling was fortunately finished some time

1. A royal mansion at Pyrgo in the liberty of Havering-atte-Bower, Essex, was used in the late Middle Ages as a dower house for the queens of England. In 1559 Queen Elizabeth granted the manor to Sir John Grey. The old mansion was torn down in 1770 and replaced by a new building. See HW to Mann 25 May 1765; Thomas Wright, *The History and Topography of the County of Essex*, 1836, ii. 430–1; George Terry, *Memories of Old Romford and Other Places within the Royal Liberty of Havering-atte-Bower*, 1880, pp. 20–1; Joseph H. Pemberton, 'Havering-atte-Bower,' *Essex Review*, 1899, viii. 188.

2. Catherine of Valois (1401–37), Queen of Henry V. Evidence that she ever used Havering has not been found. At the time of Owen Tudor's courtship of Catherine the house was probably occupied by Joan of Navarre, the widow of Henry IV, who died at Pyrgo in 1437.

3. Owen Tudor (d. 1461), m. (ca 1429) the widowed Queen Catherine.

4. Of seven scenes from HW's *Mysterious Mother* (ante 18 Feb. 1776 and n. 23).

5. 'For 36 yards of blue Indian damask for the Beauclerc Closet: 18-18-0' (*SH Accounts* 16).

6. 'In the window is a lion and two fleurs-de-lis, royally crowned, ancient, but repaired and ornamented by Price; and, being bearings in the royal arms, serve for Beauclerc' ('Des. of SH,' *Works* ii. 503). The glass was bought in by Lord Waldegrave at the SH sale xxiv. 54, but was subsequently removed.

7. HW is harking back to Mason's remark in the preceding letter, 'I do not expect you to put them up in the Beauclerk Tower.' Whether he understood Mason as meaning actual drawings (ante 21 June, n. 9) is not clear, but no drawings by Mason were placed in the Tower.

8. Jane Pope (1742–1818), noted for her soubrette parts.

9. Little Strawberry Hill.

10. Of *The Mysterious Mother*.

ago. My plasterer is turned raving Methodist, and has sent me a frantic letter[11] without sense or grammar, but desiring leave to open me a new plan of the gospel. I am glad he had no *new light* about making stucco!

Those gentry the Methodists will grow very troublesome, or worse; they were exceedingly unwilling to part with that impudent hypocrite Dr Dodd, and not less, to have forgery criminal. I own I felt very much for the poor wretch's protracted sufferings[12]—but that was not the motive of their countenance; I cannot bear a militant arch-inquisitor,[13] or an impostor in a tabernacle. Thank you for your reply to the former,[14] etc.

I have no more *Gazettes littéraires,* or *politiques.* Linguet, the outcast of France, has published one[15] here that makes some noise; part is satire on us, part panegyric,[16] but in general very superficial. I have an anecdote apropos to him that is very curious. I will tell it you some day or other, but as it is a secret, I must not communicate it to the post office.

They have sent me from town a fourth volume of the *Archæologia,*[17] or old women's logic; the first paragraph[18] is as complete nonsense as my plasterer's letter.

Don't let this horrid weather[19] put you out of humour with your *Garden,* though I own it is pity we should have brought gardening to perfection, and have too bad a climate to enjoy it. It is strictly true

11. Missing.

12. Dodd's trial was held on 22 Feb. 1777, but a legal technicality delayed the sentence until 26 May. The attempts of Johnson and others to obtain a pardon for him added to the delay, and he was not executed until 27 June.

13. The Archbishop of York. See *ante* 26 May and 10 June 1777.

14. As reported by Mason *ante* 21 June 1777.

15. The first volume of *Annales politiques, civiles, et littéraires du dix-huitième siècle* was published in Paris and London in 1777. The author, Simon-Nicolas-Henri Linguet (1736–94) was a lawyer and controversialist who was in continual difficulty with his country's government.

16. Such as Linguet's 'Tableau de l'Angleterre' in *Annales,* i. 249–318.

17. Published 1 July 1777 (*Public Advertiser*).

18. Of the first article in the volume, 'A Further Account of Some Remains of Roman and Other Antiquities in or near the County of Brecknock in South Wales,' by John Strange (1732–99): 'Though many circumstances particularly favour the researches of the early antiquaries in all countries; yet the attempts of the latter are not altogether useless, and deserve the more encouragement, as they are commonly attended with greater difficulties' (*Archæologia,* 1777, iv. 1–2). HW has noted opposite this in his copy (now WSL), 'This first sentence is absolute nonsense.'

19. 'Persons conversant in rural affairs say that the harvest will be later this season than for fifteen years, as it is so long since we have had so wet a summer' (*Public Advertiser* 9 July 1777).

this year as I have often said, that ours is the most beautiful country in the world, when framed and glazed; but remember you can make the sun shine when you please, and as much as you please, and yet the verdure of your garden will be ever green. You are an excellent parish priest, catechize and make terriers I believe in perfection; but pray do not forget poor poetry, your natural vocation, as you have done so long; but you must be everything, an inventor of musical instruments, a painter, and a law suitor—

Besides a hundred freaks that died in thinking.[20]

Well, I cannot help loving you with all your faults and all your perfections.

I am just now in great trouble, though a little relieved today by a better account. The Duke of Gloucester is extremely ill,[21] and my poor niece in despair![22] They are coming if they can to England for a little time, as the heat of the south is too mighty for him. How dear has ambition cost her! Adieu.

As it is right to be impartial, which I am not naturally, I must tell you that at the end of the new *Archæologia* there is a very good essay on ancient castles,[23] with very curious matter, by a Mr King.[24] I don't know who he is,—but it rains again, and there is no bearing it.

From Mason, Sunday 27 July 1777

Printed from MS now WSL.
Address: The Honourable Horace Walpole, Arlington Street, London.
Postmark: ROTHERHAM 29 JY.

Aston, July 27th, 1777.

Dear Sir,

FOR the last fortnight of fine weather I said to myself, 'Lounge, sleep, and be idle, break not thy repose even by writing a letter.'

20. 'Besides ten thousand freaks that died in thinking' (Dryden, *Absalom and Achitophel,* l. 552).

21. 'Yesterday an express arrived at St James's, from Rome, with an account of the Duke of Gloucester being dangerously ill, that his death was hourly expected' (*London Chronicle* 3–5 July 1777, xlii. 24). See HW to Lady Ossory 6 July 1777. A circumstantial account of the Duke's illness and its political implications is given in *Last Journals* ii. 51–68.

22. Dr Jebb gave her little hope for the Duke's recovery; her son, Prince William Frederick was ill; and the hostility of the King made her future prospects uncertain. See *Last Journals* ii. 52–4.

23. Pp. 364–413.

24. Edward King (ca 1735–1807), F.R.S., F.S.A. HW later exchanged a few letters with him.

I did so, but a great thunder-storm[1] after drowning me fourteen good acres of hay, and afterwards leaving them to rot under a cold dun sky, has driven me again to my fireside and to my *portfeuille,* where I find your favour of the 6th, to my shame, unanswered. You, who care not a rush about your own hay, will not call the spoiling of mine any judgment upon me, for my *accidie,* which Chaucer's parson will tell you is one of the deadliest of the seven deadly sins[2]. My quondam patron and patroness[3] are gone to Hornby Castle, and have called my curate Alderson thither. I conjecture the thunder-storm would just give them the meeting about Ferrybridge,[4] which would serve to corroborate her Ladyship's good opinion of the north, especially as it has been succeeded by such cold and comfortless weather. I suppose my Lord and Lady Carmarthen[5] are of the party and a pleasant one I trust it is. Had I not reason when I pronounced that paw[6] word independency[7] to the Archbishop, to be proud that I could pronounce it?

Nobody sends me anything but you. It was but yesterday that the *Epistle to Dr Shebbeare*[8] reached Aston, and that not sent to me but to Mr Verelst. There are good lines in it, and a happy mixture of the careless and serious, the burlesque and heroic. The ode, too, has its merit, but it seems *manqué,* all the lines in Horace are not alluded to, as *nomen tulit ab Africa,* and *Carthaginis flammæ impiæ,*[9] etc., which in these kind of imitations ought always to be observed. Tell me whether this criticism be not a just one. You should have contrived to have let me had [*sic*] a copy of this, because I ought not to come after an East India governor[10] in early intelligence of this sort.

What a glorious figure does Great Britain as Empress of the Sea, make in the papers of the last week![11] I fancy we shall hear in a short

---

1. On 23 July (*London Chronicle* 31 July–2 Aug. 1777, xlii. 114).
2. The fourth sin in *The Parson's Tale* is 'accidie,' or sloth.
3. Lord and Lady Holdernesse.
4. A hamlet in the West Riding of Yorkshire, on the south bank of the Ayr river.
5. Lord Holdernesse's daughter.
6. 'Improper, naughty, obscene' (OED).
7. See *ante* 21 June 1777.
8. Mason's *Epistle to Dr Shebbeare. To which is added, An Ode to Sir Fletcher Norton, in Imitation of Horace Ode VIII, Book IV. By Malcolm MacGreggor, of Knightsbridge, Esq.; Author of the Heroic Epistle to Sir William Chambers, etc.* Publication was announced 2 July 1777 (*Public Advertiser*). Since this letter was sent by

the post, Mason conceals his connection with these satires, as he did in his letters concerning the *Heroic Epistle* and *Heroic Postscript.*
9. 'Non incendia Carthaginis impiæ
   eius, qui domita nomen ab Africa
   lucratus rediit, clarius indicant
   laudes—'
        (Horace, *Odes* IV. viii. 17–20.)
('—Nor the burning of wicked Carthage, disclose more gloriously the fame of him who came back home, having won his name from Africa's subjection'—trans. C. E. Bennett.)
10. Harry Verelst was governor of Bengal 1767–9.
11. 'The power of Great Britain never received such insults in any former war,

time that Dublin[12] is in the possession of the provincials. I had rather
it were Edinburgh for the sake of my Scotch bookseller. After Great
Britain I think Mason versus Murray[13] makes no contemptible éclat,
'tis quite a pleasure to see one's name so public.[14] My lawyers[15] give
me a pleasant account of my Lord Chancellor's[16] decision, who acquitted the said Murray of a contempt of his court because he was advised to it by an attorney. Hence in chancery as at St Omer's[17] you may
do what you please provided you have the opinion of a Doctor to support you. And I suppose our attorneys are full as good as their
casuistical divines, at least his Lordship thinks so. I should be glad to
hear in your next what accounts there are of the D⟨uke⟩ of Gloucester, and pray send me all the ⟨?news⟩[18] you can, and *Gazettes littéraires* when you can spare them. Were you to send packets to Mr
Verelst's house in St James's Square with a card to Mr Manesty[19] saying only, 'Mr Manesty is desired to forward this parcel to Aston the
first time he sends anything down to Mr Verelst,' I should receive them
safe and with little trouble to your servants.

Yours very sincerely,

W. MASON

as in the present with the Colonies. Their privateers beset our coasts so diligently, that even a company out upon a party of pleasure in the west, were near falling into their hands. Where is that vigilance and activity that for ages distinguished the naval force of this once formidable country?' (*Public Advertiser* 18 July 1777).

12. Alarming news about Ireland appeared continually. The *Public Advertiser* on 16 July reported: 'Dublin has been thrown into the utmost consternation by the appearance of the American privateers on this coast. A stop is put to all trade.'

13. See *ante* 26 May 1777 and n. 2.

14. 'Yesterday morning [Friday 11 July] came on the famous cause between the Rev. Mr Mason, executor of Mr Gray, and a bookseller. After many arguments it was determined in favour of Mr Mason' (*London Chronicle* 10–12 July 1777, xlii. 48). By this decision Mason established his property in the three poems by Gray ('The Death of Hoel,' 'On the Death of Richard West,' and 'Epitaph on Sir William Wil-

liams') that he had printed for the first time in *Mem. Gray.* In 1778 Murray brought out a new edition omitting the three poems, with an explanatory 'Advertisement.' The Chancellor's decision of 11 July 1777 was apparently an interim decree, for the final decree in Mason's favour was not granted until 1779 (*post* 1 Aug. 1779 and n. 4). The case, which established an important point in copyright law, is cited and summarized in *English Reports* xxix (*Chancery* ix), 47, Carnan vs Bowles (1786).

15. 'Mr Attorney-General, Mr Solicitor-General, Mr Parry, and Mr Fitzherbert were counsel for the plaintiff in this cause' (*London Chronicle,* loc. cit.).

16. Lord Bathurst.

17. The Jesuit college for English Catholics, founded at St Omer by the Rev. Robert Parsons in 1592.

18. Word lost when the seal was broken.

19. Presumably Verelst's steward or secretary.

To Mason, Monday 4 August 1777

Printed from Mitford i. 303–6.

Strawberry Hill, Aug. 4, 1777.

YOU know I do not stand upon debtor and creditor with you, but should have indulged my pleasure of writing to you if I had been master of a moment's leisure or peace of mind. The various distresses and misfortunes of my family have engrossed me entirely. My nephew continues to fluctuate between violence and stupidity; as the last is not alarming, and there are scarce hopes of any comfortable recovery, I am inclined to wish it took place totally. In the mean time his affairs are as distracted, and have driven me into a paper war with his agent.[1] The Duke of Gloucester is still exceedingly ill;[2] Dr Jebb flatters us he shall bring him to England, but promises nothing more. The Bishop of Exeter [who] has been dying these nine months at last seems recovering.[3] All these calamities and their consequential details have left me no time for amusement or attention to anything else, and unless American privateers attack Hampton Court, I shall forget almost that there are thirteen colonies. In good truth they seem fully able to take care of themselves, nay, at leisure to return our invasions. If they burn Edinburgh, I shall not cry fire. Lord John Cavendish is returned from a visit to his sister[4] in Ireland, and gives a droll description of Viceroy Buckingham's[5] entrenchments,[6] which are not quite so strong as dictator Washington's, except in gin shops. The

1. Carlos Coney (fl. 1774–81), son of Edwin Coney, High Sheriff of Norfolk, 1734 (*Miscellanea genealogica et heraldica*, 1877, new ser., ii. 545; *English Reports* ci. 899). HW considered him a 'rascal' (HW to Mann 26 Feb. 1781).

2. 'No accounts have been received from the Duke of Gloucester since the 27th ult. dated the 15th. The above accounts mentioned his Royal Highness as being a little better, but in a very low state of health; they also mentioned the arrival of Dr Jebb and Mr Adair the same day' (*London Chronicle* 2–5 Aug. 1777, xlii. 122).

3. These hopes were ill-founded. Bishop Keppel, HW's nephew by marriage, died 27 Dec. 1777.

4. Lady Elizabeth Cavendish (d. 1796), m. (1743) the Hon. John Ponsonby (1713–89), Speaker of the Irish House of Commons 1756–69 (Burke, *Peerage*, 1953, p. 196, *sub* Bessborough; Robert Beatson, *Political Index*, 1806, iii. 343).

5. John Hobart (1723–93), 2d E. of Buckinghamshire, had succeeded Harcourt as Lord Lieutenant of Ireland 18 Dec. 1776.

6. 'His Excellency the Lord Lieutenant, in order to secure the shipping in the [Dublin] harbour from any hostile attempts from the American privateers cruising at this time in the channel, sent yesterday from the arsenal in the castle ten pieces of cannon, under the care of two detachments of artillery, and parties of the eleventh regiment of foot, one of which has raised a battery of four long six-pounders at the extremity of the North Wall, and the other a battery of six cannons at the Pigeon House, on the South Wall' (*London Chronicle* 8–10 July 1777, xlii. 40).

rest of the encampment consists in three tents. The Ossianites rave against Howe.[7] Madame de Noailles[8] the ambassador's wife arrives today[9] with a sprig, I believe, of rue in her mouth merely to keep her from laughing.[10] Cunningham[11] sailed from Dunkirk with orders to be very civil till in wide ocean,[12] but mistook the channel for it, and made nine prizes,[13] which if he sent to Dunkirk will obtain his pardon. I heard this morning that France has fifteen thousand men in India,[14] who I suppose have orders not to take Bengal within sight of the French coast. A good courtesan[15] told me last night, as a counterpoise to all these *unforeseen accidents,* that Lord Chatham has had a fall from his horse, in a fit.[16]—The bells are ringing—perhaps on that account.

I have no more *Gazettes littéraires* yet, but I have a new work that I will lend you, that you will read, though very tiresome and ill written, printed here by some of the excrement of Paris; it is called *Mémoires secrets pour servir à l'histoire de la république des lettres en France depuis 1762 jusqu'à nos jours.*[17] It is a journal of all the

7. 'Accounts that General Howe had marched, but found General Washington so strongly entrenched that he did not dare to attack him, and had marched back to New York. . . . This news was a deep blow to the Court, and the Scotch [the 'Ossianites'] declaimed with the greatest violence against the Howes' (*Last Journals* ii. 39–40).

8. Charlotte-Françoise de Hallencourt de Dromesnil (b. 1745), m. (1762) Emmanuel-Marie-Louis (1743–1822), Marquis de Noailles, ambassador to England 1776–8.

9. According to the *Public Advertiser* (30 and 31 July) she arrived in London 27 July and was to be presented at Court 31 July.

10. It was believed that France was treating with America and that the arrival of Mme de Noailles was designed to mask her country's hostile intentions towards England. See *Last Journals* ii. 40.

11. Gustavus Conyngham (ca 1744–1819), American naval officer. See *Dictionary of American Biography.*

12. 'A gentleman just returned from France says he saw Cunningham's privateer sail out of Dunkirk last Tuesday. . . . Cunningham has given bail *not* to commit any *hostilities* in the European seas' (*Public Advertiser* 28 July 1777).

13. The *Public Advertiser* of 29 July lists three vessels captured by Conyngham, one of which was retaken by its crew; corroboration of HW's 'nine' has not been found. He repeated the story in *Last Journals* ii. 40.

14. 'A letter from a gentleman at Bombay, December 1776, says, "There are no less than seventeen French bottoms on the coasts of Malabar and Coromandel and in the river of Bengal, to the great detriment of the East India Company"' (*Public Advertiser* 5 Aug. 1777).

15. That is, one in favour in Court circles. Not identified.

16. 'From Hayes in Kent we hear, that the Earl of Chatham, taking an airing on Sunday last [27 July], fell from his horse. Immediate assistance was procured, and it is said that his Lordship had not received any material hurt' (*London Chronicle* 29–31 July 1777, xlii. 111).

17. The first four and a half volumes were by Louis Petit de Bachaumont (1690–1771); the continuation was begun by Mathieu-François Pidansat de Mairobert (1707–79), who prepared the first eight volumes (1777) for the press. On the title-page the work was said to have been printed in London by a John Anderson, but it probably was actually printed in Amsterdam

minor politics, literature, theatric anecdotes, scandal and fashions of that country, and as all those heads compose much of their politics, it is the history of everything but their foreign politics. There are eight thick duodecimos, ill written, with no judgment, and very partial, almost against everybody and thing, however it shows them, and that they make little better figure than we do, though we are so low! I think a man of sense and taste should blush to be talked of in either country. I think you are too difficult however about the ode and the *Epistle to Shebbeare,* which will survive when all our trash is forgotten. What do you think of the immortal lines on Cox's Museum?[18] I beg your pardon too if I cannot see the sin of omission in some lines of Horace not being paraphrased in so heinous a light. The author does not profess a translation, and surely was at liberty to take only what parts he found to his purpose. If I had time, I dare to say I could prove to you that the ode is a stricter imitation than those of Pope; but alas! I have otherguess *besogne;*[19] however, to show you I have not totally abandoned all the occupations I love, I will mention an instance I chanced upon t'other day of the barbarity of the French language in poetry. I happened to open a volume of Voltaire

(BM Cat.; DU DEFFAND iv. 478). The collection was completed in 1789 and consisted of 36 volumes. HW owned at least nine volumes (sold SH v. 160 and 194).

18. 'So when great Cox, at his mechanic call,
    Bids orient pearls from golden dragons fall,
    Each little dragonet, with brazen grin,
    Gapes for the precious prize, and gulps it in.
    Yet when we peep behind the magic scene,
    One master-wheel directs the whole machine:
    The self-same pearls, in nice gradation, all
    Around one common centre, rise and fall:
    Thus may our state-museum long surprise;
    And what is sunk by votes in bribes arise;
    Till mocked and jaded with the puppet-play,
    Old England's genius turns with scorn away'
    (*Epistle to Dr Shebbeare,* ll. 204–15).

James Cox (d. ?1792: GM 1792, lxii pt i. 579) was a jeweller, silversmith, and mechanician in Shoe Lane, Fleet Street. When it was proposed to open the interior of India to British commerce, Cox constructed ingenious mechanical toys and jewels of precious stones and metals, which he hoped to sell to the Indian princes. War prevented the sale, and Cox tried to make up his losses by exhibiting the objects in a museum in Spring Gardens. In 1773 he obtained a private act of Parliament that permitted him to dispose of the collection, consisting of 56 pieces valued at £197,500, by a lottery, which was conducted in 1775. See N&Q 1860, 2d ser., ix. 367; 1864, 3d ser., v. 305–6. In his notes to the *Epistle to Dr Shebbeare* HW calls the above passage 'a far more brilliant piece of poetic machinery than what it describes; nor perhaps was so difficult an enterprise ever achieved in verse as this clear, concise, harmonious and humorous description. When the justness of the simile is added, it may be pronounced a *chef-d'œuvre* of poetry' (Mason's *Satirical Poems* 122).

19. That is, other kinds of business.

at Lord Ossory's,[20] and found this beginning of a scene in one of his plays:

Enfin donc désormais—[21]

Match me that hemistich if you can in a tragedy of the Sauromatæ.[22]

Garrick is dying of the yellow jaundice on the success of Henderson[23] a young actor from Bath—*Enfin donc désormais* there must never be a good player again. As Voltaire and Garrick are the god and goddess of Envy, the latter would put a stop to procreation, as the former would annihilate the traces of all antiquity, if there were no other gods but they.

I do not wonder you have had such bad crops both in your meadows and in chancery; consider how long since any sun shone on either. My *Hayssians*[24] have cost me as much as if I had hired them of the Landgrave. One would think the elements this summer came from Scotland too; and I am surprised Sir John Dalrymple or Macpherson has not told us from the *dépôt des affaires étrangères,*[25] that the sun is an enemy to English constitutions. *Vivent les brouillards!* I will finish with anticipating the best trait in the books I promise you. The witty Piron[26] made a visit to that old bigot, the Archbishop of—not York, but Paris,[27] soon after issuing a thundering mandate against some French Whigs, of which his Grace had certainly not written one word. He asked Piron, *'L'avez-vous lu?'—'Oui Monseigneur, et vous?'*[28]

Yours ever,

H. W.

20. HW promised Lady Ossory 19 July 1777 that he would be at Ampthill 'Tuesday sennight,' that is, 29 July.

21. 'Enfin donc désormais tout cède à la nature' (*Les Pélopides*, 1771, V. ii. 1).

22. Or Sarmatians: a wandering tribe of barbarians (OED *sub* 'Sarmatian').

23. John Henderson (1747–85), the 'Bath Roscius.' His first London appearance was on 11 June 1777 at the Haymarket, and it won for him immediate acclaim. 'In . . . testimony of his success, it is to be remarked that no actor was ever more generally the subject of conversation than Mr Henderson' (*Public Advertiser* 19 June 1777).

24. HW made the same pun in his letter to Conway 10 July 1777.

25. Where they obtained the state papers that they used in their histories.

26. Alexis Piron (1689–1773), dramatist and poet.

27. Christophe de Beaumont du Repaire (1703–81), Abp of Paris 1746–81.

28. The anecdote appears in Bachaumont *sub* 10 Jan. 1766 (vol. ii, 1780 edn, pp. 282–3). It was not a 'thundering mandate' that occasioned Piron's remark, but an address requesting services for the repose of the late Dauphin's soul.

To Mason, Thursday 18 September 1777

Printed from Mitford i. 306–7.

Strawberry Hill, Sept. 18, 1777.

YOU will not suspect my silence of idleness, I am but too apt to overwrite to any one I have so perfect a friendship for. I only suppress my communicative disposition when I have nothing to say but what would grieve those that feel for me. The dangerous illness of the Duke of Gloucester, and the dreadful situation of my niece (and have not I another nephew besides!) have kept me in such agitation between hopes and despair, that I have had no peace or leisure; the present moment is very favourable; the Prince has mended amazingly; he has had a most gracious letter from the King,[1] and so I hope I shall be at liberty to be a mortal again, and not anxious about princes.

This is not my immediate motive for writing, but to tell you an amazing piece of news that I have this moment received from town. The dinner-bell had rung—where? at Nuneham. The Earl[2] did not appear. After much search he was found standing on his head in a well, a dear little favourite dog upon his legs, his stick, and one of his gloves lying near;[3] my letter[4] does not say whether he had dropped the other —In short, I know no more. I will behave as well as I can on all national misfortunes, and so I proceed to tell you with a proper degree of affliction that a victualler[5] is come in who reports that the loquacious Howes have miscarried in their attempt on Philadelphia, and are believed to be gone to Boston:[6] that the provincials have

1. 'His Majesty protested "that his affection for his dear brother *had never been altered,* and never should cease; and that, lest anxiety should augment his danger, his Majesty, in case of a fatal termination, gave his dear brother his royal word that he would take care of his *family"'* (*Last Journals* ii. 55). That the King did not intend any favours to the Duchess, however, is shown in an exchange of notes with Lord North 29 Nov. 1777. North reported that the Duke had requested 'that his Majesty would, in some way or other, secure a provision to the Duchess of Gloucester in case of his demise,' to which the King replied, 'I should have thought that the very handsome proposal delivered this day by you in my name to the Duke of Glouces-

ter would have deserved in turn at least the civility of not applying for a public provision for a person who must always be odious to me' (*Corr. Geo. III* iii. 499–500).

2. Earl Harcourt.

3. The accident happened on 16 Sept. A more circumstantial account is given in *Harcourt Papers* iii. 146–8.

4. The letter has not been found.

5. A supply-ship.

6. 'The whole month of September had passed without any intelligence of or from the Howes. They had promised to write on making good their landing, but had not communicated to administration a syllable of their plan' (*Last Journals* ii. 45). The newspapers of 18 Sept. reported, 'By letters received from Glasgow . . . we learn that

abandoned Fort Edward,[7] it is said; and that, I suppose, the silent modest humble General Burgoyne[8] has not yet finished his concise description of the victorious manner in which he took possession of it, for said description is not yet arrived.[9] My dinner-bell rings, and lest my servants should suspect an accident, I must finish; did you receive the *Gazettes littéraires* which I left where you ordered a month ago?[10]

To Mason, Sunday 21 September 1777

Printed from Mitford i. 308–10.

Strawberry Hill, Sept. 21, 1777.

THIS is but a codicil to my last, but I forgot to mention in it a new discovery that charms me more than Harlequin did at ten years old, and will bring all paradise before your eyes more perfectly than you can paint it to the good women of your parish. It will be the delight of your solitude, and will rival your own celestinette. It is such a perfecting of the camera obscura, that it no longer depends on the sun, and serves for taking portraits with a force and exactness incredible; and serves almost as well by candlelight as by day. It is called *the delineator*,[1] and is invented within these eighteen months

the *York*, Captain Macvey, was arrived at that place from New York; that she sailed from thence the 10th of August, at which time no official advice had been received from Lord or General Howe of their having done anything new. But the preceding day a brigantine arrived there, which had spoke with the Grand Fleet off Philadelphia, of whom he learnt that they had made several feints in order to land, which had had the desired effect; for on August 2, General Washington crossed the Delaware with all his army and marched to Philadelphia. Lord Howe with his fleet stood to the east, supposed for Boston' (*Public Advertiser* 18 Sept.; also *London Chronicle* 16–18 Sept. 1777, xliii. 278). The story was substantially true (Washington's letters of 1–3 Aug. 1777, *Writings of George Washington*, Washington, 1931–44, ix. 1–10).

7. One of the chain of forts along the Hudson, about 12 miles north of Saratoga. 'Another vessel is likewise arrived . . . and

brings advice, that on Gen. Burgoyne's approach with his army to Fort Edward the rebels abandoned it and set it on fire' (*London Chronicle* 16–18 Sept. 1777, xlii. 278).

8. John Burgoyne (1722–92), general and dramatist. In *Last Journals* ii. 41 HW comments on the 'ridiculous bombast' of his dispatches. See also *post* 5 Oct. 1777 and 12 Feb. 1778.

9. Burgoyne's rather restrained account of the evacuation of Fort George and Fort Edward, in a letter to Lord George Germain dated 30 July, reached London 25 Sept. (*Public Advertiser* 26 Sept.) and was printed in the newspapers 29 Sept.

10. A lapse of memory: HW has in mind Bachaumont's *Mémoires secrets*, which he had promised Mason 4 Aug. 1777. See *post* 21 Sept. 1777.

———

1. 'Optical instrument or accurate delineator, entirely obviating the defects of

by a Mr Storer,[2] a Norfolk man, one of the modestest and humblest of beings. Sir Joshua Reynolds and West[3] are gone mad with it, and it will be their own faults if they do not excel Rubens in light and shade, and all the Flemish masters in truth. It improves the beauty of trees,—I don't know what it does not do—everything for me, for I can have every inside of every room here drawn minutely in the size of this page. Mr Storer fell as much in love with Strawberry Hill as I did with his instrument. The perspectives of the house, which I studied so much, are miraculous in this camera. The Gallery, Cabinet, Round Drawing[-room], and Great Bedchamber, make such pictures as you never saw.[4] The painted glass and trees that shade it are Arabian tales. This instrument will enable engravers to copy pictures with the utmost precision: and with it you may take a vase or the pattern of a china jar in a moment; architecture and trees are its greatest beauty, but I think it will perform more wonders than electricity, and yet it is so simple as to be contained in a trunk, that you may carry in your lap in your chaise, for there is such contrivance in that trunk that the filbert in the fairy-tales[5] which held such treasures was a fool to it; in short it is terrible to be threescore when it is just invented; I could play with it for forty years; when will you come up and see it? I am sure you will not go back without one.

I fear I was a little indelicate about Lord Harcourt's death, but I am so much more glad, when I am glad, than I can be sorry, when I am not, that I forgot the horror of the father's exit in my satisfaction

the camera obscura, being used without the assistance of the sun in the day-time, and also by candle-light, for drawing the human face, inside of rooms or buildings, also perspectives, landscapes, foliage and fibres of trees and flowers, exactly representing the true outlines, lights, shades, and colours' (*British Patents*, progression number 1183). The description is dated 4 March 1778.

2. William Storer (fl. 1777–85), optician, of Saham Toney, near Swaffham, Norfolk, author of *Syllabus to a Course of Optical Experiments, on the Syllepsis Optica; or the New Optical Principles of the Royal Delineator Analysed*, [1782]; listed among the bankrupts for March 1785 (GM 1785, lv pt i. 238). See *post* Appendix 4.

3. Benjamin West (1738–1820), painter. See *post* ii. 33 n. 11.

4. If any drawings were made of SH with the 'delineator,' they have not been discov-

ered. A camera obscura, perhaps Storer's, was sold SH xix. 27*.

5. HW is thinking of *La Chatte blanche* by Marie-Catherine-Jumelle de Berneville (d. 1705), Comtesse d'Aulnoy. The White Cat presents a prince with a walnut which, when opened, discloses a filbert. On opening this the prince finds a cherry-stone, and the process continues until he draws out of a grain of millet a cloth on which are painted all the birds, beasts, and fishes of creation, also rocks, trees, and fruits, portraits of all the rulers in the world, their wives and mistresses, etc. See *Contes de fées tirées de Charles Perrault, de Mme d'Aulnoy, et du Prince de Beaumont*, 1882, pp. 249–51. HW frequently alludes to this story. His copy of Mme d'Aulnoy's *Tales of the Fairies*, 3 vols, 1721, was sold SH iii. 73.

at the son's succession; like the two universities, my congratulations to the reigning sovereign are much more hearty than my *luctus*[6] for the departed one. I leave it to Lord Holderness and Lord Suffolk to pretend they are sorry that they have a competitor less for the Garter.[7]

Are not you content with Lord Abingdon's pamphlet?[8] are you not more? are you not glad he has so well puffed away Burke's sophistries? who would have thought of this little David? I am sure I should not have been surprised if I had seen him knocking down a blackbird with a sling; my Lord's Grace of York will not be pleased.[9]

As I am got far enough from the paragraph about Lord Harcourt, may I ask if you do not feel a little satisfaction in the idea of our meeting at Nuneham?[10] I am sorry I am threescore upon that account too, at that age one has not a vast many reasons for wishing to live long, but as loss of friends is the great bitter of old age, it is equally reasonable to like to enjoy their happiness. I am sure Lord Nuneham will have been exceedingly shocked; he is all good nature, and was an excellent son, and deserved a fonder father. I hear Mrs Montagu made a high-flown panegyric two days ago, on the late Earl. The poor man had not an idea; but Bishop Hurd dined at the same place, and I suppose she thought it necessary for a muse to sing the praises of all royal governors and preceptors.[11] It was at Cambridge's,[12] I was asked

6. HW sent a letter of condolence to the new Lord Harcourt 28 Sept. 1777.

7. Suffolk was elected K.G. 3 June 1778, but was never installed. Holdernesse never received the Garter.

8. *Thoughts on the Letter of Edmund Burke Esq. to the Sheriffs of Bristol*, by Willoughby Bertie (1740–99), 4th E. of Abingdon, 1760; published 6 Sept. 1777 (*Public Advertiser*). HW has noted on the title-page of his copy (now WSL) 'September 1777.' That he read the pamphlet carefully is shown by his numerous marginalia. The nature of the pamphlet is shown in its conclusion: 'The dagger uplifted against the breast of America, is meant for the heart of Old England. *Non agitur de vectigalibus, Libertas in dubio est.*' HW wrote of Abingdon: 'He was a singular young man, not quite void of parts, but rough, wrong-headed, extremely underbred, but warmly honest. He had been bred at Geneva, and had thoroughly imbibed principles of liberty. He was a sportsman, and is ridiculed by Voltaire in one

of the cantos of the *Guerre de Genève* [Canto III, ll. 194–228, *Œuvres*, ed. Moland, ix. 538–9]. . . . His pamphlet was bold and spirited and severe, and much above what was expected from him, the arguments being shrewd and clear, and destructive of Burke's sophistry' (*Last Journals* ii. 43).

9. Alluding to Markham's sermon attacking the Whigs (*ante* 26 May 1777 and n. 9) Abingdon wrote, 'As to *allegiance to the State*, though it be the sanctified phraseology of an Archbishop, it is, like the "Whiggism" he censures, allegiance "run mad".' (*Thoughts on a Letter of Edmund Burke*, pp. 15–16). Markham is also attacked in footnotes on pp. 16 and 63. See *post* 24 Sept. 1777 and n. 4.

10. Mason visited Nuneham and probably SH the following month (see *post* 24 and 26 Oct. 1777).

11. Lord Harcourt had been governor to the Prince of Wales 1751–2. Hurd on 5 June 1776 had been appointed preceptor to the Prince of Wales and the Duke of

to dine there, but excused myself, for I have no pleasure in laughing at people, and am only weary when they are acting affected parts.

PS. I recollect that they were the *Mémoires de Bachaumont* and not the *Gazettes littéraires* that I sent you last: did you receive them?

From MASON, Tuesday 23 September 1777

Printed from MS now WSL.
Address: The Honourable Horace Walpole, Arlington Street, London.
Postmark: ROTHERHAM 27 SE.

Aston, Sept. 23d, 1777.

Dear Sir,

ONE reason of my late silence was the alarming uncertainty which the papers constantly put me in concerning an event[1] which I knew your tenderness for your relations deeply interested you about. Relations are not 'those cordial drops,' which as somebody says,

—————Heaven in our cup has thrown
To make the nauseous draught of life go down.[2]

At least I don't find them so, no more than you yourself; for all my summer has been dawdled away in finding out the best way to be serviceable to a near one of my own,[3] and I doubt without much effect. I was once asked why I did not marry again.[4] My answer was that I could not find a woman that had the qualifications of a certain female whom the person who asked me knew. 'The qualifications of her! Why, she is old, ugly and a termagant into the bargain!' 'No matter for that! She was born in a boat; her mother was drowned; and she has no relation or country in the world. Those are the qualifications I require in the wife of my bosom.' And here endeth my chapter on the subject of relationship.

York. See *ante* 5 April 1777 and n. 23. Mrs Montagu's regard for Lord Harcourt seems to have been inspired by his love for animals, to which she pays tribute in a letter to Mrs Carter of 18 Sept. 1777, quoted in Reginald Blunt, *Mrs Montagu, Queen of the Blues,* [1923], ii. 36–7.

12. In Twickenham.
———
1. The illness of the Duke of Gloucester.

2. John, Earl of Rochester, *A Letter from Artemisa in the Town to Cloe in the Country,* ll. 44–5.
3. In a letter of 15 Aug. 1777 Mason complained to Alderson of the 'fatigues' that came from his hospitality to various relatives.
4. Mason's wife, Mary Sherman, whom he married in 1765, died in 1767 aged 28 (Draper, *Mason* 68–70).

I wish at your leisure you would sully a vessel[5] or two of paper with giving me the birth, parentage and education of General Burgoyne. At present I know little of him but as an orator; that consciousness of Christianity which he talks of in his proclamation in the very same breath that he threatens to give a stretch to his savage allies,[6] makes me think that one might compose a good liturgy for the use of the King's friends who, like the General, I trust, have the same consciousness of Christianity, and who like him can reconcile the scalping-knife with the gospel. I am told that General Haldimand[7] now made Governor of Quebec,[8] was the first person who laid a plan before government for employing these Indians, and that it was rejected.[9] His promotion shows that government has had the grace to change its mind, even if the *Gazette* had not told us so before.[10] Pray were not the Spaniards as defensible in employing dogs against the Americans[11] as we are?—but I scorn the word *we*, I am not, I cannot submit to call myself, an Englishman.

What an inconsistent creature is man! Poor Lord Harcourt! I fear he was so good a courtier that he would not have hesitated a moment

5. Defined by Francis Grose (*Provincial Glossary*) as 'half a quarter of a sheet' in earliest (1790) example cited by OED.

6. 'Every species of provision brought to my camp will be paid for at an equitable rate, and in solid coin. In consciousness of Christianity, my Royal Master's clemency, and the honour of soldiership, I have dwelt upon this invitation, and wished for more persuasive terms to give it impression; and let not people be led to disregard it by considering their distance from the immediate situation of my camp. I have but to give stretch to the Indian forces under my direction, and they amount to thousands, to overtake the hardened enemies of Great Britain and America' (*London Chronicle* 5–7 Aug. 1777, xlii. 130).

7. Frederick (later Sir Frederick) Haldimand (1718–91), K.B., 1785; Maj.-Gen., 1772; Lt-Gen., 1777; commandant in Florida 1766–78 (DNB; William A. Shaw, *The Knights of England*, 1906, i. 173).

8. He was offered the post 10 Sept. (*Public Advertiser* 12 Sept.) and formally appointed 20 Sept. (*London Chronicle* 20–23 Sept. 1777, xlii. 289), but did not enter upon his duties until the following summer (Jean N. McIlwraith, *Sir Frederick Haldimand*, Toronto, 1912, p. 117).

9. Haldimand had recommended the employment of Indians in a letter that he sent to Jeffrey Amherst 15 Dec. 1774 (cited in Justin H. Smith, *Our Struggle for the Fourteenth Colony*, New York, 1907, i. 78), but there is no reason for believing that he was the first to make such a proposal. Gage in a letter to Sir Guy Carleton, 18 Aug. 1775, described his efforts of the past year to bring about an alliance with the Indians (Allen French, *The First Year of the American Revolution*, Boston, 1934, p. 403). Both the English and French had used Indians in the Seven Years' War. See Cobbett, *Parl. Hist.* xix. 507–12.

10. The *London Gazette* of 5 Aug. reported Burgoyne's employment of 'about 3000 savages.'

11. Mason is perhaps thinking of a passage in Robertson's *History of America*, under date of 24 March 1495: 'The body [of Columbus's forces] which took the field consisted only of two hundred foot, twenty horse, and twenty large dogs; and how strange soever it may seem, to mention the last as composing part of a military force, they were not perhaps the least formidable and destructive of the whole, when employed against naked and timid Indians' (1777 edn, i. 127).

about giving his vote for scalping his brethren in Canada, and yet he dies in the humane act of saving a dog from drowning.

I received about a fortnight ago six volumes[12] of *Mémoires secrets,* etc., for which I return you many thanks, and will take care to bring them back to you when I come to London, but as they laid long at Mr Verelst's in St James's Square, this will not be the way of any speedy conveyance to me, which I hoped it would.

Lord Rockingham and his party are good Christians and can forgive their enemies, whatever other folks are. At York races they all dined at the Archbishop's public dinner, and gave for a reason that his Grace made them the first visit at their lodgings. So you may call them rogues, rascals, or what you please, only visit them afterwards and they will be as merry as grigs with you. Seriously speaking I hardly know a more ridiculous proceeding than this, their recession[13] was hardly more so. Had they avoided this visit, his Grace's mitre would have sat awkwardly upon him for life. As it is he must write another sermon before he meets with that contempt which every true Whig ought to give him, but where is such a Whig to be found? I see 'An Unconnected Whig' has published something.[14] Is it worth the reading? My paper is more than full, so I remain, dear Sir,

Yours most cordially,

W. M.

From MASON, Wednesday 24 September 1777

Printed from MS now WSL.
Address: The Honourable Mr Walpole, Arlington Street, London.
Postmark: ROTHERHAM 29 SE.

Aston, Sept. 24th [1777.][1]

BUT what will it[2] cost? is it in a maker's hands? and can one have it down and know how to use it, without being shown? Not that

12. HW (*ante* 4 Aug. 1777) mentioned eight volumes, but two may have been lost in the post. The entry in the SH sale catalogue (v. 194) shows that vols 1 and 3 were missing in 1842.

13. See *ante* 17 Feb. 1777.

14. *An Unconnected Whig's Address to the Public upon the Present Civil War,* published 17 Sept. 1777 (*Public Advertiser*). See *post* 5 Oct. 1777. The author is unidentified.

1. Added in pencil by HW.

2. Storer's 'delineator' (*ante* 21 Sept. 1777).

I believe above half of what you tell me. For I have arguments *a priori* (which I learnt when I was at the university) to prove that it can't take likenesses or delineate the human figure, unless that figure undergo first the chemical process which Medusa was so much skilled in and be converted into immovable stone. But this is no disparagement to the instrument, but to the human figure which ought not to have pulsation and such other matters as will make it commit the crime of false drawing, whether it will or no. Therefore I still long to see it and would even give my celestinette for it unseen, for my celestinette is now above two years old.

I cannot say but I do feel the satisfaction you speak of about going to Newnham etc., etc., etc. And I have other satisfactions of a more patriotic nature, which though they signify nothing, as there is no such thing as patriotism in this our day, yet somehow or other they please one like the filbert in the fairy-tales³ if they are not quite so substantial as your delineating trunk. What would I give to see it for half an hour? I am hardly got far enough from my paragraph of mortality to recur to the trunk, but no matter!

I have never yet seen my Lord Abingdon's pamphlet except an extract in the newspaper about the Archbishop.⁴ I am not clear whether said Earl did not dine with the Archbishop, at the reconciliatory dinner which I mentioned in my last. It would have been right to do so as a party man, in order to make the Archbishop's definition⁵ the more true, which I should think was the reason which weighed with the rest of them.

This being a codicil like yours requires no formal signature.

3. See *ante* 21 Sept. 1777, n. 5.

4. Two extracts from Lord Abingdon's *Thoughts on the Letter of Edmund Burke* were published in the *London Chronicle* 2–4 and 4–6 Sept. 1777, xlii. 225–6, 233–4. In the second the following footnote is quoted: 'I am aware how much I here differ from the very able prelate, who is for harnessing church and state together, like coach and horses, that he as one of the drivers may enjoy the smack of the whip; a smack which he cannot forget, and which he gave me reason to remember when I was at Westminster School; but as I am now out of his clutches, so I hope I am out of his books too, at least such as are akin to his political sermons. *Vide* Archbishop of York, *Sermon*, p. 10.'

5. Markham had said: 'Parties once had a principle belonging to them, absurd perhaps, and indefensible, but still carrying a notion of duty, by which honest minds might easily be caught. But they are now combinations of individuals, who instead of being the sons and servants of the community, make a league for advancing their private interests' (*Sermon*, 1777, p. 21).

To Mason, Sunday 5 October 1777

Printed from Mitford i. 314–7.

Strawberry Hill, Oct. 5, 1777.

THERE is nothing so unfortunate as to be a philosopher and a wise man, and a reasoner, and to know what can and cannot be done. If invention had not preceded demonstration, we should by this time have understood the whole system of the universe, but have thought it impossible to alter or improve anything in our world. This is my opinion, and you may confute it by argument if you please. I who have a sovereign contempt for Euclid, and Newton, and Locke, and admire nothing but original genius, and hold that everything will be found out at last, as flying, living forever, etc., trust to none of my senses, having seen Jonas[1] perform what I did not believe, when I saw, and heard Le Texier[2] be a dozen persons at once. In short it is a joke to say anything is impossible. The delineator does perform wonders; and though from my own immachinality I can do little or nothing with it,[2a] which has abated something of my enthusiasm, you who will be able to work wonders with it, are to blame to contest its possibilities. As I tell you I don't know how to manage it, you may swear I cannot describe or give directions for conducting it. It cost me ten guineas, and I believe they are thrown away, for in a twelve-month it will certainly be brought to greater perfection. In one point you are very right, one must be as motionless as Lord Abercorn,[3] or the least vibration of the features spoils the portrait. In good truth though I stared like the mob at the witchery of this new instrument, yet if it had not been so mysteriously involved in a box, I am not sure it would have surprised me more than any reflection painted on a diminishing mirror. The child has had his plaything broken to see what it was made of, and is weary of it; however I think it will answer admirably for taking the insides of buildings, and near prospects, and

1. A sleight-of-hand artist who enjoyed a vogue from 1768 to ca 1773. See Thomas Frost, *The Lives of the Conjurors*, 1881, pp. 122–5.
2. See *ante* 18 Feb. 1776.
2a. Others were baffled by the delineator; in 1782 Storer wrote that he had 're-

ceived several accounts that the most ingenious opticians abroad could not work the instrument' (*Syllabus*, p. 51).
3. Examples of his 'Castilian pomp' and laconic style are given in his GM obituary, 1789, lix pt ii. 961.

statues, and vases, and be of great help to engravers, and it does serve without the sun.

Lord Harcourt has given away at least fifty thousand pounds to his daughter and younger son.[4] I hold it very right not to heap all on heirs apparent, and yet loving the new Earl, and not caring a straw for the brother and sister, my concern for the father is not at all augmented. I had too the same reason that you hint at for being glad our friend is in possession. He had told me his intentions for you,[5] but not knowing whether he had mentioned them to you, I was trusty you see, and did not divulge them even to you,—but it was a charming thought, and I hope the well will not be stopped up.

You ask the history of Burgoyne the pompous. He is a natural son of Lord Bingley,[6] who put him into the entail of the estate, but when young Lane came of age the entail was cut off.[7] He ran away with the old Lord Derby's daughter,[8] and has been a fortunate gamester. Junius was thought unjust,[9] as he was never supposed to do more

4. By Lord Harcourt's will, proved 27 Sept. 1777, £32,000 were left outright to Colonel William Harcourt, and £2000 were left to be invested for the benefit of Lady Elizabeth Harcourt (1739–1811), who had married (1763), Sir William Lee of Hartwell, Bucks (photostat of copy of will; GEC, *Comp. Baronet.* iii. 112).

5. The reference to the well suggests that the new Earl's intentions had to do with some landscaping. Mason on his visit to Nuneham assisted in alterations of the terrace (*post* 26 Oct. 1777).

6. Robert Benson (ca 1676–1731), cr. (1713) Bn of Bingley; chancellor of the Exchequer 1711–3; P.C. 1711–4, 1730–1; treasurer of the Household 1730–1. Burgoyne was legally the son of John Burgoyne and Anna Maria Burnestone. HW's account of his paternity (which gains some support from Bingley's will: see next note) is disputed in E. B. de Fonblanque, *Political and Military Episodes . . . Derived from the Life and Correspondence of John Burgoyne,* 1876, pp. 4–8. HW's story is upheld in *Hadden's Journal and Orderly Books,* ed. Horatio Rogers, Albany, N.Y., 1884, pp. 388–91, and in Hoffman Nickerson, *The Turning Point of the Revolution,* Boston, 1928, pp. 461–2.

7. Lord Bingley in his will (dated 27 June 1729), after providing for his wife and his illegitimate daughter, Mary Johnson, left to Burgoyne's mother, Anna Maria Burgoyne, two houses and 'an annuity of £400 per annum . . . for her separate use, over which her husband shall have no control.' Most of the residue of the estate was left to his legitimate daughter Harriet and her heirs, with remainder to Mary Johnson and her heirs male, and 'in default of such issue, to the use of my godson, John Burgoyne . . . (which godson I desire may take the name of Robert Benson if my estate comes to him) for the term of his natural life' (*The . . . Registers of the . . . Abbey of St Peter, Westminster,* ed. Joseph L. Chester, 1876, pp. 331–2; photostat of Lord Bingley's will). 'Young Lane' was Robert Fox-Lane (1732–68: see GEC ii. 178 n.), Harriet's son and Lord Bingley's only legitimate grandchild, at whose majority the contingent heirs were cut off.

8. Lady Charlotte Stanley (d. 1776), youngest dau. of Edward Stanley, 11th E. of Derby; m. (1743) John Burgoyne.

9. Junius had intimated that Burgoyne was not above 'taking his stand at a gaming-table, and watching with the soberest attention for a fair opportunity of engaging a drunken young nobleman at piquet' (*The Letters of Junius,* ed. C. W. Everett, 1927, p. 133).

than play very well. I have heard him speak in Parliament,[10] just as he writes; for all his speeches were written and laboured, and yet neither in them nor in his conversation, did he ever impress me with an idea of his having parts. He is however a very useful commander, for he feeds the *Gazette* and the public, while the Howes and the war are so dumb.

I have read the 'Unconnected Whig,' and recommend him to you; he does not waste words like the unmerciful hero of the last paragraph. It is a short, clear strong picture of our present situation and its causes. I see no fault in it, but its favour for the Rockinghams,[11] the most timid set of time-serving triflers that ever existed; why should not he dine with his Grace? Do not all Lord Rockingham's politics begin and end with dinners? Is not decency their whole wisdom? when they shunned Wilkes, could they avoid the Archbishop? I would lay a wager that if a parcel of schoolboys were to play at politicians, the children that should take the part of the Opposition would discover more spirit and sense. The cruellest thing that has been said of the Americans by the Court, is, that they were encouraged by the Opposition. You might as soon light a fire with a wet dish-clout. Adieu.

From MASON, Wednesday 22 October 1777

Printed from MS now WSL.
Address (in Lord Harcourt's hand): ⟨The Honourabl⟩e Horace Walpole, Strawberry Hill, Twickenham. ⟨Free Har⟩court.
Postmark: ABINGDON 23 OC. FREE.

Nuneham, Oct. 22d, 1777.

HERE am I with the Isis before me drawing its line of silver through the greenest meadow in the world. A glorious wood to my left, and another glorious wood to my right; Abingdon spire[1] there, Radcliff Library[2] there, etc., etc., etc.[3] Yet here am I without

10. Burgoyne was M.P. for Midhurst 1761–8 and for Preston borough 1768–92 (*Members of Parliament*, pt ii, 1878, pp. 132, 140, 191).

11. At pp. 32–3. HW's favourable attention was caught by the epigraph from Algernon Sidney, 'Civil War is a disease, but tyranny is the death of a free state,' and engaged on p. 11, where Sir Robert

Walpole is praised. HW's copy is now WSL.

1. The spire of St Helen's Church in Abingdon, Berks, about three miles west of Nuneham.

2. The Radcliffe Camera, Oxford, about eight miles north of Nuneham.

3. Repeated fifteen times in MS.

my delineator. O that you would lend me yours! I would pawn my machinality upon it that I could put it together without any directions, yet if there be printed directions in the trunk, so much the better. And then as to the trunk, I would take as much care of it as King James II of humane memory did of his when he was about to be shipwrecked,[4] and I would bring it safe to you back in less than a fortnight with the *Mémoires secrets,* which your charity blest my solitariness with at Aston. And I will give you the heel piece of one of the Royal Martyr's boots which he lost before the gates of Hull[5] (the place of my nativity) and which has been lain up in lavender in our family ever since. And as the Oxford coach goes the Henley road through Brentford every day there is no doubt but the trunk would arrive here with the utmost safety. But I will say no more on the subject, only that if what I have said and what I have promised is not enough to move your compassion, you must be as obstinate, as mulish 'as a King's favourite, or as a *.'[6]

My Lord Harcourt, who will be my surety for the safety of the said trunk, sends his best compliments and thanks for your agreeable letter. I am, whether you grant my petition or not,

Your most faithful and obliged servant,

W. MASON

To MASON, Wednesday 24 October 1777

Printed from Mitford i. 318–20.

Arlington Street, Oct. 24, 1777.

YOUR letter's date made it still more welcome than their predecessors. I wish myself with you without envy, and think of Nuneham with more pleasure than I dare tell Lord Harcourt.[1] I am delighted too with the prospect of seeing you so soon. My letter's date tells you

---

4. See HW to Mason *ante* 2 March 1773 *bis* and n. 8a.

5. Presumably on 23 April 1642, when the governor of Hull ordered the gates to be closed before Charles I.

6. 'Like a King's favourite — or like a King' (Pope, *Satires of Dr John Donne, Dean of St Paul's, Versified,* ii. 78).

---

1. That is, he will find Nuneham a pleasanter place to visit now that the present Earl's father is dead. See *ante* 21 Sept. 1777.

why I do not instantly obey you. I am here and must be so some days, and the delineator is locked up at Strawberry, or I hope you do not think I am so selfish as to prefer a plaything to your amusement. I will send it the moment I return merely to satisfy you, for Mr Storer has already improved his idea so much, as to obviate I believe most of your objections. He is making me another, and honestly offered me to change it for me[1a]—and he has made a stand to it too, that remedies many inconveniences; but that I have not got yet, nor just now can I attend but to the present occupation.

The Duke and Duchess arrived yesterday.[2] His R. H. is and looks better than I expected, not pulled though pale; his leg is still swelled and he is lame,[3] but it has not opened; and his voice is strong and spirits good. The Duchess looks in health, but is much leaner and looks older. I have not seen them a moment alone, for they have not been a moment alone; all I know is, the Duke has written to ask when.[4] The answer was not come half an hour ago. It is decent I should stay two or three days; and then if I was great enough to be proud of lowering myself, I should say, I shall return to my plough. No, nor am I one of those, who, though so great, ought to be sent to plough.

I am much obliged to you for your offering,[5] yet though I like the occasion of its becoming a relic, I cannot accept it. Lord Harcourt has given me the glorious and immortal spurs of King William;[6] can I receive his uncle's boot-heel into the same sanctuary! when you want to be a Cardinal, you shall present it to his Grace of York, or to any of the *et ceteras*[7] that you do not see from Nuneham.

1a. 'Out of fifty delineators which I sold on the first construction, I had forty-six sent me to alter' (Storer's *Syllabus*, p. 50).

2. 'Yesterday [23 Oct.] arrived at Gloucester House his Royal Highness the Duke of Gloucester, attended by the Duchess and the rest of his train' (*Lloyd's Evening Post* 22–4 Oct. 1777, xli. 399).

3. 'On the 25th of August he was seized [at Trent] in the most dangerous and violent manner, with excruciating pain in his thigh and leg' (*Last Journals* ii. 53).

4. According to HW (*Last Journals* ii. 60), on the 25th 'the Duke wrote to Lord George Germaine, to desire he would ask the King when his Royal Highness might have leave to pay his duty to the King.'

5. The heel of Charles I's boot (*ante* 22 Oct. 1777).

6. 'The spurs worn by King William at the Battle of the Boyne, preserved in an Irish family, and given to the late Earl of Harcourt when Lord Lieutenant, and by the present Earl to Mr W., in a red leather box lined with green velvet' (*Des. of SH*, 1784, p. 77). The spurs were kept in the glass cabinet in the Great North Bedchamber. HW thanked Harcourt 8 Oct. 1777 in extravagant terms. Doubtless Harcourt showed the letter to Mason. The spurs were sold SH xvi. 86. They are now (1953) in the possession of the Earl of Enniskillen.

7. See *ante* 22 Oct. 1777. HW presumably means the place-giving Tories.

Pray tell Lord and Lady Harcourt that I have been a perfect courtier[8] for them, and said everything in the world, and am commanded to return everything in the world. I was impatient lest all England and still more, all Scotland should be beforehand with me in addresses; one Englishman[9] offered one this very morning—*mais attendez-moi sous l'orme*. There we shall talk more at our ease.

From MASON, Sunday 26 October 1777

Printed from MS now WSL.
Address: The Honourable Horace Walpole.

Nuneham, the day after his Majesty's happy accession,[1] 1777.

LORD Harcourt has fancied my presence so necessary towards completing some alterations he has made on his terrace[2] that I have not been able to persuade him to let me leave this place before next Wednesday or Thursday, when I am obliged to go to town before I can visit Strawberry Hill, on business[3] which I will tell you when I have the honour to see you, which I hope will be very soon. In the mean time, if anything calls you to town, I am to be found at my good host's in Curzon Street[4] as usual.

I am charmed with the fair bearer[5] of this note and wish I was a

8. To the Duke and Duchess of Gloucester.

9. 'Soon after the news [of the Duke's return] arrived at the Queen's Palace, a Great Personage [George III] sent a message to inquire after his Highness's health, couched in terms of the most tender affection' (*Lloyd's Evening Post* 22–4 Oct. 1777, xli. 399).

1. On 25 Oct. 1777 George III celebrated the seventeenth anniversary of his accession.

2. 'We have had but two days' rain or rather nights since I left Aston, and since I have been here I have been out four hours every morning executing an approach to a grotto' (Mason to Alderson 26 Oct. 1777). 'In the church [at Nuneham] there is a barrel-organ, upon which is set Mr Mason's music for the responses to the Commandments, and his Sunday hymns. The adjoining flower-garden was formed

by him, and he suggested the alterations on the north terrace' (George Simon, Earl Harcourt, 'Description of Nuneham Courtenay in 1806,' *Harcourt Papers* iii. 201).

3. In his letter to Alderson of 26 Oct. Mason mentions meeting him 'in town . . . to settle matters with Lord Holdernesse' in connection with his approaching presentation, 17 Dec. 1777, to the rectory of Langton-upon-Swale, Yorks, of which Holdernesse held the advowson. Mason continued to hold this living with that of Aston until his death (R.F. Scott, *Admissions to the College of St John the Evangelist in the University of Cambridge*, pt iii, Cambridge, 1903, pp. 530–1; *Vict. Co. Hist. Yorks, North Riding*, i. 186).

4. Richard Stonhewer.

5. Probably Jane Fauquier; see *post* 17 Sept. 1778 and n. 13, and HW to Harcourt 18 Oct. 1777.

Petrarch that I might fall in love [with] her, and why not without being a Petrarch? for 'tis surely more natural for an old widower[6] to fall in love with a young maid than for a young bachelor to be enamoured with an old married woman who had borne as many children as our gracious Queen Charlotte,[7] which I think was that poet's case.[8] Yet putting love out of the question, I may surely in all reason admire a beauty that can only be exceeded by its accompaniments of good nature, affability and modest simplicity. I would call it innocence were it not too unfashionable a thing, and what I believe no young lady, so advanced in years as she is (for I suspect she is almost seventeen) can possibly be suspected of. Certain it is, we have a brace of very accomplished ladies now in the house who seem to have got rid of all that long before they came to her years of discretion; but I only say *seem* for I would not speak with precision on such a delicate subject for the world.

Breakfast will permit me to add no more at present than that I am, dear Sir,

Very faithfully yours,

W. MASON

To MASON, Saturday 17 January 1778

Printed from Mitford i. 321–3.

Arlington Street, Jan. 17, 1778.

I HAVE not written to you since you went as I had nothing to tell you; and I write improperly now, when one is probably at the eve of having something to say,[1] but the fish I have to fry is of another kind. Can it be true that you have an opera coming on the stage, and

6. Mason first wrote 'old man.'

7. Twelve of her fifteen children had been born by 1777.

8. In Susanna Dobson's *Life of Petrarch Collected from* [J.-F.-A. de Sade's] *Mémoires pour la vie de Petrarch*, 1775, Laura was alleged to be the daughter of Audibert and Ermessenda de Noves, married to Hugues de Sade, and the mother of ten children (Dobson, edn of 1777, Dublin, i. 22 and 293). Sade's identification is not now ac-

cepted. See Edward H. R. Tatham, *Francesco Petrarca, the First Modern Man of Letters: His Life and Correspondence*, 1925–6, i. 245–8.

1. Lord Cornwallis and other officers had recently arrived on leave from America, and on 17 Jan. Cornwallis was closeted with the King for five hours. See *Last Journals* ii. 91.

that you never mentioned it to me? Had I torn Orpheus piecemeal, I could not be more unworthy of musical communication. Am I so untunable that I must not hear airs unless I can sing them? Yes, you have written an opera, and it is called *Sappho*,[2] and I suppose Mrs Montagu is to be first woman. Lord Strafford is my authority: and yet I can scarce think you would have been so basely unfriendly; if you have, I wish your celestinette may be broken about your ears, or that Lady Rockingham[3] may desire a rehearsal at our [?her] own house in the morning, and make the poet and the whole orchestra wait till nine at night.

Knapton is dying,[4] but the promise to Sandby[5] is superseded, *de par le roi*, because it dates from the Duke of Grafton.[6]

General Howe has been to take another look at Washington[7] and passed eldest[8] again. The town of Froome,[9] concluding *Burgoyne*

2. Mason's libretto was to have been set to music by Giardini (*post* 24 Jan., 12 Feb., 14 Aug. 1778), but nothing seems to have come of the plan. It was first printed in Mason's *Poems*, 1796–7 (Gaskell 37), and is in the collected edition of Mason's *Works*, 1811, ii. 319–61. In 1809 an Italian translation by T. J. Mathias was published in London.

3. Mary Bright (d. 1804), m. (1752) Charles Watson-Wentworth, 2d M. of Rockingham.

4. George Knapton (1698–1778), portrait painter; surveyor and keeper of the King's pictures 1765–78. He did not die until Dec. 1778.

5. Paul Sandby (1725–1809), R.A., painter, engraver, and caricaturist.

6. 'Instances of the King's loving to assume the donation of all places though not in his gift, and of his resentment to the Duke of Grafton. Old Knapton, surveyor of the King's pictures, was dying this winter. Lord Hertford, Lord Chamberlain, had promised the reversion to Paul Sandby, at the Duke of Grafton's request when first lord of the Treasury. Lord Hertford was now reminded of that promise, but said he must speak to the King, who wished that [Richard] Dalton, his favourite artist, should have it; and he said to Lord Hertford, "If *the Duke of Grafton* promised it to Sandby, he shall *not* have it; *I command* you to give it to Dalton" ' (*Last*

Journals ii. 113). The King's resentment against Grafton was caused by Grafton's repudiation of the administration more than two years before. See *ante* 27 Oct. 1775.

7. *Last Journals* ii. 91 shows that HW is referring to a dispatch from New York dated 15 Dec. 1778: 'Yesterday morning a sloop arrived here from Philadelphia . . . and by letters from thence we learn . . . that Washington is strongly intrenched at a place called White Marsh, about fifteen miles from Philadelphia . . . ; that his excellency General Sir William Howe, finding it impossible to bring the rebels to an engagement, arrived at Philadelphia last Tuesday' (*Public Advertiser* 17 Jan.). 'Another look' perhaps alludes to a recent newspaper comment: 'And what must the King of Prussia think of General Howe, who drew up his army in the front of Washington's lines, *looked at him,* then wheeled to the right about and–*decamped?*' (*Public Advertiser* 6 Jan. 1778). See also *post* 4 Feb. 1778 and n. 15.

8. A term borrowed from loo. 'He who is eldest hand [the first one dealt] hath the privilege of passing by the benefit thereof, that is, he hath the advantage of hearing what every one will say, and, at last, may play, or not play, according as he finds his game good or bad. If the eldest says he passes, the rest may choose whether

was a Frenchman by his name, made great rejoicings on his being taken prisoner.[10]

I heard last night that Voltaire is dead;[11] now one may buy his works safely, as he cannot write them over and over again.

You shall not hear a word more from me till you clear yourself about the opera. Should it prove true I shall never believe a syllable more about your idleness, nay shall conclude that everything that appears, is yours, and I am sure that will be full vengeance.

PS. Pray did you write *The Roman Sacrifice*,[12] the last new tragedy? It was detestable.

From MASON, Tuesday 20 January 1778

Printed from MS now WSL.
Address: The Honourable Horace Walpole.

Aston, Jan. 20th, 1778.

PACIFY yourself, my good Sir. I have not written; I am only writing an opera, and what I have written of it, I here send you; desiring, if you do not absolutely condemn both the intention and execution, to seal it up and send it to Mr Giardini.[1] He has already seen the whole plan and he must now see an act to tell me whether it will suit his purpose. As to yourself, you know enough of the lady's story,[2] fully to comprehend the drift of these pages which contain her catastrophe. But I know you rather want to know *why* I have undertaken to write an opera, than *how* I have written it. But this is a long story and relates to a little shoemaker of Aston. Mr

they will play, or no' (*Complete Gamester*, 5th edn, 1734, pt ii, p. 18: quoted by Mrs Toynbee x. 177).

9. Probably Frome in Somerset. The source of this story has not been found.

10. Burgoyne surrendered to Gates at Saratoga 17 Oct. 1777.

11. 'Letters from Paris mention the death of the celebrated Voltaire at his villa of Fernay' (*Public Advertiser* 28 Jan. 1778). These reports were premature; he died at Paris 30 May.

12. A tragedy by William Shirley (d. 1780), first acted 18 Dec. 1777 at Drury Lane (Genest vi. 5). It had only four per-

formances and was never printed. HW went to it to see Henderson. See *ante* 4 Aug. 1777 and HW to Lady Ossory 23 Dec. 1777.

1. Felice de Giardini (1716–96), violinist and composer. He came to London ca 1750 and immediately won considerable fame. From 1774 to 1780 he was the conductor of the Pantheon concerts. See Grove's *Dictionary of Music*.

2. Mason's libretto derives from the legend of Sappho's hopeless love of Phaon and her leap from the Leucadian rock.

Stonhewer will tell you the particulars,[3] and how my little shoemaker and this opera become so intimately united.

Now, don't talk to me about the author of *Caractacus*, and that he ought to write nothing but what is equal, if not superior to *Caractacus*. If you prevent me from writing operas I'll write nothing but ballads. 'Agreed, if they be political ones, as many as you please.' And don't say that a grave divine turned of fifty debases his cloth by telling a love story. Leave that argument for the bishops to handle. I have made up my conscience as to that matter. Besides if the bishops condemn me on this head they will nevertheless admire my learning, for all the fragments of Sappho will be translated and find their place in this drama. For instance, this third act opens with one of them: Δέδυκε μὲν ἀ σελάννα καὶ πληΐαδες, etc.[4]

Upon the whole then I recommend this poor innocent thing to your mercy as a critic, not as if it had my last hand, and its last polish, yet in such a state as will admit of little improvement except in particular lines and words; about this latter I mean to be peculiarly careful in order to make the language as soft and consequently as fit for music as possible, for I am persuaded this matter has never yet been sufficiently attended to by the few of our poets who have written professedly for music.

Pray put up the letter to Giardini, etc., in the packet before you seal it.

I shrewdly suspect some dark practice in this death of Lord Pigot.[5] Pray tell me what you hear of that matter, and of all others, for now the political as well as natural frost is thawed. Dear Sir,

Yours most truly,

W. MASON

3. No record of these particulars has been found. Mason apparently planned to apply the proceeds from the opera to charitable purposes. See *post* 6 Feb. 1778.

4. 'The radiant queen of night retires,
   And quits her silver car;
  The Pleiads veil their lambent
   fires . . .'
            (*Sappho* III. i. 1–3).
A footnote in the printed edition of the play acknowledges that the opening lines are 'a kind of paraphrase' of Sappho's fragment, and the note refers the reader to 'the edition of Pindar and other lyric poems by H. Stephens.' This is *Pindari Olympia . . . cæterorum octo lyricorum carmina*, ed. Henricus Stephanus [Henri Estienne], 1566, ii. 64; cf. *Lyra Græca*, ed. J. M. Edmonds, 1928–31, i. 262.

5. Pigot's death in India was reported in the *Public Advertiser* 16 Jan. 1778. See *post* 4 Feb. 1778.

To Mason, Saturday 24 January 1778

Printed from Mitford i. 325–9.

Jan. 24, 1778.

I RECEIVED your act[1] late last night, and though I have run through it but once, I am impatient not only to pardon you, but thank you. I can forgive you anything but idleness; and music, which your words always are, has charms to soothe even me. The language is so harmonious, that I think as I did of Dryden's *Ode*,[2] that it will be more melodious unset than when adapted. Yet if you can rival Dryden, Giardini cannot paragon Handel. I am, I know, a most poor judge of musical composition, yet may not I ask if Giardini possesses either force or simplicity?[3] Your act is classic Athenian—shall it be subdi-di-di-vi-vi-vi-ded into modern Italian?[4]—but it is too late to ask that question.

I shall now mention a very few criticisms.

The language is so sweet, that my soul that loves chiaroscuro as a contrast at least wants a little more sombre, and the place I would allot for it is Sappho's speech after the vision. The parts of Metastasio[5] (I do not compare you down to him) that please me most are his long soliloquies of accompanied recitative in last acts; they give scope to the poet, the passions, the actress, and the composer. I would not have Sappho determine at once, but struggle with love, fear, hope, despair, and when she doubts obeying the god, thunder may mark his anger, and decide her, for she obeys a dream too suddenly, though classic times may justify her more than a modern would be justified.

As you are sublime in choruses, why have you only one in an opera,

---

1. The third and final act of *Sappho*; see preceding letter.

2. *Alexander's Feast; or the Power of Music. An Ode in Honour of St Cecilia's Day*, 1697. At the time of its composition it was set to music by Jeremiah Clarke, later by Thomas Clayton, and in 1736 by Handel, whose version was very popular throughout the eighteenth century. See Hugh Macdonald, *John Dryden: A Bibliography of Early Editions and of Drydeniana*, Oxford, 1939, pp. 59–60.

3. Burney had a different opinion: 'Of [Giardini's] . . . compositions vocal and instrumental I shall say nothing here, lest my praise should be too much for others and too little for himself' (*General History of Music*, 1776–89, iv. 523).

4. HW means that Giardini would separate the text into recitative, airs, duets, choruses, etc.

5. Pietro Metastasio (1698–1782), poet and librettist.

—in a Greek opera? They are simple and yet give variety; sure a hymeneal chorus is necessary.[6]

I have an objection, which is odd, even to the parts I have *not* seen, but you hint (by Sappho in her female dress)[7] at her being disguised as a man in a former act.[8] Will not *that* be a little too characteristic, and give a handle to buffoonery in the learned part of the mob?

I have few verbal criticisms to make, though I could commend a thousand passages, particularly the two lines on Alpheus,[9] and the exquisite first air. I am not quite pleased with *down, down, down,* as a little too artificial, and then *down* should not come in the very next line,[10] and in a sense that is the very opposite to the former sense, and shows we express a precipitate fall and the softness of repose by the same sound.

I do not quite approve so forced an expression as *downcast tenderness,* and I cavil at

> I *feel* that full, that heart*felt* tenderness
> That blesses those who never *felt* distress,

and would rather change *heartfelt,* which has a German sound. In the second line *felt* is most sonorous.

I have literally but one more qualm: when Sappho dedicates her lyre, she says it is *far sweeter than the harp.*[11] This methinks is too nice a distinction for a person in her situation to make, and fitter for a commentator's note than a woman on the point of destroying herself. Yes, I see another, that I have just cast my eyes on; Sappho must not utter the word *requiem;*[12] in short, Metastasio may use such an anachronism, but Musæus[13] must not, shall not.

I shall send the act and the letter to Giardini, as you order, though

6. Mason seems to have followed HW's advice. In the printed version of Act III there is a final chorus and also a four-line chorus, beginning 'Holy Hymen,' at the end of Scene v (Mason's *Works* ii. 356).

7. The stage direction at the beginning of the act concludes: 'Sappho in her female habit comes out of one of the caves unattended' (ibid. ii. 349).

8. HW's assumption was correct. In the fifth scene of the first act, ll. 5–6, Sappho assumes 'the vestments of a shepherd' in order to spy on her lover Phaon, whom she believes unfaithful (*Works* ii. 331).

9. 'Where Alphæus dare not lave,
   To mix with hers his amorous wave'
   (*Sappho* III. ii. 7–8).

10. The printed version of the play shows that Mason made alterations in accordance with HW's criticisms in this paragraph and the two following ones.

11. See *post* 6 Feb. 1778, n. 3.

12. The anachronism does not appear in the printed version of the libretto.

13. Mason. See *ante* ? Nov. 1776.

with regret I own: for I doubt his music will not have that majestic greatness and distinctiveness that are necessary to let the words be understood. Add that our singers want more to be taught to articulate than to sing. All the women jabber, and bad as his taste was, Beard[14] did more justice to sense than any of our performers, for though he laid a stress on every syllable, yet at least the audience, such as were capable, could suppose the right accents. In short, I wish your opera could be accompanied only by the lyre and the tibia.

There is no new event. The Parliament has done little or nothing, as they wait for Lord George to lead up the Blues.[15] I have no time for details, and, in truth, I am thinking more of *Sappho* than of the nation, and am happy when I can amuse myself with reading anything but politics, which I am sure nobody will ever read after the day they are published; but indeed who does write what is readable? I have got two more volumes of Shenstone's correspondence,[16] and they are like all the rest, insipidity itself. Home's *Alfred* died three days old;[17] *The Battle of Hastings* is to appear this evening;[18] the child of as feeble a parent. Garrick has been *reading* plays at Althorpe[19] à la Texier,[20] and been adored as usual; yet I do not believe he succeeded half so well in the women. He goes on writing his wretched epilogues too,[21] for he cannot sit down with the *strulbruggism* that he had the sense to take up.

There is a Mr Potter[22] too, I don't know who, that has published

14. John Beard (ca 1716–91), actor and singer.

15. 'Both Houses met, but little was done, in the absence of Lord George Germaine, who was not expected in town till the 26th' (*Last Journals* ii. 92). The Secretary's absence was occasioned by the death of his wife 15 Jan. The expression 'to lead up the Blues' alludes to Germain's notorious refusal to advance with the British cavalry ('the Blues') at Minden (ibid. ii. 88).

16. *Select Letters between the Late Duchess of Somerset, Lady Luxborough, Miss Dolman, Mr Whistler, Mr R. Dodsley, William Shenstone, Esq., and Others*, ed. Thomas Hull, published 22 Jan. 1778 (*Public Advertiser*). More than half of the letters were written by Shenstone, and most of the remainder to him. HW's copy does not appear in the SH records.

17. *Alfred*, by John Home, author of *Douglas*, was first acted at Covent Garden 21 Jan. 1778 (*Public Advertiser*). It was performed three nights (Genest vi. 18). HW's copy of the second edition, 1778, is now WSL. On the title-page HW has noted, inaccurately, 'Acted but once.'

18. At Drury Lane (*Public Advertiser*). It was acted twelve times (Genest vi. 7). The author was Richard Cumberland. HW's copy is now WSL.

19. Althorp, the seat of Earl Spencer, near Northampton. Garrick's correspondence shows that he was visiting there in the previous December (*Private Correspondence of David Garrick*, 1831–2, ii. 286).

20. See *ante* 18 Feb. 1776.

21. He wrote the Epilogue to *Alfred*.

22. Rev. Robert Potter (1721–1804). His Æschylus introduced him to the London world where he was patronized by Mrs Montagu, attacked by Johnson, and approved by HW.

a translation of Æschylus,[23] and as far as I have looked is a good poet. I am sure he has taste, for in his preface he speaks like an initiate of *Elfrida* and *Caractacus*.[24] I am delighted with *Prometheus*, though I do not approve of a mad cow for first woman.[25]

To Mason, Wednesday 4 February 1778

Printed from Mitford i. 329–32.

Arlington Street, Feb. 4, 1778.

I SHALL be sorry if you depend on me for your winter provision of news, I know so little, and the papers so much, that I could only repeat their information with not half their eloquence. All last week I was confined with a great cold which I thought it impossible for me to catch, not having had a genuine one these five or six years; I mean, not more than what I call a cold when I want an excuse for not doing what I have not a mind to do; I was blooded in spite of the gout's teeth, and yet am well again.

I hear you have finished a third book of the *Garden,* thank the Muses you seldom do anything when you have nothing to do.[1] It seems I am to learn your deeds from second and third hands.

As I suppose you care more about authors than politicians, I shall begin with the former. *The Battle of Hastings*—or rather one side of it, for not a Norman appears, has been acted. I have not seen it; the accounts are a little like a charade, for they say, the first part makes one cry, the latter laugh, and the whole sleep. It will soon be gathered in due chronologic order to its predecessor *Alfred.*

I forgot till I had filled my sheet[2] to answer your question about Lord Pigot, and then it was not worth while to tap a new page, as

23. Publication of *A Translation of the Tragedies of Æschylus* was announced 23 Dec. 1777 (*Public Advertiser*). HW's copy was sold SH v. 45.

24. '. . . An amiable writer of our own [age], by an happy effort of "heaven-born genius," . . . [has] united the powers of the three illustrious Grecians, and has charmed us with the tenderness of Euripides in *Elfrida,* with the force of Æschylus and the correctness and harmony of Sophocles in *Caractacus,* adding from his own stores a richness and a grace with which the severity of the Athenian drama was unacquainted' (*A Translation of the Tragedies of Æschylus,* p. xxiv).

25. Io, who was transformed into a heifer and driven mad by a gadfly. In *Prometheus* she appears in human form.

1. *Sic* in Mitford; a semicolon seems to be needed after 'Muses.'

2. Of his letter of 24 Jan. 1778.

the account was contradicted. It is now confirmed.[3] I know no more than you see in the newspapers, and thence you will collect that there has been more than meets the ear.[4]

The enigma of the day, as he has oft been, is Lord Chatham. He has quarrelled with General Rockingham on the question of independence,[5] and in a manner declared off, yet he is expected today in the House of Lords to anathematize the new levies.[6] There is much talk too of his coming into place,[7] which I doubt; everybody must have discovered that his crutch is no magic wand, and if the lame leads the blind it is not the way of shunning a ditch. Charles Fox has tumbled old Saturn[8] from the throne of oratory, and if he has not all the dazzling lustre, has much more of the solid materials. They say nothing ever excelled his oration against the *unfortunate minister*,[9] who was truly unfortunate that day, for had Lord George been present,[10] the thunder had fallen on him. Charles's speech on Monday[11] was as marvellous for method and memory, and was really un-

3. 'Dispatches were received at the India House on Saturday last, from Madras, containing authentic advices of the death of Lord Pigot, on the 11th of May, after a long and severe illness' (*Public Advertiser* 2 Feb. 1778).

4. There is a long and circumstantial account of Pigot's death, which occurred while he was under confinement at the behest of insubordinate members of the Council of Madras, in the *Public Advertiser* 3 Feb. 1778, where it is stated that an inquest was in progress but that no verdict had been reached. A verdict of wilful murder was ultimately rendered, but nothing came of the inquiry instituted by the East India Company.

5. Rockingham was convinced of the necessity of recognizing American independence. Although Chatham had opposed England's conduct of the war, he was unwilling to relinquish the English claim of authority over the Colonies. See *Correspondence of William Pitt, Earl of Chatham*, ed. W. S. Taylor and J. H. Pringle, 1838–40, iv. 489–92; *Memoirs of the Marquis of Rockingham and His Contemporaries*, ed. George Thomas, Earl of Albemarle, 1852, ii. 348–9; *Last Journals* ii. 92–3.

6. Early in 1778 efforts to raise new regiments were made, but the legality of taking these steps without the consent

of Parliament was challenged, especially in a motion for an inquiry made by Lord Abingdon and scheduled to be debated 4 Feb. 1778 (*Last Journals* ii. 101; Cobbett, *Parl. Hist.* xix. 629).

7. 'It is whispered that Lord Ch——m is to come in alone, without making terms for any of his party; and the only thing he has asked, is to give his eldest son a seat at the Board of Trade or Admiralty. It is also whispered that the first act of his administration will be to repeal all the acts against America since the year 1763' (*Public Advertiser* 2 Feb.).

8. That is, Chatham.

9. '27th [Jan. 1778] . . . . Charles Fox, in an admirable speech, attacked Lord North on having called himself *an unfortunate minister*, and proved that all the disgraces had happened by ignorance, blunders, and misconduct, not by misfortune' (*Last Journals* ii. 94). The occasion of the speech was the debate on Fox's motion to have copies of Burgoyne's instructions submitted to the House of Commons (Cobbett, *Parl. Hist.* xix. 644–5).

10. Lord George Germain had been expected in Parliament on the 27th, but failed to appear. See *ante* 24 Jan. 1778.

11. 2 Feb. 1778. The speech in support of his motion 'that no more of the old corps [regiments of the standing army] be

answerable, for not one of the ministers knew what to say, and so said nothing, and that silence cost them many votes. In short the minority amounted to above an hundred and sixty,[12] in which were several Tories. It is supposed the inquiries will be put to a violent death, which will be very weak, for the people are contented with whatever is discussed and voted, but grow impatient when their ears are stopped by force.

The new levies are like Glendower's—he can stamp and call spirits from the vasty deep; but they don't come,[13] consequently they will not go. I fancy the American war is pretty near an end, I mean as to attempting more than keeping what remains. I don't think there will be a French war *yet*,[14] unless we chance to go together by the ears at sea. However it hangs by a thread.

Having now given you the quintessence of my intelligence you see it would not have made one more letter than it does. I shall reserve a vacuum for what may pass today in the Lords; but I have very rarely known a much expected debate answer. Chance is as much mistress of orators as of generals; and the prepared engagements of both, frequently turn out like Sir W. Howe's two *surveys*[15] of Washington's army.

5th.

Lord Chatham did not appear, they say he has the gout, but I suppose not so bad but he could hobble to the end of the park[16] if he

sent out of the Kingdom' is summarized in Cobbett, *Parl. Hist.* xix. 672–83. HW described it in his memoirs as 'a speech of two hours and forty minutes, in which he recapitulated the events, history, and misconduct of the war with astonishing memory and method' (*Last Journals* ii. 99).

12. 'For Mr Fox's motion 165; against it 259' (Cobbett, *Parl. Hist.* xix. 683).

13. *Henry IV*, pt i, III. i. 53–5. 'The subscriptions themselves were much ridiculed: . . . few or no men were to be gotten' (*Last Journals* ii. 103).

14. 'The stocks continued to fall on apprehensions of a war with France, yet there did not seem to be much cause for those fears. The French, it is true, continued arming, and it was believed had concluded a treaty with the Americans; but the probability was that it was solely a transaction of trade' (*Last Journals* ii. 89). The Franco-American treaties of alliance were signed

6 Feb. 1778 (see *post* 18 Feb. 1778, n. 16). Opposition to the new levies for the American war was largely grounded in fear that a war with France would find England depleted of troops and unable to defend herself at home.

15. See *ante* 17 Jan. 1778 and n. 7. A recent comment in the newspapers may have suggested the expression 'two surveys' to HW: 'A correspondent observes, that Gen. Howe *looked* at Washington's camp in the Jerseys, but did not think it *prudent* to *attack* it. He has now looked *again* upon it near Philadelphia, and returned under the same apprehension' (*Public Advertiser* 2 Feb. 1778).

16. That is, through St James's Park to the Queen's House (Buckingham House), the royal residence granted to Queen Charlotte by Parliament in 1775. HW means that Chatham could be persuaded to form a new government.

was much entreated. I have heard of nothing particular that passed in either House, but have seen nobody that was in either; in good truth I am little curious about debates. The ruin has gone a great deal too far to make Parliament of any consequence; speakers may amuse themselves with filling up the interstices of events, but when a house is falling does one care who painted the staircase? Yes, Lord Chatham does. Because he once raised the building a storey higher, he thinks he could do as much when the foundations have given way. Adieu! I long to see your *Garden.* I am forced to read the newspapers or my eyes would starve, yet it is feeding them with offals.

From Mason, Friday 6 February 1778

Printed from MS now wsl.
Address: The Honourable Horace Walpole, Arlington Street, London.
Postmark: ROTHERHAM 9 FE.

Aston, Feb. 6th, 1778.

I KNOW thee and the wickedness of thy heart! You would have my opera turned into a tragedy. I know the speech of *Sappho* would be much better if turned as you would have it. But if three drops of cold water which had never been mixed with the unchaste wave of Alphæus[1] is not a sufficient cure for the most outrageous love that ever was, there is no faith in mythology. All the rest of your criticisms I submit to, and kiss the rod. I even will expunge the line about the harp,[2] though it is a verbatim translation of a fragment of Sappho.[3]

As to Giardini, look you, if I did not think better of him than I do of Handel, my little shoemaker would not have had the benefit he will have (I hope) from this labour of my brain. Let Handel's music vibrate on the tough drum of royal ears; I am for none of it.

However as I am now fully employed in writing a Fast Sermon[4] for

---

1. See *ante* 24 Jan. 1778, n. 9.
2. 'Far sweeter than the harp' (*ante* 24 Jan. 1778).
3. The Sapphic fragment reads: 'Πόλυ πάκτιδος ἀδυμελεστέρα . . . Χρύσω χρυσοτέρα (*Lyra Græca,* ed. J. M. Edmonds, i. 224)—'than the *pektis* sweeter in tone . . . than gold more golden.' The precise meaning of 'pektis' is unknown (Curt Sachs,

Real-Lexikon der Musikinstrumente, Berlin, 1913).
4. The King on 23 Jan. had proclaimed that Friday 27 Feb. would be observed as a general fast, when prayers would be offered for 'a special blessing on our arms, both by sea and land,' in the American war (*Public Advertiser* 26 Jan. 1778).

York Minster, music and operas must be lain by for a season. I hope however you have sent the act to Giardini, otherwise he will think I have cheated him.

Will you be at *Elfrida* on Saturday night?⁵ and will you clap like a dragon? I have taken more pains in fitting it for the stage than I did about *Caractacus*. On Wednesday I go to York, pray remember

to direct to York, to

Yours most faithfully,

W. MASON

From MASON, Sunday 8 February 1778

Printed from MS now WSL.
Address: The Honourable Horace Walpole, Arlington Street, London.
Postmark: ROTHERHAM 11 FE.

Aston, Feb. 8th, 1778.

I AM much obliged to you for your letter received today. Your news about *The English Garden* has been told you as imperfectly as that of the opera. It is far from finished and not even fit for anybody's inspection at present. When it is, you shall hear more from me. I now write to tell you a story which I think I have told you before, but which the debate which I read in the papers about Lord Abington's motion[1] makes me think ought to be more public. 'In 1745 when the rebels were at Derby and subscriptions were going on in London, a certain (then) barrister[2] at Lincoln's Inn was called upon by a parish officer[3] for his name, etc. He was treated as a man should be that solicits an illegal unconstitutional subscription. The rebels retreated from Derby. The barrister flew immediately to the parish officer's

5. 'The dramatic poem of *Elfrida* is also preparing with alterations for representation by the author. The music composed entirely new by Signor Giardini' (*Public Advertiser* 2 Feb. 1778). *Elfrida* was first acted at Covent Garden 21 Nov. 1772 (Genest v. 360–1), but it had been prepared for the stage without Mason's knowledge, and the version failed to win his approbation. See *ante* 1 Dec. 1772.

1. The motion to inquire into the legality of levying troops with money raised by private subscription and without the consent of Parliament. See *ante* 4 Feb. 1778.

2. HW has inserted 'Ld Mansfield' above this.

3. Henry Gally (1696–1769), D.D., divine and classical scholar; rector of St Giles-in-the-Fields 1732–69.

house to put down his name. The p.o. was from home, had locked up the book, a blacksmith was called for to break open the bureau, and the name was inserted.'⁴ This parish officer lived either in Long Acre or Great Queen's Street. This I had from good authority two years ago and was told the fact might yet be authenticated.

Adieu.

I wrote a long letter two posts ago.⁵

To Mason, Thursday 12 February 1778

Printed from Mitford i. 334–7.

Arlington Street, Feb. 12, 1778.

I HAVE received two letters from you, one of the 6th and another of the 8th, but not the long one you mention; for the first was but of 25 lines, and the latter of 23, neither of which I should think a long one from anybody from whom I liked to hear at all, much less shall you pretend that one page is to pass for length; yet I conclude you have written none that I have not received. However I answer you immediately that you may ascertain the fact, and I wish for the future you would keep the dates of the letters you do write, long or short.

I will not talk now of the story you mention, which I not only know, but remember happening. *Basta!* there will be a time.¹

I am dismally afraid I shall not be able to go to *Elfrida* on Saturday.² My cold, that I thought gone, is worse, with the addition of a

---

4. 'An old story was revived at this time, which was very true. In the Rebellion, Dr Gally, minister of his parish, went to him [Lord Mansfield] on his rounds, with the book of subscriptions for raising forces. Lord Mansfield refused to subscribe; but as soon as the rebels retreated from Derby, Lord Mansfield sent for the book; and the parish officer not being at home, Lord Mansfield had his burse broken open and his subscription entered into it' (*Last Journals* ii. 107–8). Mansfield lived at No. 56, Lincoln's Inn Fields, St Giles-in-the-Fields, ca 1739–ca 1755 (Survey of London, vol. 3, *The Parish of St Giles-in-the-Fields*, pt i, 1912, pp. 88–9). The story was probably as baseless as another charge against Mansfield, of supposed Jacobitism,

that was officially investigated in 1753 (John, Lord Campbell, *The Lives of the Chief Justices*, 1849–57, ii. 370–5).

5. Apparently the letter of 6 Feb.; see HW's reply. There was a daily post to and from Rotherham (*Royal Kalendar*, 1778, p. 124).

---

1. Possibly a hint that he was inserting the story about Mansfield in his memoirs.

2. HW apparently had not noticed the announcement in the *Public Advertiser* on the day before this letter that *The Duenna* and *The Norwood Gypsies* would be played on Saturday 14 Feb. and that *Elfrida* would be presented 'as soon as possible.' See Mason's reply, *post* 23 Feb.

sore throat. I have not been out of my doors these two days, and as putrid sore throats are very rife, of which one of Lord Bute's daughters is dead,[3] I am afraid of ripening mine to one. I am a little sorry you bestow your words, not only on folk that cannot act, but on voices that cannot articulate.[4] If *Sappho* is to be sung, I wish it were by Italians, for from the pains they take to speak English, they pronounce more distinctly than our natives.

I sent your act to Giardini, and wish he may make it discourse most eloquent music.[4a] His violin[5] to be sure will make a long soliloquy— but though I like Handel, I am not bigoted. I thought Dryden's *Ode* more harmonious before he set it than after, yet he had expression; and I prefer Charles Fox's native wood-notes to Burke's feigned voice,[6] though it goes to the highest pitch of the gamut of wit.

Apropos, his last Friday's parody of Burgoyne's talk with the Indians,[7] was the *chef d'œuvre* of wit, humour, and just satire, and almost suffocated Lord North himself with laughter; as his pathetic description of the barbarities of the Cis-Atlantic army

Drew iron tears down Barré's cheek.[8]

3. Lady Augusta Stuart (1749–78), m. (1773) Andrew Corbet. She died 5 Feb. See Collins, *Peerage*, 1812, ii. 579; *Annual Register*, 1778, xxi. 225.

4. HW had no high opinion of either the Covent Garden or the Drury Lane company. See *ante* 8 Oct. 1776.

4a. *Hamlet* III. ii. 374–5.

5. According to Burney, Giardini, who delighted in long, brilliant cadenzas, was 'the greatest performer in Europe' on the violin (*History of Music*, 1776–89, iv. 521).

6. HW probably means that Burke forced his voice in Parliament. In a letter to Charles O'Hara 18 Jan. 1766, commenting on his first attempt to speak in the House of Commons, Burke wrote, 'I find my voice not strong enough to fill the House; but I shall endeavour to raise it as high as it will bear' (unpublished text kindly supplied by Mr Ross Hoffman and Mr Thomas W. Copeland).

7. At the beginning of the campaign of 1777 that led to his defeat at Saratoga, Burgoyne invited the Indian allies of the British to his camp on the Boquet river, and on 21 June he addressed them on the conduct expected of them. The speech is summarized in GM March 1778, xlviii.

122–3, and there is a circumstantial account of it and of the Indians' war-feast by an eyewitness, Thomas Anburey, in his *Travels through the Interior Parts of America in a Series of Letters*, 1789, i. 280–302. Burke's parody was part of his speech on 6 Feb. in advocacy of his motion that all governmental papers relating to the military employment of Indians be laid before the House. 'He supported the motion with his usual ability in a speech of great length (near three hours and a half), which excited so much applause that many gave it a preference to any other he had ever spoken' (*Annual Register*, 1778, xxi. 110).

8. Paraphrased from Milton, *Il Penseroso*, l. 107. 'He then grew serious; and as the former part had excited the warmest and most continued bursts of laughter even from Lord North, Rigby, and the ministers themselves, so he drew such a pathetic picture of the cruelties of the King's army, particularly in the case of a young woman [Jenny McCrea] on whose ransom, not beauty, they quarrelled, and murdered her, —*that he drew iron tears* down Barré's cheek' (*Last Journals* ii. 104–5).

I wish I could give you an idea of that superlative oration. He was pressed to print it, but says he has not time during the session.⁹ How cold, how inadequate will be my fragment of a sketch from second, third and thousandth hands; yet I must send you a bit of a daub with probably even the epithets wrong or misplaced, though each was picturesque. Well, though I can neither draw nor colour, *invenies etiam disjecti membra.*¹⁰ Hurlothrumbo¹¹ exhorted seventeen Indian nations, who so far from understanding the Hurlothrumbic dialect, are probably almost as ignorant of English; he exhorted them by the dictates of *our* holy religion, and by their reverence for *our* constitution, to repair to his Majesty's standard. Where was that? said Burke: on board Lord Dunmore's ship;¹²—and he exhorted them (I suppose by the same divine and human laws) not to touch the hair of the head of man, woman or child, while living, though he was willing to deal with them for scalps of the dead,¹³ being a nice and distinguished judge between the scalp taken from a dead person and the head of a person that dies of being scalped. Let us state this Christian exhortation and Christian injunction, said Burke, by a more familiar picture; suppose there was a riot on Tower Hill, what would the keeper of his Majesty's lions do? would he not fling open the dens of the wild beasts, and then address them thus? 'My gentle lions, my humane bears, my sentimental

9. The speech was not printed in full; summaries are given in Cobbett, *Parl. Hist.* xix. 694–99, and *Annual Register,* 1778, xxi. 110–14.

10. 'Invenias etiam disiecti membra poetæ' (Horace, *Satires* I. iv. 62). ('You will recognize a true poet even if he is dismembered.')

11. The central character in a bombastic play of the same name by Samuel Johnson of Cheshire (1691–1773), produced at the Haymarket in 1729 (Genest iii. 247). HW also calls Burgoyne 'Hurlothrumbo' in his letter to Lady Ossory 3 Nov. 1777.

12. In 1775 Lord Dunmore's war against the Indians on the western frontier was ended by a treaty arranged by his agent, John Connolly, and by virtue of this, in spite of his previous hostility, Dunmore tried to enlist the aid of the Indians on the side of the British. See 'A Narrative of the Transactions . . . of John Connolly,' *Pennsylvania Magazine of History,* 1888, xii. 310–24, 407–20; C. M. Burton, 'John Connolly, A Tory of the Revolution,' *Pro-*

ceedings of the American Antiquarian Society, 1909, n.s., xx. 70–105. Opposition to Dunmore in Virginia during this early stage of the Revolution forced him to take refuge on a man-of-war, from which he directed raids against the rebels, and from which he issued a proclamation 'given under my hand, on board the ship *William,* off Norfolk, the 7th day of November [1775],' bidding all persons capable of bearing arms to resort to the King's standard (*American Archives,* ed. Peter Force, Washington, 1837–53, 4th ser., iii. 1385). In 1776 Dunmore was decisively defeated and forced to retire from the Virginia coast, and by early 1777 he was in England (*Public Advertiser* 30 Jan. 1777).

13. 'In conformity and indulgence to your customs . . . you shall be allowed to take the scalps of the dead when killed by your fire and in fair opposition, but on no account or pretence or subtlety or prevarication are they to be taken from the wounded or even dying' (Burgoyne's speech as reported in GM 1778, xlviii. 123).

wolves, my tender-hearted hyenas, go forth; but I exhort ye, as ye are Christians and members of a civilized society, to take care not to hurt man, woman or child,' etc., etc. Barré's codicil was to threaten to paste on churches this memorable talk under the injunctions of the bishops for a fast.[14] Gov. Johnstone[15] said he rejoiced there were no strangers in the gallery, as Burke's speech would have excited them to tear the ministers to pieces as they went out of the House;[16] the ministers are much more afraid of losing their places. Eloquence, like music, is too much improved in our days to have any of their old effects on the passions of a large audience.

Voilà a truly long letter. I leave the application to your conscience.

To Mason, Wednesday 18 February 1778

Printed from Mitford i. 337–41.

Feb. 18, 1778.

I HAVE two small morsels of news to tell you, and do not know which you will choose to hear first. As you cannot choose without knowing, it would be vain to wait for your answer, especially as I cannot state them without preferring one to the other. Iricisms, it is true, are not out of fashion. *Nos seigneurs* the peers will not vote truisms to be true, lest they should betray the weakness of the nation,[1] though those truisms, and the reason for not asserting them, are given in every newspaper,[2] which newspapers are read in every coffee-house in

---

14. 'One gentleman . . . wished it to be printed and affixed to all the church-doors which contained the proclamation for a general fast' (*Annual Register*, 1778, xxi. 110).

15. George Johnstone (1730–87), naval officer; governor of West Florida 1763–7; M. P. Cockermouth 1768–74, Appleby 1774–80, Lostwithiel 1781–4, Ilchester 1784–7.

16. 'A member of great distinction and in high office congratulated the ministers upon admitting no strangers on that day into the gallery, as the indignation of the people might have been excited against them to a degree that would have endan-

gered their safety' (*Annual Register*, loc. cit.).

---

1. At the debate (2 Feb. 1778) on the state of the nation, Lord Suffolk 'threw out hints that the inquiry would betray the *weakness* of the kingdom to foreign Courts' (*Last Journals* ii. 100; cf. Cobbett, *Parl. Hist.* xix. 659). Lord Sandwich expressed the same fear on 11 Feb. (*Last Journals* ii. 109).

2. There are accounts of the debate of 11 Feb. in the *London Chronicle* 10–12 Feb. (xliii. 151–2) and in *Lloyd's Evening Post* 11–13 Feb. 1778, xlii. 145–6.

Paris.³ Ergo their Lordships suppose that France supposes herself to know nothing but what appears in the *Votes*.⁴

As a loyal subject and freeman of Parnassus, I must believe that you interest yourself more in Heliconian affairs than in the politics of the *late* empire of Great Britain. I therefore announce to you the arrival of Voltaire at Paris.⁵ Yes; there he is. Probably⁶ *recalled from exile to raise a regiment of infidels for the defence of holy church.*⁷

The other event would not be worth mentioning, but for its novelty. In that light, to be sure, no parallel instance is to be found in ancient or modern history, whether Ammonite, Jewish, Chaldean, Egyptian, Chinese, Greek, Roman, Constantinopolitan, Frank, French, British, Saxon, Pict, Ossianite, Mogul, Indian, or English (all which I have examined carefully this morning to no purpose)—nay in the *Tales of the Fairies*,⁸ in which I am still more deeply versed, I find nothing similar. You perhaps, who have all ecclesiastical history at your fingers' ends, may recollect something approaching to the transaction of *yesterday the 17th of February,* a day of confession and humiliation, that will be remembered as long as the name of England exists.⁹ Yesterday, Feb. 17, did the whole administration, by the mouth of their spokesman, Lord North, no, no, not resign; on the contrary, try to keep their places by a full and ample confession of all their faults, and by a still more extraordinary act,—by doing full justice both to America and to the Opposition,—by allowing that the former are no cowards, nor conquerable,¹⁰—that they are no rebels, for the

3. Furthermore, as Mme du Deffand wrote HW, 'Le *Courrier de L'Europe* nous traduit tous vos discours du Parlement' (DU DEFFAND v. 19).

4. *Votes of the House of Commons*, a serial publication authorized by the Speaker of the House of Commons. Like the official *Journals*, it gives no details of the debates.

5. Voltaire's arrival at Paris on 10 Feb. was announced by Mme du Deffand to HW in her letter of 11 Feb. (DU DEFFAND v. 17). See GM 1778, xlviii. 109–10; *Annual Register*, 1778, xxi pt ii. 1.

6. HW doubtless wrote 'there he is, probably' etc.

7. If this is a quotation or paraphrase it has not been found.

8. By the Comtesse d'Aulnoy (*ante* 21 Sept. 1777 and n. 5).

9. On 17 Feb. Lord North introduced his proposals for conciliation of the Colonies, including the appointment of commissioners who would have full power to treat with the Colonies collectively or separately, recognition of the *de facto* authority of Congress, consideration by Parliament of the repeal of all acts since 1763 that had been obnoxious to the Colonies, and a system of voluntary contributions for defence instead of compulsory taxation for revenue (Cobbett, *Parl. Hist.* xix. 762–7; *London Chronicle* 19–21 Feb. 1778, xliii. 177–8).

10. Lord North's speech as reported in the public press was more guarded: 'Our

new commissioners are to treat with the Congress or anybody; and by asking pardon by effects, i.e. the cancelling all offensive acts, and by acknowledging the independence of the thirteen provinces, not *verbally* yet *virtually*. These were Lord North's words.[11] To the Opposition full justice is done; for if the administration has been in the wrong from beginning to end, their opponents must have been a little in the right.

The faults of the administration, according to their own calculation, are *two:* one of being misinformed,[12] the other of persisting in a mere point of honour.[13] Some will perhaps think they have been guilty of two more;—the destruction of twenty-four thousand lives on their own side,[14] and Lord knows how many thousands on t'other, with the burning of towns, desolation of the country, and the expense of above thirty millions of money;[15] the second consists of two parts,— rejection of all proposals of accommodation offered by the Opposition, and the delay of offering terms themselves, till they knew it was too late; for Lord North was asked if he did not know that the treaty between the Americans and France is signed?[16] He would not answer till

army is great, our navy is great . . . but the resistance of America is greater, and the war has lasted longer than any friend to this country could wish . . . and I do not think that it will end in this campaign,' whereupon he proceeded to assure the House of his confidence, ultimately, in complete victory, though he felt that it might require three or four more years of war (*London Chronicle*, loc. cit.).

11. These words do not appear in the reports of Lord North's speech, but they fairly represent his meaning. 'As the deficiency of powers in the former commissioners had been objected to, so the Congress had raised a difficulty, on pretence of the non-admission of their title to be independent states. . . . Should the Americans now claim their independence on the outset, he would not insist on their renouncing it, until the treaty had received its final ratification by the King and Parliament of Great Britain' (*Annual Register*, 1778, xxi. 132).

12. 'I own I thought that the war would soon have ended. . . . I will never own that administration has deceived the public' (North as reported in *London Chronicle* 19–21 Feb. 1778, xliii. 178).

13. 'I never thought taxation a sufficient object for the contest. . . . But I fought for the dependence of America' (ibid. xliii. 177).

14. On 16 Feb. 1778 in the House of Lords the Duke of Richmond declared, 'There appears to be lost by death, desertion, captivity, or otherwise, 24,917 men' (Cobbett, *Parl. Hist.* xix. 745).

15. Richmond on 19 Feb. estimated the expenses of war to that day at 'near 33 millions' (ibid. xix. 748).

16. 'Mr G. Grenville . . . concluded by informing the House, that he had seen an extract of a letter from Doctor Franklin, mentioning the treaty between America and the Court of Versailles' (*London Chronicle* 19–21 Feb. 1778, xliii. 178). The 'treaty' was actually three treaties: one of 'amity and commerce,' one of 'conditional and defensive alliance,' and an 'act separate and secret' (providing for slight alterations in the other two treaties, at the behest of Spain). They were signed at Paris 6 Feb. 1778, though not ratified by the United States until 4 May or by France until 16 July 1778. The texts in French and English, with notes, are given in *Treaties and Other International Acts of the United States of*

Sir George [Savile][17] hallowed out, 'An answer, an answer, an answer!'
His Lordship then rose, could not deny the fact, but said he did not
know it *officially;*[18] that is, I suppose, it does not stand on the votes of
the parliament at Paris.

What shall I say more? though this is not half of that ignominious
seventeenth of February. The measure passed *nemine contradicente.*
The Tories gulped their shame,[19] the rest *pocketed.*[20] *Note.* The Opposition approved an attempt at peace, though a hopeless one. Charles
Fox congratulated himself on having converted Lord North. The
papers will tell you the rest. If anything could deepen this recantation of wilful criminality it is that it was extorted at last by the
urgency of the moment, in short, to prevent this pretended spirit of
pacification from being anticipated by France's notification of her
alliance with the American states to all Europe;—what if by a declaration of war! Her troops are in full march to the coast,[21] the Duc de
Lauzun recalled hence[22] and ordered to be in France by the 26th.
How one blushes to be an Englishman! to be a countryman of the
majority! I have no comfort but that I am not a Scot.

A night's rest has not dissipated the astonishment of mankind.
Everybody that comes in stares, and cannot express himself. Who
can at once reconcile a supplication of alliance with the high and

America, ed. Hunter Miller, Washington,
1931–48, ii. 3–47. See Samuel F. Bemis,
*The Diplomacy of the American Revolu-
tion,* New York, 1935, pp. 58–65.

17. Mitford reads 'Savage'; corrected by
Cunningham. Sir George Savile (1726–84),
8th Bt, was M.P. Yorkshire 1759–83.

18. 'Mr Burke then spoke to draw an
answer from the minister relative to that
treaty; as did Sir George Savile. This made
Lord North declare that he knew nothing
of it but by common report, and that the
ministers of France had denied it some
time ago' (*London Chronicle,* loc. cit.).

19. 'The Tories, who could not like concessions so inadequate to their hopes, and
so repugnant to their highflown attachment to the Prerogative, seeing the intemperate zeal of the Opposition, were
ashamed to mark themselves as an obstinate
and weak party, which they would be if
they separated from the Court when approved by the Opposition' (*Last Journals*
ii. 116).

20. 'Pocket. . . . To take or accept (an
affront, etc.) without showing resentment;
to submit to, endure meekly, "swallow" '
(OED *sub* 'pocket' v., 3a).

21. Mme du Deffand had written HW
10 Feb. 1778: 'Nous faisons partir tous nos
officiers de terre et de mer pour la Bretagne'
(DU DEFFAND v. 17). Similar reports from
Paris circulated at this time and were
quoted in the English press: 'Troops are
defiling towards Brittany and Normandy,
where we already have an army under the
command of Count Maillebois' (*Public Advertiser* 19 Feb. 1778).

22. Armand-Louis de Gontaut (1747–93),
Duc de Lauzun, 1766, Duc de Biron, 1788.
His recall was apparently countermanded,
for he remained in England during February to provide the French ministry of
foreign affairs with notes on England's
colonial policy. He was summoned to
Versailles in March 1778. See Gaston Maugras, *Le Duc de Lauzun,* 1893–5, ii. 155–7.

mighty states of America, with a total improbability of obtaining it? and the faintest hope of peace, with a prospect of a war with France? How, an acknowledgment of independence, with a pretension of supplies, or a suspension of the war for a year and a half, with any intention of renewing it, when the Americans shall have had time to settle their government and recruit? but who *can* digest all the contradictions into which the government plunges every day?

Who can believe what I have read in the papers today?—that one Hutton,[23] a Moravian, has been dispatched to Paris to fling himself at Dr Franklin's feet[24] and sue for forgiveness? it is said that the man fell on the Doctor's neck with tears and implored peace. What triumph on one side! What humiliation on the other! Will princes still listen to those vile flatterers who fascinate them with visions of empire, that terminate in such mortifications? for the philosopher replied, 'It is too late.'[25]

One cannot rein one's pen at such a moment: it runs away with moralities; but I will stifle commonplace reflections. Shall I not appear a trifler if I can mix anything else with such thoughts? yet having crossed over into a fourth page, I will fill up the remainder with two bagatelles; one was a story related in the House of Commons. Somebody passing along the road in Scotland, heard great outcries and lamentation and complaints of violence. He stopped to inquire the cause; another person replied, 'Oh, they are only making volunteers,' i.e. pressing volunteers.

I have waded through *Alfred*.[26] The author says it has been ob-

23. James Hutton (1715–95), leader of the English Moravians.

24. Benjamin Franklin had been in France since Dec. 1776 as one of the three members of the American commission to arrange a treaty of alliance. Hutton's ostensible purpose in visiting Franklin was to discuss Moravian affairs in America, but at the same time he endeavoured to bring about a reconciliation between England and the Colonies. Franklin described the meeting in a letter to David Hartley addressed from Passy, 12 Feb. 1778: 'An old friend of mine, Mr Hutton, a chief of the Moravians, who is often at the Queen's palace and is sometimes spoken to by the King, was over here lately. He pretended to no commission, but urged me much to propose some terms of peace, which I avoided' (*Writings of Benjamin Franklin,* ed. Alfred H. Smyth, 1905–7, vii. 104). Hutton was back in England by 1 Feb. 1778, as Franklin's letters to him dated 1 and 12 Feb. make clear. See ibid. vii. 98–101 and Daniel Benham, *Memoirs of James Hutton,* 1856, pp. 511–3.

25. 'A correspondent says, that Dr Franklin was lately applied to in order to find out if there was yet a possibility for matters to be accommodated between Britain and the United States of America. When lo! the answer was (O mortifying!) "No, it was *too late,* for that the States had entered into other connections"' (*Public Advertiser* 19 Feb. 1778).

26. Publication of John Home's *Alfred* was announced 14 Feb. 1778 (*Public Advertiser*).

jected that he has tamed a legislator into a lover in a novel,[27] but he pleads that Alfred had probably been in love.[28] The same excuse would apologize for representing the Duke of Marlborough, not as a hero but slabbering in his dotage. In the play itself I found this line, and have written in the title-page as a motto,

> I shall surprise you much; my name is Alfred;[29]

mine is

Yours most sincerely,

H. W.

PS. Pray tell me you receive this.

From Mason, Monday 23 February 1778

Printed from MS now WSL.
Address: The Honourable Mr Horace Walpole, Arlington Street, London.
Postmark: YORK 25 FE.

York, Feb. 23d, 1778.

Dear Sir,

AS many millions of thanks are due to you for your two letters of the 12th and 18th, particularly for the last, as there have been millions of money spent in order to persuade the Americans to permit us to acknowledge their independency. But I have hardly time to pay you and nothing but thanks to pay you withal. I am deeply engaged in my Fast Sermon[1] which is to be preached on Friday and not half finished yet. My text is taken out of the Book of the Lamentations of the Prophet Jeremiah and is as follows:

27. 'It has been alleged . . . "that the hero, the legislator, is degraded to a lover, who enters the Danish camp, from a private, not a public motive" ' (*Alfred,* p. vi).

28. 'Alfred was a young man, when he fought the battle of Ethendune. . . . Is it improbable to suppose, that a young hero was in love?' (ibid. p. vii).

29. What HW wrote in his copy of the play was the correct line, ' "It will amaze thee much: my name is Alfred," *v.* p. 57 and preface p. vi.'

1. See *ante* 6 Feb. 1778. The sermon, which was preached 27 Feb., was not printed. That it was political in tone and strongly anti-administration is clear from this letter and *post* 13 and 16 March 1778, HW to Stonhewer ca 10 March, and Mason's correspondence with Alderson.

Abroad the sword bereaveth,
At home there is as death—[2]

which you perceive runs very musically and even lyrically.

'Twas when the seas were roaring
With hollow blasts of wind.[3]

If all my periods have as fine a rhythmus, I don't doubt the sermon will have an uncommon effect on the ears of our *Lord* Mayor[4] and aldermen. To be serious, I mean to write it with care, lest I should find it necessary to print it, for this is a Tory town,[5] though there is a Rockingham Club[6] in it; and I question not but they will be ready to misrepresent it. However *macte virtute*. This is no time to be mealy-mouthed in.

My very principal virgin[7] is within a few weeks of her time, and Elfrida herself[8] is obliged to go to Bath perhaps to lie in too, so I fancy the representation of my tragedy will be postponed till next winter,[9] and will probably be performed in the Opera House[10] which Sheridan and Harris[11] have bought.[12] I am rather pleased at this, as

2. Lamentations 1. 20.

3. John Gay, *The What D'Ye Call It*, II. viii. 22–3.

4. In 1389 King Richard II bestowed upon the mayor of York and all his successors the right to the title of Lord Mayor, a title that until recent times has been shared only by the Lord Mayor of London. See Charles Brunton Knight, *A History of the City of York*, York, 1944, p. 239; William Hargrove, *History and Description of the Ancient City of York*, York, 1818, i. 308.

5. In his memoirs for Oct. 1776 HW wrote: 'The Mayor and Corporation of York voted an address to the King on the victory at Long Island. This showed the incapacity of Lord Rockingham to be at the head of an Opposition. He had last year neglected to get an address against the war from the county of York, where he had the greatest influence' (*Last Journals* i. 577–8).

6. The Rockingham Club in York seems to have been in existence at least as early as 1756. See George Benson, *An Account of the City . . . of York: from the Reformation to the Year 1925*, York, 1925, p. 76.

7. Presumably Ann Catley, who had led the chorus of British virgins in earlier performances (Genest v. 361; *ante* 19 Nov. 1773). At the time of her death in 1789 she had had eight children by Maj.-Gen. Francis Lascelles, who had married her in 1784 (DNB).

8. Mrs Hartley. '*Elfrida* is obliged to be deferred (on account of Mrs Hartley's illness) till further notice' (*Public Advertiser* 21 Feb. 1778).

9. The revised *Elfrida* was first performed 23 Feb. 1779 (Genest vi. 95).

10. In the Haymarket: variously known as the King's (or Queen's) Theatre, the Italian Opera House, and the Opera House. It was built by Vanbrugh and opened 9 April 1705 (*London Past and Present* ii. 199). *Elfrida* was not performed there, but at Covent Garden (Genest, loc. cit.).

11. Thomas Harris (d. 1820), proprietor and manager of Covent Garden 1774–1820.

12. 'Sheridan . . . in partnership with Harris of Covent Garden, in 1778 gave £22,000 for the Opera patent and undertook a rental of £1200 a year' (Henry Barton Baker, *The London Stage: Its History and Traditions*, 1889, i. 243). The transfer of ownership of the Opera House was not

it will be more likely then and there to have fair play. I write this on a sheet of paper on which my friend Mr Burgh had previously transcribed the story[13] I mentioned to you. If you are curious to have it better authenticated, we will examine Martyn Luther's works[14] for the purpose. Pray don't count the lines in this letter to twit me for my brevity, for indeed I have nothing more to say, and what with twice-a-day prayers, chapters and settlings of fines and visits from the gentry of the place who always make them at the most inconvenient times, I am really almost as fully and as usefully employed as if I was Sir Gray Cooper.[15]

Believe me ever yours,

W. Mason

To Mason, Wednesday 4 March 1778

Printed from Mitford i. 344–7.

Arlington Street, March 4, 1778.

IT is not from having anything new to tell you that I write you a few lines, but to ask how I may send you half a dozen more *Gazettes littéraires,* for I conclude your Varelsts are in town. There is no hurry

completed until June 1778 (*Annual Register*, 1778, xxi. 188). Sheridan sold his share in 1781 (Walter Sichel, *Sheridan*, 1909, i. 529).

13. Resembling HW's *Mysterious Mother*. Burgh has written on one page of Mason's letter: 'The following tale is extracted from a book entitled "Meditations of a Divine Soul or the Christian's Guide amidst the Various Opinions of a Vain World," printed in London for John Kersey, 1703, octavo—the tale is ascribed to Martin Luther but without any reference to the portion of his writings from which it is taken—

"I knew a young man in the city of Erfurdt who used his utmost efforts to debauch a damsel that waited upon his mother; insomuch that this gentlewoman, being informed by the same damsel of her son's design, resolved to prevent him, and to that purpose laid herself down on the maid's bed. Some time after, the son being

ignorant of what had happened, went to bed to his mother, who likewise burned in lust, and so satiated his lewd desires; whereupon she conceived, and having brought forth a daughter, caused the infant to be nursed and educated in another place. In process of time the mother took her daughter home, as if she were the child of a stranger, who was of so delicate a complexion, and of so obliging a behaviour, that the son fell in love with her, and married her with the mother's consent, neither of them knowing anything at all of the matter; so that she was his daughter, sister and wife. But the judgment of God soon overtook the mother's horrid crime, and fell heavy upon the son for his former wickedness—." ' The author of the *Meditations* was Charles Povey (ca 1652–1743).

14. The story occurs several times in Luther's table-talk. See Luther's *Werke: Tischreden*, Weimar, 1912–21, i. 82, iii. 501.

15. Sir Grey Cooper (ca 1725–1801), Bt,

about them, they will always be equally new to you, and not be much
so neither; you will find in them the following pretty riddle, which I
had seen before:

> Eloigné de l'objet que j'aime,
> Lui seul calme mon ennui;
> Il est plus beau que l'amour même
> Mais elle est plus belle que lui.[1]

The word is a *portrait* and is rather too enigmatic, for one must
know the solution, to find any sense in *elle*. I have translated it, but as
we have no genders it is impossible to render *lui* and *elle;* my imitation perhaps makes it too clear:

> From the dear object of my dreams
> Removed, I still that object see;
> As fair as love itself it seems:
> Yet she is fairer still than he.

I wish you would try it; you will have better success. I have made
another enigma on the same subject, but cannot tell whether it is
good or bad, for how can one tell whether a riddle is difficult to guess,
when one knows the subject beforehand? but do not I lay you under
the same difficulty, *le voici!*

> I counterfeit all bodies, yet have none,
> Bodies give shadows, shadows give me one
> Loved for another's sake, that person yet
> Is my chief enemy whene'er we meet;
> Thinks me too old, though blest with endless youth,
> And like a monarch hates my speaking truth.[2]

The two middle verses are very bad I know.

I agree with you; there is no harm in Mrs Elfrida Hartley's pregnancy, your drama could not be well represented by the set at
Covent Garden; not that the union of the two companies[3] will make
one good, yet will be a better than the worse half. However I doubt
whether the old saying will prove true in your case, that *ce qui est
différé n'est pas perdu*. My reason I gave six weeks ago to Le Texier;

joint secretary of the Treasury 1765–82,
hence at this time directly employed by
Lord North.

1. *Gazette littéraire* June 1777, v. 432.

2. Printed in *Works* iv. 405, there titled
'A Looking Glass.' Drafts of both riddles
in HW's hand are now in the BM.

3. Of Covent Garden and the Opera
House. See *ante* 23 Feb. 1778, n. 12.

he was consulting me whether I thought it would be advantageous for him to take the Opera House on the present plan (on which the other managers have outbidden him). I replied, *'Oui, tant qu'il y ait de l'Angleterre.'*

The two conciliatory bills[4] are so very yielding, that nothing but the immediate dread of a French war, or the impossibility of raising money to maintain the armies and fleets in America,[5] could have reconciled the Court to such vast concessions, if they are sincere in the desire of treating, which, notwithstanding wiser men than I believe them, I doubt.[6] I can see obvious reasons for seeming to treat.[7] I hear none to persuade me that the Americans will treat. Lord Carlisle is named one of the commissioners, and is very fit to make a treaty that will not be made.[8]

Voltaire came to Paris without leave, but they say has received an indulgent promise from Monsieur de Maurepas[9] that he shall not be molested.[10] His chief object was to get a new play acted, which he

4. Lord North's proposals for conciliation (*ante* 18 Feb. 1778 and n. 9) were embodied in two bills: (1) 'A bill to enable his Majesty to appoint commissioners with sufficient powers to treat, consult, and agree upon the means of quieting the disorders now subsisting in certain of the colonies, plantations, and provinces of North America.' (2) 'A bill for declaring the intentions of the Parliament of Great Britain, concerning the exercise of the right of imposing taxes within his Majesty's colonies, provinces, and plantations in North America' (*Journals of the House of Commons* xxxvi. 712). The bills were read for the first time 19 Feb. and passed 2 March (ibid. 712 and 780). On 5 March they were debated in the House of Lords and passed 9 March (*Journals of the House of Lords* xxxv. 345, 356).

5. 'The difficulty of raising money . . . easily reconciled Lord North to a plan that he hoped, by holding out peace, would raise the stocks' (*Last Journals* ii. 112).

6. 'The bills when brought in were so delusive that there was great reason to doubt whether the Court was sincere or not in their hopes of pacification' (ibid).

7. 'The inquiries in both Houses which some at least of the ministers had encouraged . . . had laid open such errors, profusion, misconduct, and misfortunes

. . . that the Court had found great desertion was spreading amongst its standing army of mercenaries in the House of Commons. . . . Overtures of peace might stifle those inquiries, and would secure the most candid, who conscientiously wished for a pacification' (ibid. ii. 111).

8. 'His Majesty named Frederic Earl of Carlisle as one of the commissioners, a choice universally ridiculed, particularly by Burke and Governor Johnstone in the House. Lord Carlisle was a young man of pleasure and fashion, fond of dress and gaming by which he had greatly hurt his fortune, was totally unacquainted with business, and though not void of ambition, had but moderate parts, and less application' (ibid. ii. 122).

9. One of Louis XVI's chief advisers (*ante* 6 Sept. 1775, n. 9a).

10. 'Sa Majesté demanda si l'ordre qui défendait à Voltaire de revenir à Paris (ordre donné sous le ministère de M. de Saint-Contest) avait été levé. Quoique le roi n'eût rien ajouté de plus, on se pressa de rapporter ce discours à M. de Voltaire, et de le lui rapporter de la manière du monde la plus alarmante. Le vieux malade en fut vivement affecté; mais l'intention du roi n'avait jamais été de l'affliger, et, grâce à l'empressement de Mme la Comtesse Jules de Polignac, appuyée des bontés de

calls *Irène;*[11] it was *Alexis Comnène,* but the latter word sounded too harsh.[12] He has half dispatched himself with reading this piece to the actors,[13] and thinks of nothing else except of being received by the King and Queen, which Madame du Deffand who has made him two visits[14] thinks he will not obtain.[15] I should like to have been present at this interview of the two only surviving lilies of the *siècle de Louis Quatorze,*[16] yet he is more occupied with the dandelions of the present age.

I am very thankful for the extract Mr Burgh gave himself the trouble to send me, and am satisfied. Mrs Delany[17] had heard of and insisted on seeing the tragedy. I knew how it would shock her devout delicacy. She returned it with compliments, but was sorry the subject would condemn it to oblivion—perhaps so, and its more intrinsic demerits, but I do not think being acted will save many of its contemporaries! I am impatient to see your sermon—did you observe a passage in the Fast-service that has diverted people much, as it came out just after the *nemine contradicente* on the pacific bills?[18] 'Then all the people shall say *after the minister,* turn us O Lord, and so shall we be turned.'[19]

I am tempted to sign my name in French, for the pleasure of quoting the following lines from Voltaire's *Indiscret,*[20] the ridiculous parts of which suit me exactly;

TRASIMON.

—Le vieux Seigneur Horace

M'a prié—

DAMIS.

Voilà bien de quoi je m'embarrasse.
Horace est un vieux fou, plutôt qu'un vieux seigneur
Tout chamarré d'orgueil, pétri d'un faux honneur,

la reine, il ne tarda pas à être rassuré' (Grimm, *Correspondance* xii. 54, under date of Feb. 1778).

11. Acted 16 March 1778 (Voltaire, *Œuvres,* ed. Moland, vii. 315).

12. HW learned this from Mme du Deffand, ?Feb. 1778 (DU DEFFAND v. 19).

13. See Mme du Deffand to HW 22 Feb. 1778 (DU DEFFAND v. 20).

14. On 14 and 21 Feb. 1778 (ibid.).

15. Ibid. v. 21. The King and Queen

continued to take no official notice of Voltaire's presence in Paris.

16. An allusion to Voltaire's history with this title, published in 1752.

17. Mitford reads 'Delane.'

18. Lord North's conciliatory bills.

19. The rubric and text are from the Commination Service in the Book of Common Prayer.

20. First acted 1 Aug. 1725 (Voltaire, *Œuvres,* ed. Moland, ii. 243).

Assez bas à la cour, important à la ville
Et non moins ignorant qu'il veut paraître habile.[21]

HORACE

To MASON, ca Monday 9 March 1778

Missing; mentioned *post* 16 March.

From MASON, Friday 13 March 1778

Printed from MS now WSL.
Address: The Honourable Horace Walpole, Arlington Street, London.
Postmark: YORK 16 MR.

York, March 13th, 1778.

Dear Sir,

I HAVE often tried but could never make a riddle in my life. Therefore I will not attempt to correct yours, but I have a better reason still. If I was to do it, 'tis ten to one but you have forgot that ever you writ them, and consequently would not understand my corrections. You have served me in a similar sort once or twice before.[1] Nay, when I had the effrontery to make an alteration in your tragedy which alteration you approved,[2] you yet gave that alteration up merely because you had forgotten what that alteration was, which had it been attended to would have secured your *Mysterious Mother* from the devout delicacy of Mrs Delany. Nay, would have made it *pit, box and gallery*[2a] with any tragedy ancient as *Elfrida,* or modern as *The Battle of Hastings.*

Now to show you how much I hold *your* critiques[3] in devout memorial, I give you to know that I have locked up my sermon in

21. *L'Indiscret,* Scene iii, ll. 13–18. A copy of this quotation in HW's hand is on a scrap in the BM, Add. MSS 37728 fol. 38v.

1. See *ante* 17 Sept. 1773.
2. See *ante* 11 May 1769 and head-note to 8 May 1769.
2a. See *ante* 3 March 1775 and n. 13.

3. Sent in a letter of ca 10 March 1778 apparently addressed to Stonhewer, and transmitted by him to Mason with the sermon. HW recommended various alterations if the sermon was printed, which he thought inadvisable unless it was 'much clamoured against.'

my bureau till that goodly time *shortly* comes when we shall all be absolutely ruined, all but the said sermon which then will shine forth with redoubled lustre. But I also give you to know that when it does come forth, every iota of it must stand as it is, for I hear it has been taken down in shorthand. And there is a man here,[4] the son of a certain baronet[5] (who did in safer times what Dr Dodd was afterwards hanged for,[6] and who is now as he ought to be a Privy Councillor)[7] who is highly incensed at the said sermon. He wrote against Price[8] but was not read,[9] and he aims at a place or pension because his father does not give him *de quoi vivre;* and I question not is the person who has called himself the congregation of York, *vide Morning Post*, March 10th.[10] Now this being the case you see there can be no softenings whatever, which I am sorry for, more on your account than my own, for I should certainly have spared Sir John Dalrymple had I then known (which his preface has since taught me) that you gave him recommendatory letters to France.[11] However, as I said be-

4. Henry Goodricke (1741–84), of Ribston, Yorks; M.P. Lymington 1778–80 (GEC, *Complete Baronetage* ii. 137; C. A. Goodricke, *History of the Goodricke Family*, 1885, p. 37). See *post* 21 March 1778.

5. Sir John Goodricke (1708–89), Bt; M.P. Pontefract 1774–80, Ripon 1787–9; minister to Sweden 1758–64, envoy extraordinary to Sweden 1764–73. See GEC, loc. cit.; D. B. Horn, *British Diplomatic Representatives 1689–1789*, 1932, p. 143.

6. Dr Dodd was hanged for forgery. Substantiation of Mason's charge against Sir John Goodricke has not been found.

7. Goodricke became a member of the Privy Council in 1773 (GEC).

8. *Observations on Dr Price's Theory and Principles of Civil Liberty*, York, 1776.

9. On the contrary, the pamphlet was applauded in both the *Critical Review* (1776, xlii. 71) and the *Monthly Review* (1776, lv. 239), and Roland Thomas, in *Richard Price, Philosopher and Apostle of Liberty*, 1924, p. 75, remarks that 'perhaps the most popular of all the replies to Price was that by Goodricke.'

10. On 9 (not 10) March the following ironical 'card' was printed in the *Morning Post:* 'The congregation, who assembled at the cathedral church in *York,* on the forenoon of the late Fast Day, present their compliments to the Rev. Mr *Mason,* and beg leave to return him thanks for the

meekness, *piety,* and *moderation* of his sermon. They esteem it a signal instance of propriety, and good sense, that the preacher's discourse, offered up in the presence of the Deity, should accord so justly with the prayers of the day; and they flatter themselves, that Mr *Mason* will continue to fill his holy function with that *moderation,* patient *meekness, generosity* of *mind,* and *good-will* towards all men, for which he is so remarkably *distinguished.* At the same time that they pay this grateful tribute of deserved applause, they rejoice that they have it in their power to distinguish, in this public manner, the *man,* who, having felt the disappointment of a *court,* could rise superior to it, by acting the part of a *consistent* member of the church, free from *party,* free from *prejudice!*

'York, March 10 [*sic*], 1778.'

11. In his Preface, describing his efforts to gain access to the French archives, Dalrymple wrote: 'Mr Stanley gave me a letter of introduction to the Duke of Choiseul. . . . Lord Harcourt and Mr Walpole, considering the cause of letters to be the cause of England, seconded my request' (*Memoirs of Great Britain*, i. p. v). See *post* 16 March 1778, where HW states that Dalrymple must have been referring to his cousin, Thomas Walpole.

fore, my unfortunate sermon is safe under lock and key and shall remain so as long as possible, perhaps forever, unless I be in self-defence
forced to produce it.

Pray, is this triumph of the minority[12] any triumph at all? And
what say you to Mrs Macaulay's late volume,[13] to whom also you gave
recommendatory letters to France? I beg your pardon, I believe it was
Lord Harcourt and not you.[14]

If you will please to send the *Gazettes littéraires* to Mr Stonhewer's,
with directions to Charles Carter, my painting servant, to send them
to me by the York fly, I shall have them speedily. I left him in town to
perfect himself in drawing at the Academy, and anything you choose
to send he will convey speedily to me. I am tired to death of my residence, the cold of the Minster is intolerable. I wish they would tax
deans and chapters and make them as unprofitable as pensions[15] that
I might have an excuse for shrinking myself into my rectorial shell.
—By the way, I meant nothing in the way of *nolo episcopari*[16] in the
sentence of my sermon which you objected to.[17] I only did not wish
to be a ways and means man or a Doctor Price. A man may be a good
bishop and be neither of these characters.

So no more at present from

Yours enti⟨rely,⟩[18]

W. ⟨MASON⟩

Pray erase with a pen[19] (if you do not immediately burn this letter)
the *scandalum magnatum* contained in the sentence about the
Baronet.

12. See *post* 16 March 1778, n. 17.

13. Catharine Macaulay's *History of Eng-land from the Revolution to the Present Time, in a Series of Letters to the Reverend Doctor Wilson*, was published 3 March 1778 (*Public Advertiser*).

14. Both Lord Harcourt and HW gave Mrs Macaulay letters of recommendation. See *Harcourt Papers* viii. 105–13; *post* 16 March 1778.

15. An allusion to the motion (9 March 1778) of Thomas Gilbert, M.P. for Lich-field, that during the war a tax of twenty-five per cent be laid on the incomes of placemen and pensioners. See Cobbett, *Parl. Hist.* xix. 873; *Last Journals* ii. 129–30.

16. 'I do not wish to be a bishop.' 'It is a prevailing vulgar error, that every bishop, before he accepts the bishopric which is offered him, affects a maiden coyness and answers *nolo episcopari*. The origin of these words and this notion I have not been able to discover; the bishops certainly give no such refusal at present, and I am in-clined to think they never did at any time in this country' (Edward Christian's note in his annotated edition of Sir William Blackstone's *Commentaries on the Laws of England*, Portland, 1807, i. 380).

17. In his letter to Stonhewer ca 10 March 1778.

18. MS torn where the seal was broken.

19. HW did not do so.

To Mason, Monday 16 March 1778

Printed from Mitford i. 348–52. It did not go through the post; see *post* p. 372.

[Arlington Street,]
Monday night late, March 16, 1778.

I HAD not seen the *Morning Post,* when I dissuaded publication; you certainly have had provocation, if you are inclined to take it. I trust at least your testimony will not be lost—perhaps the present instant is not the fittest, as the French ambassador's declaration[1] has engaged all attention; I mean as far as a first moment can do, for in two days I suppose we shall be as thoughtless as ever—nay, they who should be most alarmed, seem besotted—indeed they had little way to go—but an old regiment is to sail tomorrow for Halifax.[2] I went out of town on Saturday morning not knowing of the French declaration; it followed me to Strawberry that night, yet as if I were a minister, I did not return till this afternoon; and as both Houses are sitting could get no further intelligence. I shall probably hear something before this sets out, but what can I learn that I do not know? the alternative is to be buffeted by France and turn t'other cheek, or to have England and Ireland invaded—I could almost wish the storm would burst on Scotland—but who would go thither? There is one consolation however in our wretched state; it had been ten thousand times more grievous to have America conquered and England enslaved; and the guilty will now be the greatest sufferers. Nay, October was twelvemonth, I should have jumped at an option of the present moment. In short we are disgraced and ruined, and shall never be what we have been—but Scotland will not triumph—I know not whether the ministers will endeavour to hold their places six months longer by the favour of France; or whether Lord Chatham's old crutch will be sent for to draw a circle round St James's. I expect nothing but patching and botching from anybody, which will suit the insensibility of the times. There are no grounds for confidence any-

1. 'On the 13th [March], Monsieur de Noailles, the ambassador of France, delivered to Lord Weymouth a declaration from the King his master, acquainting his Majesty that the King of France had concluded a treaty of commerce and amity with the Independent States of America' (*Last Journals* ii. 131–2). See *ante* 18 Feb. 1778 and n. 16.

2. Corroboration of this report has not been found.

where. We shall moulder piecemeal into our insignificant islandhood, for it is an age for vigorous resurrection.[3] I will answer[4] the rest of your letter before I go to bed, that I may not dream of our shameful position nor have visions of revival that will never be realized.

You accuse me very unjustly of neglecting your alteration of my tragedy. I always thought it magic, to be effected by so few words, and should have adopted it, had I ever had thoughts of its being represented;[5] but nothing could induce me to venture it on the stage, not from superabundant modesty, but from the abusive spirit of the times. I have no notion of presenting one's self coolly to a savage mob to be torn to pieces—and you know I am as tender of my friends as of myself. I think this country at present in every light the sink of Europe, void of taste and of everything ingenuous. Calamity has often resuscitated its powers—but there are few or no instances I believe of an empire that has fallen by its own corruptions, replacing itself on its throne. My vanity is too proud to desire to twinkle under the auspices of Palæologi and Porphyrogeniti;[6] should I be remembered, I should wish it might be as one of the last reign.

I have entirely forgotten what Sir John Dalrymple said in his preface, but am most sure that if he quotes a Walpole as his recommender, it must have been my cousin Thomas,[7] for I never saw the wretch, nor ever had the most indirect connection with him. To Mrs Macaulay I did give a letter,[8] but am ashamed of it, as she ought to be of her foolish and absurd summary, which is a wretched compilation from magazines, full of gross mistakes, and confounding all characters, levelling all for no end or purpose, but to support so silly an hypothesis, as that no king can be a good king, because he is a king. She defends James II for the nonsensical pleasure of abusing King William,[9] and has no more idea of general merit than Sir John

3. HW perhaps means that England needs a more vigorous leadership than Chatham's crutch.

4. Mitford reads 'will go answer.'

5. For HW's more candid opinion of Mason's alterations see preliminary note, *ante* 8 May 1769.

6. The former were a line of Byzantine emperors, the latter were the children born to the royal purple of Byzantium (OED). HW seems to be using the terms as synonyms for despotism. His figure may have been inspired by Voltaire's new tragedy,

Irène (*ante* 4 March 1778), which takes place during the reign of the Palæologi.

7. Hon. Thomas Walpole (1727–1803), son of Horatio, 1st Bn Walpole of Wolterton; banker in London and Paris; HW's correspondent.

8. Perhaps to Mme du Deffand, who wrote to HW 26 Oct. 1777, 'Vous pouvez être sûr que j'aurai pour Mme Macaulay toutes les attentions possibles' (DU DEFFAND iv. 486).

9. 'James II . . . with all his faults, was a frugal prince: the revenue settled by

Dalrymple. In short, whom does she approve but herself and her idolater—that dirty disappointed hunter of a mitre, Dr Wilson,[10] and Alderman Heathcote,[11] a paltry worthless Jacobite, whom I remember, and her own grandfather Sawbridge,[12] who, *she has been told*[13] was a mighty worthy man though dipped in the infamous job of the South Sea. In short, I ran through the book,[14] had forgotten it, and only recollect it now to answer your question.

I enclose with this a letter[15] I wrote to you last week, but did not care to send by the post; you will find some curious particulars in it. I have finished certain verses[16] of which you saw part, but shall reserve them till we meet, as I shall the rest of my paper till tomorrow. By the way, I do not know who the transcriber of your sermon

Parliament on his first coming to the throne was more than sufficient to defray the expenses of his government; therefore, that bold stroke of policy, which delivered up the purse and the credit of the nation into the hands of the prince, was reserved for the immortal William, and his Whig partisans' (*History of England*, p. 79). In a letter to Lord Harcourt, 28 March 1778, Mrs Macaulay defended her many derogatory remarks on William: 'It was impossible for me to treat with approbation characters who have laid the foundation of our ruin by a funded debt, and by reducing the art of corruption into a system' (*Harcourt Papers* viii. 114–5).

10. The clergyman to whom the *History* is addressed in a series of letters: Thomas Wilson (1703–84), D.D., rector of St Stephen's, Walbrook, 1737–84. 'In the dawn of the present reign it was Dr Wilson's fortune to preach very early before the new King, whose favour was not conciliated by the means which were taken to obtain it. Dr Wilson's sermon was couched in terms of flattery so gross, as to be noticed with some degree of censure' (*European Magazine*, 1784, v. 250). Wilson's admiration for Mrs Macaulay was such that in 1774 his house in Bath was placed at her disposal; in 1777 he had a marble statue of her erected within the altar-rails of St Stephen's, but when she married William Graham in Dec. 1778 Wilson was so vexed that he had the statue removed. For Mrs Macaulay's catalogue of Wilson's virtues see her *History of England*, p. 2.

11. George Heathcote (ca 1700—68), alderman of Walbrook 1735–49, lord mayor of London, 1742. See Alfred B. Beaven, *The Aldermen of the City of London*, 1908–13, ii. 127; J. G. White, *History of the Ward of Walbrook in the City of London*, 1904, p. 267. 'Mr. Alderman Heathcote was a very worthy and a very honest man, unbiassed by party prejudice, and steady to the true interests of his country, which he understood better than almost any member of the two Houses I ever had the honour of conversing with' (Macaulay, op. cit. 411).

12. Jacob Sawbridge (d. 1748), a director of the South Sea Company in 1720 (GM 1748, xviii. 333).

13. 'I cannot leave this subject [the 'South Sea Bubble'] without informing you, my friend, if the concurrent testimony of all his cotemporaries has not yet reached your ears, that my grandfather, though carried along with the tide of other men's iniquity, was so perfectly free from any intention or inclination to defraud the public, that he was never once accused of being let into the secret practices of Knight, and other of the guilty directors, that he always publicly and privately exclaimed against every unfair means taken by the direction to give an unnatural rise to the stock' (Macaulay, op. cit. 306–7).

14. HW's copy was sold SH v. 51.

15. Missing.

16. Not identified.

is, nor guess what you mean by 'the triumph of the minority,' unless you allude to their carrying one question against Lord North for a tax on places.[17] It would have been a greater blow to the Crown than they will ever give, even if they become the majority; but they lost it the next night, on the report,[18] and will take care not to carry it, if ever they are ministers.

17th.

Lord Stormont is recalled,[19] for we are to be angry, since being tame would not do. Dr Franklin is to be received at Versailles today as ambassador.[20] A message is to be delivered to each House today, and the majority in each is, I suppose, to answer, 'We will assist you to chastise France for having been forced by you to pick up what you threw away.' Lord North had the modesty yesterday to recommend unanimity and to affirm he keeps his place from a point of honour.[21] Burke made a fine application of Lord Bedford's[22] answer to King James, 'I had a son who could have advised your Majesty'[23]—'America could have assisted your Majesty.'[24] Charles Fox's reply was in a

17. Gilbert's proposal to lay a tax on all places and pensions (*ante* 13 March and n. 15) 'was voted against Lord North in the committee, by a majority of eighteen' (*Last Journals* ii. 130). The vote was 100 to 82 (Cobbett, *Parl. Hist.* xix. 873).

18. When the committee reported the motion to the House 10 March it was defeated by a vote of 147 to 141 (ibid.).

19. 'In the House of Lords yesterday [17 March], Lord Weymouth acquainted their Lordships, that he was directed by his Majesty to lay before them a declaration made to him by the ambassador [Noailles] from the Court of France. . . . His Lordship was further directed to acquaint the House that, in consequence of this declaration, his Majesty had sent immediate letters of recall to the British minister at Versailles' (*Public Advertiser* 18 March 1778).

20. 'Authentic advices from Paris say . . . that the 17th of March . . . was fixed for Dr Franklin to make his *public entry* into that city as minister plenipotentiary from the Thirteen Independent States of America; that he was to be received publicly at Court in that character' (ibid.).

21. 'If a resignation of his place could in any wise tend to extricate the nation from its present difficulties, he had often declared . . . that he would most willingly resign; but as it would be cowardly to give up in the hour of danger, and . . . a resignation at that crisis would create confusion in the ministry, his honour, his pride, and his duty to his country, convinced him that he ought not to go out of office' (*London Chronicle* 14–17 March 1778, xliii. 264).

22. William Russell (1616–1700), 5th E. of Bedford, cr. (1694) D. of Bedford.

23. 'We are told, that the King [James II] under some distraction of mind . . . earnestly applied himself to the Earl of Bedford, father to the executed Lord Russel, saying, "My Lord, you are a good man, and have a great influence;—you can do much for me at this time." To which he answered, "I am an old man, and can do but little"; then added with a deep sigh, "I had once a son,—who now could have been very serviceable to your Majesty' (Laurence Echard, *The History of the Revolution*, 1725, p. 190).

24. Burke's speech has not been preserved. It was delivered 16 March 1778 on the occasion of Grenville's motion that

rougher style.[25] The stocks are not of the heroic majority,[26] yet, I believe the ministers will stay from arrant fear at St James's till they are torn out of it. That will be a poor compensation and an useless precedent, for posterity, with all its reading, is never the better for example. James II could read, but could not remember even what he had seen.

Well! I must finish, though my pen's tongue could run on forever. I feel all sort of feelings, none comfortable, but that we shall be despicable first before we are slaves; the contrary would be more mortifying. France has a right to humble us. The true English who are in America have behaved like Englishmen, without any Scot-alloy. The victories of France will be over Scots. Dr Franklin's triumph has been over a Scot ambassador.[27] Pursue this idea, we shall have occasion to pay ourselves with leathern coin.

PS. Let me know the moment you receive this packet. I add a French tract[28] which you must take care to return, though I understand little of it. The *Gazette littéraire* will show you how it relates to their present musical contests.[29] What I understand is able and full of address, but surely the irony is above most readers. I shall be glad to have all my gazettes again when you come this waywards.

papers relating to the treaty between France and America be laid before the House of Commons (Cobbett, *Parl. Hist.* xix. 908–9).

25. '16th [March]. . . . Mr Burke, Mr Dunning, and Mr Fox, particularly the latter, censured Lord North most severely for ignorance and for the situation into which he and the ministers had brought the nation, and with great contempt for proposing unanimity' (*Last Journals* ii. 132).

26. 'The present situation of our affairs he [Burke] declared to be to the last degree desperate. The stocks, the political pulse of the nation, were so low, that they plainly demonstrated the weakness of the state' (Cobbett, loc. cit.).

27. Stormont.

28. Possibly, as Mrs Toynbee suggests, J. J. Barthélemy's *Entretiens sur l'état de la musique grecque vers le milieu du IVe siècle avant l'ère vulgaire*, sent to HW by Mme du Deffand 4 March 1778 (DU DEFFAND v. 24). The *Entretiens* were later reprinted as Chap. 27 of Barthélemy's *Le Voyage du jeune Anacharsis*, 1788 (Maurice Badolle, *L'Abbé Jean-Jacques Barthélemy (1716–1795) et l'hellénisme en France dans la seconde moitié du XVIIIe siècle*, [1926], p. 396).

29. The contest between the supporters of Gluck and the supporters of Piccinni was at its height at this time. See DU DEFFAND v. 9 and 19; Grove's *Dictionary of Music sub* Gluck and Piccinni; Gustave Desnoiresterres, *Gluck et Piccinni 1774–1800*, 1872; E. Thoinan, *Notes bibliographiques sur la guerre musicale des Gluckistes et Piccinnistes*, 1878.

From MASON, Saturday 21 March 1778

Printed from MS now WSL.
Address: The Honourable Horace Walpole, Arlington Street, London.
Postmark: YORK 23 MR.

York, March 21st, 1778.

I HAVE just now received the parcel very safe, with the two delightful letters enclosed; while I continue here anything will be forwarded to me safely and expeditiously by sending them to Charles Carter.

I am not so easily provoked as to change my mind for a flam in the *Morning Post.* I will at least stay to see who prints on the occasion[1] before me; those that have preached before the Lords and Commons, not to mention St James's, ought to take precedency of the press before him that only discoursed my Lord Mayor of York.[2]

The man I meant is a Mr Goodrick, son of a baronet, one of Lord Bingley's heirs.[3] He married a Dutchwoman[4] and wants to go abroad as an envoy.

Pray out of all charity and goodness write frequently to me at this crisis, though I can send you nothing in return. The more disinterested and like the tenor of the times will be your correspondence. The post gives me not a moment more, and I must conclude.

Yours as always,

W. MASON

To MASON, Thursday 26 March 1778

Printed from Mitford i. 356–8.

March 26, 1778.

THOUGH you have desired me to write often at this crisis, and though I am never penurious of my ink, I waited till I could send you something more than rumours. The darkness has not hung

1. The general fast of 27 Feb. 1778.
2. As Mason did (*ante* 23 Feb. 1778).
3. Sir John Goodricke m. (1731) Mary Johnson (later Benson), illegitimate daughter of Robert Benson, Bn Bingley, by a daughter of James Sill, mercer of Wakefield (GEC, *Complete Baronetage* ii. 137; see also *ante* 5 Oct. 1777, n. 7).
4. Henry Goodricke m. (ca 1764) Levina Benjamina Sesster of Namur in Flanders (GEC, loc. cit.).

long without a thunder-clap. France has stopped all our shipping in their ports,[1] and the omniscient Lord Stormont himself has learnt *that* piece of news at Boulogne, being detained there by the embargo.[2] It is also expected that the Spanish *chargé des affaires*[3] will today or tomorrow compliment the King with an acknowledgment of the states of America,[4] as civilly as Monsieur de Noailles did. It is even said that Portugal allows their title.[5] Well, say you, and are not people frightened? what is to be done? Frightened; yes; some are,— some that are guilty and more that are innocent, most, not at all; for folly, that sees a ghost, always tumbles down a precipice that is before its eyes. But you *will* have some answer, and I *must* tell you what is to be done; that is, I must foresee, *not* what can be done, but what will be. I believe the oracle at Hayes has been consulted,[6] but not having received *carte blanche*,[7] shrouded its dignity in ambiguity.[8]

1. 'Extract of a letter from Dover, March 24. "You may assure your readers that an embargo is laid on all English merchant vessels in the ports of France"' (*Public Advertiser* 27 March 1778).

2. 'Some accounts say, that Lord Stormont is detained at Bologne; others say that he is very ill. The indisposition of Lady Stormont is said by others to have delayed the arrival of his Lordship' (*Lloyd's Evening Post* 25–7 March 1778, xlii. 293). Stormont arrived in London 27 March (ibid. 27–30 March 1778, xlii. 297).

3. Apparently Francisco de Escarano, secretary to the Spanish embassy under two successive ambassadors, Masserano and Almodóvar. In 1778 he is listed as 'minister resident' (*Royal Kalendar* 1777 and 1778, *Court and City Register* 1778 and 1779).

4. 'There is not the smallest doubt but Spain will, as heretofore, in every instance, second the views of her sister France' (*Public Advertiser* 26 March 1778). Events proved that Spain was not ready for such definite action.

5. This rumour was soon denied. 'The last advices from Lisbon, it is said, contain satisfactory accounts of the intentions of that Court in case a rupture should happen between France and Great Britain' (*Lloyd's Evening Post* 25–7 March 1778, xlii. 293). Portugal had been allied with England against Spain since 1640.

6. On 15 March 1778 Lord North wrote to the King that 'the present ministry cannot continue a fortnight as it is, and there is nothing which seems so likely to stem the first violence of the torrent as sending to Lord Chatham' (*Corr. Geo. III* iv. 56). Subsequent letters from North show that various efforts were made to ascertain the terms on which Chatham would enter the ministry (ibid. iv. 59–72).

7. In his reply to North's letter of 15 March the King had said, 'I declare in the strongest and most solemn manner that though I do not object to your addressing yourself to Lord Chatham, yet that you must acquaint him that I shall never address myself to him but through you and on a clear explanation that he is to step forth to support an administration whenever [?wherein] you are to be first lord of the Treasury and chancellor of the Exchequer' (ibid. iv. 57).

8. On 16 March North wrote to the King that Chatham 'wishes to speak to his Majesty in order that his plans may not be misrepresented; that he expects to be a confidential minister, that he must have the appearance of forming the ministry; that the most important offices being filled with efficient men, Lord Chatham's desire would be in everything to attend to the wishes of his Majesty' (ibid. iv. 59). But on 19 March North admitted that Chatham 'must be the head of any administration in which he acts, and it would be vain and useless to expect him on any other footing' (ibid. iv. 68).

Perhaps today more humble ambassadors[9] have been sent: I vow I do not know there have, but the event I guess. The god himself taking the form of his *pythonisse,* and enveloped in flannels,[10] that are the symbols of vast vigour of mind beneath, will go to Buckingham House, and finding full acquiescence to all his terms (by taking care to ask none really unpalatable) will then present a long list of names that are to be substituted to the proscribed. Lord Rockingham shall go to Ireland, the Duke of Richmond[11] shall be this, Charles Fox shall be t'other, Mr Burke something else, etc., etc., etc. I mean after Lord Camden, Lord Shelburne,[11a] Barré,[12] Dunning,[13] and perhaps the Duke of Grafton[14] have been appointed to the essential posts. 'Certainly,' will be the answers, 'all are very proper.'[15] Madam, the priestess, then notifies to all the nominees the graces she has bestowed, and orders them to take possession of their several departments. They all laugh in her face and call her a foolish old beldame, and thus a weak opposition is more weakened. *The most concerned* is not very sorry,[16] the only moment is lost; France will tell you the rest.

I sit resigned to our fate, for when one can do no good, and is but

9. That is, members of the Opposition. On 21 March North informed the King that he had 'just heard in great confidence that the Opposition . . . have just come to a resolution of submitting themselves absolutely to Lord Chatham, and that Lord Granby is to set out tomorrow morning to make in all their names an offer of all their services and attachment.' To this the King replied, 22 March, 'I am extremely indifferent whether Lord Granby goes or does not go with the abject message of the Rockingham party this day to Hayes; I will certainly send none to that place' (ibid. iv. 70, 72). North seems to have been misinformed, for the Rockingham Whigs remained resolutely opposed to Chatham's principle of insistence on American dependency. There was no 'abject message.' See *Memoirs of the Marquis of Rockingham,* ed. George Thomas, Earl of Albemarle, 1852, ii. 348–9.

10. Because of his gout. When Chatham did appear in the House of Lords on 7 April 1778 he was 'covered up to the knees in flannel' (ibid. ii. 352).

11. Charles Lennox (1735–1806), 3d D. of Richmond, 1750; HW's friend and correspondent.

11a. William Petty (1737–1805), styled Vct Fitzmaurice 1753–61; 2d E. of Shelburne, 1761; cr. (1784) M. of Lansdowne; statesman.

12. Barré, who entered Parliament through the influence of Shelburne, first attracted attention in the House of Commons by an attack on Chatham in 1761, but later became one of his most faithful supporters.

13. Also one of Chatham's followers, and a member of Parliament through the interest of Shelburne.

14. This Opposition peer was frequently associated with both Chatham and the Rockingham group.

15. The King's 'Sketch of a strengthening of the administration,' 15 March 1778, lists Shelburne as a secretary of state, Barré as a commissioner to the Colonies or secretary-at-war, and Dunning as attorney-general. See *Corr. Geo. III* iv. 55–6.

16. That is, the King. The remark is perhaps explained by an anecdote in *Last Journals* (ii. 145) where HW says that 'early in the winter the King had had the folly and indecency to say to Lord George Germaine, "I may be got the better of by the American rebels, but I will not by the English rebels" '—i.e., the Opposition.

an individual, it is impertinent to be anything but passive. I am less alarmed too than I should be, because I had the same apprehensions above thirty years ago, and because I had then thirty years longer to live than I have now. In youth too imagination's wing flies as far as it can. Experience tells one that all does not happen that may. I think I shall outlive the storm and talk over the ruins; but in truth I believe they will be considerable. France seems to have waited with wise phlegm for the fullness of time, and we may expect that her blows will be stunning. My idea is that she will invade us here ostensibly, more effectually in Ireland,[17] in America and in the East; if she has success in all, and we none, why then Lord Mansfield will shake off his mortal coil,[18] and persuade himself that he always meant the destruction of the house of Hanover, not its *unbounded* elevation.[19] These are my sober cool opinions; I shall be glad to be a lying prophet, for Jeremiah himself was a sad fellow if he comforted himself under captivity with the honour of having predicted it.

Yours ever,

H. W.

To MASON, Wednesday 8 April 1778

Printed from Mitford i. 358–61.

Arlington Street, April 8, 1778.

THOUGH my daily fellow-labourers[1] of this morning will give you a minute account of the great event of yesterday, I should

17. 'Mr Conolly, speaking [18 March] of the present state of Ireland, was very clear in his opinion: he said, if the French land in the south, every man there will join them; and if the Americans land in the north, they will be as gladly received there by the Presbyterians' (*Last Journals* ii. 142).

18. The troubles occasioned him by the unsuccessful war. HW believed that Mansfield was one of the foremost instigators of the conflict and had been consistently pusillanimous. See *Last Journals* ii. 106 and *passim.*

19. In a conversation with the Duke of Gloucester in Oct. 1777 HW had said: 'Sir, I believe that when Lord Mansfield found he could not restore the House of Stuart, he determined at least to do all the hurt he could to your Royal Highness's family, and therefore turned to the history of Charles I, and advised your brother to take every step that was reproached to that Prince' (ibid. ii. 66).

1. The newspapers.

be a very negligent gazetteer if I took no notice of it. Lord Chatham
fell in the Senate—not by daggers nor by the thunder of Lord Suffolk's eloquence.[2] He had spoken with every symptom of debility, repeated his own phrases, could not recollect his own ideas, and which
was no new practice, persisted in our asserting sovereignty over
America, *though he could not tell by what means.*[3] It was only new
to confess his ignorance. The Duke of Richmond answered him with
much decency and temper,[4] though Lord Chatham had called *pursuit
without means,* timid and pusillanimous conduct.[5] The Earl was
rising to reply, but fell down in a second fit of apoplexy,[6] with strong
convulsions and slabbering at the mouth. I do not doubt but the
Morning Post will allow the Duke more rhetoric than it ever acknowledged, in order to ascribe Lord Chatham's fall to his Grace's
invectives[7]—but he, who is all tenderness and sensibility, was so affected, that at night the Duchess desired me not to name it—yet
Lord Chatham is not dead and today is better, if existing after two
strokes can be called so. To be sure his biographer would have a
fairer field, had he died in his vocation.[8] In truth, I see no good he
could have done, since he has embraced the idea of still conquering
America—but much harm he must have occasioned had the Court
adopted him. Now I reckon him politically dead;[9] he will probably

2. Suffolk had attacked Chatham in the
House of Lords the preceding December.
'Lord Suffolk had the indecency to tell
Lord Chatham [11 Dec. 1777] that he only
wanted the House to sit, because *he was
sure he would be allowed to give his advice
nowhere else.* This brutality to an old man
who had made so great a figure, from so
stupid a creature, was severely treated in
the public papers' (*Last Journals* ii. 84) .

3. 'I am not, I confess, well informed of
the resources of this kingdom; but I trust
it has still sufficient to maintain its just
rights, though I know them not' (Cobbett,
Parl. Hist. xix. 1023).

4. Richmond is reported to have said:
'Not one of your Lordships has a more
grateful memory of the services performed
for his country by that noble Lord [Chat-
ham], than I have: he raised its glory, reputation, and successes to an height never
before experienced by any other nation. His
Lordship's name . . . will ever be dear to
Englishmen' (ibid. xix. 1027–8).

5. Chatham had risen to speak in reply

to Richmond's speech in support of his
motion that the King be informed of the
true state of the nation, in which Richmond demonstrated the country's poverty
of means for the prosecution of a war.
Chatham 'feared there was something in
the dark . . . which caused such pusillanimous, such timid, such dastardly councils' (*London Magazine,* 1778, xlvii. 214).

6. The first had been in the preceding
summer (see *ante* 4 Aug. 1777 and n.
16).

7. As HW expected, the pro-ministerial
Post did not neglect the opportunity of attacking Richmond: 'The sudden indisposition of Lord Chatham saved the Anglo-
Gallic Duke of R——d such a Parliamentary flogging as he never experienced, and
which his consummate vanity and impudence justly merited' (*Morning Post* 9
April).

8. That is, addressing Parliament.

9. This was the King's opinion, too. He
wrote Lord North on 8 April: 'May not
the political exit of Lord Chatham incline

neither recover strength or faculties, his family will if possible prevent his reappearance, and the Court will scarce inoculate a half-dead skeleton on their other infirmities. Lord Chatham certainly went to the House to express resentment at their having only dabbled with him indirectly, but his debility or perhaps some gleam of hope of being yet adopted, moderated his style—his water-gall[10] Lord Temple was at his elbow.

I can tell you nothing definitive on war or peace. Pacification with France, and even with America, has been much sounded these last days—probably to prop the stocks—but the selection of Governor Johnstone for one of the commissioners,[11] who even during all the late debates anathematized American independence, implies not only adherence to sovereignty but no thoughts of change—of Johnstone it is enough to say that though a Scot in opposition, he never lost sight of the promised land.[12]

You may thank me for so much politics when I am overwhelmed with other business, and have even the militia on my hands; my nephew is suddenly come to himself again—only to his former self; but I must not tap this chapter—I should be endless. He is gone to take the command of the Norfolk militia,[13] and I am commissioned to dissuade him![14] *De profundis clamavi!*[15] well, fortune has some justice and dispenses antidotes with poisons. The Duke of Gloucester's children are to have a Parliamentary provision, and considering everything, a very decent one.[16] There is one thorn removed; I have re-

you to continue at the head of my affairs?' (*Corr. Geo. III* iv. 102).

10. 'A secondary or imperfectly-formed rainbow' (OED). HW once described Temple as 'the absolute creature of Pitt' (*Mem. Geo. II* i. 135).

11. The five commissioners appointed to treat with the Colonies (see *ante* 4 March 1778, n. 4) were Lord Carlisle, William Eden, Sir William Howe, Lord Howe, and George Johnstone.

12. 'To this moment he [Johnstone] had long been in violent opposition, had ridiculed Lord Carlisle egregiously (indeed both were equally mean in consenting to go together), and had even very lately declared strongly against the independence of America, which could not make him a welcome negotiator there; but the great salary drowned all reasons' (*Last Journals* ii. 157).

13. Lord Orford was Lord-Lieutenant of Norfolk 1757–91, and *ex officio* colonel of the county militia (GEC). See HW to Mann 9 April 1778; R. W. Ketton-Cremer, *A Norfolk Gallery*, 1948, pp. 170–1, 183. The county militias had been called out late in March because of the critical state of affairs with respect to France (*Last Journals* ii. 153).

14. See HW to Hertford 5 April and HW to Mann 9 April 1778.

15. 'Out of the depths have I cried,' the first words of Psalm 130.

16. '[April] 2nd. Lord North waited on the Duke of Gloucester, and told him that the King now intended to perform his promise of providing for his Royal Highness's children; that the next day, or as soon after as could be, his Majesty would send a message to Parliament to ask provision for his own children and for the

course to my old anodynes, quartos, whenever I can snatch a moment.
I have gone through Mr Pennant's Welsh tour[17] which is a patchwork
of all sorts of shreds stitched together with unpronounceable words,
of DDwrr'rs and no vowels, so I do not remember much of what
I cannot articulate. I have dipped into Mr Warton's second volume[18]
which seems more unentertaining than the former. I perceive he
excommunicates Rowley totally.[19] Lord Hardwicke is to present us
on Saturday with two volumes of *State Papers*[20]—but with due cir-
cumspection keeps back his by far most curious letters.[21] I have a long
conversation with Dr Robertson to relate to you, but must reserve
for some moment of more leisure.[22] It would not be time lost to come
to me for a week and hear me exhaust my wallet—you must not reckon
upon too distant moments! my tattered frame grows weaker and
weaker. I waste as few minutes as possible, but constant application
of the mind to some duties or other will impair a memory that is enclosed in so frail an *étui*. Have you seen *The Old Baron*,[23] a Gothic
story, professedly written in imitation of *Otranto*, but reduced to
reason and probability![24] It is so probable, that any trial for murder

Duke's. For his own sons he should ask
£10,000 a year each, and for his daughters
six; for the Duke's son, Prince William,
£8000, and Princess Sophia, four' (*Last
Journals* ii. 156). The message was read
8 April and the bill authorizing the annuities was debated and passed in both
Houses 10 April 1778 (Cobbett, *Parl. Hist.*
xix. 1059–68).

17. Thomas Pennant's *Tour in North
Wales* was published 26 March 1778 (*Public Advertiser*). HW's set of Pennant's
works (10 vols) was sold SH iv. 6.

18. Publication of the second volume of
the *History of English Poetry* on 6 April
1778 was announced in the *London Chronicle* 26–8 March, xliii. 300. HW's copy was
sold SH v. 63.

19. He denies the authenticity of Chatterton's Rowley poems on pp. 139–64.

20. 'On Saturday next [11 April] will
be published in two volumes quarto . . .
*Miscellaneous State Papers from 1501 to
1726;* selected from the Paper Office, the
British Museum, the Hardwicke and other
valuable collections' (*Public Advertiser* 7
April 1778). HW's copy is now wsl. Both
volumes have numerous annotations by
HW.

21. Presumably those of his father, the

Lord Chancellor, whose letters might con-
firm HW's low opinion of him. The collection concludes with 1726, two years after
the future Chancellor became attorney-
general, but none of his letters are included.

22. See *post* April 1778.

23. Clara Reeve's *The Old English Baron*
was published 31 March 1778 (*Public Advertiser*). HW's copy was sold SH vi. 56.
This was actually the second edition (first
London edition) of a novel that had first
appeared in 1777 (*Critical Review* August
1777, xliv. 154) with the title *The Champion of Virtue*, printed by W. Keymer at
Colchester.

24. 'This story is the literary offspring of
The Castle of Otranto, written upon the
same plan, with a design to unite the most
attractive and interesting circumstances of
the ancient romance and modern novel.
. . . To attain this end, there is required
a sufficient degree of the marvellous, to
excite the attention; enough of the manners of real life, to give an air of probability
to the work; and enough of the pathetic,
to engage the heart in its behalf. The
book we have mentioned is excellent in
the two last points, but has a redundancy
in the first' (*The Old English Baron*, pp.
iii–v).

at the Old Bailey would make a more interesting story. Mrs Barbut's fragment[25] was excellent. This is a *caput mortuum*.[26] Adieu. I have not a quarter of a minute to say more.

To MASON, Saturday 18 April 1778

Printed from Mitford i. 361–4.

Strawberry Hill, April 18, 1778.

I AM come hither like a good Christian to pass in retreat the holy week before Easter, and the unholy week of Newmarket, which has almost beaten Easter out of the calendar, and to which yet I would give a scripture appellation, and call it the *passover*. In these ten days I shall probably fulfil my promise of sending you the heads of my interview with Dr Robertson: but I will tell you first the little else I have to say. Most people expect a French war—I still doubt it, I do not very well know why, but it does not seem a very decisive age; the Turks and Russians have not yet drawn blood.[1] I take the Emperor[2] to be the most impatient to be a Cæsar,[3] and his mother I suppose is very ready to employ him at a distance from home.[4]

The commissioners are gone,[5] and Mr Adams[6] is arrived at Paris.[7]

25. 'On the Pleasure Derived from Objects of Terror; with Sir Bertrand, A Fragment,' published in J. and A. L. Aikin's *Miscellaneous Pieces in Prose*, 1773, pp. 119–37. The author, Anna Letitia Aikin (1743–1825), m. (1774) Rev. Rochemont Barbauld, was acquainted with HW and visited SH (HW to Lady Ossory 14 June 1774).
26. Used in the figurative sense of 'worthless residue' (OED).

1. In spite of the peace treaty of Kuchuk-Kainardji signed in 1774, hostility between Turkey and Russia continued. Throughout the first few months of 1778 the newspapers reported military preparations by both nations. For the background of the conflict see Sir Bernard Pares, *A History of Russia*, New York, 1926, pp. 262–8.
2. Joseph II (1741–90), Holy Roman Emperor 1765–90, serving as co-regent with his mother, Maria Theresa, until her death.
3. At the time of this letter the newspapers carried many rumours of Joseph's preparations for war against Prussia. When the childless Maximilian Joseph (1727–77), Elector of Bavaria, died 30 Dec., Austria laid claim to parts of his territory. Frederick the Great resisted the Emperor and the so-called War of the Bavarian Succession broke out. It was terminated by the Peace of Teschen 13 May 1779. See HW to Mann 17 and 27 March 1778; Harold Temperley, *Frederic the Great and Kaiser Joseph*, 1915; Saul K. Padover, *The Revolutionary Emperor, Joseph the Second, 1741–1790*, 1934, pp. 130–58.
4. Joseph's policies were continually at variance with Maria Theresa's. See Padover, op. cit. 68.
5. 'Extract of a letter from Portsmouth, April 16. "On Tuesday evening came here

As we do not know the amount of their treaty, all we do is in the dark. I suspect that Dr Franklin has duped Governor Johnstone,[8] and yet many a dishonest man has been made a fool, as well as many an honest one.

The Opposition are notoriously split into two factions.[9] Lord Shelburne heads the Chathamites, and puts me in mind of a French beggar, who asked charity as one of the *quinze-vingt aveugles*.[10] 'Why,' said the person he applied to, 'you are not blind!' '*Hélas, non, Monsieur,*' said the fellow, '*je ne suis qu'un aspirant.*'

The Foleys[11] are at last likely to lose their cause[12] by the indecent impetuosity of their partisans.[13] If you have not seen it in the papers, you will— Oh! I have begun my letter on a torn sheet, but I cannot write it over again, and so shall proceed—yes, you will thank me for an admirable *bon mot* of George Selwyn; when the Foleys had

the Earl of Carlisle, Governor Johnston, and [William] Eden, Esq.; and this morning they embarked on board his Majesty's ship *Trident*'' (*Public Advertiser* 18 April 1778). The other commissioners, the two Howes, were already in America.

6. John Adams (1735–1826), second President of the United States, 1796–1800, had been elected a commissioner to France by the Continental Congress 28 Nov. 1777, in the place of Silas Deane.

7. 'By a gentleman lately arrived from France we are informed, that his Excellency Mr Samuel [*sic*] Adams was just arrived in Paris, express from the Congress, invested with full power to ratify the treaty of Commerce and Alliance entered into between the Court of France and the Congress' (*Public Advertiser* 17 April 1778). Adams had no such powers. See *post* 4 July 1778, n. 13.

8. HW believed that Franklin encouraged Johnstone to seek a place on the commission to America 'either seeing that Johnstone's principles could veer to any point of interest, or to prevent success to the negotiation by so unwelcome a mediator' (*Last Journals* ii. 158).

9. Led respectively by Chatham and Rockingham.

10. Pensioners of the charitable institution, the Hospice des Quinze-Vingts, founded by Louis IX for the relief of the destitute blind.

11. Thomas Foley (1742–93), 2d Bn Foley,

n.c., 1777, and his brother, Edward Foley (1747–1803) (GEC; GM 1803, lxxiii pt ii. 695).

12. The estate left by Thomas Foley (1716–77), 1st Bn Foley, was so entailed that his extravagant elder sons were unable to settle their debts. Thereupon they claimed that their father had intended to change his will, and with the help of other members of their family and of interested friends they applied to the House of Lords for relief. See *Journals of the House of Lords* xxxv. 341–4; *Last Journals* ii. 133–4.

13. '9th [April]. The Chancellor had drawn a plan for giving some satisfaction to Lord Foley and his brother, on which the Lords seemed willing to pass it: yet the friends of the Foleys had not stuck entirely to the Chancellor's plan; the two other law Lords not being present, and the Foley squadron having a majority of one present, would not consent to adjourn as the Chancellor desired, he pleading fatigue. They behaved most indecently, especially Lord Derby, and even the Duke of Richmond was too earnest for proceeding that very day. The Chancellor complained grievously of the usage, and many that wished well to Lady Foley were yet shocked; at last Lord Sandwich, who declared he had been rather disposed to grant the bill, broke out against the indecency of his friends, and moved to have the bill sent back to the judges, to which the House agreed' (*Last Journals* ii. 161).

more chance of cancelling their father's will, he said, "The new testament will now be more favourable to the Jews than the old."

There is a pretty poem just published called *The Wreath of Fashion;*[14] it is written by one Tickell,[15] a son of Addison's friend.[16] He has been an assistant at Eton,[17] and wrote this winter another poem at least as good, called *The Project.*[18] The conclusion of the new is very inferior to the rest, and ends absurdly, like Anstey's on Lord Tavistock,[19] with a hemistich;[20] and as absurdly with a panegyric on that water-gruel bard Shenstone, who never wrote anything good but his *Schoolmistress.*[21] The *Wreath* is a satire on sentimental poets, amongst whom, still more absurdly, he classes Charles Fox, but there is a great deal of wit *par-ci par-là*. He calls sentimental comedies, *dramatic homilies;*[22] says Lord Palmerstone[23] *fineers*[24] (what an admirable word!) rebuses and charades with chips of poetry;[25] and when

14. *The Wreath of Fashion; or, The Art of Sentimental Poetry* was published 11 April 1778 (*Public Advertiser*). HW wrote 'April' on the title-page of the copy in his collection, 'Poems of George III' (now in the Harvard Library).

15. Richard Tickell (1751–93), poet and satirist, brother-in-law of R. B. Sheridan.

16. Thomas Tickell (1685–1740), poet; Addison's literary executor. Richard Tickell was his grandson, not his son; his father was John Tickell (1729–82), eldest son of the poet. See Richard Eustace Tickell, *Thomas Tickell and the Eighteenth-Century Poets (1685–1740)*, 1931, facing p. 256.

17. Tickell was at Eton from 1765 to 1768 (R. A. Austen-Leigh, *The Eton College Register 1753–1790*, Eton, 1921, p. 517), but he does not appear in the lists of Eton assistants (ibid. pp. xxiv–xxv).

18. *The Project, a Poem*, dedicated to Dean Tucker, was published 25 Feb. 1778 (*Public Advertiser*). HW wrote 'Feb.' on the title-page of his copy (now in the Harvard Library).

19. *On the Much Lamented Death of the Marquis of Tavistock*, 1767. HW's annotated copy is in the Harvard Library. Francis Russell (1739–67), styled M. of Tavistock, son of the 4th D. of Bedford, died of a fall from his horse 22 March 1767. Anstey's lines 'were written and published within a few hours after the fatal accident' (*The Poetical Works of the Late Christopher Anstey with Some Account of the Life*

and *Writings of the Author by His Son, John Anstey*, 1808, p. 130). The elegy was published anonymously. It concludes:
'There culls each fragrant flower, to deck the tomb
Where generous Russel lies.'

20. 'For mute the swain, and cold the hand, that wove
Their simple sweets to wreaths of artless love—
Simplicity with Shenstone died!——'

21. *The Schoolmistress, a Poem*, 1742.

22. 'First, for true grounds of sentimental lore,
The scenes of modern comedy explore;
Dramatic homilies! devout and sage,
Stored with wise maxims, "both for youth and age"'   (ll. 23–6).

23. Henry Temple (1739–1802), 2nd Vct Palmerston, 1757; lord of the Admiralty 1766–77, and of the Treasury 1777–82.

24. 'Early form of *veneer*' (OED, which quotes Tickell). The earliest example of the word is dated 1708.

25. 'With chips of wit, and mutilated lays,
See Palmerston fineer his *bouts rimés*.
Favourite of every Muse, elect of Phœbus,
To string charades, or fabricate a rebus' (ll. 97–100).
Palmerston contributed five *bouts rimés* and a poem on an assigned subject,

lord of the Admiralty, like Ariel wrecked navies with a song[26]—
sure that is an excellent application.

I have very near finished Warton,[27] but antiquary as I am, it was
a tough achievement. He has dipped into an incredible ocean of dry
and obsolete authors of the dark ages, and has brought up more rubbish than riches, but the latter chapters, especially on the progress
and revival of the theatre,[28] is [*sic*] more entertaining; however it is
very fatiguing to wade through the muddy poetry of three or four centuries that had never a poet.

Have you heard how Voltaire has been at his own apotheosis? he has
literally been crowned with laurel in a side box at his *Irène*,[29] and
seen the actors and actresses decorate his bust with garlands on the
stage.[30] As he is so very old one must excuse his submitting to this
vanity; nay it must have been moving,—yet one is more charmed
with the *violette, qui se cache sous l'herbe*.[31]

As Lord and Lady Strafford are to drink tea here this evening I shall
desire my Lord to frank this modicum, that you may not pay for a
scrap that has nothing in it. My conversation with the Scottish historian[32] is as little worth, especially after I had prepared you for
expecting it. When do you quit your cathedral for your parish? I
shall not leave my little hill for the dinner at the Royal Academy on
Thursday,[33] only to figure the next day in the newspapers in the list
of the Mecænases of the age. Lady Di Beauclerc has drawn the por-

'Beauty,' to the first volume of *Poetical Amusements at a Villa near Bath*, Bath, 1775. HW thought some of Palmerston's verses 'very pretty' (HW to Conway and Lady Ailesbury 15 Jan. 1775), but of others had written Mason that they 'are not worth sending' (*ante* 27 May 1775). Some verses by Palmerston that are not in the *Poetical Amusements* are printed in *Harcourt Papers* viii. 136–45.

26. ' 'Twas Palmerston repelled each hostile wrong,
      Like Ariel, wrecking navies with—
      a song' (ll. 103–4).

27. That is, the second volume of *The History of English Poetry*.

28. Sections ix, xii, xv, and especially xvi have material on the history of the drama.

29. First acted at Paris 16 March (GM 1778, xlviii. 149). On 30 March Voltaire attended the sixth performance. 'As soon as he was seated in his box, the Sieur Brizard appeared, holding a crown, which he placed on his head. M. de Voltaire stretched out his hand, and perceiving the honours that were intended him, removed it, saying, with an affecting tone, "Ah! my God, you are resolved to kill me" ' (ibid. 150).

30. 'The new tragedy was played with more spirit and accuracy than it had ever been before. As soon as it was over, an unexpected and . . . still more interest-ing scene succeeded. The curtain was drawn up, and all the actors and actresses were seen surrounding the bust of M. de Voltaire, and placing by turns some crowns of laurel on his head' (ibid.).

31. Mme de Sévigné to Mme de Grignan 1 Sept. 1680 (*Lettres de Madame de Sévigné*, ed. Monmerqué, 1862–6, vii. 52).

32. Robertson. See following letter.

33. 23 April 1778: the annual dinner held on the eve of the public opening of the exhibition.

trait of the Duchess of Devonshire and it has been engraved by
Bartolozzi.[34] A Castalian nymph conceived by Sappho and executed
by Myron[35] would not have had more grace and simplicity; it is the
divinity of Venus piercing the veil of immortality, when

rosea cervice refulsit,
Ambrosiæque comæ divinum vertice odorem
Spiravere.[36]

The likeness is perfectly preserved, except that the paintress has lent
her own expression to the Duchess, which you will allow is very
agreeable flattery; what should I go to the Royal Academy for? I shall
see no such *chef d'œuvres* there.

To Mason, April 1778

Printed from MS of HW's draft or copy now wsl. First printed (incompletely)
in *Works* v. 653–5; not in Mitford; first complete printing in Toynbee x. 224–6
and *Supp.* ii. 156–7. MS bequeathed by Mrs Damer to Sir Wathen Waller, 1st Bt;
sold Sotheby's 5 Dec. 1921 (Waller sale), lot 40 (with Mason's letters to HW of
1 Aug. 1756 and 15 and 24 March 1796), to Maggs; offered separately in Maggs Cat.
No. 425 (Summer 1922), lot 1839; offered again in Maggs Cat. No. 464 (1925), lot
1690; not further traced until bought by wsl from Elkin Mathews, Aug. 1947.
There is no evidence that HW sent the letter to Mason.

Dated by first paragraph of preceding letter.

Headed by Mary Berry: To the Reverend William Mason.

Endorsed by HW: N.B. I wish some time or other that this letter should be
printed, as it contains some curious anecdotes that are strictly true. Hor. Walpole.

To Mr Mason.

THE purport of Dr Robertson's visit was to inquire where he
could find materials for the reigns of King William and Queen
Anne, which he means to write as a supplement to David Hume.[1]

34. Francesco Bartolozzi (1727–1815), engraver, born in Florence; came to England as engraver to the King in 1764; an original member of the Royal Academy. The engraving here mentioned is reproduced in Mrs Steuart Erskine, *Lady Diana Beauclerk: Her Life and Work*, 1903, p. 169. The original drawing is now in the Yale Art Gallery, the bequest of Wayland Wells Williams. See illustration.

35. Myron (fl. 5th cent. B.C.), Athenian sculptor. 'The nymph-like simplicity of the figure is equal to what a Grecian statuary would have formed for a dryad or goddess of a river' (*Anecdotes, Works* iii. 400).

36. 'Her neck gleamed with a rosy hue and her ambrosial locks breathed forth a heavenly odor' (*Æneid* i. 402–4).

1. Hume had written the *History of England from the Invasion of Julius Cæsar to the Revolution of 1688*, 1754–63.

GEORGIANA, DUCHESS OF DEVONSHIRE,
BY LADY DIANA BEAUCLERK, 1778

I had heard of his purpose, but did not own I knew it, that my discouragement might seem the more natural. I do not care a straw what he writes about the Church's wet-nurse, Goody Anne; but no Scot is worthy of being the historian of William, but Dr Watson.[2]

When he had told me his object, I said, 'Write the reign of King William, Dr Robertson! That is a great task! I look on him as the greatest man of modern times since his ancestor William Prince of Orange.'[3] I soon found the Doctor had very little idea of him, or had taken upon trust the pitiful partialities of Dalrymple and Macpherson. I said, 'Sir, I do not doubt but King William came over with a view to the crown. Nor was he called upon by patriotism, for he was not an Englishman, to assert our liberties. No; his patriotism was of a higher rank. He aimed not at the crown of England from ambition, but to employ its forces and wealth against Louis XIV for the common cause of the liberties of Europe. The Whigs did not understand the extent of his views, and the Tories betrayed him. He has been thought not to have understood us; but the truth was, he took either party as it was predominant, that he might sway the Parliament to support his general plan.' The Doctor suspecting that I doubted his principles being enlarged enough to do justice to so great a character, told me he himself had been born and bred a Whig, though he owned he was *now* a moderate one—I believe a very moderate one.[4] I said Macpherson had done great injustice to another hero, the Duke of Marlborough, whom he accuses of betraying the design on Brest to Louis XIV.[5] The truth was, as I heard often in my youth from my father, my uncle[6] and old persons who had lived in those times, that the Duke trusted the Duchess[7] with the secret, and she her sister the popish Duchess of Tyrconnel,[8] who was as poor

2. Robert Watson (ca 1730–81), LL.D., historian; author of *The History of the Reign of Philip the Second, King of Spain*, 1776, which HW admired (HW to Lady Ossory 23 Dec. 1776).

3. William I (1533–84), Prince of Orange, called William the Silent; opponent of Spanish rule in the Netherlands, and the founder of the Dutch republic; great-great-great-grandfather of William III.

4. HW repeated this to Pinkerton (*Walpoliana* i. 29).

5. A letter from Marlborough to the exiled James II in 1694, concerning a projected British expedition against Brest, is described by Macpherson as treasonable

(*The History of Great Britain from the Restoration to the Accession of the House of Hanover*, 1775, ii. 67). For a discussion and dismissal of this and similar charges against Marlborough see Winston S. Churchill, *Marlborough, His Life and Times*, 1933–8, ii. 92.

6. Horatio Walpole (1678–1757), cr. (1756) Bn Walpole of Wolterton; statesman and diplomatist; 'Old Horace.'

7. Sarah Jennings (1660–1744), m. (1678) John Churchill, cr. (1702) D. of Marlborough.

8. Frances Jennings (ca 1649–1731), m. (1) (ca 1666) Sir George Hamilton, Count Hamilton of France; m. (2) (ca 1681) Rich-

and as bigoted as a church mouse. A corroboration of this was the wise and sententious answer of King William to the Duke, whom he taxed with having betrayed the secret. 'Upon my honour, Sir,' said the Duke, 'I told it to nobody but my wife.' 'I did not tell it to mine,' said the King.[9]

I added, that Macpherson's and Dalrymple's invidious scandals really serve but to heighten the amazing greatness of the King's genius; for if they say true, he maintained the crown on his head, though the nobility, the churchmen, the country gentlemen, the people were against him, and though almost all his own ministers betrayed him. 'But,' said I, 'nothing is so silly as to suppose that the Duke of Marlborough and Lord Godolphin[10] ever meant seriously to restore King James. Both had offended him too much to expect forgiveness, especially from so remorseless a nature. Yet a re-Revolution was so probable, that it is no wonder they kept up a correspondence with him, at least to break their fall if he returned[11]

ard Talbot, cr. (1685) E. and (1689) D. of Tyrconnell; for many years Lady of the Bedchamber to Mary of Modena, wife of the exiled James II; 'la belle Jennings' of Gramont's *Mémoires*. Both of her husbands were Roman Catholics, and John Evelyn, speaking of her visit to England in 1675 after the death of Count Hamilton, describes her as 'now turned Papist' (*Diary*, ed. Austin Dobson, 1906, ii. 387). HW in his copy (now wsl) of the SH edition (1772) of Gramont, p. 193, noted: 'Frances, daughter of Richard Jennings of Sandridge, Hertfordshire, was first married to George Hamilton, and afterwards to Richard Talbot, Duke of Tyrconnel. She had children by both husbands, and dying March 6, 1730, was buried in St Patrick's, Dublin, *v.* Lodge's Irish peerage in Parsons Earl of Ross. She was sister of Sarah Duchess of Marlborough, who trusting her with the secret of King William's design on Brest, she betrayed it to the French Court. Before her death she was so reduced by misfortunes and extravagance that a woman appearing in white weeds, and called *the White Widow,* at the new Exchange in the Strand, and selling millinery goods, was universally believed to be the Duchess of Tyrconnel. I remember her coming when I was a boy to my mother at Chelsea to solicit a pension, and her eyes being dim

and she full of flattery, she commended the beauty of the prospect—but unluckily the room in which they sat, looked only against the garden wall. Hor. Walpole.' HW told the story of the 'White Widow' to Thomas Pennant, who inserted a garbled version of it in *Of London* (HW to Mary Berry 17 July 1790, BERRY i. 93–4 and n. 18).

9. Whatever HW's source, the anecdote appears to be spurious. The design against Brest was not formed until 1694; Marlborough had been excluded from the Council and the Court in Jan. 1692, and he was not in the King's grace again until 1695. See Churchill, loc. cit.

10. Sidney Godolphin (1645–1712), cr. (1684) Bn Godolphin of Rialton, and (1706) Vct Rialton and E. of Godolphin; lord high treasurer 1700–1 and 1702–10. After the Revolution the political allegiances of both Marlborough and Godolphin were anything but steady.

11. Substantially the same explanation of Marlborough's conduct has been urged by Mr Godfrey Davies ('Macpherson and the Nairne Papers,' *English Historical Review,* 1920 xxxv. 376): 'I prefer to believe that Marlborough tried to purchase his pardon in the event of a Jacobite restoration by the most harmless acts of disloyalty which would achieve the end in view.'

—but as they never did effectuate the least service in his favour, when they had the fullest power, nothing can be inferred but King James's folly in continuing to lean on them. To imagine they meant to sacrifice his weak daughter[12] whom they governed absolutely, to a man who was sure of being governed by others, one must have as little sense as James himself had.'

The precise truth I take to have been this. Marlborough and Godolphin both knew the meanness and credulity of James's character. They knew that he must be ever dealing for partisans, and they might be sure, that if he could hope for support from the General and the Lord Treasurer, he must be less solicitous for more impotent supporters. 'Is it impossible,' said I, to the Doctor, 'but they might correspond with the King even by Anne's own consent? Do not be surprised, Sir,' said I: 'such things have happened. My own father often received letters from the Pretender,[13] which he always carried to George II, and had them endorsed by his Majesty.[14] I myself have seen them countersigned by the King's own hand.'

I forgot another story[15] that I will tell you. When my father acknowledged his daughter Lady Mary,[16] and grew excessively fond of her, the Duchess of Buckingham,[17] who was always teasing him to *restore* her brother,[18] asked him significantly if he remembered *what* was not thought too great a reward for Lord Clarendon[19] for bring-

12. Queen Anne.
13. James Francis Edward Stuart (1688–1766), Chevalier de St George; 'the Old Pretender'; son of James II.
14. 'I do remember that more than once he received letters from the Pretender himself . . . Sir Robert always carried them to George II, who endorsed and returned them' (*Reminiscences Written by Mr Horace Walpole in 1788*, ed. Paget Toynbee, 1924, p. 93). See also HW to Mann 30 June 1742, n. 38.
15. That is, HW forgot to tell Robertson. This and the following anecdote are marked for omission by Miss Berry, who has noted on the MS: 'These anecdotes omitted here [*Works* v. 651–3] because printed in the *Reminiscences*'—i.e., *Works* iv. 308 n., 316 (*Reminiscences*, ed. Toynbee, pp. 76 n., 93). The omitted passage ('I forgot . . . believe in spirits') was first printed in Toynbee, *Supp.* ii. 156–7.
16. Lady Maria (or Mary) Walpole (ca

1725–1801), natural daughter of Sir Robert Walpole by Maria Skerrett (later Lady Walpole), m. (1746) Charles Churchill (ca 1720–1812), son of Lt-Gen. Charles Churchill by Anne Oldfield the actress. On 8 Feb. 1742 Sir Robert Walpole obtained a patent legitimatizing her and permitting her to take rank as an earl's daughter, an act which gave great offence (see HW to Mann 9 Feb. and 8 April 1742).
17. Lady Catherine Darnley (ca 1682–1743), natural dau. of James II by the Countess of Dorchester; m. (1) (1699) James Annesley, 3d E. of Anglesey; m. (2) (1706), as his 3d wife, John Sheffield, cr. (1703) D. of Buckingham.
18. Her half-brother, the Old Pretender, whom the Duchess 'never ceased labouring to restore' (*Reminiscences*, ed. Toynbee, pp. 91–2).
19. Edward Hyde (1609–74), cr. (1660) Bn Hyde and (1661) E. of Clarendon; Charles II's lord chancellor 1658–67.

ing back the royal family? He asked, 'What?' She replied, 'Allowing the Duke of York to marry his daughter'[20]—he smiled, and restored the son no more than Lord Godolphin did the father.

Lord Godolphin had taken such affection for Sir Robert, that as he was dying at the Duchess of Marlborough's house at St Albans,[21] nobody being in the room, but the Duchess, Sir Robert and my mother, Lord Godolphin said to the Duchess, 'Madam, if there is such a thing as a possibility of spirits returning from the other world, I shall certainly appear to you, if you should ever abandon this young man,'—pointing to Sir Robert—her Grace did not believe in spirits.

In short, I endeavoured to impress the Doctor with proper ideas of his subject, and painted to him the difficulties, and the want of materials—but the booksellers will *out-argue* me, and the Doctor will forget his education—*panem et circenses*, if you will allow me to use the latter for those that are captivated by favour in the *circle*,[22] will decide his writing and give the colour. I once wished he should write the history of King William, but his *Charles V* and his *America* have opened my eyes,[23] and the times have shut his. Adieu!

To MASON, Tuesday 12 May 1778

Printed from Mitford i. 364–8.

May 12, 1778.

I NOW and then write a letter for, rather than to you: that is, when they will bear delay and be equally fresh, and when they contain anecdotes that I do not care to send by the post if they are too personal, and I have not a prospect of sudden conveyance. The following will have all these ingredients, and will rather be an epitome of the manners of the time, than a letter. The characteristics

20. Anne Hyde (1637–71), m. (1660) James, Duke of York, later King James II.

21. Holywell House, the seat of the Jennings family, where Sarah, Duchess of Marlborough was born and where she and the Duke occasionally lived. Godolphin died there 15 Sept. 1712 (Sir Tresham Lever, *Godolphin: His Life and Times*, 1952, p. 251).

22. That is, the Court party; but Robert-son did not succumb to its blandishments or to those of the trade.

23. See *ante* 18 Feb. 1776, n. 14, and 10 June 1777. HW's regard for Robertson revived somewhat with the publication of his *Historical Disquisition concerning the Knowledge which the Ancients Had of India*, 1791 (DALRYMPLE 210), 'a sensible work' (BERRY i. 294–5).

of the age are frenzy, folly, extravagance and insensibility; no wonder when such stars are predominant, that Ruin both stalks on, and is not felt or apprehended.

About ten days ago I wanted a housemaid and one presented herself very well recommended; I said, 'But young woman, why do you leave your present place?' She said she could not support the hours she kept, that her lady never went to bed till three or four in the morning. 'Bless me child,' said I, 'why you tell me you live with a bishop's wife, I never heard that Mrs North[1] gamed or raked so late.'[2] 'No, Sir,' said she, 'but she is three hours undressing.' Upon my word, the edifice that takes three hours to demolish, must at least be double the time in fabricating! would not you for once sit up till morning to see the destruction of the pyramid and distribution of the materials? Do not mention this, for I did not take the girl and she still assists at the daily and nightly revolutions of Babel.

On Tuesday I supped after the opera at Mrs Meynel's[3] with a set of the most fashionable company, which take notice I very seldom do now, as I certainly am not of the age to mix often with young people. Lady Melbourne[4] was standing before the fire, and adjusting her feathers in the glass, says she, 'Lord! they say the stocks will blow up: that will be very comical.'

These would be features for comedy, if they would not be thought caricatures, but today I am possessed of a genuine paper that I believe I shall leave to the Museum,[5] and which though its object will I suppose tomorrow become record,[6] cannot be believed authentic an hundred years hence. It would in such a national satire as

1. Henrietta Maria Bannister (1750–96), m. (1771) Brownlow North, successively Bp of Coventry and Lichfield 1771–4, Worcester 1774–81, and Winchester 1781–1820.

2. Lady Mary Coke described Mrs North as an inveterate gambler (MS Journal 11 Oct. 1776) and wrote of her: 'I've long thought her a very indecent woman and no doubt her extravagance and every part of her conduct must be very provoking to all the Bishop's family' (ibid. 26 Nov. 1778).

3. Anne Boothby-Skrymsher (ca 1737–1814), 2d wife (1758) of Hugo Meynell of Bradley, Derbyshire, and Quorndon, Leics, 'long esteemed the first fox-hunter in the kingdom' (John Nichols, History . . . of the County of Leicester, 1795–1815, iii pt

i. 101, iv pt i. 178; GM 1814, lxxxiv pt ii. 676). The Meynells lived in Hill Street, Berkeley Square.

4. Elizabeth Milbanke (1752–1818), m. (1769) Peniston Lamb, cr. (1770) Lord Melbourne, Bn of Kilmore (I.), (1781) Vct Melbourne (I.), and (1815) Bn Melbourne (U.K.). Her husband's peerages are said to have been 'due to her brilliant qualities' (DNB sub William Lamb). See GEC; Mabell, Countess of Airlie, In Whig Society 1775–1818, 1921, p. xii.

5. The British Museum.

6. The Foley estate bill (see ante 18 April 1778) was not voted on until 15 May, and was then rejected (Journals of the House of Lords xxxv. 495).

Gulliver be deemed too exaggerated; in short Lord Foley and his brother have petitioned the House of Lords to set aside their father's will, as it seems he intended to have raised an hundred thousand pounds to pay their debts, but died before he could execute his intention. All the ladies, Melbournes, and all the bishops' wives that kill their servants by vigils are going about the town lamenting these poor orphans, and soliciting the peers to redress their grievances; but no words, no ridicule can attain to the ridiculous pathetic of the printed case itself, which now lies before me,[7] and of which the four first lines are these—upon my honour they are exactly these:

'The present Lord Foley and his brother Mr Edward Foley having contracted large bond debts to the amount of about ——£[8] and encumbered themselves by granting annuities for their lives to the amount of about seventeen thousand four hundred and fifty pounds a *year*, explained their situation to their father the late Lord ——'

Poor unfortunate children; before thirty, the eldest had spent an estate (to the possession of which he was not arrived) of twenty thousand a year—at least, forfeited his father's affections, who left him but six thousand a year and a palace;[9] and the youngest brother had been dipped in the same extravagance with him, and the legislature is desired to set aside so just a punishment, and if it does will deserve that every lad in England should waste his father's estate before his face, —tell it not in Gath, where all the shekels that ever were in the country would give no idea of the debt, though Jews are the creditors. Burn your sermon instead of printing it; do you think you can preach up to the enormities of the times? Hyperbole is baffled, and if the fine ladies of Jerusalem were so gallant that the prophets were obliged to pass all bounds of decency in censuring Duchess Aholah and Countess Aholibah,[10] where would they have found figures even in Eastern rhetoric to paint the enormity of two sons *explaining to their father* that they paid seventeen thousand pounds a year to usurers for money they had borrowed to pay gaming debts? and what tropes, what meta-

---

7. No other record of it at SH has been found.

8. 'The debts . . . are supposed to amount to near £220,000' (*Journals of the House of Lords* xxxv. 467).

9. Witley Court, Worcs, chief seat of the Foleys, is described in *Vict. Co. Hist. Worcs* iv. 372–3.

10. The sisters who 'committed whoredoms in Egypt' in the parable of Aholah (Samaria) and Aholibah (Jerusalem), Ezekiel 23.

phors drawn from asses[11] would describe a sanhedrim that suffered such a petition to be laid before it?

These have been my collections in a single fortnight in the flagrancy of a civil war. History shall not revert to Athens for decrees against diverting the revenues of the theatre to the service of the state.[12] London shall be the storehouse hereafter, whence declamations shall be drawn on the infatuation of falling empires; nay, so potent is the intoxication that in two companies this evening I have been thought singular for seeing *this petition* in the light I do; at York perhaps I may not be held so antediluvian in my opinions. With such obsolete prejudices I certainly am not very proper at modern suppers, yet with such *entremets* one would not wholly miss them. Nations at the acme of their splendour, or at the eve of their destruction, are worth observing. When they grovel in obscurity afterwards, they furnish neither events nor reflections; strangers visit the vestiges of the Acropolis, or may come to dig for capitals among the ruins of St Paul's;[13] but nobody studies the manners of the pedlars and banditti, that dwell in mud huts within the precincts of a demolished temple. Curio[14] and Clodius[15] are memorable as they paved the way to the throne of Cæsar, but equal scoundrels are not entitled to infamy after

11. Aholibah 'doted upon their paramours, whose flesh is as the flesh of asses' (Ezekiel 23.20).

12. HW presumably has in mind the laws against diverting the Theoric fund, a sum set aside by the Athenian state for the support of religious festivals, to any other purpose. Attempts to apply the fund to military purposes were central issues at the time of the ascendancy of Philip of Macedon and were supported by Demosthenes. Despite the state's need of money a law was passed making it a capital offence even to introduce a motion to encroach on the Theoric fund. The essentially religious nature of the festivals financed by this fund was ignored by eighteenth-century historians. Thomas Leland, for example, wrote: 'But, as relaxations of all kinds degenerate sooner or later into license, the people became so intoxicated at length with the gay scenes with which riches and politeness entertained them, that no public emergencies

could induce them to resign these distributions; and we shall soon see them forbidding any man, on pain of death, to move for restoring what was now called the theatrical money, to the military, or any other public service' (Thomas Leland, *The History of the Life and Reign of Philip, King of Macedon*, 2d edn, 1775, i. 135–6; HW's copy, 1758 edn, was sold SH i. 102).

13. 'At last some curious traveller from Lima will visit England and give a description of the ruins of St Paul's, like the editions of Balbec and Palmyra' (HW to Mann 24 Nov. 1774).

14. Caius Scribonius Curio (d. 49 B.C.), whose debts, according to Plutarch, were paid by Cæsar and who henceforth devoted himself to Cæsar's advancement. He is also credited by Plutarch with introducing Mark Antony to licentiousness.

15. Publius Clodius Pulcher (ca 93–52 B.C.), whose armed bands kept Rome in a turmoil that prepared for Cæsar's assumption of supreme power.

a constitution is overturned; what we shall retain, I do not conjecture. The constitution might recover, the nation cannot: but though its enemies have miscarried in their attacks on the former, is there sense or virtue enough left to restore it, though the assailants have betrayed such wretched despicable incapacity? unless sudden inspiration should seize the whole island and make it with one voice invite Dr Franklin to come over and new-model the government, it will crumble away in the hands that still hold it; they feel, they own their insufficiency. Everybody is sensible of it, and everybody seems to think like Lady Melbourne, that if we are blown up it will be very comical.

To Mason, Friday 15 May 1778

Printed from Mitford i. 368–71.

Strawberry Hill, May 15, 1778.

I HAVE gulped my anger at your silence, or at least adjourned it till I have less disposition to speak, that I may chat with you on all that has happened since I wrote last Saturday.[1] The first thing I heard on landing in Arlington Street was Lord Chatham's death,[2] which in truth I thought of no great consequence, but to himself; for either he would have remained where he was, or been fetched out to do what he could not do,—replace us once more on the throne of Neptune. The House of Commons has chosen to make his death an epoch, which is to draw the line between our prosperity and adversity. They bury him,[3] and father his children.[4] In this fit of gratitude two men chose not to be involved, but voted against attending his funeral;[5] one

1. Probably a mistake for 'Tuesday': i.e., the preceding letter. See *post* 24 May *ad fin*.
2. Chatham died at Hayes 11 May.
3. 'Last night the House of Commons unanimously voted an address to his Majesty, that he would be graciously pleased to give orders that the late Earl of Chatham should be buried, and that a monument should be erected to his memory in Westminster Abbey, with an inscription thereon, expressing the sense of this country of his eminent services, and of the irreparable loss it sustains by his death, at the public expense' (*Public Advertiser* 12 May 1778).
4. 'Mr T. Townshend . . . moved [13 May], "That an humble address should be

presented to his Majesty . . . to request that his Majesty would be graciously pleased to make such a lasting provision for the family of the late William Pitt, Earl of Chatham, as his Majesty, in his wisdom and liberality, should think fit" ' (*Lloyd's Evening Post* 13–15 May 1778, xlii. 457). The motion was carried unanimously (Cobbett, *Parl. Hist.* xix. 1228) and the King gave his assent. The sum of £20,000 was voted for the payment of Chatham's debts, and an annuity of £4000 on the earldom (*Journals of the House of Commons* xxxvi. 991 and 1006–7; *Annual Register*, 1778, xxi. 188*).
5. Twenty peers voted against Lord Shel-

was the Archbishop of Canterbury, who owed the tiara to him;[6] the other, Lord Onslow,[7] who formerly used to wait in the lobby to help him on with his greatcoat.

Yesterday teemed with events: a compromise on the Irish bills[8] was made and broken.[9] Then Sir George Saville moved for taking off pressures from the Roman Catholics,[10] which charmed every soul on both sides,[11] and I suppose the papists will soon be admitted *ad eundem*.[12]

Next arrived General Burgoyne.[13] I don't know whether he was surprised or not, but he received a prohibition of appearing at Court;[14] and a board of general officers is appointed to sit on his con-

burne's motion that the House of Lords attend Chatham's funeral, defeating it by one vote (Cobbett, op. cit. xix. 1234).

6. Elsewhere HW had written: 'Dr Frederic Cornwallis . . . was preferred to the primacy by the Duke of Grafton, who had a friendship for the Bishop's nephew, Earl Cornwallis' (*Mem. Geo. III* iii. 158), and this is confirmed by Bishop Thomas Newton in his autobiography (*Lives of . . . Pocock . . . , Pearce . . . , Newton . . . , and Skelton*, ed. Alexander Chalmers, 1816, ii. 163). See Alfred W. Rowden, *The Primates of the Four Georges*, 1916, pp. 322–5.

7. George Onslow (1731–1814), 4th Bn Onslow, 1776, cr. (1801) E. of Onslow; notorious for his desertion of Wilkes, 'the first of his more open treacheries' (C. E. Vulliamy, *The Onslow Family*, 1953, p. 157.)

8. Bills to remove restrictions on Irish trade. They were first introduced by Lord Nugent, 2 April 1778, and were supported by Edmund Burke in spite of the opposition of his Bristol constituents. See *Annual Register*, 1778, xxi. 172*–174*; *Last Journals* ii. 172; W. E. H. Lecky, *History of Ireland in the Eighteenth Century*, 1892, ii. 177–80.

9. On Wednesday 13 May Lord North wrote to the King that the House of Commons 'went into the second reading of the Irish importation bill, which was interrupted and postponed to Friday upon an intimation given to the House that a compromise was likely to take place between the friends and the opposers of the Irish bills' (*Corr. Geo. III* iv. 141). As a result of the compromise it was thought 'necessary to give up for the present most

of the advantages that were originally intended for . . . [Ireland]. Some enlargement however was given to the linen trade . . . and some openings given in the African and West India trades which did not before exist. Thus the measure, at its final transit through Parliament, might be rather considered as an opening to future service, and an earnest of good intention, than as affording any immediate benefit' (*Annual Register*, 1778, xxi. 192*).

10. 'Sir George Savile made a motion, "That leave be given to bring in a bill for the repeal of certain penalties and disabilities provided in an act of the 10th and 11th of William III, entitled an act to prevent the further growth of popery' (*Public Advertiser* 15 May 1778). On the 1778 relief act for Roman Catholics see W. J. Amherst, *The History of Catholic Emancipation*, 1886, i. 91–121; Philip Hughes, *The Catholic Question 1688–1829*, 1929, pp. 145–6.

11. Savile's motion was carried unanimously (*Public Advertiser* 15 May 1778).

12. I.e., 'ad eundem gradum,' 'to the same rank or degree' (as in a university).

13. 'Yesterday [Thursday 14 May] morning at nine o'clock General Burgoyne arrived in town from Rhode Island, but last from Portsmouth, at which place he landed on Wednesday at noon' (*London Chronicle* 14–16 May 1778, xliii. 466). After the defeat at Saratoga, Burgoyne was allowed by the American Congress to return to England as a prisoner on parole.

14. 'On Thursday evening Lieutenant-General Burgoyne, by order of the King, was sent for to the Queen's Palace, and held a conference with his Majesty for upwards of two hours; but was not at Court

duct.[15] Luckily we have enough to spare, though French and Spaniards should land in twenty places; for next came an account of Marshal Broglio[16] being appointed commander-in-chief on the coasts of the ocean. The *ubi* of the Toulon squadron is not ascertained.[17] That of Brest has thirty frigates,[18] and the Spanish ten thousand men on board,[19] so you may prophesy at your pleasure.

I say nothing of an interlude which nobody has leisure to think on, and is a great way off in a certain little empire we have, or had, called India, where Mr Hastings[20] had deposed General Clavering[21] by the plenitude of his power before the latter's death.[22]

yesterday. . . . General Burgoyne, it is said, is not expected to appear at the levee, until a general court-martial is held on the business at Saratoga' (ibid. xliii. 470).

15. On 14 May Lord Amherst wrote to the King: 'I will get the earliest and best information I can of what has been the custom and rule observed on a similar occasion of putting an officer under arrest, and who should properly perform that duty, which I will have the honour of laying before your Majesty . . . as well as of what generals, the board of inquiry may consist of' (*Corr. Geo. III* iv. 142). A court of inquiry was appointed and later reported that 'in his [Burgoyne's] then situation, as a prisoner on parole to the Congress . . . they could not take cognizance of his conduct' (*Annual Register*, 1778, xxi. 196*). Burgoyne, anxious to justify himself, sought a court-martial, but was refused on the same grounds. He then requested a public inquiry into his conduct, and on 26 May defended his actions in the House of Commons (ibid.; Cobbett, *Parl. Hist.* xix. 1176). See *post* 31 May 1778.

16. Victor-François (1718–1804), Duc de Broglie, 1745; Maréchal de France 1759–89.

17. Late in April news of the departure of the fleet from Toulon reached England (*Corr. Geo. III* iv. 122) and occasioned a great outcry from the Opposition because an English fleet had not sailed to meet it (Cobbett, *Parl. Hist.* xix. 1131–6). The newspapers at this time were publishing rumours and speculations about the destination of the Toulon fleet.

18. The exact size of the Brest fleet was given variously in the newspapers at this time. When it finally sailed against

Keppel's ships it consisted of thirty-two ships of the line (*post* 18 July 1778, n. 5).

19. Rumours concerning the Spanish armament circulated in the press. This particular report has not been found, but in the *Public Advertiser* of 12 May 1778 it was said that 'twenty-one ships of the line, with a body of 18,000 land forces, are now ready to sail from Cadiz.' Spain actually maintained neutrality until June 1779.

20. Warren Hastings (1732–1818), governor-general of India 1773–85.

21. Sir John Clavering (1722–77), commander-in-chief of the Bengal army and member of the governing council established by the Regulating Act of 1773. Rivalry between Hastings and Clavering came to a head in June 1777 when Clavering attempted to seize the government on the strength of a conditional resignation by Hastings, tendered in error by Hastings's London agent and later repudiated by Hastings, whose suit to recover his office was upheld by the supreme court of Calcutta. See G. B. Malleson, *Life of Warren Hastings*, 1894, pp. 272–82; Sophia Weitzman, *Warren Hastings and Philip Francis*, Manchester, 1929, pp. 102–5.

22. Clavering died 30 Aug. 1777 (Hastings to Lord North 7 Sept. 1777, printed in Weitzman, op. cit. 328; Sir Philip Francis to General Carnac 30 Aug. 1777, ibid. 331). News of Clavering's death reached England early in April 1778 (*Corr. Geo. III* iv. 99). Protests by Clavering and Francis against Hastings had also recently arrived (ibid. iv. 143; Lucy S. Sutherland, *The East India Company in Eighteenth-Century Politics*, Oxford, 1952, p. 333).

I thought these accidents were sufficient for one week, and came out of town this morning as tranquilly as if I were a minister; so I hold my own philosophy full as high as any stoic's in Yorkshire. It does require some command of temper to sit still and see a general wreck approaching,—I mean for one that expects and thinks on it. I know I might go to Ranelagh, and Newmarket, and exhibitions, and say, with Pope,

Whatever is, is right.[23]

But I am forced to seek other consolations; and as I have not the spirits of youth, I have recourse to age, and comfort myself that my time cannot be long whether I survive my country or the constitution, the former of which is alternately shaken or attempted to be propped by experiments on the latter; but it is idle to dream on old maxims. A great convulsion is at hand, and new eras find new levels. Old folks should not trouble themselves with great epochs at the end of their lives, but set themselves apart till they are swept to the ancient mass to which they belonged.

I have long taken my doctor's degree in Strulbruggism, and wonder I concern myself about the affairs of the living. Good night, I will go and converse with the dead.

From Mason, Sunday 24 May 1778

Printed from MS now wsl.
Address: The Honourable Horace Walpole, Arlington Street, London.
Postmark: ROTHERHAM 28 MA.

Aston, May 24th, 1778.

I HAVE got a quire of much smaller paper[1] than I formerly used, though not quite so small as that you write letters upon,[2] and I am in great hopes it will make me a much more punctual correspondent to you and the rest of my friends, for when a man has nothing to say (which is usually my case) there is nothing so formidable as seeing a

---

23. *Essay on Man* i. 294.

1. Mason habitually wrote to HW on a half-sheet of post paper that, folded into two leaves, measures approximately 7½ by 9¼ inches. This letter was written on a half-sheet of foolscap folded into 6¼ by 7¾ inch leaves.

2. HW's letters to other correspondents at this time are also written on paper of foolscap size.

huge quarto page, big enough for the types of a Scotch historian,[3] lie before one in expectation of being filled. I know I have frequently taken one of those out of my *portefeuille,* and put it in again through pure disgust at its magnitude. Pray, who is your stationer? His Majesty has been mine a great while (through the mediation of Mr Auditor Stonhewer)[4] but I'll turn him off and take yours—and yet when one considers that it is the only thing by which he has ever benefited me, or will be likely to benefit me, this would be quarrelling with one's bread and butter.

Thus the apologetical first page, the most difficult to write in a whole letter, is fairly filled, and the second begun. Shall I fill this with a threnody on the two earls[5] which have lately left my stationer in the lurch? Their characters are too dissimilar to be hitched into the same rhymes, and yet they both agreed in one virtue, that of a most profound loyalty. The latter of these with whom only I was acquainted, lamented the republican spirit that was abroad in the last conference I had with him. I did not ask him what he meant by it, because I was sure he could not tell me. But are you not charmed with the Cavendishes getting up to praise the dead statesman,[6] whom I know they hated as cordially as the King hates them? I always thought Lord John rather a modest man till this event. And are not you charmed too with the political wisdom of Sir George Saville who chooses this very moment to indispose the whole body of dissenters towards him and his party by rising up the champion of the papists? Bad as I esteem the reigning ministry I actually like them better than the Opposition. I mean the Rockingham part of it, and yet all my friends are included in that part.

Pray give me an account of the funeral, and if you have time order your gardener to pluck a bouquet of onions and send it with my compliments to Lord John that he may put them in his handkerchief

---

3. Robertson's, Dalrymple's, and Macpherson's histories were published in large quartos.

4. Stonhewer was auditor of excise 1772–89 and apparently furnished Mason with stationery from his office.

5. Chatham and Holdernesse; the latter died 16 May 1778.

6. On 13 May Lord John Cavendish urged the House of Commons not to allow 'the descendants of that great man, to whom this country owed its greatest glory, to be exposed to want' (Cobbett, *Parl. Hist.* xix. 1226). Two elder brothers of Lord John, Lord George (d. 1794) and Lord Frederick (1729–1803), were also members of Parliament, but Lord John seems to have been the spokesman of the family (Francis Bickley, *The Cavendish Family,* 1911, pp. 225–6; G. H. Guttridge, *English Whiggism and the American Revolution,* Berkeley and Los Angeles, 1942, p. 51).

to weep with greater facility. I am sick of my friends, my country, and myself. They say we are to be invaded. I am as impatient to be so, as the old nun, in the *Pucelle,* was to be violated.[7] Well; but if we are not invaded, will you meet me in a little time at Nuneham? I mean to go there the middle of next month and stay till August. I had once thought of passing through town, but the absence of my curate, I believe, will prevent me, for he is now setting off with Lord H.'s corpse to Hornby,[8] and is to return to town to settle some affairs relative to the lease of Sion Hill with the Duke of Northumberland.[9] You may well believe that I can contentedly stay here, when I reflect that a great part of the trouble and attendance that now falls upon him would have been my lot had things been as they once were. But my little quarto page happily releases you from more of my prate, and leaves me no room to say how much I am yours.

You talked in your last of a letter you had written *last Saturday.* I hope you was only *ironing,*[10] for I have only received one since I came hither from York.

To Mason, Sunday 31 May 1778

Printed from Mitford i. 376–80.

Strawberry Hill, May 31, 1778.

I AM glad you have deigned to answer me at last, for there is no conversation when only one talks. I was almost sorry that I had not begged you to order your executor to send me word you was dead, and that I need not write any more. But, my good friend, you are full as great a contradiction as Lord John,[1] or any Catholic Whig[2] upon earth. You write once in a quarter, and yet complain of my

7. Apparently he is thinking of the conclusion of Canto XI of Voltaire's *La Pucelle d'Orléans:*
'Sœur Rebondi, qui dans la sacristie
A succombé sous le vainqueur impie,
Pleurait le traître en rendant grâce au ciel;
Et, mesurant des yeux le criminel
Elle disait d'une voix charitable
"Hélas! hélas! nul ne fut plus coupable." '
8. Holdernesse was buried at Hornby 1 June 1778 (GEC). Mason officiated at the funeral (see *post* 1 July 1778).

9. The details of the business have not been found. The Duke of Northumberland owned Syon House, near Holdernesse's Syon Hill.
10. I.e., joking. HW probably meant the letter of Tuesday 12 May, written with no 'prospect of sudden conveyance,' which Mason had perhaps not received by 24 May.

1. Cavendish. See preceding letter.
2. 'Papists and liberty are contradictions' (*post* 8 Nov. 1783).

small paper; I fixed upon this little quarto for substantial reasons. I am too apt to write too much to those I love, and prescribed myself this size that I might not weary them, and it holds all one has to say to those one loves not, and yet seems to contain a decent quantity.

I should like to accept the assignation you give me, and will if I have the least encouragement, but I have had no invitation; and though I do not at all know why, am a little suspicious of not being in the most perfect favour.[3] As this is by no means positive, I take no notice, because it is not at all on my side, and it[4] shall revive whenever it pleases, as my regard is just the same. If we should not meet I think you cannot refuse coming to me for a few days. Consider, I have turned that corner beyond which every hour is *lucrum*,[5] and that I and everybody else think I have lived long enough—though I am not so old as Sam. Martin counts me.[6] The talisman is removed[7] that prohibited your access to this part of the world, though surely Twickenham is a kind of country to so near relation of Pope as you are by the side of your virgin-mothers;[8] let me have the satisfaction of seeing you here, whither very few are pressed to come. We have a thousand things to talk over, and are almost reduced to be the only two of the same opinion, for what those you call your friends[9] mean, indeed I do not guess, it is most charitable to think they have no meaning. I used to fancy that calamity would bring us to our senses —it must bring our senses too. The two alternatives now are desola-

3. On 26 May HW had written to Lord Harcourt: 'As you have flattered me with the honour of a visit [to SH], may I ask if Sunday or Monday next will be agreeable to your Lordship and Lady Harcourt?' Harcourt's reply is missing. On 8 June 1778 Mason wrote to Harcourt of HW's suspicion that he was not 'in the most perfect favour,' adding 'yet he holds this by no means positive, and says handsome things of your Lordship. I send you this by way of a hint, that you may either regard or not' (*Harcourt Papers* vii. 58). The following undated extract preserved by Mitford (see *post* Appendix 1) seems to be Harcourt's reply: 'Mr Stonhewer has invited himself to meet you at Nuneham. Mr Walpole shall be asked to be of the party— *quel mouche lui piquait*, when he took it into his head that my regard for him was lessened? He is mistaken, for I have a great esteem for him and am perpetually raising marks of his for me. I should really like to call on him much oftener than I do, but there is nothing I dread so much as being *de trop*, and he is so very apt to be *tired of people*, and I have so much sense as to think it by no means improbable that I may appear very tiresome, and therefore frequently pass his door when I had much rather knock at it' (Add. MSS 32563 fol. 102). HW soon received an invitation to Nuneham; see next letter.

4. Mitford reads 'and that it.'

5. I.e., gain.

6. See *ante* 2 March 1773 *bis*.

7. By Holdernesse's death.

8. That is, they were both sons of the Muses. HW also compares Mason with Pope *ante* 27 March 1773, ?Nov. 1776, 13 March and 4 Aug. 1777.

9. The Rockingham Whigs.

tion, or a shameful peace: bankruptcy with either, only a little nearer, or a little farther off; it is actually come out on the agitation of the changes in the law[10] that at £60 per commission, the Chancellor[11] reaped seven thousand pounds last year by bankruptcies. Those changes were to have taken place last Thursday, but I do not hear they did. Thurloe is to be Lord Chancellor or Lord Keeper, I do not know which. Wedderburne sits down with the Attorney's place,[12] a disappointment[13] and I suppose a full promise.[14] Norton[15] threatened to impeach him if peered, for telling the Chief Justice[16] that Lord North would pay him out of the Treasury seven thousand pounds for the prothonotary's reversion. Thus justice makes a rope of one rogue, instead of using two ropes.[17]

I shall certainly not go to the funeral[18]—I go to no puppet-shows, nor want to see Lord Chatham's water-gall Lord Temple hobble chief mourner. I scarcely inquire after the House of Commons, which is a scene of folly and billingsgate. Burgoyne has tried to be the pathetic hero,[19] and was forgotten for three hours, while Temple Lut-

10. That is, in the appointive legal offices of state. The King wished to make Thurlow Lord Chancellor. His promotion from the attorney-generalship was suggested by the King as early as 15 March 1778 (*Corr. Geo. III* iv. 55), but difficulties arose in the redistribution of places (ibid. iv. 95–6, 102, 110–1, 114–8, 147–50, 158–60).

11. Lord Bathurst.

12. 'It is said that the following law changes are settled to take place in the course of the week, viz. Edw. Thurlow, Esq., to be Lord Chancellor, with a peerage; Sir Fletcher Norton to be Chief Justice of the Court of Common Pleas; Alexander Wedderburne, Esq., to be Attorney-General. Other accounts say, that Mr Attorney-General is appointed Lord Keeper, *pro tempore*' (*London Chronicle* 26–8 May 1778, xliii. 510). Norton was not promoted; Thurlow, the attorney-general, was made Lord Chancellor. 'The Lord Chancellor and Lord Keeper . . . differ only in this point, that the Lord Chancellor hath also letters patent, whereas the Lord Keeper has none' (Robert Beatson, *Political Index*, 1806, p. 317).

13. He wished to be 'placed upon the Bench and in the House of Peers at the same time with Mr Thurlow' (Lord North

to George III, 18 April 1778, *Corr. Geo. III* iv. 115).

14. Wedderburn was not raised to the peerage until 14 June 1780. North's reasons for the delay are given in the letter cited in the preceding note.

15. Sir Fletcher Norton, Speaker of the House of Commons.

16. Sir William de Grey (1719–81), judge; Kt, 1771; chief justice of the Common Pleas 1771–80; cr. (1780) Bn Walsingham.

17. I.e., one rogue hangs another. The application is not clear, since the preceding sentence has not been confirmed or explained. There were four prothonotaries in the court of Common Pleas (*Royal Kalender*, 1778, p. 102).

18. Chatham's, which took place 9 June.

19. '26th [May]. General Burgoyne appeared in the House of Commons, which was so exceedingly crowded that they were forced to turn out the strangers, though Burgoyne begged they might stay and hear his defence. Vyner, after asking him some questions on the affair of Saratoga, moved for a committee to inquire into his conduct. Burgoyne seconded him, gave an account of his conduct, said nothing hard on General Howe, did great justice to the Americans, and complained much of his

terel and Lord G. Germaine scolded like two oyster-women; the first tried to be sent to Newgate, and the latter grasped his sword, and then asked pardon for having been grossly affronted.[20] Lord Barrington implored Madam his country's tears for declaring he was retiring from her service to virtuous privacy.[21] It is pity she did not order him to be buried at the public expense; Lord Sandwich has run the gauntlet in the Lords for all the lies he has told all the winter about the fleet,[22] and does not retire, but I am sick of repeating what you must be sick of reading. An invasion will have some dignity; but to see a great country gambol at the eve of ruin like a puppy on a precipice! Oh! one cannot buffoon like Lucian when one wants to speak daggers like Tacitus, and couch them in a sentence without descending to details.

I had rather talk on less interesting subjects, and will tell you a good *bon mot*. *Marie à la Coque*[23] has had an outrageous quarrel with Miss Pelham[24] on politics, or rather at Miss Pelham, who did not reply. This occasioned Lady Mary's notes being mentioned, which

being forbidden the King's presence' (*Last Journals* ii. 179). In his speech Burgoyne described himself as a man 'whose faculties, far too weak for such shocks, are almost unhinged by a succession of difficulties abroad, that fall to the lot of few, and whose disappointments and anxieties have been consummated by the unexpected reception he has met at home' (Cobbett, *Parl. Hist.* xix. 1186).

20. Luttrell compared Burgoyne's conduct with Germain's at Minden (see *ante* 24 Jan. 1778, n. 15), whereupon Germain replied that he 'despised' Luttrell, but 'old as he was, he would meet that fighting gentleman and be revenged.' On being called to order, Germain apologized to the House. 'Mr Luttrell was then called upon. He said, if after being insulted for doing his duty, he was to be committed for delivering the sentence of George II [in Germain's court-martial], he should prefer being committed, to giving up the privilege of Parliament. . . . Lord George Germain rose to make a second apology, which was fairly and particularly addressed to the honourable gentleman, for . . . feeling himself hurt by the charges stated against him' (Cobbett, *Parl. Hist.* xix. 1199–1202).

21. Lord Barrington, the secretary at

war, 'declared his intention of retiring, and quitting his seat in Parliament; but he still kept his office till the King should be ready to appoint a successor' (*Last Journals* ii. 182). See *Corr. Geo. III* iv. 150–1. The secretaryship was vacated by Barrington in December and given to Charles Jenkinson (*Annual Register*, 1778, xxi. 224).

22. Sandwich's conduct of the Navy was severely castigated in the House of Lords 25 May by the Duke of Richmond. See Cobbett, *Parl. Hist.* xix. 1145–61.

23. Lady Mary Coke. 'Marie Alacoque, a native of Burgundy, born in [1647]; entered the convent of the Visitation de Ste Marie de Paray-le-Monial in 1671; died in 1690. She was an enthusiast and a visionary. This, together with the similarity of sound, led Horace Walpole to speak of Lady Mary Coke under that name, she being also given to visions and enthusiasms, though not, however, of a religious sort' (Mrs Toynbee's note, x. 255). HW uses the same phrase to Mann 15 Feb. 1776.

24. Frances Pelham (1728–1804), second daughter of Henry Pelham. There are numerous stories of her extravagant gambling and ungovernable temper; for references see MONTAGU i. 53.

she signs as Duchess of York,[25] Maryc, the c[26] passing for a flourish,[27] if you do not go to law with her. On this, Burke said to Miss P., 'Upon my word you will be a match for her if you sign Frances P.'

There was more humour in a reply of Lady Harrington's[28] t'other day. Mrs St John[29] had asked Lady Anna Maria[30] to a ball without her mother, who would not let her go. The next time they met, Lady H. made excuses, but said she never allowed her daughter to go to balls without her. Mrs St J. replied, as her Ladyship suffered her to go the opera without her, she had hoped she would not have been more strict about a private dancing. Instead of knocking her down, as might have been expected, Lady Harrington looked her all over, and then with a face melted to compassion, said in a soft voice, and very slowly, 'Mrs St John, if you *could* have a child,[31] I am sure you would think as I do!' Imagine this addressed to a porpoise covered with flowers and feathers! but I would in vain divert you, I do not feel cheerful, though, as I told you in a former letter, I had rather see my country humbled than insolently enslaved. Nay, I think with comfort on a time which I shall not see, when the absurdity of the present age will be painted in its true colours. The mind never rests on the unhappy point; it prefers a non-existent scene to disagreeable sensations; I feel my own folly; were I to leave England as happy or as glorious as I have known it, would it always remain so? Is not it enough that the mischief is falling on the heads of its authors? what period equalled the disgraces of the last six or eight months? shall the innocent mix sighs with the guilty? who will doubt where the blame is due? all the Robertsons and Humes of the Highlands cannot whitewash the four last years; nor, which is more delightful, can they plunder and disgrace America, as their chiefs have undone Eng-

25. See *ante* 9 Aug. 1774, n. 9.

26. Mitford reads 'Marye . . . e'; emended by Mrs Toynbee.

27. HW comments on Lady Mary's royal signature in a note on his letter to Mann of 2 Feb. 1774.

28. Lady Caroline Fitzroy (1722–84), m. (1746) William Stanhope, 2d E. of Harrington, 1756.

29. Barbara Bladen (b. ca 1733), eldest daughter of Colonel Thomas Bladen of Glastonbury Abbey, Somerset; sister of Harriet, Countess of Essex; m. (1771) Hon. Henry St John, 2d son of John, 2d Vct St John (J. H. Jesse, *George Selwyn and His*

Contemporaries, 1882, i. 258; Burke, *Peerage sub* Bolingbroke; GEC *sub* Essex; J. B. Whitmore and G. R. Y. Radcliffe, *A Supplementary Volume to the Record of Old Westminsters,* [?1937,] p. 17).

30. Lady Anna Maria Stanhope (1760–1834), youngest daughter of William, 2d E. of Harrington; m. (1) (1782) Thomas Pelham-Clinton, styled E. of Lincoln 1779–94, 3d D. of Newcastle, 1794; m. (2) (1800) Lt-Gen. Sir Charles Gregan Crawfurd.

31. There had been a rumour the preceding summer that Mrs St John was pregnant (Jesse, op. cit. iii. 201).

land. Seven Jameses were not worse politicians than the whole nation is; nor is there a more indelible mark of reprobation on the Jews. I would fain persuade myself that the seeds of tyranny will not thrive in this country, though all the inhabitants sow them. Every attempt chokes the seedsman; I hope we shall be a proverb, as Ireland is, for not producing venomous animals!

Remember that if I write on small paper I write a very small hand, and that this very letter would make forty, if I scrawled a large character like dukes and old earls, who allow as much room to every word as to their coach and six. I don't want news, but you can say nothing that I shall not be glad to read.

To Mason, Friday 26 June 1778

Printed from Mitford i. 383–5.

Strawberry Hill, June 26, 1778.

Mʀ NICHOLL[1] has been here, and tells me he has seen you, and that you have not been well, for which I am very sorry indeed. He says York disagreed with you, and that you will go thither no more in winter.[2] The rest of his account was much more welcome: that you have made charming progress in your third book, and inserted divine lines on Gray.[3] Them I do thirst to see, and trust I shall ere many moons have put on their nightcaps; for Lord Harcourt has asked me to meet you at Nuneham. When it is to be I don't know, for they are going or gone into Sussex; but if you can cast a figure and guess, I beg you to give me a hint, though nothing shall prevent my being faithful to that assignation, but my lord and master, gout, whose commands however I do not expect.

Well; the signal is fired. Admiral Keppel[4] has had a smart skirmish with three frigates of the Brest squadron,[5] and has sent one of them

1. Norton Nicholls.
2. Mason continued to go to York in the winter (post 12 Nov. 1779).
3. The first sixty-two lines of the third book of The English Garden are a tribute to Gray.
4. Hon. Augustus Keppel (1725–86), admiral; cr. (1782) Vct Keppel; appointed commander-in-chief of the Grand Fleet 22 March 1778.
5. An early report of Keppel's engagement with the French 17–19 June 1778 appeared in the Public Advertiser 26 June. More circumstantial details were given in letters from Keppel to the Admiralty printed in the London Chronicle 27–30

in.[6] They fired first,[7] and yet seem to have provoked him, that they may plead we began the war. I trouble myself mighty little about what their majesties the kings of Europe will say on these punctilios over their coffee. We, the Achivi, are to be the sufferers,[8] and particularly we the Achivi of these islands. In truth Agamemnon himself[9] will be no great gainer, nor be gathered to the Atridæ with quite so many crowns on his head as they bequeathed to him, and he will wish he had not worn that of Caledonia!

I know nothing else; but what a volume in that *else!* you bards that can prophesy with the lyre in your hand have

ample scope and verge enough[11]

for pouring out odes full of calamity and of *funera Dardanæ genti*.[12] Distress is already felt; one hears of nothing but of the want of money; one sees it every hour. I sit in my blue window[13] and miss nine in ten of the carriages that used to pass before it. Houses sell for nothing, which, two years ago, nabobs would have given lacs[14] of diamonds for. Sir Gerard Vannecks's[15] house and beautiful terrace on the Thames, with forty acres of ground, and valued by his father[16]

June 1778 (xliii. 617). On 17 June the English Channel fleet observed that it was being reconnoitred by two French ships. Since Keppel's instructions had read, 'In case any French frigates of war should attend upon the fleet, or appear to be watching your motions, you are to oblige them to desist, and on their refusal, to seize them and send them to England' (*Sandwich Papers* ii. 9), Keppel ordered them to be pursued, and that same evening one of them, the *Licorne*, was overtaken. The next day, before surrendering, it fired a broadside at its English escort. The second frigate, later found to be the *Belle Poule*, engaged its pursuer in a battle and escaped to a French port. On 19 June Keppel's fleet sighted a third French frigate, the *Pallas*, and captured it without resistance. See ibid. ii. 9 and 94–8, and W. L. Clowes, *The Royal Navy*, 1897–1903, iv. 14.

6. News of the capture of the *Pallas* had not yet reached England.

7. HW may not have known that a warning shot had been fired at the *Licorne* during the pursuit on 17 June, and an-

other on 18 June, before the French vessel returned fire (W. L. Clowes, loc. cit.).

8. 'Quidquid delirant reges, plectuntur Achivi' (Horace, *Epistles* I. ii. 14: 'Whatever folly kings may commit, the Achæans are punished'). The allusion is also in HW's letter to Mann 17 March 1778.

9. George III.

11. Gray, *The Bard*, l. 51 (*scope* for *room*).

12. 'Disasters to the Trojan people' (Horace, *Odes* I. xv. 10–11).

13. The bow-window in the Breakfast Room. From it HW looked east to the road that ran from Twickenham to Teddington, Hampton Court, and Kingston.

14. Lac, lakh; Anglo-Indian for 100,000 (OED).

15. Sir Gerard Vanneck (ca 1743–91), 2d Bt, 1777; merchant; M. P. Dunwich 1768–90 (GEC, *Complete Baronetage* v. 98).

16. Sir Joshua Vanneck (d. 1777), cr. (1751) Bt; 'a mighty international financier of Dutch extraction, who had interests in every part of western Europe and America' (L. B. Namier, 'Brice Fisher, M. P.: A Mid-Eighteenth Century Merchant and his Con-

at twenty thousand pounds, was bought in last week at six thousand. Richmond is deserted; an hundred and twenty coaches used to be counted at the church door, there are now twenty; I know nobody that grows rich but Margaret.[17] This halcyon season has brought her more customers than ever, and were anything to happen to her, I have thoughts, like greater folk, of being my own minister and showing my house myself. I don't wonder *your Garden* has grown in such a summer, and I am glad it has, that our taste in gardening may be immortal in verse, for I doubt it has seen its best days! Your poem may transplant it to America, whither our best works will be carried now, as our worst used to be. Do not you feel satisfied in knowing you shall be a classic in a free and rising empire? Swell all your ideas, give a loose to all your poetry; your lines will be repeated on the banks of the Oroonoko; and which is another comfort, Ossian's dirges will never be known there. Poor Strawberry must sink in *fæce Romuli;*[18] that melancholy thought silences me. Good night.

From Mason, Wednesday 1 July 1778

Printed from MS now WSL.

Wentworth Castle, July 1st, 1778.

I HAVE had no occurrence on my progress or pilgrimage through this Valley of Life (to speak in the style of John Bunyan) worth mentioning since I wrote last, except peradventure the attending at Hornby Castle, and saying 'dust to dust' over Lord Holdernesse's remains[1] might be thought worth the notifying to you; but when I consider that you did not seem to interest yourself much in the funeral of Lord Chatham I suspect my poor Earl's would not be

nections,' *English Historical Review*, 1927, xlii. 525). Sir Joshua and his family were painted on the terrace of the villa at Putney by Arthur Devis in 1752. The figure at the extreme right has been called HW, but it is almost certainly one of his cousins, Thomas or Richard Walpole, both of whom married daughters of Sir Joshua. The picture is reproduced in Sacheverell Sitwell, *Conversation Pieces*, [1936], facing p. 49. It is described in Sydney H. Pavière, *The Devis Family of Painters*, Leigh-on-

Sea, 1950, p. 58, and is now (1953) owned by Miss Helen Frick at Prides Crossing, Mass.

17. Margaret Young, HW's housekeeper at SH, who prospered by the 'vails' given her by visitors.

18. 'The dregs of Romulus' (Cicero, *Epistulæ ad Atticum* II. i. 8).

1. On 1 June 1778 (*ante* 24 May 1778, n. 8).

thought of much consequence by you. Indeed, nobody of any rank ever seems to have stolen out of life, in a more incog manner, than he has done, for all-Frenchman as he was, Voltaire would hinder his being talked about,[2] even on his darling Continent. So that what with Lord Chatham's death here, and Voltaire's death there, his memory seems to have slipped between two stools, and so rest his soul, if Dr Priestly[3] chooses to let him have one,[4] whether material or not is not in his case much material. Excuse the pun for the sake of the sense if you be candid enough so to do.

My expedition to Nuneham is put off *sine die*. It is not the fashion to begin one's summers till autumn, and Lord Harcourt, you know, always chooses to be in the fashion. Next year I trust our summers will be in the winter, for as our days are in the night, and consequently our noons at midnight, our seasons are but half the thing during the present *ton,* and I like consistency in all matters. I hope, however, to pass some of my dog-days about the beginning of next December at Strawberry, and have made up a light fustian frock for the purpose.

My present noble host[5] you know is the very reverse of all this. His seasons go by clock-work and that clock-work as old as Tompion's.[6] I came here last Monday and shall return to my flock on Saturday. His Lordship and her Ladyship are much yours and bid me say so. The latter I think a most excellent woman, and somewhat different from the *de la Coque* you mention,[6a] but I think I can account for this difference in a manner not very flattering to the sex.

Sappho[7] is almost finished, and satisfies me better than my own things usually do, but I fear I grow like old fathers who like their children whom they get after fifty, much better than those they got at five and twenty, because they are proofs of their vigour. To be sure in the eye of episcopacy, I might full as venially have begot a child upon the body of my chambermaid as this upon my brain. A parson writing an amorous opera is a phenomenon more horrid I trust in that eye than the growth of popery. But *macte virtute,* the deed is done, and I am ready to abide by the consequences.

2. Voltaire had died in Paris 30 May.

3. Joseph Priestley (1733–1804), LL.D.; theologian, reformer, and scientist.

4. Priestley's *Disquisitions Relating to Matter and Spirit,* in which he denied the essential difference between soul and body, had appeared the preceding December.

5. Lord Strafford.

6. Thomas Tompion (1639–1713), 'the father of English watchmaking.'

6a. She was Lady Mary Coke's sister.

7. See *ante* 20 and 24 Jan. 1778.

Pray send me all the anecdotes you have concerning the latter end of Voltaire and tell me whether opium or old age killed him;[8] for I do not depend on newspapers when I am able to get Madame du Deffand's intelligence at such a second-hand as yours. I rest in hopes that we shall meet at Nuneham the beginning of September, for I fancy by that time his Lordship will be there to pluck his first violets.[9]

I am as always,

Yours most truly,

W. MASON

To MASON, Saturday 4 July 1778

Printed from Mitford i. 387–91.

July 4, 1778.

CHILDREN break their playthings to see the inside of them. Pope thought superior beings looked on Newton but as a monkey of uncommon parts;[1] would not he think that we have been like babies smashing an empire to see what it was made of? Truly I doubt whether there will be a whole piece left in three months, the conduct bears due proportion to the incapacity. You ought to be on the spot to believe it. When Keppel's messenger Mr Berkeley[2] arrived, neither the First Lord of the Admiralty nor the Secretary[3] was to be found![4] and now Mr Keppel is returned[5] we learn that the East and West India

8. A report that Voltaire died of an overdose of opium, inadvertently taken, appeared in the *Public Advertiser* 10 June 1778. See *post* 4 July 1778 and n. 21.

9. 'I will wait on you in September, and stay with you till my town winter commences, which is about the time of your Lordship's summer solstice, that is to say the middle of October' (Mason to Harcourt 11 July 1778, *Harcourt Papers* vii. 60).

———

1. 'Superior beings, when of late they saw
    A mortal man unfold all nature's law,
    Admired such wisdom in an earthly shape,
    And showed a Newton, as we show an ape'
        (*Essay on Man* ii. 31–4).

2. Hon. George Cranfield Berkeley (1753–1818), cousin of Admiral Keppel; naval officer; admiral, 1810.

3. Philip (later Sir Philip) Stephens (1725–1809); M. P. Sandwich 1768–1806; secretary of the Admiralty 1763–95; cr. (1795) Bt.

4. 'Lord Sandwich was in the country when Mr Berkley arrived [26 June], who immediately went off post to him with his dispatch' (*London Chronicle* 25–7 June, xliii. 614).

5. 'Extract of a letter from Portsmouth, June 28. "Yesterday arrived at St Helen's Admiral Keppel, with the *Pallas* and *Unicorn* [*Licorne*] French frigates, and all the fleet except two"' (*Public Advertiser* 30 June 1778).

fleets, worth four millions, are at stake, and the French frigates are abroad in pursuit of them.[6] Yesterday the merchants were with Lord North to press Keppel might sail again against a superior fleet![7] forty thousand men are on the coast, and transports assembling in every port,[8] and nothing but incapacity and inability in all this, and not a grain of treachery.

General Howe is arrived and was graciously received.[9] The agreeable news he brought is, that Clinton[10] for want of provisions has abandoned Philadelphia[11] and marched through the Jerseys to New York without molestation, on condition of not destroying Philadelphia.[12] The Congress has ratified the treaty with France,[13] and intend to treat the commissioners[14] *de haut en bas*[15] unless you choose

6. This is confirmed by an unsigned letter to Lord Sandwich (*Sandwich Papers* ii. 101).

7. Keppel wrote to Sandwich from St Helens 2 July 1778, 'I don't wonder at the alarms of the merchants, and wishing the fleet at sea; but when they do that they should hope also that it is in force for the services required of it. The King's councils have determined twenty-four ships' force sufficient. I will sail when I am joined by that addition of ships' (*Sandwich Papers* ii. 105).

8. HW says in *Last Journals* ii. 188 that the Court received this intelligence, which probably arrived in 'some dispatches . . . from Paris . . . forwarded by a messenger to his Majesty at Windsor' on 29 June (*Daily Adv.* 30 June). The story seems not to have been printed in the newspapers.

9. 'Yesterday morning [2 July] about six o'clock Gen. Howe arrived at Hampton Court . . . after which he waited on the King at Kew, where he had a private conference with his Majesty' (*London Chronicle* 2–4 July 1778, xliv. 10).

10. Sir Henry Clinton (ca 1738–95), K.B., 1777; Lt-Gen., 1777; Gen., 1793. He succeeded Howe as commander-in-chief of the British forces in America in May 1778.

11. The evacuation did not take place until the middle of June, and since Howe sailed from Philadelphia 24 May he could have reported it only as a plan. Rumours of the evacuation were current in England at this time: 'We learn that on the 24th of May a council of war was held at

Philadelphia, when it was determined to evacuate that place, which began on the 25th, by embarking the troops for New York, which was accomplished by the 5th of June' (*Lloyd's Evening Post* 1–3 July 1778, xliii. 15).

12. There was no such agreement. The British army during its march across New Jersey was harassed by the American forces, and on 28 June 1778 a battle was fought at Monmouth Court House (or Freehold). See *post* 25 Aug. 1778; *Annual Register,* 1778, xxi. 220*–226*; William S. Stryker, *The Battle of Monmouth,* ed. William S. Myers, Princeton, 1927; Leonard Lundin, *Cockpit of the Revolution: The War for Independence in New Jersey,* Princeton, 1940, pp. 396–400.

13. 4 May 1778 (*Treaties and Other International Acts of the United States of America,* ed. Hunter Miller, 1931–48, ii. 29–30).

14. Sent under the terms of Lord North's Conciliatory Bills. General Howe's place was taken by Clinton. See *ante* 8 April 1778, n. 11.

15. The commissioners showed themselves prepared to make great concessions. On 9 June they sent the Congress a polite letter, to which they received a reply 'that the acts of the British Parliament, the commission from their sovereign, and their letter supposed the people of those states to be subjects of the crown of Great Britain, and were founded on the idea of dependence, which was totally inadmissible' (*Annual Register,* 1778, xxi. 218*).

to believe the *Morning Post,* who says five provinces declare for peace.[16] I told you lately my curiosity to know what is to be left to us at a general peace. The wisest thing the ministers could do would be to ask that question incontinently. I am persuaded in the present apathy that the nation would be perfectly pleased, let the terms be what they would. A series of disasters may spoil this good humour, and there often wants but a man to fling a stone to spread a conflagration. The Treasury is not rich enough at present to indemnify the losers of four millions; the stockholders[17] are two hundred and forty thousand, and the fraction, forty thousand, would make an ugly mob; in short, tempests that used to be composed of irascible elements never had more provocation than they are likely to have; such is the glimpse of our present horizon. Now to your letter.

If your Mæcenas's[18] fame is overwhelmed in Lord Chatham's and Voltaire's, it is already revenged on the latter's. Madame du Deffand's letter of today says, he is already forgotten.[19] *La Belle Poule*[20] has obliterated him, but probably will have a contrary effect on Lord Chatham. All my old friend has told me of Voltaire's death is that the excessive fatigues he underwent by his journey to Paris, and by the bustle he made with reading his play to the actors and hearing them repeat it, and by going to it and by the crowds that flocked to him: in one word the agitation of so much applause at eighty-four threw him into a strangury, for which he took so much laudanum that his frame could not resist all, and he fell a martyr to his vanity;[21] nay, Garrick, who is above twenty years younger, and full as[22] vain, would have been choked with such doses of flattery; though he would like to die the death.

You, who are not apt to gape for incense, may be believed when

16. 'Some accounts say that five of the Colonies, others only three, have consented to receive the Conciliatory Bill' (*Morning Post* 3 July 1778). The report proved wrong.

17. In the East India Company. HW wrote in his memoirs 2 July 1778, 'The ministers were under the greatest apprehensions for the West and East India fleets, now expected home, and reckoned worth four millions.' On the 6th he wrote, 'The West India and Jamaica fleets arrived. It was very astonishing that France had not endeavoured to intercept them' (*Last Journals* ii. 189).

18. Lord Holdernesse.

19. 'Voltaire est oublié comme s'il n'avait

pas apparu' (Mme du Deffand to HW 28 June 1778, DU DEFFAND v. 53).

20. The frigate that escaped from Keppel (*ante* 26 June 1778, n. 5, and DU DEFFAND v. 54).

21. Mme du Deffand had written of Voltaire 31 May: 'Il est mort d'un excès d'opium qu'il a pris pour calmer les douleurs de sa strangurie, et j'ajouterais d'un excès de gloire, qui a trop secoué sa faible machine' (DU DEFFAND v. 46). HW's remarks to Mason incorporate information he had from other letters of Mme du Deffand between 10 Feb. and 31 May 1778.

22. Previously printed 'and as full as.'

you speak well of *Sappho*. I am sorry I must wait for the sight till Lord Harcourt proclaims summer. I enjoy the present, which I remember none like, but even this is clouded by the vexation of seeing this lovely island spoiled and sold to shame! I look at our beautiful improvements, and sigh to think that they have seen their best days. Did you feel none of these melancholy reflections at Wentworth Castle? I wrote the Earl a letter[23] two days ago that will not please him, but can one always contain one's chagrin when one's country is ruined by infatuation? No, we never can revive! We killed the hen that laid the golden eggs! The term *Great Britain* will be a jest. My English pride is wounded, yet there is one comfortable thought remains— when liberty was abandoned by her sons here, she animated her genuine children, and inspired them to chastise the traitor Scots that attacked her. *They* have made a blessed harvest of their machinations. If there is a dram of sense under a crown, a Scot hereafter will be reckoned pestilential. Methinks the word Prerogative should never sound very delightful in this island; attempt to extend it and its fairest branches wither and drop off. What has an army of fifty thousand men[25] fighting for sovereignty achieved in America? retreated from Boston, retreated from Philadelphia, laid down their arms at Saratoga, and lost thirteen provinces! nor is the measure yet full! such are the consequences of our adopting new legislators, new historians, new doctors! Locke and Sidney, for Humes, Johnsons and Dalrymples! When the account is made up and a future historiographer royal casts up debtor and creditor, I hope he will please to state the balance between the last war *for America*[26] and the present *against it*. The advantages of that we know, Quebec, the Havannah, Martinico, Guadeloupe, the East Indies, the French and Spanish fleets destroyed, etc., etc.; all the bills *per contra* are not yet come in! Our writers have been disputing for these hundred and sixty-six years[27] on Whig and Tory principles. Their successors, who I suppose will continue the controversy, will please to allow at least that if the ministers of both parties were equally complaisant when in

23. Missing.
25. In Feb. 1778 the Duke of Richmond had said that 'from the returns it appears the greatest number of land forces serving in North America in 1777 consisted of 48,616 men, including officers' (Cobbett, *Parl. Hist.* xix. 744).
26. The Seven Years' War, 1756–63.

27. HW probably means since James's accession and the union of the crowns in 1603, but his calculation is nine years off. Or he may be thinking of the political controversy that raged in 1612 over the marriage-contract of the Elector Palatine and James's daughter Elizabeth.

power, the splendour of the Crown (I say nothing of the happiness of the people which is never taken into the account) has constantly been augmented by Whig administrations, and has faded (and then and now a little more) when Tories have governed! The reason is as plain: Whig principles are founded on sense; a Whig may be a fool, a Tory must be so: the consequence is plain; a Whig when a minister may abandon his principles, but he will retain his sense and will therefore not risk the felicity of his posterity by sacrificing everything to selfish views. A Tory attaining power hurries to establish despotism:[28] the honour, the trade, the wealth, the peace of the nation, all are little to him in comparison of the despotic will of his master, but are not you glad I write on small paper!

To Mason, Thursday 16 July 1778

Printed from Mitford i. 391–3.

Strawberry Hill, July 16, 1778.

THOUGH it is a most anxious moment I do not write to tell you or talk of politics; most men in these regions expect news of a battle at sea: I do not. As we have nothing left to save but ourselves, *I wish theirselves*[1] would leave themselves and us that little.

Jean-Jacques is certainly dead[2] as well as Voltaire; poor Charon! Fanny, blooming fair,[3] died here[4] yesterday of a stroke of palsy. She had lost her memory for some years, and remembered nothing but her beauty and not her Methodism. Being confined with only servants,

28. 'The Tories . . . are so absurd as to regret the national freedom, the sole source of the wealth on which they fatten. . . . Had the Tories succeeded at the Revolution, or accession, this fair country would have been another Spain, the desolate abode of nobles and priests' (*Walpoliana* i. 96–7).

1. The King and his Scottish advisers and favourites.

2. Rousseau died 2 July at Ermenonville. His death was reported to HW by Mme du Deffand in her letter of 5 July.

3. Lady Frances Shirley (ca 1706–78), dau. of 1st E. Ferrers, was the subject of the

popular song, 'When Fanny blooming fair,' alleged to be by Chesterfield, but more probably by Thomas Philips (Robert Dodsley, *A Collection of Poems*, 2d edn, 1748, i. 337–8; R. S. Cobbett, *Memorials of Twickenham*, 1872, p. 69; Roger Coxon, *Chesterfield and His Critics*, 1925, p. 168). HW included her in his 'Parish Register of Twickenham,' written about 1758:
'Where Fanny, ever-blooming fair,
Ejaculates the graceful prayer,
And, 'scaped from sense, with nonsense smit,
For Whitfield's cant leaves Stanhope's wit'
                                        (*Works* iv. 383).

4. Lady Frances lived in Heath Lane Lodge, Twickenham (Cobbett, loc. cit.).

she was continually lamenting, 'I to be abandoned that all the world used to adore!' She was seventy-two.

I received a letter[5] this morning from the engraver[6] of Johnson's *Poets* to inquire if I knew of any portrait of Dyer or Mallet.[7] If the latter is one of Johnson's *poets*,[8] I do not wonder Gray was not.[9]

The sun seems to be the only prince that is generous and sticks by us in our distress. People of all ages call it an old-fashioned summer, such as we used to have ten or twenty years ago, when you are to suppose they were young. I that do not haggle about my three scores, do not remember any such summer these fifty years. It is Italy in a green gown.

Mr Nicholl[10] and I went last week to see the new apartment at Osterley Park.[11] The first chamber, a drawing-room, not a large one,[12] is the most superb and beautiful that can be conceived, and hung with Gobelin tapestry,[13] and enriched by Adam in his best taste, except that he has stuck diminutive heads in bronze,[14] no bigger than a half-crown, into the chimney-piece's hair. The next is a light plain

5. Missing.
6. Perhaps John Hall (see following note), but there were several other engravers for the edition of the *Works of the English Poets* (1779–81) for which Johnson engaged to do the *Lives*. It was advertised as 'ornamented with heads of the respective authors, engraved by Bartolozzi, Sherwin, Hall, Collyer, Cook, and Walker' (*Public Advertiser* 7 May 1777). See Boswell, *Johnson* iii. 111.
7. The portrait of Dyer used in the *Works* was engraved by John Hall (1739–97), appointed in 1785 historical engraver to George III. No portrait of Mallet was included.
8. Johnson had a moderate opinion of Mallet's worth: 'As a writer he cannot be placed in any high class. There is no species of composition in which he was eminent' ('Life of Mallet'). For HW's low opinion of Mallet see his letters to Mann 9 Nov. 1744 and 17 May 1749, and *ante* 21 July 1772. The poets included in the edition were selected by the booksellers, not by Johnson.
9. Gray was included in the *Lives*, but Johnson's views on Gray were doubtless no secret even before the *Life* appeared in 1781. In 1775 he said of Gray, 'Sir, he was

dull in company, dull in his closet, dull everywhere. He was dull in a new way, and that made many people think him great. He was a mechanical poet' (Boswell, *Johnson* ii. 327).
10. Norton Nicholls.
11. The seat of Robert Child, the banker, in Heston, Middlesex. Originally built ca 1577 for Sir Thomas Gresham, it was remodelled and decorated 1760–80 by Robert Adam for Child. See HW to Lady Ossory 21 June 1773; Arthur T. Bolton, *The Architecture of Robert and James Adam*, 1922, i. 279–302; Peter Ward-Jackson, *Guide to Osterley Park*, 1953.
12. After his earlier visit HW said it was a room 'worthy of Eve before the Fall' (to Lady Ossory 21 June 1773).
13. Executed in the Gobelin shop of Jacques Neilson (1714–88) after designs by François Boucher (1703–70). See Bolton, op. cit. i. 291–5 (with photographs); J. J. Marquet de Vasselot and Roger-Armand Weigert, *Bibliographie de la tapisserie des tapis et de la broderie en France*, 1935, p. 49.
14. The heads 'are inlaid in coloured composition, not bronze, and they are repeated, in a different material, in the frieze above the doorcases' (Ward-Jackson, op. cit. 14).

green velvet bedchamber.[15] The bed is of green satin richly embroidered with colours, and with eight columns; too theatric, and too like a modern head-dress, for round the outside of the dome are festoons of artificial flowers.[16] What would Vitruvius[17] think of a dome decorated by a milliner? The last chamber, after these two proud rooms, chills you: it is called the Etruscan,[18] and is painted all over like Wedgwood's ware, with black and yellow small grotesques. Even the chairs are of painted wood. It would be a pretty waiting-room in a garden. I never saw such a profound tumble into the bathos.[19] It is going out of a palace into a potter's field. Tapestry carpets, glass, velvet, satin, are all attributes of winter. There could be no excuse for such a cold termination, but its containing a cold bath next to the bedchamber:—and it is called taste to join these incongruities! I hope I have put you into a passion.

To Mason, Saturday 18 July 1778

Printed from Mitford i. 393–6.

Strawberry Hill, July 18, 1778.

AS I was going out this evening I was stopped in Twickenham, and told that France has declared war.[1] I knew the Brest squadron was at sea,[2] and that Admiral Keppel, by letters received from him at the Admiralty on Thursday, is off the Land's End in hourly expecta-

15. The walls were of green velvet (Bolton, op. cit. i. 296).

16. Ibid. i. 295–7.

17. Marcus Vitruvius Pollio (fl. 1st century B.C.), Roman writer on architecture.

18. On Adam's interest in Etruscan design see Bolton, op. cit. i. 296–300. The illustrations on pp. 298–9 show that the room remains as HW describes it.

19. After quoting this passage Mr Ward-Jackson comments: 'Whether we agree or disagree with this stricture, the Etruscan Room is an interesting experiment and remains the only surviving example of a type of decoration which Adam employed in several houses' (Guide to Osterley, p. 17).

———

1. 'On Saturday morning between three

and four o'clock, a messenger arrived express at the Admiralty, and went to the two secretaries of state, with dispatches from France, said to be an account of the French court having made a declaration of war in form against Great Britain on Tuesday last' (Public Advertiser 20 July 1778), an erroneous report. Although there was no exchange of explicit declarations, and communications were not broken off, both England and France considered themselves at war. As HW wrote Mann: 'We are in the oddest situation that can be; at war in fact, but managed like a controversy in divinity' (4 Aug. 1778).

2. The Brest fleet, commanded by Comte d'Orvilliers, had sailed 8 July (Sandwich Papers ii. 10).

tion of being joined by three or four men-of-war,[3] which will make his fleet thirty ships of the line,[4] with which he was determined to seek the enemy, who have thirty-one,[5] two of fifty guns, and eight frigates. Thus the battle may be fought as soon as war is proclaimed; and thus our ministers may have a full prospect of all their consummately wise measures may produce! What can be expected from two wars, when one has been so ignominious?—With an army of fifty thousand men[6] against a rabble, and without being beaten, they have lost a whole continent, and near half that army,[7] and retreated from place to place. Not one general has gained any reputation; our only fleet on this side of the world is to decide whether the two islands[8] are not to be fought for on land. Thus have we, the people, been gamed for; and some few of us against our wills! It is very hard, especially on us that remember other days! I know not what Lord Mansfield's reflections are when he recollects his sagacious journey to Paris[9] to convince the French cabinet that it was against their interest to protect the Americans, and his famous passage of the Rubicon.[10] I should be sorry to feel what he ought to feel even on the score of folly,—indeed *defendit numerus;*[11] and all that may be left to us few, may be to meet him, *torva tuentes*[12] like the ghost of Dido.

England will one day recollect it had a minister, to whom it owed |

3. On board his flagship, the *Victory*, 16 July 1778, being then off the Eddystone light, 14 miles SW. of Plymouth, Keppel wrote to the Admiralty: 'The prevailing calms, I imagine, detain the *Centaur* and *Vigilant*. . . . This junction and the *Shrewsbury*'s will make the fleet twenty-nine ships' (ibid. ii. 119). On the following day he reported that the *Shrewsbury* had come up with him and that the other two ships were in sight (ibid. ii. 123).

4. The reinforcements that arrived 17 July made Keppel's fleet twenty-nine ships of the line, but another ship joined him 21 July (ibid. ii. 372).

5. D'Orvilliers sailed with 32 ships, but two parted from the fleet, and when the fleets came together in a skirmish on 27 July (see *post* 10 Aug. 1778) there were 30 ships on each side (*Sandwich Papers* ii. 10).

6. See *ante* 4 July 1778, n. 25.

7. The Duke of Richmond in a speech in the House of Lords 7 April 1778 reported 'that the loss of men by death, deser-

tion or otherwise in North America . . . had in the land forces amounted to 19,381, besides 5336 prisoners; and that there were at that time 4639 sick' (Cobbett, *Parl. Hist.* xix. 1016).

8. England and Ireland.

9. See *ante* Oct. 1774.

10. In the debate after the second reading in the House of Lords, 28 March 1774, of the bill 'to discontinue . . . the landing . . . or shipping of goods, wares, and merchandise, at the town and within the harbour of Boston' (*Journals of the House of Lords* xxxiv. 99). Lord Mansfield, supporting the bill, 'discovered himself the true instigator of violence, which he first endeavoured to colour with all the obscure chicanery of law, and at last avowed, declaring that the bill was as decisive *as passing the Rubicon*' (*Last Journals* i. 322).

11. 'There is safety in numbers' (Juvenal, *Satires* I. ii. 46).

12. 'Staring wildly' (*Æneid* vi. 467, where the form used is 'tuentem').

twenty years of prosperity and happiness, and who left it a motto that would have preserved such halcyon days. *Quieta non movere*[13] was as wise a saying as any my Lord Bolinbroke[14] bequeathed to my Lord Bute.[15] I do not know whether it is true, what has been said, that my father on being advised to tax America, replied, 'It must be a bolder minister than I am.'[16] But that motto of his spoke his opinion.

Well; war proclaimed! and I am near sixty-one; shall I live to see peace again? and what a peace! I endeavour to compose my mind, and call in every collateral aid.—I condemn my countrymen, but cannot, would not divest myself of my love to my country. I enjoy the disappointment of the Scots, who had prepared the yoke for the Americans, and for our necks too. I cannot blame the French whom we have tempted to ruin us: yet, to be ruined by France!—There the Englishman in me feels again. My chief comfort is in talking to you, though you do not answer me. I write to vent my thoughts, as it is easier than brooding over them, but allow that it is difficult to be very tranquil when the navy of England is at stake. That thought annihilates resentment—I wish for nothing but victory, and then peace, yet what lives must victory cost! nor will one victory purchase it. The nation is so frantic, that success would intoxicate us more; yet calamity, that alone could sober us, is too near our doors. Resignation to the will of heaven is the language of reason as well as of religion, when one knows not what would be best for us. It is a dilemma to which the honest are reduced; our gamesters[17] are in a worse situation. The best they can hope for, is to sit down with the *débris* of an empire. What a line they have drawn between them

13. 'The great principle on which Walpole conducted himself, seems to have been his favourite motto, *quieta non movere*, not to disturb things at rest' (William Coxe, *Memoirs of the Life and Administration of Sir Robert Walpole, Earl of Orford*, 1798, i. 753). See also *Walpoliana* i. 88.

14. Henry St John (1678–1751), cr. (1712) Vct Bolingbroke; author of essays and tracts, including 'The Idea of a Patriot King.'

15. For comment on Bute's alleged influence on the education of George III when heir-apparent see Romney Sedgwick's Introduction to the *Letters from George III to Lord Bute 1756–1766*, 1939, and L. B.

Namier, *The Structure of Politics at the Accession of George the Third*, 1929.

16. 'Sir Robert Walpole is said to have had much clearer and juster notions concerning the means of making the British colonies pay the mother country for their defence, and even contribute to her opulence. A scheme for taxing them having been mentioned to him during that war with Spain which broke out in the year 1739, he smiled and said, "I will leave that for some of my successors, who may have more courage than I have, and be less a friend to commerce than I am"' (*Annual Register*, 1765, viii. 25).

17. The administration.

and Lord Chatham! I believe it was modesty made them not attend his funeral.[18] Will the House of Brunswick listen again to the flatterers of prerogative? My time of life, that ought to give me philosophy, dispirits me. I cannot expect to live to see England revive. I shall leave it at best an insignificant island. Its genius is vanished like its glories, one sees nor hero nor statesman arise to flatter hope. Dr Franklin, thanks to Mr Wedderburne, is at Paris;[19] every way I turn my thoughts, the returns are irksome. What is the history of a fallen empire? A transient satire on the vices and follies that hurried it to dissolution. The protest of a few that foretold it, is not registered. The names of Jefferies[20] and two or three principals satisfy the sage moralist who hurries to more agreeable times. I will go to bed and sleep if I can. Pray write to me; tell me how you reconcile your mind to our situation. I cannot. Two years ago I meditated leaving England if it was enslaved. I have no such thought now. I will steal into its bosom when my hour comes, and love it to the last.

From Mason, Sunday 19 July 1778

Printed from MS now WSL.
Address: The Honourable Horace Walpole, Arlington Street, London.
Postmark: ROTHERHAM 23 JY.

Aston, July 19th, 1778.

IN one of your unanswered letters[1] (I am ashamed to look at its date and say which, for I have three before me) you talk of my having finished my third book, and of my having been ill, neither of which are true, though I thank heaven only for the falsehood of the last. The truth is I showed Mr Niccols (when he was at York) an exordium written I believe above five years ago, which I believe you have seen, and I turned a slight cold into a sickness to avoid doing the hospitable honours of my post in too great a degree, for *entre*

18. Their refusal is reported *ante* 15 May 1778.

19. That is, Wedderburn's attack on Franklin at a meeting of the Privy Council in Jan. 1774 forced the Americans to seek French aid; see *ante* 23 March 1774 and n. 13.

20. George Jeffreys (ca 1648–89), cr.

(1685) Bn Jeffreys; chief justice of the King's Bench 1683–5; lord chancellor 1685–8; archetype of the 'hanging judge.'

1. That of 26 June 1778. Mason wrote HW on 1 July from Wentworth Castle, but had not received HW's letter, presumably directed to Aston.

nous that said Mr N. (but I beg it may go no further for the honour of the cloth) drinks like any fish,—though perhaps you have not discovered it, and it is happy for him that Mr Gray cannot.[2]—Now both this poetical communication and this plea of sickness were mere subterfuges to avoid something worse, i.e., hearing the eternalities of his foreign tour[3] and saving myself from a morning headache. Yet either your having mentioned my finishing the book, or this wonderful fine weather, or a new bower (already half covered with woodbine) which I made only two months ago, and in which I now write this letter—one, or all of these causes collectively have actually made me resume the work, and I do verily believe that I shall get the whole of it into a readable condition by the time we meet at Nuneham, which I hope will be in September.[4]

Pray ask Madame du Deffand whether Rousseau really died of eating strawberries,[5] and in the mean time do not commit any fruit-debauches of the same kind. You are apt to sin in this way—or if you do, take St Paul's advice and 'use a little wine for your stomach's sake and your often *gout* infirmities.'[6] I do not wish you to do the honours to Nicchols in claret that I did in port, yet as far as half a pint may go, or a third of a bottle, especially after your raspberries, I hold to be salutary.

Nothing can be so provoking as this fine weather. It comes on purpose to convince one that one's country is the finest climate in the world, just when one should be learning to forget that it is one's country. Last year I would have suffered it to be a province of France with ten times the complacency. I console myself at present with thinking it is too good for those that govern it, and therefore the better it is, the greater will be their loss. But what do I gain by that? Ay, there's the rub! a rub that takes the skin off one's very shin-bone.

2. Gray, who was notoriously abstemious, had a high regard for Norton Nicholls, whom he had first met in 1762 when Nicholls was an undergraduate at Cambridge, and whose studies he had thereafter directed. See *Gray's Corr.* ii. 851–2. Mason's remark about Nicholls should be viewed in the light of their mutual antagonism, probably originating in jealousy of Gray's friendship, that is apparent in Nicholls's reminiscences of Gray (ibid. iii. 1293–5).

3. See *ante* 7 May 1773.

4. Mason was at Nuneham by 17 Sept., for HW addressed a letter to him there. On 27 Sept., 'the first evening' of his return home, HW wrote to Lord Harcourt thanking him for his hospitality during his four-day visit.

5. This pleasantry is so obscure HW missed it (*post* 24 July 1778). Nothing about strawberries appears among the accounts of Rousseau's death.

6. 'Drink no longer water, but use a little wine for thy stomach's sake and thine often infirmities' (1 Timothy 5.23).

Pray, do you think it possible to procure me one of the prints of Lady Di's drawing of the Duchess of Devonshire?[7] I should think you might have interest enough with the designer to obtain it. I hear the plate is in the possession of the Duchess of Marlborough.[8] If you succeed, pray bring it with you to Nuneham.

We are in the *ton* here I can assure you. An old maid in a neighbouring village, from which she hardly ever stirred, is broke for £6000. She had no visible way of spending it but in turning ivory.[9]

I expect Giardini here some time next month ⟨in⟩ order that he may comprehend the full meaning of the words he is to set.[10] I am clear, if he will but be docile, which he promises to be, that he will do it more justice than any of our English composers.

I have taken again to my old-sized large paper and the consequence is that I cannot fill it. 'No matter' say you, 'I have had full enough and will suffer you to conclude yourself,

My most faithful servant,

W. MASON'

To MASON, Friday 24 July 1778

Printed from Mitford ii. 1–5.

Strawberry Hill, July 24, 1778.

YOURS of the 19th I did not receive till yesterday.[1] I do not write again so soon to answer it, but on a subject very foreign to all my last, and which I will tell you presently, when I have replied to a few of your articles.

I did not discover, and certainly did not suspect, a Bacchanalian disposition in a certain person,[2] for we dined together but once. We

7. See *ante* 18 April 1778 and *post* 24 July 1778.

8. Lady Caroline Russell (1743–1811), m. (1762) George Spencer, 4th D. of Marlborough, brother of Lady Diana Beauclerk.

9. 'The turner is a very ingenious business, and brought to great perfection in this kingdom. . . . Turners differ among themselves according to the materials they use; some turn wood, others ivory, tortoise-shell, etc.' (R. Campbell, *The London Tradesman*, 1747, p. 243). The old maid apparently turned ivory as a hobby.

10. Mason's *Sappho:* see *ante* 1 July 1778 and *post* 14 Aug. 1778.

---

1. When HW was in London (COLE ii. 103).

2. Norton Nicholls.

think alike on that subject, I assure you, but I will reserve it for our meeting.

Madame du Deffand said nothing on the strawberries and cream, nor if I asked her would she probably remember to answer. She never interested herself about Rousseau, nor admired him. Her understanding is too just not to be disgusted with his paradoxes and affectations, and his eloquence could not captivate her, for she hates eloquence. She liked no style but Voltaire's, and has an aversion to all modern philosophers. She has scarce mentioned Rousseau, living or dead;[3] and D'Alembert was egregiously mistaken in thinking she wrote my letter to him;[4] Rousseau would have been still more offended had he known how very little she ever thought on him. She was born and had lived in the age of true taste, and allowed nobody but Voltaire to belong to it. She holds that all the rest have corrupted their taste and language. La Fontaine is her idol; that is, simplicity is.[5]

But I shall not forget to answer you on the article of strawberries and cream. How very kind to caution me against them; and how kindly I take it! In truth I am very temperate now on that head, as well as on all others. I eat very little cream, remembering that my stomach is not so young as it was; but for wine, I am persuaded fruit never hurts me, unless wine is poured on it. Yet the other day I did drink two

3. On 5 July Mme du Deffand wrote HW: 'La feuille du jour dit la mort de Jean-Jacques. Je ne sais si cela est vrai' (DU DEFFAND v. 57). The death of Rousseau is not mentioned again in her letters.

4. HW's letter from the King of Prussia to Rousseau. See COLE i. 110–1 and 'Short Notes,' GRAY i . 41. 'As soon as the letter made a noise, I was so afraid of affecting to write French better than I could, that I mentioned everywhere, and particularly to M. Diderot at Baron Holbach's, that the letter had been corrected, though I did not tell by whom, for fear of involving others in a dispute; but I never, as M. d'Alembert has falsely asserted, avowed that I had had any assistance in the composition, which would have been an untruth' ('A Narrative of What Passed Relative to the Quarrel of Mr David Hume and Jean-Jacques Rousseau, as far as Mr Horace Walpole Was Concerned in It,' Works iv. 251). Helvétius had 'pointed out one or two faults in the French' and

Hénault 'changed the construction of the last phrase' (ibid. iv. 250). D'Alembert had written to Hume 4 Aug. 1766: 'On dit ici comme une chose très certaine que c'est Madame du Deffand qui lui a inspiré cette méchanceté . . . ; on ajoute que c'est elle qui a revu et corrigé la lettre pour le style' (The Letters of David Hume, ed. J. Y. T. Greig, Oxford, 1932, ii. 432). See Hume to HW 20 Nov. 1766. On the importance of the King of Prussia letter in the Hume-Rousseau quarrel see Frederick A. Pottle, 'The Part Played by Horace Walpole and James Boswell in the Quarrel between Rousseau and Hume,' Philological Quarterly, 1925, iv. 351–63; Margaret Hill Peoples, 'La Querelle Rousseau-Hume,' Annales de la Société Jean-Jacques Rousseau, 1927–8, xviii; Henri Guillemin, Les Philosophes contre Jean-Jacques: 'cette affaire infernale,' l'affaire J.-J. Rousseau–David Hume, 1766, 1942.

5. See DU DEFFAND i. 119, iv. 116.

glasses. The excessive heat of the nights had exhausted me so much, that I had recourse to that cordial, and it quite restored me; it would not unless a novelty. I beg your pardon for talking on myself, but gratitude opened my heart. I feel your goodness with great satisfaction, for it could please me in no form more than yours; and I wished to prove to you that one you regard, is not childish.

I doubt much whether I can get you a print of the Duchess of Devonshire: certainly not before winter, for Lady Di is at Brighthelmstone; but I will try then; she had not many proofs for herself, and I know had not one left. Everybody, from taste or fashion, tore them away. The Duke,[6] her brother, paid for the plate, and would suffer, I think, but two hundred impressions to be taken. I promised the Duke of Gloucester to beg one for him, which perhaps will not be refused. If I can obtain two, the second is yours. I have set my own in a frame I trust you will like, as it harmonizes with it amazingly, though rich.[7]

I have been two days in town.[8] What I could collect was, that the Congress will not deign to send any answer to the commissioners;[9] that Lord Howe refused to act as one of them,[10] and that the bear and the monkey[11] have quarrelled.[12] That the Americans have sent an

6. George Spencer (1739–1817), 4th D. of Marlborough.

7. 'A print by Bartolozzi of Georgiana, Duchess of Devonshire, from the drawing of Lady Diana Beauclerc; in a frame with Wedgwood's cameos, and two flies engraved and painted by Hill' ('Des. of SH,' Works ii. 425). It was sold SH xi. 108 to Miss Burdett Coutts.

8. 22 and 23 July 1778 (HW to Bedford 22 July and to Cole 24 July 1778).

9. 'Mr Eden in a letter to his brother Sir Robert, in London, dated the 18th of June, says "they had made their overtures to the Congress, but had received no answer of any kind when the packet sailed"' (Lloyd's Evening Post 20–22 July 1778, xliii. 79). A detailed account of the reception of the commissioners is given in Annual Register, 1778, xxi. 217*–20*. See Last Journals ii. 190–1.

10. 'Monday, 8th [June]. Wrote a letter for Lord H[owe] to the new commissioners, communicating his intention to decline from serving in the new commission, and also to the Secretary of State [Germain] for the same purpose' (The American Journal of Ambrose Serle, Secretary to Lord Howe,

1776–1778, ed. E. H. Tatum, Jr, San Marino, California, 1940, pp. 307–8). Howe was vexed because Lord Carlisle had been named first commissioner (ibid. 308; Carl Van Doren, Secret History of the American Revolution, New York, 1941, pp. 66 and 93).

11. Governor Johnstone, who was notoriously gruff, and Lord Carlisle, whose foppishness was the subject of much contemporary satire (e.g., Nos 5473-5 in BM, Satiric Prints v. 286–9).

12. This proved to be only rumour. On 18 June William Eden wrote of the pleasant relations that existed among the members of the commission, though he then acknowledged that Johnstone's 'feelings at present are roused beyond his power to govern them; and though he will wish to go on with us as pleasantly as he has done thus far, I cannot answer for his doing so' (quoted by Van Doren, op. cit. 96). A later attempt by Johnstone to negotiate secretly with the Americans embarrassed the commission, but this could have no bearing on the rumour current in July.

expedition to Florida,[13] and that Washington's army is reduced to seven thousand and is very sickly;[14] one should think the two last circumstances were invented to balance the others, but surely our ministers ought at last to exaggerate on the other side, that things may seem to turn out better than was expected rather than worse, as hitherto they have contrived to make them appear.

France has *not* declared war;[15] and if the Brest fleet did sail it was not a stone's throw.[16] I imagine they wait for news of D'Estains,[17] before they take the last step, or they will draw Keppel aside, and then set forth an embarkation. I sometimes hope peace is not impossible. It cannot be half so bad as a new war in our present situation. It would at least give us time to prepare for war. We are come to the necessity of fortifying the island, or it may be lost in a single battle. When we have no longer the superiority at sea, it would be madness—it would—it is madness to have no resource, no spot where to make a stand—but what signify my politics? who will listen to them?

It is not unlucky that I have got something to divert my mind: for I can think on other subjects when I have them. I am at last forced to enter into the history of the supposed Rowley's poems. I must write on it, nay, what is more, print, not directly, controversially, but in my own defence. Some jackanapes at Bristol, I don't know who, has published Chatterton's works;[18] and I suppose to provoke me to tell the story, accuses me of treating that marvellous creature with con-

13. A land force of between two and three thousand men and a small naval force went to Florida in June 1778, but after a skirmish retired to Georgia. See Wilbur H. Siebert, *Loyalists in East Florida*, Deland, 1929, i. 56–9; Charles L. Mowat, *East Florida as a British Province 1763–1784*, Berkeley and Los Angeles, 1943, p. 122.

14. Despite the losses suffered at Valley Forge, at the time of the British evacuation of Philadelphia Washington's effective force was 'near 14,000 Continental troops, fit for service' (report of the council of war, 17 June 1778, in *Writings of George Washington*, Washington, 1931–44, xii. 77).

15. See *ante* 18 July 1778, n. 1.

16. On the day before this letter the French and English fleets had come in sight of one another some seventy-five miles west of Ushant, and on 27 July, after four days of manœuvring, fought a sharp but

indecisive action (*Sandwich Papers* ii. 10). See *post* 10 Aug. 1778.

17. Jean-Baptiste-Charles, Comte d'Estaing (1729–94), Vice-Adm., 1777; commandant of the Toulon fleet, which reached the Delaware on 8 July. See John J. Meng, *D'Estaing's American Expedition 1778–1779*, New York, 1936; *Sandwich Papers* ii. 285–6. 'A correspondent assures us, on the faith of a friend at Paris, that the French cabinet have judged it prudent to wait the arrival of intelligence from Count d'Estaing, before they determine how to act with Great Britain, for the late national insult off Brest' (*Public Advertiser* 16 July 1778).

18. *Miscellanies in Prose and Verse by Thomas Chatterton*, 1778. The editor, who signed his Preface 'J.B.,' was John Broughton (d. 1801), a Bristol attorney. See 'Short Notes,' 1778, Gray i. 50; Chatterton 177 n. 1.

tempt; which having supposed, contrary to truth, he invites his readers to feel indignation at me.[19] It has more than once before been insinuated that his disappointment from me contributed to his horrid fate.[20] You know how gently I treated him.[21] He was a consummate villain,[22] and had gone enormous lengths before he destroyed himself.[23] It would be cruel indeed if one was to be deemed the assassin of every rogue that miscarries in attempting to cheat one;[24] in short the attack is now too direct not to be repelled. Two months ago I did draw up an account of my share in that affair.[25] That narrative and an answer to this insult which I wrote last night[26] I will publish,[27] signed with my name, but not advertised by it. It will reach all those that take part in the controversy, and I do not desire it should go farther. These

19. 'One of his [Chatterton's] first efforts, to emerge from a situation so irksome to him, was an application to a gentleman well known in the republic of letters; which, unfortunately for the public, and himself, met with a very cold reception; and which the disappointed author always spoke of with a high degree of acrimony, whenever it was mentioned to him. . . . Perhaps he [the reader] may feel some indignation against the person to whom his first application was made, and by whom he was treated with neglect and contempt' (*Miscellanies . . . by Thomas Chatterton*, pp. xviii–xxi). HW's copy is now WSL; HW has written 'Mr H. Walpole' in the margin opposite 'a gentleman' etc. See CHATTERTON 345 and illustration.

20. Notably in the account of Chatterton's career supplied by George Catcott and printed by John Langhorne in his review of Tyrwhitt's edition of the Rowley poems (1777) in the *Monthly Review*, 1777, lvi. 323: 'In 1770 Chatterton went to London, and carried all this treasure with him, in hopes, as we may very reasonably suppose, of disposing of it to his advantage; he accordingly applied, as I have been informed, to that learned antiquary, Mr Horace Walpole, but met with little or no encouragement from him; soon after *which*, in a fit of despair, as it is supposed, he put an end to his unhappy life.' See E. H. W. Meyerstein, *A Life of Thomas Chatterton*, 1930, pp. 274–7.

21. HW consulted Mason and Gray early in the Chatterton affair. Both pronounced

the Rowley specimens forgeries and advised him to return them without any further notice (Tyson to Cole 4 Feb. 1779, cited by Meyerstein, op. cit. 262; *post* 28 Aug. 1778). HW then 'wrote him a letter with as much kindness and tenderness as if I had been his guardian' (HW to Bewley 23 May 1778, CHATTERTON 127).

22. 'He possessed all the vices and irregularities of youth, and his profligacy was, at least, as conspicuous as his abilities' (*Miscellanies . . . by Thomas Chatterton*, p. xviii). See Meyerstein, op. cit. 77 and COLE ii. 205.

23. 24 Aug. 1770.

24. As Chatterton had tried to cheat HW with his list of 15th-century painters at Bristol and the 15th-century verses of his own composition.

25. HW to Bewley 23 May 1778.

26. *A Letter to the Editor of the Miscellanies of Thomas Chatterton.* '1778. At the end of July wrote my answer to the editor of Chatterton's works' ('Short Notes,' GRAY i. 50).

27. Two hundred copies of the pamphlet were printed at the SH Press in Jan. 1779 ('Short Notes,' GRAY i. 51; *Journal of the Printing-Office* 19; Hazen, *SH Bibliography* 116–8), to be distributed to friends and others interested in the Chatterton affair. HW's annotated copy is now WSL; see CHATTERTON 348–50. The *Letter* was subsequently reprinted, with HW's permission, serially in the GM for 1782, and it is included in HW's *Works* (iv. 206–20).

things I will have transcribed, and ask your leave to send you before they go to the press.[28] I am in no hurry to publish, nor is the moment a decent one, yet I embrace it, as I shall be the less talked over. I hate controversy, yet to be silent now, would be interpreted guilt; and it is impossible to be more innocent than I was in that affair. Being innocent, I take care not to be angry. Mr Tyrwhitt, one of the enthusiasts to Rowley, has recanted and published against the authenticity of the poems.[29] The new publisher of Chatterton's undisputed works, seems to question the rest too,[30] so his attack on me must be mere impertinent curiosity; one satisfaction will arise from all this: the almost incredible genius of Chatterton will be ascertained. He had generally genuine[31] powers of poetry; often wit, and sometimes natural humour. I have seen reams of his writing, beside what is printed.[32] He had a strong vein of satire too, and very irascible resentment;[33] yet the poor soul perished before he was nineteen![34] He had read, and written, as if he was fourscore, yet it cannot be discovered when or where. He had no more principles than if he had been one of all our late administrations. He was an instance that a complete genius and a complete rogue can be formed before a man is of age. The world has generally the honour of their education, but it is not necessary; you see by Chatterton, that an individual could be as perfect as a senate! Adieu!

28. There is nothing in the correspondence to indicate that HW sent them to Mason.

29. In an *Appendix*, published separately before 10 June 1778, to his *Poems Supposed to Have Been Written at Bristol by Thomas Rowley* (HW to Cole 10 June 1778, COLE ii. 90; Meyerstein, op. cit. 463). HW's copy of the *Appendix* is now WSL; see CHATTERTON 357. See also *ante* 17 Feb. 1777 and n. 4, and L. F. Powell, 'Thomas Tyrwhitt and the Rowley Poems,' *Review of English Studies*, 1931, vii. 314–26.

30. 'With respect to Rowley's poems, the prevailing opinion seems to be, that they were actually written by Chatterton: for though the antique manner in which they were clothed, had served greatly to disguise them, yet it could not but be observed that the smoothness of the versification, and the frequent traces of imitation of later writers, were utterly inconsistent with the idea of their being the productions of the fifteenth century' (*Miscellanies . . . by Thomas Chatterton*, pp. x–xi).

31. Dr Chapman suspects that 'generally' is a mistake of HW's or Mitford's.

32. Presumably he was shown them by Percy and Lort. 'Dr P. and Mr L. have collected everything relating to him that can be traced, and all tends to concentre the forgery of Rowley's poems in his single person' (HW to Bewley 23 May 1778, CHATTERTON 131).

33. He employed it against HW in his 'Memoirs of a Sad Dog,' which HW had just read in the *Miscellanies*, pp. 198–202. At p. 198 HW appears as 'the redoubted Baron Otranto, who has spent his whole life in conjectures.' HW has noted in his copy, 'Mr H.W. author of *The Castle of Otranto*.' See also CHATTERTON 345.

34. Chatterton died almost three months before his eighteenth birthday.

To Mason, Monday 10 August 1778

Printed from Mitford ii. 6–9.

Strawberry Hill, Aug. 10, 1778.

I DID not write to you on our naval skirmish,[1] because I had nothing to add to what you saw in the papers. It is evident the French had orders to risk nothing, and accordingly they got out of the scrape as fast as they could, yet they pretend that our fleet retired first.[2] If it had, we should have taken as much pains to charge Mr Keppel as they could.[3] The consequences are and probably will be good. Their flight will not encourage them, and it has saved our East India fleet, which is all come in.[4] I have heard enough to make me change my mind about Spain,[5] who I believe will join in the *mêlée*, unless we are awed into peace, which I cannot but suppose is the meaning of the war going on in this equivocal shape. I expect to hear some *beau matin* that everything is compromised. There are reasons both good and bad why it ought not to surprise one.

I have lengthened my Chattertonian pamphlet, and now think shall not publish it. It will clear me whenever it does appear, and I have rather more respect for posterity than for the present generations, who have evidently lost all ideas of right and wrong; but I will say no more on two topics of so little worth as the present age and myself.

In lieu of everything else, I here send you an original indeed,—the

1. Off Ushant, 27 July 1778, an indecisive encounter described in Palliser's letter to Sandwich ca 31 July 1778 (*Sandwich Papers* ii. 131–2) and discussed in detail in A. T. Mahan, *Major Operations of the Navies in the War of American Independence,* Boston, 1913, pp. 82–97.

2. 'The English admiral . . . availed him of the darkness of the night to effect his retreat' (quoted from the *Supplement to the Gazette of France* in *Public Advertiser* 7 Aug. 1778 and in *London Chronicle* 6–8 Aug., xliv. 131). Mahan (op. cit. 97) considers that the English claim is supported by the stronger evidence.

3. 'The Court affected to be greatly disappointed at not having gained a complete victory, in order to blame Keppel' (*Last Journals* ii. 195). Keppel's adherence to the

Rockingham faction made him an object of suspicion to the ministerial party (*Sandwich Papers* ii. 3), but the correspondence of George III fails to bear out HW's charge.

4. See *ante* 4 July 1778. '7th [August]. Account of the arrival at Portsmouth of eleven East Indiamen, for which there had been great apprehensions. Keppel had sent five ships to meet them, on hearing the French had dispatched six to intercept them. Thus had all the fleets come in, reckoned worth four millions' (*Last Journals* ii. 195–6).

5. 'Spain continues to disclaim hostility, as you told me. If the report is true of revolts in Mexico, they would be as good as a bond under his Catholic Majesty's hand' (HW to Mann 31 May 1778). Spain continued its devious course of diplomacy

preface to Rousseau's *mémoires*,[6] which is got out, though the work itself is I believe not yet published.[7] The style, the singularity, the intolerable vanity, speak it genuine,—nay, so does the laboured eloquence, which would be sublime if it were not affected frenzy, and worse. I wish you not to give copies, because, should it be discovered, I should be said to have spread it to his prejudice;[8] yet I have none, nor am angry with him by the common rule, because I offended him. So far from it, I have always allowed his masterly genius, and was only angry with him for his own sake, that he who was born to be superior in common sense should have stooped to build his fame on paradox, and seemed to choose rather to be talked of for the singularity of his writings, than for their excellence; but this preface goes farther, much farther.—He aims at being the capital figure at the last day. I send it to you, shocking as it is: *la voici*.[9]—

Je forme une entreprise qui n'eut jamais d'exemples, et dont l'exécution n'aura point d'imitateurs. Je vais montrer à mes semblables un homme dans toute la vérité de la nature, et cet homme c'est moi.

Moi seul je sens mon cœur et connais les hommes; je ne suis fait comme aucun de ceux que j'ai vus; j'ose croire n'être fait comme aucun de ceux qui existent; je ne vaux pas mieux ou moins, je suis autre; si la nature a bien ou mal fait de briser le moule dans lequel elle m'a jeté, c'est ce dont on ne peut juger qu'après m'avoir lu. Que la trompette du jugement dernier sonne quand elle voudra je viendrai, ce livre à la main, me présenter devant le souverain juge. Je dirai hautement, voilà ce que j'ai fait, ce que j'ai pensé, ce que je suis; j'ai dit le bien et le mal avec la même franchise; je n'ai rien tu, rien déguisé, rien pallié; je me suis montré coupable et vil quand je l'ai été; j'ai montré mon intérieur comme tu l'as vu toi-même, être éternel; rassemble autour de moi l'innombrable foule de mes semblables; qu'ils écoutent mes confessions, qu'ils rougissent de mes indignités, qu'ils gémissent de mes misères; que chacun dévoile à son tour

until June 1779, when it finally declared war on England.

6. The *Confessions*. The preface, which had been circulating in manuscript, had been sent to HW by Mme du Deffand (DU DEFFAND v. 64). The existence of the *Confessions* had been common knowledge since 1770, and after Rousseau's death there was much gossip and speculation about the final disposition of them. See Grimm, *Correspondance* xii. 132; L. P. Bachaumont, *Mémoires secrets*, 1780–9, xii. 33, 51, 59; Elizabeth A. Foster, 'Le Dernier séjour de

J.-J. Rousseau à Paris 1770–1778,' *Smith College Studies in Modern Languages*, 1921, *passim*; Pierre–Paul Plan, *J.-J. Rousseau raconté par les gazettes de son temps*, 1912, pp. 137–45.

7. The first edition of the *Confessions* did not appear until 1782.

8. Because of HW's 'Letter from the King of Prussia to Jean-Jacques Rousseau.'

9. The text copied out by HW is closer to Bachaumont's (op. cit. xii. 55–6) than to the published edition; the differences among the various texts are slight.

son cœur aux pieds de ton trône, et qu'un seul te dise ensuite, je suis meilleur que cet homme-là.

What can one see in this rhapsody of insufferable pride but a studied delirium, an arrogant humiliation, a confession turned into a bravado, —and for what theatre! and before whom! Cartouche[10] might have proposed to talk in such a style at the day of judgment. Think of the audacious insect allotting to himself a mould made on purpose, intending to be the orator of that moment, and demanding to have all mankind judged by comparison with him! To meditate a gasconade for the end of the world!

Suppose, instead of her modest contrite deportment, Mary Magdalen had stalked into the hall of the Pharisee with the air of a streetwalker and had bawled out: 'Let the trumpet sound. I declare myself the greatest strumpet in Jerusalem. Here is the list of my whoredoms, who dares own as much? and yet who are chaster than I?'[11] I hope a friend of ours[12] will be cured of his enthusiasm to this new Erostratus, who has burnt the temple of modesty to make himself talked of.[13] Here I finish; it is impossible to add anything that would be of a piece with this rant.

From Mason, Friday 14 August 1778

Printed from MS now WSL.
Address: The Honourable Horace Walpole, Arlington Street, London.
Postmark: ROTHERHAM 17 AU.

Aston, August 14th, 1778.

I WILL say nothing about our naval skirmish nor our land preparations, except that our poor country, from being once a well-bred gentleman is now turned a downright blackguard. A gentleman when he has received an affront sends his challenge and then fights his duel.

10. Louis-Dominique Cartouche (ca 1693–1721), celebrated French thief. An English account of his career, *The Life and Actions of Lewis Dominique Cartouche,* 1722, is attributed to Defoe.
11. This passage, after 'Pharisee,' was omitted by Mitford, and was first printed by Mrs Toynbee from Mitford's MS transcript (Add. MSS 32563 fol. 50).

12. Lord Harcourt. His enthusiasm for Rousseau is reflected in Brooke Boothby's letter to him of 10 Aug. 1777 (*Harcourt Papers* viii. 211–5).
13. Herostratus was an Ephesian who set fire to the Temple of Artemis at Ephesus on the night that Alexander the Great was born, 356 B.C., in order to immortalize himself.

A blackguard in similar circumstances drives his fist directly at the jowl of his adversary and waives the ceremonial of the challenge. I leave you to make the application, only I protest that had Keppel been victorious I should have hesitated about ringing the three cracked bells in my country steeple, for I can never think a fair victory can be gained over an enemy before war has been declared. Perhaps I am too punctilious. No matter. We have *not* been victorious, so we won't dispute about it.

Your extract from Rousseau is indeed *sui generis* and I thank you a thousand times for it. Poor man! I always pitied him, even when I admired him the most, and I admired him the most in his letter to David Hume,[1] when he was certainly the maddest, as, from this foretaste of his memoirs, I conclude they will at least in this, equal that letter. I shall read them with avidity, whenever they reach my hands, because they will give me those humane emotions of pity, which many of his other works have given me, and I will never believe with you that his was either *studied delirium* or *affected frenzy*[2] till I am absolutely compelled to it, and this for the sake of that compassionate feeling which his writings do and will excite in me, so long as I can believe them written by a madman in good earnest. Prove him a pretender to insanity and the charm vanishes. I shall then regard his eloquence, as little as I do Chatterton's poetry.

I hope you will think a second time, before you resolve *not* to publish what you have written on this latter subject. I think that to say something about it to the world, is a duty you owe to yourself. I shall hope therefore you will bring the MS with you when we meet next month at Nuneham, and that you will publish it some time before Christmas. I have an hypothesis of my own concerning those poems which I think I could make out to be at least highly probable. Viz., that they were originally all written in modern English and antiquitized[3] after. Had I his modernisms now published,[4] I would take one

1. On 15 July 1766 Hume wrote to Hugh Blair: 'Today I received a letter from him [Rousseau] which is perfect frenzy. It would make a good eighteen-penny pamphlet. . . . He there tells me that D'Alembert, Horace Walpole and I had from the first entered into a combination to ruin him' (*Letters of David Hume*, ed. J. Y. T. Greig, 1932, ii. 63). Hume printed Rousseau's letter in his *Exposé succinct de la*

contestation qui s'est élevée entre M. Hume et M. Rousseau, 1766, translated into English in the same year as *A Concise and Genuine Account of the Dispute*, etc. See *Letters of David Hume* ii. 385–401.

2. Phrases used by HW in his letter of 10 Aug.

3. This nonce-word does not appear in the OED. That Mason has oversimplified Chatterton's creative process is demon-

of them and antiquitize it in two manners, *à la* Chaucer and *à la* Chatterton, and I am persuaded that these two specimens would prove the matter clearer than all the critical arguments that either have or will be produced, and yet I think that T. Warton has done enough in that way[5] to convince even the president of the Antiq[uarian] Society[6] (if such president were ever capable of conviction) that he was, of all forgerers, the most palpable. All this however no more detracts from his poetical abilities than Rousseau's insanity does from his oratorical.

I am waiting here a visit from Giardini, in order to give him all the lights I can for the proper music to *Sappho,* but whether he will come before or after York races, i.e., this next week or the fortnight after, I am yet ignorant. At all adventures I hold myself in readiness to meet you at Newnham the middle of September if not sooner. Though I have a visit to pay in Shropshire[7] in my way, and mean from thence to come by Birmingham and the Leasows.[8] All this however shall be lengthened or shortened according to your time of going to Nuneham, where I promise myself the greatest pleasure in meeting you. Believe me, dear Sir,

Yours very cordially,

W. MASON

Mr Palgrave is with me and desires his best compliments.

strated by Meyerstein's study of the materials of the Rowley poems (*A Life of Thomas Chatterton,* 1930, pp. 170–205).

4. The *Miscellanies in Prose and Verse.* See *ante* 24 July 1778.

5. In Section viii of the second volume of the *History of English Poetry* Warton argued that the Rowley poems were forgeries.

6. Jeremiah Milles, who had recently 'been at Bristol to procure proofs to support the authenticity of Rowley's poems' (COLE ii. 92). At the end of 1781 Milles published his edition of the Rowley poems 'with a commentary in which the antiquity of them is considered and defended.'

7. Probably to his friend John Mainwaring (ca 1724–1807), fellow of St John's College, Cambridge, 1748–88, and rector of Church Stretton, Salop, 1749–1807; subsequently (1788–1807) Lady Margaret professor of divinity (COLE ii. 252–3; Venn, *Alumni Cantab.*). Mason was visiting Frederick Montagu at Papplewick, Notts, on 2 Sept. 1778, and wrote from there to Alderson: 'I mean to leave this place tomorrow and to proceed through Nottingham to Derby, Burton, and Litchfield in my way to Mainwaring.'

8. Shenstone's *ferme ornée* had passed to Edward Horne (1740–1807), high sheriff of Shropshire, 1780, who rebuilt the house 1776–8. In 1778 he sold the Leasowes to John Delap Halliday (1749–94), brother-in-law of the 5th E. of Dysart. See N&Q 1867, 3d ser., xii. 288–9; J. B. Blakeway, *The Sheriffs of Shropshire,* Shrewsbury, 1831, p. 209; *Scots Peerage* iii. 410.

From MASON, ca Saturday 22 August 1778

Printed from MS now WSL. Dated conjecturally from HW's reply, *post* 25 Aug. *Address* (in unidentified hand): The Honourable Horace Walpole, Arlington Street, London.
Postmark: ROTHERHAM (date illegible).

EPISTLE
TO THE HONOURABLE HORACE WALPOLE

To brand imposture, to detect a knave,
Who else might slink secure into his grave,
Some years ago, my Walpole! had its merit,
While yet remained a gleam of public spirit.
  When Douglas[1] plucked the mask from Lauder's face,[2]
Douglas was thought to do a deed of grace;
When a like touch of his Ithuriel's spear[3]
Bade Archy Bower in full-blown fraud appear,
And from a martyr, change into a cheat,[4]
Full sure the Doctor did a doughty feat.
Egregious Scot![5] who hot in truth's defence,
Beat up his namesake's stews for evidence;[6]
And, though each rogue was of his mother nation,

1. John Douglas (1721–1807), D.D., divine and pamphleteer; F.R.S. and F.S.A., 1778; Bp of Carlisle 1787–91, of Salisbury 1791–1807.

2. William Lauder (d. 1771), who in 1750 published a pamphlet, *An Essay on Milton's Use and Imitation of the Moderns in His Paradise Lost*, to which Johnson wrote the Preface, 'in full persuasion of Lauder's honesty' (Boswell, *Johnson* i. 228–30). Other readers were suspicious of Lauder, but Douglas's *Milton Vindicated from the Charge of Plagiarism* (in the second edition entitled *Milton no Plagiary*) was the decisive demonstration of Lauder's imposture.

3. 'Him [Satan] thus intent Ithuriel with his spear
    Touched lightly; for no falsehood can endure
    Touch of celestial temper . . .'
              (*Paradise Lost* iv. 810–2).

4. Archibald Bower (1686–1766), a Scottish Roman Catholic who entered the Society of Jesus in 1706, left it and the Roman Catholic Church in 1726 and professedly became a member of the Church of England. He undertoook a *History of the Popes*, allegedly designed to refute the doctrine of papal supremacy, but at the same time conducted a private correspondence with the provincial of the English Jesuits and represented himself as secretly Catholic in his sympathies. When the letters were discovered, Bower claimed that they were forgeries. Douglas exposed him in a pamphlet entitled *Six Letters from A——d B——r to Father Sheldon, Provincial of the Jesuits in England*, 1756.

5. Douglas was the son of a Fifeshire merchant.

6. 'Mother Douglas kept a house of civil reception at this time in Covent Garden, and the Doctor in the heat of his controversy with Bower accused him of having been seen coming out of a bawdy house in that quarter' (Mason's note). See Douglas's *Six Letters*, p. 30.

Disdained to give their lies a dispensation—
Egregious Scot! if fame my verse can give,
Long as that verse (at least) thy name shall live.

But times are changed, ev'n Douglas' self must own,
Since Scottish kingcraft reassumed the throne.
Now Bower and Lauder, were they both alive,
With wit would figure, and by parts would thrive.
Ill-fated pair! whom that blind midwife Time
Dragged into birth some years before their prime;
And ruthless Death drove to the realms of night
Some years before our glorious fifty-eight[7]—
Else, worthy pair! crowned with a Court's attention,
Macpherson's self had got but half your pension,[8]
And still inspired by hunger's urgent call,
Created every month a new Fingal.

Ah burn then, Horace! thy ill-timed defence.
Truth, dressed in all thy native eloquence,
Will naught avail. Thou stand'st (as I am told)
Indicted for a crime, full ten years old,[9]
'For that, not having 'fore thy eyes the fear
Of Grub Street, thy proud heart disdained to hear
A stranger boy, who sent thee a rich store
Of Saxon, Norman, and heraldic lore;

7. The meaning of this line is obscure. Bower lived until 1766 and Lauder until 1771, although he emigrated to Barbados many years before. Mason seems to have combined an echo of the 'Glorious Eighty-Eight' of King William, a reference to the great victories of the Seven Years' War (which he has put in '58 instead of '59), and a reference to the ascendancy of Bute.

8. Mason seems to mean that George III would have rewarded Lauder and Bower even more bountifully than Macpherson. In Feb. 1776 HW wrote, 'Macpherson, the Ossianite, had a pension of £600 a year from the Court, to supervise the newspapers, and prevent the publication of truth or satire' (Last Journals i. 524). He again wrote, 4 Dec. 1781, that Macpherson 'had a pension of £800 a year from Court for inspecting newspapers, and inserted what lies he pleased, and prevented whatever he disapproved from being printed' (ibid. ii. 387). The £800 seems to have rep-

resented the combined income from Macpherson's pension and a sinecure, as is shown in a memorandum from Lord North to George III, 26 March 1782: 'Mr James Macpherson has for many years been a most laborious and able writer in favour of Government. . . . Almost all the good pamphlets on the side of administration were the production of his pen. When Lord North succeeded the Duke of Grafton, he found Mr Macpherson on the private list of pensioners. He is now in possession of a pension of £500 a year, and has lately lost the place of secretary to the province of West Florida, worth near £300 a year' (Corr. Geo. III v. 414). Nothing has been learned concerning Macpherson's reported 'inspection' of newspapers, which according to HW printed a 'daily column of lies' supplied by him. See HW to Lady Ossory 7 Jan. 1782 and post 26 Nov. 1781.

9. Chatterton's applications to HW were in 1769.

With manie a rime, coygned by thilk craftie Skylle,
As cherisonde[10] the herte of gode Deane Mylle;[11]
Nay turned him, on this wicked town, to graze,
Without his pittance or of pence or praise;
Because (I blush the reason to repeat)
Only, because you thought the boy a cheat.'
'I think so still.'—'This, Sir, is no denial;
'Tis pleading guilty; it impedes your trial;
Disown the general charge, and let us bring
The council of our Sov'reign Lord the King,
Ev'n Sawney's self,[12] in his new silken gown,
To prove the fact, as plaintiff for the Crown.

The Attorney-General's speech in our next.

To MASON, Tuesday 25 August 1778

Printed from Mitford ii. 11–14.

Arlington Street, Aug. 25, 1778.

YOU have put an end, my dear Sir, to my thoughts of publishing my narrative, for you have said in four lines all that I have been trying to say in thirty pages, so my *native eloquence* which your partiality honours,[1] proves what I have long suspected it was, only easy verbiage. In the early part of my life I wished to have it known that I was not a fool—doctors differ on the method and on the success: now, when I was grown much more indifferent to fame, you have bestowed on me more than I should ever have presumed to ask. I am now like

10. 'Cherisonde, pleased or comforted. Chatterton made the noun Cherisaune, and I on equal authority have made the verb' (Mason's note). Mason is referring to 'cherisaunei,' in the first line of the 'Entroductionne' to *Ælla*. Chatterton, apparently misled by a misprint in Kersey's *Dictionarium Anglo-Britannicum*, wrote it for 'cherisaunce,' the correct Middle English form (E. H. W. Meyerstein, *A Life of Thomas Chatterton*, 1930, pp. 171–2).

11. See *ante* 14 Aug. 1778, n. 6.

12. Alexander Wedderburn, who had been made attorney-general in June 1778.

1. In l. 30 of the preceding 'Epistle to the Honourable Horace Walpole.' HW writes as though he expected Mason to publish the verses, and it appears that Mason actually printed at least the first section, for a proof-sheet of the 'Epistle' that included Mason's note on Bower and Douglas was found in Mitford's copy of Mason's Dufresnoy (*Catalogue of . . . the General Library of the Late Rev. John Mitford*, sold Sotheby and Wilkinson April–May 1860, lot 1240).

people that have a ticket to Richmond Park[2] which they lend to others when they can go in without, by being known to be in favour with the proprietor,[3] or like country squires returned for two places, who make their option for the county, and resign their family borough, on which perhaps there is not a tenement left standing. I choose my niche in your verses; and my namesakes, my uncle, my cousin[4] and his son,[5] shall be welcome to all the memory that shall remain of writings under the appellation of H.W. reserving only what is said of individual me in the life of Gray, whose monument,[6] by the way, I shall visit tomorrow.

I must not say more of your poetry, because it is the only poetry of yours to which I may be partial, but when I have told you how exceedingly I am flattered by being immortalized in it, you may be sure I am content with my patent. I must too say no more because without blending myself with you at least indirectly, I know not how to comment, and I should be the falsest, as well as the vainest of mortals, if I made the smallest comparison between us. I hope you think I know enough of poetry not to confound the genuine heir of the right line with a maker of prose; for poet, Phoebus knows I am not, and if I do not waive every sort of pretension it is only that you may not have bestowed an encomium on a subject totally worthless.

I should have replied to your last sooner if I had been sure that you were not set out on your tour.[7] I shall be ready to set out for Nuneham whenever I receive my summons.

It is but this moment that I am come to town, and would fulfil the duty of gratitude, before I inquired about the new engagement in America.[8] For the *Gazette* account,[9] I do not understand it, which is being a good subject, for like other such relations, it is only meant to confound. All I do know is that on Sunday night the undisciplined[10]

---

2. The right of the public to free passage through Richmond Park was recognized in a legal verdict handed down in 1758. But the admission of carriages was restricted to those who obtained tickets of admission from the Ranger. See H. M. Cundall, *Bygone Richmond*, 1925, pp. 38–9.

3. The King.

4. Horatio Walpole (1723–1809), 'Pigwiggin,' son of 'old Horace'; 2d Bn Walpole of Wolterton, 1757; Bn Walpole of Walpole, 1797; 1st E. of Orford (n.c.) 1806.

5. Horatio Walpole (1752–1822), 2d E. of Orford (n.c.), 1809.

6. See *ante* 8 Oct. 1776 and *post* 28 Aug. 1778. The monument was unveiled 6 Aug. 1778 (GM 1778, xlviii. 387).

7. See *ante* 14 Aug. 1778.

8. The indecisive battle of Freehold (New Jersey), or Monmouth Court-House, 28 June 1778.

9. Sir Henry Clinton's account of the battle was printed in a *London Gazette Extraordinary* 24 Aug. 1778.

10. I.e., indiscreet enough to acknowledge that affairs in America were going badly.

courtiers spoke of it in most dismal terms. If I guess right Washington was ill served,[11] and thence, and by the violent heats,[12] could not effect all his purpose; but an army on a march through a hostile country, that is twice beaten back, which is owned,[13] whose men drop down with heat,[14] have no hospitals, and were hurrying to a place of security,[15] must have lost more than 380 men.[16] In fact they were hurrying whence they could not stay into the last trap. They will be starved into surrender or desperation at New York; and D'Estain is blocking up our port and fleet,[17] and a swingeing lie will the *Gazette* have to tell, if both army and fleet are taken.

The papers say that Keppel and Palisser[18] have fought a duel,[19] I do not know how truly. The reason given in the papers[20] is *not* the true if another that has been whispered is; namely that Palisser did not obey Keppel's signal,[21] though the former at first behaved bravely; and is

11. HW could have read in the *Public Advertiser* of 24 Aug. 1778 that General Charles Lee of the American army 'was accused of misconduct,' and that Lord Stirling, another of Washington's generals, was 'under arrest.' The report concerning Stirling was erroneous, but it was true that Washington was incensed by Lee's behaviour in the battle.

12. 'The heat of the weather was intense, and our men already suffered severely from fatigue' (Clinton's letter to Germain, *London Gazette Extraordinary* 24 Aug. 1778).

13. '23rd [Aug.] Colonel Patterson arrived from New York with an account that Sir Henry Clinton, in his march from the Jerseys to New York, had been attacked by Washington and twice beaten back' (*Last Journals* ii. 197, which continues with a passage that is close to the rest of this paragraph). Clinton's narrative fails to credit the Americans with these successful thrusts, but they are confirmed in an American account published in the London newspapers at this time. See, e. g., *Public Advertiser* 26 Aug. 1778.

14. According to Clinton's return of the killed, wounded, and missing, 59 enlisted men died of fatigue during the battle. There were probably more who died in the course of the retreat from Philadelphia to New York. See W. S. Stryker, *The Battle of Monmouth*, Princeton, 1927, pp. 258-9.

15. New York.

16. Clinton's return totalled 358. The

accuracy of his figures, however, has been questioned. See Stryker, op. cit. 259-60.

17. 'On the 7th [July], D'Estaing's fleet . . . appeared off New York. Lord Howe formed the line within Sandy Hook' (*Public Advertiser* 24 Aug. 1778). 'In consequence of the accounts which were circulated yesterday relative to the blocking up of Lord Howe's fleet at New York, stocks have fallen one and a half per cent' (ibid. 25 Aug. 1778).

18. Sir Hugh Palliser (1723–96), Bt, 1773; Rear-Adm., 1775; Vice-Adm., 1778; Adm., 1787; lord of the Admiralty 1775–8; commander of a division and third in command under Keppel in the Channel fleet, 1778.

19. 'A report is current of a duel being fought between two officers who commanded our late naval engagement off Brest' (*London Chronicle* 22–5 Aug. 1778, xliv. 190). Shortly after the Ushant action there were 'rumours at Portsmouth and Plymouth and veiled references in the London press, to a misunderstanding between Keppel and Palliser' (*Sandwich Papers* ii. 192). The report of the duel was false.

20. The *London Chronicle* (loc. cit.) stated that the quarrel was 'in consequence of some reflections thrown out on a great officer, respecting the equipment of the fleet.'

21. This charge was later brought out into the open. Palliser demanded that Keppel publish a denial, and upon his refusal

not suspected of want of spirit, but of Mindenian finesse,[22] and that by secret order of the trident-bearer.[23] Keppel was much insulted at Plymouth,[24] by the same direction as supposed; and that provocation may have brought out what was at first suppressed.[25] However I affirm nothing of all this, though I have heard enough by different channels to incline me to believe there is an appearance of foundation in the groundwork; though it is impossible to conceive that revenge could have blinded an old politician,[26] so far as to have made him lose all sight of the advantage that would have accrued even to himself from a victory.

In short, disgraces and misfortunes thicken so fast, that I believe there will be no time to unravel half, while there is an opportunity, supposing there were one. History will be forced to poke and patch out scraps, and when the whole is a heap of ruins, some David Hume will be [?moved] to compose a system of wise and virtuous motives, which always tend to produce folly and crimes, and then the induction will be, that nobody should be wise and virtuous. Adieu! Adieu!

PS. You may imagine I am impatient for the sequel.[27]

From Mason, ca Tuesday 25 August 1778

Printed from MS now WSL. This sequel to *ante* ca 22 Aug. was carried to HW by Alderson. See *post* 28 Aug.

'It hurts me[1] (gentlemen upon the jury)
It hurts my finer feelings, I assure ye;
To try the strength of my forensic arts,

instituted court-martial proceedings against him. The court met at Portsmouth 7 Jan. 1779, and on 11 Feb. exonerated Keppel. See HW to Mann 5 and 29 Jan. and 11 Feb. 1779.

22. That is, behaving like Lord George Germain at Minden in 1759. See *ante* 16 Dec. 1775, n. 8.

23. The King.

24. This is not corroborated by the letters that passed between Keppel and Sandwich or by the letters of the King.

25. Possibly for strategic reasons. 'If Keppel wished for an official inquiry into Palliser's conduct (and we can find no evidence that he wanted this at the time) he was

perfectly right to keep silent about it, since a court-martial at that time would have delayed the sailing of the fleet, giving the French command of the sea and delivering the year's trade into their hands' (*Sandwich Papers* ii. 192).

26. Palliser was senior professional member of the Board of Admiralty and a supporter of the ministerial party. He was also two years older than Keppel, though junior to him in rank.

27. To the preceding 'Epistle.'

1. The 'Attorney-General's speech,' a continuation of *ante* ca 22 Aug.

Against a man of the defendant's parts;
Who, had he lived in the third Richard's reign,
Had been Lord Steward, or Lord Chamberlain.
I say it hurts me much, that such a man
Should draw his line on this contracted plan;
So falsely delicate; so over-nice;
To deem poetic forgery a vice.
To this all poets plead prescription[2] wholly
I won't except old Ossian, or old Rowley;
Whether they lived, is immaterial quite,
A want of being bars no claim of right.[3]
Not to discriminate is mighty odd,
'Tween Thomas Chatterton, and Doctor Dodd.[4]
Pope said, 'tis true, when Pope possessed that name,[5]
He thought a lie in verse and prose the same.[6]
But will his friend Lord Mansfield find it law?
In Pope's Reports 'tis not the single flaw:
There are who do not by his code abide,
Which reads, that "Murray is his country's pride."[7]
Lawyers there are, and on that side am I,
Who ground it on his privilege to lie,
Yet still demur, whether such power extend
To vest for life his leasings [8] in his friend.
But waiving this, as one of Pope's old flaws,
I enter on the merits of the cause.
        'A youth is dead. Felo de se, or not,
By p—x or poison,[9] matters not a jot.

2. The word is here used in its legal sense of 'uninterrupted use or possession from time immemorial, or for a period fixed by law as giving a title or right,' or in the derived sense of a 'claim founded upon long use' (OED).

3. 'The Attorney's assertion seems to militate a little against common sense, it is nevertheless good law. It may be argued "that a man who was never alive, was incapable of committing a forgery." But the question here is not of competency but of right. A married man may be incompetent to beget children, but the right to beget them legally is still in him. The case is exactly parallel, both rights being dormant' (Mason's note).

4. Dr William Dodd, the forger, executed in 1777. See *ante* 13 March and 6 July 1777.

5. Of poet.

6. 'See Pope's Epistle to Doctor Arbuthnot, v. 339' (Mason's note).

7. ' "Where Murray long enough his
        country's pride
   Shall be no more than Tully or than
        Hyde"
                (Pope, Epistle 6th, v. 5[2–]3)'
                        (Mason's note).

8. Lies.

9. 'Mr Cross [an apothecary who was

A youth is dead, who might have been alive,
Had the defendant found him means to thrive;
Lodged him at Strawb'ry Hill, in decent dress,
And made him the corrector of his press.
Why did he not?—His reason I repeat,
Only because he thought the youth a cheat.
　'Ridiculous!—If pleas so very weak
Be held admissible, led Campden[10] take
The steerage of the state, for North and I
Will yield the office mighty readily.
Who'll fit your fleets to give the French a beating,
If you prohibit them the right of cheating?
Or one sound loaf for all Coxheath[11] procure?
I'll answer for my countryman—not Muir.[12]
Your camps must starve; your navy be undone;
Expedients fail ye; and contractors shun.
Where will you find, I pray, so great a novice,
Will serve without his perquisites of office?
Who, without plate, and — pounds a day,
Will beg your pardon from America?[13]
That man must be a brahmin, or a dervis
Who will not sip the sweets of secret service.
　'His Grace of Richmond plagued us all last year
With calculations;[14] making it appear,
In spite of all the trifling sums we granted,

a friend of Chatterton] says he had the foul disease which he would cure himself and had calomel or vitriol of Cross for that purpose' (quoted from Lort's memorandum by Meyerstein, *A Life of Thomas Chatterton*, p. 441).

10. Lord Camden was in opposition to the government's American policies.

11. One of the temporary military camps established to meet the threat of a French invasion. Coxheath is near Linton, four miles south of Maidstone, Kent. The encampment is described in the *London Chronicle* 21–3 July 1778, xliv. 78.

12. 'A man who after gaining 50 per cent by his contract for rum, now furnishes all the camps with bread' (Mason's note). Hutchinson Mure (ca 1711–94), trader;

associated with Richard Atkinson (see *post* 28 Feb. 1782; GM 1794, lxiv pt ii. 771; E. E. Curtis, *The Organization of the British Army in the American Revolution*, New Haven, 1926, p. 85).

13. According to the schedule of payments drawn up by William Eden, one of their number, the peace commissioners to America were to receive an annual salary and allowance amounting to £6225 (Carl Van Doren, *Secret History of the American Revolution*, New York, 1941, p. 83).

14. During 1778 the Duke of Richmond had frequently addressed the House of Lords on the state of the nation, and had supported his arguments with an impressive array of figures. See Cobbett, *Parl. Hist.* xix *passim*.

How much our army and our navy wanted.
He missed the mark, ev'n grant his reasoning true;
I have a greater want than these in view.
Poor if we be in land and water fighters,
We're poorer still in ministerial writers.
Broad-tongued Shebbeare like ev'ry other dog
Has had his day; Johnson is grown a log;[15]
Home and Macpherson now their weambs[16] are full[17]
Grow very indolent and very dull.
To own the truth, we Scots have found a way ⎫
To get for all we publish double pay   ⎬
And write at once for Cadell,[18] and Sir Gray.[19] ⎭
For this sage end, we ne'er condense our sense,
But spread o'er quartos our thin eloquence;
Scorning in pamphlet channels to confine
The torrent of our energy divine;
While English readers hate a bulky book,
And leave the lake, to tipple at the brook.
But he the youth whose loss we now deplore,
Which loss we lie at the defendant's door,
Was Bristow born, yet 'tis by all agreed
He'd parts might figure ev'n beyond the Tweed.'

To be continued,[20] but I know not when, for I am at present much interrupted, and am besides preparing for my journey. If the person[21] who brings this should chance to meet with you at home he will tell you all I know of myself, and of my motions, nor is he ignorant of the contents, for I know he may be trusted. I would not wish you to write here to me again, but in about a fortnight from this time, I hope to be at a place[22] where I would much rather meet you than your letter, though I should like to meet both, or your letter a day before you.

15. Since his *Taxation No Tyranny* Johnson had written nothing likely to give aid and comfort to the administration.

16. 'A Scottish name for bellies' (Mason's note).

17. Both Home and Macpherson had pensions from George III.

18. Thomas Cadell, the elder (1742–1802), bookseller and publisher.

19. Sir Grey Cooper, one of the joint secretaries of the Treasury, 1765–82, and thus one of the dispensers of royal patronage.

20. Mason did write a continuation, the text of which is printed in Appendix 4. Whether HW ever received a copy of the continuation is doubtful.

21. Alderson (*post* 28 Aug. 1778).

22. Nuneham.

GRAY'S AND MASON'S MONUMENTS
IN WESTMINSTER ABBEY

To Mason, Friday 28 August 1778

Printed from Mitford ii. 14–18. Misdated by Mitford 'Aug. 2' at beginning of letter, but correctly dated at the end.

Aug. 28, 1778.

I HAVE seen Gray's monument.[1] The absolutely necessary position is very disadvantageous to it, and prevents any grace in the outline; his nose is a little too aquiline, but both his head and the Muse's are well executed; her body is a little flat, and her legs, from the same want of place, too small and crowded; your epitaph and friendship are the most shining ingredients.

When I mention your friendship for him, I recollect that I was too much intoxicated in my last with your partiality to me. I mean that I did not receive it with humility enough; but in the satisfaction of being recorded by you, forgot how little I deserve it. As there has been so much of blamable in my life, I am conscious that I ought to desire to be spoken of by my enemies, and not by my friends, that the truth may be told, not palliated. To ask that, would be an artful way of avoiding it. I have been told that what I begged you to say of my being the first to blame in my differences with Gray,[2] persuaded some that the reverse was true. I am sure *that* was not my intention; and I would say it still more strongly, if it would not look affected. I have a horror for any praise that one does not deserve; humility is next to vainglory, if it is put on, and has no merit but in avoiding impudence. Simplicity is the medium to be sought, and silence about one's self the surest way of being simple. A corner in your writings which you have allotted to me, I am not lowly enough to waive: but

1. In Westminster Abbey. 'The cenotaph is placed immediately under that of Milton, and represents, in alto-relievo, a female figure with a lyre, as emblematical of the higher kinds of poetry, pointing with one hand to the bust above, and supporting with the other a medallion, on which is a profile head inscribed, "THOMAS GRAY." On the plinth is the following date: "He died July 31, 1771." The sculpture was executed by that eminent artist Mr Bacon [John Bacon (1740–99), R.A.], in Newman Street, at the joint expense of Dr James Browne, Master of Pembroke College, Cambridge; Richard Stonhewer, Esq., auditor of Excise; and the author' (Mason, *Works* i. 141). In a manuscript note in his own copy of his edition of the correspondence (ii. 386), now WSL, Mitford has written: 'Mason mentions in one of his MSS that this monument cost more than a hundred pound.' The profile head of Gray on the medallion closely resembles Carter's engraving (*ante* 16 July 1773, n. 13). See illustration.

2. See *ante* 2 March 1773 *bis* and *Mem. Gray* 41.

I have regard enough for you to desire that you should never say anything of me that you may be ashamed of; remember, your writings will be standards, and remember too that Pope's blindness to Bolinbroke took off the edge of half his satires. I shall not suffer you to hurt your own fame in compliment to me, early and late have I despised Cicero's *orna me*.[3] Has one better claim to praise one has not earned, than to money one has stolen? and to beg one's friend to lie for one! no, my dear Sir, there are a few honest good men that deserve such verses as yours,—I should think I robbed them, while they want your praise.

I had written thus far, when I received your second part by Mr Alderson; you desire me not to write, but to bring you my answer, and odd as the request is, I shall obey it for two reasons; the first is, that the impression of your seal is so sharp, that I am convinced all or most of those you send by the post have been opened.[4] The second is that your modesty would not permit me to tell you to your face how much I am charmed with your poetry. You have an original talent for this style, that without resembling either, is much more like Horace's than Pope's was; and instead of piddling with petty dunces, you gibbet greater dunces and much greater rogues. Nay you do, what history cannot, for you record their villainies, and if history's majestic gravity could contrive to register them, yet nobody would read what ought to be enrolled only by the ordinary of Newgate, but when you make your readers laugh at our state culprits they will remember them.

There are two odd rencontres in your second part that I must mention: you have introduced the Duke of Richmond, who is one of the virtuous few that is worthy of such a pen as yours, and was in my eye in the foregoing page,[5] and you have brought in Pope, and Lord Mansfield, which I have done too in my narrative,[6] as you will see, though for a different quotation; but in short, you have made my

3. 'Load me with honours.' 'The most conspicuous and glaring passion of his soul was the love of glory and thirst of praise' (Conyers Middleton, *Life of Cicero*, 1741, ii. 517).
4. HW seems to have suspected that the seals were broken and the impression then forged, or else that the wax was softened enough for the letters to be opened and resealed. The cover of Mason's letter of ca 25 Aug. (carried by Alderson) is missing.

5. 'There are a few honest good men that deserve such verses as yours.'
6. 'Mr Pope, I know, laments the misapplication of talents, enumerates the deserters from Helicon, and tells us "How many Martials were in Pultney lost;" but this was irony and compliment, and Pope himself would have been sorry that his friend our great Chief Justice, "He with a thousand arts refined," should have quitted the bar, and been nothing but

narrative useless; you have anticipated it by inspiration, and Apollo has made you prophet as well as a poet. I that knew all the circumstances have told tediously what you, by magic I think, have set in a ten times clearer light and compendiously. And as I owed to you and Gray the confirmation of my doubts at first, you have told all that is necessary of my story for me and made it entertaining. Remember this is not to flatter you and draw more panegyric from you; you have justified me in as innocent a transaction as any of my life, and I am more than satisfied, and the best way of thanking you is to be jealous of your honour and to turn it on more meritorious objects. I do not deserve praise; to justify the innocent is worthy of you,— if I was not irreproachable on the article of Chatterton I assure you I would tell you so, for instead of being pleased with your defence, it would aggravate my contrition, and, therefore, I beg you will never put me to shame. My parts are moderate and I trouble my head little about them; but I would give a pound of them if I have so much, for an ounce more of virtues. The crisis of this country will soon put all men to the test; brand the guilty and reward the good; and since the fountain of honour[7] is now the channel of corruption, wrench the chalice from his hand and dispense the waters to the deserving. The moment is coming I think when the constitution may be restored though not the empire. If they who call themselves patriots, flinch from their duty, they will deserve your lash, still more than the present crew. I have no great hopes, though the moment is so propitious (as it is a repetition of precedent lessons) for showing that the folly of tyranny leads directly to the destruction of darling prerogative. I have sometimes thought, so servile has been the copy, that Lord Mansfield has drawn out the steps of James II, and recommended them one by one, in order to ruin the house of Hanover by the same manœuvres that paved their way to the crown. Or he was a woeful, or a most presumptuous politician, to flatter himself he could succeed where Jefferies and Jesuits failed. In short, he and the Scotch have no way of redeeming the credit of their understandings, but by avowing that they have been consummate villains. *Stavano bene; per star meglio, stanno qui.*[8]

---

poet laureate' ('Letter to the Editor of the Miscellanies of Chatterton,' *Works* iv. 214). The first quotation, 'How many Martials,' is from the *Dunciad* (iv. 170). The second should read, 'He with a hundred arts refined' (*First Ode of the Fourth Book of Horace*, l. 15).

7. The King.

8. 'They were well, but trying to be better, they are here.' In *Spectator* No. 25

To Mason, Thursday 17 September 1778

Printed from Mitford ii. 20–2. This letter was sent to Mason at Nuneham in the form of a postscript to a letter to Lord Harcourt, 17 Sept. 1778. The postscript begins, 'Your Lordship authorizes and therefore I presume to add the following words to an Israelite indeed.'

To Mr Mason.

VIDE in my writing-box a long letter[1] that will clear me from your accusation,[2] and the reasons why I choose to bring it myself;[3] moreover I have waited time out of mind for Mr Alderson.[4] I pressed him to come and see my house and flattered myself that would be a temptation, but he is a priest,

And Strawberry must yield to Sion Hill.[5]

As to wanting the conclusion, I do ardently, especially if it is *ad infinitum;* do you think I can have enough of you, of you *issime?* do you imagine I have no self-love? am I so accustomed to flattery as to be surfeited with it? am I to be praised in every magazine like Garrick and Dr. Johnson; and if not satiated with panegyrics, do I write them on myself, like the former?[6] do I not know that a line of yours will preserve me like a fly in amber? what do you think is come to me? in short in self-defence I must tell you why I did not send away my letter. I have done such justice on myself in it, on your account, that my modesty would not hold out; and though I shall be rigorously just enough to trust you with my confession, I could not bring myself to stand in a sheet before the clerks of the post office, and I am too idle to write a letter over again—so much for that.

Addison mentions 'an Italian epitaph written on the monument of a valetudinarian: "Stavo ben, ma per star meglio, sto qui" ' ('I was well, but trying to be better, I am here').

---

1. That of 28 Aug. 1778.
2. Which was, apparently, that HW owed Mason an acknowledgment of the second instalment of Mason's 'Epistle' to him. The 'accusation' may have been in a missing letter or in a message transmitted by Harcourt.
3. That is, when he goes to Nuneham on 21 Sept. (see HW to Harcourt 17 and 27 Sept. 1778).
4. To carry HW's letter to Mason.
5. Probably an echo of the opening stanza of Lord Bath's 'Strawberry-Hill, a Ballad,'

'Some cry up Gunnersbury,
   For Sion some declare . . .
But ask the beaux of Middlesex,
   Who know the country well,
If Strawb'ry-Hill, if Strawb'ry-Hill
   Don't bear away the bell?'
6. As in the prologue described *ante* 27 Feb. 1777.

I sit feeling and handling and probing myself from hand to foot and putting myself to pain, in trying if the gout is gone. I am just like Harlequin, when he was tickling himself to death.[7] If it does not come before Monday, I shall think myself safe. I was rejoiced to be got home; but when I came up into the blue room,[8] and found Lord Harcourt's letter,[9] I was out of my wits; yet I do not despair, as the journey has shifted the seat of the pain,[10] which I always reckon a good symptom. I have begged the prayers of Lord Harcourt and his congregation, but I will have none of yours: they are not worth a straw. Should we be in such a dismal situation, if you could have prayed us out of it? The English clergy have prayed for popery[11] and slavery,[12] and drawn down miseries on us, that will not be suspended for your deprecations, because folly and iniquity are punished by their natural consequences.

My commission to you shall be to lay my homage at Miss Fauquier's[13] feet, which will make it more agreeable. I shall be very happy or very miserable on Monday on all your accounts, as no party could be assembled more to the liking of my heart, but I must not trespass too much in a postscript, for which I again beg Lord Harcourt's pardon. You will oblige me, dear Sir, if you will drop in conversation that Lady Craven has lately allowed me to print *at my press,* her translation of the *Somnambule;*[14] and pray observe if no one in the company seems to feel a *soupçon* of remorse.[15] I shall not tell you why, but I have my reasons.

7. In *Arlequin empereur de la lune* Harlequin avows his determination to die for love, and remembering that the ancients mention that men can die of laughter, he attempts to tickle himself to death. See C. W. Beaumont, *The History of Harlequin,* 1926, p. 69. HW's early passion for harlequinades is mentioned in his letter to Montagu 22 Sept. 1765, and *ante* p. 328.

8. The Breakfast-Room.

9. Missing.

10. 'The motion of the chaise has removed the pain into my foot' (HW to Harcourt 17 Sept. 1778).

11. An allusion to the allegedly Catholic sentiments of the supporters of the administration, such as Archbishop Markham (*ante* 26 May 1777).

12. It was HW's (and the Opposition's) fixed belief that the administration, especially in its conduct of the American war,

threatened the liberties of all Englishmen.

13. Jane Georgiana Fauquier (d. 1823), m. (1787, as his 2d wife) George Venables-Vernon, Lord Vernon, Lady Harcourt's brother. She is frequently mentioned in the *Harcourt Papers.* See HW to Harcourt 27 Sept. 1778.

14. *The Sleep-Walker.* '24 June 1778. Resumed the press. Began to print *The Sleep-Walker,* a translation of the *Somnambule* of M. de Pondeveylt [Pont-de-Veyle] by and for Lady Craven, who acted it at her house at Benham Place, Bucks. 30 August. Finished *The Sleep-Walker,* 75 copies' (*Journal of the Printing-Office* 18–19). See Hazen, *SH Bibliography* 114–6.

15. HW means Lady Harcourt, whose poems he wished to print at the SH Press. See *ante* 3 Sept. 1773 and HW to Lord Harcourt 27 Sept. 1778.

From MASON, Wednesday 7 October 1778

Printed from Cunningham vii. 139. The MS, which was franked by Lord Harcourt, was sold at Puttick and Simpson's Dec. 1848 (Hodges sale) for 16s.; sold again at Puttick and Simpson's 9 May 1851, lot 92, to John Bullock; sold at Sotheby, Wilkinson, and Hodge's 4 Feb. 1876 (Bullock sale), lot 248; not further traced.

Nuneham, Oct. 7, 1778.

I SEND you, with this, a short account[1] of an old play[2] in Lord Harcourt's library, with an extract from it, which will show you how similar the story is to your *Mysterious Mother,* or rather to my alteration of it.[3] I look upon it as a curious discovery, but which affects your tragedy no more than Aaron Hill's *Fair Inconstant,* or his *Athelwold*[4] (for he wrote two on the same subject) does my *Elfrida.*

W. MASON

To MASON, Sunday 11 October 1778

Printed from Mitford ii. 22–5.

Strawberry Hill, Oct. 11, 1778.

A THOUSAND thanks for the trouble you have given yourself, and the information you have sent me;[1] it fully satisfies me, at least till my next visit to Nuneham. I own there is an idea in the play you describe, which had it come into my hand, I should certainly have adopted:—the mother's intention of meeting her own husband and

1. Missing.

2. HW does not identify it in his reply or in his later comments on the play, but it may have been the anonymous *Fatal Discovery, or Love in Ruins,* 1698, which David Erskine Baker mentions in the article on *The Mysterious Mother* in *Biographia Dramatica,* 1782, ii. 248–9, as closely resembling HW's plot though the mother's guilt is 'softened.' Baker's article is reprinted in the preface to the pirated Dublin edition of *The Mysterious Mother,* 1791. HW has unfortunately not annotated the article in his copy of *Biographia Dramatica,* now WSL. Another play with a similar plot is Robert Gould's *Innocence*

Distressed, or the Royal Penitents, printed in 1737. See *The Castle of Otranto and The Mysterious Mother,* ed. Montague Summers, 1924, p. lvi.

3. See *ante* 8 May 1769.

4. *Elfrid, or the Fair Inconstant,* by Aaron Hill (1685–1750), was produced unsuccessfully at Drury Lane in 1710. Later Hill rewrote it and, as *Athelwold,* it was presented in 1731, when it again failed (DNB; Genest ii. 432–3, iii. 327–8). Mason's treatment of the story bears little resemblance to Hill's (Draper, *Mason* 174).

————

1. Missing (*ante* 7 Oct. 1778).

not her son.[2] However as you have, by a *coup de baguette,* obviated the shocking part, I trouble myself no farther. I never had any difficulty of adopting your corrections, but because my original view was to paint the height of repentance for real guilt; whereas any palliative admits a degree of weakness in the Countess, and makes her rather superstitious or delicate, than penitent upon reason;[3] but however as I am tired of the subject I will not tire you upon it. If ever the play is acted, it must be with your improvements, which I will print with it. So I will whether it is acted or not:[4] for such marks of your genius should not be lost, though you want not other proofs; and it will please me to have furnished you with the materials. I grow tired to death of my own things, and hate to talk of them.

Lady Laura,[5] who carries this, will tell you how many accidents prevent my obeying Lord and Lady Harcourt, and accompanying her.[6] I have lost near £700 by a clerk,[7] and I am on Tuesday to sign a family compact with my nephew,[8] by which, some time or other, I shall get the fortune my father left me, which I never expected,[9] so the balance of events is in my favour, and then the deuce is in it if I am to be pitied.

Lady Laura will describe to you a most brilliant fête that I gave her and her sisters[10] and cousins[11] last Thursday. People may say what

2. Mason had urged this in his proposed alterations (*ante* 8 May 1769).

3. See *ante* 11 May 1769.

4. HW never printed Mason's alterations.

5. Lady Elizabeth Laura Waldegrave (1760–1816), m. (1782) George Waldegrave, styled Vct Chewton, 4th E. Waldegrave, 1784.

6. To Nuneham (HW to Harcourt 9 Oct. 1778).

7. 'I am come to town this morning on disagreeable business with my brother, and which will cost me some hundreds of pounds, a clerk in our joint office having chosen to dispose of some money entrusted to him, à la macaroni' (HW to Harcourt 9 Oct. 1778). HW shared with his brother Sir Edward the proceeds from the collectorship of customs. See 'Account of my Conduct,' *Works* ii. 364–5; 'Short Notes,' GRAY i. 15.

8. Lord Orford's request that HW assist him in settling his affairs according to the terms of Sir Robert Walpole's will is the subject of HW's letter to him of 5 Oct. 1778.

The details of the compact, however, are not mentioned, though apparently HW reluctantly consented to the sale of the Houghton pictures (HW to Mann 11 Feb. 1779).

9. Of the £5000 which HW was to have by his father's will he had received by 1782 only £1000 ('Account of My Conduct,' *Works* ii. 365), and there is no reason to believe that he ever received any more of it.

10. Lady Charlotte Maria Waldegrave (1761–1808), m. (1784) George Henry Fitzroy, styled E. of Euston, 4th D. of Grafton, 1811; and Lady Anna Horatia Waldegrave (1762–1801), m. (1786) Hon. Hugh Seymour Conway (later Lord Hugh Seymour) (Collins, *Peerage,* 1812, iv. 246).

11. Anna Maria Keppel (1759–1836) m. (1790) William Stapleton, and Laura Keppel (1765–98), m. (1784) Hon. George Ferdinand Fitzroy, 2d Bn Southampton, 1797 (BERRY i. 119 n. 11, ii. 136 n. 3). Their sister, Charlotte Augusta (b. 1771) was probably too young to attend the fête.

they will, but splendid as it was, I am not of opinion that this *festival of nieces* was absolutely the most charming show that ever was seen. I believe the entertainment given by the Queen of the Amazons to the King of Mauritania in the Castle of Ice, and the ball made for the Princess of Persia by the Duke of Sparta in the Saloon of Roses were both of them more delightful, especially as the contrast of the sable Africans with the shining whiteness of the Thracian heroines, and the opposition between the nudity of the Lacedemonian generals and the innumerable folds of linen in the drapery of the Persian ladies, must have been more singular than all the marvels in the Castle of Strawberry last Thursday. To be sure the illumination of the Gallery surpassed the Palace of the Sun; and when its fretted ceiling,[12] which you know is richer than the roof of paradise, opened for the descent of Mrs Clive in the full moon, nothing could be more striking. The circular drawing-room was worthy of the presence of Queen Bess, as many of the old ladies, who remember her, affirmed, and the high altar in the Tribune[13] was fitter for a Protestant king's hearing mass than the chapel at Lord Petre's.[14] The tapestry bed in the great chamber[15] looked gorgeous (though it had not an escutcheon of pretence like the Duchess of Chandos's[16] while her father and brother are living[17]) and was ready strewed with roses for a hymeneal; but alas! there was the misfortune of the solemnity! Though my

12. Modelled after that of one of the side aisles of Henry VIIth's chapel in Westminster Abbey. See 'Genesis of SH' 78.

13. Also called the Cabinet and the Chapel. 'On the right hand stands an altar of black and gold, with a marble slab of the same colours, taken from the tomb of two children of Edward III in Westminister Abbey' ('Des of SH,' *Works* ii. 471). See 'Genesis of SH' 78.

14. Robert Edward Petre (1742–1801), 9th Bn Petre, a Roman Catholic, had recently offered the hospitality of his house at Thorndon, Essex, to the King and Queen when they visited the camp at Warley Common. The invitation was accepted for 19 Oct., and Lord Petre's elaborate preparations became the talk of the town (Lady Mary Coke's MS Journal for 28 Sept., 7 and 19 Oct. 1778; *Last Journals* ii. 200; Maude D. Petre, *The Ninth Lord Petre*, 1928, pp. 39–48).

15. The Great North Bedchamber, or State Bedchamber, 'hung with crimson Norwich damask' ('Des of SH,' *Works* ii. 494). For the bed, see illustration *ante* p. 42.

16. Anne Eliza Gamon (d. 1813), m. (1) Roger Hope Elletson (d. 1775); m. (2) (1777) James Brydges (1731–89), 3d D. of Chandos.

17. Her father was Richard Gamon (ca 1717–87) of Datchworthbury, Herts, and of Grosvenor Square; her only brother was Richard (later Sir Richard) Gamon (1748–1818), cr. (1795) Bt. An escutcheon of pretence is the small escutcheon bearing the arms of an heiress placed in the centre of her husband's shield. Placed on her husband's shield it pretended to something she was not entitled to represent so long as her father and brother were alive. See A. C. Fox-Davies, *A Complete Guide to Heraldry*, [?1929], pp. 536, 542.

nieces looked as well as the houris, notwithstanding I was disappointed of the house of North to set them off,[18] and though I had sent out one hundred and thirty cards, in this region there are no swains who are under my own almost climacteric.[19] I had three Jews of Abraham's standing, and seven Sarahs who still talk of the second temple.[20] The rest of the company were dowagers and maidens, with silver beards down to their girdles; Henry and Frances, whose doves have long done laying;[21] the curate of the parish;[22] Briscoe, the second-hand silversmith;[23] Mr Raftor; and Lady Greenwich[24] in a riding-dress, for she came on her own broom. You may perhaps think that some of the company were not quite of dignity adequate to such a high festival, but they were just the persons made the most happy by being invited; and as the haughtiest peers stoop to be civil to shop-keepers before an election, I did not see why I should not do, out of good nature, what the proudest so often do out of interest. I do not mention two ancient Generals, because they have not been beaten out of America into red ribbands,[25] nor a Judge [Perryn],[26] who had

18. Presumably the elder daughters of Lord North: Lady Catherine Anne North (1760–1817), m. (1789) Sylvester Douglas, cr. (1800) Bn Glenbervie; and Lady Anne North (1764–1832), m. (1798) John Baker-Holroyd, cr. (1781) Bn and (1816) E. of Sheffield. In a marginal MS note in his copy of the correspondence Mitford has written, 'Not famous for their beauty.'

19. HW, at 61, was within a year of his grand climacteric.

20. Zerubbabel's Temple in Jerusalem (Ezra 3. 8–13). HW's Jewish guests probably included the Prados of Twickenham and the Frankses of Richmond and Isleworth (*post* 4 May 1783; COLE ii. 373 and nn. 23, 25).

21. Richard Griffith (d. 1788) and his wife Elizabeth Griffith (ca 1720–93), whom he married (1751) after a long engagement, had published anonymously in 1757 the first two volumes of *A Series of Genuine Letters between Henry and Frances*, which was said to be a selection of their correspondence before their marriage. The letters, which are excessively sentimental, achieved great popularity. Two additional volumes, relating to their marriage, were published in 1766, and two more in 1770. See J. M. S. Tompkins, *The*

Polite Marriage, Cambridge, 1938. The Griffiths were probably at this time neighbours of HW's, but no mention of their house has been found.

22. Josiah Disturnell (ca 1747–1834), curate of Twickenham 1776–82 (R. S. Cobbett, *Memorials of Twickenham*, 1872, p. 126).

23. Stafford Briscoe (ca 1713–89), who had been an eminent silversmith in Cheapside and who had at Twickenham 'a neat and convenient family-house . . . the gardens of which . . . have ever been noticed by all passengers, for their remarkable neatness, and the taste in which they are laid out' (Edward Ironside, *The History and Antiquities of Twickenham*, 1797, p. 84; cf. GM 1789, lix pt ii. 1150; Cobbett, op. cit. 105).

24. Lady Caroline Campbell (1717–94), elder sister of Lady Mary Coke; m. (1) (1742) Francis Scott (ca 1721–50), styled E. of Dalkeith; m. (2) (1755) Hon. Charles Townshend (1725–67); cr. (1767) Bns of Greenwich.

25. An allusion to General Howe, who had become a Knight of the Bath 13 Oct. 1776. (*Last Journals* i. 577 and GEC).

26. (Mitford reads 'Persin'; emended by Cunningham.) Sir Richard Perryn (1723–

solicited me to invite his daughters,[27] and brought them on my sending a very civil card, and yet did not so much as write an answer or
thank me—but I really believe it was from mere stupidity. If I could
grudge your staying at Nuneham, I should regret your not being
here in such noble weather. Come however as soon as you can and
stay as long.[28]

By the rise of the stocks, and the wonderful hide-and-seek of the
fleets I suspect some treaty is brewing;[29] it cannot be so scandalous
but it will go down: and therefore it cannot be worse than the
nation deserves. If anything prevents it, it will be the declaration of
the Spanish ambassador,[30] that King Carlos[31] will never acknowledge
the independence of America till King George does, which I suppose
the latter will not do, if even the King of Monomatapa or the King of
Mechlemberg[32] will encourage him to go on—besides it is a heavenly
sight to see soldiers, and not see an enemy! and a more heavenly sight
to see a puppet-show,[33] and to lock up one's son, who is of an age to
enjoy one![34]—and yet what command of one's passions to put off a

1803), bencher of the Inner Temple, 1770; baron of the Exchequer, 1776; Kt, 1776. The Perryns' house at Twickenham was at the junction of the roads leading to Whitton and to Isleworth (R. S. Cobbett, op. cit. 97, 363; DNB).

27. Of whom the eldest was Mary (d. 1834), who m. (1788) Alexander Hatfield, and the youngest Frances, who m. (1781) John Edward Maddocks (GM 1781, li. 242; 1788, lviii pt ii. 657; R. S. Cobbett, op. cit. 97).

28. HW wrote to Lady Ossory 21 Oct. 1778, 'A fortnight ago I gave my nieces a most brilliant assembly. My whole castle was illuminated, and the palace of Armida was not more enchanting.' He explains to her that her recent affliction—the death of Lord Ossory's sister, Lady Holland—prevented him from sending her 'a considerable chapter' about his fête. That recital went to Mason instead. In his letter to Harcourt of 9 Oct. 1778 he refers only briefly to the fête.

29. 'A correspondent observes that within these few months the three per cent consol. have risen upwards of six per cent: if therefore the public funds are a true political barometer, there must be some secret negotiation for peace; and indeed the indecisive operations of the two grand

fleets [i.e. of England and France] seem to countenance this opinion' (Public Advertiser 7 Oct. 1778). The rumour seems to have been without foundation.

30. Pedro Jiménez de Góngora (d. 1794), Duque de Almodóvar del Rio; diplomatist and author; Spanish ambassador to England 1778–9 (Enciclopedia universal ilustrada, sub Jiménez; HW to Mann 27 March 1778, Mann to HW 3 July 1779).

31. Charles III (1716–88), King of Spain 1759–88.

32. HW is emphasizing England's desperate lack of allies. Monomotapa was a native empire of Eastern Africa in the Mozambique-Zambezi region. Queen Charlotte was from Mecklenburg-Strelitz, a very small grand-duchy.

33. On 28 Sept. 1778 the King and Queen set out on a visit to the camps at Winchester and Salisbury, returning to Windsor 2 Oct. Elaborate reviews were held at both camps. They are described in London Gazette 29 Sept.–3 Oct. and 3–6 Oct. 1778.

34. The Prince of Wales was at this time sixteen. 'As the public may be at a loss to account why the Prince of Wales did not attend his Majesty to the review of the camp, the following anecdote may be relied on:—The Prince of Wales and Bishop of Osnaburgh had leave to attend his

review for a christening!35—what pity gazettes-extraordinary were not in fashion, when two shillings were issued out of the exchequer to Jack of Reading, for getting on the table and making the King sport. This was in the reign of Edward II, and is only recorded in a *computus* still extant.36 Adieu.37

From Mason, February 1779

Printed from MS now WSL. The date of the note is between 11 Feb., when Admiral Keppel was acquitted of the charges brought against him by Palliser (see *ante* 25 Aug. 1778, n. 21), and 20 Feb., when Mason's verses were printed in *Public Advertiser*. Mason's mention of his 'care' of his 'child *Elfrida*' and of HW's 'thought' suggest that the note was written in London.

Address: The Honourable Horace Walpole, Arlington Street.

Ye courtly heroes who so boldly vote
To cut America's collective throat
And hope to tear her limb from limb asunder
With Johnson's,[1] Eden's and Lord Carlisle's thunder,
Your threats are vain, your very looks are fibs.
Cowards! ye quake at crackers and at squibs,[2]

Majesty, and beds ordered at Winchester for their reception; but a certain Scotch privy councillor of great weight in the cabinet, so strongly represented the danger of his Royal Highness becoming popular at this crisis of impending ruin, that our good Queen resolved to go in his stead' (*Public Advertiser* 6 Oct. 1778). The privy councillor was presumably Lord Mansfield.

35. On 8 Oct. the King and Queen stood sponsors to the new-born daughter of the Duke and Duchess of Chandos (*Public Advertiser* 10 Oct. 1778); on 9 Oct. it was announced in the *Public Advertiser* that the 'review of the camps at Warley Common and Coxheath by their Majesties, which was to have been the ensuing week, is by order of the King put off till the week after.'

36. HW's source has not been found, but T. F. Tout ('The Westminster Chronicle Attributed to Robert of Reading,' *The Collected Papers of Thomas Frederick Tout*, Manchester, 1932–4, ii. 293) speaks of two Johns of Reading attached to the

royal household in the reign of Edward II, one the king's merchant, another a purveyor of lodgings and harness for the king's horses and carts.

37. Here occurs a break in the extant correspondence until the following February. At the end of his brief entry for Oct. 1778 HW has written in his *Last Journals* (ii. 200): 'I was very ill to the end of the year.' From the beginning of November to 24 Dec. he was unable to write, though he dictated a few letters to Lady Ossory, Mann, Cole, and others. This attack of gout lasted fourteen weeks ('Short Notes,' GRAY i. 51).

———

1. Properly Johnstone's, the allusion being to the three members of the ill-fated peace commission sent to America in 1778.

2. 'Guns were discharged by the servants of some of the great lords in the Opposition, and squibs and crackers thrown plentifully by the populace' (*Last Journals* ii. 247).

Trembling lest every stone the rabble darts³
Should break the casement of your guilty hearts.

I have put your thought into careless verse;⁴ if you think it will do,
I leave you to do what you please with it⁵ for I have not a moment's
time. The care of my poor child *Elfrida* engrosses all my attention.⁶

To MASON, May 1779

Missing. See following letter.

From MASON, May 1779

Printed for the first time from MS now WSL. The approximate date is indicated
by HW's 'Short Notes' for 1779: 'At the end of May wrote a commentary and
notes to Mr Mason's later poems' (GRAY i. 51)—that is, the notes printed in
Toynbee's edition of Mason's *Satirical Poems*. An incomplete draft of the notes
is now WSL. This letter was presumably a response to a request from HW.
Address: The Honourable Mr Walpole, Arlington Street.

Monday morning.

SIR W.¹ was born in Yorkshire, went to Sweden² and from thence
to China.³ He had the order (a Swedish one)³ᵃ long before he as-

3. The houses of Palliser, Lord George Germain, and others who were regarded as Keppel's enemies were stoned after his acquittal (ibid. ii. 247–8).

4. HW's 'thought' was presumably communicated in conversation.

5. The verses, entitled 'An Epigram on the Late Rejoicings' and signed 'Squiblerus,' were printed in *Public Advertiser* 20 Feb. 1779.

6. The revised version of *Elfrida* was first presented at Covent Garden 23 Feb. 1779 and was acted five times (Genest vi. 95). Publication of the text was announced in the *Monthly Review* for March, with the comment: 'The author of *Elfrida* apparently entertains a very mean idea of the modern stage, since, in order to render his drama, as he supposes, more theatrical, he has made it infinitely less classical' (lx. 233).

1. Sir William Chambers. HW's first note on the *Heroic Epistle* begins: 'Sir William Chambers was born in Yorkshire, was

early in his life in Sweden, and afterwards in China. The Order of the Polar Star is a Swedish order often bestowed on literati and artists, and was conferred on Sir William some years before he assumed the title, which, he said, he did at the desire of King George' (Mason's *Satirical Poems* 53).

2. Chambers was born in Sweden, of Scottish ancestry, but his father had estates in Yorkshire, and he was brought to Ripon at the age of two and there educated (Thomas Hardwick, 'A Memoir of the Life of Sir William Chambers' in *A Treatise on the Decorative Part of Civil Architecture by Sir William Chambers*, revised and edited by W. H. Leeds, 1862, p. 1).

3. At the age of sixteen Chambers sailed as a supercargo in a ship of the Swedish East India Company that visited China.

3a. Mason is correcting HW's (and apparently his own) notion that the order was Polish (see *ante* 17 May 1772 and n. 6a).

sumed the title,[4] and this he said he did at the express direction or advice of his R——l patron here.[5]

For the clan of M.[6] consult Burnet in King William's time, who tells the story how they were employed in a massacre which they executed with so much cruelty[7] that the name was taken from them, and the clan unclanned. They were restored to their name, etc., by an act of Parliament about four years ago. Mr S.[8] will examine both Burnet and the Statutes for both these particulars, but I fear he won't be able to send you his notices immediately, as he is at present much engaged.

4. Chambers 'Sir-Williamized' himself the next year after receiving the Order of the Polar Star in 1771 (*ante* 9 May 1772, n. 15).

5. Before George III ascended the throne, Chambers acted as his instructor in architecture. He later became the King's private architect, and, successively, controller and surveyor-general of the Board of Works. Through the influence of the King, in 1768 Chambers was made treasurer of the newly established Royal Academy. See Hardwick, op. cit. 3–4.

6. MacGregor. Mason adopted the pseudonym of 'Malcolm MacGreggor' for his *Ode to Mr Pinchbeck* (1776), and the *Epistle to Dr Shebbeare* and *Ode to Sir Fletcher Norton* (1777). HW's first note on the 'Advertisement' to the Pinchbeck ode reads: 'As the author had in the *Heroic Postscript* ironically assumed the title of Sir W. Chambers's bard, and affected in the same tone to celebrate the King and administration, he here adopts a Scottish name, as that nation was peculiarly distinguished by the royal countenance; and calls himself MacGregor, a clan that for their infamous barbarities had been deprived of their appellation by act of Parliament in 1633. It was restored to them in 1661 for their loyalty and attachment to

the Crown; was again suppressed in 1693 on account of a horrid massacre committed by the same clan; and as George III was fond of subverting the acts of K. William, and of copying those of the Stuarts, the MacGregors were reinstated in 1776' (Mason's *Satirical Poems* 94). The reinstatement occurred in 1775, by act of 15 Geo. III, c. 29.

7. Mason apparently had in mind the massacre of Glencoe in 1692, when soldiers of the Crown slew some thirty or forty of the Macdonalds of Glencoe in spite of their submission to King William. Contrary to Mason's statement, the MacGregors were not concerned in the massacre, nor does Burnet connect them with it. The suppression of the clan in 1693 was a punishment for 'depredations and robberies' that they were alleged to have committed (*The Acts of the Parliaments of Scotland*, 1814–75, ix. 324–5; Bishop Burnet's *History of His Own Time*, ed. Sir Thomas Burnet, 1724–34, ii. 88–90; John Paget, *The New 'Examen,'* ed. W. S. Churchill, 1934, pp. 35–79; Amelia G. M. MacGregor, *History of the Clan Gregor*, 1898–1901, ii. 451–3).

8. Probably Stonhewer. If the 'notices' were sent to HW, they have not been found.

To Mason, July 1779

Missing.

From Mason, Sunday 1 August 1779

Printed from MS now WSL.
Address: The Honourable Horace Walpole, Arlington Street, London.
Postmark: ROTHERHAM 4 AU.

Aston, August 1st, 1779.

I RECEIVED your melancholy (a King's friend would call it a *croak-ing*[1]) letter, the day after my arrival here after a long journey in which I saw many places and liked a few.

I can tell you nothing, except that I am here a week longer, and then to York, where I hope to keep a regular correspondence with you, if a correspondence will be feasible. Till the 8th a letter will find me here and on the 11th at York.

I am charmed with the notes, which will answer my purpose and posterity's exactly. I do not think I shall have occasion to add above one or two.[2]

Adieu, my dear Sir, this is merely to tell you where I am and where I am going, indeed I can tell you nothing else and I fear you must be the chief informer during our next suite of correspondence.

Pray give me joy of the conclusion of my chancery suit[3] and be-lieve me

Most faithfully yours,

W. Mason

1. Probably an allusion to Dean Tucker's 'Thoughts on the Present Posture of Affairs, July 24, 1779. By the Dean of Glouces-ter,' which appeared in the *London Chron-icle* 27–9 July 1779 (xlvi. 92–3) and the *Public Advertiser* for 29 July 1779. The Dean, a 'King's friend,' calls malcontents 'croakers.'
2. There are no notes in Mason's hand in either the first or the final draft of HW's notes on Mason's satires.

3. The final decree in Mason's suit against John Murray (*ante* 26 May and 27 July 1777) was granted 13 July 1779. Murray was required to pay the costs of the suit and to give Mason £3 represent-ing the profit from his printing of the three poems by Gray of which Mason owned the copyright (chancery papers in the Public Record Office, C 33/452, pt 2, fol. 486–7: information kindly supplied by Miss N. J. M. Kerling).

WALPOLE'S HOUSE IN BERKELEY SQUARE

To Mason, Monday 9 August 1779

Printed from Mitford ii. 26–9.

Strawberry Hill, Aug. 9, 1779.

I KNOW how to wish you joy on the conclusion of a suit in chancery for I have just carried one there, and may say with truth what never could be applied before to law, *veni, vidi, vici*. My cause was commenced, heard and decided in two months, my palace in Berkeley Square is adjudged to me with costs, and the title bettered by that ordeal,[1] and so I am rejoicing, as the ministers on the arrival yesterday of the Jamaica fleet,[2] when neither I nor they know whether in two months any property may be worth sixpence. Nobody at your distance can conceive how much is at stake from total and general incapacity. Two dotards[3] are at the head of the only fleet and only army that are to decide our fate; and Lord North with that *bonhomie*, for which a child is whipped when it shouts on setting its own

1. Since the lease on HW's Arlington Street house was to expire in 1781 ('Account of My Conduct,' *Works* ii. 365), he began looking about for a new one well before that year. In the autumn of 1778 he initiated the purchase of a house in Berkeley Square that had belonged to Sir Cecil Bisshopp (d. 1778), Bt, and on 2 Nov. 1778 signed an agreement with the auctioneer to buy it for £4000 (not including the fixtures, which were 'to be taken at a fair valuation'). But there was a delay owing to a disagreement among Sir Cecil's heirs as to how they should receive and share the purchase money, and on 7 May 1779 HW entered a complaint at the Lord's Chancellor's office to which the Bisshopps were required to reply. On 21 July the Master of the Rolls heard the case and pronounced a decree in HW's favour (chancery papers in the Public Record Office; HW to Lady Ossory 24 July 1779). The house was at No. 40 (afterwards No. 11) Berkeley Square; it was torn down in 1937. HW took possession 14 Oct. 1779 (HW to Lady Ossory 14 Oct. 1779).

2. This was only part of the large and valuable fleet of merchant vessels from the West Indies whose arrival had been anxiously looked for during the past

several days. 'The account of the arrival of the Bristol share of the Jamaica fleet seems certain; it will be very happy if the rest arrives safe; I hope Lord North will defer sending the account of the rest till he can accompany it with the certainty of the news; on this occasion I am happy he did not wait for that' (the King to Lord North, *Corr. Geo. III* iv. 408–9). The fleet was safe in the Channel by 7 Aug. (*Public Advertiser* 9 Aug. 1779). According to the GM (1779, xlix. 420), the fleet that arrived at this time numbered 125 vessels.

3. Hardy and Amherst. Admiral Sir Charles Hardy, the younger (ca 1716–80), Kt, replaced Keppel as commander of the Channel fleet in March 1779. Hardy came from retirement to assume the command, no other eligible officer on the active list having been willing to accept the appointment, out of sympathy for Keppel, recently cleared of the charges brought against him by Palliser. See *Sandwich Papers* ii. 196, iii. 3–4. Jeffrey Amherst (1717–97), cr. (1776) Bn Amherst, was commander-in-chief of the army from 1778 to 1782. HW resented the fact that Amherst had been chosen instead of General Conway (*Last Journals* ii. 139).

frock on fire, cries, he expects the French every day.[5] I remember a story of General Nieberg,[6] governor of the last emperor,[7] and who lost the first battle[8] against the King of Prussia.[9] He wrote to the Queen of Hungary these words; 'Je suis faché de dire à sa Majesté que son armée est battue, et tout par la faute de son serviteur Nieberg.'[9a] The Queen who had not contributed, repaired the misfortune.

In one word I assure you I hope, though I do not believe, that the invasion will be in Ireland,[10] not England. I wish this because it would be vain to wish that Scotland were south of both. I have no ill will to poor Ireland, but Ucalegon[12] is at least one door farther off than one's own. I saw a letter but two days ago from Dublin which says there is not a shilling to pay the small army there:[13] they are hiding their plate and flocking to the capital, where there is no army to protect them.[14] London will be in the same case; is to be left to

5. HW amplifies this in his letter to Lady Ossory 7 Aug. 1779.

6. Wilhelm Reinhard (1684–1774), Graf von Neipperg; Austrian field-marshal.

7. Francis I (1708–65), Holy Roman Emperor 1748–65; husband of Maria Theresa; eldest son of Leopold, Duc de Lorraine, whom, as Francis Stephen, he succeeded in 1729 in the duchy, which he subsequently was obliged to exchange for Tuscany as part of his marriage pact. Neipperg in 1723 was made his tutor, and remained his friend throughout his life. See Constant von Wurzbach, *Biographisches Lexikon des Kaiserthums Oesterreich*, Vienna, 1856–91, *sub* Neipperg.

8. Mollwitz, in Lower Silesia, 10 April 1741.

9. Frederick II (1712–86), the Great; King of Prussia 1740–86.

9a. HW had apparently seen a French account of Neipperg's letter of 23 April 1741 to Maria Theresa (printed in *Mitteilungen des K. K. Kriegs-Archivs*, n. s., ii, 1888). In the course of a lengthy apology Neipperg admitted that his own inexperience ('meine Unerfahrenheit') was largely responsible for the defeat at Mollwitz (p. 204).

10. Lord North wrote the King ca 30 July 1779 that he thought the French 'intention to invade that Kingdom [Ireland]

very probable, and he has no doubt but they will accompany their invasion with an offer of independency, liberty of religion, and freedom of trade' (*Corr. Geo. III* iv. 402).

12. 'Iam proximus ardet
Ucalegon' ('Already neighbour Ucalegon burns')
(Virgil, *Æneid* ii. 311).

13. 'Lord North has the honour of sending to his Majesty a packet of accounts which he has received from the Lord-Lieutenant in consequence of applications from hence; by which accounts it appears that the Treasury of Ireland is at present very low indeed, and by an abstract made from all the accounts it appears that if all their payments in that kingdom are strictly and without a single exception confined to such military service as cannot be postponed, there will probably be a deficiency of about £27,000 Irish or £25,000 English' (Lord North to the King ca 30 July 1779, *Corr. Geo. III* iv. 401–2).

14. For an account of the defenceless state of Ireland at this time, except for volunteer companies, see Hist. MSS Comm., 12th Report, App. x (Charlemont MSS), 1891, p. 50; Francis Dobbs, *A History of Irish Affairs, from the 12th of October 1779 to the 15th September 1782*, Dublin, 1782, p. 9; *post* 21 Oct. 1779.

old vain Northumberland[15] and his constables, when the emperor of America[16] takes the field with all his guards. Lord Amherst in the mean time has begun works at Chatham, that cannot be finished in ten years,[17] and then will be commanded by all the hills around:[18] I could tell you forty parallel anecdotes, which if they do not terminate in total destruction, will never be believed, though every step of the last five years have marched towards them. Russia, Sweden, Denmark, Holland, fold their arms and cry, we have insulted them all so much, that they must sit still till we are humbled. *That will happen,* we shall take a panic at once, and sign anything; or on the first unexpected and indecisive success flounder on in obstinacy. This reduces one barely to wish for favourable events, with the reversion of chance; for one knows not what to wish coolly. Fortune can scarce dovetail good and bad circumstances so as to repair and strengthen the country and constitution; which if not restored together, the former will at best but languish and never revive; but it is in vain to skim one's thoughts, they boil over, and it is as well to finish now as write on. I will talk as if I did not see further than, I was going to say, most of those who have conducted us to the precipice, but some of them, believe me, are soundly alarmed. They do see at last that a bribe in hand was not worth two estates in the bush. Well! *parlons comme si de rien n'etait.*

I was lately at Beddington[19] and saw there a print I never met with

15. Hugh Smithson (later Percy) (ca 1714–86), 2d E. of Northumberland, 1750; cr. (1766) D. of Northumberland; Lord Lieutenant of Northumberland, 1753–86, and of Middlesex, 1762–86; Master of the Horse 1778–80. Northumberland was active in forming volunteer companies in Middlesex and promoted a plan of instructing citizens in the use of arms. See *London Chronicle* 13–15, 17–20, and 22–4 July 1779, xlvi. 42–3, 59, 78; *Public Advertiser* 10 and 13 Aug. 1779; *Corr. Geo. III* iv. 392. When Northumberland became Master of the Horse in 1778, HW remarked on his pride and vanity: 'The Duke of Northumberland, in imitation of his wife's grandfather, Charles, the proud Duke of Somerset, intended not to use the King's liveries but when waiting on his Majesty; but the King insisted on his always using them' (*Last Journals* ii. 212).

16. George III.

17. Presumably designed to be part of the 'Chatham lines,' the series of fortifications around the dockyards and military edifices, begun in 1758 and not finished until 1807 (*Murray's Handbook for Travellers in Kent and Sussex*, 1858, p. 47). A redoubt on the summit of the hill at the south-east extremity of the lines was known as 'Amherst's Redoubt' (W. H. Ireland, *England's Topographer, or a New and Complete History of the County of Kent*, 1828–30, iv. 352).

18. The northern boundary of the parish of Chatham is the Medway river, 'near which in the vale, the town of Chatham and the dockyard are situated, whence the chalk hills rise suddenly on all sides' (ibid. iv. 346).

19. In Surrey. An account of Beddington Manor and its owners, the Carew fam-

before. It is a mezzotint of a Sir Nicholas Carew,[20] who lived temp. Geo. I, and never did anything but sit for that print,[21] yet you know how inestimable an unique print—which however is not unique, is to a collector. There are at least five more in the house, and perhaps the plate,[22] or I should not be so audacious as to beg one. In short I should be greatly obliged to Mr Fountaine[23] if he would give me one. An attorney[24] lives in the mansion, who might be ordered to deliver one to Mr Thomas Walpole,[25] who lives at Carshalton, not two miles from Beddington. They are all framed and glazed. I do not want their accompaniments[26] nor the print much, if pasted on cloth, though I would deign to accept one so, if no other is to be obtained.[27] Adieu! I have survived many dark moments, and think, I do not know by what luck, that you and I shall still meet again and pass some agreeable hours. When one reasons, one has few hopes; but a superstitious confidence always carries me to incline to expect that things will end to please me; and as I have found that my star knows much better than I do what is best for me, I commend myself to it, and beg it will mend the scene, as it did after the conquest of New York.[28]

ily, is given in E. W. Brayley, *A Topographical History of Surrey*, 1850, iv. 51–6. See also HW to Lady Ossory 14 July 1779.

20. Sir Nicholas Carew (1687–1727), cr. (1715) Bt; M. P. Haslemere 1708–10 and 1714–22, Surrey 1722–7 (GEC, *Complete Baronetage* v. 26).

21. Which was by John Faber, Jr, 1723. It is described in John Chaloner Smith, *British Mezzotinto Portraits*, 1883, i. 321, where it is stated that only one copy of the print was known, presumably HW's copy, which was sold London 495. However two copies of the print appeared in two sales of Smith's prints: Sotheby's 24 March 1887, lot 648, and 3 Feb. 1896, lot 52.

22. HW was right. See *post* 21 Aug. 1779. HW was particularly anxious to have the print because an earlier Nicholas Carew was one of his ancestors. See HW to Lady Ossory 14 July 1779.

23. Dr John Fountayne (1714–1802), Dean of York (see *ante* 9 Sept. 1772, n. 3), nephew through his mother, Elizabeth

Carew, of Sir Nicholas Carew (Joseph Foster, *Pedigrees of Yorkshire Families*, 1874, ii *sub* Wilson of Leeds). Fountayne's cousin, Sir Nicholas Hacket Carew (ca 1716–62), in his will devised all his estates, which ultimately included Beddington, 'to devolve on the eldest and other sons of his cousin, Dr John Fountain, Dean of York, in tail-male' (Brayley, op. cit. iv. 56).

24. Presumably William Pellatt, who was living in 1797 (Brayley, loc. cit.; GM 1797, lxvii pt i. 174).

25. HW's cousin, the banker. HW had dined with him at Carshalton in July (HW to Lady Ossory 14 July 1779).

26. I.e., the glass and frame.

27. Mason's successful embassy is reported *post* 21 Aug. 1779.

28. A revival of confidence followed the English victories at Long Island and New York in August and September 1776. For HW's comments see *Last Journals* i. 574–6, 587.

To Mason, Wednesday 18 August 1779

Printed from Mitford ii. 29–31.

Strawberry Hill, Wednesday night late, August 18, 1779.

ALL is true that you will see in the papers of the *Marlborough*, *Isis* and *Southampton* being chased by the French and Spanish fleets of 60 or 63 sail, as the former were going to join Sir Charles Hardy.[1] Today came another express that the united squadron was off Falmouth on Saturday.[2] They are probably come to seek and fight our fleet, which if not joined by those three ships consists of but thirty-six,[3]—on whom depends our fate!

I could give you details of unreadiness at home that would shock you, miracles alone can counteract it, and them have we merited? If Hardy does not vanquish to deletion of the enemy, shall we be bettered? if he does, will foolhardiness be corrected by success? turn whither you will, whence is salvation to come to a nation so besotted? I will give you a sample of what the victors would reserve for those they deem their worst enemies, the friends of their country. The

1. 'Late on Monday [16 Aug.] evening Sir Jacob Wheat, first lieutenant of his Majesty's ship the *Marlborough*, arrived express at the Admiralty office, with an account that early on Saturday morning last, the *Marlborough*, on her way to join Sir Charles Hardy, saw a large fleet, much to the southward of Scilly, which the captain imagining to be the French and Spanish squadrons, he sailed as near them as he prudently could, in order to ascertain what and who they were. As soon as they espied him, a signal was given to chase. . . . The French ship which gave chase was accompanied by four others, and the *Marlborough*, being at that time joined by the *Isis*, *Southampton*, and *Cormorant* [a sloop], made the best of her way back. . . . The commander of the *Marlborough* dispatched his first lieutenant to Plymouth in the *Cormorant* with the news, and sailed onward with the *Marlborough*, *Isis*, and *Southampton*, in order to reinforce Sir Charles Hardy . . . The captain of the *Marlborough* in his dispatch sent word, that as near as he could ascertain,

the number of the combined fleets of France and Spain was 60 sail' (*London Chronicle* 17–19 Aug. 1779, xlvi. 162). The *Public Advertiser* (18 Aug. 1779) reported the enemy's fleet to consist of 63 ships of the line. Actually it numbered 66 (Georges Lacour-Gayet, *La Campagne navale de La Manche en 1779*, 1901, p. 23).

2. According to a letter from Falmouth dated 16 Aug., printed in the *London Chronicle* 19–21 Aug. (xlvi. 176), the fleet first appeared off Falmouth at noon on Sunday 15 Aug. The object of the combined fleets was to cover an invasion from Havre and St Malo, but sickness, lack of provisions, and various mischances brought about an abandonment of the plan (*Sandwich Papers* iii. 6–7; Lacour-Gayet, op. cit. 23–5).

3. This agrees substantially with the published line of battle of the English fleet (*London Chronicle* 17–19 Aug., xlvi. 168; *Lloyd's Evening Post* 18–20 Aug. 1779, xlv. 174), which listed 37 ships of the line, including the *Marlborough* but not the *Isis* or *Southampton*.

Bishop of Oxford,[4] once a writer in patriot opposition,[5] wrote t'other day to his friend and patron my brother,[6] that Lord Harcourt had invited him to dinner, treated him most benignantly, and not mentioned a word of politics; 'surely,' added the meek apostle, 'if there were a toleration of patriots, Lord Harcourt would be entitled to the benefit of it'[7]—That is St Dominic[8] would not cut his host's throat, if the Holy Office[9] ever pardoned, but it does not; and Lord Harcourt must die though he has banqueted a bishop.

It is such wretches and their blundering politics, that in nineteen years have changed a glorious empire into a wide heap of ruins. Amidst these calamities and public woes, I am trembling for Mr Conway, who is chained to a rock.[10] I am anxious about the Duke of Richmond, who is exiled to Exeter,[11] and may be exposed to the first descent with a handful of men, but

God and good angels fight on Richmond's side.[12]

His virtues shine the brighter from the cloud of filth that is thrown on them, and a nation cannot be destroyed without its being remembered who would have saved it. History may flatter contemporaries, but as the dead have no places, no pensions to bestow, truth revives

4. John Butler (1717–1802), D.C.L., Bp of Oxford 1777–88, of Hereford 1788–1802.

5. In his *Address to the Cocoa-Tree, from a Whig*, 1762, Butler attacked Bute and the conduct of the ministry after the accession of George III, but during the American war he transferred his political allegiance to the Court and published a number of pamphlets, signed 'Vindex,' on behalf of the administration. He was rewarded for his services by the bishopric of Oxford.

6. Sir Edward Walpole, who had asked HW to recommend Butler to Lord Hertford, the Lord Chamberlain, for a King's chaplaincy. See COLE ii. 283 and *Last Journals* i. 103.

7. HW repeated this story in a letter to Harcourt, Oct. 1779.

8. St Dominic (ca 1170–1221), founder (1216) of the Order of Preachers (Dominicans) that opposed heresy. The conduct of the various courts of the Inquisition was largely committed to Dominican friars.

9. The Inquisition (OED *sub* 'office' 8d).

10. Jersey, of which Conway was governor 1772–95. Early in May 1779 Conway went there upon reports that an attack on it was being planned by France. An unsuccessful attack took place before his arrival. See HW to Mann 9 May 1779. Conway remained there until Nov. 1779, organizing defences (HW to Mann 31 Oct., to Lady Ossory 21 Nov. 1779).

11. HW apparently suspected malice in the assignment of Richmond's Sussex militia to Exeter. Richmond had recently been outspokenly critical of the defence plans of the King and Lord Amherst, and had expressed an unwillingness to regard them as orders that should be obeyed (*London Chronicle* 31 July–3 Aug., xlvi. 106). The King was anxious to remove Richmond from his Lord-Lieutenancy (*Corr. Geo. III* iv. 407–8 and 418), but Richmond retained it. In a public address at Lewes on 26 Aug. Richmond expressed his resentment over the sending of his militia out of its own county (*Lloyd's Evening Post* 30 Aug.–1 Sept. 1779, xlv. 212).

12. *Richard III*, V. iii. 176.

the moment its enemies are in the grave, and then the bones of the *ultimi Anglorum* will be selected and enshrined by poor weeping posterity. You see I am seeking consolation among the relics of my few friends; cold comfort, a vision of honorary tribute to be paid to the ashes of heroes in a little northern island, that has no pride to live on but the memory of virtuous patriots! Those of happier days will be remembered too! and my father's favourite sentence of *quieta non movere* will appear to have been replete with as much wisdom as Lord Mansfield's schoolboy quotation of the Rubicon being passed.[13] Adieu.

From Mason, Saturday 21 August 1779

Printed from MS now WSL.
Address: The Honourable Horace Walpole, Arlington Street, London.
Postmark: YORK 23 AU.

York, August 21st, 1779.

Dear Sir,

I HAVE procured you a Sir Nicholas Carey of the Dean of York,[1] as good an impression, I believe, as the plate was capable of giving and ready for a *portfeuille,* having no canvas to incommode you at your next print shearing. I will send it rolled on a stick by the first person I hear of going to town.[2]

By the papers of the two last posts I am led to expect something has been already done which will decide whether poor England is mistress of the seas or no.[3] I wait a line from you with impatience, for I know you don't stand on the punctilio of letter for letter, which to me, who have no news to pay with, would be worse than the posting tax.[4] I hope however this ensuing race week, and Lord John Cavendish's company whom I expect today, may make my next more worth postage; in the mean time thanking you for all your favours, I rest, or rather sleep,

Sincerely yours,

W. Mason

13. See *ante* 18 July 1778, n. 10.

1. See *ante* 9 Aug. 1779.

2. Mason ultimately sent the print by coach (*post* 14 Sept. 1779).
3. There were false reports of an en-

To MASON, Monday 23 August 1779

Printed from Mitford ii. 32–3.

Arlington Street, Aug. 23, at night.

YOU may think what you please, but I am grieved to say that even more than the empire of the seas is at stake! At present the combined fleets are gone or blown from Plymouth,[1] and the bells at Richmond rang last night as if they were gone to the bottom. The only conclusion to be drawn at this moment is, that they will fight Sir Charles Hardy before their embarkation takes place. By what I see much is to be apprehended from so little being apprehended, and from the unaccountable intentions of a landing. You would[2] scarce believe half I could tell you. I did indeed this morning as I came to town, meet thirty-six carriages with ammunition going to the west,[3] not post, and yesterday they worked all day at the Tower,[4] though Sunday. Is it pleasant to know that the fate of one's country may be decided in few weeks? My opinion is that the enemies will strike in every place they can. They threaten Minorca,[5] and the French minister at Florence[6] sent an order to the Great Duke[7] by his *valet de chambre*

gagement either being fought or about to be fought between the English fleet and the combined fleets of France and Spain. See *London Chronicle* 19–21 Aug. 1779 (xlvi. 171) for a collection of rumours.

4. A new and unpopular tax on the use of post-horses had recently been imposed (*Public Advertiser* 2 July 1779; HW to Lady Ossory 6 July 1779).

1. 'On Sunday [22 Aug.] an express arrived from Vice-Admiral Shuldham, at Plymouth: the particulars which have transpired are, that the united fleets of France and Spain, after having continued within a few leagues of Plymouth for several days, had suddenly disappeared on Wednesday the 18th' (*London Chronicle* 21–4 Aug. 1779, xlvi. 182).

2. Mitford reads unintelligibly, 'unaccountable intentions of a landing takes place, you would' etc. Cunningham and Toynbee omit all the words between 'apprehended' and 'you would.'

3. 'Yesterday morning early, thirty thousand stand of arms were sent off from the

Tower in wagons, as is said to arm the tinners in Cornwall' (*Public Advertiser* 24 Aug. 1779). According to the *London Chronicle* 21–4 Aug. 1778 (xlvi. 183) the wagons in the train numbered 40.

4. 'A large train of artillery is now getting ready at the Tower, to be in readiness to be sent to any part of the kingdom on the first notice' (*Lloyd's Evening Post* 23–5 Aug. 1779, xlv. 185).

5. 'They write from Toulon, that it is now generally known that the fitting out of the squadron at that port . . . has for its object the conquest of Minorca, in conjunction with some Spanish forces from Malaga and Barcelona; which business they expect to be ready to commence the beginning of September' (*Public Advertiser* 20 Aug. 1779). See Mann to HW 7 Aug. 1779. The recovery of Minorca, captured by England in 1708, was one of Spain's objectives in this conflict, and was achieved in 1782.

6. Joseph-Pierre-Balthazar-Hilaire de Puget (1727–ca 1800), Marquis de Barbantane; envoy from the court of France to the

not to admit English vessels into Leghorn,[8] and it is supposed a like message has been delivered at Naples, though perhaps in a more decent manner.

You will see in the papers Lord Sandwich's incredulity of Sir Jacob Wheate's account[9] of the combined fleets; when he gave the same relation to Neptune[10] himself and happened to say, they were superior to ours, the quick answer was, 'Oh, yes, I suppose they have four or five ships more.'

I have not time nor disposition to write more; even now I have written affectedly, for I have suppressed the various kinds of indignation I feel, and I cannot write long to you unnaturally, yet it is below a man to rail, when England totters to its foundations. Disgraced it is forever! in what piteous condition it may emerge I know not—if it does emerge—if it does not, happy they who do not live to see its utter destruction.

Yours to the last,

H. WALPOLE

Grand Duke of Tuscany, 1766–84 (*Recueil des instructions données aux ambassadeurs et ministres de France,* vol. xix, 1912, p. 146).

7. Leopold II (1747–92), Grand Duke of Tuscany 1765–90, Holy Roman Emperor 1790–2.

8. 'Monsieur de Billeraye, lately Marquis de Barbantane's *valet de chambre* whom he left here when he went to France, to take care of his letters, received by the last French courier some copies of the French king's manifest, which he distributed to many people. The same person last Sunday delivered a paper to the Secretary of State to the following purpose: that the Court of Versailles having determined to besiege Minorca at the same time that the Spaniards besieged Gibraltar, the English would consequently have no other port in the Mediterranean to resort to, but that of Leghorne. His most Christian Majesty therefore insisted that

the Great Duke, notwithstanding his neutrality, should positively refuse admission in that port to all British ships and vessels, otherwise he would send a fleet thither to block up Leghorne' (MS letter of Sir Horace Mann to Lord Weymouth, 3 Aug. 1779, in Public Record Office, State Papers 98, Tuscany, vol. 82 fol. 384–5.)

9. Sir Jacob Wheate (ca 1746–83), 5th Bt, 1760; naval officer; Lt, 1765; Commander, 1779. When dispatched to the Admiralty with intelligence of the enemy he was serving as Lieutenant on the *Marlborough.* See *ante* 18 Aug. 1779. HW is apparently alluding to a charge made against Sandwich in an open letter to him published in the *Public Advertiser* for 23 Aug., signed 'Unanimous'; but Sandwich's letter of 17 Aug. to the King shows that he accepted Wheate's report (*Corr. Geo. III* iv. 411).

10. The King.

To Mason, Sunday 5 September 1779

Printed from Mitford ii. 34–5.

Strawberry Hill, Sep. 5, 1779.

WHAT can I write when I know nothing, and believe little that I hear? Winds and naval manœuvres I do not understand. Everybody contradicts everybody, and each new moment the last. Last week the enemies were between our coast and our fleet,[1] and that was bad. Now our fleet is at Portsmouth,[2] and the enemies nobody know[s] where, and this is bad. Sum total—we are in a very bad condition, where nothing mends it; it is lucky for you that I cannot crowd my thoughts into a letter, nor can choose to which to give the preference. It is almost insupportable to see England fallen so low. Fallen! it dashed itself down—no laws of gravitation could have thrown it so low in a century. It *would* strip itself of men, arms, wealth, fleets, to conquer what it possessed. It would force its friends to be its foes, that it might plunder them and prevent their continuing to enrich it, and then when a neutral power[3] much more inclined to peace than war, would have extinguished the conflagration—bounce! you may be our enemy too if you please. There!

There's room for meditation even to madness! I am very far from well in body too. All the summer I have been tormented off and on with the gout in one of my eyes, which is now quite removed, but in the garb of rheumatism has fallen on my hip,[4] and confines me to my house, so that I am a chaos of moral reflections. I am trying to extract an elixir of resignation, but as Cato and Brutus themselves allow one not to be perfectly philosophic, that is, indifferent to the ruin of one's

1. On 2 Sept. 1779 Sandwich wrote to Hardy: 'I am made very happy by finding that you are got within the enemy's fleet' (*Sandwich Papers* iii. 88).

2. 'On Friday afternoon [3 Sept.] Sir Charles Hardy arrived off the Isle of Wight with the fleet under his command, and dropped anchor at Spithead' (*London Chronicle* 4–7 Sept. 1779, xlvi. 226).

3. Spain. Even before hostilities with France broke out, Spain tried to bargain with England, offering neutrality in exchange for Gibraltar. When war with France began, Spain persistently offered to mediate, her object continuing to be the recovery of Gibraltar. See Samuel Flagg Bemis, *The Diplomacy of the American Revolution*, New York, 1935, p. 78.

4. The 18th century's discrimination between gout and rheumatism seems to have been Cotton Mather's, that rheumatism was 'gout's younger brother' (Otho T. Beall and Richard H. Shryock, *Cotton Mather, First Significant Figure in American Medicine*, Baltimore, 1954, p. 128). Rheumatism was 'nearly akin to the gout' (*Encyclopædia Britannica*, Edinburgh, 1773, iii. 124, *sub* 'Medicine'), as Johnson's *Dictionary*, 1755, also suggests.

country, I am in a very Christian mood about personal sufferings, but cannot find a text in the New Testament that bids me not care what becomes of England when I am gone; unless silence gives consent. Adieu!

Yours most cordially,

H. Walpole

To Mason, Tuesday 14 September 1779

Printed from Mitford ii. 35–7.

Strawberry Hill, Sep. 14, 1779.

I RECEIVED the print of Sir Nicholas[1] last night by the coach, and thank you kindly.

I have not written very lately for two reasons. When disgrace arrives from every quarter, from east, west, south, what is to be said? secondly, I have been very ill, and have now only the use of one hand. First I had a disorder in my bowels, then an inflammation on my hip which ended in the gout in my elbow, knee and left hand. The two first went off so very quick, that I flattered myself the whole would—now I am hoping I shall be quit for one hand which is tolerably bad indeed. In one word and without deluding myself, but for the moment, it is evident that my constitution is extremely impaired, and presents but a melancholy prospect for the rest of my life, which my increasing weakness will not probably allow to be long. Life, which I liked as well as most men, was indeed never less *aimable*. To linger on in illness were a pitiful wish to form, and to outlive the prosperity and glory of one's country were meaner still to wish. Wishing in fact decides nothing, and it is silly to say anything about it, but, when the cast of one's mind is forced on those reflections, one is a very disagreeable correspondent.

That *ignis fatuus* of a brighter period, Lord Temple is dead. He was thrown out of a chaise on a heap of bricks, fractured his skull, was trepanned and died.[2]

My indisposition will prevent my visit to Nuneham this month,

1. Sir Nicholas Carew (*ante* 9 Aug. 1779).

2. 11 Sept. 1779 (*Public Advertiser* 14 Sept.). There is a circumstantial account of his death in the *London Chronicle* 14–16 Sept., xlvi. 263.

which I had promised. I shall take care how I promise unless what I should not be sorry to be hindered from executing.

It is ridiculous in gouty sixty-two to make engagements, or undertake a journey, when at least one ought to put into one's chaise, a crutch, an hour-glass and a death's head. My heart to the last will hover about Nuneham, as one of the few spots it still dearly loves, for its own beauties and its excellent possessors. I can frame visions of how happy, how delighted I should have been, had they enjoyed it some years ago, when you, more Orpheus than Orpheus himself, would have made the groves dance after your lyre and pencil, and rendered it what we fancy Penshurst[3] was, but was not,[4] and would have found a Sacharissa congenial to her Waller.[5] I should have been proud to have been pursuivant to the house of Harcourt, and—but adieu visions, I must form no more, and what is the theatre on which any man could form them now! Oh, what a weight of lead is the ruin of one's country.

From Mason, Saturday 18 September 1779

Printed from MS now WSL.
Address: The Honourable Horace Walpole, Arlington Street, London.
Postmark: YORK 20 SE.

York, Sept. 18th, 1779.

Dear Sir,

I AM very sorry to find that your old enemy the gout has attacked you so early in the year, the winter was usually the time for his campaigns. I wish he may behave like the French and run away from you after he has just threatened what he is able to do with you.[1] Am not I a true prophet with respect to these said French? Did not I

---

3. Penshurst Place, Kent, famous for its connection with the Sidney family, into whose possession it came by grant of Edward VI. Sir Philip and Algernon Sidney were born there.

4. 'This morning we have been to Penshurst—but oh! how fallen! The park seems to have never answered its character' (HW to Bentley 5 Aug. 1752).

5. Penshurst's beauties were celebrated by Edmund Waller (1606–87); see HW to Cole 11 Nov. 1780 (COLE ii. 240 and n. 16).

Some of Waller's best-known lyrics are in praise of 'Sacharissa,' Lady Dorothy Sydney (1617–84), who married (1) (1639) Henry Spencer, 1st E. of Sunderland, and (2) (1652) Robert Smythe. HW is of course referring here to Lady Harcourt.

1. The combined fleets of France and Spain had sailed away from Plymouth without striking a blow. See *ante* 21 and 23 Aug. 1779.

say they would prove our superiors in folly? and have they not done so? But they have disgraced us and robbed us of our naval honour; that is a matter we are too wise to regard. We are like Palgrave's old uncle who on asking his neighbour why he parted beds with his wife and was told it was because she stank, 'Pshaw,' said the old man, 'I would never mind a little stink.' Is not this a good story and is it not well applied?

As to myself, though tolerably well in health, I have not spirits enough in this dull place to do anything to the various unfinished things which I ought to finish, and therefore I have taken up your trade of book-making and have interleaved our old church anthem-book, in order to write little anecdotes about the composers out of the *opus magnum* of your friend Sir John Hawkins.[2] Don't abuse me. You have taken painting anecdotes to yourself, pray let me deal in musical ones. Dr Johnson, you know, has all poetical ones in fee simple,[3] therefore I have nothing left me of the liberal arts but music, and that I will make the most of, and as Lord Orrery said that you could throw spirit into a catalogue[4] I shall aim at as arduous a thing and endeavour to throw spirit into an anthem-book.

I forget whether I told you in my last that this ancient city is at present honoured with the company of Anti-Sejanus.[5] By pushing the *jus divinum* of tithes a little too far with his parishioners at Simon-burne[6] they have made the place too hot to hold him,[7] and therefore

2. See *ante* 29 Feb. 1776. This was the beginning of a work on church music which Mason published in 1782. See *post* 24 Feb. 1782 and n. 6.

3. The first four volumes of Johnson's *Prefaces* (*Lives of the Poets*) had appeared late in the preceding March (Boswell, *Johnson* iii. 380 n. 3).

4. At the beginning of his edition of the *Life of Monmouth* Orrery refers to HW as 'an honourable author, who in a just piece of criticism has exhibited so spirited a manner of writing, that he has given wit even to a dictionary, and vivacity to a catalogue of names, and has placed our royal and noble English writers in a more learned and eminent light than they have ever appeared before' (*Memoirs of the Life of Robert Cary . . . Earl of Monmouth,* ed. John, Earl of Corke and Orrery, 1759, p. i).

5. James Scott (1733–1814), D.D., divine and political writer. In 1765, under the patronage of Lord Sandwich, he wrote a series of letters against Lord Bute, published in the *Public Advertiser* under the signature 'Anti-Sejanus.' 'These letters unfortunately were never collected; but many of them were published in 1767, in a work called *A Collection of Interesting Letters.* His intention in writing them was not so much to serve a party, as to expose the mischief of favouritism. He chose therefore the signature of Anti-Sejanus, Sejanus having been the great favourite of Tiberius, who advanced him to the highest situation in government' (Nichols, *Lit. Anec.* ix. 725). See *Mem. Geo. III* ii. 191.

6. Scott was presented to the rectory of Simonburn in Northumberland in 1771, through the influence of Lord Sandwich. 'It was Dr Scott's misfortune to succeed

he has flung himself into York in imitation of the Royal Martyr.[8]
Who knows but there may be a time when his patron[9] or even his
patron's patron[10] may follow his example. However let them come
as soon as they please. I can tell them they must expect no favour from
Anti-Sejanus. He will arm every coffee-house in the city against them,
for he already abuses them like fury.[11] This however I have only from
hearsay, for I have the prudence to keep out of his way, lest I also
should be abused because I was once a courtier and a King's chaplain.[12]

I hope in your next to hear a better account of your health, which
I am more earnest to hear than of a better account of my country,
because the former is within the lines of possibility and the other
not. Adieu, my dear Sir, and believe me to be ever

Most truly yours,

W. MAS⟨ON⟩

To MASON, Tuesday 28 September 1779

Printed from Mitford ii. 39–40.

Strawberry Hill, Sept. 28, 1779.

THOUGH I am vexed at your lying fallow, I know not how to reprove it. With what spirit could an African Homer have finished
an Hannibaliad when *delenda esset Carthago?* Horace and Virgil

a clergyman [Henry Wastell] who was so
totally negligent of his temporal affairs,
that although he had held the living upwards of 52 years, it produced less to him
at his decease, than it did at his induction.
A number of surreptitious moduses [mone-
tary payments in lieu of tithes] had crept
in . . . and the parishioners had been so
accustomed to pay to the rector just what
they pleased, that they looked upon his
[Scott's] demands as oppressive and illegal;
they therefore threatened him that they
would lay all their corn-lands down with
grass, if he would not take what they were
disposed to give him for their tithes' (Nichols, *Lit. Anec.* ix. 726–7; cf. *A History of
Northumberland,* vol. xv, ed. Madeleine H.
Dodds, Newcastle, 1940, p. 189). Scott filed
a bill in the court of Exchequer to sub-
stantiate his claim. The litigation was
destined to go on 'for more than 20 years,

at the expense of more than £10,000'
(Nichols, *Lit. Anec.* ix. 727).
7. 'Dr Scott was, as may be supposed,
pursued with the utmost rancour and
malevolence during his litigation with his
parishioners; all which he bore with the
utmost composure, until a desperate attempt was made upon his life' (ibid.). He
later removed to London, where he remained until his death (Dodds, loc. cit.).
8. Charles I, who established his court
at York in 1642.
9. 'Lord Sandwich' (HW's interlinear
note).
10. The King.
11. 'He [Scott] had promises in abundance from Lord North, but they were none
of them fulfilled' (Nichols, *Lit. Anec.* ix.
726).
12. 1757–72. See *ante* 17 May 1772.

could prank away because they shared in the spoils of their country, yet you might imitate a worthier Roman, and instead of turning your harp into a harpsichord,[1] you might like Tully, write *de finibus bonorum et malorum*,[2] if the latter should meet their deserts; one would think it likely, when Anti-Sejanus begins to demolish the statues of Sejanus.[3]

I am sorry Paul Jones[4] has exchanged *the Friths*[5] for the coasts of Yorkshire[6] for both reasons.[7]

America is again to be conquered, Sir George Collier[8] having, like the man-mountain Gulliver, destroyed the whole naval force of the colonies at Penobscot,[9] which being a famous port, of which I had never heard, I suppose is the Plymouth of Blefuscu.[10] There is a post

1. HW uses this phrase in a letter to Nuneham 17 July 1773, where he connects it with Roderick O'Connor, presumably the 12th-century Irish king who in 1175 acknowledged Henry II, King of England, as his liege lord, thus 'turning his harp into a harpsichord.'

2. Cicero's ethical treatise *On the Ends of the Good and the Evil*.

3. That is, Sandwich.

4. John Paul Jones (1747–92), American naval hero, who had harried the coast of Scotland in the spring of 1778 (Don C. Seitz, *Paul Jones: His Exploits in English Seas during 1778–1780*, New York, [1917], pp. 3–25). As a result of his success Jones went to Brest to solicit a larger ship. After many disappointments, with the help of Benjamin Franklin he obtained a French vessel, which he renamed the *Bonhomme Richard*. With this and a small squadron he sailed from Groix Roads, near L'Orient, on 14 Aug. 1779 on a cruise around the British Isles which considerably augmented his fame. By the middle of October he was off the east coast of Scotland, sailed up the Firth of Forth to Leith, thereby causing great excitement, but turned back without doing damage. See Gardner W. Allen, *A Naval History of the American Revolution*, Boston, 1913, ii. 439–88.

5. A not uncommon variant of 'Firths.'

6. 'Extract of a letter from Newcastle, Sept. 25. "The little squadron commanded by Paul Jones, after leaving the Firth of Forth, directed its course along the coast southward, and excited no small fears in the inhabitants along-shore as they

passed"' (*London Chronicle* 25–8 Sept. 1779, xlvi. 304). On 23 Sept. Jones fell in with a fleet of merchantmen escorted by two British ships of war, the *Serapis* and the *Countess of Scarborough*. The merchant vessels escaped, but a battle ensued between Jones's ships and the British escorts in which Jones was the victor. His *Bonhomme Richard* being damaged, he allowed it to sink and completed his cruise in the *Serapis* (Allen, op. cit. ii. 456–80; Seitz, op. cit. 41–58).

7. That is, HW would be sorry to see Yorkshire attacked, but thought that Scotland deserved it.

8. Sir George Collier (1738–95), Kt, 1775; Commander, 1761, Rear-Adm., 1793, Vice-Adm., 1794. From March to Sept. 1779 he was acting commander-in-chief while awaiting the arrival of Vice-Admiral Arbuthnot, appointed in February to succeed Vice-Admiral Gambier. See *Sandwich Papers* iii. 119–21.

9. On 19 July 1779 a naval expedition sailed from Massachusetts against a British post in Penobscot Bay, Maine. The squadron, consisting of nineteen vessels, was pursued by Collier, and the colonists abandoned their ships and destroyed them to prevent their falling into his hands. See Allen, op. cit. ii. 419–38. Collier's account of his victory appeared in the *London Gazette Extraordinary* 24 Sept. 1779.

10. The island empire 'situated to the north-north-east side of Lilliput,' whose fleet Gulliver captured single-handed (*Gulliver's Travels*, Pt I, Chap. v).

however lost of great consequence, but if the *Gazette* does not own its importance, nobody will mind it.[11]

When do you look southward? I am removing into my new house[12] and am much pleased with it; of myself I can only say that for these two days I have mended. I am taking the bark, and think it is of service, but I have more ground to recover than is likely at sixty-two and with so weak and shattered a frame, though the foundation is so strangely strong.

They are still writing *éloges* and verses on Voltaire at Paris, which would not be worth telling you, but as it has occasioned an admirable *bon mot* of Madame du Deffand; she said that Voltaire *subissait le sort des mortels, d'être après leur mort la pâture des vers*.[13] There is no adding anything to this, but that I wish you were here.

To Mason, Thursday 21 October 1779

Printed from Mitford ii. 40–1.

Berkeley Square, Oct. 21, 1779.

PERHAPS you have been expecting that the combined fleets would take Ireland[1]—perhaps they may, though not so easy, when a nation knows how to assert its rights;[2] but in the mean time the Irish have chosen to take their kingdom into their own hands. They have twenty-eight thousand men in arms,[3] *a committee* of whom attended

---

11. HW possibly alludes to Grenada, taken by the French 4 July 1779. 'The loss of Grenada will be more severely felt here than if all the Leeward Islands were taken, the fee-simple or proprietary of this island being mostly in London merchants' (*Public Advertiser* 27 Sept. 1779). The loss of Grenada had been recorded in the *London Gazette* 18–21 Sept. 1779, but without comment on its seriousness.

12. In Berkeley Square.

13. In Mme du Deffand to HW 18 Sept. 1779, DU DEFFAND v. 175.

---

1. HW had written Mann on 11 Oct.: 'In my own opinion, the principal effort will be against Ireland.'

2. Buckingham, the Lord Lieutenant of Ireland, opening the Irish Parliament on 12 Oct. promised that 'his Majesty will

most cheerfully co-operate with his Parliaments in such measures as may promote the common interests of all his subjects' and entreated the members to show their 'honourable support of his Majesty's government.' An address of thanks was moved as a matter of form, but a lively debate followed the motion and both Houses voted to include in their addresses the statement: 'It is not the temporary expedients alone, that can save this nation from impending ruin, but a free trade only' (*London Chronicle* 19–21 Oct. 1779, xlvi. 377, 380–1).

3. Volunteer organizations to defend Ireland against invasion sprang up throughout the country in 1778, and these were strengthened in the late summer of 1779 because of rumours that the combined fleets of France and Spain would strike at

the address to the Castle.4 I dare to say Mr Edmund Burke does not approve of these proceedings, for the twenty-eight thousand are all Protestants.5 He would, I suppose, have liked better the advice of the Honourable and Right Reverend Father in God, Dr Frederic Hervey,6 Bishop of Derry, who told a person I know that he had proposed to the administration in England to take off the test from the Roman Catholics; and though it was rejected, he told another person that it was to be taken off.7

It looks as if the naval campaign were over,8 but I do not know. The re-settlement of the administration on the old bottom, only with some crossing over and figuring in, which you see in all the papers, I am told will take place.9

You perceive by my date that I am removed into my new house. It is seeming to take a new lease of life. I was born in Arlington Street,10

Ireland. See *ante* 9 Aug. 1779; W. E. H. Lecky, *A History of Ireland in the Eighteenth Century*, 1892, ii. 222–40; Francis Dobbs, *A History of Irish Affairs*, 1782, p. 10. According to a conservative estimate in the *London Chronicle*, loc. cit., the armed societies at this time were 'above 14,000 strong.' Lecky says that the number of volunteers 'under the pressure of imminent danger had risen to about 42,000' (op. cit. ii. 234), and HW revised his estimate upward to 40,000 when he wrote to Mann 31 Oct. 1779.

4. The Lord Lieutenant's residence at Dublin. HW's 'committee' was the entire body of the Dublin volunteers. On the occasion of the address from the throne on 14 Oct., 'the whole of our city volunteers . . . appeared under arms, and completely lined the streets from the Paliament House to the Castle' (*London Chronicle* 21–3 Oct. 1779, xlvi. 386).

5. 'For at least the first three years of their existence, the Irish volunteers were essentially a non-Catholic body' (Patrick Rogers, *The Irish Volunteers and Catholic Emancipation*, 1934, p. 57). Catholics, however, supported the volunteer movement (ibid. 63). Burke, whose wife and mother were Catholics, took an active part in the struggle for the relaxation of Catholic disabilities, and was accused of being himself a Catholic, a charge which HW appears to have believed (*Last Journals* ii. 141, 311).

6. Frederick Augustus Hervey (1730–1803), D.D., 4th E. of Bristol (Dec. 1779); Bp of Cloyne, 1767, of Derry, 1768.

7. HW gives a somewhat more circumstantial reference to this in his letter of 14 Oct. 1779 to Lady Ossory, but does not identify his informants. The Bishop's advocacy of a more liberal policy towards Catholics is discussed by W. S. Childe-Pemberton in *The Earl Bishop: The Life of Frederick Hervey, Bishop of Derry, Earl of Bristol*, [1925], i. 238–41.

8. Both the combined fleets and the English fleet were in harbour. Though HW had no way of knowing it, the enemy had abandoned the plan of an invasion some three weeks before this letter.

9. Rumours about changes in the cabinet were reported in the *Public Advertiser* 19 Oct.; *Lloyd's Evening Post* 15–18 Oct., xlv. 373; and *London Chronicle* 14–16 Oct., xlvi. 368. The rumours proved substantially accurate: Stormont and Hillsborough were made secretaries of state (*Lloyd's Evening Post* 27–9 Oct., xlv. 413, 415, and GM 1779, xlix. 567), Carlisle became first lord of Trade (*Lloyd's Evening Post* 5–8 Nov. 1779, xlv. 445), and Bathurst became president of the Council (*Public Advertiser* 25 Nov. 1779). Speculation continued, however, for several weeks. See *post* 16 and ca 19 Nov. 1779.

10. See 'Short Notes,' GRAY i. 3.

lived there about fourteen years,[11] returned thither, and passed thirty-seven more;[12] but I have sober monitors that warn me not to delude myself.

My four nieces[13] are at Nuneham. I saw Mrs Harcourt[14] on Tuesday at Sion Hill, come up to kiss hands for Gen. Burgoyne's regiment;[15] no doubt to the great joy of Bishop Butler.[16] What charming children the little Carmarthens[17] are.

I shall return to Strawberry on Monday for about a week, and then be chiefly in London. You will not tell me your own intended motions, and therefore I shall leave you to your own vagaries.

I heard t'other day of *The World As It Goes,* a poem published last spring,[18] but which I had never seen. It is by that infamous Combe, the author of *The Diaboliad.* It has many easy poetic lines, imitates Churchill,[19] and is full as incoherent and absurd in its plan[20] as the worst of the latter's. I do not wonder that it made no noise.[21] Adieu! I send no compliments to your anthems, for I am not in charity with them.

11. Until 1732, when Sir Robert Walpole moved to Lord Ashburnham's house on the east side of St James's Square (Gray i. 56), where he lived until 1735. He then moved into Downing Street (Gray i. 11).

12. In 1742 HW and his father returned to Arlington Street (Gray i. 12), to live in the house (later No. 5) which was to be HW's London residence until his removal to Berkeley Square.

13. Three of them were the Ladies Waldegrave, as is shown by HW's letter to Lord Harcourt Oct. 1779. The fourth was probably Anna Maria Keppel (see *ante* 11 Oct. 1778).

14. Mary Danby (1749–1833), m. (1) (1772) Thomas Lockhart (d. 1775); m. (2) (1778) Hon. William Harcourt, brother of Lord Harcourt, 3d E. Harcourt, 1809 (GEC; John Fisher, *The History and Antiquities of Masham and Mashamshire,* 1865, p. 283).

15. 'Yesterday Colonel Harcourt kissed his Majesty's hand at St James's on being appointed to the command of General Burgoyne's regiment of light horse [16th Light Dragoons]' (*Public Advertiser* 22 Oct. 1779. For the letters that passed between Burgoyne and two successive secretaries at war, Lord Barrington and Charles Jenkinson,

leading to Burgoyne's disgruntled resignation, see GM 1779, xlix. 531–4.

16. See *ante* 18 Aug. 1779 for Butler's remark about Lord Harcourt.

17. Lady Holdernesse's grandchildren: George William Frederick Osborne (1775–1838), 6th D. of Leeds, 1799; Mary Henrietta Juliana (1776–1862), m. (1801) Thomas Pelham, 2d E. of Chichester, 1805; and Francis Godolphin Osborne (1777–1850), cr. (1832) Bn Godolphin of Farnham Royal.

18. Publication was announced 21 May 1779 (*Public Advertiser*).

19. Edmund Cartwright in the *Monthly Review* also thought that the imitation of Churchill was unfortunate (*Monthly Review,* 1779, lxi. 109–10; B. C. Nangle, *The Monthly Review . . . Indexes,* Oxford, 1934, pp. 8, 225).

20. 'The Satiric Muse presents herself to the poet and gives him a visionary representation of "the world as it goes," filled with groups of mercenary courtiers, ladies of easy virtue, oppressors, misers, hypocrites, etc.' (*Critical Review,* 1779, xlvii. 473).

21. But there was a second edition in 1779. HW's copy of it with notes throughout is at Harvard.

From MASON, Friday 12 November 1779

Printed from MS now WSL.
Address: The Honourable Horace Walpole, Berkley Square, London.
Postmark: YORK.

York, Nov. 12th, 1779.

Dear Sir,

AS I could not precisely tell you how I was to regulate my motions after the end of my residence, which concluded yesterday,
I deferred writing till the present moment when I have to tell you
that my motions will be no motions for three months to come, as
the Dean and chapter have allowed me to take another residence
immediately, by which means I save the expense and trouble of
removing my family,[1] and lay up for myself a year and three quarters
of liberty, a great sum you will say of such a commodity which is
at least equivalent to what the whole nation may promise itself the
enjoyment of. However this be, I shall hope that while I remain
in durance you will relieve and console me with your letters which,
though I do not expect that the events which they relate will be of
a comfortable cast, yet still they will be my very best amusement.

My Lord Carmarthen called upon me the other day in his return
from the East Riding of this great county, where he had reviewed
the whole coast,[2] and found it so totally defenceless that he had given
a ball at Beverley on the occasion; he had withal added twenty men to
the militia and by the addition of two captains had metamorphosed
a paltry battalion into a complete regiment, a very great military
manœuvre, and which I doubt not will be attended with the most
salutary consequences to this part of the island, especially as the
corps with which they are to be embodied is at Coxheath.[3] From
York he retired to Kiveton,[4] where if he pleases he may make another
ball and invite Lady Conyers[5] to it, who I don't doubt will be pleased

1. His servants.
2. Lord Carmarthen had been named
Lord Lieutenant of the East Riding of
Yorkshire in July 1778 (Collins, *Peerage*,
1812, i. 260). His departure on a recruiting tour of Yorkshire was reported in the
Public Advertiser 21 Oct. 1779.
3. 'The Marquis of Carmarthen has obtained permission of his Majesty to raise a
company of grenadiers, to be incorporated

with the Yorkshire Buffs (East Riding
militia) now encamped at Coxheath, to consist of 120 men' (*London Chronicle* 12–14
Aug. 1779, xlvi. 145).
4. Kiveton Park, 8 miles E. of Rotherham; the seat of the Duke of Leeds.
5. Lady Holdernesse's daughter and Lord
Carmarthen's divorced wife, who held the
title of Baroness Conyers s.j.

with such a fête, for you must know at Lady Holdernesse's request I have lent her my parsonage to reside in while Mr Byron[6] is raising recruits at Sheffield and Rotherham.[7] This was by no means a pleasant sacrifice to make on my part, but I fancy you will think with me that as Lady Holdernesse asked it I could not decently refuse.

I am at present revising and correcting a verse translation of Fresnoy's *Art of Painting*[8] which I began when I was a boy at the university and have since at the intervals of five and sometimes ten years proceeded upon. I believe I shall now complete it, and I fancy you will like it as well as a thing so very didactic will be capable of being liked.[9] I forget whether I ever showed you any part of it.[10] If not, pray do not set your stomach ag⟨ainst⟩ it, for one day or other you must swallow the whole dose.

I congratulate you on your removal to Berkley Square. May you enjoy the comforts of your new situation as long as the Phidian work which is placed in the center of that square[11] continues to be its chief ornament. This is a new prayer of my own which I offer up even with more zeal than I do that which the wisdom of the legislature has lately tagged to that about wars and tumults.[12]

Amen.

6. John Byron (1756–91), son of Adm. John Byron, m. (1), June 1779, Lady Amelia Darcy, Bns Conyers, and (2), 1785, Caroline Gordon, by whom he was the father of Lord Byron, the poet (GEC *sub* Leeds; Collins, *Peerage*, 1812, vii. 110; G. F. Russell Barker and A. H. Stenning, *The Record of Old Westminsters*, 1928, i. 154–5).

7. Byron was an army officer from 1773 to 1780 (Barker and Stenning, loc. cit.).

8. *De arte graphica*, by Charles-Alphonse Dufresnoy (1611–65), posthumously published at Paris in 1668.

9. See *post* 5 and 28 Feb. 1781.

10. There is nothing in the correspondence to indicate that he had. In 1768 when Mason showed Warburton 'a first sheet of the translation of Fresnoy, which I printed in octavo, some years before I corrected and published the whole in 4to,' Warburton replied, 'The specimen vastly exceeded my expectation. It will be a noble thing. . . . I think this translation will do you as much honour as anything you have written. You have gained what you aimed at, to have it read like an original'

(Mitford MSS in BM, Add. MSS 32563 fol. 18–20).

11. 'In the centre of the square was an equestrian statue of George III, in a Roman habit, "in the character of Marcus Aurelius." It was executed by Beaupré under the direction of Wilton for the Princess Amelia, who placed it in 1766' (*London Past and Present* i. 165). J. T. Smith describes it as 'that miserable specimen of leaden-figure taste' (*Nollekens and His Times*, 1828, ii. 181). It was removed early in the 19th century.

12. The text of 'a prayer to be used every day next after the prayer in time of war and tumults, in all cathedrals and collegiate and parochial churches and chapels within England and Wales and the town of Berwick-upon-Tweed, during the present troubles' is printed in the *Public Advertiser* 9 Aug. 1779. The last sentence begins, 'Turn, O Lord, the heart of his [the King's] rebellious subjects in America, and let neither our unhappy divisions, nor our other manifold sins and provocations, obstruct his designs for the

To Mason, Tuesday 16 November 1779

Printed from Mitford ii. 44–6.

Berkeley Square, Nov. 16, 1779.

MR STONHEWER wrote to you on business[1] and could not get an answer, and was seriously alarmed that you was ill; I did not know whither to direct till you told me yesterday that you are hoarding a reversion of holidays at York; not very agreeable to me, who do not reckon on what is to accumulate; but in short, it is well you please me so much, for you often provoke me; so you do in translating Fresnoy. I do not care whether I shall like it or not; you will no doubt improve a middling poem, and what then? you will not insert a thousand new lights and ideas that you would have conceived if you had written a new poem on painting, which you understand better than Fresnoy. A mighty merit it would have been in Raphael, after the *Transfiguration*[2] (pray mind that word) to have copied Giotto! You are original, and I will like none of your copies. I do feel for the adulteration of your parsonage; it is monstrously unpleasant to have one's house tumbled and dirtied by strangers— and yet I do not see how you could refuse.

What can I tell you of news and politics? just now we are arrived at a moment of *grim repose.*[4] The combined fleets have not come forth— I imagine from much sickness and mortality.[5] Sir Charles Hardy is crowing upon what may very properly be called his own dunghill.[6] Though the French have given us many sound blows,[7] they have certainly not come half up to their boasting and possibilities—yet it is likely that they will wind up the campaign with the capture of

public good, nor bring down thy judgments upon us.'

———

1. The letter is missing.
2. Raphael's last masterpiece, now in the Vatican Gallery, commissioned by Cardinal Giuliano de' Medici for the Cathedral at Narbonne.
4. 'Regardless of the sweeping whirlwind's sway,
    That, hushed in grim repose, expects his evening prey'
    (Gray, *The Bard,* ii. 2, ll. 13–14).

5. HW was right. See *Sandwich Papers* iii. 9.
6. His fleet, which had sailed with orders to cruise wherever Hardy judged best 'for the protection of the trade and coasts of Great Britain and Ireland and for defeating the designs of the enemy' (ibid.).
7. Notably in the West Indies, where St Vincent and Grenada had fallen to the French.

New York and Arbuthnot's fleet,[8] which will make our obstinacy for the recovery of America still more heroic. Firmness retires, where practicability finishes, and then obstinacy undertakes the business.

Ireland I believe will be brought to the same consistence, not with so much system and intention of driving it into rebellion, but—however we have so many data to go upon, that there would be no great honour in foretelling misfortunes.

There is another, and as yet little cloud about the sun, that may join and make other tempests come to explosion. Lord Gower[9] has declared for resignation;[10] Lord Weymouth wavers.[11] I believe they have touched at many ports[12]—I should be glad to see them shut out everywhere; whoever is betrayed and deserted by them, has at

8. Marriot Arbuthnot (ca 1711–94), Rear-Adm., 1778. He was appointed to the command of the North American station in Feb. 1779 and arrived in New York 25 Aug. 'The present rumour is that D'Estaing has taken Long Island, and blocked up Admiral Arbuthnot;—but the account comes from France' (HW to Mann 12 Nov. 1779). The rumour proved groundless. D'Estaing's sailing from the West Indies to the North American mainland caused alarm in England, but after participating in the unsuccessful siege of Savannah he returned to France. See Sandwich Papers iii. 122; HW to Lady Ossory 14 Oct. 1779.

9. Granville Leveson-Gower (1721–1803), styled Vct Trentham 1746–54; 2d E. Gower, 1754; cr. (1786) M. of Stafford; P.C., 1755; lord privy seal 1755–7 and 1784–94; Master of the Horse 1757–60; Master of the Wardrobe 1760–3; lord chamberlain 1763–5; lord president of the Council 1767–79 and 1783–4.

10. From the presidency of the Council. Dissatisfaction with the conduct of the administration prompted his decision to resign (Lord North to the King ?Sept. 1779, Corr. Geo. III iv. 443–4; post ca 19 Nov. 1779).

11. Thomas Thynne (1734–96), 3d Vct Weymouth, 1751; cr. (1789) M. of Bath; lord of the Bedchamber 1760–3; Master of the Horse to the Queen 1763–5; Lord Lieutenant of Ireland, April–July 1765; P.C., 1765; secretary of state for the north, Jan.–Oct. 1768; for the south, 1768–70 and 1775–9. Earlier in the month the King was hopeful that Weymouth would be willing to accept another office in the administration, but when on 5 Nov. the King wrote to offer him the presidency of the Council in exchange for his post as secretary of state, Weymouth firmly declined. See Corr. Geo. III iv. 473–4.

12. I.e., had attempted to ally themselves with various factions. Charles Jenkinson, the secretary at war, reported to the King on 4 Nov. a conversation he had had with Wedderburn, the attorney-general: 'He told me he had seen the Chancellor [Thurlow] with whom he had had some conversation, and who had said that he did not know whether Lord Weymouth would resign or not, as he had not had any talk with him upon it, but that he was of opinion that he ought not; I conceive that much more passed between them, and I think they are well together. He told me he had seen Lord Gower; and I found they had had a great deal of conversation together; he endeavoured to justify Lord Gower in the step he had taken. . . . I begin however to think that there is a plot forming to get wholly rid of Lord North; how many are as yet concerned in this, I will not presume to say' (ibid. iv. 471–2). On 11 Nov. Jenkinson reported that Gower had had a long conversation with the Duke of Grafton (ibid. iv. 482). One of the reasons for the King's plea that Weymouth remain in the administration was that this 'would remove the appearance of any concert with Lord Gower' (ibid. iv. 474).

least the merit of not being a traitor and running away.[13] Distress and dissatisfaction do begin to murmur everywhere. Men do perceive that they cannot live upon loyalty and dissipation. General Bourgoyne flatters himself that everybody will forget their own sorrows to be occupied with his.[14] I will allow Lord Gower and Lord Weymouth to be mightily touched for him, but beg to be excused myself. I cannot forget how ready he was to be a great favourite.

I have very lately heard an account of the eruption of Vesuvius,[15] and one part that was quite new to me. The people rose and were on the point of burning the theatre where the King[16] was at the opera—enraged at his insensibility.

Thank you for your prayer and your excellent account of Lord Carmarthen's review and ball.

To Mason, ca Friday 19 November 1779

Printed from Mitford ii. 46–9. Dated approximately on the assumption that the postscript was written on the day following the rest of the letter.

Berkeley Square, Nov. I don't know what day.

IF you can be content with anything but news as fresh as mackerel, I will tell you as pretty a story as a gentleman can hear in a winter's day, though it has not a grain of novelty in it but to those who never heard it, which was my case till yesterday.[1]

When that philosophic tyrant the Czarina[2] (who murdered two emperors[3] for the good of their people, to the edification of Voltaire,

13. 'I cannot say that I approve of the conduct of Lord Gower, Lord Weymouth or even the Chancellor; the two first desert your Majesty in the moment of difficulty and danger; by their resignation they render that administration still weaker, which they declare to be too weak already to carry on the business of government' (Jenkinson to the King, 7 Nov. 1779, ibid. iv. 475).

14. Burgoyne's reluctant resignation deprived him of emoluments to the amount of £3500 a year (GM 1779, xlix. 562).

15. In Aug. 1779. HW heard it from the younger Horace Mann, who repeated an account given to the elder Mann by Sir William Hamilton. Another account was sent by Hamilton to Sir Joseph Banks, who printed it in *Philosophical Transactions of the Royal Society of London*, 1780, lxx pt i. 42–84. See HW to Mann 12 Nov. 1779.

16. Ferdinand IV (1751–1825), K. of Naples 1759–1806, and, as Ferdinand I, K. of the Two Sicilies 1815–25.

1. HW's source for this and the following story of the Czarina has not been found.

2. Catherine II (1729–96), 'the Great'; Empress of Russia 1762–96.

3. Catherine was suspected of complicity in the murders of Peter III (1728–62) and Ivan VI (1740–64).

Diderot and D'Alembert[4]) proposed to give a code of laws that should serve all her subjects as much, or as little as she pleased, she ordered her various states to send deputies who should specify their respective wants.[5] Amongst the rest came a representative of the Samoieds; he waited on the marshal of the diet of legislation, who was Archbishop of Novogrod.[6] 'I am come,' said the savage, 'but I do not know for what.' 'My clement mistress,' said his Grace, 'means to give a body of laws to all her dominions.' 'Whatever laws the empress shall give us,' said the Samoied, 'we shall obey, but we want no laws.'[7] 'How,' said the prelate, 'not want laws! why you are men like the rest of the world, and must have the same passions, and consequently must murder, cheat, steal, rob, plunder,' etc., etc., etc. 'It is true' said the savage, 'we have now and then a bad person among us, but he is sufficiently punished by being shut out of all society.'

If you love nature in its *naturalibus,* you will like this tale. I think one might make a pretty *Spectator* by inverting the hint; I would propose a general jail delivery, not only from all prisons, but madhouses, as not sufficiently ample for a quarter of the patients and candidates; and to save trouble, and yet make as impartial distinc-

4. Catherine 'corresponded with Voltaire and D'Alembert. She invited the latter to assume the place of tutor to the Grand Duke, her son. She tendered him a munificent salary of twenty-five thousand livres. . . . To Diderot she also made the most liberal offers. She purchased his library at an enormous price. She allowed him to retain it in his possession, and gave him a salary as her librarian' (Samuel M. Smucker, *Memoirs of the Court and Reign of Catherine the Second, Empress of Russia,* New York, 1859, pp. 79–80). See du Deffand i. 298, 299; ii. 214.

5. Catherine's commission for the codification of Russian law, representing all classes of society and all nationalities of the empire, met in Moscow for the first time 10 Aug. 1767. The final session of the plenary committee was held 29 Dec. 1768, but sub-committees continued their work until 1774. The project fell far short of its grand design. See Sir Bernard Pares, *A History of Russia,* New York, 1947, pp. 242–4; S. M. Solov'ev, *Istoria Rossii,* [ca 1900], vi. 347–50.

6. Daniil Andreievich Sechenov (1709–

67), who took the name in religion of Dimitri; Bp of Nizhni Novgorod and Alatyr, 1742, of Riazan and Murom, 1752, Abp of Novgorod, 1757, and Metropolitan of Novgorod and Velikie Luki, 1762–7. He was a friend of Catherine and officiated at her coronation. In 1767 he was appointed delegate from the Holy Synod to the committee for the codification of the laws, and gave the opening address at the convention. HW is wrong in describing him as the marshal of the diet. The marshal was Alexander Ilich Bibikov (1729–74), soldier and diplomat (*Russkii biograficheskii slovar,* vi. 394–5; information kindly supplied by Dr Andrew Lossky).

7. A variant of this story of the Samoyeds appears in William Tooke's *Life of Catharine II,* 1800, i. 437: 'The deputies of the Samoyedes alone had the courage to speak freely. One of them stood up in the name of his brethren, and said:—"We are a simple and honest people. We quietly tend our reindeer. We are in no want of a new code; but make laws for the Russians, our neighbours, that they may put a stop to their depredations."'

tion, to confine the virtuous and the few that are in their senses, but I am digressing, and have not yet told you the story I intended; at least, only the first part.

One day Count Orlow,[8] the Czarina's accomplice in more ways than one, exhibited himself to the Samoied in the robes of the order,[9] and refulgent with diamonds.[10] The savage surveyed him attentively, but silently. 'May I ask,' said the favourite, 'what it is you admire?' 'Nothing,' replied the Tartar, 'I was thinking how ridiculous you are.' 'Ridiculous,' cried Orlow angrily; 'and pray in what?' 'Why you shave your beard to look young, and powder your hair to look old.'

Well! as you like my stories, I will tell you a third, but it is prodigiously old, yet it is the only new trait that I have found in that ocean the *Bibliothèque des romans*,[11] which I had almost abandoned; for I am out of patience with novels and sermons, that have nothing new, when the authors may say what they will without contradiction.

My history is a romance of the amours of Eleanor of Aquitaine,[12] Queen of our Henry II. She is in love with somebody who is in love with somebody else. She puts both in prison. The Count falls dangerously ill and sends for the Queen's physician.[13] Eleanor hears it, calls

8. Grigorii Grigorievich Orlov (1734–83), Count, 1762; leader of the conspiracy that dethroned and murdered Peter III in 1762, and favourite of Catherine.

9. When she ascended the throne, Catherine invested Orlov in the order of St Alexander (*Memoirs of Catherine the Great*, trans. Katharine Anthony, New York, 1927, p. 271). The badge of the order was worn on a flame-coloured ribbon, and the ceremonial costume consisted of a mantle of red velvet with white facings, a silver jacket, and a black hat with a white feather (Sir Bernard Burke, *The Book of Orders of Knighthood and Decorations of Honour*, 1858, p. 231).

10. 'Gregory Orlof displayed the utmost pomp and magnificence when on his travels. He appeared at Paris in a coat all the buttons whereof were large diamonds, and with a sword having the hilt also set with diamonds' (Tooke, op. cit. ii. 90). See Mann to HW 27 June 1775.

11. The *Bibliothèque universelle des romans* was published periodically from 1775 to 1789, in 112 volumes. HW had eighteen volumes, sold SH v. 116. 'On y donne une

analyse raisonné de tous les romans anciens et modernes, français ou traduits dans notre langue; on y joint des anecdotes et des notices historiques et critiques concernant les auteurs ou leurs ouvrages, ainsi que les mœurs, les usages du temps, les circonstances particulières et relatives, et les personnages connus, déguisés ou emblématiques. Ce recueil, compose de seize volumes par année, parait périodiquement, comme le *Mercure*, le 1er et le 15 du mois' (Grimm, *Correspondance* xi. 307). HW subscribed in 1776 on Mme du Deffand's urging (DU DEFFAND iv. 308, 316).

12. Eleanor (ca 1122–1204), dau. of William X, Duke of Aquitaine; m. (1) (1137) Louis VII, King of France; and (2) (1152) Henry Plantagenet, who became (1154) King Henry II of England. For an account of some of the amorous tales about Eleanor (not including HW's) that were current in the Middle Ages, see F. M. Chambers, 'Some Legends Concerning Eleanor of Aquitaine,' *Speculum*, 1941, xvi. 459–68.

13. In the story, Eleanor is jealous of a Comte de Ponthieu, who is enamoured of Amélie de Vermandois. The physician is

for the physician and gives him a bowl which she orders him to prescribe to the Count, the doctor hesitates, doubts, begs to know the ingredients,—'Come,' says her Majesty, 'your suspicions are just: it is poison—but remember, it is a crime I want from you, not a lecture, go and obey my orders: my captain of the guard and two soldiers shall accompany you, and see that you execute my command, and give no hint of my secret, go, I will have no reply.' The physician submits, finds the prisoner in bed, his mistress sitting by. The doctor feels his pulse, produces the bowl, sighs, and says, 'My dear friend I cannot cure your disorder, but I have a remedy here for myself,' and swallows the poison.[14]

Is not this entirely new? It would be a fine *coup de théâtre,* and yet would not do for a tragedy, for the physician would become the hero of the piece, would efface the lovers: and yet the rest of the play could not be made to turn on him.

As all this will serve for a letter at any time, I will keep the rest of my paper for something that will not bear postponing.

20th.

Come, my letter shall go, though with only one new paragraph. Lord Weymouth has resigned, as well as Lord Gower. I believe that little faction flattered themselves that their separation would blow up Lord North, and yet I am persuaded that sheer cowardice has most share in Weymouth's part. There is such universal dissatisfaction, that when the crack is begun the whole edifice perhaps may tumble, but where is the architect that can repair a single storey? The nation stayed till everything was desperate before it would allow that a single tile was blown off.

---

one Marileif. See the *Bibliothèque* for July 1779, ii. 68–82.

14. HW has taken a few liberties with the original, in which the doctor is represented as saying nothing to the Count, but, after drinking the poison, says to the guards, 'Allez dire à ceux qui vous envoient que si je n'ai pu obéir, leur secret, du moins, meurt avec moi' (ibid. x. 84).

To Mason, Monday 29 November 1779

Printed from Mitford ii. 49–53.

Berkeley Square, Nov. 29, 1779.

I DESIRED Mr Stonhewer on Saturday to write to you, and to tell you why I could not.[1] From him or from the newspapers, who know everything as well and as soon as anybody, you will have learnt that the edifice of the majority does not, like the chief temple of the Philistines, rest on two slight pillars, which being removed, the whole fabric fell to pieces; but when pilasters take themselves for buttresses, no wonder they are mistaken. Such has been the fate of the Lords Gower and Weymouth, and I wish everybody saw them in as contemptible a light as I do. The last has attempted to avoid no degree of shame, for he is actually run away to Longleat.[2] However they do not give up the game, but have a matador still to play a *black ace*.[3]

So you think that we are still living on Thursday's debate and division![4] you are extremely mistaken, good Sir, we have fresh events every morning, not revolutions indeed, nor sea-fights, nor rebellions —all in good time. But we can furnish you every day with occurrences so strange and unexpected, that you folks in the country would live on a single one for three months—come what do you like? what do

1. HW was suffering from an acute attack of gout (HW to Mann 28 Nov. 1779).

2. 'The Lords Gower and Weymouth found that nobody had been frightened but themselves. What the latter feared, no mortal can guess' (HW to Mann 28 Nov. 1779).

3. The matadors, the highest ranking cards in quadrille (or ombre), are spadille, the ace of spades; manille, the deuce of spades or clubs, when spades or clubs are trumps, or the seven of hearts or diamonds, when hearts or diamonds are trumps; and basto, the ace of clubs. HW's application of the figure is not altogether clear, but the black ace may be Thurlow, the Lord Chancellor, whose 'swarthy complexion matched well with his keen black sparkling eyes and bushy eyebrows' (DNB). Thurlow's association with Gower in a

scheme to overthrow North is discussed in North's letter to the King 30 Nov. 1779 (*Corr. Geo. III* iv. 500–2).

4. The King opened Parliament on Thursday 25 Nov. The Earl of Chesterfield then moved the customary address of thanks, but the motion was vigorously opposed by members of the Opposition, including Rockingham and Richmond. The division, however, showed 82 lords for the address and only 41 against it. See *London Chronicle* 25–7 Nov. 1779, xlvi. 507–9. The resignations of Gower and Weymouth had been expected to precipitate 'a very considerable defalcation from the standing majority' (HW to Mann 28 Nov. 1779), but the vote in both Houses on the address showed the administration still to be firmly entrenched.

you choose? Is not a sudden death very comfortable in a long winter's evening over a sea-coal fire? or is a duel more to your taste? what young profligate would you wish hurried out of the world in an instant—I mean only as a beautiful flower that would close a sermon delicately, that you are composing on the debaucheries and gaming of the age? would not there be still more dignity in it, if he were a young peer? or shall he be a fashionable orator? or a grave judge—or shall he be all three? you are a little difficult Mr Mason, and yet in these times much may be done to serve a friend, or what think you of a single combat seasoned with a little spice of premeditated assassination *à la* Sam Martin,[5] which pray observe does not signify Saint Martin.

Well then I will try to please you if I can. Know then that on Saturday night one of his Majesty's chief justices in eyre,[6] after having vented a warm philippic on Thursday *against* the administration,[7] and after having retired to his house at Epsom[8] on Friday,[9] attended only by four virgins, whom he had picked up in the Strand,[10] and after having supped plentifully on the said Saturday on fish and venison,

5. HW's detested 'reversionary heir,' who practiced firing at a target for some months before challenging Wilkes to a duel. See *ante* 2 March 1773 *bis* and nn. 19–21.

6. Thomas Lyttelton, 2d Bn Lyttelton, appointed chief justice in eyre of the counties north of Trent 18 Nov. 1775.

7. Lord Lyttelton's speech is reported in Cobbett, *Parl. Hist.* xx. 1038–45, and in abbreviated form in *London Chronicle* 27–30 Nov. 1779 (xlvi. 516–7), where the warmth of his language is apparent: 'The noble lords . . . smile at what I say; let them turn their eyes on their own weak, ill-judged, and wretched measures, and then let them declare in their consciences which is most fitly the object of contempt, my openly and unreservedly speaking my real sentiments in Parliament, without regard to any personal consideration, or their consenting, in a moment of public difficulty and danger, to pocket the wages of prostitution, and to sit either in sullen silence, or, what is still more criminal, to rise and palliate the calamitous and disgraceful situation of the British empire.' Other examples of Lyttelton's independence appear in Cobbett, *Parl. Hist.* xx. 455–64.

8. Pitt Place, near Epsom, Surrey, described in Reginald Blunt's *Thomas, Lord Lyttelton: The Portrait of a Rake*, 1936, pp. 263–5.

9. The party assembled at Epsom on Saturday 27 Nov. (ibid. 186–7; Thomas Frost, *The Life of Thomas, Lord Lyttelton*, 1876, p. 348). Writing to Mann 28 Nov. 1779 about Lyttelton's death, HW admitted that he might not be 'very accurate in dates.'

10. Described in HW's letter to Mann 28 Nov. as 'a caravan of nymphs.' The party assembled at Pitt Place on the day of Lyttelton's death comprised Hugh Fortescue, cr. (1789) Vct Fortescue; William Wolseley, subsequently admiral of the red squadron; Frances Cavendish, who married (1769) Frederick Flood, cr. (1780) Bt of Ireland; and Eliza, Christina, and Margaret Amphlett, 'daughters of a respected neighbour of Lord Lyttelton's residing at Clent, near Hagley Park,' and distant relatives of Lyttelton (Blunt, op. cit. 194). 'The ages of the girls were 19, 17, and 15' (ibid. 194–5). See Frost, op. cit. 344. There are reasons for suspecting that the Amphlett girls were not models of prudence (*Delany Correspondence* v. 497–8; Blunt, op. cit. 188, 194–5, 197).

finding himself indisposed, went to bed, rung his bell in ten minutes, and in one minute after the arrival of his servant, expired;—but what signifies sudden death without forewarning? he had said on Thursday that he should die in three days, had dreamt so and felt it would be so; on Saturday he said, 'If I outlive today I shall go on,'[11] but enough of him: my next event is worth ten of this.

As Lord Lyttelton had spoken *against* the ministers, Mr Adam,[12] nephew of the architects, spoke *for* them. It is supposed that whenever Scotland was dissatisfied with—pho! I mean not satisfied by Lord North, Adam was delegated to run at him:[13] and now and then might have a plenary indulgence from the Pope for talking the language of opposition, in order to worm out secrets—poor souls! as if they had any!

Well, on Thursday he made a most absurd speech in favour of the Court,[14] which Charles Fox tore piecemeal with infinite humour and argument, which tortured the patient so much that next day he asked an explanation.[15] Fox assured him he had meant nothing personal, but had a right to dislocate his arguments, and he was satisfied,

11. This is one of several versions of the story of Lyttelton's death, and not the best authenticated (see Blunt, op. cit. 186–98). HW's account agrees substantially with the story told a few months later by Lyttelton's uncle, Lord Westcote, purportedly based on conversations with members of the Pitt Place party: 'In the evening of the following day, being Friday, he told the eldest Miss Amphlett, that she looked melancholy; but, said he "You are foolish and fearful, I have lived two days and God willing I will live out the third." On the morning of Saturday [before the party set out for Epsom] he told [the three Miss Amphletts] that he was very well, and believed he *should bilk the ghost'* (ibid. 186–7). See *post* 11 Dec. 1779.

12. William Adam (1751–1839), politician, son of Robert and James Adam's brother, John; M. P. Gatton 1774–80, Wigton 1780–6, Elgin 1786–90, Ross-shire 1790–4, Kincardineshire 1806–12; solicitor-general, 1802; attorney-general, 1805; P.C., 1815.

13. 'Adam, the Scot . . . often attacked the Court, though, as was suspected, either by direction to get into the councils of the opponents, or instigated to vent particular discontents of Lord Bute, Lord Mansfield, or some of his countrymen against Lord North' (*Last Journals* ii. 209).

14. Professing himself unconnected with any party, Adam spoke against a change of ministry on the grounds that the present cabinet was not solely to blame for the nation's difficulties, included men of ability, and was not likely to serve the state better if staffed with new officials (Cobbett, *Parl. Hist.* xx. 1101–4).

15. Fox is said to have declared that if he were a minister and heard any such defence as Adam had made of Lord North, he would reply: 'Begone! begone, wretch! who delightest in libelling mankind, confounding virtue and vice, and insulting the man whom you pretend to defend, by saying to his face, that he certainly is infamous, but that there are others still more so' (ibid. xx. 1118). The letters that passed on this occasion between Adam and Fox were later published in the newspapers, with an account of the duel drawn up by the seconds, Humberston and Fitzpatrick. See, e.g., *Public Advertiser* 2 Dec. 1779 and *Annual Register*, 1779, xxii. 235–6.

but on Sunday he sent a Scotch major[16] to Fox to complain of the state of the debate in the newspapers, and to desire Mr Fox would contradict and declare his good opinion of him. Fox returned for answer that he was not responsible for accounts in newspapers; that it was harder still if on their misrepresentation he must give a good character of any man they abused: he again declared he had intended no offence, and that Mr Adam was welcome to show that declaration to anybody. After consult had,[17] Adam returned that Mr Fox must print that recantation. 'Hold,' said Fox, 'not so far neither'—Oh! I forgot the principal circumstance of all, Adam added that his *friends* would not be satisfied under less than publication. At eight this morning they went into Hyde Park, Fox with Fitzpatrick, Adam with his Major Humerstone for seconds; Adam fired, and the ball wounded Charles Fox's side, though very slightly; he then fired, missed, and said, 'Now, Mr Adam, are you satisfied?'

Near as you are to the Tweed you will not guess the reply, 'No,' said Adam, 'you must still print your letter.' Nothing could be more unjust, more unfair; they had fought because Fox would *not* consent to that pretension; Fox with the same firmness and temper with which he had conducted himself through the whole affair peremptorily refused, and the bloodhound again fired, but missed, and then Fox fired into the air and it ended.[18]

An odd circumstance larded this history. Humerstone was waiting for him at Fox's house, and so was Sheridan;[19] when Charles was come home and had dispatched the bravo, Sheridan said, 'Pray who is that ill-looking fellow? he looks like the carrier of a challenge.'

Well, I am sure I have made amends for having been punished by the gout, and here too have I been writing in bed till eleven at night, but thank you I am better and was in the other room from twelve till six today, when my pains returned; yet finding them easier at nine, I was eager to be the first to tell you two such strange events. Half the town have been reading the latter correspondence in Charles Fox's room the whole morning, and I received it piping hot,

16. Thomas Frederick Mackenzie Humberston (ca 1753–83), major in the 78th (later 72d) regiment, 1779; Lt-Col., 1780. He died of wounds received while fighting in India.

17. *Sic;* 'consult' as a noun occurs in *Paradise Lost* i. 798.

18. Fox and Adam later became friends. See Lord John Russell, *The Life and Times of Charles James Fox,* 1859–66, i. 220.

19. Richard Brinsley Sheridan, the dramatist.

except that I have abridged it a little, from a very accurate reporter. Adieu, or the bellman[20] will be gone.

From MASON, Tuesday 7 December 1779

Printed from MS now WSL.
Address: The Honourable Horace Walpole, Berkley Square, London.
Postmark: YORK.

York, Dec. 7th, 1779.

Dear Sir,

I CANNOT enough thank you for your most friendly attention to me in combating even pain itself to give me pleasure by your correspondence. I assure you the pleasure I receive is great and I only lament that I can make you no return, for the dulness of this place is inconceivable. We are however going to bestir ourselves a little, and there are wheels in motion towards bringing this large county together to a general meeting;[1] whether the measure will be carried into execution I am not yet certain. If it is, it will have this merit, that it arises entirely from a set of private independent gentlemen without any lordly leader whatever.[2] Its object will be to consider the critical state of our landed property etc., and to petition

20. The collector of letters for the post, who signalled his approach by ringing a hand-bell.

———

1. This county meeting was to set off 'a political agitation on a scale surpassing anything which was reached until the crisis of the Reform Bill of 1832' (George Otto Trevelyan, *George the Third and Charles Fox*, 1927, ii. 206). The Yorkshire Association, which took form at this meeting, has been studied in detail by Herbert Butterfield (*George III, Lord North, and the People, 1779–80*, 1949). One of its leading spirits and its historian was the Rev. Christopher Wyvill (1740–1822), political writer and leading advocate of Parliamentary reform. 'Mr Mason, to whom the editor [i.e., Wyvill] had not then the honour to be known, and to whom therefore no explanation of the plan proposed had been sent, with a zeal which well accords with his usual vigour and public spirit, had also given his unsolicited support' (Christopher Wyvill, *Political Papers*, [1794–1802], iii. 113). For the correspondence and advertisements that preceded the meeting of Dec. 1779 see ibid. iii. 107–72 and *post* 28 Dec. 1779. Also see G. S. Veitch, *The Genesis of Parliamentary Reform*, 1913, pp. 55–8.

2. There are no peers among the proponents of the county meeting as listed by Wyvill. On 10 Dec. 1779 Mason wrote to Alderson: 'I am embarked in a business that will take up much of my time this month, as I am one of a committee formed here to call a county meeting, and we are now employed in sending out hundreds of circular letters. How the matter originated I cannot at present explain, but of this be assured, that it is formed by independent private gentlemen and that no lord is the first mover.'

and perhaps remonstrate accordingly. I hear you say, what will all this signify? Have you not petitioned and remonstrated before? and pray what came of them? True, and as little will come of what we shall now do.—I know all this; yet it will show that we have not absolutely lost all feeling, and it will tend to put certain folks[3] still more in the wrong.

Last post brought me a weighty packet from my friend Fraser, so heavy that I wonder he was not ashamed to load the post with it. All however is not gold that is ponderous, 'twas Mr Eden's letters to Lord Carlisle,[4] and I have read them and am not comforted by them so much as his correspondent was either by them or his new sinecure.[5] He tells us on the comfortless side that the combined fleets are much larger than ours[6] and in the very next page to comfort us that our present fleet is beyond compare the best in the world.[7] Throw such comfort 'to the dogs, I'll none of it.'[8] All I can learn from it is that though we are already taxed more than ever we were, we are capable of paying still greater taxes, and therefore we ought to pay them freely without any retrospect to those who have of late imposed them to such ineffectual purpose. Suppose Lord Lyttleton had recovered the breaking of his blood-vessel[9] and a physician had told him, 'My Lord, you lost two quarts of blood and the weakness of your blood-vessel was occasioned by your debaucheries. You ought therefore to go on in your debaucheries because the human body contains many gallons of blood.' His Lordship perhaps might have approved the advice, but I trust the nation are not all [of] them Lord Lyttletons.

—O mercy on me! a letter just come from Alderson and he tells me that the west wind which blew so violently on Thursday night has tore off a great deal of my fine Westmoreland slate, that the slate in falling has broken all the panes in the very window of that best bed-

3. Probably an allusion to Rockingham and his followers, whose policies Mason considered ineffectual. See *post* 25 and 28 Dec. 1779.

4. Publication of *Four Letters to the Earl of Carlisle from William Eden, Esquire,* was announced in the *Public Advertiser* 24 Nov. 1779. It is an octavo volume of 163 pages.

5. Carlisle had been appointed first lord of Trade 10 Nov. 1779 (*London Chronicle* 9–11 Nov., xlvi. 454).

6. 'It must also be confessed, that the united fleets of our enemies exceed in number, and in the aggregate of their apparent strength, any naval force that we are yet able to produce' (*Four Letters,* p. 45).

7. 'The bravery and excellence of her mariners . . . may, without any colouring of national prejudice, be called peculiar and unrivalled' (ibid. 46).

8. 'Throw physic to the dogs, I'll none of it' (*Macbeth* V. iii. 47).

9. See *ante* 29 Nov. 1779.

chamber where my Lady Conyers and Mr Byron conjugally reposed.[10] That not only my Lady but even her military spouse were greatly alarmed and obliged to quit their apartment, and that it still rains so violently that it is doubted whether the roof can be repaired before the inside ceiling is damaged.[11] To this sad detail I hear you cry very composedly, 'A just judgment!' However I find they are not so frightened but they will still keep their headquarters at Aston, though Mr Byron has received orders to remove his recruiting party[12] to Beverley, which by the nearest roads (which are now impassable) is fifty miles, and by York above eighty. No matter, his Majesty's service will go on full as well as ever it did for all that, and so ends my Aston Gazette Extraordinary.

Believe me, dear Sir,

Most cordially yours,

W. MASON

Pray in return give me a better account of your gout than I have of my house.

To MASON, Saturday 11 December 1779

Printed from Mitford ii. 56–7. The first sentence shows that the letter was dictated.

Berkeley Square, Dec. 11, 1779.

THE very morning after I wrote to you last, the gout seized my right hand and still keeps possession, not that I have had anything particular to tell you; the papers are full of, and accurate enough in debates, and by them majorities are no whit affected. The two seceding Lords[1] made a very silly figure; one has seceded from his own secession and speech,[2] and the other from his secession into the

10. See *ante* 12 Nov. 1779.
11. Mason replied to Alderson 10 Dec. 1779: 'My house I leave entirely to your management, it is not the house it once was to me and I could, I believe, bear to hear it was even blown down with much philosophy. I wonder, however, if slates were wanted, you did not think of un-roofing a useless chaise-house in the fold-yard and converting . . . the slates to a more material purpose.'
12. See *ante* 12 Nov. 1779.

1. Gower and Weymouth.
2. On 1 Dec. 1779 Gower voted with the administration against the motion intro-

country. McDonald,[3] the former's son-in-law has made as absurd, though not as black a figure as Adam; he abused Lord North in very gross, yet too applicable terms,[4] and next day[5] pleaded he had been drunk, recanted, and was all admiration and esteem for his Lordship's talents and virtues;[6] so much for Parliament!

Lord Harcourt has told you a better anecdote[7] than any of these: there is no improving upon it.

You bear the effects of the storm with great philosophy indeed; some folks, I see, push old proverbs to both extremities and can touch nothing, but they bring a *new* house upon their heads. Old ones, however more solid, tumble too at a certain fatal touch. The removal of the south terrace at Windsor[8] has endangered, ay, cracked that whole range of buildings, and the grantees of the lodgings have removed their goods and furniture lest all should be crushed.

I am glad you have tasted of Mr Eden's four plates of *blanc-*

duced by Lord Shelburne that the ministers should be censured for their conduct of Irish affairs. He thus 'seceded from his secession' from the ministry. In his speech, however, he acknowledged that charges of neglect urged against the ministers were 'strictly true' (Cobbett, *Parl. Hist.* xx. 1175), and therefore his vote was not consistent with his sentiments.

3. Archibald Macdonald (1747–1826), Kt, 1788; cr. (1813) Bt; admitted to Lincoln's Inn, 1765; called to the bar, 1770; M. P. Hindon 1777–80, Newcastle-under-Lyme 1780–93; solicitor-general 1784–8; attorney-general 1788–93; lord chief baron of the Exchequer 1793–1813; P.C., 1793. He married (1777) Lady Louisa Leveson-Gower (1749–1827), eldest dau. of Lord Gower by his second wife.

4. On 6 Dec. 1779, speaking in the House of Commons, Macdonald accused North 'of being lazy, indolent, and incapable; of being evasive, shuffling, cutting, and deceptious; of being plausible and artful, mean, insolent, confident, and cowardly; of being a poor, pitiful, sneaking, sniveling abject creature, fraught with deceit, and one whom no man of honour could support or trust as a minister or an individual' (Cobbett, *Parl. Hist.* xx. 1228).

5. It was two days later, 8 Dec. 1779 (*Public Advertiser* 9 Dec. and Cobbett, *Parl. Hist.* xx. 1241).

6. 'Mr Macdonald apologized to Lord North for some hasty expressions which had fallen from him on the 6th. He could now affirm that they were totally ill-founded, and that in his cooler moments, were directly contrary to his real opinion, never having had any reason for entertaining any such sentiments respecting the noble Lord. It was a natural infirmity which suddenly hurried him sometimes to go beyond the limits of his own judgment' (Cobbett, loc. cit.).

7. On 8 Jan. 1780 Mason wrote to Lord Harcourt: 'I should have thanked you sooner for your account of the episcopal fête, had I not been so fully employed, as you know' (*Harcourt Papers* vii. 62). This presumably alludes to the story that HW here mentions, though further information about the 'episcopal fête' has not been found. Harcourt had apparently told HW that he had related it to Mason.

8. The construction of lodges for the Queen and the princesses outside the castle grounds to the south was begun in 1778. The King is reported to have had a hand in the design of the new buildings. The lodges were completed in 1782, but in 1823 were removed in the course of large-scale renovations. See R. R. Tighe and J. E. Davis, *Annals of Windsor*, 1858, ii. 537–8; W. H. St John Hope, *Windsor Castle: An Architectural History*, 1913, i. 347–8.

manger stewed with caraway comfits.⁹ Though they must have soon palled your stomach, never was such an insipid *entremets* dished up by a gentleman confectioner.

Mr Tickell's hodge-podge of partridges and House of Commons¹⁰ is as silly, though afterwards, here and there, there are eight or ten pretty lines. I have read Sheridan's *Critic*,¹¹ but not having seen it, for they say it is admirably acted,¹² it appeared wondrously flat and old, and a poor imitation;¹³ it makes me fear I shall not be so much charmed with *The School for Scandal,* on reading, as I was when I saw it.¹⁴

If you can send us any stories of ghosts out of the north, they will be very welcome; Lord Lyttelton's vision¹⁵ has revived the taste, though it seems a little odd that an apparition should despair of being able to get access to his Lordship's bed in the shape of a young woman, without being forced to use the disguise of a robin redbreast.

If your county remonstrate, it will be met halfway by the south;

9. HW's copy of *Four Letters to the Earl of Carlisle from William Eden,* 1779, is now wsl. HW has written 'November' under 1779 on the title and annotated the tract throughout. The tone of his notes may be gauged by his comment on p. 61, 'There is scarce anything but declamation in this second letter.' On pp. 94–5 Eden says, 'England . . . does not, under all her burthens, yet exhibit any one symptom of internal decay.' HW has noted on this: 'Yes, evidently in the diminution of the value of lands and houses, and in the vast number of houses to be let.'

10. Publication of Richard Tickell's *Epistle from the Honourable Charles Fox, Partridge-Shooting, to the Honourable John Townshend, Cruising,* was announced in *Public Advertiser* 9 Dec. 1779. HW's fully annotated copy is now at Harvard in his 'Poems of George III.'

11. HW must have read it in manuscript, for the first edition was not published until 1781 (*The Plays and Poems of Richard Brinsley Sheridan,* ed. R. Crompton Rhodes, Oxford, 1928, ii. 260; Iolo A. Williams, *Some XVIIIth Century Bibliographies,* 1924, p. 222). The prologue to *The Critic* was written by Richard Fitzpatrick, Lady Ossory's brother-in-law. See HW to Lady Ossory 6 Dec. 1779.

12. The play was first presented at Drury Lane 29 Oct. 1779 with King as Puff and Miss Pope as Tilburina. 'The whole was excellently acted' (Genest vi. 125).

13. Of the Duke of Buckingham's *Rehearsal.* In writing to Lady Ossory about *The Critic* 13 Jan. 1780, HW acknowledged that 'my being ill versed in modern dramas, most of the allusions must have escaped me.'

14. See *ante* 16 May 1777 and HW to Jephson 13 July 1777. HW had read *The School for Scandal* by May 1780 (*post* 19 May 1780).

15. According to Lord Westcote (see *ante* 29 Nov. 1779, n. 11), Lyttelton three days before his death reported the following dream: 'He said he thought he was in a room which a bird flew into, which appearance was suddenly changed into that of a woman dressed in white, who bade him prepare to die, to which he answered "I hope not soon, not in two months." She replied: "Yes, in three days"' (Reginald Blunt, *Thomas, Lord Lyttelton,* 1936, p. 186). Other accounts of the dream are discussed by Blunt, op. cit. 187–98. Lyttelton told his friends that a robin had flown into a room where he was conversing with an acquaintance a few days before his dream (ibid. 186, 188).

they talk of a like rebuke from Hampshire,[16] where there is already a sturdy opposition to the Court candidate,[17] as there is in Devonshire too.[18] Ireland I fear is going much faster, but with what are not we threatened? Yet perseverance in the American war is at this moment avowed![19] Is it possible to write on, when one has told you the excess of distraction?

To MASON, Saturday 25 December 1779

Printed from Mitford ii. 58–9.

Berkeley Square, Christmas Day, 1779.

I SUPPOSE this will find you like a true reformer in the midst of anathemas and minced pies. I am sorry the great barons who would not budge a foot while they had any dormant hopes of favour, are coming to put the sickle into the fruits of your plough.[1] Mr Fred. Montagu was so obliging as to call on me and offer to carry any letter to you: but, at that time I was not able to scratch out a line, as I do now, even with a swaddled hand, and in truth with so much difficulty that I could engrave as expeditiously: I have had a relapse, though a slight one, and called it only a *codicil* to my gout: Mr Gibbon[2] said very well, 'But I fancy it is not in consequence of your *will*.' Lord Bristol has outran me, and leaves an Earl-Bishop[3] and a Countess-

16. On 3 Jan. 1780 'a petition from Hampshire on the plan of that from Yorkshire was voted at a meeting at Winchester' (*Last Journals* ii. 263).

17. Sir Richard Worsley (1751–1805), 7th Bt; M. P. Newport, Isle of Wight, 1774–84, Newton 1790–3 and 1796–1802; P.C., 1779; F.R.S. and F.S.A. Though already holding a seat in Parliament, he offered himself as successor to Sir Simeon Stuart, 3d Bt, who had died 19 Nov. 1779, M.P. for Southampton county. On 24 Dec. 1779 HW noted: 'Court lost Hampsh. election; Sir R. Worsley giving up before end of the poll' (*Last Journals* ii. 260). The victorious candidate was Jervoise Clarke Jervoise (GM 1780, l. 627; 1808, lxxviii pt i. 90). In Parliament the Opposition made political capital of Worsley's failure (Cobbett, *Parl. Hist.* xx. 1271–2). See also *post* ii. 147.

18. Deputies from the committees of several counties, cities, and towns met in London in March 1780 (Wyvill, *Political Papers* i. 116–29).

19. In the debate on the army estimates, 8 Dec., Lord George Germain declared that 'as far as he knew the American war was not abandoned' (Cobbett, *Parl. Hist.* xx. 1249).

1. The county meeting at York held on 30 Dec. 1779 was attended by the Dukes of Devonshire and Rutland, and Lords Rockingham, Effingham, Scarborough, Egremont, and Fitzwilliam (Wyvill, *Political Papers* i. 46).

2. Edward Gibbon, the historian, who during this period called on HW 'once or twice a week' (*post* 27 Jan. 1781).

3. At the death of Augustus John Hervey,

Duchess.[4] Have you seen in yesterday's *Public Advertiser* a good collection of applications to public characters from *Tom Thumb*,[5] like those with which we were so pestered last year from Shakespeare?[6] The last, on the bigamist maid of honour I have just mentioned, is one of the happiest quotations I ever saw:—

> A maid like me heaven formed at least for *two;*
> I married him—and now I'll marry you.[7]

I find the graving-tool too laborious, and must quit it, and as I have given my secretary leave to go and keep his Christmas, this must be only a note, not that I had anything new to tell you if I could have continued.

Yours, etc.,

Horace Walpole

From Mason, Tuesday 28 December 1779

Printed from MS now wsl.
Address: The Honourable Horace Walpole, Berkley Square, London.
Postmark: YORK 3⟨0 DE.⟩

York, Dec. 28th, 1779.

I AM shocked to think that when you put yourself to so much pain in writing to me I should not be more frequent in my return of letters. But if ever any man had a good excuse I have one at present.

Earl of Bristol, 22 Dec. (*Public Advertiser* 23 Dec. 1779 and HW to Lady Ossory 23 Dec. 1779), the earldom devolved upon his brother, the Bishop of Derry.

4. Elizabeth Chudleigh.

5. The collection was communicated to the *Public Advertiser* by 'J.B.' (possibly Boswell, at that time a frequent contributor to this paper), who thus introduced his quotations: 'I was much pleased with the *Modern Characters from Shakespeare* which appeared in your paper last year; and indeed it was wonderful to observe the coincidence between so many of his portraits and living characters existing so

long after his decease. But . . . this felicity is not altogether peculiar to Shakespeare; for I have found in Henry Fielding's *Tragedy of Tragedies, or the Life and Death of Tom Thumb the Great*, a considerable portion of the same excellence,' etc.

6. At least two of these collections were issued as pamphlets, *Modern Characters from Shakespeare, Alphabetically Arranged*, 1778, and *Modern Characters for 1778: By Shakespeare, Part II*, 1778. The latter has been attributed to the Rev. Cutts Barton (ca 1707–80), for whom see Venn, *Alumni Cantab.*

7. *Tom Thumb the Great*, II. x. 38–9.

Look only at the enclosed list,[1] the last that will be published, count only the names and consider how very active a small committee must have been to have collected these in the space of a fortnight. I do not think that any measure of the kind was ever carried on to *this point* with greater success; but beyond *this point* I can frame but little conjecture. The great barons pour in upon us tomorrow, to do precisely what you say they will do.[2] Could this have been prevented (and yet all that we could do, was done to prevent it[3]) I have no doubt our conclusion would have been as prosperous as our beginning. What this conclusion turns out to be, you shall hear as soon as I know it. Excuse the greatest haste and believe how heartily I wish you a speedy recovery.

From MASON, Friday 31 December 1779

Printed from MS now WSL. All but the close, signature, and postscript is in the hand of an amanuensis.

1. Preserved with the MS. It is an advertisement, apparently clipped from a York newspaper, addressed 'To the nobility, gentlemen, clergy, and freeholders of the county of York. The death of the late respectable High Sheriff of this county [Thomas Duncombe: GM 1779, xlix. 567] having rendered it impracticable to obtain a county meeting, called in the ordinary mode, with that expedition which the distress of the country requires, the undernamed gentlemen, conceiving it to be the duty and interest of every independent person, in times of national distress especially, to exert his best endeavours, that measures for the public good may be concerted and carried into effect, do earnestly request the nobility, gentlemen, clergy, and freeholders of the county of York to meet at the Assembly-Room in York on Thursday the 30th of December 1779 at ten o'clock in the forenoon, to consider what measures may be expedient in the present critical situation of public affairs.' There follow the names of 209 signatories (also given in Wyvill, *Political Papers* i. 2–4). Mason has placed an x beside his own name and beside that of Harry Verelst.

2. That is, win popular approval by their support of the meeting, though they had not the courage to initiate it. See *ante* 7 Dec. and 25 Dec. 1779. Mason enclosed in this letter another clipping giving the names of 26 of the 'great barons,' headed: 'The following members of both Houses of Parliament, who have property in Yorkshire, have expressed their approbation of the ensuing county meeting, and many of them have engaged to attend.' For the names of the peers who actually attended, see *ante* 25 Dec. 1779, n. 1.

3. What was done is not clear. At the opening session Wyvill said that 'the idea of calling a meeting of the county of York had originated, not, as the enemies of the measure had asserted, with Lord Rockingham, nor yet with any other member of either of the two Houses of Parliament, but with a few private country gentlemen of the North Riding, who were totally free from all party influence, and equally unconnected with the leaders of administration, and their opponents' (*Political Papers* i. 9–10). See *ante* 7 Dec. 1779, n. 2, and *post* 4 Jan. 1780.

Address: The Honourable Horace Walpole, Berkley Square, London.
Postmark: YORK 3 JA.

York, December 31st, 1779.

Dear Sir,

ALL that I can have time to tell you more than you will read here
in print[1] is, that there was a very slight opposition[2] began by
Mr Cholmley[3] (who married Smelt's daughter[4]) and seconded by a
schoolboy declamation of Mr Drummond's.[5] Smelt himself (warm
from the royal bosom of his gracious master[6]) gave us a long harangue
beginning with a string of egotisms, and afterwards resigning in form
his own pension,[7] then declaring *totidem verbis* that instead of de-
creasing the power of the Crown we ought to give it a great deal more
power; that the King was the soul of the state, the best patriot, nay
the only patriot in the nation; that we ought to be taxed a great deal

1. The enclosure (presumably a copy of the petition described in the next note) is missing.

2. To the petition presented for their approval to the freeholders of York at the county meeting on 30 Dec. 1779. The petitioners requested that 'before any new burthens are laid upon this country, effectual measures may be taken . . . to inquire into and correct the gross abuses in the expenditure of public money; to reduce all exorbitant emoluments; to rescind and abolish all sinecure places and unmerited pensions; and to appropriate the produce to the necessities of the State, in such manner as to the wisdom of Parliament shall seem meet' (Wyvill, *Political Papers* i. 9).

3. Nathaniel Cholmley (1721–91), M. P. Aldborough 1756–68, Boroughbridge 1768–74; High Sheriff, co. York, 1754 (Joseph Foster, *Pedigrees of the County Families of Yorkshire*, 1874, iii *sub* Cholmley).

4. Anne Jessie Smelt, m. (1774, as his third wife) Nathaniel Cholmley (Foster, loc. cit.). She was the daughter of Leonard Smelt (ca 1719–1800), member of an old Yorkshire family; deputy governor (through his friendship with the governor, Lord Holdernesse) to the Prince of Wales and Prince Frederick 1771–6; deputy ranger of Richmond Park, 1800.

5. Perhaps Robert Auriol Hay-Drum-

mond (1751–1804), eldest son of the Hon. Robert Hay-Drummond, Abp of York (1761–76), and heir of his father's estate at Broadsworth, Yorks; 10th E. of Kinnoull, 1787; P.C., 1796; Lyon King of Arms, 1796.

6. 'Mr Smelt's character sets him above most men, and does great honour to the King, who calls him his "friend," and has drawn him out of his solitude (the life he had chosen) to enjoy his conversation every leisure moment' (*Delany Correspondence* v. 380). See also Fanny Burney's *Diary*, *passim.*

7. Smelt declared that on resigning his deputy-governorship of the princes he had refused a pension, but 'he was followed by the solicitations and commands of his gracious master, to which he no longer could make resistance. "Whether the annual payment that is made to me," said Mr Smelt, "be within the description of pension, I do not know. People may, perhaps, look on me as a pensioner, but the stipend which I receive is not upon the pension list; it is paid from the privy purse of my benevolent master; but I am henceforward indifferent to whatever construction may be put upon it, for from this moment I shall cease to receive it; I resign it back—and now, Sir, I am an independent man" ' (Wyvill, op. cit. i. 14–15).

more (for which he was hissed by the yeomanry[8]); that all our calamities arose from the Opposition, who tore off the sacred veil, which always ought to envelop the sovereign, and a great deal more trash, which served the cause he meant to attack more than any other speech could have done. He was afterwards ridiculed paragraph by paragraph by Mr Spencer Stanhope,[9] member for Carlisle, with great effect. Sir G. Savile being called upon by one of the praters,[10] of which there were a great many, gave us an excellent speech, and though the petition was carried nem. con. there were two faint noes by Smelt and his friend Matt. Dodsworth,[11] on which I wished to call a division, but without effect. You will find by the resolves that we are still as active as if the petition was yet in embryo, and shall continue so till Easter Tuesday, so that it is hardly possible this petition can be treated as others have been, especially if other counties join, of which we have the most sanguine expectations. The spirit, if not the exact letter of Smelt's speech will, I hope, soon be published,[12] and if anything can, it will astonish you by its impropriety. He has torn the veil with a vengeance.

Yours in great haste,

W. MASON

8. According to Wyvill, when Smelt said that 'one of the greatest misfortunes of this country was that no minister was found sufficiently firm to keep up the taxes in the time of peace to the greatest height of a war establishment,' he was 'interrupted by a violent hissing throughout the room' (op. cit. i. 21).

9. Walter Spencer Stanhope (1749–1821), M. P. Carlisle 1775–80, 1802–12, Haslemere 1780–4, Kingston 1784–90, Cockermouth 1800–2. See Foster, op. cit. ii *sub* Spencer Stanhope, and *Members of Parliament*, pt ii, 1878, pp. 150, 169, 184, 196, 202, 216, 259. Stanhope's speech is reported by Wyvill, op. cit. i. 35–8.

10. 'Sir George Savile . . . now came forward and said, that he had not originally intended to have spoken, but that being so urgently called upon by one of his constituents, he should now deem silence a species of high treason against the majesty of the people' (ibid. i. 32).

11. Presumably Matthew Dodsworth (d.

1805), member of a prominent Yorkshire family of Thornton Watlass. See Foster, op. cit. iii *sub* Dodsworth of Thornton, and GM 1805, lxxv pt i. 86.

12. *The Speech of Leonard Smelt, Esq., Delivered by Him at the Meeting of the County of York, December 30, 1779*, York, 1780. The prefatory advertisement announced: 'This speech was not taken down in short-hand; it is not therefore pretended that it is a faithful copy of every identical word that was delivered by Mr Smelt in every sentence; but as it was put together from the notes taken by several gentlemen present, and as these notes were put into the hands of the editor, who can himself boast a tolerably good memory . . . the public may rely upon its authenticity in point of argument and of sentiment.' The preface and the footnotes reveal the purpose of the publication: to demonstrate the King's insistence upon the royal prerogative. Mason is believed to have played a part in the publication (Davies, *York*

Pray show this to Lord Harcourt. I have not time to write more and for this you see I have used an amanuensis to copy what I had before written to another correspondent.

Press 286) and the conjecture seems sound in view of this letter and another to Harcourt 8 Jan. 1780: 'I hope soon to send you the Count's [Smelt's] speech in full, with notes *variorum*' (*Harcourt Papers* vii. 63). Smelt later published his own version, *An Account of Some Particulars Relative to the Meeting Held at York, on Thursday the 30th of December, 1779, 1780*, which only served to show that his sentiments, although heightened in the Opposition version, were not unfairly represented.